Another Day in Paradise

Mark Reece

Raider Publishing International

New York   London   Johannesburg

First Printing

Songs Mentioned:
Harmony By Elton John
Many too Many By Genesis
Ordinary World By Duran Duran

ISBN: 1-935383-94-9
Published By Raider Publishing International
www.RaiderPublishing.com
New York London Johannesburg

Printed in the United States of America and the United Kingdom

This book is dedicated to Katie, Ellie and Beanie.
With all my love forever.

A special thanks to Neil, Kat, Darren, Graeme, Simon, Anne, Max, Michele, Denise, Adam and Vanessa for all their help along the way, and to those of my friends and family who stood by me.

Another Day in Paradise

Mark Reece

SECTION ONE

For those that know,
You know who you are

EXETER, 14 JULY 2008

Reed looked out of the small tinted window of the tour bus. It was raining; the swirling spray from the motorway traffic blurred his vision of the outside world. He knew where he was exactly. He'd travelled the same journey hundreds of times before but not in the same circumstances. Reed knew every turn, every rise, every fall and all the undulations in between. That was experience from the previous decade or two. He didn't have to look out of the window; he could tell where he was by the pressure on his body as his weight transferred from one side to another. Down the dip, up the other side, into the long left hander, a sharp right, then over the rise and down the fast left curve, passing the "Well Hung Meat" sign and onto the straight, watching out for the rain stream opposite the farm gate. He looked out of the window again and half smiled to himself as he confirmed where he was. In his M3, he could hit the rev limiter in sixth if it was dry on this section.

The tour bus rattled on. The back axle sounding like it was dry of oil, groaning with all the effort of keeping up a steady sixty mph. A plastic cup rolled back and forth irritatingly in the aisle, the smell of warm stale air all about. Reed never liked being a passenger, but this was different again. This time he was confined to a small space, sat upright with no fresh air. His knees pressed against the partition wall in front, he was beginning to feel heady and sweaty. The oncoming of carsickness just a few weak swallows away. The journey would take just over an hour and Reed was only twenty minutes into it. He took a few deep breaths and tried to think about what had just happened. At that moment, he thought his life was over. Everything was on the line. His marriage of twenty-three years to his beautiful Catherine, his two daughters, his life's work, everything that he'd strived for, probably all gone in a moment of complete madness outside of his control.

Reed thought of all his friends and family. What would they think? How was he going to face them with any dignity ever again? And Catherine, his beautiful Catherine. She'd been through so much and now this. Would she still be there for him and what about the girls? Reed's mind was racing backwards and forwards as he tried to reconcile his situation.

The tour bus slowed to a halt in the traffic. The rain had stopped and Reed could see Marsh Barton disappear in the distance as they got going again. The kangaroo starts and sharp stops making every passing moment a step closer to regretting what he had eaten for breakfast that morning.

A distant muffled voice shouted, 'Ten minutes lads.' Ten minutes passed in a blink of an eye and the bus stopped abruptly outside a huge red stone building, the brakes hissing as it did so. The portcullis opened in front of the bus with a wood splitting sound of age-old hinges. Backwards and forwards shunting carried on whilst Reed could only imagine what lay ahead. A few more tight manoeuvres and the bus slowly passed through the entrance tunnel with barely six inches gap either side. Reed looked at the red sandstone walling and thought of the Parson and Clerk, a rocky outcrop just off Holcombe Point. It was the same reddish brown colour and texture. It was a happy thought of a summer's day amid a brilliant blue sea. It quickly passed.

The driver stepped out of the cab greeted by a security guard.

'How many?'

'Four,' he replied. 'Okay, on you go.'

Up the hill they chugged and came to a halt outside a grilled and battered entrance door. Reed looked up at the chilling words chiselled deep into the cold grey granite lintel above the doors. Devon County Prison. *What the fuck am I doing here*, he asked himself. His anger still vehement from the court barely a few hours earlier. Key, Lord, Hutchings, Davis and McKinney weren't going to get away with this, not if Max would get his way. But how? He didn't know. He would find a way. Of that he was sure. Whatever it took, however long, he would have the last say.

The guard opened the cubicle door and cuffed Reed as he stood ready to go. Out of the Reliance van, he looked up all around. Tall walls, razor wire loops hung from every possible wall top and fence. All windows were covered with bars. Barbed wire everywhere. There would be no getting out of here when you passed "GO."

Another guard walked forward and ordered Reed and his

fellow travellers up the concrete stairs. Twenty steps up around the right angle and up another ten steps to a grilled gate. Reed noticed the smell of damp and stale air again as he walked into the reception area. Everything was well used. The paint on the walls was faded and flaky, the lino tiles on the floor were ripped and worn looking like they'd been put down some time in the sixties.

Reed sat down on a threadbare cushioned chair and leant forward, supporting his chin on his steepled fingers. *God, this is awful*, he thought. He couldn't do fourteen months of this.

'Reed,' shouted someone from beyond a hatch.

'Yes,' he replied looking around for the speaker.

'Through the open door, please Reed,' he said firmly.

A prison officer asked Reed to stand by the wall.

'What height are you?'

'Five-foot-eight.'

'Weight? Stand on the scales.'

'Twelve and a half,' replied Reed.

The guards had taken all of Reed's possessions from him when he had been sentenced and then sent him down to the cells under the court. Everything had been sealed in a plastic bag all noted and numbered. Reed now saw the same bag on the desk in front of him. He had only taken to court his brown leather document case that Catherine had given him some ten years earlier, his mobile phone and his wallet. He had passed his house keys and car keys over to the barrister's PA, so that his car could be collected and driven back to his home.

The prison officer barked at Reed. 'Get in there and strip off. Put your clothes on the rail. What size are you? You look medium.' It didn't matter what he answered, he was going to get what he was given, whether it fitted or not.

A set of prison issue clothing was handed over. A pale blue T-shirt with HMP Exeter on it, a pair of cheaply made grey tracksuit pants, a pair of grey boxer shorts and a grotty pair of socks.

'Shoe size?' bellowed the prison officer. *Christ, I'm standing three feet in front of you,* Reed thought. *There is no need to shout.*

'Eight,' came the reply.

Reed looked at his clothing. It was all well worn, frayed at the edges, stained and looked like it had been washed in grey water. Who'd worn them before didn't bear thinking about.

A pair of new size-eight, black Doctor Marten style shoes with no laces were thrown at Reed's feet.

'Okay,' said the guard. 'We need to deal with all this.' He pointed at Reed's personal belongings.

The leather document case was upturned and shaken ; the contents strewn across the desktop. Everything was detailed, listed and bagged. Next was Reed's wallet with the same procedure. 'The maximum value you can take into the cell is a hundred pounds. What's this watch worth?'

'About fifteen hundred quid,' said Reed.

'Well you're not taking that in. That's currency.'

Reed said nothing.

'Would you like to take ten numbers off your mobile phone?'

Reed switched on his mobile and took ten numbers that he thought might be useful and wrote them down on a scrap piece of paper.

'Right then, write down on this sheet all those numbers you want to ring. Those will be the only numbers you can call whilst you are here, just ten that's all.' He only wanted to ring one.

'I'm glad you said that. I thought you meant, write down the numbers that you couldn't remember.' Most of the important numbers, Reed could remember. He even had a good recall of fourteen digit international numbers.

Reed rewrote the preferred telephone numbers on the official form, then signed off his personal belongings and was ushered into the next room.

Another guard addressed Reed.

'Drugs?'

'No.'

'Alcohol?'

'No.'

'Special medication?'

'No.'

'Depression?'

'No.'

'Disability?'

'No.'

'Fainting?'

'No.'

'Fits?'

5

'No.'

'Diabetes?'

'No.'

'HIV?'

'No.'

He thought he could have answered some of the questions with "not yet", but thought better of it.

'Okay, sign here and here and then wait over there.'

A prison orderly walked up to Reed with a clear plastic bag.

'This is your kit,' said the orderly. 'Look after it. It's all you'll get.'

Reed surveyed the contents. A dirty, bobbly, nylon pillow case, two grubby looking pale green sheets, two well worn woollen blankets, a dented metal flask and a pale blue plastic mug, a tube of unbranded toothpaste, a toothbrush with about ten bristles, a dark green small hand towel, a pale blue plastic bowl and a set of white plastic cutlery. All the fabric smelt, nothing looked new; it was all the kind of thing you would throw out. Reed thought, *I don't deserve this. This is so wrong.* Another prison officer walked over to Reed.

'Come with me please.' He used the word' please' - that was a first.

Reed followed the officer through the back of the reception area, down the seven stairs, along the corridors to a locked steel gate. The walls were tall, painted in vile gloss beige to half way, with an equally disgusting brown to the lower part. Above, fluorescent strip lights lit the brick arched ceiling some flickering intermittently, their lenses filled with dead flies and bugs. The officer opened the gate and locked it behind Reed as he passed through, the clash of locks and bars echoing all about. The corridor was dimly lit and there was that distinct smell all about him.

Reed followed the guard into an office and sat down alongside the cluttered desk.

'Right, we need to get you through here as soon as we can. Is this your first time?'

'Yes,' said Reed.

'I thought so,' said the guard. 'We need to fill in a few forms; you need to speak to Helen in counselling. Have you had anything to eat?'

'No.'

'Okay, I'll get you some food. I'll also get you an emergency phone card, so that you can call your wife?'

'Yes, my wife,' said Reed.

Reed answered the questions on the various forms and the prison officer allocated Reed a prison number – VN7708. 'This number will stay with you and will always be your reference,' he said.

'Look, this looks very bad for you at the moment, but believe me it will get better. You may not think that now, but it will. Right now, you are an emotional mess. You don't know your arse from your elbow. Take my advice. Don't feel sorry for yourself. Stand up, face it and deal with it. There are some very nasty people in here and you need to keep out of trouble. Don't stare at any one, keep yourself to yourself and that will help.. I'm not going to put you in with a crack head or a pisshead. I will put you in with someone similar to yourself.'

Reed hadn't thought about sharing, let alone being put in with a crack head. It wasn't something he had ever thought about. This was a different world to what he was used. There would be no comfortable king size bed to sit with the children reading books. Reed thought about Catherine and his two young daughters and started to cry. He just couldn't stop himself. He never cried, but this was raw angry emotion flooding out.

Reed wiped his eyes and five minutes later the guard lead him through to the counsellor.

'Hi, I'm Helen. I would like to check how you are and ask a few questions. Can I get you a cup of tea?'

'Yes please, white, no sugar, thank you.'

'Okay, you've been sentenced to fourteen months. That means that you will serve a maximum sentence of seven months provided you stay out of trouble. You should be eligible for eighteen day early release and possibly HDC tagging.'

Reed nodded, he didn't have a clue about all this. He hadn't once considered this outcome. His legal team had never talked through this possible scenario. He wondered how he was going to survive the first week let alone seven months, and this was before he had even got onto the landing where his cell would be.

'Do you have any history of depression?' asked Helen.

Reed shook his head. 'No.'

Helen looked at Reed and told him the same as the guard. 'You will come to terms with it, it's not going to be easy, but stay strong for your family. Are you married? Children?'

Reed nodded and wanted to say, yes, married to Catherine for twenty-three years with two young daughters aged two and seven, but before he could speak, the tears flooded out uncontrollably.

Helen leant across the table. 'Come on, you've got to keep your head up, walk forward. It's what your family would want.'

Reed controlled himself and managed to finish the interview without a further breakdown but it was so difficult and he felt so pathetic.

'Come on, drink your tea, and I'll take you through,' said Helen. 'Do you want to ring your wife?' She said, 'I'll get your emergency phone card.' Reed stood in the corridor and waited for Helen to return. The nerves and the anticipation were almost overwhelming.

She handed him the card. 'Lift the handset and dial your number, then press hash and then dial the code in the envelope.'

Reed followed the instructions and Catherine picked up the phone. Through the tears they managed to say enough to console each other, but realistically they were both wrecked. Catherine told Reed to stay strong for his girls. Keep your faith. We love you and always will, whatever. It meant everything. The credit on the payphone was racing down and Reed tried to say as much as he could. 'Bye, I love you.' The phone went dead and the line sounded the continuous tone. He stared at the telephone, nothing. This was it, the talking was over, now he had to walk the path.

'Okay, Reed, follow me.' The niceties if there were any, now dispensed with. More corridors, more gates and up ahead the increasing sound of the animals.

The door opened on to the landing of B Wing, Reed stared through. Ahead several prison officers were leaning over the railings looking down the stair well. Inmates were shouting and swearing down below. *This is it*, Reed thought. His worst nightmare.

Reed approached the door to cell B4-5 as the prison officer unlocked the door and beckoned Reed inside. Nothing was said.

The steel door shut with a heavy thud as Reed turned around and stared at it for what seemed an age.

'Hello,' said a voice from the top bunk. 'I'm Karl.'

8

Reed looked at Karl and extended his hand 'I'm Max.'

Karl swivelled off the bunk and jumped down onto the dark green lino floor.

The cell was fifteen feet long and nine feet wide. At the far end was a small window, three-foot wide and two-foot high, with two sets of steel grills. The cell door was solid steel with a massive lock and a narrow archer's type window in the upper centre measuring two inches wide and ten inches high. On the outside of the door was a steel flap which the guards could open to see what was going on inside.

Even with the light on, the room was dimly lit. It wouldn't improve much with daylight. On one side of the cell were two bunk beds, a small locker and a couple of corner shelves. On the other side of the cell were a table and two chairs. A doorway led to the loo and a small wash hand basin – the en suite, if you like. A CCTV camera was fixed in the top right hand corner and that was basically it. An empty corner shelf fixed to the wall with a socket and aerial jack. Nothing else.

'How long are you in for?'

'Fourteen months. And you?'

'I'm on remand, got in a couple of hours ago,' said Karl. Max didn't really know what that was but didn't say anything.

'I got stopped for drinking and driving whilst disqualified. I've got to go back to court next Monday for sentencing.'

Reed looked at Karl. 'I've been sentenced to fourteen months,' he said quietly and then after a short pause he continued, 'but they've just told me I will serve a maximum of seven months less an early release of eighteen days. I should be out by the end of February.' Christmas in prison. It was a sobering thought. He didn't understand how it all worked, but that was what he'd been told. It was now 14th July 2008 and February 2009 seemed a long way away. The conversation was slow and painful for both of them. Neither wanted to speak, they were tired and frightened of what lay ahead and there was along way to go.

By the time Reed had got into the cell, it was near 10:00 pm. He'd been in custody since 1:00 pm and hadn't eaten anything. The promise of food never materialised, the officers couldn't care less. He was weary as he made the bed and climbed in.

Lying there, with his hands behind his head, staring at

the underside of the mattress above, he thought about the hundreds of villains that had laid in the very same spot , murderers, rapists, paedophiles, fraudsters, they'd all been there before him. Just twenty-four hours earlier Max and Catherine had been special guests at the back stage party of the Duran Duran concert in Birmingham. Simon Le Bon was a good customer of Max's and it just couldn't seem possible that he could go from kissing Simon's supermodel wife, Yasmin to where he was now in less than a day. It was mad. Someone had burnt the paint off the lattice frame and bedposts and scratched "Reggie woz 'ere 1963".

TEIGNMOUTH, OCTOBER 1974

It was nearing the end of October 1974, Reed had been at Teignmouth Grammar School for nearly two months and he liked it. It was a lot better than a boy's boarding school and there was the added attraction of girls, something he had not really experienced before. It usually took twenty to twenty-five minutes to walk home and quite often there was a pretty girl walking in front of him along the way. She was in the same year as Reed, but in a different class. He didn't know who she was. There were about six hundred pupils at the school and in the third year, there were three classes with about thirty in each class with equal numbers of boys and girls. Reed was in 3M, situated in the lecture theatre next to the Biology laboratory.

Once out of the school gate, there was a steep hill to the right, which followed the main road up to the Haldon Moor. Reed would walk up the hill, passing the school playing fields and hockey pitch, until it flattened off after about half a mile and then take the first turning right into New Road. The worst part of the trek home was over. Max strolled past the new bungalows lining the left hand side of the road with the older detached properties on the lower right hand side of the hill. Between the houses and looking down the hill, he could see the harbour in the distance with all the small boats moored up and a cargo ship being piloted into the estuary. The view went out of sight as Max passed the end of the detached houses and now he could see the outline of the Notre Dame Convent School for Girls just beyond the stone boundary wall which was lined with masses of mature trees of all types. There was no pavement on the right hand side of the road at this point, just a low stone wall so Reed crossed the road at the junction of Buckeridge. There would be four left hand turnings into modern estates before Reed got home. The ribbon development of bungalows on his left resumed as he stepped back onto the pavement. Max's mother's red Triumph Spitfire was parked in the driveway of the third bungalow. It was Mrs. Zachiry's house, probably built in the mid to late 1960s and by the looks of it, not touched since. Mrs. Zachiry was a retired head mistress, a widow and lived alone. The yellow paint on the woodwork was faded and riddled with moss. Reed didn't know how long she'd lived on her own but he didn't particularly like going into the house. The bungalow had a light smell of cat's wee and generally bad odour. It was an old person's smell and it was quite nauseating especially with the sun shining through the window.

Max's mother noticed him walking up to the gateway and beckoned him into Mrs. Zachiry's house. Reed didn't want to go in, but his mother insisted. The old lady was sitting in her chair in the lounge, with a china tea set placed on a tray on the occasional table in front of her.

'Hello, Max, good day at school? Take a seat, love. Would you like a cup of tea?'

Max sat down and accepted her offer. Mrs. Zachiry was a friend of Max's mother and like most of his mother's friends was a little bit strange to say the least. She was seventy-six years old and must have been at least sixteen stone standing no more than five foot four. Her legs were like huge tree trunks and she displayed her underwear under her cotton floral patterned dress as she awkwardly poured the tea. Max averted his gaze until Mrs. Zachiry said, 'There we are Max. Sugar?'

'Yes, two please.'

Max picked up the cup and saucer and began to stir his tea with the teaspoon.

'That's an unusual way to stir your tea Max.'

'I've always done it like this,' he replied.

Max held the spoon with his thumb and forefinger of his right hand gripping the spoon a third of the way down from the top and then used his first finger which he placed on the end of the spoon and rotated the spoon to stir the sugar in the tea.

Mrs. Zachiry and Max's mother rattled on about some inane rubbish for about twenty minutes when she turned to Max

11

and asked if he would like to play a game of Scrabble. Before he could answer, Mrs. Zachiry had the Scrabble box pulled out from under another table and started laying out the pieces around the board.

'Pick a letter Celia.' Max's mother dipped her hand into the bag and pulled out a letter, then passed the bag to Max who did the same. Mrs. Zachiry chose her letter and they all placed them face up on the playing board.

'Nearest to A to start,' said Mrs. Zachiry, which meant Max's mother would kick off.

Max's father used to enjoy playing Scrabble and often saw it as a major victory when or if he beat his friend Alan. Max would usually play with the pair of them, but his chances of winning were slim. He was getting better at it, but he couldn't beat his father just yet. Maybe it wouldn't be a good idea if he did.

Half way into the game, Max's mother turned to Max and said, 'Mrs. Zachiry is a fortune teller. She has hidden powers you know. Yes, true she does.'

Max thought for a moment, saying nothing not wanting to be drawn into a conversation. What a load of nonsense. Another of mother's nutty friends. It wasn't just Mrs. Zachiry either. All his mother's friends were completely off the wall. He didn't think that any one of them was normal.

'All right then,' said Max looking at Mrs. Zachiry. 'Who's going to win this game?'

'You are,' she replied. 'You are.'

She was right. Max won the game emphatically. He shrugged and thought, *Perhaps the old bat is a fortune teller; perhaps she does have special powers.* He didn't believe in it, but he had won the game. Maybe, maybe not.

Mrs. Zachiry leant forward and with a smile asked Max if he would like her to tell his fortune.

'Don't worry darling, I'm not going to tell you anything bad.'

EXETER, JULY 2008

Reed woke up, it was early. The scenery hadn't changed. The jangle of the guard's keys unlocking and locking doors reverberated around the landings outside his cell. An alarm was sounding from one of the cells. Commonly known as the room service button, residents could press the red button if they were in distress. A red light system would relay the cell identity to the landing staff. The guards weren't that quick at responding, usually because of the abuse of the system by the crack heads. God help you, if you had a real problem. You'd probably be dead by the time they got off their backsides.

Neither Reed nor Karl had a watch. Reed's faithful Omega Seamaster had been taken from him at reception. There was no clock in the cell, so they didn't know what time it was and in truth, they didn't know what day of the week it was. Max filled the basin with lukewarm water and stared at himself in the reflection of a makeshift mirror made from an upturned biscuit tin glued to the bricks with toothpaste. What he could make of it, he didn't look good. Inmates all around were shouting abuse at each other, banging on their doors and generally making a nuisance of themselves. It was the pre breakfast frenzy. A guard unlocked Reed's door. Nothing was said. The two men just looked at each other. *What next,* they thought.

Max opened the door and looked out onto the landing; it was a scene he'd only previously watched on television. He saw other inmates carrying their blue plastic bowls down the central staircase, their footsteps sounding like numerous *glockenspiels*.

'Hey Karl, come on its breakfast. Take your bowl with you,' he said looking for some moral support. They followed the queue down to the servery. A kitchen orderly ticked off their name as they entered the serving area. A bowl of Rice Crispies, two pieces of warm, limp toast, two individual margarine tubs, a tea bag, a sachet of sugar and a small packet of whitener. That was it. Back up the stairs and returning to the cell, Reed saw other offenders filling their flasks with hot water at the boiler. Following their lead, he did the same and returned to the relative safety of the cell. It was like indoor camping, thought Reed. Everything felt soggy or damp. Both of them quickly realised that the tea was undrinkable with the whitener, which meant pouring some of the milk out of their cereal bowl into their plastic mugs, but it took several days for them to think of it. Maybe too many other worries on their minds. Twenty-three hours per day, the pair of them were locked up. There was no air, no books, just the slow passage of time for them to think about their plight.

13

The door was unlocked again. Guards were shouting, 'Exercise, exercise, exercise!' It had to be 10:45 am. That's what it said on the timetable stuck to the cell wall. Reed followed the men down the stairs to an assembly area and waited for the prison officer to open the blue steel gate. Looking around, it didn't look good. He could almost see the tension all about him. Soon they were out in the open walking along a designated path to an exercise yard known as the playground. The area was square with thirty feet tall close mesh fencing along its perimeter, topped with razor wire. In the centre was a huge pole, which held the cross wires supporting the steel netting that covered the whole area. The entrance gate was occupied by four prison officers who blocked the exit physically. Outside the playground perimeter fencing stood another three prison officers with Alsatian dogs. It would be fair to think it wouldn't be easy to escape from the exercise yard but it had been done in the past. Inside the fencing were three paths arranged in diminishing circles like an archery target with grassed areas between each path. There were eight randomly placed old wooden park benches dotted around and a small terraced area with four picnic benches.

By the time Reed and Karl arrived, there were already a hundred or so prisoners walking the paths in groups, couples or on their own, all going in the same anti-clockwise direction. Nobody went the opposite way. It took one hundred and fifty seconds to walk the one hundred and fifty paces around the outer circle. That meant Reed had to walk the outer path twelve times to do a slow mile.

Looking around was intimidating enough, but Reed remembered the advice when he came in the night before. Keep yourself to yourself. Standing amongst murderers, psychopaths, bank robbers and violent criminals was not what Reed had expected, but here he was and he had to keep his wits about him. The whole situation was highly charged and even on day one, he could sense that it could kick off at any time. Reed didn't want to be amongst it, if it did.

He thought back to when he was at Teignmouth Grammar School. There was quite a lot of ill feeling between the grammar school and the secondary modern at Westlawn. It was made worse by the fact the schools were next to each other on a hillside. The grammar school sat above Westlawn, so naturally looked down on the secondary school. The lower exit from the

Grammar school was along a path that ran alongside Westlawn where all the hard nuts would "screw you out" as anyone walked by. They were angels compared to the animals in the exercise yard. The whistle blew and Reed walked back towards his cell. There was no getting away from it. This was real and it was happening to him now. It was no dream. If only it was.

At that moment, someone dropped a table leg out of one of the cells above and a scuffle broke out in front of him. There was shouting and jeering. Reed couldn't see clearly but he could see the length of wood being violently raised and thrashed down onto the head of another inmate. The whistles were blowing and the guards raced through the crowd pushing everyone aside as they did so. A clearing like the parting of the Red Sea opened up before Reed as he looked down at a body lying awkwardly on the concrete path, his head bleeding profusely and his face covered in blood. He was still alive, but he didn't look too clever. The dogs kept everyone back and order was restored. It was all over in fifteen seconds. The job had been done. It was frighteningly, that quick. The medics arrived and tended to the injured prisoner, but Reed was gone, hurried back to his cell. Typically, no one knew who had done it and the screws didn't ask either. Just another day in paradise. The weapon was thrown to one side, blood spattered.

Reed was terrified. He wasn't a violent man and he was physically shaking. His palms were sweating as he lay down on his bunk. *Fucking hell*, he thought. *This is worse than a zoo full of wild animals that haven't been fed for a week.*

Karl leant on the wall with his forehead pressed against the cold bricks. 'Jesus Christ,' he said. 'That was close. Do you think he'll be okay?'

'Who knows? I'm just glad we're back in here.'

When Reed came through reception the night before, he had nine pounds in his pocket. The money would be put on his prison account from which he could buy whatever was listed on the canteen sheets. If Reed enrolled in education, he would earn seven pounds fifty per week and that would be added to his account. How he spent the money was up to him, but his priority was to get some credit on his phone account. He wanted to speak to Catherine but this seemed unlikely for at least a few days. Lunch passed uneventfully. Reed collected his pressed steel tray and passed it to the servers who slopped the chef's special onto it. An apple and four slices of bread followed. *Great*, thought

Reed as he passed the queue of crack heads lining up at the happy hatch for their methadone. By the length of the queue, it appeared that everyone on the wing were druggies. Their faces drawn, their eyes sunken and dark, their appearance ragged and dirty and their hair greasy and matted. *What a state to get in,* thought Reed. Looked like something out of Auschwitz.

Max and Karl spent four days in cell B4-5 on B Wing before being transferred to A3-036 on A Wing. In that time, they spent most of the long hours in silence, but when they did speak, it was usually about their wives and family, what they were doing, how they were coping. It was awful, but they couldn't do anything about it. Reed knew all about Karl's family, how many children, how many brothers and sisters, what they did for a living, what they did at Christmas, and even what position Karl's wife Lisa liked best. It was bizarre; here were two men twenty-four years apart discussing the sex life of Karl's wife.

TEIGNMOUTH, OCTOBER 1974

Mrs. Zachiry took Max's right hand and turned it over so she could look at the palm. 'Hmm,' she sighed. 'Well you've got a nice long life-line and you don't look like you're going to have a problem with your health. That's good. You're going to have two children. You won't have to get married but you will marry at the age of twenty-four to the sister of a friend. You will go overseas a lot; I see a lot of oceans. You will change direction in your career in later life. You will never want for money. One of your children will have red hair, and I see a green car in the New Forest.' A lot of information to take on board in less than a minute.

Max confined every detail to his memory and mulled over the information in his mind. For now, it was just a fun thought. It couldn't possibly come true, could it? Max's mother passed him the house key and he let himself out, thanking Mrs. Zachiry as he shut the door behind him. Reed carried his books in a black Adidas hold-all, which he threw over his shoulder as he walked back down the drive and out onto the pavement, then turning left, he followed the pavement on the left hand side of the road going home. He crossed the first turning left, Ashley Way, which lead to a grocers and small post office from where

16

he did his paper round, then walked another five hundred yards crossing Mandelin Drive, by Johnny Johnsons garage, then up the hill another three hundred yards passing Higher Woodway Road on his left and Lower Woodway Road on his right. He looked all ways, crossed Higher Woodway and continued the slight uphill along New Road. St. Mawes Close was the last left turning before Reed's house, which he could now see the entrance in the distance. He was two hundred yards from home, when a blue Peugeot 504 Estate nosed out of a private drive barely ten feet in front of him. Max heard the car coming down the drive, so he wasn't startled by it. The car stopped at the road and then pulled out turning right down the hill. He watched it as it drove away in the distance. There was a family of six in the car. Behind the driver was the girl that Reed had seen walking in front of him on his way home. She looked through the side window at Max, smiled and half waved. He turned his head and watched the car drive off into the distance. Was she just being polite or did she simply recognise the school uniform and acknowledge it?

The private drive was shared by two houses, so the mystery girl had to live in one of them. Reed smiled to himself, walked the last two hundred yards, home and walked down the drive. As he passed the garage, he looked in through the window at his father's new white Jaguar E Type waiting for its next outing. Popper, his faithful Siamese cat, was yowling at his feet. It was five past six and Reed's mother had not arrived home yet. His father usually got home at about twenty past six. It was critical that his mother was home before his father. Reed opened the back door, letting Popper in and went up to his bedroom and got changed, not noticing...

NEWTON ABBOT, CHRISTMAS 1968

The helicopter circled high in the sky over Courteney Park. Reed watched it intently as it flew in and out of sight behind the trees and then gently approached a flat area in the centre of the park, landing perfectly on its skids.

It was just before Christmas 1968, Max and his brother Neil had broken up from Buck House and were now on their

Christmas holidays. It was Reed's father's busiest time of the year. He would make more money in the two weeks leading up to Christmas, than he would in the whole of January and February. It was vitally important that the Christmas trade was a good one. Every year he would want to better last year and this year was no exception. A good result would be takings of five thousand pounds in the first week and seven thousand pounds in the week leading into Christmas Eve. During the Christmas week, the boys reluctantly went into work with their father. They hated it, but amused themselves as boys do. They'd go over to the market and crawl under the stall holder's trestles and then look up girls' skirts. It passed the time of day and they never got caught.

Father Christmas stepped out of the helicopter in his full red and white suit and white beard, and then reached back into the Perspex bubble for his Christmas sack. He reached back again and with his arms outstretched, helped a little girl out onto the grass below.

By this time, quite a crowd had gathered of more than a hundred small children, some with parents. The town mayor greeted Father Christmas and his small helper, whilst the children went up to them and collected small gifts.

Max and Neil waited patiently in the anxious queue, Max holding Neil's hand just as mother had ordered. Neil was only six and a half years old, eighteen months younger than Max.

Max looked keenly at Father Christmas and wished him Happy Christmas.

'And what would you like Father Christmas to bring you this year, boys?'

'Well, I would like Scalextric, and Neil wants - what is it that you want, Neil?' asked Max.

'I'd like the Battle Station Hornby train set,' said Neil.

Father Christmas smiled at the two boys and said, 'Well, I think those are on my list too. I don't think I've got those with me today, but I might have something else for you.'

Father Christmas reached down into his sack, found two presents for Max and Neil, and put them in their hands.

'Happy Christmas,' he said.

'Thank you very much,' replied the boys. 'Happy Christmas.'

The two boys went and sat on a park bench a short

distance away and watched Father Christmas hand out the remaining gifts and then pack away his sack into the helicopter. The little girl waited until she was lifted back into the cockpit and waved excitedly as the rotors lifted the machine off the ground. The children shouted and waved and the helicopter turned and disappeared out of sight. It would be another thirteen years before Max would meet Father Christmas again.

EXETER, JULY 2008

The officer opened the prison cell door and confirmed Reed and Karl's names, and then continued into the room and checked the bars on the window. It was a security check.

'This is a working prison, which means that you have to work. If you don't want to work then you can lie in bed all day but you won't get paid, okay?'

They didn't reply.

He continued, 'Today, you will be visited by the prison chaplain, the nurse, probation and the custody management unit. CMU will be discussing your sentence, early release and HDC tagging. The nurse will give you a brief examination. Any drugs?' The officer looked up and the cellmates shook their heads. 'Okay, the chaplain will be with you in about ten minutes. Tomorrow, if you want to work, you will need to report to the Learning Zone. Movement to Labour at 8:45 am. Queue on A1 landing and wait to be called through. Okay?' The guard turned to go.

'Any news on a TV?' asked Karl.

'Sorry, no TVs at the moment. You're first in line when one becomes available.' It was a standard answer. He turned the latch to lock and shut the door.

'Looks like we've got something to do then,' said Max.

CMU were the last of the days' visitors and marched Reed down to C Wing. A barrage of questions followed, and Reed was really none the wiser. He'd been sentenced to fourteen months of which he would have to serve half. He could get a further eighteen days early release, and possibly early release on HDC tagging.

19

'What's HDC?' Reed asked.

'Home Detention Curfew.'

'Okay, what's that?'

'This your first time in trouble with the police, in prison?'

'Yes,' Reed replied, 'I'm not intending making a habit of it.'

'Okay, if you are eligible. Do you have a home to return to?'

'Yes.'

'Any trouble with violence or police action at the house?'

'No.'

'How long have you lived at the address?'

'Twenty-three years.'

'That should be okay, then. Do you have a land line?'

'Yes.'

'Right, well subject to the probation and HDC being okayed, we will issue you with an early HDC tagging. You will need to wear a strap on your ankle for the period from the early release date to the end of your conditional release date or seven months less eighteen days. You will be curfewed to the address from seven at night to seven in the morning. You may be able to vary those times but that will be down to the Governor and you.'

'So when will I get HDC?' asked Reed.

'We will confirm all of that to you in writing tomorrow. It will be in the internal post.'

The last resident had left a calendar on the wall of the cell. Reed looked at it as his mind tried to work out how long he would be there. He was sentenced on the 14 July 2008, for fourteen months; less seven months would be 13th February 2008 less eighteen days. "D" day would be 27th January 2009. That meant Christmas in prison, it was a chilling thought. From where Reed sat, 27th January 2009 might as well have been life. Yeah, it was a lot better than fourteen months but he just couldn't see how he was going to last that long.

Reed remembered something about risk assessment and something about being released sooner than the eighteen day early release. It was all a bit too much to take in. His solicitor and barrister had never mentioned any of this because they believed Max wouldn't be going to prison. Reed climbed back on to his bed and waited for Karl to return.

'That was quick.'

'Yeah,' replied Karl, 'they just confirmed that I'm on remand until next Monday and then I will be sentenced.'

'Right okay, they didn't say what your likely sentence would be?'

'No, they didn't know about that, so I will just have to worry about it for a few days more. When do we get our proper phone credit, I want to phone Lisa?'

'I don't know,' said Reed shaking his head. 'I hope it's soon. I'll ask the PO when he comes back. In fact, let's make some notes on what we need to ask.'

TEIGNMOUTH, NOVEMBER 1974

Reed stood in the queue, dinner tickets in one hand and his cutlery in the top pocket of his blazer. The prefects monitored the line and kept them in check. Reed had his back to Paddy Harris as his hand gripped Reed's shoulder.

'Do you want any lunch today?' and before he could answer he said, 'Well come on, move on.' The raised voice attracted the attention of the two girls standing in front of Reed and they turned around to look.

'Hello,' said the one on the right, 'I live down the road from you. I'm Carolyn, but I get called Caro.'

'Yes, I know. Hi, I'm Max.' Reed already knew who she was. He'd taken the trouble to find out earlier that day.

The queue moved forward and Caro and Max collected their lunch and sat at different tables with their respective friends. Max looked up in her direction every now and then, but never caught her eye. Caro looked across, Max was busy laughing and joking with his friends. Maybe she would talk to him later.

ILFORD, JUNE 1975

Donald Key looked at his watch as he sat outside the director's office. It was ten past five. The traffic was always heavy on a Friday night. He didn't want to be home late tonight.

He had plenty of work to be getting on with at home. He had the bead blasting man coming over on Saturday to take the paint off the XK120, which was partially stripped and still needed loads of the remaining small pieces of trim and fittings removed. He had to get a replacement gas bottle for his welder so that he could heat up some bolts to remove the front suspension. The hire shop would be open at eight o'clock in the morning. The front bumpers needed to come off, the lights, the screen and the dashboard all had to come out and it was obvious that most of it would be seized tight. He thought he would squirt some WD40 on the fixings when he got home. Karen wouldn't be too pleased, but nothing new there. His two boys were too young to help, but he would like them to help him when they got a bit older.

'Ah, Don, sorry to keep you waiting, come on in, sit yourself down. Thanks for coming up.'

'Thanks.'

'I've got to be gone fairly quick tonight Don, and I'm sure you don't want me to keep you anyway,' said Alan. 'I don't know if you know, but Gary is moving on, he's moving to the Frankfurt office. He's been here ten years now and he thinks it's time for a change.'

Don nodded, 'Yes, I'd heard something, but not any detail.'

'Look, would you be interested in taking his job, Head of Photographic quality control. It would be your first managerial position. We know you have the ability and we would like you on board. You'll be answerable to me directly, but I would be expecting you to show initiative, keep me updated, but try to solve problems on your own accord. Obviously, if things get difficult, then my door's always open. You worked closely with Gary, so you know what it's all about. I don't need to explain it all. Do I? There will be an increase in your salary and a bonus scheme based on throughput volume. We can discuss the details after the weekend. Do you want to think about it?'

'Er, no, I don't need to think about it. I would like to give it a go. Yes, I'd like to accept your offer. Thank you,' said Don.

Alan stood up and offered his hand out to Don and he shook it. The deal was done. Alan, now in his early sixties was the area director of Kodak and ran the biggest facility in the UK. He'd been in charge at Ilford for fourteen years since his promotion in 1961. He needed a good man to oversee the quality control and Don was the obvious choice.

'Don, are you still fiddling about with those old cars?' enquired Alan.

'Yeah, nothing much though,' replied Don keen to play it down.

'Well, have a good weekend. Karen okay? And the boys?'

'Yes, they're fine thanks.'

'Good, then I'll see you on Monday.'

Don ran down the stairs to the rear entrance and flung open the door. The cold November night took him by surprise. There was a frost already forming on the screen of his Triumph Dolomite and the heater took ages to work. Don started the engine and got back out of the car to scrape the screen and then set off into the commuter traffic. It was twenty past six, it was dark, and at this rate he was going to be up all night if was to be ready for the bead blaster in the morning. He pulled up outside his three bedroom semi-detached house, locked the car and hurriedly walked up to the front door. The light was on in the front room.

TEIGNMOUTH, OCTOBER 1974

Reed's mother arrived home just after 6:30 pm. Max was sat down in front of the TV with Popper on his lap. He'd lit the fire, got the extra coal in and stacked some dry logs by the hearth. Celia struggled with the shopping bags unseen by her son. She was seven months pregnant and expecting her third child - a new baby brother or sister for Max and Neil.

Max got up, helped his mother with the shopping and started putting things away in the larder.

'Your father's going to be a bit late tonight, he's had to go and see a customer.'

It wasn't true, but Celia believed it. She had no reason to doubt her husband. Whilst he had cheated on her once before, that was a long time ago and besides, she was expecting their third child in a couple of months and all the talk was about a little girl and everything was luvvy-duvvy. Celia had wanted a little girl and so had Max's father, but they didn't know what it

23

would be. Reed's mother had overdone it eating for 'two' and with two months to go, she was enormous and very uncomfortable. Twelve and half years had passed since Neil was born.

Derek got home at about ten p.m. Max had already gone to bed but he heard his father's Volkswagen Caravanette's distinctive air-cooled engine chug to a halt. He heard the back door shut and muffled talking in the kitchen. The conversation raised and lowered and then there was quiet. Max could guess what his mother had been saying, but at least it didn't seem that it would escalate to any violence. The expectation of another child was keeping them together. Reed's father was desperate to have a daughter and how he wanted to call her Jemima. Max's bedroom was above the kitchen, not that he could hear much below, but their talking had kept him awake.

Max drifted off to sleep, huddled under several layers of blankets and an eiderdown. It was a big detached house and Max's father never liked putting the central heating on. He was a believer in the old fashioned mode of putting more clothes on if you were cold. Max could count on one hand the number of times that he'd washed in hot water at home. It didn't make any sense to Max. Why have those new cars and not have the heating on. The only time it was on was when some of father's friends came around for dinner.

The cold made the house a bit spooky. It was a 1930's house built in dark brick with Tudor style black and white panelling in part with a huge oak front door and leaded windows. The Reeds had moved in during the summer of 1970. Celia had known nothing about it until Max's father told her he had a surprise for her.

Derek had fiddled everything to get the mortgage, and somehow his accountant had managed to get the application agreed. Through the large front door was a wooden herringbone polished floor in the hallway leading left to a downstairs cloakroom and adjoining WC. Off the hallway was the breakfast room and doorway to the kitchen. Above the doorway was the servant's bell box. A rear passage led to the back door and a walk in larder pantry. There were three further reception rooms downstairs. A large dining room, a study and a beautiful lounge. A conservatory lead from the study and all the major rooms faced south with a spectacular unobstructed view of the harbour, the estuary and the bay. Upstairs, there were five bedrooms all fitted with fashionable vanity suites, a separate WC and family bathroom. It was a very nice house by any standard. The house sat in an acre and a half of its own grounds with open farmed fields to the south and east, the tennis court to the west, with the front of the house facing north. There were various outbuildings by the kitchen and a greenhouse where Max's father grew tomatoes.

On a good day, you could see Start Point to the South-West and Portland Bill to the east. From his bedroom window, Max's father could see his boat moored just off the Salty. A few years earlier Donald Crowhurst's ill-fated Teignmouth Electron had started out on his attempt at the *Daily Express* Round the World Yacht race. Max and Neil were there on the back beach waving him off along with hundreds of others that day. Crowhurst's children were there too and Max remembered thinking they were the same age as him.

The house was littered with spectacular wall clocks, grandfather clocks, antiques and paintings. By 1973, Reed's father had become very successful and money was in evidence all about the house.

EXETER, JULY 2008

Reed jotted down a few notes with the shortened broken pen to ask the P.O. when he next came around on his visit. That all went out the window when Max and Karl were overwhelmed by the guard delivering the television. It was like a gift from Heaven. Something to do, watch the box. The prison officer went back out onto the landing and came back with two emergency canteen supplies, sealed in separate plastic bags.

'Smoker?'

'Yes,' said Karl.

Max's face dropped. *No, not a smoker*, thought Reed. Karl hadn't mentioned smoking up to that point. Max didn't smoke, never had, never even tried, didn't drink and here he was, sharing a small cell with a smoker who had just been caught for drink driving whilst disqualified having been sentenced to an eight month suspended sentence only two months beforehand for the same offence. It could have been so much worse though.

He looked at his canteen bag and surveyed the contents.

A packet of bourbon crème biscuits, two chew bars, a Kit Kat, a Twix, two sachets of Nescafe coffee, a packet of Cheesy Wotsits, two envelopes with four sheets of writing paper, a one litre bottle of lemon squash. That was it! No pen to write a letter. No emergency phone card.

Karl didn't get any sweets or biscuits, just tobacco and a packet of Rizlas, but no matches! *No lighting up tonight*, Reed thought thankfully.

Max looked blankly at the screen. Karl was obsessed with the soaps, Emmerdale, Coronation Street and East Enders, all based on people in pubs, people outside pubs, screaming, shouting, arguing. It was the same story on all of them. Karl's life revolved around the soaps at night when he was home. It opened Max's eyes. He couldn't believe anyone could be so taken in by it. *Each to their own*, he thought.

The night passed and Max was woken at 6:30 am by the prison officers opening and closing gates, doors and jangling keys. Max turned over and tried to blank out all the noise, but it was useless. The crack heads were getting restless, shouting out for their meds. The banging on the doors got louder and more frequent. Soon enough the whole B Wing was drumming to the sound of plastic cups, bowls and fists banging against the steel cell doors. Bloody animals, worse than animals. In fact, it was probably being cruel to animals saying that. You couldn't get away from the noise; it was relentless and driven by desperation and addiction.

The noise began to dwindle as the guards started unlocking the cells. The druggies legged it to the happy hatch as Max and Karl dived in to the canteen for breakfast. The same menu as yesterday. A bowl of damp cornflakes and two slices of limp cold toast, which they carried back to their cell. It never got any better.

At 8:45 am, Max went off to Labour and found himself doing a literacy and numeracy test. Questions for the numbskull, one, two, three. Once Max had arrived at the learning zone, he would be locked in until 10:30 am, and then he could return to his cell. Exercise was at 10:45 am. Karl had now got a lighter, so making up for lost time, he was now getting into full cigarette production. He was a gentle guy and did his best to smoke near the window, but if you are not a smoker, it's just not nice.

Whether or not it was the clubbing the day before or something else, Max didn't know but Karl declined going to exercise and Max went out on his own.

The stroll around the outer circle in the exercise yard was time to get some fresh air, feel the warmth of the sun on your back and if it rained, it didn't matter. It was away from the smoke and the stale air. Max didn't know whether it was the water or the soap, but whatever the number of times he washed his hands or face, he still felt greasy and dirty. It was disgusting.

He sat down on an empty bench leaning forward with his elbows on his knees staring at the ground in front of him. A few moments passed and Max was so engrossed in thought that he hardly noticed someone come and sit down beside him.

'Nice day today, isn't it.'

'Yes,' said Max. 'Typical, when we've had such a crap summer so far, then get locked up in here and the sun comes out.'

'What are you in for?'

'It's a long story.'

'They always are. I'm Tom Clock,' he replied.

'Max Reed.' They shook hands.

'Max Reed? Ah, you're the Ferrari guy on the television the other night?'

'Well I didn't see it, but yes that was me.'

'Well you shouldn't be here. They'll ship you out pretty quick. They won't want you here. What cat are you?'

'I'm a category D prisoner whatever that means,' said Max.

'Yeah, they'll ship you off to Channings Wood or Leyhill, probably Leyhill because that's an open prison for white collar crime, nothing violent. Exeter's a Cat B remand prison, so the worst of the worst are here. See that old guy over there with the grey hair? Standing up?'

'Yeah.'

'He went over to Thailand, found himself a wife and brought her back here, tied her up and carved her up. He's in for life.'

'Jesus, no,' said Max.

'See the little guy with his own clothes on, with the purple shirt. He's just come back from court this morning. He came home from work early one day found his wife in bed with someone else. He went into the garage and got a can of petrol, doused his wife and set fire to her. He's got to be in his sixties, he'll probably not get out in his lifetime. The two guys over there with their shirts off?'

'Yeah.'

'They got let out two months ago after serving thirteen years for armed robbery. You would have thought that would have taught them a lesson. They're now in on remand for four armed robberies and grievous bodily harm (GBH). They're happy though. They're institutionalised. Can't cope out in the open. They're expecting seventeen years.'

'What about you?' Max asked. A brave question considering he'd just met the bloke, but he looked okay.

'Be careful who you ask that question. Some may not want to be asked, some will undoubtedly lie and others you may not want to know the answer. I'm on remand for originally GBH, but they've reduced that to ABH (actual bodily harm). I've been here for three months, so if it takes a couple more months to go to court, I should be able to walk free having already served the sentence on remand.'

'What about your wife, children?'

'Well, she's out of the picture, but I still want to see my kids and probation will have a lot to say about that. We'll have to see how it goes. Here, this will make you laugh, that guy over there with the red hair?'

'Yeah.'

'He's an alcoholic; he'd been drinking, broke in to someone's house late at night and went into the sitting room and helped himself to the drink and got completely hammered. In the morning, the owner came downstairs dressed in his uniform, he was a copper, and matey boy was sparko'd on the settee.'

Max laughed, 'So what will he get?'

'Oh, I don't know. He's a nice guy though.'

The whistles blew and Max stood up alongside Tom and made for the 'playground' exit.

Tom asked Max whereabouts he was and Max told him he was on B Wing.

'Yeah, they'll be watching you on the CCTV for a few days and once they consider you not being a suicide risk, they'll move you onto C Wing. You might go to A Wing, but I doubt it. What's your palmate like?'

'He's okay, harmless, came in at the same time as me.'

'They'll probably keep you together and move you at the same time. They won't split you up if you're getting on okay.'

'Ah, that's good.'

'Yeah, you'll be okay; you've just got to get through it. It's not going to be easy. You don't fit the description. You're like a fish out of water here. If you get to Leyhill, you'll be all right. Speak to your personal sentence officer and they'll speak to CMU.'

HENLEY ON THAMES, MAY 2000

Ted Little sat at his desk, a cup of milky coffee in one hand and a copy of Top Marques magazine in the other. It was a Monday morning at the beginning of summer 2000. A few months earlier Ted had started his own business in partnership with a long term school friend from Dulwich College, James McAfee. James was the son of a successful banker in the City and provided the finance. Both of them were twenty-six years old and full of energy and blind innocent ignorance. Having not had any experience in business on their own before, everything was new to them. Ted had worked for the last four years at Coys Motoring Department in Kensington, under the watchful eye of Graham Lord and had learned from his experience in the auction department. Effectively, Little was a runner. Do this, do that, push this, push that, fetch the tea etc. He had no direct contact with the clients either on the sales side or the purchasing side. Obviously, he got to know who was who. Who had the great cars, who had the big collections, but he couldn't really speak to them unless they spoke to him or he was instructed to do so. A puppet that's all.

The specialist motoring auction industry was a hard place to be. There were some shrewd operators out there and it was a very small market, albeit world-wide. All the top dealers knew who had the right cars and with values then reaching in excess of ten million pounds for a single car, it could be quite lucrative if you got your sums right.

Ted's office was a two room rented suite above the pub on the High Street in Henley on Thames. Suite was too grand a term for it, but that's what it said on the estate agent's blurb. James had the front room overlooking the road and Ted's office looked out over the car park and the bins behind. Both offices were fairly spartan in finish with just the essential office equipment, minimal furniture and the only giveaway they were trading in prestige cars were a few cheap randomly hung fading prints on the walls. The 1970's floral patterned carpets and yellowing paintwork would hardly inspire anyone into parting with their hard earned cash for their new car. There were no showrooms. All of Ted's cars at that time were customer cars or James' father's cars. Not really the basis of a good business, but a start nonetheless.

James leant against the door jamb of Ted's office dolled up to the nines in his blue and white striped shirt, navy trousers and brogues. He *was* Mr. Label if ever there was one. 'I've just spoken to Lawrence; he's a friend of my dad's. He wants a 355 Spider for his son's twenty-first birthday next Saturday. Do you know of anything? It's got to be yellow.'

'A bit short notice isn't it? He didn't wait for a response. I'll see what I can find.' Ted looked at his Patek wristwatch. 'Nearly time for lunch. I'll chase it after lunch,' he replied

This was the first real enquiry that Wedgewoods had taken and it was 12.15 pm, plenty of time to get on the phone before most people would grab something to eat. If Reed had a strong enquiry like that, he would be on it like a flash, seamless phone call after another until he found something or exhausted his enquiries. Ted was completely different, and James' playboy lifestyle showed an almost nonchalant attitude to his chosen career. Neither of them really knew what they were doing. They were just going through the motions. They looked good in their tailored suits, tiger eye cufflinks and silk ties. They felt good. They were good. They were businessmen running their own business and they liked playing the part, sales weren't important. A two hour lunch was par for the course. That's what real businessmen did.

EXETER, JULY 2008

CMU shoved the paperwork under the door of the cell. Reed heard the whoosh of the envelope sliding across the floor and got up from his bed to pick up the papers.

'It's my sentence report,' said Max slowly looking at the title lettering.

'What's it say?' Karl didn't move from his facedown position on the top bunk.

30

'I don't know. I'm just reading it.'

Reed read the Release Dates Notification Slip to himself.

Start of sentence date 24/07/2008, number of days in sentence 427, sentence expiry date 13/09/2009, conditional release date 12/02/2009, HDC eligibility date 29/10/2008 and licence expiry date 13/09/2009. Your sentence dates with all adjustments are shown above. Release on HDC is subject to an assessment. Please sign in the box below and return to your landing officer.

Reed read it three or four times, but he wasn't sure exactly what it meant. What he thought it meant was that provided he passed the necessary assessments, he could go home on tagging on the twenty-ninth of October. So, after being sentenced to fourteen months imprisonment in court, it was possible that he would be out after serving fourteen weeks. He couldn't believe it. Had they made a mistake? Was this the start of the mental torture?

Fourteen weeks was still a long time, but Reed could get his head around that. Fourteen months was a different thing altogether.

If he wanted anything in prison, he couldn't just ask for it. He had to fill in an application form detailing the information required and then hand it in to the landing officer between 8:15 am and 8:30 am. Hopefully he would get an answer the following day.

Reed filled out the application form asking for an appointment to see CMU, and placed it on the table.

The door crashed open. Reed jumped. 'Pack your things lads; you're moving – five minutes, 'A' Wing.' The cell door slammed shut.

Max and Karl looked at each other. After four days, they had just got settled and were a little more secure. Now what? 'A' wing. Tom Clock had said that was unlikely. They didn't have time to worry about it.

The guard lead the two of them down the landing through the steel caged doors and onto the hub. More keys, more locks, more bars.

'Wait here.' The guard swapped with another prison officer from 'A' Wing and ushered Max and Karl down the spiral staircase and onto Level 3. Squeezing past the landing office, the three of them stopped at cell A3-036.

'Right, in you get,' ordered the guard.

Max and Karl walked in and the door slammed behind them. It was disgusting, dirty socks and pants on the floor, dirty old bed linen strewn everywhere, a plastic bowl full of dog ends, rubbish and dirt all over the floor, the sink was full of grime. It was revolting. You wouldn't want to walk through it let alone live in it.

Reed looked at the toilet; there was crap all around the rim and over the seat hinge. The 'U' bend was black. It was enough to turn your stomach, and the smell. Well the smell of urine and stale smoke was overpowering.

Karl looked at Max. 'At least we've got a TV.'

The B4-05 cell was effectively two rooms as it had a separate WC and sink, but A3-036 was a single cell and had the toilet and the sink within the one area. The thought of having a crap whilst your pad mate was also in the cell was both funny and horrible at the same time.

The pair of them shared the duties, Reed drew the short straw and cleaned the toilet and the sink with the limited available cleaning equipment found behind the loo, and Karl did the floor, walls and surfaces. There were curtains made from bed linen hanging over the grilled unglazed windows, which Karl ripped down. Let there be light! There was one table, one locker and no chairs. All of it was rough. The television sat on top of the locker alongside the cell door, and only one pillow.

It took four hours to make the cell habitable, and that was in an area of fifteen foot by eight foot. Karl switched on the TV.

'No TV tonight, some bastard's wogged the fucking aerial.'

'I don't bloody believe it!' came the despondent reply.

Reed resigned himself to yet another long night and started counting the bricks.

PAU - FEBRUARY 2004

Jacques clicked on the start button and the five pages of text and photographs silently struggled out of the printer. He didn't speak the best of English but if he read it slowly, he could understand the basis of the text. EBay wasn't new to Jacques, he would quite often surf the motoring pages on the French site and had in fact bought a few items, giving him a feedback score of four. He wasn't bothered, feedback wasn't important to him as a casual buyer. The items he had bought arrived as described and on time, so he considered it a good service.

He read through the item description and slowly translated the English text. Judging from the pictures, it was exactly what he wanted. It was the right model year, the right colour combination exactly the same as the one he'd bought new in 1981 when he was eighteen and that was twenty-four years ago. Maybe it was rose tinted glasses and all that, but it still looked a great bike. He was getting excited thinking about it. However, he was concerned about the location of the bike. Newton Abbot, Devon, UK, and he was in Pau in the far south west of France. The advert read delivery possible.

Jacques thought about it for a while. He didn't think that the vendor would deliver the bike eight hundred kilometres or more. Maybe he would drive to Calais with a van. Yes, maybe he could do that. *Where is Newton Abbot anyway*, he thought. He switched the computer back on and immediately scrolled down to google.fr and typed in Newton Abbot, UK. He clicked on the Google map and a map of the UK south west peninsular came into view. Newton Abbot looked like it was about fifty or sixty kilometres north of Plymouth. The dotted lines on the map indicated that there was a Brittany ferry from Roscoff. Maybe he could drive to Roscoff. Maybe Plymouth. Maybe the seller would deliver the bike to Roscoff. It sounded like a lot of work for an old bike even though it did look like new. He'd deal with it later; he had a lot to do that day. Besides, the eBay auction was a ten day auction and still had eight days to run. Plenty of time to put a bid on it.

Saturday was normally Jacques day off but there were a few too many people away on holiday and his boss had asked him if he wouldn't mind covering the Saturday morning. He would work the half day finishing at one o'clock, but get paid for a full day. It seemed fair to him.

He'd worked for DHL in Pau since 1998, it was a no brainer. The pay was pretty good and whilst his wife Antoinette was bringing up their youngest child, she couldn't work, so Jacques was the bread winner. Yes, they could do with more money, but they were comfortable.

Antoinette had given him the green light to get a bike, but she couldn't see the fascination herself, although she did have fond memories of them both motorcycling in their late

33

teens. At the end of the month, Jacques would get the performance results of his depot and everyone in the organisation would be paid a bonus. Last year, they had beaten their target by one hundred and twenty percent and he had a windfall of three and a half thousand Euros. They were expecting to achieve a much better target bonus this year, so hopefully, he should get at least three and a half thousand Euros but maybe he could get a little bit more. For now, the double pay on Saturday was very welcome.

EXETER - JULY 2008

More keys jangling, more doors crashing shut, room service alarms bleeping, canteen staff slamming down towers of steel preformed trays. It wasn't Radio Two, not even Radio One. Another morning at Her Majesty's pleasure in one of Britain's finest hotels. Reed wondered if they would hang, the "no vacancies" sign out over the front door.

That morning, the guards would unlock five hundred and nine men in a jail designed to accommodate four hundred and ninety. Such was the overcrowding that the staffing levels and security were seriously flawed. If anything sparked off at opening times, it could get very difficult.

Reed handed in his applications to the landing officer, one to see the CMU and the other for some phone card credit, and then took his bowl down to the canteen and stood in line. In the distance, the crack heads lined up outside the hub gate jittering for their morning slow down fix at the happy hatch. Karl was back down the line as Reed returned to A3-036 and placed his cereal filled bowl onto the table. He needed some hot water to fill his flask. The boiler was on the landing ten feet from his door. He picked up the flask and turned towards the door, just as the Pheasant burst through the door and rammed Reed up against the back wall, pinning him to the spot with his forearm across his throat. Reed didn't struggle. He thought about it, and then thought better of it.

'Know who I am? I'm the Pheasant and I run this fucking jail. Got it? It's my gaff. You fucking answer to me, nobhead.'

Reed nodded, all bug eyed. He had no idea who the

34

Pheasant was, but he knew now.

'You want anything, you come to me. Burn, works, stuff, you fucking get it from me, you cunt. You wanna do anything, you ask me. You go against me. You in the yard yesterday?'

Reed nodded.

'Well, that's what happens when you upset the Pheasant. So we know where we stand.' The pheasant took his forearm away from Reed's throat, still looking at Reed six inches from his face.

He was so close that Reed was finding it difficult to focus on him. He'd never forget that face or the vile smell of his warm breath. Cold grey, bulging, piercing eyes, angular jaw line, fair hair shaved at the sides, long at the top pulled back over his head into a small bun tied at the rear centre of his head. He had a white sallow complexion, a couple of day's stubble and a chiselled Roman nose.

He stood about five ten, maybe six foot, was solidly and squarely built, big arms, big chest, thick neck, not fat. He obviously worked out, he was a powerful man and he was evil.

The Pheasant moved away from Reed and then gently straightened Reed's T-shirt and stroked out the creases across Reed's shoulder.

'See, no harm done. We have an understanding.'

Reed didn't realise it was a question.

He raised his voice and repeated, 'We have an understanding?'

'Yes, we do,' Reed croaked.

'Good, then we'll get along just fine. Best mates eh?'

Reed nodded, daring not to do anything else.

The Pheasant cracked a smile, opened his eyes wide and said, 'Now, I've got your attention haven't I?'

'Yeah', said Max and calmly sat down at his desk. The whole incident no more than a passing couple of minutes.

The Pheasant turned and walked out the door, barging past Karl as he returned with his breakfast, knocking him against the door frame as he did so and spilling his milk and cornflakes over Karl, down his front and all over the floor.

'What's he doing in here?'

'Karl, you don't want to know.' Reed rubbed his neck. It felt like he'd had the cartilage crushed in his throat. He needed a drink. His heart still pounding. If he had pockets, he would have stuck his hands in them, he was trembling that much.

Reed picked up his flask and went to the boiler, his hands shaking as he filled it to the brim, constantly looking around and behind him. Ten minutes and he needed to be in the education department. He scoffed his breakfast and took a few swigs of tea, grabbed his paperwork and shot off the landing, down the stair well and waited in the queue.

There was a small corridor between the lower landing and the exit for the yard between A Wing and the education block. A guard had unlocked the door to the yard and was holding the gate closed with his foot from the outside whilst chatting to a couple of prisoners standing at the front of the queue.

When commanded, the prisoners would walk through the gate, thirty meters across the yard, up the twenty steps and through another guarded, gated entrance to the education block.

There was shouting on the landing above as a prisoner was racing down the stairs, more *glockenspiels*. A couple of prison officers were wobbling in pursuit. More guards were joining the race. The inmate charged towards Reed, barging past him and the rest of the queue, arriving at the gate with such force that it swung open and slammed the guard against the wall behind him. Five overweight guards roared past Reed, the first one being tripped up. They all fell to the ground in a big heap, nobody helped, the inmates just laughed. The prisoner was confronted by more guards in the yard, there was fighting and then he was easily pushed to the ground, face down with a guard's knee across the back of his neck and three other bodies keeping him pinned down. He was shouting out as he was cuffed and led away to solitary. God knows, what it was about.

Reed had been confronted by a psychopath before breakfast, witnessed an ugly fight and it wasn't even 9:00 am. The animals were wrestles. What next?

TEIGNMOUTH, NOVEMBER 1974

When Max was at Buck House, he never had a good report. He'd lost count of the number of beatings he had at the hands of his father because of it. Hands, slippers, canes and even the strap. Every end of term, something to look forward to when he got home.

His father had always said Max was thick, a complex he held for many years after. He thought he *was* thick. The reality was that he wasn't thick, quite the contrary, he just didn't apply himself. In contrast, his younger brother Neil was father's blue eyed boy and always had a good report with glowing comments from the headmaster.

Derek had always said, 'I don't know what I'm going to do with you Max.' Always ramming home the point that, 'do you have any idea how hard I work to pay those school fees?'

Max never had a reply and knowing the length of his father's fuse, he was never likely to either.

But when Max got into Teignmouth Grammar School, it was all change, a double whammy. Firstly Max got in which was something his father was immensely proud of, but secondly there were no more school fees to pay. Derek would only see one Teignmouth Grammar School report.

Caro met Reed at the school gate and they ambled home together, feverishly talking about this and that. All her family, his family. All the usual stuff. Max couldn't tell her everything, some things were better not said, but he told her the good things, sadly that didn't take long. It was the beginning of a relationship that at the time would transcend all others and last many years. They agreed to meet the following morning, at the bottom of her drive. It was early days.

Autumn merged into winter, Reed was fourteen in mid November. Christmas was on its way; Neil would be back from boarding at Buck House in a few weeks time. The old man was leaving Max alone and Max was sill riding the crest of the wave having made it into the Grammar school.

Reed liked Caro a lot. She was a pretty girl, mousey shoulder length hair parted at the side, blue eyes, a small turned up nose, nice body, a little bit shorter than Max and she was easy to talk to. He could talk to her about anything really and they'd spend hours together listening to music, doing homework, revising. Max had got to know Caro's family and often stayed for lunch or tea at the weekends. On occasion, Caro would help Reed with his weekend paper round. They just liked each other's company. It didn't stop Reed from going out with other girls or off with his mates, but she was always there for him and him for her.

Max liked Caro's parents. They were nice normal

people. They didn't shout at their children, they didn't seem to argue. It was a world away from the knife edge life that Reed had survived for the last fourteen years. He wished that if only his family could have been the same.

HENLEY ON THAMES, MAY 2000

Ted Little leafed through the Ferrari section of the Top Marques magazine carefully reading every advert looking for a Yellow Ferrari 355 Spider for his customer. All the private adverts with pictures had red 355's or the occasional black, but no yellow. He must have read it three or four times before realising that nobody had one. In some respects, that was good news, because if he couldn't find one easily, then it would mean that it wouldn't be that simple for the customer either.

He started calling the dealers asking the same questions over and over again.

Someone was being served at the parts counter. Mike turned to the customer and said, 'I'll be with you in a minute, I'll just answer this call, good afternoon Velodrome, how can I help you?'

Ted Little asked to speak to someone in sales.

'Which department do you want, cars or bikes?'

'You do bikes as well, what sort of bikes?'

'All sorts, mainly competition off road, a few sports bikes and some classic stuff as well.'

'Oh, that's interesting. It's the car side I'm interested in though today.'

'If you would like to hold the line a moment, I'll try to put you through to Max.'

Mike pressed Max's line and he picked up.

'Yes Mike.'

'I've got a car enquiry for you.'

'Okay thanks, put him through.'

'Hello, can I help you,' said Max.

'Well, yes I hope you can. I'm calling from a company called Wedgewood's in Henley on Thames. We sell prestige cars and we have a customer looking for a yellow 355 Spider, but it must be yellow.'

'Well, I haven't got one in stock. I have several 355's

but not a yellow Spider. Do you have a price range?'

'I suppose £75,000 would be the ceiling,' said Ted.

'Do you have a spec in mind?'

'No, I think anything will do within reason.' He didn't know because he hadn't asked his customer the question. He was just guessing.

'At £75,000 you won't get a right hand drive car. I don't think you'd get a high mileage early 1995 car for that sort of money. Would you be okay with left hand drive?' Max asked.

'I'd have to check, but I think that would be okay. The customer has several homes abroad. I'd have to ask,' said Ted.

'I was with a customer last week and he had a 1999 355 Spider in yellow with dark blue leather, dark blue roof, challenge rear grill and a sports pipe. He was considering selling it. I think it had done about eight and a half thousand kilometres, roughly five thousand miles. It was a manual car. If that's any good to you, I can call him and check.'

Ted liked the sound of the car and asked Max to ring the customer and give him a call back. Max took his number down, cut the connection, and immediately pecked out the number for Christian.

'Good afternoon, Testastretta.'

'Hi, is that you Chris?' said Max.

'Yes.'

'It's Max.'

'Oh, hi Max, how are you?'

'Fine, where's Claire today?'

'Oh, she's just gone off to post some parts etc.' said Chris. 'She'll be back in a minute! What can I do for you today?'

'Have you still got that yellow 355 Spider?'

'Yes, I have.'

'Could you tell me all about it?'

'Yes, I'll just go and get the file.' Max listened to Chris moving around his office opening and shutting a filing cabinet. 'Right then, it's a 99 on a 'T', eight and a half thousand kilometres, MOT'd two weeks ago, Full Ferrari service history with Zoller Ferrari, last serviced two months ago with Zoller at seven thousand four hundred and eleven kilometres with the belts done at the same time. Giallo fly yellow, dark blue leather, piped yellow, blue carpets, red callipers, challenge grill, manual oh and electric seats. Paint is excellent, needs nothing, nice car.'

Max asked, 'What do you need for it?'

'As much as I can get. It's not my car, it's here on sale or return, but it is for sale.' Chris forgot to mention the sports pipe.

'What will you take?'

'I suppose it's got to be £70K.'

'That's probably a bit too much for my man.'

'Well, where do you see it?'

'Sixty five.'

'Yeah, I don't think I can do it for that, I'll see what I can do. Give me five minutes and I'll give you a call back.'

Max put the phone down and Mike buzzed him.

'Yes, Mike.'

'It's Ted Little for you.'

'Okay thanks, put him through. Yes, Ted.'

Ted confirmed that the spec was okay and left hand drive was not a problem. 'Look, if we do a deal, I'll need the car ready to go this Saturday.'

'Okay, well, I've just spoken to the customer and he said he'd call me back. As soon as I know what the position is, I will call you.'

'Okay, thanks,' said Ted and ended the call.

Max's line was buzzing, it was an internal call. 'Yes, Pete?'

'What's the stand in value on the SP5?'

'From memory, I think I wrote it back to twelve and a half. I'll check in a minute.' Max was turning the pages of the stock book. 'Yes, it's twelve thousand five hundred. It's not on the system yet, but Kevin will put it on later today or tomorrow.'

'That's good,' said Pete.

'Got something cooking?'

'I've got a guy, been in twice already and he's got a 916 SPS and he doesn't like it. He's quite tall and it's hurting his neck riding it, so he wants out of it, and fancies our 888.'

'What's he valuing the SPS at?'

'Well, he paid £21,750 from Riders for it, two months ago and he's hardly done a couple hundred miles on it.'

'Finance?'

'He says not, but obviously, I'll check.'

'Have you got anybody for it?'

'I might have, but I wouldn't want you to think it's a straight in and out.'

'Have you discussed figures?'

40

'Yes, I'm looking at obviously a backward deal. Our bike plus £3,000.'

'Would he do it for that?'

'Yes, I think he would. Does the 888 need anything?'

'The back tyre looks like it's getting a bit low, it definitely needs a battery and an MOT, and it's had a recent service, so not much. Just a pdi (pre delivery inspection). If we've got that much in the deal, we'll put a new tyre on it and keep the old one. If you do the deal, make sure you put that on the service works sheet.'

'Yes, okay.'

'Pete?'

'Yes, obviously chip him if you can, let me know.'

'Of course.'

Max put the phone down. He trusted Pete, he was a good guy: he'd worked for Max from the start. They'd both been at Teignmouth Grammar School together and Max had gone out with his wife before Pete and Penny had met. Ultimately, Max wanted to step back from the front line and hand over the reins to Pete when the time was right. That wasn't now but hopefully some time in the future.

Pete had worked at TVM Yamaha for many years until they'd gone bust in the late 1980's and then gone to work for the Mitsubishi dealer in Torquay. A slight product change to say the least. After a few years, he moved on to Volvo Exeter.

When Max had started the business in 1987, he was operating out of a small unit on the outskirts of the town. Pete had rolled up on his Triumph Tiger one afternoon. Max recognised him immediately even though it had been a good ten years since the last time they'd seen each other.

Pete was fed up at Volvo, and liked the idea of a change, but he was comfortable there and he wasn't about to risk all for a change. Or at least, that was what Max thought.

The conversation revolved around old times, old bikes, do you remember when stories, but after a while the pair of them were talking seriously about Pete joining Max. The worry for Max was that he didn't want to take on Pete and then have to lose him because the business couldn't afford him. Max deliberated for about a week and rang Pete.

'Life's too short Pete, come and sell some bikes for me.'

Pete didn't hesitate and that was the start of some wonderful years.

41

Chris rang back from Testastretta, 'Max, when would you be looking to do the deal?'

'Well, if the guy accepts it, then it will be in the next couple of days. I'd come up on the train. Could you collect me from Paddington or is it easier to get a cab?'

'Graeme's away at the moment with our supplier, so it would be better to cab it.'

'Okay, so what's it got to be?'

'I can do it for sixty-nine thousand five hundred.'

'Sounds like sixty six to me.'

'Look, Max, I haven't got a lot in it. It's not my car, you know how it works; they always want more than it's worth.'

'I'll go to sixty eight thousand and confirm it later one way or the other.'

'You're a hard man Max; okay give me a buzz later.'

'Will do, bye.'

Max put the phone down.

'Yes, Mike.'

'It's Ted on the phone.'

'Thanks, put him through. Hi Ted.'

'Hi, any news on the 355?'

'Yes, I can definitely offer you the car. It needs nothing.'

Max read out the full specification and confirmed Ted could have it in two days.

'How much do you need for it?'

'Seventy four thousand,' said Max.

'Oooh, that's a bit tight.'

'Yeah, I could probably squeeze him up a bit; can you give me a little off that?'

'Such as?'

'Would you take £73,500?'

'Are you offering £73,500?'

'Yeah, okay, £73, 500,' said Ted.

'Okay, we have a deal.' Max took down all Ted's details and wrote out a contract as they talked and agreed to meet Ted at his office in Henley-on-Thames two days later at 2:00 pm. No two-hour lunch for Ted then, that day.

Max rang Chris at Testastretta just before closing time and confirmed the deal and asked Chris to make sure he had all the documents. Max stood up, stretched out his arms, switched off all the electrical equipment and walked into the showroom. Pete was packing up his day-to-day diary.

'Good day?' asked Max.

'Cor yeah, you should have seen the bird that came in earlier, Oh, absolutely stunning. Legs up to here, tits out here. I think Mike was having a wank somewhere; he was gone for ages.'

Max laughed.

'No seriously, the Ducati guy is bringing the SPS in tomorrow morning, so I'm hoping that's a deal. A couple of good enquiries. Plenty on the go. I'll tell you in the morning,' said Pete. 'You?'

'I've done a 355 on the phone, so should complete that in a couple days.'

'Well not a bad day then?'

The pair of them walked down the showroom, locked the doors, set the alarm and stepped out into the evening light.

EXETER, JULY 2008

Reed quickly realised that the only way to get through the prison sentence was to fill his day with all the offers available to him. Do as many courses on offer however menial. There was the BICS cleaning course, Men's Health, Food hygiene, Manual handling, Gym. He enrolled in them all. He could also do art, IT, library etc but they would possibly cross over with the courses. The first step was the literacy and numeracy test that he got 100% in. Not difficult. The examiner looked at the results and asked Reed, 'Have you done this before?'

'No,' replied Reed.

'I don't know if it would interest you, but we could do with someone like you to help some people with their learning. All you'd have to do is be on hand to assist them. You know, don't give them the answers; just try to tease it out of them. It would mean you coming in for an hour or so, sort of every other day and then help them with their letters in the library on a Friday.'

'Yeah, fine by me,' said Reed, anything to get me out of that cell.

'I'll speak to the head of education, and they'll pop a note under your cell door in the next couple of days. You'll still

43

be able to do your courses. It shouldn't affect that.' The day passed more quickly, Karl didn't go out into the playground, but Tom Clock was there. They sat on the same bench and passed the time of day. A gaggle of Russians strutted past, two Slovaks, a Moroccan awaiting deportation and Shooey the ex British ABA boxing champion who'd also represented Great Britain in the 1984 Olympics. The variety was fascinating.

'How's your pad mate?' asked Tom.

'He's okay; he's just being a bit lazy at the moment. He'll be fine.'

'Any news on your transfer?'

'No nothing yet.'

'You'll get it soon enough. This is a harsh prison for a hard crime. Your crime is nothing. It's not right that you're here. The punishment doesn't fit the crime. You'll go soon.'

'So how does this all work then?'

'What do you mean?'

'Well the prison categories . . .'

Tom interrupted, 'Well, this is a Cat B remand prison, so prisoners are kept here if their crimes are serious enough, or if they're considered a danger to the public, between the time they're charged and the time they go to court, so that's the first bit, the remand. As a Cat B prison, it will hold serious offenders, murderers, violent criminals, armed robbers, gbh, abh, lifers, paedophiles, it's got the lot. This isn't a maximum security prison, that's a Cat A or Cat AA. Dartmoor used to be a Cat A, but now it's a Cat B. Channings Wood is a Cat C and Leyhill and Ford are Cat D's.'

Reed listened intently. 'All the courts local to Exeter will use Exeter as the remand and first point sentencing prison, so if you get sent down at Exeter, Plymouth, Truro or Bridgwater, you're most likely to come here. Exeter will then hold you for a few weeks and CMU will then distribute you through the prison network depending on availability and your category.'

'And what about the prisoner category?' asked Reed.

'Well, they're much the same. Cats A to D.' Tom leant forward with his elbows on his knees and his hands outstretched before him. Spreading his four fingers, he tapped out.

'Cat A, the lunatic fringe, rag heads terrorists, serial rapists, murderers, multiple lifers. Cat B and C is the most common ranging from serious drink driving offences, to manslaughter, murderers, sex offenders, and violent crime. Cat D

44

is minor non violent generally white collar crime, fraud that sort of thing. So you being a Cat D prisoner you should be in a Cat D prison. Cat D prisons are open prisons, so there are no cells, you get a room. You are more or less free to come and go. You get your own single room and your own key, basically home from home. Serving time at a Cat D is not like serving a sentence in a Cat A, B or C, it's a lot softer, more of an inconvenience to you than a sentence.'

Tom rolled a cigarette lit up and took a drag, 'You know, this must have been a bloody awful place when it was built. No electric, no toilets in the cells, just buckets.'

'Looks like mid nineteenth century,' said Max.

'Yeah, I think it was 1870 or thereabouts. Someone was saying that the nonce wing still has buckets.'

'Nonce wing?' asked Reed.

'Yeah, it's where all the kiddie fiddlers are. D Wing. It's over the back of C Wing. You can't get to it. You know when you go to the gym? There are the gates on the right with the caged tunnel?'

'Yeah.'

'They call it the hamster run. That's it. It goes down to 'D' Wing. They're completely separated from the rest of us, otherwise they'd get killed. Any violent criminal in here would rip them apart. As far as they are concerned, their crimes are one thing, but the nonces shouldn't be on this Earth.'

Tom looked across at the centre pole. 'There used to be a huge oak tree in the middle there. It's where they used to hang people.'

Reed liked his casual chats with Tom. He was an old hand, he knew all about what was going on around him.

The guards blew their whistles and shouted A Wing, C Wing. Tom and Reed stood up and followed the crowd back down the steps and onto A Wing.

'See you tomorrow Tom.'

'Yep, I'm not going anywhere,' he replied with a wry smile.

Reed went up the two flights of steep steps to his landing and waited for the guard to open his cell door.

Tom was on C Wing, so he walked through A Wing, through the hub, past the hub office and onto C Wing.

Reed opened the flap on the archer's window and could see Karl lying on his bed. No change there. The guard opened the cell door. Reed shuffled in. Surprisingly the TV was on! Bargain Hunt was on.

'Hey, what happened there then?' asked Max looking at the television.

'I smiled sweetly at Mrs. Naylor and she said she pinched the aerial off someone else!'

'Great.

'And we've got some chairs too.' said Karl.

'Oh, that's all right then. At least we can sit down and eat. Things are looking up.'

PAU - FEBRUARY 2004

Jacques didn't have broadband. They didn't have it where he lived. They were still on the slower speed dial up, which was fine for ninety nine per cent of his surfing but it was a real problem if he was trying to bid on an online auction, usually because by the time the page refreshed, if he was nearing the end of the auction, it will have probably finished and left him out in the cold.

He figured out that if he was to try to win an item, he would need to bid his maximum amount fifty seconds before the end of the auction. Then, by the time the page refreshed, he would have about five to eight seconds left to see if he was the high bidder. Another fifty seconds and he'd know if he'd won the item.

He clicked on "Mes favorites" and the eBay item popped up on the screen. Thirty-two minutes remaining and it was already at three thousand seven hundred and seventy Euros and hadn't reached its reserve. There were over thirty bids. He wasn't the only interested party. Obviously, these bikes were quite desirable and this model maybe more so because it was the same bike that was used on the bob sleigh run in the James Bond film *For Your Eyes Only*.

He thought about it for a moment and reckoned that the reserve would be four thousand Euros or just below. There was no gauge to measure it by, there were so few available these days, but surely it couldn't be five thousand Euros could it, he thought.

He looked at his watch. It was just gone 8:30 in the evening. He looked back at the screen, twenty-eight minutes remaining. Auction end nine pm CET, Paris. He'd go back to his computer in twenty minutes.

TEIGNMOUTH, DECEMBER 1974

Max's father had a half day on Thursdays so he collected Neil from school at the end of the autumn term. It was December seventeenth 1974. Max was still at school until the following day, but he was looking forward to seeing Neil. It had been five weeks since he was home during the half term break.

'How goes it bro?' Neil asked out of parental earshot.

'Yeah fine. What about you?'

'Yes, I'm okay.'

'Anything new at Bucks?'

'No still the same,' Neil replied.

'What about Guss? Still taking the pictures?'

'What do you think? Yeah of course he is. That Brett business hasn't stopped him. Benjamin took over up the Lobster Pot for a couple of weeks, but Guss has been up there ever since. He's still up to his tricks. Stromberg's gone.'

'Yeah, Mum told me. What happened there?'

'I don't know. Something to do with something he did when he was in Stockholm. Nobody has told us. What about here?'

'It's been okay. They've not been arguing, so that's good news. We went fishing Sunday. God it was boring. Bloody cold as well. Father lost one of his rods over the side. We had a good race with Restless on the way back from Thatcher Rock.'

'Who won?'

'Restless, by about a boat length. It was good though. We were flat out. I saw Hopper yesterday, he asked when you'd be back.'

'I'll pop over tomorrow, if we're not doing anything,' Neil said.

Restless was a pleasure boat now, but in its heyday was a fast launch boat built at Morgan Giles boatyard on the Teign. It had now been converted for fee paying passengers tripping around the bay and into Brixham. Max's father's boat had been built in 1972 by Harry Sealey's boat builders, again on the Teign. Everyone knew each other on the back beach at Teignmouth, it was fun friendly rivalry.

'Mother's been getting fatter by the day. They're going

47

on about it all the time.'

'When's it due?' Neil asked.

'A couple of weeks, I think. When are you going back?'

'I think it's the sixth January.'

'Well, we've got a while then. It said on the news, it might snow at the weekend. I don't think we have to go into the shop next week, but I know there's a large delivery of coal coming and couple loads of logs. We'll have to unload that lot and chop the logs if we want some money for Christmas. I think he said the coal's coming Monday and the logs Wednesday or Thursday.'

EXETER, JULY 2008

The day had come and gone and Reed was resigning himself to thinking that he would serve his sentence in its entirety in Exeter's B Cat prison. He had got used to the regime. It was not a lot different to Buck House in many ways, same incarceration, the room mates were a bit livelier though. CMU had told him that he would be shipped out on the Friday after he had arrived. It was now Sunday, nearly a week later and CMU were saying Monday or Tuesday but not with any conviction. Mind games. He didn't trust them; in fact, he really didn't feel he could trust anyone after what he had just been through.

Karl was pleased because it meant he didn't have to cope with the possibility of a new hairy arsed inmate to take Reed's place. *Just get through it*, he thought. *Just get through it. Ignore the inner rage and deal with it.*

The day had started all too early, in fact just before 3:00 am. Max heard Karl get down uneasily from his upper bunk and shuffle the four feet to the loo, the first of many sorties that night. It was unusually quiet except for the muffled groans from Karl as he tried unsuccessfully to slow down the massive back pressure in his system. And then it started, like machine gun fire, a thousand rounds in a minute, an upside down firework display going off in the bowl. The noise of whooshing air, exploding gases and the splattering of violent diarrhoea as it smashed against the sidewalls and splashed at full throttle into the waiting U-bend. It went on for ten minutes or so, sporadic shots accompanied by long sighs and deep intakes of breath. Then, in the middle of it all, Karl giggled uncontrollably like a nervous hyena.

No matter how hard Max tried to remove himself from the ordeal, it wasn't going to work. In such a confined space, the first wave of gas bellowed from the bowl like a gale force wind, rushing over Max's hidden face, but inevitably the odour broke through like a cloud of mustard gas in world war one, creeping upon him invisibly but somehow slightly warm. There were three more visits to the loo that night all vying for the best performance and all enough to turn your stomach. Eventually, Max fell asleep, but the bombing raid was all too evident the following morning.

'Hi, I'm Reed and you are?'

'Blake,' came the reply.

'First things first. I'm not here to write a letter to your girlfriend or wife. That's your job, but I will help you. Who's it to?'

'Lilla.'

'Have you made a start?'

Blake pulled a piece of paper from his back pocket and handed it to Reed. There were three lines of writing on it. The writing was appalling and the spelling hopeless.

A lot of prisoners are the same – soft centre with a hard exterior. Get through to their soft side and you can reveal a totally different person to the grade one haired, tattoo riddled, muscular thug. Often, they've had the worst of upbringing and society hasn't been kind to them. Crime, for them is a way of life. Often said, but rarely thought about seriously.

Reed looked at Blake. 'I think the best thing is to start again. What do you want to say to her?"

'I want to tell her I love her, I miss her and I'm sorry,' he said sheepishly.

'Will she be there for you when you get out?'

'Oh yeah 'course.'

'How long are you in for?'

'Five years. GBH and robbery. It's the second time. We robbed a post office and I gave the guy a bit of a slap.'

'Okay, well let's get going.'

Reed helped Blake write his letter. A single A5 size page with large lettering took nearly half an hour and there was still a queue out of the door when he sent Blake on his way.

The letter writing helped Reed, because he got to know

49

more people on the wing and that way they were less scary. Also, they needed Reed. The word got out, Reed was a novice, but he was an okay guy. Reed wasn't a criminal in their eyes, he was a straight guy. He wasn't muscled with tattoos, he didn't have a grade one haircut, he spoke well, he didn't swear. He was like their brief.

For the remainder of Reed's time on A Wing, life was less heart in mouth. Reed no longer felt that he was at the bottom of a shark and barracuda infested pool trying to reach the surface with his air tanks empty. It wasn't so frightening. He was still wary, but he had come to terms with it. The sharks had confidence in him.

Now he had prisoners coming to his door, asking for legal letters to be read and explained to them, drafting short replies, answering questions. He thought he'd heard everything but the answers the remand guys had for their actions were as far fetched as you could possibly get. It was amazing, funny almost, but the thing is, a lot of them would get away with what they had done, or the charges would be dropped or lowered. It was a game to them. A3-036 during association breaks, free time breaks, had fast become a drop in citizens' advice bureau.

Reed didn't do it for nothing. Every man had his price, but in a market place with no money, currency was canteen, and canteen was tea bags, fresh milk, biscuits, chocolate etc.

The screws turned a blind eye. Reed was providing a service and the prisoners were going away happy. On the last day in "A" Wing, a real thug showed up at Reed's door, darkening the cell as he did so. Karl was lying face down on his top bunk as usual, sleeping through his sentence.

'Hey mate.' His voice sounded totally at odds with his appearance.

'Yeah,' said Reed, looking up.

'I've had a letter from my missus. Can you read it to me? I've got four sachets of sugar; that okay?' He couldn't read or write.

'Yes, that's fine; sit yourself down.'

Reed took the envelope, opened the letter, and turned it over.

'It's from Lucy.'

'Yeah, that's the missus.'

'Okay, here goes.

'Dear Si, I hope everything is okay with you. I miss you

a lot. I saw your mother today and she sends her love. I also saw Dave. He brought round more of the money. He says he'll bring the rest of it next week. I need to know what you want me to do. Please ring me on my mobile when you get your phone credit. I have put a £10 postal order in. I'll send more next week. I s'pose you're missing East Enders. What's your cellmate like?'

'I went shopping with Di and Trix yesterday. We had a great time. Trix had away about five hundred quid's worth. I bumped into Shazza, she sends her love, cow!

'When we got home last night, we'd had a few drinks. Di and Trix left about nine. I was feeling so hot. I couldn't stop thinking about you. I went upstairs and put on your favourite outfit. You know the black one. Black basque, black stockings, and those tiny black panties you bought me and my highest heels. I felt so sexy. I stood in front of the mirror pretending you were with me. I started lightly fondling my nipples and then slipping my fingers inside my top. My nipples were standing up like organ stops. I was aching for you. I felt everywhere and then slid my hands into my panties the way you like it and fingered my clit imagining you were there licking me. I was so horny. I laid on the edge of the bed, got the vibe out, the one with the rabbit. That just blows my mind. I pulled my panties to one side and fucked myself, slowly at first then quicker and quicker. You were there. You were with me. I had a huge orgasm. You were completely spent. You held me in your arms and I fell asleep. I know you can't read this but it turns me on knowing someone will read it to you.

'Gotta go, Trix will be here in a minute.

'Love you babe.

'Lucy. Loads of kisses etc.'

Reed said, 'That's it.' The letter had been difficult to read. It was basically one sentence from beginning to end, no punctuation, no capital letters, no full stops, and the spelling was atrocious but they all got the drift.

Si looked at Reed. 'She's a dirty bitch my missus, thanks for that. My pad mate's having a shower in a minute, I need to sort this out,' he said looking down. There wasn't a dry eye in the house.

Si left Reed's cell, his dick pointing the way to his own apartment further along the landing.

Reed looked at Karl. 'I think I've definitely heard it all now.'

They laughed. It kept them smiling all day. *Incredible,* he thought. His facial expression said it all.

PAU, FEBRUARY 2004

Jacques was elated. He'd gone back to his computer with three minutes to go. The bidding had gone over four thousand Euros and the green numbering indicated that the reserve price had been met. He'd worked out the time remaining and tapped in four thousand seven hundred and fifty Euros with fifty seconds to go. The dial up speed refreshed the page with ten seconds left, Jacques was the highest bidder at four thousand two hundred and sixty Euros. He clicked refresh again and fifty seconds later the page refreshed showing the auction had ended. Jacques had won the item, but there must have been some last minute bidding which upped his winning bid to four thousand six hundred and ten Euros.

He quickly emailed the seller, giving him all of his details, address, telephone number, mobile number and asked him to call. He said he could speak a little English, but noted that the seller could speak a little French as shown on the advert.

He knew that Antoinette wouldn't have wanted him to spend as much as that, but it was done. He was happy. He had enough to send the seller a deposit as a gesture of good faith and would be able to sort out the balance when he got his bonus, at the end of the following week. Hopefully he would get more than the three thousand five hundred Euros he'd got last year. He'd make it up to Antoinette later.

What Jacques couldn't have realised at the time was that in pressing that button he had started a chain of events that was going to change his life and others for the better forever.

EXETER, JULY 2008

Catherine couldn't get to visit Max in the first two weeks of his imprisonment. They had spoken on the phone a couple of times, but it was short and difficult. Catherine was hurting. She felt betrayed. Her marriage of twenty-three years seemed

52

irreparably damaged. She wanted to trust Max, she wanted to believe what he was saying but he had kept everything from her. Max had kept it all to himself. She'd had no idea what was going on, and she would have been the only person that could have helped him. She had a legal mind. Her father was a solicitor, her brother was a solicitor, and her brother in law was a principal partner in one of the big London law firms. She had worked with her father for fifteen years. She kept asking herself why Max hadn't turned to her for help. He was a brilliant dad, a faithful partner, worked hard and had a great sense of humour and he was well liked by his friends. Why didn't he confide in her? So many questions and no answers.

Maybe that was an issue for another day. All she knew now was that he was suffering and she couldn't do anything about it. She couldn't imagine what it would be like for him. Maybe he deserved to be punished, she didn't know, but not what he was experiencing now. She had spoken to Max's solicitor several times and met him at his office in Cardiff. They'd gone through everything but he really didn't inspire her with any confidence. She could understand what had happened, that was the easy bit. She knew Max would not have done anything criminal with intent, but somehow if it was going to happen, it would happen to Max. And the funny thing was that her perception of Max's solicitor, the answers he gave her and the flippant manner in which he dismissed questions with off the cuff weak and unconvincing answers lead her to think that perhaps Max had not had the best advice. If Max had, as she thought, taken his solicitor at his word, which she was sure he would have done, then the writing would have been on the wall right from the start.

Catherine arrived at the prison and parked her Land Rover in the overcrowded car park. The back end was sticking out, but she couldn't do anything about it. She thought to herself. She looked up, God, what a place and that was just from the outside looking in. Max was on the other side. All visitors report here the sign proclaimed. Catherine passed over the correct paperwork and sat in the waiting room like a second class citizen. She was fifteen minutes early.

On the other side of the prison, Max's cell door opened.

'Reed, visit, out,' said the landing officer just like that.

Max followed others down to the visits hall and queued in the hallway behind the locked door. Ahead, lay the checkpoint and the visiting hall beyond.

Visitors were called through one at a time into the search lobby. The drugs dog walked around Catherine as the guard patted her down. The dog indicated the presence of drugs.

The guard looked at Catherine. 'You will have to have a closed visit.'

'What do you mean?' said Catherine.

'The dog is indicating drugs on you.'

'I've never taken drugs in my life.' Catherine was incensed.

'You can still have the visit but it will be reduced to one hour and it will be closed behind glass,' said the prison officer.

Catherine was distraught, but any visit was better than no visit.

Max crossed the checkpoint and signed the entry form into the visits hall. He couldn't see Catherine anywhere. There were loads of visitors sat at fixed tables all around the room but Catherine wasn't at any of them. A guard caught Reed's attention and showed him into a closed room. He sat down. Catherine was sat tearfully opposite. A fixed pane of glass separated them. It was like something out of an American thriller. Totally unfair.

They talked, they cried, they talked more and they cried more. The hour passed in a blink of an eye. The guard came and took Reed away. Catherine cried as Max was lead back out of the hall. She walked back to the car and sat in the driving seat for several minutes gathering her thoughts and composing herself.

Reed had got as far as the area beyond the checkpoint. Closed visits were not good news.

'Shirt off,' ordered the guard.

'What?' Reed replied. There was no point being civil to them, they weren't worth it.

'You heard, step into the cubicle and take your shirt off.' Max did as he was told, but he was boiling inside. The guard was an arrogant twat, he thought.

'Shoes.' He took his shoes off and put them to one side.

'Socks.' Reed removed his socks.

Soon enough he was naked, standing in front of the two guards.

'Turn around.' Max turned around.

'Hands up above your head.' Max did as he was told.

'Touch your toes.' Max turned around, his eyes wild

with anger. 'What do you mean, touch my toes? Are you some kind of fucking pervert?'

'Do as you're told and do it now.'

Max turned around and touched his toes, then stood up and looked over his shoulder. One of the guards was putting on a pair of rubber gloves.

'Jesus Christ, what now,' Reed spat out.

The guard replied, 'If you don't like the job, don't do it! Now crouch down.'

The guard placed one hand on Reed's left shoulder and ran his other hand along Reed's backside.

'Right get dressed and stand over there.'

Reed was seething and did his best to fix a stare that said it all to the guard. The guard looked away. Reed considered the indignity of it all. He'd said it many times before, but he didn't deserve this. If you hadn't been through it, you cannot imagine the mental torture of it. The feeling that you just want to batter the guy to a pulp. Max was totally enraged within.

Reed said to himself, *I've got to get through this; beat the bastards.* He smiled. *Always look on the bright side of life, di dum, di dum, di dumpty dumpty dum. Always look on the bright side of life.*

BUCKFASTLEIGH, APRIL 1982

Sunday mass was heavy duty religion. One and a half hours of full on prayer, sanctimony and hymns all conducted in Latin. A small congregation of maybe less than fifty sporadically filled the public seating area. Ahead of them lay the extravagances of their faith. Sixty monks stood in their tiered stalls, flanked by the full school choir on the public side and the hierarchy of the abbey on the altar side.

Father Abbot walked down the aisle, in full regalia swinging the incense bowl forward and back creating a small smoke screen along his path. The smell wafted across the assembled onlookers as he returned to his position behind the altar holding his palms up in prayer.

Leo Easton absorbed the spectacle in his new itchy clothes. At the signal, he would take his confirmation and receive his first Holy Communion. This was a big day for Leo and it meant everything to his parents Jane and Peter. Being life long practising Catholics, they'd been coming to the abbey for over fifteen years since they moved down and knew nearly every monk on a first named basis. Jane Easton worked in the abbey half a day a week changing the flowers and replacing the candles. Peter wasn't quite so faithful to the cause, but he went along with it and he knew how important it was to Jane.

Leo stepped out into the aisle, half knelt facing the altar and made the sign of the cross over his heart with his right hand. Two other children joined him as he walked towards the step at the end of the stalls. The adults queued two by two behind them down the aisle.

Leo walked forward and knelt on the cushion before Father Abbot, his beautiful robes finished in white silk and red braids festooned in gold embroidery.

'Corpus Christi.'

Leo repeated the words and stood up crossing his heart once again and exiting to the right of the altar, walking behind the stalls and returning to his seat.

ILFORD - JUNE 1975

Alan Hemmings pondered over his decision to promote Don and was pleased that he'd accepted it so readily. He felt that Don was a company man just like himself and one day he'd probably take over at the top, just like he'd done all those years ago. Mind you, it was a more difficult job every year. Technology had changed all that. Computers, machinery, everything was moving so much faster and with less and less labour input. Kodak was still the market leader but others were there to take the mantle should they fall.

Don gave Karen a cuddle from behind and leant over her shoulder and gave her a kiss on the cheek.

'I've got some good news,' he said.

'Don't tell me, you're going to have a night in with me and the children.'

'Well not quite, I've got promoted at work. I'm taking over Gary's job.'

'That's fantastic Don, well done. Let me pour us both a drink,' said Karen.

'To us,' Don said, and they clinked their glasses.

'Are you working on that heap of rubbish tonight?' asked Karen.

'Yeah, I'm afraid so, I've got the guy coming tomorrow.'

'Well don't get involved in anything now, tea will be ready in about twenty minutes, Oh and there's a letter on the side for you.'

Don went upstairs and got changed into his old clothes and left a pair of overalls on the banister as he walked through to the kitchen. Karen was laying the table.

'Don, give the boys a call.'

Everyone sat at the table and chatted away. Karen tapping the boys plates asking them to eat their greens.

'What was in the letter?'

'I don't know, I haven't opened it yet,' Don replied. He did know what was inside, but he hadn't told Karen yet. The news of his promotion could well throw a bit of a spanner in the works. He had just accepted a promotion at work, which would mean a significant increase in his salary and a bonus on top of that. Gary had told him what he was being paid so Don was expecting at least that. For now, the letter could wait.

Don cleared the plates and placed them in the sink. Karen would finish them off. Don went back out into the hallway and climbed into his overalls. It was cold outside and Don really didn't want to start climbing around the front garden in the dark with a lead light in his hand, but it had to be done. One day, he thought to himself, he might be able to do this sort of thing in a more professional manner, or better still, pay someone else to do it.

Don had finished packing away all his tools by 12:30 am. Karen had gone to bed two hours ago and she was less than happy. He pulled the tarpaulin back over the XK120 and quietly let himself back into the house.

He spilt the Swarfega over the draining board as he washed his hands, using a nail brush to shift the stubborn oil stains under his finger nails. He pulled off his overalls and sat down at the kitchen table and opened the letter. It was from his solicitor.

Dear Don, Further to our conversation on Monday, I have pleasure in confirming a few details that I hope will satisfy your requirements. I have checked with Company's House re the use of Donald Key Restorations Ltd and confirm that this corporate identity is available should you choose to incorporate it. There would be a one off fee of one hundred and seventy-five

Pounds.

Alternatively, you could buy a Limited Company off the shelf for twenty-five *pounds and then use it accordingly. For example ABC Ltd T/A Donald Key Restorations*

You will also need to set up a PAYE scheme and VAT registration in due course.

If you would like to think about it for a while and then give me your instructions, I will be pleased to oblige.

Yours sincerely, Matt.

Don read the letter a couple of times. The promotion had come at just the wrong time. It would be difficult to convince Karen. It would be a risk and the only savings they had were wrapped up in the Jaguar XK120 in the garden. They could go to the bank; they had a little equity in the house. Maybe he would register the name and not trade the company. He could call Matt after the weekend. He was tired and he had to be up early in the morning. Now was not the time.

WANDSWORTH, MAY 2000

Max walked up the platform, through the turnstile and then turned right under the huge black electronic notice board looking for the exit to the taxi rank. Having been at the front of the train, he was first off and quickly found an empty taxi.

Leaning in through the passenger window, he asked the driver, 'Hi, do you know Testastretta, the Ferrari dealer in Wandsworth?'

'Yeah, mate, in you get.'

Max stepped in to the back of the cab and made himself comfortable.

'Long stay?' the cabbie asked.

'No, I've just come up to London to collect a car, that's all.'

'A Ferrari?'

'Yes, a 355,' said Max.

'Sounds good to me.'

'Yes, they are, I'm a dealer, so it's just a case of collecting the car and selling it on and hopefully making a profit.'

'What a great job.'

'It has its moments,' Max replied.

Chris at Testastretta was waiting outside his premises warming up the Ferrari when Max arrived. It looked fabulous. The exhausts were steaming. Max went into the office and collected the documents, paid Chris and asked if he could just photocopy the log book and the service coupon from the service book. Chris handed him the spare keys and he set off the short distance to Henley on Thames.

Driving down Wandsworth Road Max picked up his mobile and dialled Ted Little.

'Ted, it's Max, if the traffic is okay, I will be with you in about forty-five minutes. I'm in the car now, everything works properly, so you've got nothing to do to it. It's been valeted so it's ready to go.'

'Fantastic,' said Ted, 'I'll see you shortly, I'll get the kettle on.'

Max had driven hundreds of supercars and knew what to look for, how to listen to the car and how to treat it when he was doing a delivery. Gone were the days when he had to try to impress anyone. This was a profit centre and had to be looked after. Just be careful with it and get it safely to the customer.

Max pulled over into a bus stop just outside Henley and lowered the electronic roof. The car looked stunning as he drove the last few hundred yards into the town.

Ted Little hurried down the stairs of his office and strutted out to the edge of the road as if he was hailing a cab, and Max pulled up to the kerb alongside him.

The pair of them chatted, whilst Ted took a cursory look around the car.

'Looks a hundred per cent,' said Ted convincingly, not really knowing one end of a car from another.

'It's fabulous, difficult to fault really.'

'Yes, I agree, that's what we want. You can leave it there if you like, and come up to the office.'

Max raised the roof, locked the car and climbed the stairs into Ted's office.

'Please take a seat.' Max sat down and looked around as Ted returned with a tray of drinks and a few cookies on a plate.

'Milk?'

'Yes please.'

'Tell me when to stop.'

'That's fine.'

'Sugar?'

'No thanks,' Max replied.

'Well thanks for bringing the car up. You've saved our lives. I am sure that our customer will be delighted,' Ted smiled.

Both of them talked for fifteen minutes or so, then Ted signed the Velodrome contract and handed Max a cheque for seventy three thousand five hundred Pounds.

Max took a good look at the cheque, the words, the numbers, the date, the signatures, and the payee. All was okay. He noted the cheque number was 000001 and thought to himself, this is their first cheque, I need some security here.

'Look Ted, I'm quite happy to let you have the car on a cheque but I'll keep the log book, the service book and the spare keys until the cheque clears. I've got a copy of the documents that I can let you have. It's a lot of money, I'm sure you understand. You know how it is.'

Ted accepted Max's demands and both of them chatted for a while longer. Ted wanted a stock of similar cars and asked Max to help him.

'Well, let's get this one done and dusted and we'll take it from there,' said Max.

'Do you get involved in any classic stuff?' asked Ted.

'We've done a few classic cars. I'd like to do a few more. I've got some good customers. Are you looking for anything in particular?'

'I took an enquiry yesterday from an Ameican guy who was in South Africa. He's looking for some very special stuff, pontoon Testarossa, GTO, short wheel base, plus a load of moderns as well, 550 Mararello etc.'

'Sounds like quite a shopping list,' said Max, 'have you checked him out?'

'Yes, he appears to be legit . . . we've got all his numbers, addresses etc.'

'What's he do?' asked Max.

'Well, I didn't quite understand it, but basically he's an international currency dealer.'

Max rounded off the conversation and said, 'If you need any help on that one, let me know, if you need anything else, just give me a call.'

Max stood up and offered out his hand shake and then thanked him. His train was leaving in thirty-five minutes and he didn't want to miss it.

It would be quite a long day by the time he got home, but it was worth it. He'd just made five and a half thousands profit on one car without having to spend a bean on it. Generally, the bikes back at the garage would struggle to net five hundred Pounds and Pete had to sell forty bikes per month just to stand still. The Ferrari business was a welcome bonus so Max was keen to market himself and the company and capitalise on it.

Fortunately, Velodrome had five thousand square feet of underground parking where Max was operating the Ferrari side of the business and it was working well. Max was attracting customers from all over Europe and they were flying into Exeter and viewing the cars he had available. He wasn't selling a huge volume but it was building slowly, so it was going in the right direction.

Initially, Velodrome didn't do any work on the cars, Max used the authorised Ferrari agent in Exeter. He'd got a good deal with the service manager, so all Velodrome's Ferrari's were going back and forth from Newton Abbot and Exeter for service work, warranty work, repairs etc. It would be fair to say that at that time, Velodrome were selling more Ferrari's than the official authorised dealer.

Max used to look at Isca Ferrari's premises and think, what a waste! All the kit and nobody to run with the ball. He got on well with the service manager and together they kept Velodrome's customers happy.

Earlier in the year, Max had ordered two Ferrari 360 Spiders on the same day. The cars hadn't even been announced but he thought that there was every chance that Ferrari would create a convertible version of their latest model. He paid his deposits and hoped the car would be produced. Nobody else had done the same thing, so Max would be the first customer to receive the new cars if and when they came out. The service manager had confirmed to Max that the cars were ordered on the system, so should Ferrari press the button, and then it was all systems go.

Ted Little wanted some more cars, that was good, and he had an interesting potential client in the guy from South Africa and that could be a lot better. Max thought about whom he could speak to about the GTO etc. No one person came to mind immediately but he'd been a member of the Ferrari Owners Club since the mid eighties and he'd got to know a lot of owners, a lot of cars and how these rare cars tended to come on to the market.

He remembered speaking to a guy at Birtsmorton Court several years earlier. If he remembered correctly, he was Welsh, had quite a large collection of old Ferraris. He would be a good starting point. He'd got his number somewhere. He thought he'd give him a call.

TEIGNMOUTH, JANUARY 1975

Caro waved Max goodbye and watched him walk off towards his house. He didn't turn around once. It was a bitterly cold January day in 1975. She stood still in deep thought at the end of the private drive leading up to her home. Max didn't seem the same. She wondered whether he was not telling her something. He was usually such a jolly person, laughing, joking, and pulling her leg. A real nice person to be with, but today he was different. Very different. They hardly spoke at all on the way back from school. All of her efforts to start a conversation were met with short or single word replies. Something wasn't right. He was miles away.

It was getting dark as Max opened the back door and was greeted by a yowling Popper.

'Do you want some bickies, Pop?' Max asked in a sort of babyish voice.

Max went to the larder and found the Go Cat box and emptied the remainder of the contents into Pop's bowl. His motors were running as he gnashed away at his food.

Nobody was home. Neil had gone back to Buck House the week before, father was at the shop and he didn't know where his mother was. He switched the kettle on and got his cup from the mug tree, stopping to look out the window as he did so. The kitchen light shone across the terrace in front of the rose bed. There was a hedgehog scuttling across the slate slabs.

He finished making his tea and went into the breakfast room and picked up the coal bucket. Congratulation cards littered the window sills, television and bookshelves. There were baby clothes, towels, various paraphernalia and a neatly stacked tower of towelling nappies on the dining table.

Max cleared the grate from the night before and emptied it into the dustbin outside, then set about making the fire and lighting it. He stood in front of it, warming his hands, as it popped and spat, lowering more coal into strategic spots as the fire took hold. Like many, life at home was different to life at school. Going to school was a release, a relief from what was happening at home behind closed doors. Nobody breathed a word.

Ferris was born five days earlier on the tenth of January. A little healthy boy 10lbs 2oz; well maybe not so much of the little, but nonetheless a healthy boy about the same size and look as a Christmas turkey thought Max. His mother didn't have the best of deliveries, but she was okay. Max assumed that was where she was, at the hospital, probably getting a check up. She had only been out two days.

Max sipped his tea and opened his school bag looking for his history homework. It wouldn't take long, ten minutes, quarter of an hour maybe. He was still in his uniform with his blazer on as he put his exercise book on the kitchen side and leaning over on his left elbow, he started scribbling away. He stopped for a while then thought, then fired off a few more lines. He never tried that hard, he just did what he had to do. He stuck his hand in the biscuit jar and pulled out a McVities Digestive and dunked it in his tea, then twirled his fountain pen in his fingers, a Parker 45 Flighter, black barrel, brushed silver cap with gold arrow clip. It was a good looking pen, he thought. His parents had bought him the pen as a gift for getting into the Grammar School and unbeknown to him at the time he would keep the same pen for the rest of his life. Max finished his homework and chucked his books back into his bag. He pulled at his left lapel of his blazer and slid his pen into his inside pocket.

He needed to get changed. Popper jumped onto the bed and Max sat down beside him stroking him as he did so. He pressed 'Play' on his cassette player and started listening to Elton John's Goodbye Yellow Brick Road album.

The night before, his parents had started off on each other. They'd been shouting, screaming and for the first time he'd heard his father use the 'f' word. His mother was supposed to be staying in bed being looked after herself, but she wasn't, she was up and about as if nothing had happened. Harmony, harmony, harmony. The tape stopped. He shook his head and breathed out a sigh. The silence was beautifully still.

'Just you and me Pop,' he said. 'Just you and me.'

The back door opened downstairs and Max's mother carried Ferris up to his room and placed him into his cot.

'Hello, luv, are you all right?'

'Yes, fine thanks, where've you been?'

'I had to get some baby stuff, you know and I got some cartridges for you. They're in my bag downstairs.'

'Okay, thanks.'

'Right, I'll go and put some tea on before your father gets back.'

There was no mention of the previous night. Everything was hunky dory. Life on a knife edge continued. It was as it always was. Nobody said anything.

The phone rang as Max was walking down the hallway. He lifted the receiver and answered it, 'Teignmouth 3601.'

'Hello Max, it's Auntie Pauline, is your mother home?'

'Yes, I'll just get her for you.'

Pauline was Max's mother's best friend. She'd known her since she was a teenager growing up in Topsham. Max didn't particularly like her. There was something about her. She was always talking about business, deals, and houses, and endlessly referring to so-and-so getting divorced or some bloke going off with another one of her friends.

She was a tall slim woman in her mid thirties with short red hair. In many ways, she reminded Max of Queen Elizabeth I or Mary Queen of Scots. She had two daughters and a son and they were great as was their father, Ralph, but she was a wicked witch. Max thought that, in many ways, Pauline was jealous of his mother who was younger at thirty four, attractive, lived in a large beautiful house, and had a successful go getter husband, nice cars and a good lifestyle. Pauline had the same, but two levels down. Her house wasn't quite so nice, her husband wasn't quite so dynamic, his business wasn't as glamorous and whereas the Reed's cars were all new, Pauline's were getting on a bit. Her E-Type was a 1968 black roadster and she'd only bought it because Derek had bought a new V12. It was a strange sort of keeping up with Jones' type situation.

Max handed the phone to his mother and went off to the kitchen and pinched another biscuit. Derek, his father opened the back door and walked into the kitchen and placed a bottle of Bells onto the side.

No pleasantries. 'Where's your mother?' He didn't sound good. Max sensed the atmosphere. *Oh no, not again*, he thought. It didn't look good. He could feel his heartbeat pick up.

Derek walked through the hallway and into the study.

Celia was slumped to the floor, back against the wall sobbing, her knees huddled up to her face, the phone hanging on its curly wire from the desk above. Derek picked up the phone and said 'Hello, hello, hello.'

There was no one there.

Celia screamed, 'Why, why do you do it to me?'

He couldn't handle Celia's nagging questions whether it was about business or anything else.

Max's mother was raving at him, they were fighting and Max tried to intervene. His father was a powerful man and had a temper like no other. He ran upstairs shouting and crashing around. Fifteen years of pressure, stress and a rocky marriage and finally, it had come to this.

The row raged on for a couple of hours, tea was burnt. There were smashed plates all over the kitchen floor, furniture knocked over. A gravy smeared, broken Denbeigh plate lay on the carpet in the breakfast room. Max picked it up noticing the long strands of his mother's hair stuck to it. Father had knocked his mother about and still she would not go quiet, still she kept arguing. Max felt hopeless.

The back door slammed and Max's mother went next door to the neighbour. All was quiet.

The television was on; Derek poured himself another whisky and sat down in his leather winged back chair, dishevelled with beads of sweat on his forehead. A pompous man with an RAF handlebar moustache and a pink bow tie was chatting away on 'Call My Bluff'. Derek had locked the back door.

Derek got up and changed channels on the television as Big Ben chimed out the Ten O'clock News. There were no lights on anywhere in the house, just the flickering light of the TV.

Max sat quietly in the corner of the breakfast room, experience had taught him not to say anything, do anything, even move. Anything could and would set him off.

Upstairs and unheard, Ferris was awake and beginning to cry. He was due his feed.

Max wanted to go to bed, but didn't want to get up out of his chair and draw attention to himself. If he was in bed, he could get away from it, pull the blankets over his head, Popper would lie alongside him and together they could forget it all.

There were footsteps outside on the pathway between the breakfast room and the garage. Max's mother walked past to the back door and tried the handle. The 'old man' was no longer drinking from the tumbler; he was swigging from the bottle. Max had never seen his father like it before, he was scared. Mother tried forcing the door and then came to the window.

'Will you please let me in,' she said firmly.

'Are you going to stop nagging me?'

'Are you going to tell me what's going on?'

'Let me in,' she demanded.

'Let me in.' She shouted and started banging her fist on the window.

'Ferris needs feeding and changing, let me in.'

'Max, let your mother in.'

Max got up and went through the kitchen to the back door and unlocked it.

'Thanks, love,' she said, switching on the lights and went straight upstairs and dealt with Ferris. Half an hour later and she was back downstairs and confronting Derek, pointing her finger in his face. It was incessant; it was vehement, spittle spraying from her mouth with the ferocity of the verbal onslaught. Max was cowering in the corner opposite the pair of them.

Celia backed off and stood up. Four hours earlier, her best friend told her that she'd been having an affair with her husband. She was wild. Derek made as if to stand up and reached into his pocket. Max thought that this was it. Any moment he would have to jump in between them and attempt to prevent his mother from being pummelled. And then it all changed, his father didn't get up; he reached deep into his pocket and pulled out a revolver. A small black revolver. He pointed it at Max's mother. *Jesus Christ, this is just too much*, Max thought, his heart racing, his mind in overdrive.

Celia ran down the hallway. Derek sped after her and Max after him. His father shoved Max to the floor as he slammed the breakfast room door behind him. Celia screamed, 'NO, NO, NO, noooo,' and then Max heard the single sharp crack. All was quiet again except the muffled sound of the television. Max crawled under the dining table. *Oh my God*, he thought. There were no lights on, he couldn't see anything and he was petrified. Was he next? He moved to one side and hid out of sight behind the television.

The breakfast room door opened and his father hurriedly sidestepped into the kitchen and unhooked his car keys, walking out through the back door and leaving it to swing in the breeze. After a minute or so and hearing no footsteps, Max slowly got up from behind the TV and crept into the larder quietly. Looking out of the small window, he saw his father turning left out of the driveway. He breathed a sigh of relief. Ferris was crying in the distance.

PAU, FEBRUARY 2004

'Ah. Bonjour, puis je parle a Jacques s'il vous plait?'
'Oui, c'est moi.'
'D'accord, je m'appelle Max. Je vous avez vendu la moto Yamaha XT cinq cent. Parlez vous Anglais.'
Jacques replied, 'A little.'
'Comme mon francais,' said Max.
Both men spoke to each other for five minutes or so. Max agreed to send Jacques his bank details for a five hundred Euro deposit. Max had told Jacques that he had some other bikes to deliver in France.
'Vous etes de Paris,' asked Max.
'Non, non, j'habite pret de Pau sud ouest France. Est ce que c'est une probleme pour vous?'
'Je ne sais pas, a ce moment, c'est possible, mais c'est beaucoup des kilometres,' said Max.
It was a long way. There were three bikes to deliver to Paris and Max asked if Jacques could come to Paris as well. That would make it a lot easier.
'Qu'est ce que c'est la prix?'
'A Paris – trois cent euros.'
'Et Pau?'
'Je pense six cent euros.'
'Okay,' Jacques said. 'Six cent euros est okay, pour moi. Quand vous transportez les autres motos?'
'Le semaine prochaire, possible Mercredi ou Jeudi.'
Max had been selling bikes in France for a couple of years and had carved out a bit of a niche market for himself. His conversational French was getting a bit better, helped by Catherine giving him a "Speak French" CD the previous Christmas. Max was always difficult to buy presents for. She would always say what do you buy the man who has everything?

67

The French CD was something he would use. On his long foreign trips, he would slide the CD into the head unit and "repeat after me". To date, his French was based on his memory of 'O' Level French some thirty years ago.

Most Frenchmen could speak a little English, but it was important to try to speak their language. It showed the buyers that Max was making every effort to make it easy for them.

Max agreed to deliver the bike to Pau on the following Thursday. It would be a long few days, but it would be well worth it in more ways than one. Jacques would pay the balance and the transport costs in cash Euros on delivery. He'd asked about the bike and Max assured him that he would not be disappointed. It looked better in the real than it did in the pictures. Jacques couldn't wait.

DUXFORD, JULY 2000

A White Mitsubishi Evo pulled up at the rear of Hangar Seven. Wing Commander Johnny Jenkins looked at his watch. Two minutes late. He was a stickler for time. That was the product of thirty seven years in the Royal Air Force. Now retired, Jenkins was the curator of the RAF Duxford Air museum. No longer dressed in uniform, he went over to the doorway and opened the door before the man had time to knock. He knew who he was and knew why he was there.

'Can I help you?' he said.

'Yes, I have an appointment to see Mr. Jenkins at 2:00 pm.'

'You must be Graham Lord.'

'And you must be Mr. Jenkins, pleased to meet you.'

'Please, call me Johnny; I'm past all that claptrap.'

Lord had gone to Duxford to view a couple of original but broken Spitfires, one a MK XVI and the other a late clipped wing, high speed doodle bug intercept aircraft. Both aeroplanes were disassembled and had been lying in parts in a remote building on the airfield for nearly sixty years. The museum wanted to sell the aircraft in order to fund some other projects.

Jenkins showed Graham Lord all the parts. The wings were mostly complete, the fuselage on both aircraft were on cradles. Someone had obviously done some work on them some years ago. Could have been apprentices learning their trade, thought Lord. There were boxes and boxes of parts, mostly identified with labels and numbered. The two Rolls Royce Merlin engines sat on crates at the back of the building.

Lord looked at everything. It was difficult to know what or if anything was missing.

'Do you know if anything is missing,' asked Lord.

'You're not going to get a project like this and find every last part there. Your decision has to be based on what you see. We will sell the aircraft as projects and parts. If you are missing any parts, we can help with identifying them as and when you need them.'

'What sort of history do you have for them?'

'We have log records for both of them. Both saw active service. The clipped wing is credited with at least one successful V1 doodle bug. The other one went to Holland after the war and was used by the Dutch Air Force until it was force landed in a marsh on the coast near Zandvoort.'

Jenkins looked at Lord poking about and thought to himself, he didn't look the type to be interested in this sort of thing. He was circa six ft tall, mousey brown hair, probably fourteen to fifteen stone, smart trousers and clean shoes with an expensive looking knee length wool overcoat. On the phone, Lord had been talking about restoring the aircraft himself, but he looked more like an organiser rather than a practical "hands on" man.

'Do you mind if I take a few photographs?' asked Lord.

'No, please be my guest.'

After an hour or so, both men walked back to the Hangar Seven office alongside the modern administration block discussing the various options. It was important to Lord that there would be access to enough technical support should it be needed.

Pleased to get out of the strong cold wind, Jenkins shut the office door having said goodbye to Lord. He had to take him at face value. Lord had told him that he already had a lot of personal aircraft, as did his brother. He obviously had quite a lot of flying experience, but he wasn't sure about him. The dress, the Etonian-like voice, strangely it didn't match the car. He didn't know what it was, but there was something about him, something that didn't quite click. He could be wrong of course, but his instinct was usually right. He knew he shouldn't judge a book by its cover but he'd be surprised if it went any further.

EXETER, JULY 2008

Reed ticked off the courses he had wanted to do and signed the application form the week before. Now he was studying Men's Health, Food Hygiene, Health & Safety and a couple of other courses. It was good, because it gave him something else to focus on. Whilst he was being taught, he didn't have to think about his surroundings, where he was, how much he was missing Catherine and the girls. Even in his second week of incarceration, it could still bring tears to his eyes. He didn't think that anyone could ever get used to that sort of environment. Most of the prison officers were arrogant or ignorant, not surprising considering the calibre of the people in their care, but, Reed thought to himself, it worked both ways.

If the prisoners were treated better by the guards then surely the prisoners themselves would have more respect for the officers. Maybe not. Maybe the crack heads wouldn't, maybe the violent offenders would. What Reed thought as being total hypocrisy were all the posters around the jail decrying racism and discrimination, yet he was sure that if a prison officer was outside the jail, he or she would not speak to people in the manner he'd been spoken to. He felt that in the main, he was being treated like dirt.

In order for a guard to treat him like that, he had to be prejudiced. He had to have prejudiced Reed, formed an adverse opinion, and then discriminate against him by treating him as they did. It was a farce. There were so many reasons why offences had been committed and offenders being treated badly would never help.

After two hours of talking bollocks in Men's Health, Reed had learnt all about his prostate, sexual infections, condoms, needles, hepatitis C and was glad to get some fresh air in the exercise yard at 10:45 am. Anybody who knew him on the outside would have known that he would have absolutely loved that.

Neither Tom nor Karl were in the playground that morning, so Reed did his twelve laps and sat down on the grass with his back leaning against the wire fence. He drew his knees

70

up and rested his chin on them, then closed his eyes and thought of Catherine. She was an absolute brick to be putting up with this crap. How were they ever going to get past it and overcome the horror of it all?

A few ideas came to mind but nothing of any worth. As far as Reed was concerned, Catherine had to deal with the day-to-day phone calls. She was the one point of contact and loads of their friends had called offering help and support. Even distraught friends had called. It was very comforting to know that people still cared and she wasn't alone. Her family had pulled together and her younger sister dropped everything to help. But when it all died down, there would still be the taint and he didn't know whether he could do anything about that. People forget, but Reed was quite a high profile person. A lot of people knew him and Max knew that if he had known someone with a similar history, he'd remember. Somehow, he had to think of something that would clear his name.

Reed wasn't expecting to be sent to prison so he hadn't made any preparations at all. Catherine had to take care of any outstanding business and sort out the daily problems at least for a while. She shut down the website. There was no point in customers sending money for orders if Catherine didn't know what the items were or where they were. All work in progress stopped in its tracks and motorcycle deliveries would have to be delayed until further notice. Semi completed jobs awaiting parts would have to wait. So, no cash flow. Effectively, no business.

Catherine had booked a holiday for a week in Majorca. All the family plus Reed's mother were due to fly out on the Saturday after the court case. Max insisted that she should still go. The fact he couldn't go was not a good reason for Catherine and the children not to go. She could get away from the bad publicity for a week and try to relax. Okay, she wasn't going to stop thinking about it, but hopefully she could get some peace.

The whistles blew, the guards shouted and the sheep were herded back to their stalls.

TEIGNMOUTH, JANUARY 1975

Reed crept out of the larder, being sure that his father wasn't about to return, then methodically switched on all the

71

lights as he made his way along the hallway. The lounge door was closed, and Ferris was crying upstairs.

He looked at the lounge door for what seemed like an age mentally preparing himself for what might be on the other side. He turned the brass handle slowly and quietly, then when the door was open at a jar, he reached through the gap, feeling his way along the felt flop wallpaper and switched on the lights. Looking through the gap, he moved his head from side to side trying to see if his mother was there. He couldn't see her and guessed she must have been behind the door. He stuck his head through the slightly more open door and looked around. Nothing. Max walked into the lounge, the smell of cordite in the air.

'Mum?' he whispered.

Max's mother stepped out from behind one of the curtains and took Max in her arms.

'I thought he'd shot you. Do you want me to call the police?'

'No dear.' She looked up. There was a small hole in the ceiling where the bullet had passed through.

'Has he gone?'

'Yes, he went off down the road.'

'Come on love, let's go upstairs, you need to go to school tomorrow. I'll clear up the mess. I need to sort out Ferris. Your father won't be coming back tonight.'

Max's mother was amazingly calm. She'd been knocked about so much that she'd almost become immune to it. Whilst Max and Neil were at Buck House, they were boarders, so for thirty-six weeks a year, they were away from home and they never got to hear about the rows. There hadn't been a crossed word whilst Max had been at the Grammar School so he had thought that his parents had put all of that behind them. How wrong he was.

'I've never seen him like that before,' said Max, 'and where did he get that gun from? And he never drinks, and he was drinking whisky.'

'Look Max, don't worry darling. Try to get some sleep.' She tucked him in and kissed him on his forehead, stroking his hair as she did so. Popper jumped up and settled at his side. He went out like a light.

When Max woke up the following morning, it was beginning to snow. The forecasters had been threatening it for some while but as usual, it never happened where he lived, but in the half-light, he could see small white specs floating onto the window sill. His mother was already downstairs in the breakfast room feeding Ferris when he went into the kitchen. Everything was clean and tidy and in it's place. There was no trace of the night before. Max's father was not around. He had gone and unbeknown to Max at the time, he'd never be coming back. As he got his breakfast, he felt a huge sigh of relief, for now. It was like a massive weight taken off his shoulder. It wasn't just the rows, it was the pressure and the tension. He was living life on the edge, all the time, constantly fearing that if he stepped out of line, he would get whacked. Maybe if his father could have held himself together for a few more years, he would have become a little more understanding, a little mellower and less violent, but at thirty seven years old, he still couldn't control his temper. It was as if he was schizo.

Whilst Max obviously still loved his father, he was glad to see him go the night before. He realised that he couldn't carry on like it, his mother couldn't and sooner or later, the family would be split up in one way or another.

'What's going to happen now?' asked Max.

His mother didn't know. She looked like she hadn't slept for weeks. She was only thirty four and aged twenty years overnight.

'I'll give your father a call later on. You go off to school and do your bit. Keep it to yourself. I don't want other people knowing our business.'

Max nodded and went into the cloakroom to fetch his duffle coat. The snow was beginning to settle as he went out the back door and up the driveway. Not many cars were venturing out and those that were on the road, passed slowly. Caro was standing in the usual place as Max walked up to her with his bag over his shoulder and his hands in his pockets. She tucked her arm inside his and said, 'This is nice, how are you today?'

'Yeah, fine thanks. You?'

'Never been better,' she replied.

'Good, then we're both okay then.'

It was business as usual, as if nothing had happened the night before. Caro would have been horrified if Max had told her about the fighting, the drink and the gun. Most normal people wouldn't be able to get their heads around it. The reality should have been that Max's father ought to have been in custody. He wasn't. He was with his mother's best friend.

The snow started to fall more heavily and by the time Max had got to school, everywhere was white. Every child likes the snow and Max intended to make the most of it when he got home, and the fact that it had snowed was a huge distraction for him. He really didn't think about the events of the previous night at all that day. He only thought about it again when his form teacher asked him to get a note signed by his father for a field trip due in a couple of weeks.

Max sat next to Rob in nearly all the lessons except English where Max was in the top group. Rob was a few weeks older than Max and shared the same interests. His dad, Ken, was a structural engineer in Teignmouth and he was a really nice chap. In fact, Rob's brother, sister and mother were all nice people, but he particularly liked his dad, because he had a great sense of humour, a nice smile and he always used to make fun of the two boys.

Rob lived in Stoke-in-Teignhead, a small village up the Rocombe Valley and his parents had a Devon long house with a separate garden across the road in front of the house. Ken had got planning consent to build a modern detached house in the garden and was going to build it himself.

Rob's older brother, Colin, Rob and their dad were working at weekends digging trenches, mixing concrete and general labouring on the house project. Max needed to earn some money to save up for his moped and asked Rob if his dad needed any extra hands and Rob had told him that day all was okay for Max to start the following Saturday. Max had got a new Falcon five speed racing bike for Christmas, so he would cycle the six miles back and forth to earn some money. Ordinarily, he would have to ask his father's permission but he didn't know what was happening on that point, so he told Rob that it should be all right, but he would confirm it the following day.

It had snowed all day and by the time Max got home, it must have been five or six inches deep. The fire had already been lit and the heating was on when he chucked his bag down on the kitchen floor. His mother was talking on the telephone and Ferris was asleep in the travel cot, so he switched on the kettle and made himself a cup of tea just as his mother walked in.

'Yes, please love.'

'Okay?' asked Max.

'Your father's not coming back. He's gone off with Pauline.'

74

'What do you mean, he's gone off with Pauline?'

'Well, apparently, he's been having an affair with her for some time.'

'He's always said he didn't like her. He never liked you seeing her. I don't know what he sees in her,' said Max.

'No, neither do I, but from now on, it's just going to be the four of us. I haven't told Neil yet. I'll have to speak to Father Cuthbert. I don't know what I'm going to do about money. I've got about ten pounds on me.'

Max handed her a cup of tea. In some ways, it was difficult to believe, in other ways, it was completely reasonable to believe.

'I've tried calling the shop, but he's not there, and I don't know where he's gone or what he's intending to do.'

Max was slowly coming to the realisation of it all. If his father had gone. It might not affect him too much immediately but it would later and may be for the better, he didn't know. He finished his tea, got changed and went sledging in the field in front of the house. He had a great time. Some kids who lived in the house at the bottom of the field joined in and when he came in from the cold, it was dark and he was freezing. Tea was on the table and Max and his mother sat down and quietly ate. It was different, it was more relaxed and Max liked it. He liked it a lot.

PAU, FEBRUARY 2004

Jacques answered the phone, it was Max. He had delivered the three bikes in Paris and was now heading out of the city along the Pereferique about three kilometres from Port Vancennes. It would probably take him five hours from the orbital exit if the traffic was good. The satellite navigation was indicating an ETA of ten past three, but Max would usually beat the ETA on longer distances. In anticipation, Jacques had taken the day off and he was amazed things were going so smoothly. The English guy had kept in touch, given him all the details he needed and was now on his way to his house.

At the Banque Nationale d'Agricole earlier that morning, Jacques had withdrawn the cash for the bike. He still had more than two thousand Euros left over from his bonus, so Antoinette would not be quite so annoyed that he'd spent a little bit more than he'd intended.

Max slowed for the toll barrier and took off his seat belt to slide over to the left hand booth. He pressed the button and took a ticket. Within a few minutes, he was back up to his cruising speed of 140 kph, basically flat out. The only time he'd stop would be for fuel or more toll booths. He'd never delivered a bike to the south west of France before as most of his bikes went to Paris, but he was used to travelling long distances at a high average speed. Even in a Mercedes Sprinter van, he would leave home on a Sunday, return late on a Tuesday night and have been to Paris, Frankfurt, Hamburg, Dusseldorf, Amsterdam and home delivering several bikes on the outward journey and buying a van load on the way back.

On one occasion, he'd sold a Porsche 996 Turbo to a very good customer in Paris on the Place de la Concorde. He was taking another Porsche in part exchange, a 996 C4 cabrio. By the time, he'd done all the paperwork and pulled out of the customer's private garage, it was raining and it was quarter past seven at night. Six hours later amidst rain all the way, he was tucked up in bed at home in Newton Abbot, Devon! It spoke volumes for the four wheel drive Porsche.

Max listened to the satellite navigation as it directed him towards Jacques' home.

'Take the next right, and the destination is three hundred metres on the right.'

Max pulled up outside the typical old terraced building with pale blue painted shutters, noticing the crucifix on the entrance gate. Jacques came out to greet Max.

'You are very quick.'

'I had a good run down, no problems.'

'Would you like a drink, coffee, Coke?' asked Jacques.

'Oooh, Coke would be nice. Thank you.'

Jacques returned to the house where a young woman was standing at the door. They spoke quickly and she disappeared into the house.

Max opened the rear doors of the van and jumped in. It would take ten minutes to unload, go through the paperwork, get paid, drink the Coke and go. He never spent very long with any customer. He just wanted to get the job done, get paid and get home as quickly as possible, until the next time.

Max was used to the reaction he got from his customers. Another well restored bike going to a very happy customer. It was always the same age range of customer buying a blast from the past. Max started the bike and let it warm through and then explained the starting procedure and all the controls. He always did it because Yamaha XT500s could be notoriously difficult to start, and although there was plenty of information about them on the internet, each bike was different and if he showed them how to start it, then hopefully, they would be able to get it going themselves.

Jacques sat on the bike and took it for a quick ride a short distance up the road and back by which time his wife Antoinette came out of the house with two iced Cokes in tall glasses.

'He's like a little boy,' she said.

'We all are,' replied Max.

The three of them went into the house and sat down at the kitchen table.

In broken English, Antoinette asked Max if he would like to stay for dinner, but he politely declined, explaining that he had a long way home to travel and he wanted to be home as soon as possible.

'Ce n'est pas une probleme,' she said.

'Non, merci,' replied Max.

They finished the paperwork and Max counted the money, receipting the invoice as being paid in full. They chatted for a while, half in English, half in French and Max finished by saying,

'If you know anyone else interested in these sorts of bikes, please let me know or if you know anyone who has any old sports or racing cars for sale, again let me know. I'm a keen buyer and seller.'

Jacques looked at him, and then flashed Antoinette a sideways glance.

'What sort of racing cars do you look for?'

'Well anything really, any condition, good or bad, damaged, parts missing etc.'

Jacques couldn't understand fully what Max had said but he had a good idea nonetheless.

'My father in law has an old racing car. He have the car depuis avant la guerre.'

'Since before the war?' Max said.

'Yes,' Jacques answered.

'Do you know what it is?'

'No, ce n'est pas en tres bien etat. It's not in good condition.'

'Does he want to sell it?'

Jacques looked at Antoinette again, 'Yes, I think so.' Antoinette agreed.

'Where is the car?' asked Max.

'It's about twenty-five kilometres from here.'

'Could we see it now?'

'No, I will speak to him and he will call, but his English is not so good. He will be away until the end of the week.'

Max turned the van around, waved to Jacques and Antoinette as he drove past and pressed 'Home' on the satellite navigation.

NEWTON ABBOT, MAY 2000

Nick Salmon walked into his office; it was just after 8:30 am. All his staff were trickling in and at various stages of readiness. The familiar sound of numerous computers booting up, and printer motors winding forward was sounding around him when Simon Booth caught his attention.

'Good morning Simon, good weekend?'

'Yes thanks, Nick. What about you?'

'Yes we all went down to the beach at Bantham. We had a lovely day. The kids were in swimming nearly all day. They didn't want to go home. It was beautiful down there. We had a picnic, usual thing. Anyway, anything on the prickly list this morning?'

'Velodrome.'

'Oh dear, what is it?'

'They've got a reversal on a credit posted last week, it's seventy three thousand five hundred Pounds.'

'What's the reason?'

'RDPR, refer to drawer please represent.'

'Okay, leave it to me, I'll give them a call and come back to you. How far over are they?'

'They're not, they're okay at the moment.'

Joy walked into Nick's office, 'Morning Nick, cup of tea?'

'Yes please, Joy, thank you.'

78

Joy went off to the staff kitchen and made Nick a cup of tea. She'd worked for Nick for nearly seven years. It was unusual in the bank these days as they were constantly moving people on. After the debacle of the early 1990s recession, most banks including Barclays had made a corporate decision to move personnel on quickly. It stopped managers becoming personally involved with their customers and made it easier to take hard decisions when necessary. Nick knew he would be moved on sometime soon but for the meantime, he was happy with his lot.

Joy returned with his mug of tea.

'Thank you, Joy. Could you get Max Reed at Velodrome on the phone for me please?'

Twenty minutes later Joy buzzed Nick's office.

'Nick I've got Max Reed for you on line one.'

Nick pressed the flashing button and started speaking.

'Hello Max, how are you?'

'Fine thanks Nick, and yourself?'

'Yes, pretty good. I hope you were out enjoying the weather at the weekend.'

'Well, sort of. We were running a few bikes down at St Kew in the Enduro Championships.'

'Oh, right.'

'We think we've got a one, two, but the results haven't been confirmed yet. We'll know for sure later in the week. Anyway, what can I do for you?' asked Max.

'You paid in a large cheque last week?'

'Yes, seventy three thousand five hundred Pounds, it was from Wedgewoods.'

'Well, it's gone back RDPR.'

'Okay, when will it come back round?'

'Wednesday.'

'It was a Barclay's cheque. I kept a copy of it. You couldn't do a bank to bank check for me, could you? Just find out if it's going to be okay, otherwise I'll go up and get the car if it looks bad.'

'Fax it through, I'm not promising anything, I'll see what I can do and give you a call back,' said Nick.

Max put the phone down and banged his fist down on the desk. *Great start to the week*, he thought. He found the bank's fax number, scribbled an FAO onto the photocopy of the cheque and sent it through. He decided to not call Ted Little until he'd heard back from Nick. No need to worry until you have to worry.

Max liked Nick, he was a good guy. When Max had made the move to the high street premises, he had negotiated with Nick a number of times before getting the deal that he finally settled on. Nick was no pushover, but he was a realist, he knew how things worked and that sometimes things could go wrong. Nick wasn't jumpy. He was hard but fair. He was the only bank manager that would ring up Max before he was going on holiday just to make sure that Max had enough funds available on his overdraft to allow for the next two weeks trading.

Every quarter, Max's book keeper would run off the accounts and send them off to Nick for his review, whereupon Nick would then go down to the garage, run through the numbers and then pop over to the Queens Hotel for a light lunch. It was a good relationship and it worked well.

Mike buzzed through to Max, 'It's Nick Salmon.'

'Yes. Hi, Nick.'

'Max it should be okay. I spoke to my equal at their branch and Wedgewood's have got an international telegraphic transfer on their system, which will be credited to their account some time today. The problem is that if a telegraphic transfer chap's payment comes into the UK, it will go through 'International' first and then get redistributed out to the beneficiary account the following day. The net result is that it takes a day longer to clear. I'm happy with it, so don't worry about it. I'll cover you if you run over.'

'Thanks Nick, that's good of you,' said Max and rang off.

Max was pleased that he didn't have to ask for more money, they were always banging on the door of the overdraft limit. It was the nature of the beast. The more they sold, the more money they needed to cash flow the business especially if they were selling new motorcycles and taking second hand motorcycles in part exchange.

Essentially, most new stock in the showroom would be supported by what was called a finance stocking plan backed by the manufacturer. So, if they had new motorcycles to sell, the manufacturer would insist that they used their dedicated stocking finance company. With Velodrome being Aprilia and Peugeot dealers, the preferred stocking finance company was Transamerica. In 2000, Velodrome had a stocking line of

£75,000 for Aprilia and £25,000 for Peugeot. On top of that, they had a further £75,000 with Deutsche for their range of Victory motorcycles. Add to that an overdraft facility of £120,000 and it was easy to see how much bigger the business had become since the start in 1987.

The way it would work would be relatively simple. Velodrome would order, for example, a new bike from Aprilia. If it was an RSV1000R, then the cost would be circa £8,500, so Aprilia would invoice Transamerica £8,500 on Velodrome's behalf and then get a confirmation. Usually the bike would be distributed to the dealer a few days later after the approval from TA. When the bike arrived in the showroom, Velodrome would be charged around £50 per month in arrears, whilst it sat there unless sold. The bike could sit in the showroom unsold for three months, but no matter what, when the three months was up, Transamerica would direct debit the full value of the invoice from Velodrome's bank account. This is why dealers have to move stock quickly, because they don't want to really end up owning the stock. If they own the stock, it would have to be paid for by their own cash or the bank overdraft, in Velodrome's case. If the bike was sold prior to the three months, Transamerica would direct debit the money at that point.

Now this all sounds fine if you are dealing with one bike, but in Velodrome's case, they were selling an average of forty bikes per month, of which sixty per cent were new and forty per cent were used. So, Velodrome would sell twenty-four new bikes on average, therefore, they would be direct debited by Transamerica twenty-four times on average per month each usually on different days. Add in to this mix, the likelihood of a part exchange on the outgoing new bike and what you end up with is an increase in value of the owned stock by the collective value of the used part exchanges. Hence the more successful they were in selling new machines, the more money they needed to fund the increase in the used owned stock.

The key to it was to either sell the new stock without part exchanges or have the part exchanges stand them in at a value, which would enable them to trade them out to other dealers, keeping the good part exchanges, to retail. Easy in theory but a nightmare in reality.

The other major cash flow knock was if the bike was sold on finance, which would be highly likely. Most finance companies would pay out on the BACS system (Bank automated clearing system) which is a five day inter bank payment. Typically, a customer would come in on a Saturday, sign the finance documents and take away his or her bike. Velodrome would fax a copy of the finance documents up to the finance company and in turn, the finance company would then activate the BACS payment. However, Transamerica would activate their direct debit immediately the bike left the showroom floor. So, the position would or could create a negative cash flow between paying for the bike and being paid for the bike and that would have to be met by the bank. It was juggling at it's best and it was all the time.

'Max, it's Ted Little for you.'

'Thanks Mike, put him through.'

'Hi Ted, how are you?' Max said in a rather upbeat voice.

'Ah, not too bad, not too bad. Umm, bit of a problem really.'

'Oh?'

'Yes, the cheque we gave you is going to bounce if it hasn't already,' said Ted.

Max obviously knew, Nick Salmon had already told him a few hours earlier, but he wanted to see where the conversation was going.

'Will it bounce, refer to drawer' or refer to drawer, please represent?'

'It will be the please represent one.'

'Okay, is it going to clear on its second presentation?'

'Yes it will,' said Ted.

'It better,' Max insisted, 'or I will have to collect the car.'

'No, honestly, it will be fine. Our money came in later than we anticipated.'

'There are some charges, so I'll have to recover those. It's about twenty-five pounds. That's what the bank charges me.'

'That's okay,' said Ted. 'I'm sorry about this. I wouldn't have wanted to upset our dealings for the future.'

'Ted, if you pay me and it all goes through properly, we can forget it, okay?'

Max said that, but he knew if he sold Ted another car, they would need a better arrangement than that.

As if Ted was thinking about some sort of half hearted recompense, he said, 'I've spoken to my client in South Africa.

He's interested in talking to you direct. Can you cut me in on a commission if you do a deal?'

'Yes, I can do that. No problem.' It was just what Max was hoping.

Ted gave Max all the details and finished the call by telling him to give Muzi a call today and sorry once again for the inconvenience on the 355.

Max looked at the details he'd written in his daily diary. The guy's name was Muzi Kweyaka. It didn't look like an Amercian name, it didn't look like a name he'd come across before.

The 'Muzi' looked African but the 'Kweyaka' looked like it could have been Japanese. Come to that, the 'Muzi' bit could have been Japanese as well.

Max tapped out one of the three numbers in front of him. It was the fax. He cut the connection and tried again with the second number. It was ringing.

'Hello,' a girl answered.

'Hello, may I speak to Mr. Kweyaka please?'

'Who's calling please?'

'My name is Max Reed. I'm calling from a company called 'Velodrome' in the UK.'

'I'm sorry, Muzi's not here at the moment, he'll be back in a couple of hours. You can reach him on his mobile, do you have his number?'

'Is that the 278 7036 number?'

'Yes, that's right, give him a call on that one. I will make a note that you called. Do you want him to call you back?'

'Yes, please, my number is plus-four-four for the UK, one–six–two–six–thirty–three–five thousand,' said Max. 'I'll try him, but if I don't get through he can call me later. That'll be fine. Can I just take your name please?'

'Yes, I'm Thabiso,' she said.

PAU, MARCH 2004

Olivier returned from holidaying on the south of France and was glad to be home. Even though the journey had been fairly stress free, it was very tiring. He shared the driving with his wife of sixty years. They'd only been away for a week, but like most people, it seemed like he'd never been away when he opened the front door, stooping down to pick up the post as he did so.

He'd lived in the same house all his life having been born there in 1920. In it's heyday, it had been a beautiful rambling property with numerous stone and brick built outbuildings in grounds of nearly five hundred acres.

Over the years, the buildings had become dilapidated and the house needed a serious amount of work and money spending on it. Originally, it was a beef farm with more than three hundred head of cattle and his family had grown a lot of their own crops. That was mostly before World War Two.

During the war, the farm wasn't occupied by the Germans but a lot of valuables had been looted at gunpoint by the Waffen SS and like so many, the wealth of the family had diminished to almost nothing. Through the war years, it was a miracle that Olivier and his wife had survived at all. Many of their friends and family died in the conflict, something that Olivier no longer cared to remember. He'd had relatives at Oradour Sur Glane when in the final weeks of the war, the SS shot every man woman and child in the village and then set fire to it. He'd blocked it out of his mind and with it the memories of the high life that his father had enjoyed in the 1920s and thirties where he mixed with fellow notable people of the time. His father was a keen sportsman, a self made man who had started the Cheval Train Company. He had amassed a small fortune before losing it all at the outbreak of the war.

Looking around the house there were a few relics of the past, but nothing of any value. The farm had long since ceased being a working farm and as Olivier was no longer capable of manual work he had survived the last twenty years by selling off parcels of land and also renting out some land to adjoining farmers. His two daughters had married office bound men who were not interested in farming, so he didn't have anyone to continue his line.

Olivier shuffled through the post, but before placing it on the kitchen table, he noticed a handwritten note, and obviously hand delivered, and began reading it.

'Dear Papa, I hope you had a good holiday. We are all fine. Jacques and I took the children to Verlacque yesterday and had a good time. We are having a get together next Saturday and wondered whether you and Mama would like to come along.

Please give us a call when you get the chance. All our love Antoinette, Jacques and the girls.'

Olivier passed the note to his wife and then went outside to collect their bags, returning a short while later, huffing and puffing and dropping the suitcases at the bottom of the stairs.

He steadied himself against the dining room table and thought about the time when his father's motor racing friends had once graced the table. A darkened framed sepia photograph was the only record of the occasion and he found himself staring at it as he gathered his strength. The picture had sat in more or less the same position above the fireplace for more than seventy years. He smiled to himself and walked into the kitchen.

TEIGNMOUTH - FEBRUARY 1975

Over the next two to three weeks, it became clear to Celia that her husband would not be coming home. In reality, it was to be expected.

He was a very volatile man and they had led a turbulent marriage, but knowing all that, she was still completely unprepared for her current position. She had no money. She didn't even have her own bank account.

Derek used to keep her on a very tight rein, making sure that she had just enough for the housekeeping but very little else left over for herself. Usually, they had around a thousand pounds of kitty money in the safe at home and if she needed it, she could take some from there, being sure to note what she had taken.

Since Derek had walked out of the family home, the shop had been closed with a note in the window reading, 'Gone to Tally'.

Celia had been over to the shop and seen the message but didn't know what the message meant. She didn't know whereabouts Tally was or who Tally was. Equally, she didn't have a set of keys to open the shop and get trading. If she could get in, she could make some money, after all, she had been at Derek's side running the business for nearly ten years. The bank had been on the phone asking what was going on. Reggie Kimble, their bank manager and friend was becoming very concerned. The bank was highly exposed and sooner or later, they might have to instigate recovery action, something that

Reggie was acutely aware of.

For much of the time that Celia had been working in the shop, she had been selling antiques and her experience on that side had introduced her to a lot of dealers, auctioneers and of course retail customers, so the thought had crossed her mind that if she couldn't get any cash, then she would have to start selling off the family silver. Obviously, she wouldn't get the best price for it, but she would at least get some money in, and as she put it, keep the wolf from the door.

She sat down in the kitchen and started making a list of items in no particular order and then gave them an order of merit. If she sold anything, it would have to be a cash sale, no cheques as she had no bank account. Her car was bought and paid for but the E-Type was on finance so she couldn't do anything with that, so realistically the antiques were the best way to go. There was a set of eight George III silver dinner plates in the safe worth in the trade at least £750, so that would have to be the first item to go and when that money ran out, she'd move on to the next items on the list.

She needed to sort herself out, get a solicitor, talk to their accountant and find out what her position was. Derek wasn't coming back and she wasn't having him back. Not now, not ever. This was a new beginning. Time to move on.

A week passed and there was one thing becoming very clear. There *was* no money available. The stock in the shop was covered by a debenture at the bank and that in turn was supported by a charge on the house and if that wasn't bad enough, the mortgage on the house hadn't been paid for three months. Celia had no idea. She hadn't signed any charge forms, so as joint owner, that would be something to contest, but if the bank practically owned the stock, then there would be nothing forthcoming from a voluntary liquidation. The options, if any, were limited.

She'd been advised by her solicitor that she wouldn't be forced out of the house, at least in the foreseeable future, but she would need to get down to the social services to find out what could be due to her. She still had her family allowance, but that wasn't going to pay for Neil's school fees and he still had another term to start and finish. After ten years in business and a fifteen year marriage, she had very little to show for it. Her only hope of any money would be to challenge the second charge on the house. If the social services would meet the mortgage interest, then hopefully she could see her way through it. Not easy, but possible.

She explained the situation, as best she could to Max. He more or less took it in his stride. He took the view that they'd get through it. He was confident of that.

Celia placed the carrycot alongside the chair as Father Cuthbert, the headmaster at Buck House, beckoned her to please sit down. The school matron, sat down alongside her, and they all exchanged pleasantries before turning to the matter in hand.

Both Max and Neil had been at Buck House for more than five years and it was a very expensive school particularly if you were a boarder, as most were. The fees were nearly £140 per term and that was a lot in the early seventies.

Cuthbert didn't like confrontation and after Celia had explained to him her situation, he offered to allow Neil to finish his education at Buck House until the end of the summer term 1975 free of charge. Mrs. Reed was under enough pressure, he thought, without adding to her woes. He didn't mention the fact that the current school term fees hadn't been paid, but it wasn't important now.

Max was chatting to Caro at the end of her drive as his mother drove by, then stopped, reversed up awkwardly and called Max over.

'Are you okay love?'

'Yes, I'm okay, why?'

'Okay, just checking, that's all,' said his mother.

It was nonsense of course, all she was doing was stopping to see who Max was talking to.

She craned to say hello to Caro and she in turn said 'Hi.' Max's mother went to pull away, forgetting that the car was still in reverse. Ooops, up the pavement.

'I'll see you in the morning Caro,' he said chuckling and set off home. His mother was sorting out Ferris as Max said, 'Hey, you know that sign on the shop door?'

'Yes, dear.'

'Well, it's not 'Gone to Tally', it's gone totally.'

GAUTENG , MAY 2000

Muzi read the message that Thabiso had written earlier

that day and went into the living room where she was sitting on the settee looking out over the balcony and onward towards the beautiful Gauteng Province. All around them was rolling green countryside peppered with small farms. Their ultra modern design residence sat high on the hills, just outside Atteridgeville. Muzi had gone to school locally but was now a successful businessman, having spent the best part of his adult life in Tampa, Florida where he'd learnt his trade. He'd been married in Florida to an American girl and had two children, but Thabiso, or Tabby, as he called her, had been his girlfriend for nearly three years. Muzi missed his children and hoped that one day they would come to South Africa and live with him.

'Hi, Tabby, good day?'

'Yes, honey, great day, what about you?'

'Much the same as usual. Great expectations, but no deliveries, at least not today, so far. Umm, you spoke to this guy?' he said, pointing at the notepad message.

'Yes, did he not call you?'

'I'm not sure. I haven't spoken to him, but maybe he's left a message. It's no problem; I'll give him a call in the morning. It's a bit too late now. Is this a mobile number or a land line?'

'Sorry, honey, I don't know that. I didn't ask him. He sounds like a nice guy though.'

'Okay. I'll ring him tomorrow.'

Muzi wandered off into his redwood panelled office and set down his briefcase on the large maple desk and took out a bundle of papers. He pulled up his chair and sat comfortably, leaning backwards against the sprung back, and flicked on the large television using the remote to trawl through the figures on the financial pages. Everything down. Nasdaq, Wall St, FTSE London, all down on the day's trading. Tricky world trading conditions were sending shivers through the markets. This was the third day in a row that the markets were falling.

Not to worry, he thought, and went over to his bookshelves and pulled out an old motor racing book, a copy of Hans Tanner's world renowned book on Ferraris.

He leafed through the pages and stopped at the bookmarked page, where an old black and white photograph showed the start of the 1962 Nurburgring 1000 km race. He'd looked at it dozens of times and read the accompanying passage to the point he could almost repeat it word for word.

88

He had been extremely successful in his short life. He would say, he just got lucky, but the kind of wealth he'd amassed and lost was greater than some small countries GDP – Gross Domestic Product. He knew many world leaders personally and one in particular he didn't care for at all, others were decent people trying to make a change. He'd started off making money for himself with all the trappings a young man would want, fast cars, fast women, a private jet, homes all over the world, but then he lost it all and had to start again. Now he was on the up again and this time he was determined to keep it and determined to make a change.

Thabiso called him in for dinner. Steak, he always liked steak. Muzi opened a bottle of red wine and set it on the table to breath a while. They chatted about this and that, she at one end of the glass table and he at the other.

'I spoke to your father earlier, he's still not well you know. I think you're going to have to go down to the farm and sort out a few things,' said Tabby.

'Yes, I know. I was just hoping he would get over it, but it's not looking that way, is it?'

'No, and I think you need to talk to your mother, she's not going to like it, but a few things need to be said and sorted.'

Muzi agreed, but he wasn't looking forward to it. His father had not been well for quite some time and now he was beginning to deteriorate much more quickly than before. There was a lot to sort out, the farm, the staff, the children and all his outstanding matters. And of course, a will. Muzi wasn't sure as to whether his father had written a will but he just knew that a conversation along those lines was going to be difficult. Very difficult.

If he broached the subject of the will, if there was one, he believed that his father would think that there wasn't much hope of him getting better and that's what everyone would be thinking of him. Muzi, for his part would feel difficult firstly for making him feel that way and secondly because he felt that his father would consider him as being money grabbing, which he wasn't. He couldn't win either way, but something had to be done, and as the eldest child, Muzi had a responsibility to do it. It needed a lot of thought.

He was a well educated and interesting guy, Muzi. At thirty six years old, he was intelligent, spoke several languages, slim, five foot eleven inches tall with close cropped hair, black and fun looking. He lived life on the edge; that was his business, feast and famine. Now was the time for the feast to come again.

Thabiso was ten years his junior, black and beautiful, slim and athletic. She worked out every day, dressed herself in beautiful expensive slinky outfits. She was a head turner bar none. Muzi loved her and loved looking at her. As a couple, they were the perfect match. Fast and furious.

Max took the call at 8:45 am, he had just finished his progress meeting with Pete when Muzi had buzzed him.

'Hi, Mr. Kweyaka, thank you for returning my call.'

'Hey, let's start off how we mean to carry on. Please call me Muzi. We don't stand on ceremony here.'

Max listened to his articulate American accent and said, 'Thanks, that's fine by me, please call me Max.'

'Good,' said Muzi.

'So, I spoke to Ted Little yesterday and he tells me that you might be looking for some classic cars.'

'Yes, that's right. I have some specific interests. What are you like at hunting things down? You know, long lost cars. Cars off the radar?'

'I can't say that I've had a lot of experience of trying to find cars where the current whereabouts is unknown, but to be fair, that wouldn't really stop me. Within reason, I would chase things as far as I could reasonably go, and of course, it would also depend on how obscure the car is! What do you have in mind?' asked Max.

'A lot of cars. I have a shopping list. There are some very obvious requirements and some maybe not so. I have different reasons for buying different cars. They range from a Ferrari 250 GTO to one of the three Alfa Romeo bat mobile cars, but in between, there are some fairly mundane or ordinary cars in comparison. For example I'd like a 1972 911 RS Carrera and one of the final edition Jaguar E-Type roadsters.'

Max interjected, 'How do you want to go about this? Do you want to pay me on a finder's fee, a commission, a retainer? How do you want to play it?'

'The easiest way for me, is if I give you the list of cars that I'm looking for and then when you find something, you give me the price including your slice, raise a contract and execute the deal. The details will emerge when we're close to doing a deal. I will then send you the money, you transfer the amount for the car, keeping your bit for yourself. Are you on email?'

'Yes,' said Max and gave Muzi, his email address, fax number and mobile number.

'I'll email you the list. You start searching and come back to me as soon as you have something,' said Muzi, 'and do you have a dollar account?'

'Yes, we have obviously a GBP Sterling account, a US dollar account and a Deutschemark account.'

'That's good,' said Muzi, 'most of my transactions will be in US dollars, but we do occasionally use Deutschemark, so there's options open to us there.'

'The only other thing, when you send the list, would you just confirm what you want me to do and also send me a copy of your passport or driving licence. It's just that I will need to have some kind of confirmation of who you are etc.'

'I understand, that's to be expected. I will send you a copy of my passport via the email. I don't think there's anything else for the moment, but if I think of anything, I will call you. Just one last point, what is the latest time I can call you on your mobile?' asked Muzi.

'Try me any time. If I don't answer, leave a message and I'll call you back, okay?'

'Good, let's get down to business and find me something and I can send you some money. Bye for now.'

Max and Muzi finished the call, put their respective phones down and set back in their chairs and thought about their respective conversations. Muzi liked the sound of Max. He sounded like he could work with him and Max for his part liked the idea of dealing with Muzi. It could be a match made in Heaven. Max could do with the money and Muzi wanted the cars. All Max had to do was find them.

ILFORD, JULY 1976

The alarm bell rang. It was the fourth time that week. Donald Key was getting extremely frustrated. His bonus was dependent on the volume throughput and every time there was a jam, the alarm bells would ring, the machine would have to be back cleared, reset and started again. That process could sometimes take an hour or more and Don had had enough of it. He very rarely troubled Hemmings, but he felt that he was going to have to speak to him. More and more Don had been thinking of setting up his own classic car restoration business and was worried that if he didn't do it sooner rather than later, then he'd miss the boat and maybe never have the will to leave the comfort of a well paid job with good opportunities as he had at Kodak.

He'd been in his current job as manager for just over a year and generally, it had gone very well, but the old machinery was never designed to run such high volumes hence the ever increasing numbers of breakdowns and downtime.

Everybody at Kodak knew the problems, but head office was becoming more obsessive with numbers, statistics and performance targets. It was a world away from the business he joined straight out of school.

Alan Hemmings understood Don's frustration and agreed with him on all the points he had raised. Since Gerry Hall had left, Don spoke less to Alan than before, so when they did speak it was usually serious points of discussion.

Alan could sense that he needed to sort things out, but the disruption to the line, the cost, the downtime, it would have a huge knock on effect for the business. He knew Don was right and he knew Don was not going to put up with the pressure for ever, but his hands were tied. For the meantime, he managed to placate Don and he'd gone out of the office reassured.

Don however, took a different view. He thought that any reinvestment in the line would be more than twelve months away and in that time, the machinery would really only get worse. He sat down at home in the front room with Karen and broached the subject of his own business.

He'd now restored a few cars, an MGB, a Jaguar XK120 and an AC Ace. He couldn't do all the work but he had a reasonable mechanical understanding and what he couldn't do, he could farm out. He knew some reliable suppliers and some local skilled craftsmen. He was sure he could do it.

Karen didn't agree anything in particular at that point and he wouldn't have done anything without telling her, but she did say that it would be a good idea to get a few things sorted. She was the money person and sorted out all the household finances, so the first thing to get done was a rough idea of the costs involved, what was needed and some kind of timescale. The house had a bit of equity in it, they had a small amount of savings following the successful sale of the XK120 and they could possibly get a loan from the bank.

Don spent a lot of time researching his costs, his likely financing requirement and the sort of size premises he needed. He wouldn't be able to do it from home, not if he was to do it properly. He'd had a couple of cars in mind to restore and he'd also spoken to a potential customer about restoring an Aston Martin. He was hopeful.

TEIGNMOUTH, JUNE 1975

1975 was a watershed year for Max. His father had left home and all that had gone before him had changed. His two brothers and his mother were still living in the family home, but significant things had changed. Max was expected to follow his father into the family business but that had been put into voluntary liquidation, so everything he was going to do, he no longer had to do. He was free to think about his own future. This was something that he never thought possible. He didn't know what he wanted to do, but at least now he could make up his own mind.

For much of the summer of 1975, he was working. He'd got a job as a waiter at the Elmbrook Hotel in Teignmouth. He cycled to work at seven am and did the breakfast shift and then started the evening shift at six pm. The pay was fourteen pounds per week and the tips were good. It meant that he could give some money to his mother and he could buy his own clothes, records etc. He was finding his own way. He was also out and about, spreading his wings, if you like. There were a few girlfriends that summer too, but what he really enjoyed was the freedom. He didn't have to answer to an over domineering father and the knife edge lifestyle had gone. He was more relaxed. He was a sensible lad, so he wasn't about to go off the rails, but with his father out of the picture he could do things he would never have done had his father been around.

Max was a very keen cyclist, he would at the age of fourteen cycle to Exeter and back to Teignmouth including non stop up the notorious Telegraph Hill, only stopping to say Hello to Smokey Joe who was the resident tramp at the top of the hill on the left hand side.

Mrs. Reed had managed to pull things together and take care of the day to day goings on. She obviously couldn't work, what with Ferris, but in many ways that was an enormous advantage. For a start, social services would support her as much as possible. With the well being of three children in mind, creditors were unlikely to take proceedings against her as the courts would take a dim view of a single mother being hounded. If she could slowly sell off the crown jewels and keep the family unit together, then she stood a good chance of coming out on top of the situation. The bank charge on the house was being contested on the grounds that she knew nothing about it. In other words Derek must have forged her signature. If that was true, the bank would not be able to force the sale of the house without extreme difficulty and cost.

As it stood, the house was mortgaged by a first mortgage of £10,000 and a second mortgage in favour of Barclays in the sum of £5,000. The value of the house in 1975 was £15,000. There was no doubt about the first mortgage, that was a joint mortgage and the interest on that loan was being met by social services. Some of the bank's second mortgage would be met by the banks full and floating debenture on the stock. If Mrs. Reed could satisfy the court that she knew nothing of the second mortgage, then she would not be responsible for it and therefore the bank couldn't touch her. That responsibility would fall squarely on the shoulders of her soon to be, ex husband.

Now, the fly in the ointment would be the equity in the family home. Again, if the house was worth £15,000 or more, then half of that equity belonged to Derek or his creditors, so if he came out of the business with virtually nothing then he was going to want his share. Mrs. Reed's solicitors took a different view.

The housing market at the time was not good. The proceeding two years had seen the likes of high interest rates, the oil crisis, power strikes and the notorious Red Robbo. The country was being ruled by the unions and the whole economy was in tatters. There was no confidence anywhere and most people were sticking rather than moving.

All these factors helped Mrs. Reed. She was able to take advantage of the situation she'd been thrown into. Whether it was a conscious decision or not didn't matter, but she had custody of the children and they needed a roof over their head. Social services would support her for a reasonable period and that could be for several years. Mr. Reed would have to support the children until they were eighteen and if he couldn't pay the

94

maintenance, then social services would step in. Legal aid would pay the ongoing legal costs, so all she had to do was stick it out and she'd be okay.

The legal process would be typically slow, taking months or years to resolve, so if she was lucky, the economy would lift, the housing market would pick up and the value of the family home would increase and may be enough to realise a healthy equity that would buy a smaller home outright at a later date. All she had to do was sit tight.

GAUTENG, JUNE 2000

Captain Rux sat at his desk, looking at the man standing in front of him and chewed over the question that he had just been asked. The overhead ceiling fan squeaked as it slowly rotated.

'Why?' he answered.

'I have a client who needs some information. He's asking lots of detailed questions, and he needs some answers fairly quickly.'

'What sort of information does he need?' asked Rux lazily.

'He's about to do some business with the man, all above board. A proper contractual deal, but he knows nothing about the man, and he wants to know who he's dealing with. He speaks the part, certainly sounds the part and appears to be a hundred per cent up front, but he's in a different country and can't get information easily.'

'Which country?' asked Rux.

'I'm sorry, I can't say that.'

'Where's the information going?'

'Just me and my client. That's all. No one else will know anything about it.'

Rux stood up and walked over to the window looking out over the yard and placing his hands in his pockets, deep in thought.

'You know, I've been in this job eighteen years, there's been a lot of change. I've made a lot of friends and I've lost a lot of friends, you don't forget that. I should have done like you, gone private, but I needed the security of the job for my family and now it's probably a bit too late. I don't know whether I'd have the will to take the risk now. What you are asking can't be done quickly, you know that. It takes time. Time to set up. Time to organise. I would need a few days. What sort of deal is your client doing with our man?'

'I'm not absolutely sure. He wouldn't say, but I think it's quite high value.'

'A hundred thousand, a million?'

'From what I understand, it would be millions, maybe more. It's definitely not hundreds of thousands. I mean you wouldn't need my services if it wasn't a lot of money.'

'Yeah, well you're right there. What have you got for me?'

Rux took the package and sat back at his desk without opening the brown C4 sized envelope. The name, address, phone numbers and a small photograph were laid out in a line along his desk as Rux studied the photograph intently.

'We've looked at this guy before. I recognise the face and the name seems familiar too. What does he do?'

'I'm not sure and neither is the client.'

'Hmm, what are you going to need?' said Rux looking up.

'Plain clothed surveillance, background checks, revenue, criminal records and if possible a phone tap.'

'You've got to be mad. I can't do all that. What do you think this is? It's not your personal intelligence office. I've got to work here for the government, not for you.' He raised his voice.

'Okay, okay, okay, what can you do?'

'Well, it's more about what you can do for me.'

'I've come prepared.'

'Thought you might.'

Rux took the second envelope and looked inside.

'Five thousand, okay? Five thousand now and five thousand when we get the information.'

Rux spun around on his chair and opened the top left drawer of his desk and slid the envelope in. The drawer clicked shut.

'Call me in a couple of days, I'll see what I can do for you.'

Looking around the dimly lit room he mentally took an inventory, institutional beige paint slapped on, running in places on to the floor, two basic chairs and a table, a locker, a stainless steel sink with push button taps, a stainless steel toilet with no lid or seat and the beds they lay on. That was it. Hardly home from home. Nothing to inspire him here, he thought. What am I going to do, he questioned himself? His mind raced. 'How am I ever going to walk out of here with any dignity? I've lost so much face. I could go and see everyone and tell them exactly what happened. No, that wouldn't do any good. I could have a party and then make a speech – no not really, a bit impersonal. I could take a page in the local paper and write my side of the story. None of those ideas seemed feasible. There had to be a better way. Maybe I don't have to do anything – I wish. No, that's not right. I need to do something, but I don't know what.'

Reed lay on the bed thinking way into the night; he couldn't sleep; the animals on the wing were restless. *I wonder if I could write a book*, he thought. He wasn't sure.

He mulled it around in his mind for a while. Perhaps, he could write it as a biography and identify all the individual characters he'd dealt with. He could explain how he'd ended up where he was, who had said what and why? He could write it in a manner such that the reader could make up their own minds on him and how he was treated, but do so knowing that they knew both sides of the story rather than a highly scandalised one sided affair. The idea was appealing enough, but he still wasn't sure he had the capability. Writing an essay or a letter was one thing. Writing a one hundred and fifty thousand word book was quite another. He would have to carefully consider all the characters, lead up to a plot and have a decent ending. It would be a tall order, no doubt about that.

Reed woke up, the daily racket had started out on the landing, and it must have been about six am. Jangling keys like endless wind chimes filled the air, doors slamming, people shouting. The usual dawn chorus. His mind turned to his book. *Today will be different*, he thought. Today he would take in every detail and mentally store it for recall at a later date.

Tom Clock was sitting at the bench and Reed strolled over to join him.

'What a beautiful day.'

'Another day in Paradise?' He sarcastically replied.

'Yeah, something like that,' Reed replied.

'You been to education this morning?' asked Tom.

'Yes, Men's Health, it's all about your balls etc., prostate, infections, condoms, it's got the lot. Quite entertaining really.'

'If you like that sort of thing.'

'Well, it's better than lying on the bed for twenty-three hours a day.'

'Yep, you're right on that.'

'See those guys over there with the yellow and blue squares on their tracksuits.'

'Yeah.'

'Why are they wearing those outfits? They look like court jesters.'

'They're escapees. That's what they wear if they've tried to escape. They stand out more easily to the screws so they can keep a better eye on them. The little guy escaped from Dartmoor. Obviously didn't get far enough though.'

'What about the other one?'

'He's quite astonishing. He made himself a bomb belt.'

'What?'

'A bomb belt. You know the whitener you get for your tea?'

'Yeah.'

'Well, if you light it, it burns like magnesium, really bright. What he was going to do was pack himself up with whitener, sugar and some cleaning or lighter fluid and 'bang'. Take a load of people around him as well.'

'How did the screws catch him?' asked Reed.

Whilst his cell mate was out on exercise, he mentioned the belt to one of his mates and a someone overheard. He'd ripped up his sheet and made pockets for all the sachets to be emptied into. He was nearly there. So that's why he's got his 'jester' suit on.'

'We're surrounded by bloody nutters,' said Max.

'Tell me about it,' Tom replied.

'How's your move going?'

'I haven't heard anything. My solicitor's coming this afternoon so I'm going to ask him to send a letter to the governor if that's any good. I shouldn't have to put up with this all the time. Crack heads, fights, threats, it's not right.'

'You'll be gone soon. Mark my words.'

'What about you?'

'My court case has been put back, so it looks like I'm going to be here for a while yet. I'm going to put in for a job over in the hospital. Orderly job. Supposed to be pretty cushy. It'll get me away from the idiots for a while.'

'I didn't even know they had a hospital here.'

'Yeah, it's just over the back of A Wing.'

'Ah right. Well, I hope that works out all right for you,' said Max.

It was quite warm, some of the cockerels had taken off their shirts, all puffed up for all to see. Tom went off to C Wing and Max back to A Wing. Five minutes later, the cell door opened, the guard walked in.

'Pack your stuff lads. You're being moved.'

'Where?'

'Just pack you stuff. You'll see.'

Max and Karl hurriedly packed everything up and walked outside the open door.

'Follow me.'

The pair of them did as they were told and followed the guard back down the spiral staircase and stood outside the hub office. Another guard took over and escorted them onto C Wing.

'This is your last move. This is where you'll stay now.'

Back to square one. No television, no mattress, no pillows, one locker, no chairs and it was filthy. This would be normal prison life. Most of the guards couldn't care less and it showed. Arrogance, rudeness and attitude. It would make Reed laugh. Everywhere, there were posters saying, 'Treat others like you would like to be treated'. What that really meant was, be nice to the guards and it won't be reciprocal. Even the senior officers were the same.

Max and Karl went through the same cleaning routine, the same wait for the furniture and the same wait for the television. It was almost as if it was done on purpose to grind you down. So if the guard could be believed, their last address at Devon County Prison would be C4-15, landing 4, cell number 15 on C Wing.

The regime was very slightly softer on C Wing than A Wing and it was definitely quieter. Both Reed and Karl could sleep a little more. It still had the toilet in the cell, same awful paint, same damp dark musty smell and more dead flies in the light lens but they made what they could of it.

Come opening up time, they had a new neighbour, it was Tom Clock. They all chatted together, arms trailing over the railing as they looked down the well between the landings, watching the queue for the servery to go down as they awaited their call.

When Reed got back to his cell, there was a prison officer waiting to hand him a notification slip. Reed read it carefully as he sat down to eat his evening slop.

'You are required to have a further medical with the nurse in CMU on C1 to assess your transfer to Leyhill on 5 August.'

Max read it. He'd been at this juncture before. The first night he entered the prison was on a Monday. He was told he would be out of Exeter by the end of the week. It didn't happen. Then he was told it would the following week. It didn't happen. Two and a half weeks of scary days and sleepless nights had passed and he was still at Exeter. He genuinely thought he would see out his sentence at Exeter, but now it looked like he had a piece of paper saying he was going. What remained to be seen was whether it would actually happen.

Karl was upset. He'd been through a lot with Max and it now looked like they were going to be separated, and that worried him. What was next for him?

Reed, sensing Karl's feelings, played down the transfer, so as not to upset him, saying he'd heard it all before, but secretly he was delighted. Anything had to be better than what he was experiencing now. If it all went to plan, he had four days to go. He could get through that.

The following morning Reed reported at 9:00 am to the Custody Management Unit office and waited outside, it was August 1st, Catherine's birthday. After twenty minutes waiting, a prison officer called Reed and ushered him into the nurse's office. She asked a few questions, took his blood pressure and asked him to sign a release paper. Five minutes with the nurse and it was all done.

The prison officer looked over Reed's shoulder asking the nurse if all was okay. She confirmed everything and handed the paperwork over. It was official. Reed would be transferred at 8:00 am on fifth August. No ifs or buts, it was booked.

That night, Max rang Catherine and told her the good news and wished her Happy Birthday if that was possible. She was so pleased. Anything to get him out of that hell hole.

PAU, MARCH 2004

Olivier relaxed in the warm evening sun under the portico, music playing, a glass of local red wine in his hand and a beautiful mellow feeling all about him. He looked at his family, laughing and joking before him, playing and having a good time. It hadn't been such a bad life. He had two caring daughters, two wonderful sons-in-law and four perfect grandchildren. How his own father would have liked to see the happiness that he now witnessed.

Jacques put his hand on Oliviers shoulder and offered him a top up.

'I met a man from England a couple of weeks ago. I bought a bike on the internet and he delivered it all the way from the UK.'

'What do you want a motorbike for?'

'Oh, I had one once before and I'd always regretted selling it, so the opportunity came along and I took it. And it is superb. He knelt down at Olivier's side, 'look, I don't know if you are interested, but he told me he buys old cars, racing cars, bikes etc and I wondered whether you'd want to talk to him about the car in the shippen. You know, if you wanted to.'

Olivier let out a long sigh. He hadn't seen the car for such a long time.

'You know Jacques, I can't speak English so well. I would need you to help me. I would sell it, but it's complicated. What's he called?'

'His name is Max, he's a nice man. He did everything he said he would. I think we could trust him. If you want, I can call him and see how interested he is.'

'Does he know what it is?'

'No, because I didn't tell him. I don't know what it is,' said Jacques.

'Did you tell him what condition it is in?'

'No, not really. I just said it was an old racing car and that you had owned it for a very long time.'

'How old is he?' asked Olivier.

'I'd say he was a similar age to me, early forties,

101

something like that.'

Olivier nodded and took a sip of wine.

'Good wine Jacques. I'll have a look at the car and tell you its condition. If you call your friend and ask if he would like to view it, we can take it from there. Don't tell him what it is.'

'That will be difficult, not telling him what it is and expecting him to travel a thousand kilometres.'

'If you tell him, it would be worth his while, he can make up his own mind. If he does come, then we know he's serious. If he doesn't come, then we're no worse off than we are now.'

Jacques thought about it for a moment.

'Would you want me to be the go between?'

'Yes, you know him, he's dealt with you, and he will trust you. Tell him who I am, that's fine, but ask him to come to you and then you can bring him over to me.'

'Does he need to bring money with him? I would need to tell him,' said Jacques.

'No, that wouldn't be necessary. All we need to do is let him see the car and evaluate it for himself. I don't even know if we have all the parts anyway, but let him look and see where the conversation goes. If we agree something then we can talk about how we would do it.'

Antoinette walked up to Olivier and gave him a hug. 'How's my old Papa then?'

'Less of your old,' he replied.

'Come on. Mama wants a dance.' She held out her hand and dragged him away.

TEIGNMOUTH, MAY 1976

On a Saturday, Max had been working all through the winter on Rob's dad's building site. It was hard manual work but it was good fun. The two youngsters were constantly having the piss taken out of them, but one such Saturday it was deserved.

When they were mixing concrete or mortar, one of them would shovel the aggregate into the mixer whilst the other would fetch and carry the water. The fastest way to get water was to drop a bucket into the manhole in the road and then fill it quickly from the running water.

The manhole had a grilled cover which was easy to lift off, so Rob or Max would lift it up and prop it against the wall and leave it there all day until they came in at night.

Rob's older brother John was pushing his Honda CB200 motorcycle backwards out of the passage alongside the house and fell down the manhole with the bike falling on top of him. It was very comical at the time but John didn't see the funny side of it. Max and Rob never heard the end of it. Not a Saturday would pass without some chaos being caused. They'd fall in the wet concrete, fall off the plank with the wheelbarrow full of mortar. They would always be doing something wrong, but that was boys doing boys things. Both of them stuck at it and saved towards their mopeds, knowing that they would both be sixteen at the end of the year and that meant the long awaited licence. It would mean freedom, fun and adventure.

For now, he was still 15, and it was the fantastic summer of 1976. In Formula One, James Hunt was winning in his McLaren M23 and Barry Sheene was leading the world championship on his Suzuki RG500. It couldn't have been better.

Max cycled in to work at Holcombe. He'd started working for Mervyn at the Smugglers Inn during the summer holiday. He would have gone back to the Eastbrook Hotel, but the owners had sold up and moved on, so he had looked elsewhere. The job at the Smugglers was good fun, there was a lot of banter and two of the girls from Max's form also worked there, so they all got on well together.

It was a simple job, a bit of hoovering, cleaning, dishwashing, tidying, general all round help. Mervyn recognised Max as being a good worker and offered him more hours, which he took. Anything to earn some more money. The goal to achieve was £250, that's how much he had to save. He had saved £70 from his job with Rob's dad so the remaining £180 would need to be earned over that beautiful summer. Now, that would appear to be a bit of a breeze but for the many distractions, which inevitably would cost money. Fortunately, Max was never a clothes man, a pair of jeans, a T-shirt and his Adidas trainers and that was it, (thirty years later, he would be exactly the same) but it's always easy to spend money. With cash in your pocket, there's music, going out, food, parties, it was all going on. It really was the greatest summer. Every day between shifts at the pub, Max would cycle home, pick up his swimming stuff and then cycle flat out down to the beach, park his bike by the sea wall and lead the most carefree life, spending his time on the pier beach or talking to friends on the back beach. He wished that his family still had the beach hut but that was long gone. It would have been fun to have it at a time when he could have made the most of it, but it didn't matter.

Occasionally, Max and Neil would hire a boat from Snowy Hook and head out to sea or up the river. They'd done it all before, under duress with their father, but they'd learnt what to do and how to do it, where to go and what to avoid.

Max's fathers boat, Pisces II, was still on it's same mooring, opposite the Salty and the tender punt was still roped upside down onto the back beach. Max didn't know who had bought the boat, but it was always there, he never saw it off the mooring, and unbeknown to Max, amazingly it would still be there thirty years later.

When they did hire a boat, they'd go mackerelling, swimming, diving, and have the time of their lives watching the porpoises, beaching the boat and larking about. It was Swallows and Amazons all over again.

Caro was still around, Max would still see her most days. They were good friends, nothing more. Maybe Max had thought it would become more, but as time went on, it became less likely. She had gone out with several guys and he had a number of different girlfriends over the years, and as they'd got older they were starting to drift.

It was the same with Neil. The previous summer, Neil had finished at Buck House. He was his father's blue eyed boy and Neil took his father's departure very hard. Although, he didn't say anything at the time and his actions didn't indicate anything, he was nonetheless, probably more effected by it, than both Max and his mother had realised.

It wasn't helped by the fact that Neil didn't get into the Grammar School. He was at Westlawn, so the two were separated and Neil didn't really get into the best crowd. They were nice enough boys but they weren't ideally the best for Neil. He was easily lead and started drifting away. It wasn't obvious at first, but slowly he started to become indifferent to Max. It was not cool to be associating with a Grammar School snob and it was such a shame. Neil was an exceptionally bright kid; he was a talented sportsman and did everything with ease. He could have done anything and he'd have been good at it. He was throwing it all away and he didn't know it.

Mrs. Reed was still battling away with the legal wranglings making slow headway whilst her ex husband was doing his best to make life even more difficult for her, but she had the upper hand and she was determined to hang on to it. Ferris was eighteen months old and becoming more of a character, still just as noisy, but Max thought he was becoming more interesting. He could walk, he could feed himself and throw it all over the floor. He was good fun provided Max didn't have to change his nappy. Their summer really was the most glorious summer, endless sunshine and endless fun. Max thought that he could never have had so much of a good time had his father still been around. And what of his father? What was he doing? Well, he was still with Max's mother's ex-best friend, living in a cottage in Branscombe, but he didn't seem to be making any effort to see the three boys. No Christmas cards, no birthday cards, nothing. It was if they didn't matter, they didn't register in his mind on any level. He had a new life and he was concentrating on that. His old life was past and that was that.

Max had grown in confidence tremendously in that summer as if he had previously had his wings clipped and now he was free to fly. He made the most of it. By the time he went back to school in the fifth year, he'd saved enough for his moped, the insurance and all the clobber that went with it. He'd already bought his crash helmet, having once been caught by his mother wearing it sat up in bed, reading the Gilera Motorcycles brochure for the hundredth time. He couldn't wait for the next two and a half months to pass so that he could be on the road.

He was in the Winterbourne Centre during the school morning break playing pool. Eve looked across the green baize table and caught Max's eye and that started it all. She was blonde, tall and attractive and she was new to the school. Max wasted no time and went over to her and started chatting. They got on well and started going out. It didn't last long, it never did. Maybe three weeks maybe four but certainly no more. It was funny though. Max realised that if you weren't going out with anyone, nobody was interested, but as soon as he did go out with a girl, there were other opportunities as well.

For all that though, it would all be a faded second compared with the passion of getting his moped. Hunt had won the Formula One Drivers Championship and Sheene had won the World Motorcycle Championship and for petrol heads, 1976 was one of the true great years. It was for Max too.

BRISTOL, APRIL 1999

It was a bright but cold spring afternoon when Dimo Dacari pulled into Gordano Services on the M5 at Bristol. He parked the car clear of any others to avoid door damage by careless drivers and passengers. He'd had the Porsche Carrera convertible from new having bought it from Velodrome a year or so earlier He had dealt with Ferris Reed for the whole transaction. Ferris had located the right specification Porsche from Aachen in Germany, brought it to the UK, registered it with Dimo's private registration number and taken his beloved Ferrari 355 GTS in part exchange. For Dimo, it was a nice easy deal done on the telephone from his second home in Porta Benuiz. Ferris had collected the 355 from Dimo's other home in Warwick, evaluated it, given Dimo a price to change and agreed the deal. It was one of the first prestige car deals that Ferris had done for Velodrome when he started working for Max in 1998. At the time, they couldn't afford to retail the 355 so they had to trade it out to a dealer in London by the name of Testastretta. It's how they came to meet Christian Thomas and Greg Schoolheifer. Max had described the car to Christian and they agreed a price. Max delivered the car, got paid and the deal was done.

The Discovery came to a halt alongside the Porsche and both Max and Ferris jumped out of the car.

'He must have gone into the restaurant,' said Max.

'Yes, that's okay, take your stuff and we'll go over,' Ferris replied.

They walked into the Services, looking around for Dimo. He was sat in the corner on his own next to the window sipping a cup of latte.

They'd all met before when Dimo collected the car, but now they were meeting to discuss business. Ferris had spoken to Dimo on several occasions regarding his potential involvement with Velodrome. They'd batted a few ideas around, but essentially, Dimo didn't want to get involved with the company, and he wanted to keep it simple. Max was happy with that. Max wouldn't have wanted to give anything away anyway.

Dimo was an Iranian or Persian to be accurate. He'd come to the UK in the late eighties after fleeing his own country. He'd had a building company, which went bust, and he'd lost everything. He then set up shop in the UK doing much the same thing starting with nothing. Within a few years he had successfully fought through and established a growing construction company specialising in industrial units. And then came the early 1990s crash and Dimo was too highly geared. He had too much borrowing, which was fine when business was good and units were selling but as soon as sales slowed he got into trouble. The banks saw construction and housing as a huge money loser and customers in those sectors were the first to lose their funding. It was happening all over the country. Banks were calling in managers, moving them on and changing their new managers into hatchet men. Dimo got the call and was told that the bank could no longer support his business. The fact that they had caned him on the interest payments for the last six months was just another demonstration of how the banks work. Fair-weather friends. Short term funding for what customers believe are long term projects.

Dimo hadn't learnt his lesson. He lost nearly everything the second time except this time he lost his wife as well. The children now nineteen and seventeen were more or less old enough to look after themselves. They were both in higher education. He'd managed to keep hold of the family home although some creditors were challenging that asset in the court, so he was really up against it.

His hobby at the time was clay pigeon shooting and of course he couldn't afford the shotgun cartridges.

When he bought the house, he also acquired an area of disused MOD land alongside which his wife used for her horses. The land was used during the Second World War as an underground armaments depot, with several bunkers dotted around it.

Out of the ashes of his crashed building company, he began manufacturing shotgun cartridges for his own use and quickly realised the potential profit in a larger scale operation. His ace up his sleeve was the land with the bunkers, because it enabled him to obtain the necessary licences to store explosives, underground and out of harms way. There couldn't be an objection because the government had already used the site for exactly the same purpose.

By the end of the nineties, he'd sold out the ammunition business for over five million pounds and semi retired to Porta Benuiz as a tax exile. He was allowed back into the UK for a maximum of thirty days per year.

'Look, this is the deal I'd like to do,' he said. 'If you have a customer for a car, I will pay for it. It will remain my property until you pay me for it. You get paid by your customer and you pay me. I will want to see the sales invoice and the purchase invoice and I want a twenty-five per cent commission on the margin for my trouble, paid on repayment of the initial loan. It doesn't matter whether they are new or used cars and if you want to buy a car for stock then the same applies. Just keep it simple.' Dimo finished off his latte and stood up. 'I've got to go. If you're happy with that, I'll fax over an agreement for you to sign and we can get on with it.'

They all chatted and walked back to the car park. Dimo went east and Max went west. Max told Ferris there were a few details to iron out, but essentially it was a good deal. They'd secured funding for the expensive cars and could now do it properly, rather than relying totally on sale or return customer cars. The twenty-five per cent commission was expensive borrowing, but Max would just have to factor that cost into the deal.

FORT LAUDERDALE, AUGUST 2000

The phone was ringing in Steve Majendie's office as he unlocked the door and ran in to answer it.

'Steve Majendie,' he answered.

'Hi, Steve, it's Graham, Graham Lord.'

'Oh hi Graham, how are you today? I'd just stepped into the office. What time is it where you are?'

'It's just after two in the afternoon,' said Graham.

'Okay, most of your day's work done then?'

'Yes, more or less.'

'Tell me, what can I do for you?'

'Do you have a customer for a lightweight E-Type?'

'Possibly, what's it all about?'

'It's a 1962 car, genuinely bodied by the works but not a works car. Good race history. Full comp motor on webers, peg

108

drive wheels. Full restoration by Donald Key Restorations. Proper thing. FIA papers. Needs nothing. Race ready.'

'I'm covered at sixty five thousand,' said Graham.

'Dollars or pounds?' asked Steve, 'or is that a stupid question?'

'Pounds.'

'I've got a Jaguar guy I can talk to this afternoon. He won't be up yet. It's five in the morning East coast time, but I'll give him a call and sound him out. I've sold him quite a number of cars, but I haven't spoken to him in a while. I'll get back to you. Don't do anything with it until I call you. Oh and Graham, can you email me the pics, description, etc.?'

'Of course, I'll do that straight away for you,' Graham replied.

Steve put down the phone and went off to make himself a cup of coffee. *Like the sound of that*, he thought. It was 9:20 am in Fort Lauderdale and he couldn't call his customer in Seattle for at least five hours.

TEIGNMOUTH, NOVEMBER 1976

Max walked to school with Caro as usual. It was November 17th 1976 and it was cold. It was Max's birthday and she'd got a small present for him. He opened the small gift wrapped parcel.

'Rock of the Westies, Elton John. That's fantastic, thanks. I wasn't expecting that. That's really good of you,' he said.

He leant forward and went to kiss her on the cheek. She turned just as he was about to make contact and ended up kissing her on the lips. It wasn't a full on snog, more of a soft touch. It was different, very sensual and Max sort of froze thinking he shouldn't be doing this, but it was nice. It seemed like an age, but it was momentary. They looked at each other and said nothing, both surprised. She took his left hand tightly and they carried on walking.

'I'm not walking home tonight, my mother's collecting me. We're going off to Shaldon to pick up my bike,' said Max.

'Okay, no problem,' she replied.

'I'll come up and see you later before I go out, okay?'

'All right,' said Caro and they went their separate ways to different form rooms.

Rob was sat at his desk when Max walked in.

'Hey, Maxi, the big day eh?'

Rob was three weeks older than Max, so he was already on the road with his moped. Cigs, another friend was also on the road. Rob had a Gilera Trial and Cigs had a Yamaha FSIE-DX. That was *the* bike to have. All the talk was bike talk, where they'd been, where they were going. Max couldn't wait. They talked about the evening arrangements, times etc.

Max said he would pick up his bike at half past four, go to Robs, then go home and meet at Cockwood for a meal with everyone at about eight. It sounded like he was darting about a lot and he was, but his first night on his bike was always going to be crammed.

It was a long slow day, but it was worth it. Caro walked past Max as he was waiting for his mother.

'I'll see you later,' she said and carried on home.

Max and his mother walked into TVM at Shaldon. Dave, one of the owner's, handed over Max's Gilera Trial, explaining all the controls as he did so. There was no training, just get on it and ride. Rob was already there waiting. Max used the loo to get changed out of his school clothes and set off on his new steed to Stoke in Teignhead. By now, it was already dark and the Gilera lights were no better than a flickering candle. It was also bloody freezing. Max soon realised that his gloves were as good as useless. It was only three miles to Rob's house, but in mid November on a clear night, Max's fingers were fat like Bowyers beef sausages after a couple of miles. It was so cold. Rob's mum made the boys a drink and soon Max was off on his own again back home.

He parked his bike in the back yard, frozen to the core. His mother came to the back door and looked him up and down.

'I'm freezing,' he said. 'I can't go to Cockwood like this. I'll have to find some better gloves and a scarf and a big jumper. Max ran down to Caro's as he said he would. Her family all wished him a Happy Birthday and surprisingly her younger sister Sandra hugged him and whispered something in his ear. He didn't think he heard quite right, so dismissed what she said and made nothing of it.

It was 7:00 pm when Rob and Cigs arrived at Max's house and set off to Cockwood, only stopping once at Kenton to collect Cig's girlfriend. Nicola was standing at the door waiting when the three lads walked up the path leaving their bikes parked 'ready to go' at the end of the cul de sac. On the count of three, they ran back down the path and jumped onto their bikes. Max's bike started first. He revved it up, slammed it into gear and promptly shot off across the road on the back wheel with his body flailing behind, still holding on. Max went through a small privet hedge into someone's front garden. The bike, with Max still gripped to the handlebars, fell on its side into the flower bed with the engine screaming it's head off and the back wheel firing earth all over some poor old lady's front window. In one swift continuous move, Max picked up the bike, scrambled on, shot back out through the privet hedge, across the pavement and up the road. He was gone.

Meanwhile, Rob and Cigs were almost wetting themselves with laughter. They couldn't move. Rob was crying, it was just so funny. If only Max could have seen it himself.

Not the best start. Things could only get better.

FORT LAUDERDALE, AUGUST 2000

Steve Majendie downloaded the email from Graham Lord and read the details about the lightweight E-type. It looked promising, he could make a decent margin on it if his customer went ahead. The pictures looked spectacular. Donald Key had done a fantastic job on the restoration. It'd had a complete rebuild from top to bottom, all bodywork, mechanicals and the spartan interior. There were copies of invoices, FIA passport, race programmes showing the car in battle on the front cover, loads of sundry paperwork, scrutinising tags from the early 1960s and some lovely old black and white photographs with the first owner.

Steve tapped out the number and waited for the phone to be answered.

As always, a beautiful husky voice answered, conjuring up a thousand different images in his mind as he asked to speak to Bill please.

'Who's calling please?' asked the receptionist.

'It's Steve Majendie.'

'I'll put you through to his office Mr. Majendie.'

111

'Thank you.'

Another voice came on the line, it was Jennifer, an English girl, Bill's personal assistant. 'Just putting you through Mr. Majendie.'

'Thank you,' he said.

'Hi, Steve, how are you? Long time, no hear.'

'I am very well thanks, and you?'

'Just fine Steve. Lots on, too much in fact. I'd like to take a break, but it's all happening so fast at the moment.'

'Come on Bill, you've done your bit, can't you step aside and let someone else into the hot seat?'

'Well, I'm working on it, but it's still some way off yet. Anyway, what can I do for you?'

'I have a nice lightweight E-Type available. It's a '62 car with period race history, recent full restoration with Donald Key Restorations, FIA papers, race ready.'

'Sounds interesting.'

'It's not a genuine factory lightweight, but it has all the lightweight panels. Same shape as the Dick Protheroe car. Full competition motor, all correct. It's a very nice package,' detailed Steve.

'What are you looking at value wise?'

'Seventy eight and a half thousand pounds.'

'And is that including you?'

'Yes, my commission is covered. The car is in the UK, so I don't know if you'd want to keep it there or have it over with you.'

'Would it be eligible for Goodwood?'

'Yes, I'm sure it would be.'

'Have you got some details you can email me?' asked Bill.

'Yes of course. I've got a couple of picture zip files and a detailed history with copies of the important paperwork.'

'Okay, well get those over to me, confirm the Goodwood eligibility and we can catch up later in the day. I've got a meeting this afternoon. Is it okay for me to call you at home this evening?'

'Yeah, you've got my numbers?'

'Let me just check.' There was a short pause whilst Bill typed in Majendie on his keyboard, '7740 and 6018?'

'Yes that's right.'

'Okay, I'll speak to you later. Oh, just one more thing. Is

there a time restraint on this?'

'There always is Bill. You know how it is. First come and all that. I've asked the seller to wait for me and I'll call him now to let him know I'm awaiting a response.'

'No names please Steve.'

'No, that's fine, no name will be mentioned.'

Steve put down the phone and immediately dialled Graham Lord.

'Hi Graham, it's Steve.'

Graham saw the number come up on the phone and recognised it as Steve Majendie. He wanted to sell cars to Steve, but he hated having to speak to him. He just went on and on in this long monotonous southern drawl. He couldn't get him off the phone.

'Hello, Steve. How are you?'

'Yes, fine thanks Graham. I'm calling about the E-Type. I've spoken to my client and he's going to come back to me tonight with a decision. He's in meetings most of the day, but he's a proper guy, so I expect to hear from him. Can you hold it for me until I hear?'

'Yes, that should be okay. I have some other clients I'd like to offer the car to, but I will wait until you've told me one way or the other.'

'Graham, the other thing I need to confirm is whether it's eligible for Goodwood,' asked Steve.

'Yes, it's definitely eligible. I think the car raced at the Revival two years ago, but besides that, there is a result sheet in the history paperwork somewhere with a second or third at Goodwood. I think in 1964. So it would be most definitely eligible,' Graham confirmed.

'Okay, that sounds good. It will probably be late, my time, when he gets back to me, so I'll call you tomorrow and let you know the outcome.'

'Yes, that's fine with me.' Graham put down the phone and let out a sigh of relief. A surprisingly short phone call, all things considered.

Steve typed out an email to Bill confirming the Goodwood eligibility of the car followed by a few niceties and then pressed send.

Max got back from the Anchor Inn at Cockwood at about 11:30 pm. It was a late night for a school day, but what a night. He was frozen solid, his fingers numb, but he was beaming. He was on the road and he was incredibly happy. It would be the beginning of a life long association with motorbikes and cars. An unashamed petrol head. Many who don't understand, would say, 'What's the fascination?' but they're obviously not made the same way. Once you've had a motorcycle, most will look back on it with fond memories. It's the last total freedom. You can do things on a bike and get away with things on a bike that you would never get away with in a car. There were downsides of course, a higher likelihood of getting killed being one of them, but that never really crossed Max's mind.

Because he lived less than two miles from school, Max was forbidden to ride his bike to school, which meant that he still walked in with Caro each day. He had played the cassette she'd given him for his birthday, whilst he was getting ready that morning and was humming Philadelphia Freedom as he walked down to meet her.

He was either early or she was late, but she wasn't there. He stood at the end of the drive kicking his heels when he saw her rounding the corner at the top a couple of minutes later. As she walked towards him, he thought about the kiss the day before and how much it meant to him. He wanted to do the same again as she flashed her beautiful good morning smile at him. They stood and looked at each other for what seemed an embarrassing age. There was a sort of shy awkwardness. The silence said everything and yet nothing. She took his arm and happily chirped away as they strolled on. They felt the same about each other but for some unknown reason they just couldn't seem to get it together.

PAU, MAY 2004

Two months ago, Jacques and Olivier had sat down and

talked about the old racing car in the shippen and agreed to get the English guy to come over and look at it. However it had proved difficult for Jacques to convince him, without telling him what it was. Jacques had called Olivier at least twice to ask him to change his mind on that point, but he was steadfast, sticking to his original thought that, if the man was serious, he would come.

Max had thought about it several times, usually when he was driving his many long distances, but it always came down to the fact that it was a bloody long way and it could be for nothing. He kept thinking the only positive aspect was that the French guy had owned the car since before the war. He'd been on false errands and wild goose chases before searching for supposed cars and it had come to nothing, but the more he thought about it, the more he thought there could be something to it. He made a decision. There was a customer who wanted his bike to be delivered to Limoges and it was in the right direction for Pau, so if the delivery came off, then he'd go down to meet Jacques afterwards. Get it over and done with, once and for all.

Let's get it done; no time like the present, he thought and scrolled through the J's on his mobile and gave Jacques a call.

Antoinette answered, 'Bonjour.'

'Hi, it's Max from England.'

'Hi, Max, how are you?' she said in that lovely French English accent.

'Very well thank you, and you?'

'Tres bien,' she said. 'You like Jacques?'

'Yes please.' Max could have listened to her voice all day long.

'Oh, hi Max, you okay?'

'Yes fine.' I've possibly got a delivery in Limoges next Wednesday. I thought I'd come to you afterwards. I need to confirm it but should know for definite over the weekend. Work on the basis that I'm definitely coming and if there's a change I will let you know. Is that okay?'

'Yes, that's good for me too.'

'Okay, I'll call you. Thanks, Jacques.'

The delivery to Limoges was straightforward enough so hopefully he would get some more bikes to deliver en route at the same time. He had a guy in Nantes who said he'd catch the train up to Le Mans and another customer who lived just south of Caen. So, all being well, it would be a three drop delivery at Caen, Le Mans and Limoges then on to Pau.

The good thing about multiple deliveries would be that Max would be getting paid between three and five hundred Euros per bike, so that would offset the cost of going to Pau if it all turned out to be a waste of time.

Max was still unsure about going to Pau, but he didn't want an ongoing doubt nagging away at him. It would be much more sensible to go down and have a look, make up his mind and walk away if it was no good or sort it if it was worth buying. From what Jacques had said about his father in law, he didn't have much money and the buildings were in quite a bad state so Max was sure that he'd be looking at some sort of weird French home grown contraption, which would have been typical of the time.

Jacques called Olivier and let him know that the Englishman was coming.

'So he is serious,' said Olivier.

'Yes, looks like it. He's got to deliver a bike in Limoges and then he's coming down to me afterwards,' said Jacques.

'Well, that's good. That's very good. I will make sure that he can get around the car. There's quite a lot of rubbish in there. You couldn't give me some help Jacques, could you?' asked the old man.

Jacques went over to his father in laws on the Sunday. It took nearly all day to shift all the clutter around the entrance to the shippen. There were oil drums, antiquated farm machinery, a broken down tractor, various other old hand equipment rusting away on top of which there were thick brambles and long grass. Olivier would never have been able to do it on his own.

Having got as far as clearing away the path up to the shippen, they then had the problem of trying to open the huge solid oak doors, which proved impossible on the day.

The lintel had collapsed and sagged so badly that it was resting on top of the doors and holding them closed. Jacques could just squeeze through the gap but inside was even worse, there were boxes, fruit trays, sieves, garden equipment, and more farm machinery including a huge hopper of some kind. If they couldn't open the doors, then they couldn't clear out the area around the car. He couldn't even see a car.

The building looked to be in quite a dangerous state. The doors were supporting the end wall. If they opened the doors, the end wall would collapse and then the rest of the building would probably fall down too. Perhaps they should have looked at it a

116

bit sooner, they thought. Jacques agreed to take some accro props from work and drop them over to Olivier's on the Monday evening.

NEWTON ABBOT, MAY 1999

Max rang the *Sunday Times* and asked to be put through to the Motoring Section classified advertising.

Now that he'd secured funding for the prestige cars, he was keen to run some adverts in the *Sunday Times*. He was due to fly out to Stuttgart the following week to collect a brand new Ferrari 360 Modena coupe, which was being bought for stock. He wanted to turn the car around quickly, get it advertised and get it sold. A quick sale would make some money for Velodrome and Dimo and then they could go again.

He decided to run two adverts, one advertising the Ferrari 360 and the other a general Ferrari advert asking if people were looking for anything Ferrari, and then call Velodrome. Max ran through the copy with the classifieds staff, booked a run of four weeks and paid by the company credit card.

Max was buying the 360 from Autosportivo in Germany. The guy there was Josef Norbert. He was a really nice guy and the same man that Ferris had used nearly a year earlier when they had supplied the new Porsche to Dimo. Max was due to collect the car and drive it back to the UK on transit plates. Dimo's money had arrived in Velodrome's account direct from Banque de Monaco a few days earlier and Max had transferred out the Deutschmark equivalent to Autosportivo, so all he had to do was collect it. For Max, it would be the start of a business that would be much more profitable than the bike business and get the company onto a much better financial footing.

The plan was for Max and Ferris to run the car side and leave Pete to run the core business, which was the bikes. It would mean that Max would have to go abroad a lot to all points around Europe, but if Velodrome were making money, then it had to be a good thing.

Max had started an email database and a fax database of all the Ferrari dealers and specialist Ferrari dealers around the world and had now begun sending information out to each and everyone of them, saying what he had available and asking if

117

they in turn were looking for anything in particular. What he was amazed about, was the level of response. He was getting enquiries from all sorts of people all over the world.

TEIGNMOUTH, DECEMBER 1976

Caro stood on the steps of St. Michael's church on the seafront at Teignmouth. It was Christmas Eve. She was deep in conversation with her best friend Vicky who looked quite upset. That all disappeared when Max and Rob walked up to meet them.

'Hi, all right,' said Max.

They both said, 'Yes,' accompanied by Caro saying, 'Come on let's go in, it's freezing out here.' Once a year only, that's the most likely time most of us go to church. It was the evening carol service and both Max and Caro had been to the same service the year before. Max opened the door and ushered his friends through and followed them to the pews where they sat down whispering this and that.

Rob had always fancied Vicky and this was his opportunity to be alone with her as such. Max was with Caro. Just good friends even if at times it could seem something more than that.

Whether it was the season of good cheer or something else, it was definitely good for Rob. Vicky seemed quite receptive to Rob's attention to her and after the service, the four of them all walked together to the Ship Inn on the back beach. They had a riot. The Ship on Christmas Eve was a great place to be. Everyone knew each other. All the happy reddish faces glowing, laughing and joking, frolicking and loving every minute. These were golden moments in time, which Max would remember forever.

The four of them left the pub at gone 10:00 pm. Vicky was in potentially the worst trouble if she missed the last bus. Her father was a policeman and he didn't like her being out late. Rob would be okay. He walked with Vicky to the bus stop and waited with her until she got on it.

Max and Caro walked home from the triangle up to the top of Teignmouth. About half an hour away.

'So what was wrong with Vicky earlier? She seemed

118

quite upset when we turned up.'

They were walking arm in arm, like they always used to, when she stopped and looked at Max.

'It's difficult. No, it's complicated.'

'Why? What can be complicated about our lives? It's not like we've loads to do or worries is it?'

'No, it's not like that. It's complicated because I can't tell you the whole story.'

'Try me,' said Max.

'I can't.'

'Oh go on, you've started now, you've got to tell me something.'

'Okay, I'll tell you a bit, but you mustn't say anything, ever. You promise?'

'Yes, of course, she's not pregnant is she?'

'Oh God no, it's nothing like that, thank goodness. She's very upset that's all.'

'What about?'

'She'd really like to go out with someone, but he's not interested in her or at least he's not showing any interest in her and it's really getting to her.'

'It's not Rob then?'

'No, it's not Rob, but that might help, if it happens.'

'Do I know this person?' asked Max. 'Is he in our year?'

'I don't want to say. It's not for me to say.'

'Oh right, I mean does this guy know she fancies him. Has she made it obvious?'

'Well, she thinks she has but he doesn't seem to be noticing. I don't think it's because he doesn't like her. I just think he doesn't realise. He hasn't cottoned on at all. It's quite funny really.'

'Why doesn't she ask him straight out?' asked Max.

'Well she hasn't got the nerve for that. I couldn't do it and she definitely couldn't.'

'Is this chap going out with someone else?'

'No, he's not, but he has been out with a few girls, so that's sort of adding to her upset really.'

'How long has this been going on?'

'You're not going to believe it, but she's had this thing for him since the fourth year.'

'You're joking.'

'No, I'm not, it's absolutely true,' she chuckled.

'It's Christmas as well, so she's more emotional than normal and it doesn't help that she keeps seeing him all the time at school and out on the town.'

They continued walking up Haldon Avenue and left into Lower Woodway.

'What's she going to do?' asked Max.

'I don't know. Hopefully, if something happens with Rob, it will take her mind off him. I hope so.'

'Well, I know he's interested, so it will be down to her, not him.'

They turned right at the junction of New Road and strolled slowly up the hill.

'Just a thought, why don't you ask him on her behalf or find out on her behalf. It would save her the embarrassment if he wasn't interested, wouldn't it it?'

Max walked her up to her front door and stepped inside the porch, looking in through the glass at the festive lights and the Christmas tree in the hallway.

'I can't do that. I just couldn't do it. Anyway it gets worse.' Her voice quietened as she said the last bit.

'What do you mean it gets worse? Surely it can't get any worse?' He chuckled.

'Sandra thinks exactly the same about this guy and the pair of them talk about him when Vicky comes up here. It's really difficult. I've heard Sandra cry herself to sleep thinking about him. I've been into her bedroom at night and she's been completely beside herself.

'Jeez, who is this guy? Superman?'

'No, he's just a nice chap who hasn't got a clue about what's going on around him. Well at least not as far as these girls are concerned'. She grabbed hold of him. 'Please don't go saying anything will you? I've told you in complete confidence, that's all. Don't even joke about it. They would be horrified if they knew I had told you.'

Caro's mum tapped on the glass, 'Come on you two.'

'I've got to go.'

'Yeah, okay,' said Max

She put her arms around his neck and gave him a long kiss.

'Happy Christmas Max.'

'Happy Christmas Caro.' He walked down the drive and waved before turning the corner and out of sight. Caro waved

120

back and whispered quietly, 'love you'. He wouldn't have heard her and he wouldn't have known either.

'Hi Steve, it's Bill, sorry it's so late but I wanted to get back to you on the E-Type.'

'Thanks Bill, I was hoping you would call,' said Steve.

'Is there any movement on the price?'

'What are you saying?'

'Well, if we can agree a price, then I think we could probably do a deal.'

'Okay, what sort of figure do you have in mind?'

'Sixty five.'

Steve knew that even though Bill was an exceptionally wealthy man, he always wanted a deal, which is why he'd bumped up the price to £78,500.

'Bill, you know I can't do it for that.'

'Well where's it got to be. No, tell you what, I'll go to £70,000 on it.'

'Make it £72,500 and I'll sort it all out for you.'

'Okay, that's all right. I'm away for a few days, so speak to Jennifer. Give her all the details and the wiring instructions and we'll get the money transferred. Can you sort out the collection and delivery?'

'Where do you want the car to go?' asked Steve.

'Actually don't worry about that for a minute. I'll get the money over to you. You secure the car. I'll probably keep it in the UK. I've got a good guy over there that I shall probably get to run it, but I need to speak to him first and I can't do that until after I get back.'

'Do you want the money in dollars or pounds?'

'Pounds, please Bill. I've got a UK bank account, so it would be best if you transfer the money into that account.'

'Yes, that'll be okay. We will send the money from our Barclays account in Kensington, so it should be in your account on the same day. Okay, I'm going to leave it with you and speak to you in a couple of days.'

Steve could sense that Bill was in a bit of a dash, so simply said thank you, have a good break and we'll speak soon.

He slowly replaced the receiver, sat back in his chair and rested his head on his hand. He was pleased. Bill was a good customer, made decisions quickly, always came through with the money and was easy enough to deal with if he had the right product. This E-Type was the right product, not quite the real deal, but close enough and just as importantly, it was highly eligible for the right tours and competitions throughout the world.

Steve was tired, so he decided not to call Graham Lord there and then, he'd wait until tomorrow like he'd already said.

GAUTENG, JUNE 2000

Captain Rux picked up the phone.
'We need to speak.'
'Okay, when?'
'Tomorrow afternoon. 2:00 pm. Yours?'
'Yeah, that's good for me. Got much?'
'Yeah, I've made a start. Can't talk now. Tomorrow?'
'Yeah, good.'

Rux put down the phone, gathered up the paperwork in front of him and put it away neatly in his desk drawer and then locked it.

STUTTGART, SEPTEMBER 2000

Josef was waiting at Stuttgart airport in the arrivals lounge as Max walked through carrying a small brown leather holdall. The flight was over an hour late which meant they would get held up in the city traffic.

Max placed his bag in the back of the Mercedes ML and climbed into the front alongside Josef.

'Where are we collecting the car from?'

'It's about two hours away, just outside Heidelberg, between Heidelberg and Mannheim. It's all ready for you. Only problem is that I haven't been able to get the transit plates for you. I can get it done tomorrow morning though, said Josef.

Max didn't want to wait until the following day to get the transit plates. He needed to be back in the UK. He was annoyed that he didn't bring the company trade plates. At least that would have been a number plate.

'Josef, I need to go tonight. I can't wait until tomorrow. I need to be back.'

'I'm sorry, I can't get the transit plates tonight.'

'Okay, I'll just write the trade plate number on the back of the car. Have you got a black marker pen?'

'You're joking?'

'No, I'm serious. It's 5:30 pm now, I can be in Calais before midnight and home by 4:00 am, get some sleep and back into work before 10:00 tomorrow morning.'

'You're mad Max. I don't know anybody who drives like you do. Don't you get tired?'

'Yeah, of course I do, but I find that if I take a half hour nap when I get tired, it recharges me and I can then go for another three or four hours.'

Josef turned into the garage car park. The Ferrari 360 was in the middle of the fully glazed showroom, brightly lit in front of the slightly open doors. It looked fabulous.

'All the paperwork's done Max. We just need your signature here and here,' said Helmut Kopel the garage principal, pointing at the paperwork.

Max looked around the car checking for any marks or blemishes, and then checked the leather pouch with all the manuals. Everything was there including the aluminium Ferrari torch, exactly as it should be. Max switched on the ignition and checked the digital fuel level and the mileage – 186 km. *Maranello test mileage*, he thought. It was full just as he had asked.

Helmut opened the showroom doors fully as Max wrote his trade plate number 246TT in black felt pen in the number plate recess. Josef looked at Helmut and rolled his eyes.

Max saw them and realising their disbelief said, 'It's no big deal, the French do it all the time and even if I did get stopped, the number could be traced to me anyway. I won't go back through Frankfurt and Cologne, I'll cut across to Saarbrucken and go up through Luxembourg. It's only the German police that might cause a problem. I've got all the paperwork. I'm not worried about it.'

He was a little bit concerned, but it was night time, there was still quite a lot of traffic on the road. He would just blend into the background, if that was possible with the latest Ferrari.

Max fired up the car and drove it out of the showroom into the wet evening. Josef waved goodbye as Max pulled out onto the main road and looked at Helmut, shaking his head.

'The English, they're mad.' Josef agreed.

Max wasted no time in getting the Ferrari into the outside lane of the autobahn, keeping a reasonable chipping distance away from the car in front. As the time rolled on, the traffic thinned and Max was able to light up the 360. Calais before midnight and safely home in bed just after 4:00 am. It was a good drive, no problems and Max thought that the Ferrari was a good car. Easy to drive quickly, reasonably comfortable, good lights but poor instrumentation. The digital readouts were not easy to determine quickly and the air conditioning controls were too random around the cockpit. Apart from that, would he buy one? No. The 355 was prettier and nicer to drive, more of a driver's car. None of that mattered though because it was only a potential profit centre and that's how he was thinking. The enthusiasm for those types of cars was waning. It was now an opportunity to earn some money.

Catherine placed a cup of tea on the bedside cabinet and sat down next to Max on the edge of the bed. She was five months pregnant expecting their first child. Max sat up.

'You did well last night. Weren't you in Luxembourg when you rang?'

Max played it down. 'Yes, the traffic was fairly light so I had a good run.'

Catherine was always amazed at how far Max would travel and the time it used to take. It was almost like she'd be tidying up around the house of an evening and in the same time frame, Max had crossed a continent.

'How's the junior?'

'Kicking again last night. I think it's going to be a feisty one.'

'It'll take after you then,' Max replied.

The rear gates at the garage were open ready for Max to drive straight in. The valet was waiting for him as he got out of the car.

'I think it's going to rain Primate, so do the outside first and I'll come back down and put it inside for you to finish off. They called him Primate because he was small and looked like a monkey, but he was very good at his job. He could make even the worst bike look good, so cars were a doddle for him.

124

Max walked through the showroom and into Pete's office.

'Hi,' he smiled. 'Good trip.'

'Yes very good, no problems.'

'Nice car?'

'Yes, very quick, loads of grip. You should have seen the roosters off the rear diffuser. Huge, just like an F1 car.'

'Have you heard the news this morning?'

'No, why?' asked Max.

'Okay, well I think we might have a problem.'

PAU, MAY 2004

That was the last bike off the van. The trip from Caen to Le Mans had gone perfectly but the customer was late for the meeting at Limoges and had delayed Max by nearly an hour. With at least two hours to Pau, Max wouldn't get to Jacques house until at least eight to eight thirty even if he went flat out all the way. He rang Jacques and told him he was going to be a bit late, but cut the connection before Jacques had the chance to finish the conversation.

Not to worry, thought Jacques. He'd deal with the problem when Max arrived.

Jacques got on the phone to Olivier. 'Hi, it's Jacques; he'll be here at about 8:30 am so we should be with you by nine. Is that okay?'

'Yes, of course. Have you told him about the access?'

'No, not yet. I tried, but he cut me off.'

'Okay, it shouldn't be a problem. He can crawl in there if he wants,' said Olivier.

'Okay, we'll see you later.'

The drive from Limoges to Pau was full of trepidation for Max. Was he wasting his time, or was there something real to have a go at? He'd soon find out. Two and a half months of occasional and sometimes intense thought was about to come to an end. Nothing ventured, nothing gained.

Jacques was standing at the front window as Max pulled up in the van and gestured a quick hello.

'Hi Max, good drive?'

'Yes, long, but not too bad.'

'Everyone okay?'

'Yes thank you.'

Antoinette came to the door as Max walked through the front gate. She gave Max a kiss on each cheek, which took him a bit by surprise. *Like old friends*, he thought.

'Do you have time for something to eat, Max?'

'Umm.'

Before Max could answer, Jacques suggested they quickly went over to her fathers, looked at the car and had something to eat when they got back.

'Yes, that's okay with me,' said Max.

They both jumped into Jacque's car and set off into the countryside. Jacques was a bloody lunatic at the wheel. Max went for the imaginary brake several times and winced at how close he was to the hedge. It didn't seem to bother Jacques. They drove along the country lanes for about twenty minutes and then pulled into a gated driveway. Max could see the house in the distance about four hundred yards away. There were a couple of lights on and even though it was dark, he could make out the shape of the house quite easily. It looked beautiful. There were stone buildings on the right of the drive and a picket fence on the left.

The outside light flickered on as the car stopped outside the front door.

'My father in law is called Olivier, he's over eighty and he doesn't speak English, so I will translate anything you need to know.

Max said, 'If he speaks slowly, I will try to understand him.'

'Okay, we'll see how it goes.'

'Ah, Jacques, you've brought your friend.'

'Yes, Olivier this is Max.'

'Bonsoir, comment allez vous?'

'Ca va, merci.'

Jacques looked at Max. 'We have a little problem Max. The doors to the building where the car is are stuck and we cannot open the doors to remove all the rubbish. You will be able to get in, but it's very dirty and there are lots of things in the way. And the other problem is that there is no electricity in there. We have a torch though.'

'Well, I've come all this way so we'll give it a go. Is the car covered?' asked Max.

'Yes, it's covered, many boxes and other things.'

Max was still up for it, so the three of them made their way back up the drive a short walk and then turned left between two buildings. Olivier opened the wooden gate and walked across the cobbled courtyard to two tall wooden doors, one of which was slightly open.

Jacques spoke to Olivier in French. Although Max caught a few words, the conversation was too quick for him to understand.

'In here?' Max asked.

'Yes, the car is at the back on the right hand side.'

Olivier handed the torch to Max and it went out as soon as Max took hold of it. He shook it, and it lit up again. *This is good*, he thought. He squeezed through the opening and shone the torch around the room. He didn't think it would look so good in the daylight. The first problem was to try to get past a huge oil tank that was lying across the doorway at an angle. Max had a two thousand litre one at work and this one looked bigger than that. He didn't want to try to climb over it, not least because it was so filthy, but he wasn't sure how stable it was. He shone the torch at the ground and could see a gap under the angle of the tank. He could probably get through there, he thought. He lay down on the earthen floor and pulled himself along until he could get up on the other side of the tank. He shone the torch, but with so much rubbish in there, he still couldn't see the car. A huge wooden dresser had fallen from against the wall and was only being prevented from falling to the floor by a tall feed hopper. Everything seemed to be relying on everything else for support. Max moved a load of boxes out of the way to make a clearing. He was less than four feet from the car and he still couldn't see it.

Jacques shouted, 'Are you okay; can you see it?'

'Yes, I'm okay, I'm nearly there, just need to move a few more things.'

'Okay,' said Jacques.

Max leant forward and pulled at a chrome bar, it was an old pram. A box fell down from somewhere above and deposited what he thought was a load of rotten apples over him and for a moment he lost his footing and dropped the torch and it went out.

'Are you okay?' Jacques asked again.

'Yes, I'm okay, I just dropped the torch and it's gone

out. It's all right, don't worry.'

Max was laying across 'God knows what', with his right hand searching across the floor below, wondering what he was going to put his hand into next. It was pitch black, he couldn't see a thing. He could smell the waft of oil, rat's wee and rotten fruit. It wasn't ideal.

He felt the end of the torch with tips of his fingers and tried to tap it towards him. He was at full stretch. He tapped it again and the light flickered on, dim at first, then bright, then dim and then it stayed bright. Max inched forward and leant through the gap to try to pick up the torch. He was lying on something squishy. The light was shining away from him and then he saw it. Unmistakeable. He could see the rear left wheel. There was no tyre on it, but he instantly knew what it was.

FORT LAUDERDALE, AUGUST 2000

Steve Majendie called Graham Lord and confirmed the sale of the E-Type.

'Graham, we can go ahead on the Jag. Could you please send me a contract of sale detailing chassis number etc?'

Graham replied, 'Who do you want to make it out to?'

'Umm, probably, no definitely make it out to me at SM Classics. You've got all my details haven't you?'

'Yes,' said Graham.

'Okay, email it to me and I will sign and return it to you. I'm expecting the funds into my UK account tomorrow or the day after, so if you can give me the bank details for the transfer, I can get that organised. I'm not sure about where the car is going as yet, but I will know a little more in a couple of days. Is the car okay to stay where it is for a while?'

'Yes, it should be fine. I will check for you and let you know,' Graham confirmed.

'It's a pleasure doing business with you Graham, as always. Many thanks.' Steve rung off.

Graham pressed speed dial "D". Karen picked up the phone.

'Good morning, Donald Key Restorations.'

'Hello Karen, it's Graham, is Don in?'

'Yes, just a moment Graham, I'll put you through.'

'Hi Graham, how are you?'

'Very well thank you. I've sold the E-Type.'

'That's good news.'

'I'm sending off the contract this morning, but I've dealt with the client several times before, so it won't be a problem.'

'Who's buying it?'

'I don't know. I haven't asked. I've dealt with the middleman. He's an agent for the buyer. He won't let us down.'

'Okay, that sounds very reassuring. Can I expect your commission invoice?'

'You certainly can. I'll get the payment in and all the paperwork done so it should all go through in the next few days. Can the car remain with you for a short while?'

'Yes, we've got space at the moment but it will be tight if it's still here in two weeks. Try to get it away before then if you can,' said Don.

'I'm only expecting it to stay with you for a few days. The buyer is away on a break, so I'll be told what to do when he gets back.'

'Okay, well done on that. Oh just one more thing, my Asian client is looking for a new left hand drive Ferrari 360 F1, if you know of one.'

Graham replied, 'I might be able to help on that one, but I'll have to check and come back to you.'

'That would be good. Thanks.'

Graham Lord put down the phone and made a note on his pad about the 360. He didn't know of a car but wanted to make sure Don would stick with him on it and save Don the trouble of looking elsewhere. It worked. Don was busy and hadn't got the time to chase around for a car, he'd leave that to Graham. Let him earn his money.

TEIGNMOUTH, DECEMBER 1976

Chicago were playing 'If you leave me now' on the radio. It had been No. 1 in the charts on Max's birthday and he was singing along to the tune when he saw Rob coming down the drive. He was expecting him.

'So what's wrong spunk bubble?'

'I don't know. I just can't get it going, and my spark

129

plug spanner doesn't fit that well.'

'Have you got the tea on then?'

'Yes, I can make a cup of tea.'

'You make the tea and I'll see if my plug spanner is any better than yours,' said Rob.

There was no one at home except the pair of them. Max made them both a mug of tea and went back out into the garage.

'It doesn't look like this plug has ever been out. TVM obviously didn't change it. It's so tight. Have you got a bar or something to lever it with?'

Max looked at the lawnmower, the usual source of parts. 'I'll have a look. See what I can find.'

Max came back with a length of tube and Rob had a go with that.

'So what's happening with young Valerie then?' pushed Max.

'Wouldn't you like to know?'

'So?'

'I'm meeting her later at the Dawlish Inn. She's staying with Caro tonight, so her old man won't be a nuisance. She's nice though. I hope it works out. She seems interested. You just can't tell though, can you? Women. Anyway, what happened about that girl the other night?'

'What, Bridgitte?'

'Yeah, the one at the pub, short blonde hair, real looker.'

'No, she's not interested in me, she's the sister of one of Neil's friends. Nice though. Would if I could,' Max said with a smile.

'I still can't move this at all.' Barely had he finished the sentence when the spanner jolted and he gauged his hand across the top of the cylinder head ripping his fingers and deeply cutting his palm. 'Fucking hell!' he grimaced, holding his hand out in front of him, the blood dripping onto the floor. 'God, that fucking hurt.'

'I'll see if I can find something. Come into the kitchen and we'll get it sorted. Are you all right?'

'Oooh, that hurt, I feel a bit sick,' he laboured.

'Never mind that, did you get the plug loose?' Max joked, 'I hope you haven't damaged my bike.'

'Bugger your bike.'

Max went to the first aid box. There was a knock at the front door. It was Caro.

130

'Ah, that was good timing, can you have a look at Rob's hand, he's scratched it.'

Caro sorted it out and told them she was babysitting, 'You can come down if you like.'

'Rob's going off with Vicky, so yes I'll come down in an hour if that's okay.' He needed time to have a wash thinking Caro's mum would have been none too pleased if he reeked of petrol.

It was the last Christmas they spent together. They didn't realise it at the time, so they didn't make the most of it or perhaps they did. Perhaps, just enjoying each other's company was enough. Whatever the future held, it was going to be very different.

Time was moving on. Christmas gave way to the New Year and a new Spring Term, mock 'O' Levels and decisions to be made. What did Max want to do? Did he want to stay on in the sixth form or go to technical college and if he did go, what course was he going to take? Decisions.

Almost to the day two years previously, there was no decision to make. He would be going into the family business, but that had all changed, there was no family business. Max hadn't heard from his father since, now he could do what he wanted, not what someone else wanted. But what? He didn't know.

It was easier for Caro, she wanted to go into the RAF and make a career of it, but first she'd stay on at school and do her 'A' levels in the sixth form.

Max didn't want to stay on for the sixth form, he wanted to go to pastures new. As such it was almost like approaching a fork in the road and they were getting closer to it each and every day. Caro would go left and Max would probably go right.

It was just after Ferris's second birthday when Max was sitting with Caro in the kitchen of her parent's house, nobody else was home. They were supposed to be revising, they weren't.

'Have you ever wondered if you've met the person you're going to marry?' asked Caro in a sort of sheepish way.

'Yes, I suppose I have, it's crossed my mind. Haven't thought about it seriously though.'

'You know, like how close you may have been to them, had you passed them in the street, were they standing next to you at the bus stop, and did you speak to them? That sort of thing.'

Max thought of what Mrs. Zachiry had said: "You will

131

marry the sister of a friend". Well it wasn't going to be Caro, because none of her siblings had been a friend of his before he met her. It was an interesting thought, though. A lot happens in your mid to late teens, everything goes so fast, you're always up to something, meeting different people. You could well meet someone momentarily that later you'd end up with.

Max looked at Caro. 'There's so much I want to do, getting married ties you down.'

'No it doesn't, not at all, you'd enjoy it together. See everything, do everything, experience it all together and remember it forever, whatever.'

'Well, when you put it like that, it sounds a lot better,' said Max. He continued, 'I don't know, sometimes there's that feeling of restraint or responsibility which you wouldn't have on your own'.

They didn't get any revision done. They sat idly and chatting listening to music, horse playing until late in the day. They'd had a good day like good friends do. No pressure to talk, being together was enough, more than enough.

Whether they had already met their future partner remained to be seen.

Rob's relationship with Vicky had blossomed. He was besotted, always around her place and she was so much happier. He was happy too. The Superman guy that she was so upset about hadn't disappeared from her mind. She had come to terms with it. He still didn't know even though he saw her quite a lot. Caro's sister Sandra was still head over heels with the same guy too.

Max felt that there was a certain inevitability about his immediate future. He'd always liked it at the Grammar School and the time was coming when he'd be leaving. He thought about his friends, and all the good times they'd had together, like a big happy family. By his own choice, he was thinking of moving on. It was still six months away but it would pass quickly. It was already 1977, he'd be 17 at the end of the year and he'd be in a different education environment altogether, so would Rob.

NEWTON ABBOT, JANUARY 1987

Max drove his BMW home to have some lunch, the radio was playing Foreigner's 'Cold as Ice' before the one o'clock news. The song reminded him of a time ten years earlier when he worked for John Moore at the Ness House Hotel. Max parked the car and held onto the ignition key as he listened to the local headlines. The second item rang out.

'Buck House Preparatory School, a private school run by Benedictine monks has given notice to parents of an immediate closure. The highly regarded boarding school has taught pupils from ages six to thirteen years since 1967. A spokesman for the Roman Catholic School has commented that the school had been losing pupil numbers over a period of years and was no longer a financially viable business.' The newsreader confirmed, 'There has been a lot of opposition against the closure with some parents forming a pressure group to oppose the decision.'

Max pursed his lips and thought, *Hmm, that doesn't sound right.* That sounded like a scandal is about to break, and he knew what it would be. The Catholic church didn't have to worry about the school being "financially viable"; the site on which the school was built was a huge income stream for the church. That argument was nonsense. No, there had to be a lot more to it than that. Max had left Buck House in 1974, it was now 1987; thirteen years had passed. It beggared belief that they'd managed to keep it quiet for that long. He shook his head and shut the car door. There was a fresh breeze, he took a deep breath.

HIGH WYCOMBE, AUGUST 2000

The familiar sound of the brass letterbox springing back alerted Graham Lord to the Sunday papers having just been delivered. He was single and lived alone and enjoyed his slow start Sunday mornings.

He read the front page of the *Sunday Times* scan reading the headlines and then picked through all the supplements to find the motoring section. Jeremy Clarkson's two page feature spread was always a humorous read.

He refilled his coffee cup from the cafeteria and leafed through the classifieds to the Ferrari section. Nothing, nothing, nothing, nothing, 355, 550, F40, no don't want any of those he thought to himself and then caught Velodrome's advert. Ferrari 360 Modena F1, rosso corsa, high spec, LHD, delivery mileage. POA Call Velodrome +44 1626 335000.

He outlined the advert and made a mental note to call them on Monday morning.

NEWTON ABBOT, FEBRUARY 2000

Six months earlier, Max walked across the showroom with Pete following behind. He tapped out the code on the security door and pushed it open.

'Do you want a coffee?' Pete asked.

'Yes please, that would be nice,' Max replied.

Pete walked into Max's office as he was booting up his computer and placed the two coffees on the desk mats. Every morning at 8:15 am, Max and Pete would have a sales management meeting to discuss the previous day's business and anything for the day, so that both knew what was going on and what action to take.

'So, what's the problem?' asked Max.

'I think it could be a major problem. Defra have banned *ALL* off-road motorsport because of the Foot and Mouth crisis, and it's with immediate effect.'

'Oh, bloody hell.' Max didn't swear very often, so it was more poignant that he had.

'Did they say for how long the ban is going to run?'

'No, it's immediate and there's no idea on when it could end. Some are saying it could be the end of the year,' Pete added.

Max let out a long sigh. 'That's not good, Pete, I'm going to need to think about that,' he said.

Velodrome were off road competition motorcycle dealers. They relied on sales of competition bikes, sales of accessories, parts, clothing, servicing of all things off road. They sponsored the South West Enduro Championship, they ran several competitors in the series and if the sport was banned, then effectively they had potentially little or no income. Nobody was going to buy bikes, parts, or accessories to go off road riding if you weren't allowed to ride your bike off road. Max switched on the television in his office and trawled through to the Sky News Channel. A few minutes later the presenter confirmed

Pete's earlier conversation.

'Christ, if it's not one thing, it's something else,' Max said to Pete. 'Look, you go into your office and write a list, an action plan and I'll do the same and we'll talk again after lunch.'

Max looked at Pete. 'I don't know, we could do without this.' Then held his head in his hands as Pete collected up the coffee cups and went back to his office.

Max clicked on 'Inbox' and waited for the emails to download, it took several seconds. He scrolled down the addresses and noted the one from Muzi Kweyaka.

It read. 'Dear Max, Thank you for taking the trouble to contact me earlier. I confirm my desire to start collecting a number of classic cars over the next few years and have attached a list for your interest.

In all instances, I would expect you to find an appropriate car and confirm the details to me following which I would instruct you to acquire the car or decline the offer. I have put some notes against some of the cars so as to help you with your search.

I do hope that we can do business and look forward to a fruitful relationship. Best regards, Muzi.'

Max read the email again and thought, *That looks good.* Couldn't have come at a better time. He downloaded the attachment and read through the list. There were twenty-five cars listed and a postscript on the end stating, more to follow. *Crikey,* he thought. *This could be the golden egg.*

He read the inventory one by one. They were the best cars in the world. Alfa Romeo 8C 2900, Alfa Romeo 2300 Monza Zagato, Bugatti Type 35C, Bugatti Type 51, BMW328, Ferrari 250 GTO, Ferrari 250 short wheel base, Ferrari 250 SWB Californian Spider (closed headlight), Ferrari 250 Testarossa, Ferrari 330 P3/4, Ferrari 206SP Dino, Frazer Nash LM replica, Gineta G5, Jaguar D Type, Jaguar E-Type V12 Commemorative edition, Lancia B20 Aurelia, and the list went on. There were a good thirty million dollars of value in those first sixteen cars let alone the rest of the list or come to that, more to follow. Surely, he could make some money out of that. If he'd been a cartoon character, the cash tills would have been ringing up in his eyes.

He clicked on reply and thanked Muzi for his email confirmation of their telephone conversation and added his intent to start looking straightaway.

It wasn't money in the bank, but it looked very

promising and with the current foot and mouth situation, it might be more than enough to counteract any losses Velodrome could have. Max knew that the business had to sell forty motorcycles just to break even. Lately, they had struggled to reach that number, but some of the deals in the month had been worth more than the average net profit on a deal so they were managing to keep on target. Max kept a sales chart on his office wall showing all the information month on month, year on year. Pete was responsible for keeping those targets and his commission depended on it, so it was always a constant pressure. Max's Ferrari sales were really supposed to be the profit on top of the normal business but if the foot and mouth really took hold then the Ferrari sales could be the only sales and that was a real worry. He hadn't been doing it long enough to rely on it, and also the demand on the bank account would be huge if they started selling more high value cars. It was bad enough when the average sale value was £5,000, but with the cars, the average sale value was nearer £65,000, thirteen times more.

He thought about Muzi and the potential profit he could make from some of the high value deals. A four litre Ferrari 250 GTO had sold privately in the early 1990s at the height of the boom to a Middle Eastern collector for a reputed ten million pounds. He thought it wouldn't be unreasonable to ask for a £50,000 commission on such a deal if he could pull it off. He thought about it. No, £150,000 would be more like it. The real answer was that he just didn't know what to ask or expect. This was a totally different situation and needed a completely different approach. First though, he had to find some cars. He'd had a lot of calls from his email and fax marketing and he was slowly working through those enquiries when Mike in the parts department buzzed through to him.

'Max, it's Mike, I've got a Rick Brady on the telephone for you. Ferrari enquiry.'

'Hello, Max Reed speaking.'

'Oh, hello, Rick Brady here, I noticed you had a Ferrari 360 Modean advertised in the *Sunday Times* yesterday.'

'Yes, that's right, a 360 F1, red with black leather, red callipers, challenge grills and scuderia wing badges,' said Max.

'How many miles has it done?'

'It's done 1236 kilometres. I collected the car out of the Ferrari showroom last week and it's parked in our service area at the moment. It's not registered yet.'

'What do you want for it?' asked Mr. Brady.

'The price is £109,950 registered on the road with twelve months road fund licence and number plates.'

'Would you be able to first register the car with a private number?'

'If we have the right paperwork, yes of course,' Max replied.

'Are you negotiable at all?'

'Well, maybe a little but the difficulty for me is finding another car to replace it.'

'Okay. I understand that. There's no part exchange, I'm a cash buyer. I don't need finance and I can pay a deposit on the telephone.'

Max sold the Ferrari for £107,500 and took a £7,500 deposit by credit card, which was effectively his profit on the deal. He asked Mr. Brady for all his details and faxed a contract out to him followed by the original in the post. The customer hadn't even seen the car. It was a good deal, Max had only had the car a few days and it was sold.

Pete walked in to Max's office just after 2:00 pm with his list of recommendations. Max read them through carefully. Focussed off road stock, change accessory stock, change advertising, staff numbers, service department, timescale, shift emphasis.

Max had written similar items on his list too, so both of them were thinking along the same lines.

'I think the first point we need to establish is how long this situation is going to last and we need to consider how long we are going to leave it before we start actioning some drastic measures,' said Max.

'Two weeks, a month?'

'I don't want to rush into anything. If we jump ship now and de stock, we will lose money on every bike and we're going to have to find that from somewhere. Who knows, this nonsense may only last a few weeks.

'And if it doesn't, we don't want to be six weeks down the line, because the stock's going to be worth even less. The clock's ticking. We'll be losing all ways. Stock devaluation, loss of income and maintained overheads.'

Pete hardly needed to have said. Max knew exactly where he stood. To run the company, cost £25,000 per month and that cost was going to happen regardless. On top of that, the devaluing stock would compromise the quarterly figures to the bank. Everything would and did have a knock on effect.

Max told Pete he would check out with Defra how long the problem could last and where. If there were regions around the country that didn't have the disease, then the answer would be to sell or trade out the bikes to dealers in that area, sooner rather than later.

The worst case scenario would be a full scale sale, followed by a change of direction to road bikes and scooters. It would mean changing all the accessories too. Whatever happened, they were going to lose a lot of money, so it had to be dealt with quickly.

There were a number of part exchange road bikes in the basement, which he had Primate clean up and bring into the showroom. He made room by removing duplicated competition bikes back down to the basement.

He decided not to do anything dramatic straight away and told Pete to wait a week and review it daily. See what happened. It was Russian roulette.

BUCKFASTLEIGH, JULY 1986

Father Phillip or Father Prior as his more commonly known title should be had waited nearly thirty years for the opportunity to arrive. It wasn't something he actively sought when he went into the church, but as time had gone by, he warmed to his ambition of becoming the man at the top of the tree.

Buckfast Abbey was a highly regarded Benedictine abbey for nearly eighty monks and as such had a highly prominent and respected place both in the local community and the diocese in which it served. It also had worldwide regard for its produce of Benedictine wine and honey.

Father Leo Abbot had recently died and being Abbot, the position had become vacant for a newly elected member. Being number two in the management of the abbey, Father Prior was the natural and most likely successor. He had more than thirty years experience in the Roman Catholic church having read languages at Cambridge before following the path that lead him to Buckfast Abbey in September 1966. He was well liked by his colleagues, his friends and was on first name terms with many of the local congregation. He was the ideal man for the job.

WANDSWORTH, JUNE 2000

The mood was not good at Testastretta, Chris was pacing up and down highly agitated stretching the phone to its limit as he tried to reconcile his position with his bank manager. Greg his partner was sitting down at his desk, with his head in his hands listening intently to the conversation. It didn't look good.

The bank wanted £60,000 in cleared funds before midday, otherwise they were going to bounce a cheque. Now the problem with that particular cheque was that it was payable to their principal supplier and if it did bounce, the supplier would withdraw his cars. Chris had been warned previously after a similar incident that if it happened again, then it was game over.

Chris put the phone down quietly and let out a sigh, 'They want £60,000 in cash before midday.'

'Yeah, I got the drift,' Greg replied slumping back in his chair.

'We've got nothing here to cash in quickly. Tom won't know until tomorrow if the cheque gets returned today, so I suppose we could say the customer paid us in cash and we didn't want to pay it in because of the charges. He might swallow that, but I don't think we could find the money by tomorrow either really.'

'When is the blue 355 Spider going out?' Greg asked.

'I haven't got him accepted on finance yet, it's looking okay, but I haven't had the final okay from John yet, and anyway it's one of Tom's so I don't know,' said Chris desperately.

'What if we blow a car? Get rid of it in the trade quickly, someone we know.'

'It will only buy us some time for a short while.'

'That's all we need isn't it. We just need to cash flow the banking until the money comes in for the blue car,' said Greg pushing the point.

'But suppose that car doesn't go ahead, what do we do then?'

'I think that we should worry about that if we need to. What we need to do is cover that cheque, otherwise we are completely bollocksed. Tom will be down with his posse and we'll be out of business, just like that. If we go my way, we stand a chance of carrying on,' Greg insisted. 'Otherwise we might as well put our hands up now and call it a day,' Greg replied. 'Anyway he's paid a £2,000 deposit so he isn't going to walk from that.'

'Which car are you thinking about?'

'I don't know, we don't own any of them except for the part exchanges, so it would have to be the Ferrari 456 or the Ferrari 550 Maranello.'

'Okay, who could we call that's got the money now, we've got an hour and a half to bank the money?'

'The problem is, all the usuals are in the same boat as us. I could try Dan at Ferracci and maybe Max at Velodrome,' suggested Greg.

'Okay, look, give it a try, but don't give away that we're desperate if you can.'

Greg got on the phone. Dan's number went straight to voicemail, so that didn't look very promising. He then tapped out Velodrome's number and as usual Mike picked up.

'Hi, Mike, it's Greg, can I speak to Max please?'

'Yeah, I'll put you through. Max it's Greg.'

'Hi Greg, how are you?'

'Okay thanks. Just seeing if you are looking for anything,' probed Greg.

'Yes, I am. I need another 360. Have you got anything?'

'You sold that one out of the *Sunday Times*?'

'Yes, Max replied.

Greg sensed an opportunity. Max would have been paid and got some money, so there was a glimmer of hope.

'I haven't got a 360, but I've got a lovely 550 Maranello and a 456 if you're interested,' Greg suggested.

'The 456 doesn't do anything for me and we've never had a 550. Don't think so really, unless it was cheap.' It was a throwaway line and Max didn't expect Greg to pick up on it.

'What's cheap?' asked Greg.

'Well tell me about the car first,' Max replied.

Greg filled him in on the condition, year and specification. When new it was over £170,000. A used '97 car with low mileage would have to be cheap for Max to be interested, only because he wouldn't be able to fund it otherwise.

'Seventy-five thousand,' Greg opened.

'Sorry Greg, it's not for me, I'm committed elsewhere.' It was a lame excuse for really saying, I don't want to buy it, I can't afford it. It wasn't true because Max hadn't got anything on the go that he was going to buy, but he didn't want to upset Greg by telling him he just didn't want to buy the car. 'Have you got anything else?' Max asked, and continued, 'What about the blue 355 Spider you had up there the other day?'

Greg began to answer and then said, 'Wait a minute Max, let me just speak to Chris.'

Greg held his hand over the mouthpiece and held the phone to one side as he whispered to Chris, 'He's asking about the blue 355.'

'Tell him you'll ring him back in a minute,' said Chris.

'Max? Sorry about that. Look, someone's just walked in the showroom, can I call you back in a few moments?' asked Greg.

'Yes, sure, no problem, speak to you shortly.'

Max put the phone down and thought about the 550. If he really wanted it, he could ring Dimo, but he thought better of it. He could sell the 355 Spider, but he was unsure about the 550 Maranello. Not having had one before, it was too big a risk to take and it would be unnecessary. He was better sticking with what he knew.

Greg rang back a few minutes later.

'We might be able to do something on the blue Spider,' he said. 'It would depend on you.'

'Okay, what do you want for it?' asked Max.

Max knew all the details on the car because he'd seen all the info on the car when he was last there.

'Max, we've got it up for £69,950 and we haven't got a lot in it.' Greg looked at his watch, it was just after 11 o'clock.

Max jokingly replied, 'You never have. So what do you want?'

'Sixty-three?'

Max sensed the reply as a question, never a good idea when you're trying to sell something because it leaves the seller open for a lesser bid. It's almost the same as the seller saying, 'will you give me sixty three thousand rather than saying it is sixty three thousand. The second way to say it is much more positive indicating you're not going any lower.

'Greg, I'm too far off to make it sensible for me. I'd be buying it for stock rather than a quick sale.'

'Look, Max, I'll be straight with you. I'll blow some money on the car if you can pay me before 12:00 pm. We've got another deal on the go and we need the extra money to make it work,' said Greg.

It was nonsense of course, but Greg had to give Max a believable reason for wanting the money quickly rather than telling the truth.

'So, what sort of deal are you doing?'

'We're trying to buy a Ferrari F40. It's the right car with the right mileage and the guy needs the money,' said Greg.

'Oh right then, that's fair enough. Greg, sorry to be hard, but it's £55,000 and I'll TT the money now.' Max held his breath and said nothing.

Greg ummed and ahhed and said, 'I'll call you back.' It was quarter past eleven. Chris looked at his watch.

'God, I hate all this,' he said, 'what've we got to give Tom.

'Sixty two,' Greg replied, 'and Max will give us fifty five grand before twelve.'

'We've gone from making nearly £8,000 profit on the car to making a £7,000 loss, just because the bank won't help and we can't cash flow it. Can we get the customer another car?' asked Chris.

'I don't know. Maybe. I don't even know what I'm going to say to the guy about his deposit,' Greg worried.

'We're going to have to do something in a minute otherwise it's going to be too late.'

'Do you want to try Dan again?'

'No, it's not worth it, we'd sound too desperate trying to get it done in half an hour.'

'In which case, we've either got to swallow the bitter pill now or swallow an even bitter pill tomorrow. That's the decision. I'm going to get a sandwich. I'll leave it to you. Do you want anything?'

'Cheese and pickle,' he replied.

Chris picked up the phone and called Max. They agreed a deal at £55,000 for the 355 and Max fired off a fax to the bank to exact the transfer. He then sent a copy of the fax to Chris, being careful to delete the codeword on his version.

In turn, Chris rang his bank, simultaneously sending the fax sent in by Max. His bank manager accepted the fact that Chris was going to be £5,000 light on the provision that there

142

were more funds due in later that day. The bank was not going to bounce the cheque.

Greg got back from the sandwich run, 'Done?'

'Yes, it's done. Max has sent the money.'

'Well that gets us out of the shit today, but it's going to get worse tomorrow, for sure,' Greg assured Chris.

'I know, all too well and I'm not looking forward to it. How to lose seven grand in one easy step.'

TEIGNMOUTH, JULY 1977

With 'O' levels out of the way, the summer of '77 was going to be good, not as good as the summer of '76, but Max knew he was going to have a good time. There were still goals. He had to pay his mother for a contribution towards his keep and he also wanted to change his bike for a 250cc bike when he was seventeen, and that would mean he would need to probably add £250 to the cost of his existing machine. Then, there was insurance and all the rest of it. The week before he finished at the Grammar School, he'd been down to the Ness House Hotel and had an interview with John Moore for a summer job. Max was going to run one of the snack kiosks that John had dotted around the local seaside area. He was looking forward to it. There would be very little interference from John, he'd just let Max get on with it.

The last week at school whizzed by. A few goodbyes, a few thank yous, a bit of tidying up and it was all over. No send off, a bit of an anti climax really. The end of year school photo was taken at the beginning of the summer term and that was the last record of a place in time.

Neil was working for TVM Motorcycles at Shaldon in the racing department so he was happy. Rob was working for his dad and Caro had got a job in a small department store in the town. They would all be still seeing each other right through the summer, but whereas they were quite a compact unit before, now they would start moving apart finding their own new space.

Max started his first day working for John Moore by first reporting at the hotel to collect the keys and cash float for the till. The kiosk had been fully stocked the previous day, so all Max had to do was open up and get on with it. John told him to make

143

his way over to the kiosk in Dawlish and he would be over later. It was a fifteen minute ride on Max's moped over to Dawlish and on a bright sunny day, with the smell of the sea in the air, he cherished every second of it.

Max opened up the kiosk and went inside to unlock the shutters. No sooner had he put the 'Open' sign out and he was deluged with holidaymakers. They'd all just got off a coach, wanting teas, coffees, biscuits, sweets etc. Max managed it okay. John had told him to switch on the hot water boiler as soon as he got in, and he hadn't forgotten. Good job too.

A white Jaguar XJ6 with a black vinyl roof pulled up alongside the kiosk with that lovely quality sound of tyres on gravel. Max recognised the number plate PAD525M, he'd seen it before at the hotel. It was John.

'Everything okay, Max? John asked as he sauntered up to him, very relaxed not appearing to have a care in the world.

'Yes, fine thanks. A bit of a quick start earlier. I had a coach load in. I didn't know all the prices, so I just made it up as I was going along.'

'There should be a price list board somewhere. I know I did it for you. I thought I brought it here yesterday. Maybe it's back at the hotel. I'll check.'

'I had a good look, but I couldn't see anything,' said Max.

'Well, don't worry. Let me just run through everything here.'

John gave Max the low down on all the stock, what to do and how to do it and then left him alone. He told Max that if the takings were more than £100 in the day, then he should drop it back to the hotel before going home, if it was less than £100, he could bring it with him in the morning. John's wife Jan, always made a packed lunch for the kiosk attendants so he would collect that from the hotel, hand over the takings, keep the float and then set off for Dawlish. John had also told Max that he could fill up his moped once a week and as long as he handed in a receipt to Jan on wage day, he could take the money from the day's takings. Max took that as a really nice gesture, which he hadn't asked for, but was very welcome. Petrol was a big expense.

Max really enjoyed the kiosk; it was the best job he could get. The money was good, he was well looked after and he was left alone to get on with the job. He met loads of people and that developed his confidence. It was the beach life, loads of

144

girls in bikinis; it really was a great time for him. A good laugh. John would come around in the Jag twice a week to restock and on occasion Max would sit outside with him and pass the time of day talking about this and that, bikes, sport, girls, all the important things in life. In many ways Max saw a lot of his father's nicer side in John and he liked him. He wondered whether he would have been able to sit down and have had a similar conversation with his father. He doubted it and he had felt sad about that. If ever he had children, he thought, he would want to be there for them, no matter what.

Max's mates would come over to the kiosk. Those on bikes would park up and perhaps go down to the beach and then come back later. Max would keep an eye on the bikes. It was all very casual and easy going. Radio 1 would be blaring away in the background. There was always something going on. The best day that Max had at the kiosk, he rang up £175 in the till. When it was sunny, he was busy but if it rained, it was very quiet.

Then there was the local tennis tournament. That really was a highlight. Max knew nothing about it. He'd vaguely seen some posters advertising it, but he wasn't prepared for the onslaught of girls that appeared at his kiosk on one damp morning. The tournament was a week long, knockout competition and there must have been more than a hundred taking part. When Max arrived at the kiosk, there were masses of scantily clad girls all over the place. *If only the boys could be here now*, he thought.

Once he'd opened up, they were at him straight away and because they were in numbers, they were cocky and confident, ribbing Max all the time. He took it in good humour, giving as good as he was getting, but there was one girl that did take his eye. He was a bit shy to say anything in front of all her friends and hoped she may come back on her own. Max thought she was a similar age to him, black curly hair, very pretty, slim. She was gorgeous. He didn't know her name but she stuck in his mind.

By the end of the week, a lot of the tournament players had fallen to the wayside so the numbers pestering him at the kiosk got less as the week wore on. Max was thinking about what time he was playing Rob at squash that night and J. Geils was playing 'My Girlfriend is a Centrefold' on the radio. Max was singing along to the opening bars, when he was interrupted by someone saying hello at the hatch.

145

Max turned around and she was standing there and *she* was on her own.

'Hi, sorry about that, can I help?' asked Max. He leant on the counter.

'Umm, could I have a 99 please?'

'Would you like a single or a double?'

'Single please.'

Max served her and took the money and gave her some change.

'How's the tennis going?' Max enquired. Anything to get her chatting and keep her in front of him. Then frustratingly an old bat with a brat came to the hatch and interrupted them. Max expected her to go but surprisingly she stayed.

'I've been knocked out. I got to the quarter finals but I wasn't good enough on the day to go any further,' she said.

'Oh, I'm sorry about that, but quarter finals is a good result isn't it?' Max asked.

'Yes, it's good, but I think I could have done better. I made too many silly mistakes.'

'I haven't seen you around. Are you local?'

'No, we've just moved down from Hampshire. My dad got promotion and had to move down here,' she informed Max.

'Do you like it?'

'It's different, but it's nice, I do like it. I miss my friends though.'

'Yes, I can understand that, so where are you living?'

'Teignmouth.'

'Whereabouts?'

'Higher Woodway, right at the top on the right hand side, the white house.'

'Yes, I know. I live about five hundred yards away from you as the crow flies in New Road.'

'Oh where?' she asked.

'If you are going home from here, you'd turn right into New Road and we're the first house on the left. It's about a couple hundred yards from the junction.

'Okay, I think I know where you mean,' she said.

A silver Ford Cortina pulled up and a lady wound down the drivers window.

'Hi, love, I'm late, I'm in a hurry.'

She turned to Max and said, 'It's my mother, gotta go.'

'What's your name?'

'Jenny,' she said with a smile running around to the opened passenger door.

'I'm Ma. . . x.'

She wouldn't have heard. Her mother was already turning the car around.

Wow, thought Max. *Yes, Yes, Yes. That's the one for me. Fat chance that would be, but then again, she did smile and she could have walked off when that old bat came to the hatch, and she didn't, so, so, so nothing really.* He didn't know. Maybe.

He leant on the counter with his forearm supporting him as he surveyed all before him thinking of you know who.

Max was playing squash with Rob at 6:20 pm then they were off to the fair. Anderton & Rowland would always set up on the Den at Teignmouth in the summer and Caro and Vicky said they were going, so Rob and Max had agreed to meet them at 8.00 at Caro's house, and then walk down to the town.

The four of them spent an hour or so at the fair, doing all the usual rides and stalls, bumping and whizzing. Max sat out the last ride. He felt a bit green from the previous ride. He stood at the side of the Noah's Ark watching them having fun, screaming and shouting, whirring round and round to the music and flashing colour lights. It always seemed to be the same music, T Rex, Slade etc and 'do you wanna go faster? Caro was at one end of the purple speckled swirling chair singing out loud to Band On The Run. Her hair was swinging in the wind and her smile was captivating. Max looked at her and thought how special she was. He hadn't really thought about her in that way in a while, but there and then in that situation, he was mesmerised by her cheeky smile and just how much fun she was. He loved her energy as she jumped out onto the walkway and went up to Max and grabbed his denim Wrangler jacket by the lapels and pulled him close to her and rubbed noses. He wanted to give her the most passionate kiss of his young life, but he didn't. She wanted him to give him the most passionate kiss of her young life but she didn't. Caro looked across at Vicky and she sort of looked away.

In an instant, Caro took hold of Max and Vicky's arm and with Rob on the other side of Vicky, they set off to the Ship Inn on the back beach. None of them should have been in there but Rob looked older than sixteen and those were the days when they could get away with being underage buying alcohol. The landlord turned a blind eye, more often than not. The other fact

147

was that the Ship had benches and seating outside on the beach so it was not such a big deal. Max and Rob shared the round and Rob came out with the drinks and they all sat on the beach amongst the ropes and chains and buoys and boats. Looking up the river with the moors in the distance and the setting sun beyond, casting its soft light across the shimmering water. The sound of flags and rigging mingled with the gentle lapping of the tide on the shoreline. It was cosy sat there on the beach. Max could see his father's old boat a hundred yards across the water. Max wondered whether these would be the best days of their lives.

By ten thirty, it was time to stroll home. They walked home in couples about ten yards apart along the sea front, past the Lido, over the railway bridge and up the cliff path. It was still light enough to see and the view from the top of the path was spectacular. Even though the route home would take longer than the more direct route up Barnpark and Woodway Road, it was worth it. Just before they reached Cliff Road, they had to pass through a cornfield, which was a public thoroughfare with a turnstile at each end. It had become dimpsy and a few bats were flitting about. Max and Caro watched them darting overhead, the other two were ahead of them and out of sight.

She rubbed her arms and said, 'It's getting a bit chilly.'

Max took off his jacket and offered it on to her shoulders. Refusing at first, then pulling it on, she left the collar upturned and she looked great.

Max slipped his hands inside his jacket and fastened them behind her back and pulled her close to him.

'I don't want to get cold,' he said.

She put her arms around him and held him tightly. It was now or never, Max thought, leant forward and kissed her. She put her arms around his neck and responded. It seemed to go on forever and it was beautiful. Her soft lips, the smell of her perfume, the coolness of the night, Max lost himself in the moment. She ran her fingers through his hair as his hand stroked her back up and down and over the top of her jeans. And then, just as quickly as it came, it went.

She stopped abruptly, as if someone had switched on the light and said, 'No, we can't.' She corrected herself, 'I can't, not now.' She looked to one side in the distance, still stood in front of him, stroking his chest with the palms of her hands.

'Why not?' whispered Max.

148

'I just can't, not now. I just can't, please don't push me,'
she said.

'Hey look, you know I'd never do that.'

Yeah, I know, it's just . . .'

'Look, it doesn't matter,' Max said sympathetically, but
deep inside he thought something else.

'It does,' she said. 'It does, because I don't want to leave
it like this. I love you!' She turned and faced him, and said
quietly, 'I think I always have, but I can't do anything now. I
know it sounds ridiculous, but that's because it is.'

Max thought about what she was saying, it didn't make
sense. She said she loved him, always had, but after a passionate
snog, she says she can't carry on. He hoped he wasn't sending
out a signal that he just wanted to shag her and that was perhaps
scaring her. Yes of course he did, any man would, but he didn't
honestly think that she was thinking that. No, it couldn't be that.
Maybe, it just wasn't meant to be.

Max looked at her, she had tears in her eyes. He held her
head in his hands and dried away the droplets with his thumbs.
She felt so soft, so fragile, she started to speak. 'I'm sorry.' He
placed his fingers over her lips and whispered, 'Ssshh, it's not a
problem, you don't have to explain.' He lifted her chin and
looked into her eyes, the moment had passed.

Max looked out across the field at the moonlit sea
beyond taking in the warmth of her body as he hugged her with
all the passion of a man leaving for war.

He could make out the sand banks in the estuary, the tide
had gone out.

EXETER, AUGUST 2008

Just three days and three nights and Reed would be on
his way to a hopefully better life. He had one long slow weekend
to get through followed by the Monday afterwards and that
would be it. Devon County Prison had not been for Reed, he'd
lost weight, he constantly felt dirty and he was desperately
unhappy being banged up twenty-three hours a day in the stifling
suppressing atmosphere of a small, Victorian prison cell.

Waiting for those three days to pass was going to be
difficult, but he had to do it no matter what.

The weekend timetable varied from the normal weekday schedule in that lunchtime and dinner were served a quarter of an hour earlier. 'Association', which is the free time period was at 2.00 pm, just after the screws got back from lunch. 'Association' or 'Domestics' was an opportunity for a prisoner to have a shower, clean his cell, change laundry or similar.

The prison hairdresser lived on 'C' Wing. He was a six foot, fit, black guy called Rapper Joe. He was in his mid thirties, fifteen stone and rock solid. He looked like Jimi Hendrix and he was one of the prison's larger than life characters. Reed had seen him setting out his stall the day before and he'd nodded as Max walked by.

Not only was he the wing hairdresser but he was also the main heroin dealer in the prison. Through his job, he was able to float from wing to wing plying his trade as the legitimate hairdresser and at the same time sell his extras. Before going to work, he would wrap his heroin and mobile phone in a surgical glove and stick it all up his backside. This was a regular method of concealment in the prison. Mobiles are banned and it was the easiest and best place to hide one. 'Easiest' would depend on how many times you had done it. Most first timers would have to use the margarine tubs served at breakfast as a lubricant until their rectum was more pliable. In a life of criminal innocence, Reed could hardly believe what he was hearing, but it was going on all around him, all of the time. He could rent a mobile phone on the inside for £50, complete with SIM card and charger. The thought of sticking the charger and the plug up his arse made him wince. The pheasant had offered him a phone but he hadn't accepted it, even though he would have loved to have been able to speak to Catherine and the children more often. The risk and cost was not worth it. It wasn't just the risk of being caught and losing the phone, it was the penalty too. Normally there would be an outside adjudication and forty two days added on to a sentence, but on top of that Max would then have to repay the pheasant with a new phone plus any downtime on any overdue return. In short, you'd have to get a replacement phone in from the outside and that would mean getting a phone in through the visiting hall. It didn't bear thinking about, but many prisoners were all too ready to take that risk.

Rapper Joe walked along the C2 landing. Max, Karl and Tom could have seen him from where they were standing, two landings above.

It was a beautiful summer's day outside and Reed had walked to the end of the landing to look out through the large grilled window taking in the rooftop view of the city of Exeter. He thought about shopping with Catherine, having coffee in Cathedral Yard, meeting his brothers Ferris and Neil in Starbucks, and Rob's old printing works almost directly opposite the prison gates. For a few moments, he was away from the prison and living in the outside world. It didn't last.

Max had heard a bit of a scuffle behind and below him somewhere, but unlike when he first arrived at the prison, when he would have scuttled back to the relative safety of his cell, this time he carried on looking out of the window ignoring the animals. *Let them get on with it*, he thought.

Then the screaming and the shouting started. Rapper Joe had been jumped by two cons and bundled into a cell where another prisoner was waiting. Joe put up a hell of a fight against the three determined assailants who had slowed him down by slamming the door on his head. He fell to the ground. The screws were racing through the landings and up the stairs, the alarms had been sounded. The cons jumped up and down on top of Joe's limp body until he crapped himself and out popped the mobile phone and the heroin. From start to finish, it took no more than forty five seconds, such was the brutality of the assault.

Max had run back down to his cell as an army of guards shoved everyone back into their cells and shut the spy hole flaps. Max never did know what happened to Joe, but he had seen all the blood in the entrance to the cell, he heard the screws shouting for help and he heard the ambulance arrive and go. There was a twenty-four-hour prison lock down. Max thought, *Christ, that's a guy's life down there on the floor, he is probably dead, and for what? A mobile and some heroin.* There were no values. It was horrific. Max wondered what the judiciary would think if they had to sample prison life under cover. They'd certainly have a better idea of what they were sending criminals down for. He kept thinking all the time, the punishment didn't fit the crime. The fear was still there but now he had come to expect these happenings. It was part of everyday prison life. It had become almost normal to him.

Tom had told Max that Leyhill was a better prison. An open prison, no barbed wire, more of a holiday camp than a prison. After Exeter, it seemed too good to be true.

On and off that weekend, Max still had the thought of

151

writing a book rattling around in his mind. The more he thought, the more he felt he had something to say. He considered the storyline, the characters, their plights and the overall theme and was juggling around with them. If he did make a start then he would do it at Leyhill as it would be difficult at Exeter. If, what he had heard about Leyhill was true, he would have his own room and be able to come and go as he pleased and have a bit of privacy. It was becoming more of a possibility. Just one day to go.

SLOUGH, AUGUST 2000

Graham Lord sat in his car outside Donald Key's Restorations works and picked up the newspaper he'd put on the passenger seat. It was folded on the right page face down. He pressed out the number on his key pad and waited for it to ring.

He turned down the volume on the radio as a voice answered 'Velodrome, can I help you?' It was Primate, he'd been walking past the reception desk and hearing the phone ringing and no one at the desk, he'd answered it.

'Yes, I'd like to speak to someone about the Ferrari 360 advertised in the *Sunday Times*.'

'Certainly, I'll try to put you through.'

Mike walked back into the showroom and Primate handed the phone to him. Mike mouthed to him, 'Who is it?' Primate didn't know.

Mike took control. 'Good morning, just putting you through, who's calling please?'

'Graham Lord.'

'Thank you Mr. Lord.'

Mike rang through to Max and put him through.

'Hello, Mr. Lord, how can I help?' asked Max.

'You have a Ferrari 360 advertised in the *Sunday Times*. I was wondering if you could tell me a little more about it.'

'We've sold the car I'm afraid. We've been paid the deposit, so we're just waiting for the paperwork to come through so that we can register it. Is it specifically a 360 that you are looking for?'

'Yes, I have a customer for a new delivery mileage 360.'

Max replied, 'I am due to speak to someone this

afternoon about another car, I haven't got all the details about it just yet, but it is a delivery mileage left hand drive 360 F1. Much the same as the car advertised. If that's any good to you, I can take your details and call you later.'

Graham gave Max his details and asked the simple question, 'Why Velodrome, bearing in mind you are selling cars?'

'We're principally a motorcycle dealer, that's why,' Max answered.

'Oh, that's interesting, I've got a Yamaha R1.'

'Nice bike,' said Max. 'We are mainly an off road dealer, although we are trying to reverse out of that at the moment, because of the foot and mouth disease, but hopefully we can change the stock mix and offer more sports bikes. We've had a few sports bikes over the years, Fireblades, 888's that sort of thing. You mentioned that the car was for a customer. What do you do?'

'I tend to concentrate on classic racing cars and the like, but I also get involved in classic cars and aircraft.'

Max liked the sound of the racing cars and asked Graham, 'Do you race yourself?'

'Yes, I do. I've got a few bits and pieces around me at the moment and I have a guy that works for me helping me run the cars. I'm on the lookout for a McLaren M23 if you know of one.

Max told him that he didn't ever come across that sort of thing, but he'd make a note of it and let him know if anything cropped up.

'Do you come across cars like GTOs, Testarossas, short wheel bases, that sort of thing?' Max asked.

'I've got many customers around the world for that type of car. If you are looking for something like that, I could probably help.'

'Okay, I'll have a think on that one.' Max didn't want to jump straight in with, well I'm looking for $30 M dollars worth of classic cars, he'd just spoken to him and didn't know him from Adam, so he decided to ask him a little bit more. 'So, have you always been involved in these cars?'

'No, always been interested, but no, I was originally involved in setting up Apple. Apple computers?'

'Yes, I know,' said Max.

Graham continued, 'And then I sold my shares and now

153

spend my time and money indulging myself in what I really prefer.'

Max listened intently trying to extract as much information from Graham as he possibly could without him realising it.

'So do you come from a motoring background? Was your father into motor racing as well?'

'Good God no, my father works in the City at the Bank of England.'

'Well that couldn't be any more different. How long have you been racing?'

'On and off for twenty years, I think,' Graham replied. 'Oh yes I almost forgot, I also had a short spell at Coys.'

'Just the classic stuff or moderns as well?'

Max knew a lot about motor racing so he was probing Graham without him knowing that he knew much about it.

'Mainly sixties and seventies racing cars, Formula One and Formula 2, Formula 5000 and I track day the R1. That really is a fantastic motorcycle. For the money, there is so much performance. There's nothing to touch it. It's a little bit small for me, but what a bike,' said Graham.

'Yes, it is a superb bike, we sold several when they first came out in 1998. We were importing them from Germany,' Max commented.

'What about you? Do you race?'

'We run an Enduro team here and I've raced in the South-West Enduro Championship for many years, I've done quite a bit of trials. That's the bike side and as for cars, I did Formula Ford 1600 and Formula Ford two thousand in 81 and 82 plus a bit of Formula 3 in 84 and around that time I did a bit of production saloons as well. Today, I still race my bike, a bit of production saloons with a friend of mine, hill climbs and vintage sports car stuff. I'd like to do more, but it's time and money.'

Graham was extremely articulate, very well spoken and Max guessed he'd been to public school. He aged him at about the same age as himself.

'What did you do at Coys?' Max asked.

'I was in the motoring department working on the car and memorabilia side. I did that for a few years, but just lost interest really. It wasn't for me.'

'Did you know a guy called Ted Little?'

'Yes, I did, he worked directly under me!' Graham

replied. 'You know him?'

'Well, I sold him a Ferrari 355 Spider a while back,' Max replied.

'How did you get on with him?' Graham enquired.

'Okay, we had a bit of a problem, but he managed to sort that out.'

'He's a complete wanker if you ask me. A blithering idiot.'

Max told him that he hadn't done any business with him since, but he had spoken to him a few times. Graham obviously wouldn't be inviting Ted Little around to his next dinner party. Sounded like a bit of history there.

'What sort of aircraft do you get involved in?' Max asked.

'Do you know anything about them?'

'Not really, Graham, my father had his PPL (private pilot's licence) and I did a lot of hours when I was thirteen or so, but nothing since.'

'I've got things like Stomps, Tiger Moths. My brother and I share ownership on the aeroplanes and we try to take them up as often as possible. We have about twelve at the moment but not all of them are operational. The trouble with the older aircraft is the availability of the parts. A lot of bits need to be especially made.'

'If I had the chance, I'd like to go up in a Spitfire. There's a girl somewhere that has a two seater. I think that would be fantastic,' Max enthused.

'Anne Grace has one. I know her actually, so when you're ready, let me know and I will see what I can do,' said Graham, adding, 'I have just bought two Spitfires for restoration. I haven't made my mind up yet but I think I will restore one of them and sell the other to fund the restoration. One was a Dutch Air Force plane that came down in the marshes in Holland at the end of the war and the other is a clipped wing doodle bug, you know V1 rocket, chaser.'

'Whereabouts are you based?' asked Max.

'I'm in High Wycombe in Buckinghamshire.'

'You're quite a way from me. I'm in Newton Abbot in Devon.'

'Yes, I know. I'm coming down to Devon later in the year with my lady friend. I think we're staying.' He stopped and then started again, 'Is it Holne?'

155

'Yes, Holne is near Ashburton.'

'Yes, we're staying at a hotel there for a weekend away.'

'Is it Holne Chase Hotel?' asked Max.

'Yes, it is, that's right, do you know it?' Graham asked.

'Yes, I do, it's very nice. Beautiful grounds and the chef has a good reputation. I've never stayed there but I've had afternoon tea there with my wife once or twice. I don't think you'd be disappointed,' said Max, 'it's about eight miles from where I'm sitting now.'

Max wrapped up the conversation, they'd been on the telephone for over half an hour. He had eked out as much information as he reasonably could and felt that Graham was a genuine guy and not a dreamer. There was a real possibility of him helping with the Muzi list.

Max had told Graham that he had the possibility of another 360 and he didn't have to wait for very long to find out more. No sooner had he put down the phone when Mike was buzzing him to take a call from Josef.

When Max was in Heidelberg with Josef the week before Josef had mentioned a couple more cars that might become available. The problem with getting the 360s was that they were highly desirable and were therefore fetching huge premiums. Essentially a customer would order his new Ferrari from the dealership and then have to wait up to two years for his new car. When the car arrived, he could use the car for a few weeks, do up to five hundred kilometres in it, get it out of his system, then sell the car on for twenty to thirty thousand pounds more than he had paid for it. The economy in Europe was quite buoyant at the time and the huge premiums being banded around were actually being achieved.

For Max, his job was to find a car at a reasonable premium and then find a customer willing to pay a greater premium. The reality was that there were more customers willing to pay greater premiums than there were sellers willing to sell even though they could make a good profit on their car.

There were several reasons for customers not wanting to sell their new cars, but two particular reasons were that for starters, the Ferrari 360 was an exceptionally good car probably being the most useable car that Ferrari had ever made. The quality was good, it was very quick, it was a nice looking car and it was very reliable. The other reason for not selling was that the huge premiums being obtained were achieved on the first

156

produced cars and they were generally going out to all of Ferrari's favoured customers. These customers would have been long term Ferrari owners who quite often had a number of new and classic Ferraris locked away in their garage. They could also be favoured celebrities, heads of state, captains of industry, collectors and similar types of people, and generally they didn't need the money. A £30,000 profit on a car that they'd driven for a few hundred kilometres just didn't interest them. The money was not important.

Combining these two reasons with the very low annual Ferrari production and what you have is a market with very few available cars. Now Ferrari, the factory are not stupid, they know what goes on. They know they have a highly desirable fantastic product with a brand name second to none. If you want an ordinary sports car you go and buy a Porsche. If you want something special, a real driver's car, then you have to have a Ferrari.

Ferrari deliberately keep their production volume low to maintain the desirability and keep up the exclusivity of their range. They have no shortage of willing customers and also they have an almost total contempt for their customers. The contempt runs from the factory right through the supply chain and into the individual Ferrari franchised dealers. Trying to get information about an order that you have placed for your new Ferrari is nearly always met with the usual standard answer, 'It will be here when it's here!' It's almost like they're saying, 'Bugger off and leave me alone.' Bearing in mind, the customer has paid a deposit, he or she would be entitled to know when they could expect their car, so it wouldn't be an unreasonable request. Yet, the customer is expected to accept a rather open ended delivery date. No other manufacturer could treat a customer in the way that Ferrari treat theirs and get away with it. But then again, no other manufacturer could make a sports car as good as a Ferrari with the unrivalled heritage of the Italian company.

When a new model from Ferrari is launched, the favoured few get their cars first. They would normally have a history with the company going back a long way and that history would have been based on continued ownership or buying of Ferraris. The factory would take an extremely dim view of a favoured customer if he were to take his or her car and immediately sell it on for a profit. The customer might not have that opportunity ever again, so he or she would not want to lose that. Furthermore, the franchised dealer who sold the car to the customer would prefer to have the car back to them so they can make more money from a used car sale. The whole customer dealership relationship is a very tricky one, not least because the people playing the game are often very successful and are used to getting their own way.

If a favoured customer receives their car, then it is likely that they would have their next Ferrari already on order for a year to eighteen months down the line. The dealer would agree a part exchange value on the current car so as to get it back on the next change. The customer for his part would get a guaranteed value for his car for when the new one arrived and usually this would be more or less the same as what had been paid for it. The only difference to pay would be the increased cost of the new car. In this way, owing a Ferrari is relatively inexpensive in terms of devaluation although servicing costs are high, but if your future change valuation is based on mileage done as well then the maximum likely service cost in that twelve to eighteen months would be less than £5,000.

Ferrari were notoriously slow at getting their new cars out into the market place and it was not unusual for problems with the manufacturing process to come to light when the cars were being put to the test by their new enthusiastic owners. The effect of recall problems again slowed down production, something that just would not happen with a Porsche.

The Ferrari franchised dealers themselves weren't without their problems either. They had no problems reaching their sales allocation, far from it, they could sell a lot more cars than they would receive. The factory were very dictatorial and the allocation was based on total overall performance including parts and accessory sales too. In Europe, Germany were the biggest market followed by the UK, however the UK along with all the other right hand drive markets were always the last to receive their cars, normally at least a year after the left hand drive cars had first come on to the market. This led to a lot of right hand drive market customers buying a used left hand drive car rather than waiting. Impatience ruled, and in a buoyant market economy, premiums became ever bigger.

Max had owned a Ferrari himself for nearly fifteen years and he knew how the system worked. He'd driven tens of thousands of miles in the very best of them. He had an in depth knowledge of the market and could speak to any Ferrari owner in

158

complete confidence that he knew his subject. Having raced cars for several years, he could comment on any particular Ferrari that he had driven and give a customer an honest opinion of how good it was. Like many owners, he knew more about Ferrari than the sales people in the dealerships, and frankly he had little time for most of them anyway.

It was interesting that the premium phenomena had become an ever increasing issue leading up to unprecedented levels when the 360 came out. In 1985, the 308 QV had a small capability of a premium, but the rise from then rose like an exponential curve by the time the 355 came out in 1995 and went off the scale four years later with the 360.

With so many variables relating to the materialisation of a car, Max had his work cut out to sort what was real, what was going to be real and who was just wasting his time. Some, come to think of it, quite a lot of people would ring Max and say they had a car coming. They'd ring loads of times saying it was on it's way and then he wouldn't hear from them again.

Max trusted Josef; he was a worker; he kept at it until he got what he was looking for. He'd come up trumps with the first car and Max fully expected him to come through with the second, which he could in turn then offer to Graham. He'd been offered other cars, but he couldn't tell whether they were real or not, and he didn't want to risk Dimo's money on anything that could go wrong.

Josef rang back at just after four o'clock, it was five o'clock his time and the end of the day.

'Max, I have a car for you. New, delivery kilometres, red, black leather, electric seats, wing badges, and the F1 gearbox, two hundred and fifty thousand Deutschmarks.'

Max very rarely bought anything for the asking price and managed to beat Josef down to DM248,000. Someone had once said to Max that he would never earn so much as the amount that he knocked down the price in the time taken. In other words, if someone wanted £100 for something and he managed to knock them down to £90 and it took thirty seconds to do it, then he reasoned he earned £10 in thirty seconds. There was some sense in it especially when the numbers got bigger. The same man had said to him that all things being equal there's always room for a cut. If a man wants to sell something for £100 and another man is looking for something for £100. For a middleman there would appear to be nothing in it. There's no point buying something and selling it for the same price, however it would be likely that the seller would take £95 and the buyer would pay £105. Both would need convincing but it could and would be done. So, from apparently nothing, you could have a deal and make a wage. It would be easy to throw away a deal because it didn't look feasible, but with a different view of it, there was the challenge to make it possible.

'Max, the only problem with this car is…' Max thought, *oh here we go.*

'Is that it's in Helsinki.'

'Helsinki, Finland?'

'Yes, it belongs to the CEO of Nokia. I have done business with him many times. He's a good man.'

'Okay. I'm certain I will have it, but I need to make a call first.'

Max put down the phone and immediately called Dimo and asked if it was okay to roll the first money into a second car on the basis that he wouldn't return the capital, just Dimo's share of the profit, so that Max could transfer the money from the sale of the first car directly to Josef to speed up the process. Dimo was pleased about the sale of the first car and agreed Max's plan was the right thing to be doing. The deal was done.

As promised Max rang Graham and gave him the specification of the Helsinki car. He'd asked if it was physical and based upon Josef' assurance, Max passed on the information to Graham. The car was immediately available. Graham said he would come back to Max in the morning with an answer. Max wasn't worried about it, he had several other *Sunday Times* enquiries to call back so he was confident he could sell the car.

His mind turned to the day's other worries when Pete popped into his office shortly before going home.

'How goes it?' asked Pete.

'Yes, it's looking good actually on the car front. Plenty on. Just need to get a few paid and displayed and I'll feel a lot better. What about you?'

'Quiet today. Very quiet. I caught up on a bit of paperwork. Chased a few on the phone, but not a lot doing really. What do you want me to do about the *Autotrader* advert, Sally will be here in the morning?' Pete asked.

160

SECTION TWO

MARCH 2000

'What do you think about doing a big sale ? We're going to have to do something. You know the sort of thing, half price this and that. Bargains to be had on all 2000 models?' asked Max. ' You know, something to get some money in'.

'Yeah, we could go with something like that?' Pete replied.

'I'd rather be the first to do it rather than the last and soon enough, everyone else will be doing it anyway,' said Max.

More than anything else Max was worried about the quarterly figures for the bank. If it showed the stock levels were at a high level over the three month period and low turnover, then it would indicate a sales problem with the stock mix and if they asked the question about stock then they would easily realise that the real stock value was not as per the listed figures and probably considerably less. One hundred and fifty thousand pounds of unsaleable competition bike stock could easily become half that. Wiping fifty per cent off the stock value would seriously jeopardise the business. The bank didn't like Max being involved with the cars, it was too spiky on the account with too many big swings from credit to debit. They had always said they supported the company on the forecasts of motorcycle sales not cars. At first Max would listen to them, but he was the one with everything on the line not them and right now he had to make money whichever way he could. Bikes or cars, it didn't matter as long as there was a profit.

EXETER, AUGUST 2008

The last day and night at Devon County Prison were the longest. It wasn't the end of his sentence, far from it, but it marked the end of the most severe and harrowing experience he'd ever endured. He'd experienced fear many, many times at home, at school and in competitions but all of that was a different fear. This fear was raw and wild and totally unpredictable. Everything and anything could happen in an instant. An innocent remark, a sideways glance, a misunderstanding, all of these could flick the switch in the mind of a convict and turn him into a homicidal maniac. Max was not physically equipped to deal with these people.

After the lockdown over the weekend, Max was looking forward to getting some fresh air during the playground break. All he had to do was get through the first couple of hours of education, a manual handling health and safety course and he would be there. It dragged, it was desperately boring. An hour and half film about picking things up is never going to set your imagination alight.

Mentally, he was closing down the remaining time. The last morning education, the last walk around the exercise yard, the last lunchtime and so on, then ticking the boxes, done that. He still had the worry that something inevitably might go wrong and nothing would be certain until he walked out of that red stone Victorian building and tucked himself away in the cubicle of the tour bus.

Karl hardly ever went out for exercise any more. He preferred to try to sleep in the cell. He'd become even more introvert. Max couldn't do that, he needed to get outside. He hated the horrible and constant feeling of being greasy. No air, like being stuck in a lift shaft or the same awful dirty feeling someone gets from being on the tube mid summer.

Max caught up with Tom as he walked around the exercise yard, always a mind of information. 'Three attempted suicides and one successful suicide on 'A' Wing yesterday,' Tom said.

'You're joking.'

'No, I'm not. The suicide was in the cell next to your old one,' said Tom.

'What, the two young lads?'

'Yes, I know one of them, Alan Baxter. His pad mate went to bed okay. Al heard nothing and then woke up at about six this morning and his mate was hanging from the grills in the window by a ripped down twisted sheet. He never gave the slightest clue. He was still twitching as they took him down, but it was too late, he was gone.'

'What about Alan?' asked Max.

164

'He'll probably get freed. He only had seven weeks to go and that kind of image is pretty damaging.'

'This is just so awful. Joe Public can't possibly have any idea of what goes on in these places.'

'No, but you don't have to worry about that. In less than twenty-four hours, you'll have a new postcode,' Tom mused.

Max certainly hoped so.

'I'm thinking of writing a book. If I do, I'll mention you. I'll change your name, so you don't have to worry about that,' said Max.

'What's it going to be about?'

'My experiences, why I'm here, that sort of thing. I haven't really closed it down yet, I just think I can do it and maybe when I get to Leyhill, I'll have the private time and space to start. That's of course, if you've not gilded the lily too much.'

'No, not at all. You will be able to do it there. It's not like here at all,' Tom replied.

They strolled back to their respective cells, got themselves locked in and waited for lunch. The remainder of the day passed without incident, that had to be a first, and Reed settled himself in for one more night of Emmerdale, East Enders and Coronation Street. He'd seen Tom before the cell door was locked for the night and told him he would see him before he left.

Max hardly got any sleep that night, mainly because he was so desperate to get to sleep that he couldn't. The alarms were ringing at different ends of the wing, the sound of toilets flushing, the usual jangle of keys and of course the animals. The endless noise torturing the mind. The window warriors warring through the grills.

The heavy sound of the unlocking mechanism in the door woke Max as the door swung open and a guard stepped in.

'Reed?'

It seemed like the middle of the night but it wasn't. 'Yes.'

'Get yourself packed. Five minutes.' That's all he said and slammed the door shut. Max had no idea what time it was, didn't really have time to think about it. He'd packed all his cell belongings the night before, so it was a quick teeth cleaning and shave and he was ready. Karl was still half asleep. He didn't want Max to go. He was worried about what would happen next, but he brought himself to say goodbye. They'd been through a lot together and having been thrown in at the deep end, they'd drawn strength from each other to cope with what they felt was the madness of it all.

Max tapped on Tom's cell door and opened the flap to look in. He waved and Max was gone. In less than two minutes, he was off the landing, back out through the hub along the B Wing induction unit tracing back the steps he'd made three weeks earlier when he had first arrived on that fateful day.

The leaving procedure was the exact opposite of the coming in. Max was reunited with the clothes he had on arrival and was offered a cubicle to get changed. It was less stressful than the last time he was at this juncture. A few papers to sign followed by breakfast in the reception area and then a short wait for the tour bus.

Max drank a cup of tea and ate his cornflakes in the company of a murderer and an armed robber, both of whom were being moved on to different jails for different reasons. A month earlier to the day Max and Catherine had been served a continental breakfast in a fine hotel after a night out at a concert. How things had changed.

The prisoners weren't cuffed as they boarded the tour bus, so they made their own way in and sat down in the cubicle of their choice. The guard and the driver joked with them as they awaited clearance.

'Right lads, we're going to Shepton Mallett first for Mr. Barrett, then we will take Mr. Cox to Bristol Horfield and finally Mr. Reed to Leyhill. We shall be landing at Shepton Mallett in about an hour and a half. There will be an in flight service which I'll deal with once we get out onto the motorway.' The speaker clicked off with a crackle of static.

Max got out of the bus at the Shepton Mallett lifer's prison, stretched his legs and took some fresh air. He wasn't a good traveller and the confined space of the cubicle was stifling. Another two and a half hours and he would be looking at Bristol's Horfield Category 'B' Prison. It looked just like Exeter, all red brick, grills and razor wire.

It was gone two o'clock when the tour bus turned off the M5 motorway just south of Michael Wood Services and turned right following the direction towards Wooton Under Edge. Leyhill was about two miles down the road on the right hand side. Max looked out of the window as the bus turned into the complex. There was a simple barrier like you would expect to see at the exit of a car park and that was it. No barbed wire, no high walls and fences. It was completely open. The buildings were all modern low level dark face brick, randomly dotted around the site and it was quiet. *Thank God for that*, Max thought.

AUGUST 1977

Caro was sitting at the kitchen table with her elbows on the table holding a mug of coffee with both hands and leaning forward frequently to take a sip. Her mother was at the sink chirping away, but Caro wasn't listening.

She was miles away thinking when she winced and rubbed her temple.

'Are you all right love?' asked her mother.

'Yes, I'm okay, just a sharp pain that's all. It's gone now,' said Caro.

'Do you want an aspirin or something?' her mum asked.

'No honestly. I'm fine thanks. It's gone now,' Caro replied.

Max had dropped the previous day's takings down to John at the hotel and was now riding back to Dawlish to open up the kiosk for the day. He slowed down as he neared the brow of the hill by the turning to Holcombe as there was a police accident sign mounted on the pavement. There were a few bits of debris on the road, but nothing else. He carried on, passing the Smugglers Inn on the right, his old workplace noticing Merv still had his Morris Marina TC, and smiled into his helmet. The ' TC' bit was very important to Merv.

Max had one week left at the kiosk, then a couple of weeks off before starting at South Devon Technical College. He didn't really know what he wanted to do, but liked the idea of something in the construction industry, architecture, civil engineer or structural engineer, something like that. Rob's dad was a structural engineer and Max had been down to his office a few times and quite liked the idea of it. He was hoping that he could do the OND Building course, which would give him a broad based idea of the industry and then choose something that took his liking as he went on. He needed four 'O' levels to get on the course and managed to get seven so he was in, confirmed and

167

ready to start.

Max hadn't seen Caro since the time they all went to the fair and that was a few weeks back. He'd heard she had started going out with a guy called Sam who was in the year above them at school. He still didn't understand Caro's reluctance at a relationship with him, but he didn't dwell on it. She had her reasons and that was that. There were more fish in the sea but...

Max opened up the kiosk and switched on the radio. Smiley Miley was getting people to guess the mileage on the Radio 1 road show at Torre Abbey Meadow in Torquay and The Motors were filling the airwaves with their single, Airport.

The first of the day's customers arrived, but it was a slow morning. Rob turned up after lunch.

'You heard the news?'

'No, what news?'

'Simon West was killed this morning at Holcombe.'

'How?'

'A car crossed the road to turn into Holcombe and didn't see him coming. Colin Mason was on the back. He's in intensive care,' said Rob.

'Shit!' said Max. 'I passed the accident sign on the way over here this morning. God, I can't believe it.'

'Well that might slow you down eh?'

'Yeah, that's horrible. Where've they taken Colin?' asked Max.

'Torbay, I think,' Rob replied.

'I didn't know Simon that well. Neil knew him better than me, and Colin is in the same year as him,' said Max. 'Not nice.'

It was the first time that Max had known someone of his age to die. He'd known his girlfriend. She was in the Shaldon Sailing Club when Max was there in the early seventies. He felt sorry for her. There was a period of silence whilst their eyes roved the beach. Life went on.

'On a different subject Vicky and I are going to the flea pit Friday night. Do you want to come?' asked Rob.

'What's on?' Max asked.

'Saturday Night Fever.'

'Yeah okay. I'm up for that. I've got no one to take though. Caro's off with that Sam bloke in the lower sixth,' Max said disparagingly.

'Yeah, I know. I wouldn't let it bother you though.

Move on and all that,' suggested Rob.

'Yeah, I know. I'll have to try to find something on the beach down there. Here, you hold the fort and I'll see what's about,' Max said jokingly.

'Are you going to make a cup of tea then?' asked Rob.

'Yeah, of course, anything else Sir? A free tank of petrol perhaps?'

Rob stood outside and leant up against the counter and they passed the time of day for an hour or so, scanning the scantily dressed randomly passing by.

'Who are you going to bring on Friday then?' Rob asked.

'Oh, I don't know. I'll probably come on my own.' Max replied, 'but you never know, we'll see.'

'How's things with Vicky then?'

'Yeah okay, no probs there bud.' Rob replied, 'hey I got forty six across the bridge on the way here.'

'No you didn't. Maybe with a tow.'

'Honest, I did, and it's going really well. It's probably about to blow up knowing my luck.'

'Have you decided what you're going to get next?' Max asked.

'It depends really on the money, but if I can get enough together, I'll probably get one like brother's and do a bit of a paint job on it. There's a guy that lives in the village opposite the Church House Inn. He does a bit of paintwork. I thought I'd ask him, if I get one. You?'

'Well, it'd have to be an off road bike and it's got to be a Yam, so I'm hoping I'll have enough for a DT250, if not I'll go for a DT175 but if I had the money, I'd have the 250 for a short while, take my test and buy an XT500,' said Max.

'What's the insurance on a DT250?' Rob asked.

'Dave Horn said it would be about thirty quid full comp'. I only paid seventeen pounds with the Co-op last year.'

'What's the time?' Rob asked.

'Quarter to four.'

'I had better be going. If I don't see you before, I'll see you Friday. Give me a ring in the week and I'll sort it out with you.'

'Yeah, okay,' Max replied.

Rob put on his helmet and jacket, pulled up his gloves and set off. Max waved him off and went back into the kiosk.

Another day nearly over.

Max thought about Friday night and who to take. Did he need to take anyone at all he asked himself. *Not really*, he thought. But it was always difficult going as the odd one out, especially with Rob and Vicky, because Max would normally have taken Caro to make up the four. They would have had a laugh together and gone for a drink afterwards. Max sort of felt a little bit lost really because he'd come to rely on Caro to fill in the gaps when he wasn't going out with anyone. Now that she was going off with someone else, he selfishly felt a little bit let down.

He saw Caro on the way home, she was walking up New Road about a hundred yards from her house so he stopped and took off his helmet.

She walked up to him, 'Hello stranger,' she said.

'Hi, you okay?'

'Yes, thanks.'

'I hear you have a new man,' said Max.

'Yes, Sam. He is in the lower sixth,' said Caro.

'Ah right, yes I know who you mean,' said Max. Of course, he knew who he was, but he pretended to vaguely know who she was talking about.

'Are you coming on Friday night? Flicks?'

'Umm, I'm not sure at the moment, Rob spoke to me about it earlier. We said we'd speak later in the week about it,' Max replied. He had told Rob that he would go, but Rob hadn't told him that Caro was going with her new man as well. Perhaps he didn't know, Max thought. It didn't matter that Caro had this new guy with her; that was not the problem. It was just that they were a four and now the four were a different four and Max wasn't sure that he wanted to be tagging along as number five. It wouldn't be the same.

He started his bike and put his helmet back on.

'Okay, I might see you at the end of the week then,' Max said.

'Yeah, okay then, go safely.'

'Will do, bye.'

'Bye.'

Caro watched him go up the road and turn right into the drive of his house. She looked down at the ground and gently kicked some loose gravel back onto the driveway.

AUGUST 2000

Donald Key listened to Graham Lord, jotting down the details as he did so.

'Graham, the only problem I think we might have with this one is the colour. The specification is fine, it's the red. My customer would prefer silver.'

'What about painting it?' asked Graham.

'If it's the last resort, then yes, we could do that possibly,' Don replied adding, 'I'll speak to my customer and see if I can convince him to go with red.'

'Okay, how long do you need? These cars are so difficult to find. It will be gone if we don't act relatively quickly.'

'Yes, I know.' What time is it now he asked himself. 'They're ten hours in front of us, so I won't be able to speak to him now until later tonight. I'll do what I can and call you back.'

'Good, speak to you later,' said Graham.

AUGUST 1977

Max thought about what he was doing and wondered whether it was the right thing. He didn't want to look an idiot, but nothing ventured, nothing gained. The pressure was on, albeit self induced. He put his gloves in his helmet and propped the lid on top of his bike's mirror and tentatively walked up the steps to the front door. Heart beat thumping in his jacket.

He looked around, but he couldn't see a doorbell. There was a brass knocker which he rapped twice. Nothing, no response. Phew, he thought to himself, no one in, that's that then. He tried again and a woman quickly came to the door.

She looked down at Max irritated that she had to stop what she was doing , 'Hello.'

'Hi, I just wondered if Jenny was at home?'

'Yes, she is, I'll get her for you. Would you like to come in? Who shall I say it is?' she asked. She was warming up.

'Max,' came the reply.

Max stepped into the hallway. There were a few unopened boxes by the stairs, a stuffed coat rack, a tall hallway mirror and a two tone green trimphone on a wooden shelf. There was no carpet.

'She's just coming, sorry about the mess, we're just waiting for the carpet fitter. He should have been here last week, but I expect you know what it's like, they overrun on a job and everyone else gets put back. I'm Jenny's mum, Sheila,' she said and extended her hand to Max's.

'Are you the one working in the kiosk at Dawlish?' she asked.

'Yes, that's me, just a summer job.'

'Jenny mentioned you the other day.'

'I hope it was good,' he said.

'Yes, it was,' Jenny said as she turned the top of the stairs and started walking down.

'Oh you've changed,' said her mother.

She was wearing a pair of tight blue jeans with a close fitting white T shirt and she looked terrific.

'Hi, I was passing and thought of you. Thought I'd come and say hello,' said Max. It was utter rubbish of course. He'd been sat at the bottom of the road for half an hour trying to summon up the courage to go up to her house and knock on the door.

Her mother smiled and trotted off somewhere.

'Have you got time for a drink?' Jenny asked.

'Yes, that would be nice.'

'Cup of tea, cup of coffee?'

'Tea please, no sugar.' Max followed her into the kitchen. He hadn't taken sugar in tea since his father had left home, only because his mother kept forgetting to buy it, so eventually it was easier not to have it.

'We're still trying to get sorted from the move, as you can see,' she said pointing at various packages around the room.

'It will take a while, but it looks like you're nearly there. What school are you going to?' Max asked.

'The Grammar School,' she replied, adding, 'Sixth form.'

'Oh right, I've just left there. I'm off to the Tech in a couple of weeks.'

'What's the Grammar School like?'

'Yes it's good. I really liked it, but I wanted to go to the

Tech and do something that was unavailable here.'

'What are you doing?' she asked.

Max told her what he was doing and why he was doing it and they chatted for half an hour or so, when Max came to the crunch point.

'I'm off to the flea pit tomorrow with some friends, would you like to come along?'

'Yes, that would be good. I'd like that. What sort of time?'

'It starts at 7.45 pm, so if I meet you here at seven, we can walk down. I'd take you on my bike but I haven't passed my test.'

'My mother wouldn't want me on the back of a bike anyway, so that's okay,' she said.

Max finished his tea, said goodbye to Jenny's mother and headed back to the front door.

'See you Friday.'

'Yeah, thanks bye.'

Jenny stayed at the door and waved as Max rode off.

'He seemed like a nice lad Jenny,' said her mother.

'Hmm.'

'Where did you meet him?' she asked.

'He was the guy I was talking to in the kiosk when you picked me up from tennis.'

'Oh,' she smiled, 'that's right.'

'He's just finished at the grammar school. He's going to the Tech.'

'Yes, I heard,' said her mother with an enquiring look.

'What?'

'Nothing,' her mother replied.

Max was pleased with himself. *That took some nerve*, he thought. Cold start, straight in and ask her out. Brilliant. She didn't even ask what was on.

JUNE 2000

Rux was not pleased, he'd been sat waiting in the car in the searing heat for nearly half an hour and he was beginning to get annoyed. He had the information required. It hadn't been easy to obtain. There were a few people he had to pay off along the way.

He opened the file and looked at the small passport size photograph again. Below was listed everything that was known about him. Wives, girlfriends, family, known associates. It was all there and it made good reading. Rux chuckled as he paused over certain details when there was a knock at the driver's window.

He sat up and opened the car door.

'Sorry I'm late, I got held up.'

'You could have called me,' said Rux furiously.

'Yeah, I'm sorry. Everything there?'

'Yeah, it's all there. He's being monitored.'

'By who?'

'I don't know. Too high up for me to find out. Government, I would expect.'

'Our government or elsewhere?'

'Both, I think. He's creating a bit of interest.'

'Background?'

'Yeah, it's all there. I've got a phone tap going on tomorrow night. We'll be able to cover it for seven days. Is that long enough?'

'Should be. Depends on what comes next.'

Rux handed over the file, 'Call me late Friday, we'll have the taps scripted by then, and don't forget the money.'

'Yeah okay.'

Rux climbed back into the Toyota Land cruiser and blasted down the trail leaving a reddish brown dust cloud bellowing behind him.

JULY 2000

Chris from Testastretta rang Max and told him their bad news. Chris and Greg were going their separate ways and closing the business. It was in fact a bit of a lie, because they had put the company, Testastretta Ltd into voluntary liquidation and their supplier had collected the remainder of his stock. They had nothing to sell. Chris was going to retreat to his farm in Cullompton and Greg was happy to continue selling Ferraris, but in the trade.

Chris offered Max some part exchange cars that were

currently held by the liquidator but Max wasn't interested in what they had.

'The trouble is, Max we've been hopelessly under funded. You know how it is, all these cars are big money. It only takes one or two cars to slow up on a deal and it buggers cash flow completely. I've put hundreds of thousands into this business and I've lost the lot. I'm getting out whilst I still have some sanity,' said Chris.

'I'm sorry to hear that, but to be honest with you, there but for the grace of God go I, and a load more of us as well. We're all in the same boat. There are always problems, it's never an easy ride,' Max countered.

'Well, if you're ever passing Cullompton. You've got my details, give me a call. It would be good to see you.'

'Thanks Chris, good luck and all that.'

Max put down the phone and realised immediately why it was that he got the 355 so cheap. He thought about Testastretta and their showrooms, all show and no go. Max felt sorry for Chris because he did actually like him and he was easy to deal with. He described cars properly and didn't waste people's time, he was a breath of fresh air in that respect. There was nothing up at Testastretta that Max particularly wanted so he didn't bother ringing the liquidator.

AUGUST 2000

'I'm sorry but that red 360 is no good, Graham, I spoke to my Asian customer last night and he is adamant that it must be either silver or titanium.'

'That's okay, Don,' said Graham, adding, 'I will keep looking and come back to you as soon as I have something.'

Graham Lord was a bit annoyed, because he really wanted to go back to Max at Velodrome and do a deal with him, not least, because there was the commission as well. It could open up the chance of some more business. He would call Max and let him know his client's decision.

Graham picked up the phone and spoke to Max.

'Sorry Max, but I'm not going to be able to do anything with that 360. My client wants a silver car, he's quite determined on that.'

'Okay, it's not a problem,' said Max. 'I'm going to collect the car anyway. I've had quite a few enquiries on it so I'm confident we'll get it sold anyway. I'll see if I can find you a silver car.'

Earlier that morning, Max had spoken to two different customers both enquiring about the car, so he felt he could sell it regardless of Graham's customer, but before he put the phone down on Graham, he asked him if he knew of a Ferrari 250 short wheel base California Spider.

Max had been speaking to a Swiss customer who was desperate to find this highly desirable car.

'I don't know of a car, but I do know who to speak to. How positive is your customer?'

'He seemed fairly keen on the phone. He wants a closed headlight car.'

The Ferrari 250 SWB California Spider has to be one of the all time great Ferraris if not one of the greatest cars ever. It's a sublimely beautiful Pininfarina designed two seater open top three litre V12 sports car from the late 50s, early 60s. When built, it would have been sold to royalty, racing drivers and the like. Ferrari were very low volume producers at the time, so no more than fifty five of these stunning cars were built over a four year period in two distinct body types being open headlight and closed headlight. It is generally accepted that the closed headlight, side vent car is the one to have, and if it had period race history, interesting ownership history and the very rare hard top then that would add significantly to it's value. Strangely enough, the condition of the car didn't matter too much, because most buyers are just so relieved to get a car that if it needed restoration then they would get that done. What is important in all these old cars is the matching numbers. When the car was built, all of the major components, such as the chassis, engine, gearbox, back axle etc are all numbered and the factory would have recorded all the details and have them available in the archive department at Ferrari's headquarters in Maranello, Italy. Most of the major collectors in the world would want a matching number car, which means that the numbers on the car are the same as when it was produced. This would indicate that the car would be mostly original. A non original engine would make a difference to the car's value in most instances. There are a few exceptions to the rule but there would have to be a very good reason.

Max's Swiss customer was in his early thirties, completely self made and highly successful in the specialist electronics industry. Like Muzi, he was starting to build a Ferrari collection and the 250 California was one of the first three cars that he wanted. He knew the value of the cars and he was very friendly with his local Ferrari franchised dealer, who had rung Max in the first instance as a direct response to the fax they had received mentioning; if they were looking for anything, please call.

Max was taken aback by the number of enquiries for high value cars, but he was pleased. It meant that if he pulled off just one deal, it would have a significant positive effect on his business.

Graham had told Max that he would contact a friend he had in the USA to find out if a California Spider was available. They finished their telephone call and agreed to speak again later in the day.

Things were moving quite fast. Max needed to organise the collection of the Helsinki 360, he had sold the blue 355 and that was going out, he had a customer chasing him for another 355 and he was yet to go back to Muzi about his list of wants as well. The lack of sales on the motorcycle side of the business was a financial disaster in the happening. He needed to change the stock, but at the same time, he didn't want to lose too much money and the problem was made worse by the fact that nobody knew what was going on with the foot and mouth disease. He'd spoken to Pete during their early morning meeting and they had agreed to shed the stock by the end of the following week if things didn't change. The upside would be that they could begin to buy road bike stock. The downside would inevitably produce a huge loss on the balance sheet. Something had to be done and there would be no point dragging it out for months. Max had said, 'Do it once, do it now and get on with the job, instead of worrying about the 'what if's' all the time. It had become a huge financial strain at a time when the Ferrari sales were beginning to pick up, and what Max had intended as the icing on the cake was now having to be the main profit centre. If the foot and mouth disease hadn't hit the company so hard, the bike sales would have continued to make a small profit each month keeping everyone including the bank happy and the Ferrari sales would be making a significant profit. Instead, Max had to work harder than ever, just to make ends meet. It was never easy.

The first time Max looked on a map to see where Helsinki was, he was sitting in the aircraft reading the in-flight magazine. He knew it was in Finland, but he never realised it was quite so far. There were places he was passing that he'd only heard about on the ten o'clock news. At four o'clock in Helsinki, it was pitch black. Nikki Carlson collected Max from the airport in his silver Mercedes S320 and took him straight to his home on the northern outskirts of the city. The course of the journey took Max through the centre of the city and he thought it was really beautiful. He would have liked to have been there for a few days with Catherine, but this trip, like many, didn't leave him a lot of time, especially now as he realised how far he was from home.

Nikki was a really nice guy, his girlfriend had laid on a light meal, so they all sat around the table and ate whilst finishing off the paperwork. Max had thought, at the time, what an easy deal it had been. The car was registered on Nikki's private number plate EN3, which was de registered from midnight that night. Max had to be on the ferry home from Helsinki to Stockholm at 7.00 pm, and didn't want to risk missing it, so Nikki showed Max the way back into the city and then onto the port. Once the car was out of Finland, the de registration wouldn't matter because Velodrome were the new owners and Max had all the transfer paperwork.

Max was the last car onto the ferry and what a ferry it was. The first thing that hit him was that there was a Harley Davidson motorcycle franchise in the centre of the boat and the second was that everybody on the boat all seemed to be getting completely pissed. It didn't matter how old they were, they were all legless and that was before nine o'clock. It was very strange. The boat was nicknamed "The Love Boat", and Max could see why. There was naughty goings on everywhere he seemed to look. It was worse than a teenage party.

The boat docked early in the morning and Max went up onto the deck to watch the final few miles into Stockholm. The scenery was just so beautiful. Huge tracts of water with tree-lined shores and multi-coloured traditional timber three- or four-storey water front properties.

Max drove onto Stockholm's cobbled streets looking all around at the surroundings, searching for the signpost south to Malmo. He pressed the CD open, put *ABBA's* greatest hits in the drive, touched the play button, turned up the volume and the opening bars blasted out, 'Money, money, money, must be funny in a rich man's world'. It seemed appropriate.

The drive down to Denmark had to be the most fantastic ever. There were hardly any other cars on the road at all. Maybe the odd errant Volvo, but nothing else . It was nearly all dual carriageway or very fast single lane 'A' roads, all surfaced to perfection set in beautiful countryside. Max lit up the 360 and cruised through four tanks of fuel. A Ferrari on that road at a steady one hundred and twenty to one hundred and thirty mph was outrageous fun, unlikely to be repeated.

It took two days to get back from Helsinki and Max sold the car on the way back to a shipping magnate in Nassau. He wanted the car delivered to a swanky London address. Max never even met him. It was all done on the phone and fax.

Muzi had been on the phone to the garage a few times when Max finally got to speak to him.

'Hi, I was calling to find out how you were getting on?' said Muzi.

'I've been away for a couple of days. I had to collect a 360 from Helsinki, so I'm sorry I haven't come back to you. I had a good look at the list. Does it matter which order they come in?' asked Max.

'No, not at all,' came the reply.

Muzi continued, 'It would be nice to find one of the more desirable cars but I don't mind. Some things I wanted to ask. Do you have enough room to store some of the cars for a while?'

'Yes, we do. All under cover. Depends, of course how many, but these cars are unlikely to come thick and fast, so it shouldn't be a problem. We'd probably have to work out something on the insurance if some cars were to stay a while, especially the higher value ones,' said Max.

'That's okay, because I'm not sure where I want these cars to end up. It may be that they stay in the UK. Also, I want to race some of them in historics.'

'Race them yourself?'

'No, I'll find someone to do that for me,' said Muzi.

'I'll stick my hand up for that job,' Max said.

'You had experience?'

'Yes, I used to race in single-seaters and saloon cars plus various other stuff over the years.'

'That's good. I'll take you up on that, but that's some way off. Try to find something for me. I'd like to get the show on the road.'

Muzi rang off.

Mike buzzed through to Max, 'It's Greg for you.'

'Hi Greg, how are you?'

'Not too bad, things are going through with Testastretta. I guess Chris filled you in?'

'Yes, sorry to hear about that,' said Max.

'Well, I'm trying not to dwell on it, but we've got some issues there that may cause us some problems at a later date, but hopefully they'll go away.'

Max assumed he was talking about creditors, but didn't ask.

'Are you looking for any stock?'

'Yes, but not that part exchange stock you had,' said Max.

'No, I didn't mean that. The guy that was supplying us, could be interested in doing a deal with you. It would help me too.'

'Okay, what's he got?' asked Max.

'It's all Ferrari, 355, 360, 550, the usual late model kit,' said Greg.

'Well yes, I would be interested. How do you want to do it?' Max asked.

'I think the best way, would be for you to come up to London and I'll pick you up and we'll go over to Tom's place. He's over in Essex. It's about an hour from Testastretta's on a good day.'

'That sounds good. When are you thinking?'

'Tomorrow?'

'I'll say yes, but just let me check with Pete here and I'll come back to you. What number are you on?' asked Max.

'The mobile, same number.'

'Okay, give me a couple of minutes.'

Max cut the conversation and walked into Pete's office and sat down. They had just started talking when Mike interrupted them.

'Max, Dimo's on the phone.'

'Okay, Mike put him through to Pete's line.'

'Hi, Dimo, how are you?'

'Good, thanks Max. How did you get on with the Helsinki car?'

'It's sold Dimo. I sold it on the way back. A shipping

guy bought it. It's still here at the moment but I've had the confirmation copy of the money transfer on the fax from his bank so we should be in funds in a couple of days.'

'Okay, that's good. I'm going into Sebastien's tomorrow to order the 360 Spiders. I need the specification for your two cars.'

Max had jumped the gun several months earlier and ordered two Ferrari 360 Spiders from Olympic Ferrari in Exeter. At the time of ordering the cars, he was the first on the list because the car had not been announced. Now, Max had agreed with Dimo that he would take two of the three cars that Dimo was going to order from the Ferrari franchised dealer in Marbella, Spain. Ferrari had confirmed that they were now definitely going to produce a convertible version of the 360 Modena, to be called the 360 Spider and Dimo knew the owner of Sebastien's personally, so he would get to the top of the list if he ordered the cars.

'Do you want the specification on the phone now?' asked Max.

'No, fax it over to the Spanish number,' replied Dimo.

'Okay, I'll do that tonight.'

Max put the phone down and told Pete about going to London the following day. It wasn't a problem for Pete. He knew how important it could be.

No sooner had Max walked out of Pete's office when Graham Lord was on the phone asking for Max.

'Hi Max, I think we might have something for your Swiss customer. Do you know Steve Majendie?'

'No,' Max replied.

'He's a dealer much like you and I. He's based in Florida. He was at a function recently and met a customer of his and they discussed the possible sale of his California Spider.'

'Okay, that sounds interesting.'

'First, I think we need to establish some ground rules so that there is no misunderstanding between us,' said Graham.

'Yes, that makes sense. What do you have in mind?' asked Max.

'I'd like to keep it simple. Basically if we sell a car as a result of one of us finding it and the other
selling it, then we divide the profit equally. If you need a car and I find it and you can sell it then we go fifty-fifty on whatever we make and vice versa.'

'I'd be happy with that,' said Max.

'Okay, on that basis of trust, we agree?' asked Graham.

'Absolutely,' said Max and continued. 'We can work together and hopefully make some money.'

'Well, that's the plan,' said Graham adding, 'I've dealt with Steve Majendie several times and I've just done a lightweight E-Type with him. His client with the California Spider is a guy from Long Island, New York called Tony Sangster. According to Steve, he can be quite a difficult guy to deal with. He's very tight. I'm just telling you this because you need to know the background before we launch ourselves into the melting pot. Before we start firing up Sangster, we need to be sure that your Swiss customer is capable and willing to come up with that sort of money.'

'What sort of money?' asked Max.

'That, I don't know, but talking to Steve, it's got to be somewhere around the million and a half dollar mark. What we don't want to do is wind up Sangster, because he's a funny bloke. He's a New York Jew and made his money in the newspaper business. He's got plenty of money but he's extremely difficult when it comes to him buying or selling his cars. The car though is good. It's not an original closed headlight car. It's an open headlight car that was converted by Pininfarina for the first owner in period. So I guess, it would have been done within a year or two of first delivery. It's a 1962 car, complete matching numbers, race history in period and full unbroken history. Oh yes, I nearly forgot, it's also got the original factory hardtop which is not in perfect condition but it is the original one. Sangster has amassed loads of history for the car and that would go with it, if your man goes ahead.'

Max suggested that he spoke to the two people involved in the purchase. Firstly, Sirol Lessek, and secondly, the end user Nino de Vacchi although he didn't mention either person by name. After he had spoken to them, he would go back to Graham and give him his honest opinion of now to proceed. Graham accepted that, and in turn telephoned Steve Majendie to let him know what was going on.

Max quickly wrote the fax to Dimo confirming the specification for the two 360 Spider orders for Sebastien Ferrari and stapled the 'sending receipt', to the paperwork before placing it in the Dimo Dacari file.

Max shuffled some paperwork around on his desk

looking for Sirol Lessek's number.

It was gone seven o'clock and Max was still at work and he still had to call Greg back to confirm the London trip the next day.

'Hi Sirol, it's Max.'

'Hi Max, I'm with someone at the moment. Could you call me at home later?'

'Yeah, no problem. Bye.'

The trip to London was definitely on so Max packed up his brown leather document case and drove home. Later, he called Sirol and went through the information that Graham had given him. Max wasn't prepared to tell Graham about the customer, who he was or where he was, because he wasn't at that stage a hundred per cent sure of Graham and therefore didn't want to jeopardise the good relationship he had with Sirol.

Lessek Ferrari was a well respected franchised dealer in Lugano, Switzerland and Sirol was the man at the top of the tree. He had raced in Formula 1 in the early 1970s amongst the likes of Petersen, Stewart and Fittipaldi and like many true enthusiasts, he was a really nice and generous guy. Max always got on well with Sirol and in turn, he had begun to point a few good customers in Max's direction. Nino was one of them.

Max knew the chassis number of the Spider California and gave it to Sirol to check with the factory archive department. If the car came up as a true original numbered car, then Nino would definitely want to buy it, so Sirol told Max that he would get it cleared the following day and call him back.

Max rang Graham Lord and let him know that he'd spoken to one party and was waiting for a return call and that he would call him back as soon as he'd spoken to them. He then called Greg and gave him his train arrival time at Paddington.

Graham telephoned Steve Majendie and told him things were progressing and that he would get an update in the next twenty-four hours.

AUGUST 1977

St. Scholastica's was a Benedictine convent in Teignmouth, which housed nearly twenty mainly elderly nuns. It was a closed order, which meant that the nuns lived their lives

183

behind closed doors effectively. It was a huge building and it had now become redundant to its original purpose. The nuns were being re-housed elsewhere and the convent was going to be de-commissioned. During the lead up to the closure, some of the monks had travelled to Teignmouth from Buckfast Abbey to help organise the movement of some of the more important artefacts.

Father Prior had finished his work at the convent for the day and thought he'd pay someone a visit. He closed the faded red gothic style door, marked Tradesman Entrance, behind him and walked up the hill a hundred yards to the old metal field gate opening and closing it as he passed through. It was just a short three minute walk across the top of the field. He stopped midway to look at the view, scanning the estuary and up the river Teign, and then carried on until he reached the lower garden gate. Ahead of him was a large bricked, Tudor-style detached house, which he'd visited many times before.

He walked across the lawn and up the garden steps to the terrace, following the path to the back door. He didn't need to knock, Mrs. Reed had seen him coming.

Father Prior was a very charming, well read man and both Max's parents had enjoyed his company over the years. He was a little more worldly and a little more approachable than a lot of his ilk, which made him very easy to get along with. He wasn't all religion. He was just like a very regular guy that anyone could meet in the street.

Mrs. Reed made a pot of tea and they both sat in the conservatory overlooking the garden. They talked about the usual subjects, her divorce, how she was coping, the boys and he was genuinely pleased that she was finally coming to the end of her problems and it was now time to move on. The house had been put on the market at long last, which meant she could downsize and get away from the memories. A chance for a new beginning.

AUGUST 1977

Jenny stood in the hallway looking into the mirror adjusting her top and flicking her hair into place. Her mother was standing in the kitchen looking at her remembering doing the same when she was younger.

'Oh what it is to be young and carefree,' she said.

'You are young, Mum. Maybe not carefree, but thirty-nine is not very old. Look at Dad; he's forty-three. He *is* old,' Jenny replied.

Her father quickly came in through the back door.

'I'm off, love. I'll see you about nine. I'll stop for a quick drink after okay?'

He picked up his sports bag and darted out through the door and was gone.

'I remember when your dad first asked me out. He was scared stiff. He got a friend of his to ask a friend of mine if I would be interested.'

'And what did you say?' asked Jenny.

'I didn't know who he was, so his friend pointed him out to me and I said, maybe.'

'Well, that was all right, wasn't it?'

'Yes. I suppose so. It wasn't quite like your date turning up on the doorstep and springing a surprise. Oh to be young,' she said.

'He's called Max, Mum.'

'Yes, I know, I . . .'

There was a knock at the door. Jenny's heart missed a beat. Her mother raised her eyebrows and smiled. Max could feel his heartbeat racing.

Jenny opened the door with a big smile and invited him in.

'Ah, the carpet man has been,' he said

'Yes, he came today,' said Jenny's mother as she wandered over.

'It looks good.'

Jenny took her coat off the newel post and gave a little wave to her mother.

'I'll be back at eleven,' she said.

'Okay, be careful and no later than eleven. Have a nice time.'

'Bye.'

The walk down to the town would take about half an hour. They were soon rabbiting away and by the time they arrived at the Riviera Cinema, they knew masses about each other and would have been quite happy to carry on talking rather than seeing the film. Max's friends were stood outside, he hadn't told them he was bringing someone along so it came as a bit of a surprise to some of them.

Saturday Night Fever was one of the most successful films of the time and Max liked it. He liked the music, which was different to his normal listening, and he liked the dancing although he was completely incapable of doing the same. The whole ' fever phenomena' had swept the world and everywhere you turned, there seemed to be a white suited, medallion man strutting his stuff and dance studios seemed to be springing up on every corner. Most of the songs from the sound track had gone to number one in the charts and it was a real 'feel good' time to be a teenager. Max would listen to all sorts of music, which Rob couldn't comprehend.

He'd say to Max, 'How can you possibly like *Genesis*, *Supertramp*, *Queen* and all the like and buy an *ABBA* LP or a *Bee Gees* record? It doesn't make sense'. But here he was with his girlfriend watching a *Bee Gees* soundtrack movie'

Max had no answer. If he liked the song, it didn't really matter who sang it. He didn't like Uriah Heep. Rob did.

That night changed the make up of the old four forever. It was like the parting of the old guard. Caro was with Sam, Rob was with Vicky and Max was now with Jenny.

The drifting that Max had thought to himself months earlier was now a reality. In the next few months, Rob and Max would have a completely new set of friends and the old Grammar School would be a thing of the past. He'd still remember all his friends fondly, but wouldn't really see them much ever again. Sadly, it was the same with Caro.

She had her new man, he seemed like a nice chap, and that's where she wanted to be. All four would meet again at a few parties in and around Teignmouth, but the magic of 1976 and 1977 really had gone forever. What replaced it in many ways was a lot better but it was more serious and less carefree. Things had changed.

AUGUST 2008

The tour bus stopped outside a modern low-level building. The air brakes hissed and there was movement up towards the front of the vehicle.

'Mr. Reed?'

'Yes.'

'We've arrived. We just need to do some paperwork and then you'll be on your way. A couple of minutes, that's all.'

'Okay,' Max replied. He looked out of the small window craning his neck to see as much as he could. There seemed to be signs everywhere. Sports field, Gym, C Unit, Education, Chapel, Medical Centre, Keep off the grass.

The truck door opened and Reed was released from the confines of his cubicle. *That's a relief*, he thought. It had started to rain so the prison officer beckoned Reed to run across the grass. It was the only time he did. The cool air on his face being a welcome change.

The reception procedure entering Leyhill was much the same as Exeter. The paperwork and medical was similar except that the surroundings and the prison officer's manner were so much better. The process took about an hour. Max was still not allowed to have his watch or mobile phone, but everything else was returned to him. He was issued with a photographic identity card and offered a sandwich and drink from a tall chiller cabinet. Things were definitely looking better.

After the 'signing in' was complete, a woman prison officer escorted Max casually down to the A unit. This was a modern two-storey building not too dissimilar to a small motel. The walk was no more than three hundred yards from the reception building to the A unit office, but Max was to all intent free. He could walk along the path uncuffed and take in the surroundings. The relief was immense. The concrete paths were lined with red edging bricks, as were all the roads. There were huge expanses of mown gardens, all in immaculate condition. There didn't seem to be a blade of grass out of place. There was a fish pond, garden bench seating and loads more signs pointing to tennis courts, golf course. It went on. Max couldn't believe it was a prison. It reminded him of Buck House in a lot of ways, but mostly because of the design and the landscape.

The WPO took Max into the unit office and collected a key.

'Dinner is served at 5:00 pm.' Pointing, she said, 'You'll find the canteen in that building over there. There are two entrances, one on either side. We have a roll call at 4:30 pm; you will be required to stand by your room with your identity card displayed for the duty prison officer to check. That will happen every day at 11:30 am, 4:30 pm and 8:30 pm. We don't want you going missing do we Mr. Reed?' she joked.

Max was listening intently but he didn't need to answer the question.

'I'll show you to your room where you can unpack and settle in. I need to see you at 7:00 pm outside the A unit office,' she said.

She gave Max the key when they arrived at his room. He looked up at the number on the door, AS4, turned the lock and walked in.

Mrs. Redman, the WPO smiled and said, 'Right, I'll leave you to it and see you at 7:00 pm.'

Max thanked her and closed the door, leaning his back on the inside as he surveyed all before him. He couldn't believe it. The room was fully furnished with a large picture window at the far end looking out over the beautifully manicured lawns, shrubs and trees. There were no bars on the window. He could see the low boundary fence about three hundred yards in the distance. Again, no barbed wire. He could even see the odd car pass by in the distance. It was quiet.

The room had a fourteen-inch colour television with remote, a comfortable bed, a writing desk and chair, a locker, a wardrobe and a comfortable relaxing chair. There were two pin boards on the wall. It couldn't be further removed from the experience at Exeter. *It's very welcome*, he thought. *I can cope with this.* It wasn't home comforts, but he'd slept in worse places around the world on the outside, so this would be a piece of cake. So far so good.

If the room was a revelation, then the canteen was amazing. Max had felt quite obvious standing in the queue. He was still wearing the same clothes that he'd worn in court and being quite smart, he stood out a bit. Most of the residents were wearing regulation jeans or tracksuits and he felt that he would be more comfortable blending rather than standing out as he was.

He arrived at the servery and collected a tray. There was a choice. Unbelievable, there was a choice. Chicken Korma curry, lasagne, chilli, roast duck with orange. *This isn't a prison*, he thought. *This is a bloody holiday camp.* However that thought was short lived. It wasn't quite a holiday camp, but provided Max followed the rules, he would see out the remainder of his sentence in a more civilised way. Yes, he had to comply with a lot of rules, but he was in prison serving a sentence, it wasn't going to be a free ride.

The seven o'clock meeting was a welcoming opportunity from the prison to the new intake and also a chance for the new prisoners to ask questions. The overriding points related to absconding and the many, many rules. Max couldn't possibly take them all on board at once but at least there was a reference book given out, explaining how the prison was run and how prisoners should behave. There was nothing to stop Max walking out the gate, but if he did, the maximum penalty could be two years added to his sentence, it was enough of a deterrent.

Leyhill was a working prison, which meant that every resident had to either work or be in education, and the first two weeks of Max's time would be taken up with a compulsory induction period. Mrs. Redman explained the zero tolerance rule. It was a simple rule. If an inmate stood out of line in any respect whatsoever, however minor or petty, then the prisoner would have a new postcode. There were no warnings. If Max had any sense at all about him, then he would follow the rules to the letter, enjoy what he could of the facilities and ride out this difficult period in his life.

Zero tolerance meant zero tolerance and inmates were being shipped out more or less every day. A lot of prisoners would go to Leyhill after having been in a 'bang up jail' for many years where all their decisions were made for them. If the cell door opened, then they walked out, if the cell door closed, they were shut in. As such, in a situation like that, prisoners didn't have to think. Their day was time controlled by the prison staff, they just followed along. Leyhill was very different. Prisoners had to think for themselves and be responsible for themselves and in some cases, prisoners couldn't cope. The rules combined with the freedom would be too much for them and ultimately they would be cuffed and escorted back to Reception and then shipped out to a 'bang up' prison, that's if they hadn't already legged it over the fence. For someone like Max, the thought of going back to Exeter Prison was enough of a deterrent on its own.

The regime at Leyhill was relatively easy during the induction period. Every day a prisoner would be required to report at a place at a particular time and undertake certain tasks. The induction was designed to sift the inmates and sort them into various jobs and education.

Mrs. Redman closed the meeting and left the new intake

189

to some free time to look around. The next appointment to keep would be the 8:30 pm tally roll call, so he had an hour to himself.

Internally, the building was like a school, full of notice boards, polished lino flooring and shuffling residents. They all seemed to be friendly enough. There was none of the barracuda like atmosphere that Max had just come from. This was civilised. The A unit was divided into four distinct areas being north, south, east and west corridors with the north and west being on one side of the A-unit office and the south and east being on the other. Each corridor had its own "ablutions" block and each pair of wings had a kitchen with the usual equipment. Alongside the entrance area to one side were some basic interview rooms and opposite stood the games room with snooker, pool, table football and darts. Max looked at the dartboard and thought it quite funny. If ever there was a weapon, it was a dart, but not considered so here. Things must be good.

Like being a new boy at school, it takes a while to get used to everyone and everything, but from what he had seen so far, it had to be the best he was probably going to get.

He returned to his room for the 8.30 tally and chatted briefly to his new neighbour. It had been a long day and it had been an even longer three weeks, but finally he felt he could relax, not like it would be at home, but he could kick off his shoes, sit back in a comfortable chair and listen to some music. He looked at the photographs of Catherine and the girls he'd put on the pin board and smiled. *Better times*, he thought. Three of the pictures were taken the previous summer when they rented a villa in France, and the other picture showed them all skiing in Courchevel four months before. Their smiling faces made him smile too.

Max went to the kitchen and made himself a cup of tea and returned to his room and sat at the desk, his brown leather document case lay in front of him unopened.

He didn't need to be provoked; he knew the time was right. He opened the case and took out his Mont Blanc pen looking at it carefully as he did so. It had been a present from Josef in appreciation of the business they had done together. It seemed fitting that Max had it with him now. He opened the writing pad to the first blank page and started.

'Reed looked out of the small tinted window of the tour bus. It was raining and the spray from the motorway traffic blurred his vision of the outside world' . . .

MAY 2004

It was pitch black by those doors; Jacques could only just make out Olivier's face and couldn't see Max at all. The torch had gone out again and Max was trying to get it to work, but not having much luck. He felt his way back towards the entrance doors, fumbling around in the dark. He felt the sides of the oil tank and traced his way to the underside and crawled through to the outside.

Jacques and Olivier were rambling away in French. They were speaking too fast for Max to understand.

'Are you okay Max?' asked Jacques.

'Yes, a bit dirty I think, but yes I'm okay,' he replied.

'Shall we go into the house?'

'Yes, that's a good idea. I could do with washing my hands,' said Max.

The three of them walked into the kitchen and Olivier directed Max to the sink, showing him the soap and a towel.

'Café?'

'Oui, sil vous plait,' Max replied, looking down at the state of his clothes. 'Et changes mes robes aussi,' he continued.

Jacques laughed. 'Well, you wanted to have a look.'

'Yes, I did.'

They all sat down at the table and looked at each other waiting for someone to speak first.

Max opened up, 'Well, I know what it is, or at least I think I know what it is, but how did you come by it?'

Olivier spoke to Jacques in French and Jacques replied in English, 'It's been in the family since 1932. Olivier's father bought the car direct from the man himself, he travelled to the works and agreed to take the car after it had completed in the Targa Florio.'

Olivier interjected often adding more and more information as he did so and Jacques couldn't keep up with the story, asking Olivier to slow down several times.

Jacques carried on, 'His father collected the car from Weissman in Paris and drove the car here in time for the Pau Grand Prix the following weekend. He didn't win. He retired with a supercharger problem. The car was raced many times all

191

over Europe but it never had as much success as when it was used by the factory. A couple of years after, the car was virtually redundant as a competitive car and his father was very busy at his workplace so the car never got used.

Olivier repeated something he said earlier and Jacques made the point, 'Olivier says that when his father died in 1939, the car hadn't been used for many years.'

'Okay,' said Max. 'What happened then?'

Olivier understood the question and spoke in French.

Jacques interpreted, 'When Hitler walked into Paris, we knew there was going to be problems, so we started hiding all of our valuables. We stripped the car down and put on an old Citroen body on top of it and put it up on jacks and that's how it stayed throughout the war years until some time in the 1950s.'

Olivier said a little more and Jacques in turn gave his version, 'Olivier started to restore the car in the 1950s, but couldn't find some of the parts and then lost interest. It's been here ever since.'

Max was completely fascinated. It was a fantastic story. 'What do you want to do now?' he asked.

'We would like to sell the car but we have a few problems. We know the car is not perfect and there are some parts missing, although Olivier seems to think that if he let you look, you could perhaps find them. They are here somewhere. But the major problem is that the authorities do not know that we have the car, because the records office was destroyed during the war. In France, we pay our taxes based on our assets and Olivier has never declared the car, which was perfectly okay in the early days when it wasn't worth anything but today it is worth something, so he's worried that if he sells the car and the authorities find out, then he could be liable for back taxes which could be more than the car is worth. Therefore, he'd get nothing for it. What we need is someone we can trust and we are hoping that's you,' said Jacques.

'Okay,' Max said. 'Well first and foremost, I would like to buy the car and I am more than prepared to work out some kind of way that we all benefit. I don't know what that is going to be at the moment, but I think we all need to think that one through. Who else knows about the car?'

'Nobody, not even the specialists, but we do know that they have been looking for it. Most people think the car was lost in the war,' said Jacques having conversed with Olivier.

'That's good. If it's all right with you, I'd like to come back down again in a couple of weeks and look at the car again in daylight, or with a better torch or lead light. I can see what it is, but I will need to satisfy myself exactly which one it is.'

Olivier confirmed that was perfectly acceptable. Max leant across the table and put his hand forward for Olivier to grasp with both his hands and Jacques placed his hand on top. The three had agreed that Max would buy the car, Olivier would sell it and between them, and they would keep the secret.

The trip to the South of France had been worth it, but Max realised in many ways there was such a very long way to go.

AUGUST 2000

As promised, Graham rang Steve Majendie after he had spoken to Max and was now in a position to confirm to Steve that Max's customer was serious and capable.

'Hey Graham, what if I ring you back and we have a conference call with your man?' suggested Steve.

'I don't have a problem with that, but I need you to respect the fact that he is my customer and that should any business come about now or in the future, it has to come through me,' Graham replied.

'Hey, Graham, you don't need to say that, you know how I work.'

'Better safe than sorry,' said Graham.

'Ah. No. I understand.'

Graham put down the phone and rang Max.

'Hello Max, I've been speaking to my agent regarding the California Spider and he would like to talk to you on a conference call with me as well. Are you okay with that?'

Max was happy to oblige. He waited on 'hold' for a few seconds and Graham came back on the line.

'Max?'

'Yes.'

'I have Steve Majendie on the line.'

'Hi, Steve.'

'Hi Max.'

Steve asked, 'Max, my client is the most difficult guy to

deal with. I expect Graham has filled you in on his background.'

'Yes he has,' said Max.

Steve continued, 'He wants everything his own way and he can be incredibly tiresome to deal with. How sure are you of your customer?'

'One hundred per cent,' said Max, 'he wants a closed headlight California Spider and he has the money to buy one. I've been asked to find a car and I've told him that we potentially have one. The ball is in your court.'

'Okay, that sounds good,' said Steve. 'I'll speak to Sangster and get the ball rolling, and Graham?'

'Yes.'

'I'll get back to you later with my progress so that you can let Max know. That all right with you Max?' asked Steve.

'Yes, that's fine by me.'

Graham told Max he'd call him later so they ended their call whilst Graham finished off with Steve.

Max was thinking about the profit margin he could hope to get on the car. Obviously, it would be divided in two, but he thought that $100,000 would be possible. When Graham rang back, Max asked him the question and they agreed that would be a sensible figure to add onto the sale price, but add another $50,000 to allow for any bargaining,' said Graham.

By now, Max had spoken to Sirol who in turn had received a lengthy conversation from Angelo in the Ferrari factory archive department. The car in question was a proper car, all matching numbers, known by the factory from new. He confirmed the specification and the Targa Florio history, and importantly the return of the car to the factory in 1963 for the headlight conversion. Angelo had recommended the car as being a good car to buy, but advised Sirol that all the numbers should be inspected by one of the factory experts based in North America, before any money changed hands.

It was now up to Steve to sort out his end of the deal.

Sirol had put another two customers on to Max during that earlier call, one wanting a Ferrari 250 Short Wheel Base and the other wanting a particular Ferrari 212.

All of this high-faluting talk about expensive cars didn't reflect at all in the dire sales on the motorcycle side of Velodrome. That side of the business was in 'free fall'.

The train whizzed through Reading, Max knew it would be about forty minutes into Paddington. He'd been on the phone so much that the time had passed really quickly. Greg was collecting him from the station and then it was off to Essex and hopefully the opportunity to do a deal on some late used Ferraris.

The train was on time as it pulled into the station and Max went straight to where he'd agreed to meet Greg who was standing by his car with his hand outstretched.

'Hi Max, good trip?'

'Yes, thanks. It went really quickly, I was surprised. Normally it's a real drag. Have you got a Nokia charger?' asked Max.

Greg had an in car multi-charger adaptor that fitted Max's phone so it could be recharged.

'These phones are bloody useless; my battery has the life span of a gnat,' said Max, plugging the charger into the cigarette lighter, continuing, 'So who's this guy we're going to meet?'

'His name is Tom McKinney. He imports used Ferraris mainly from Germany and he does very well at it, as you will see. It's all late model cars, 355s, 360 and 550s. He gets some heavy stuff like 288s, F40s F50s as well, but mainly the 355s and 360s,' said Greg adding, 'He's an easy guy to deal with, but don't cross him; I think he could get a little awkward if things went wrong.'

'That's fair enough. I just need some cars to sell to people. We're getting a lot of enquires and I haven't got the stock to satisfy them,' said Max.

'Well, hopefully he can sort you out with that.'

They'd been driving swiftly for around fifty minutes when Greg turned into a large gated entrance and onto a private drive lined with beech trees. Ahead he could see a beautiful country pile.

'Is this it?' asked Max.

'Yep, this is it.'

The car pulled up in the rear courtyard and a casually dressed fit looking man in his early forties opened the back door of the house and walked towards Greg's car.

'Hi Greg, good to see you,' he said, 'and you must be Max?'

'Yes.'

He held out his hand, 'Tom McKinney. You need some cars?'

'That's the plan,' said Max.

'Okay, follow me; let's see what we've got.

Tom opened up the garage doors around the courtyard with a hand held remote, each one opening slightly behind the next. In all, there were nine cars tucked away. Two five fifties and the rest were three five fives. Max looked at them all. They were all left hand drive, UK registered, taxed with full service history and had the log book V5 documents on the passenger seats. Max looked at them all carefully. They were very nice cars, and they needed nothing, no paintwork or repairs and best of all no servicing. Most of them had been serviced within two thousand kilometres of the current indicated mileage.

'What do you think?' asked Tom.

'They look good to me,' said Max.

'That's because they are. I buy them in Germany from Ferrari franchised dealers and make sure they're serviced before I collect them. They're all less than twenty thousand kilometres and unmarked,' said Tom.

'So what's the deal?' asked Max.

'How many do you want?' Tom replied.

'I'd like them all, but I can only afford to buy one.'

'How will you pay for it?'

'I've bought my cheque book with me. Greg can vouch for me.'

'No, that's fine, Greg's told me all about you,' said Tom. 'Look, if you pay me for one, you can take two others and give me a post dated cheque, say for a month's time. How's that?'

'Okay, to pay for one, but I'd prefer to pay for them as I go. I could give you a cheque for the payment of the first car dated today and take that one, and then give you two separate cheques for the other two cars, dated next week and then you bank them when I tell you I've sold the car!' Max offered.

'Yep, I'll go with that. You can take the three today?'

'Well, it's only me, so no, I'd have to organise transport,' said Max.

'No need, I'll get them dropped down. I've got some drivers, they can follow you now,' Tom answered.

'Yeah, okay, if that's all right with you.'

'Of course, let's get the job done.'

Max chose the three cars and went into Tom's kitchen and filled out the order forms, being careful to get all the information correct. Tom bought in all the service books and logbooks and handed it all over to Max. The two extra drivers arrived about twenty minutes later whilst Greg and Tom had a cup of coffee with Max.

It was a truly spectacular house, circa 1900 Victorian, probably six or seven bedrooms in the most beautiful landscaped gardens. Max reckoned it had to be worth several million pounds. *Hard to believe, but all this from selling cars*, he thought.

On that first visit Max had bought two 355 Spiders, and a 355GTS, a 98 and two '97s, registered with tax and they were great cars. He was pleased.

It was gone closing time when Max arrived with the cars back at Velodrome so he parked them safely in the service department and went home. It had been a good day. Max now had the capability of being able to offer a selection of good used Ferraris that he'd got from Tom McKinney combined with the new 360s funded by Dimo, and all the classic Ferraris through Graham Lord. It looked like he had the makings of some good business, and he needed it. They were only two months into the foot and mouth disease, but the lack of bike sales were affecting the business so badly that something needed to change quickly. The new 360s that Max had bought from Josef had sold well and he'd made a good profit, but he had to keep that going. With the used 355s, he could make a similar margin so now he had a good chance at making it work and the classic cars would become the cream.

DECEMBER 1977

The last day of term, Christmas 1977, had been an early finish. The weather had been threatening to close in and the principal of the technical college had been advised to let all students go home early. It had started snowing and the forecast suggested there could be three to four inches and drifting. The journey from Teignmouth to Torquay would normally take about twenty minutes to cover the eight miles along the spectacular cliff top coast road.

197

Max had been trail riding on his moped and now his two fifty at weekends, so the snowy conditions were really another opportunity to have some fun. A bit more adventure. His Yamaha DT250 was a dual-purpose bike equally at home on the road or a reasonable off road bike. Riding through the snow would be no big deal.

By the time he'd packed up his gear and walked down to the motorcycle bike park, all around him was white and the snowflakes were coming down thick and fast. His eyes lit up, it was magic. He didn't know why, it just was. The bike started easily and Max eased out of the college campus and followed the main road out towards Maidencombe on the Teignmouth Road.

The wind was getting up and the snow was now coming down heavily, nearing blizzard conditions, as Max pressed on out of Torquay. There were no visible road markings and the definition of the road was difficult to read. The kerb to the pavement couldn't be seen easily along the first couple of miles, but past that point, there were hedges or walls edging the road. The last thing Max wanted to do was clip a kerb, because that would have him off the bike easily. He wasn't panicking, he knew the road well, he knew where all the manhole covers were and if necessary he could describe every contour and every turning along its route. There were few cars on the road or at least few moving cars, the odd Land Rover maybe but no ordinary cars were venturing out, which meant that for the best part of his journey he was completely alone, just him and his bike. A few people were walking inappropriately dressed at the roadside. *What a wonderful day*, he thought. Max passed several randomly parked cars.

The five-mile twisting section of road from Maidencombe to Shaldon ran north along the high cliff edge with the sea on the right hand side and the land to the left. The right hand side of the road faces east and the wind and snow were blasting in from that direction with absolutely no protection. Max wasn't perturbed, it just added to the adventure of it all, even though he couldn't ride at much more than twenty miles per hour maximum. Most of the time he was doing five to ten miles per hour occasionally dragging his feet as a stabilising influence. There was over four inches of snow on the top road, with large drift banks forming in the left hand hedge forcing Max to ride more down the centre of the two lane 'B' road. Max could no longer see any other tracks from other vehicles, but the way his bike's front wheel fell into slots and followed certain paths indicated that below the soft virgin surface of the snow were more hard packed tracks. The final set of bends before dropping down the long hill into Shaldon are really quick in the dry, but with drifting snow now built up in the hedge, he could take the right hand bends by planting his bike into the embankment, and shooting the berm, hanging the back out, motocross style.

Arriving in Shaldon, a police car was parked across the road. A cold lonely figure dressed in a black cloak, cowering with his back to the wind was looking towards Max as he approached. The bobby stepped out into the road and waved Max down.

'What the hell are you doing out in this weather?' he asked aggressively.

'I'm just going home from Tech,' said Max.

He calmed down. 'Okay, I thought you were fooling about.'

'No, I'm on my way home, that's all.'

'It's Max, isn't it?'

'Yes it is'.

'I thought it was. I knew your dad'. Max didn't know whether that was good or bad.

'Oh right,' Max replied.

'Well look, go carefully, and mind all the test pilots out there. You'll be okay on your bike, but cars aren't going anywhere. There's an accident on the other side of the bridge and the run up to West End garage is impassable at Bitton Park for a car. Where do you live? Still in New Road' asked the copper.

'Yes, that's right, Butterknowle.'

'You'll be all right on that bike, probably the best transport for the job, but mind yourself. Anybody on the cliff road?'

'Not that I saw, they're all stranded on the hill between Watcombe and Maidencombe. I didn't see anything on the top at all. It's getting quite deep up there and it's drifting.'

'Okay, well, I'll let you get on.'

'Thanks,' said Max and put the bike into first gear and set off across the bridge to Teignmouth. There was carnage at the end of the bridge. About five cars had mangled themselves into each other. Max rode serenely past, through the traffic lights and along Bitton Park Road climbing the hill between the crazy, zig

199

zagged, abandoned cars, still doing no more than ten miles per hour and then arriving at the red traffic lights at the bottom of Exeter Road and keeping his momentum, he ignored the red light and turned left up the hill passing his old school on the right hand side. There was an ambulance and two police cars parked just a short way up the hill from the school with a car angled half on and half off the pavement. It looked like they'd been there for a while judging by the settled snow on the vehicles. A few people were milling around but it didn't look serious.

A few minutes later, Max parked his bike in the back yard and kicked the wall lightly with his boots to shake off the snow. He was completely white. He was dry, that was the main thing. His wax cotton Belstaff jacket, trousers and over mitts had kept out the weather and his feet were warm in his Sidi Joel Robert motorcross boots.

Max's mother and two brothers were home and the lit fire was a welcome homely sight. He got out of his motorbike gear, put the kettle on and warmed his hands on the open fire. The snow was falling heavily outside, a timely arrival for Christmas.

He leant on the window sill looking out over the wintry view of the garden sipping his tea. He needed to get some Christmas shopping done. He didn't know what to get Jenny. He'd bought her some Charlie perfume and an LP for her birthday the month before, so it wouldn't be good form to buy her something similar for a Christmas present. He saw Popper come into sight from the right of his vision, he didn't like the snow. He shook his paws every time he lifted them out of the snow. He was getting a bit old now, he'd lost a bit of weight and he was sleeping more. *Twilight years*, Max thought sadly. It didn't stop him yowling for his tea though.

It had been dark all day but now it was getting darker as the night drew in. Max was due to meet Jenny at eight o'clock at her house and then go out for a drink with some of her friends. He didn't think that the snow would stop them so carried on as arranged.

If it hadn't been snowing, he would have taken her on the back of his bike. He'd passed his test a couple of weeks after his seventeenth birthday in mid November and Jenny's mother had said it was okay to go on the pillion provided he looked after her. He had no intention of doing anything other than that, but snow on the road was probably a little bit too much of a risk to take with a passenger. In saying that she was a very good passenger, she didn't lean the wrong way or poke him in the ribs for going too fast and she wasn't very heavy, so Max didn't really notice her being there other than the fact she had her arms around him.

He knocked on the door at eight and she let him in. Her parents and brother had just gone around to the next door neighbour's house for a party.

'We've got the house to ourselves,' she said.

'Where is everyone?' Max asked.

'Next door at a party,' Jenny replied.

He grabbed hold of her, 'Come here you,' they kissed and cuddled for a while. They liked each other's company.

'Last day for you as well then,' Max said.

'Yeah, we go back on the sixth.'

'I think we're the same,' said Max adding, 'What time are we meeting people?'

'I said between half eight and nine at the Ship.'

'Okay, it will be fun walking down in the snow.'

Jenny went upstairs to get a coat and some gloves and came back down, stopping at the mirror to look at herself.

'You look fantastic, you don't need to do anything,' Max said.

'You say all the right things,' she said and kissed him.

The Ship was incredibly busy that night. It was as if everybody needed an excuse to go out and walk in the snow. There was snow, even on the beach. A couple of Jenny's new girlfriends from school came in with their boyfriends, two of whom Max had known from the Grammar School. *This is going to be a good night*, he thought. One of them was Jonathon Thomas. Max never particularly liked him, he didn't know why; he just didn't gel with him. He'd known him since they had played in the juniors at Teignmouth Golf Club. Jonathon and Max both played off a thirteen handicap when Max was thirteen and Jonathon a year older at fourteen. When Max first went to the Grammar School, the boys in his year had been called up to the nurse for the regular 'cough drop' check on their balls. For some reason 'Dick' hadn't been the year previously which is why it was a surprise to see him in the queue when he was a year above them.

Dick was a pushy sort of guy, loudmouthed and considered himself God's gift, which is why it was all the more funny when he pushed himself in towards the front of the queue. Dick was standing two in front of Max when Dave Shaw came out of the nurse's office.

'What's it like?' asked Dick.

Max was listening.

'Yeah, it's okay, she just gets you to drop your trousers and pants and gets you to cough whilst she's cupping your balls,' said Dave sniggering.

'Oh, right,' said Dick.

'The only thing is that it shows, she can tell,' said Dave.

'What do you mean?' said Dick.

'Well, she can tell!'

'Tell what?' said Dick rather snappily.

'She can tell if you've been wanking,' said Dave with a smile.

'How?' said Dick.

'I don't know,' said Dave, 'she just can!'

Dave went off back down the corridor to his classroom and Dick surreptitiously eased his way to the back of the queue. Max smiled thinking about it. Proper wanker then.

Despite Dick being there, they did have a good laugh and before long the time had passed so quickly, they were ready to go home. It had started snowing again. All the Christmas lights were on and there was a tall, decorated Christmas tree on the triangle in the centre of the town. Jenny and Max stopped and looked at it as they were walking past. They kissed under the tree and she told him 'I love you Max' and he replied 'I do too'. They'd held each other tightly and walked home.

The party was still raging away at the neighbour's house, so Jenny invited Max in for a drink. She put the kettle on and Max got the mugs out while she moved things off the kitchen table. She turned and watched him as he looked in the various pots for the tea bags. She hadn't ever felt so happy.

'In the end one,' she said.

'Right,' he replied.

'Max?'

'Yeah,' he said, looking up.

There was a delay before she spoke again. She walked the few feet across the kitchen and put her arms around his neck and looked into his eyes for what seemed an age.

'Will you marry me?'

He kissed her. 'I can't, not now, I'm making the tea.' He

didn't take it seriously, but unbeknown to him she was. They were only seventeen and they'd only been going out for four months, but she meant it and that took Max by surprise. He was incredibly flattered, amazed in fact and he loved her and she loved him, but surely it was just 'puppy love' as someone once sang? Really, it was probably more than that, but both of them wouldn't realise that until later.

She put on some music, Rod Stewarts Atlantic Crossing LP and sat down in the lounge. They soon had their hands all over each other. She was gorgeous, there was no doubting that. Her parents and brother crashed through the back door at about midnight making enough noise to announce their arrival thankfully and give Max and Jenny enough time to organise themselves before her dad entered the room.

'Hi, you two!'

'Good party, Dad?'

'Yeah, very good, thank you. Where have you been then?'

'We went down to the Ship,' said Max, 'It was good tonight, ever so busy.'

Max had got to know Jenny's dad, because he played squash at Dawlish where Rob and Max played. They'd met a few times and Jenny's dad had bought Rob and Max a drink in the bar after a game on occasion. He seemed like a nice guy.

'Right, I'd better be going,' Max said, sensing he didn't want to overstay his welcome at that time of night. Jenny followed him to the door.

'I meant what I said,' she whispered in his ear.

'I know you did,' Max replied with a smile.

'Tell me you love me,' she asked.

'I love you Jenny.' He added, 'Very much.'

She smiled. They kissed and Max turned to walk down the path. She scraped the snow off the window ledge and threw a snowball at him as he walked backwards into the road.

'I'll call you tomorrow. Night.'

'Night,' she replied and closed the door.

The walk home was no more than ten minutes and he thought about what she said. Did he love her? He didn't know. He didn't really know what being in love was. Yes he was totally infatuated with her, but he didn't know if he loved her. Did he want to be with her for the rest of his life? He didn't know that either. He just wanted to enjoy the moment. He opened the back door at home and walked in. His mother had left the kitchen light on. He took off his jacket and noticed the message on the side. Please ring Rob. He went up to bed and reminded himself to ring Rob in the morning. Two minutes and he was asleep.

'Hi Geoff, it's Max, Rob there?'

'Yeah, I'll just get him.'

There was a short wait while Geoff called for Rob.

'Hi mate, how are you?'

'Yeah fine thanks; went down The Ship last night with Jenny. I had to endure that wanker Dick all night. And you'll never guess what?' asked Max.

Rob had realised by the way he was animatedly talking that he didn't know.

'Sorry, Max, I've got something to say. Where are you?' asked Rob.

'I'm in the study,' Max replied sensing something odd.

'Max, you better sit down. I don't know how to say this bud but...'

Max sat down in the chair leaning on the desk, concerned as to what Rob was going to say.

'Caro has died. She was involved in a freak accident. A car . . .'

Rob was finding it difficult to tell Max, but he knew how close Max had been with Caro and he also knew why it was that Caro never went out with him.

'How?' asked Max disbelievingly.

'A car mounted the pavement yesterday afternoon after school. Apparently the driver wasn't speeding, but was caught out by the snowy conditions, went up the pavement and hit Caro. She fell backwards and hit her head on the wall. She hardly had a mark on her,' said Rob.

Max wiped his eyes, he could feel a lump in his throat. He'd seen the ambulance and the police cars outside the school the day before. That must have been it. And he'd ridden by and not known. *How would she have felt about that*, he thought. He hadn't spoken to her for five or six weeks and he felt bad about it. She was lying in that ambulance with no one she knew and one of her best friends had passed her by within a few yards.

'God, no, I don't know what to say Rob.'

'Do you want me to come over?'

'Give me a moment, I'll call you back.' Max's throat cracked.

'Okay, bud.'

Max sat at the desk looking at the photographs on the wall. He felt nothing. He thought about her family. It all seemed so quick. There was no lead up. It was just over, so final. Max went in to the other room and told his mother. He held himself together, forcing himself not to cry, however hard it would be. His mind turned back to her family thinking to himself that he should go down and see them. That was going to be hard, but it was what he should do. He felt guilty that he hadn't spoken to her. There would have been so many things he would have liked to have said to her, but he couldn't, not now. He wondered where she was and hoped by now she'd be in some fantastic place.

It was half an hour before Max rang Rob back. There wasn't much they could say to one another, holding back with long periods of nothing said. Rob was right in the middle of Caro's two best friends. On one hand was his girlfriend Vicky who was completely beside herself and on the other was Max, his best mate. Vicky had known the night before so her grief had a head start but Max had just found out and he still had to come to terms with it and what to do next. He thought about that sensational summer of '76 and how much fun they'd had. He always would, you don't forget things like that. He thought of the cornfield at the top of the cliff path on the walk back from the fair. It all raced back into sharp focus in his mind like instant rewind. He felt robbed. It was so unfair. She had so much ahead of her and it was just taken away in a flash. So many ifs or buts. So many things to say, so many things left unsaid. He shook his head and looked up, letting out a long sigh, flushed with emotion. He'd lost his soul mate and wondered how life could be so cruel. He'd miss her like no tomorrow.

Max plucked up the courage to press the doorbell at Caro's home. Her mother walked through the hallway and opened the internal door before opening the outside door for Max. She didn't say anything, she couldn't. She hugged Max, crying uncontrollably on his shoulder then stepped back and looked at him. His eyes had welled up, his face felt warm and his mouth was dry. He couldn't speak for fear of breaking up altogether. He managed to say 'I'm sorry.'

She took his coat and placed it over the newel post at the bottom of the stairs and went into the kitchen to make a cup of tea. Her father came out of the lounge looking totally shot and gave Max a warm hug.

'Thanks for coming Max.'

Caro's two sisters and brother were sat around the lounge in various states of despair. Max didn't know what to do or where to look next. He felt that anything was going to set him off then in an extraordinary moment, all three stood up and walked over to Max and they all put their arms around each other and said nothing. Yes, they cried, as did Max, but there was strength in their unity and they felt better for it.

After a while they managed to get themselves under control and all sat squashed together on the settee as they had done many times before when Caro and Max had babysat them. They talked as best they could, swallowing hard at times. It was the most difficult thing Max had ever done, but it had to be done, Caro would have wanted them to stay strong and be there for each other. There were long periods of silence, they all said nothing. Max had been through difficult periods in his life and this would be another one. Last time, Caro was there for him, this time she wasn't.

Max leant forward and looked around at everyone. 'She wouldn't want us to be like this, however hard it is. Whenever I think of her she's smiling and that's the way I'll always remember her, smiling, and I won't ever forget that.' It was difficult for him to say but somehow he managed to get the words out.

He closed the door behind him and stepped out into the cold night air, put his hands in his duffle coat pockets and looked up at the sky above. The stars were bright. It had stopped snowing and it was a very cold clear evening. He had so many memories of Caro and they were all good ones, but that captivating smile she flashed on the Noah's Ark at the fair that summer with her hair swinging in the wind, singing to Band on the Run. That was the memory. The ever-lasting image in his mind. He shrugged and smiled. She would always be there for him, out of sight, but never out of mind. He walked down the drive to the main road and stopped where she first flashed that everlasting smile at him. She was gone but not forgotten, he kept saying to himself.

He kicked the snow idly at his feet and whispered out loud, 'I'll miss you Caro, you know I will.' He wiped a tear rolling down his left cheek and strolled home singing her favourite song that they listened to so many times in that glorious summer of 1976.

'Harmony and me are pretty good company,

Looking for an island in our boat upon the sea!

Harmony, Gee I really love you and I want to love you forever.

Think of the never never, ever ending harmony.'

It seemed fitting. The following days were never going to be easy but they got easier as the pain slowly subsided and the memories took over from the reality. Caro's dad asked Max if he would like to say a few words at her funeral. He said he would, not because he had been asked, but because he wanted to. It was the right thing to do for a very special friend and he felt compelled.

When Max was at Buck House, he had learnt to speak publicly, it was part of the education there. At first, he would address his form from the front of the classroom, then he would move on to 'readings' in church or school assembly and then there were performances like plays and music introduction in front of all the parents. It was all designed to make pupils more confident so that they could deal with the fear of public speaking and make it more engaging. Breathing, projection, clarity; that was what the music master had always drummed into them. Max thought he'd need all that and some.

The sun shone brightly on a beautifully crisp day, the last of the snow having all but melted away as the assembled masses filed up the steps into St Michael's church. It looked like the whole of the school had assembled to pay their last respects, crammed into every last inch of space within the ivory stone pillars.

A year earlier, Max had walked up the same steps to the evening Christmas carol service. He couldn't have thought in his wildest dreams that he'd be walking up the same steps a year later to a very different tune.

He took his place on the aisle next to Rob, Vicky and Jenny in the congregation, leaning forward to look along the bench at his friends as he did so.

Max looked towards her coffin and thought of her lying there all alone with no one to hold. It seemed so remote, so cold. Jenny squeezed his hand and he felt guilty about that too.

The service started with the first hymn, which thankfully people knew, but it was hard to get the words out and then the minister followed with the service. All around him Max could hear the sorrowful sounds of crying eyes. He didn't want to hear it, he was trying to hold himself together. Jenny leant her head on Max's shoulder and put her arm around him as he put his arm around her giving her a gentle reassuring squeeze. He leant his head against hers and held his service sheet in his left hand out in front of them looking down. The time came quickly. The minister nodded at Max and beckoned him to step forward. He took a deep breath and looked up.

He croaked the first few lines, his throat running dry, nearly cracked up completely for the middle section, but managed to hold it together for the end.

We are here today to celebrate the life of our very special friend, Caro
And I can see the sadness in all your faces before me,
But that's not how you will be remembering Caro
And it's not how she will be remembering you.
Smile as she smiled, think of her as she cried with laughter.
She was a very special friend, who touched all our hearts
With her beguiling ways she lit up our world.
A world that will be all the more empty without her,
But a world so much better for having known her.
Whenever I think of her, she's smiling.
That's the everlasting image in my mind.
Whenever I think of her, she makes me smile
And that gives me strength and peace of mind.
We love you and we always will,
Wherever you are, we will be.

It was short, it had to be; Max knew it would be difficult. He knew it off by heart and delivered it from his heart. He hoped she would have liked it.

He walked up to Caro's coffin a few steps away and looked at it for what seemed like an age. It would have been only a few seconds. He placed his left hand on the lid and said quietly, 'Bye for now Caro,' then turning, walked back towards his seat sliding his hand along the length of the coffin as he did so. He stood next to Jenny and felt someone give him a reassuring pat on his left shoulder, keeping their hands there before dragging it away. It was Sam. You could have heard a pin drop. The minister finished the service and the congregation gave her a resounding send off.

People were milling around outside the church, exchanging pleasantries and their respects when Max caught Caro's father's eye. His face was flushed and burning welcoming the cool air. He walked up to Max and hugged him. Holding his hands on
Max's shoulders , he stood back and looked at him,
'Thank you.' His eyes said it all. It was all he needed to say. He swallowed hard. It said everything and it meant everything. Sadly, he could count on one hand how many times he would see him again.

MAY 2000

Dimo walked across the shiny tiles of Sebastien's glitzy Ferrari showroom and sat down in the comfortable beige leather sofa with a cappuccino in his hand, and looking at the television documentary about the old man Enzo, he saw Victor walking towards him.
'Hey, don't get up, we can sit here if you like, how are you?'
'Very well, thank you.'
'I have all the paperwork done. I just need some specifications from you,' said Victor.
Dimo pulled out the fax that Max had sent him and passed it to Victor.
'No red then?'
'No,' said Dimo.
Nearly all Ferraris are red, but none of the three cars on the fax were red, they were blue, silver and yellow.
Victor filled in the paperwork and accepted the deposit cheque for the three cars.
'When can I expect delivery?' asked Dimo.
'We will have them for you in September. September 2000,' said Victor.
'Ah, that's good,' replied Dimo. 'That's very good indeed.' He would call Max later that day and let him know.

MARCH 1978

Just over three years after Max's father had left the family home, it was now time for the rest of them to leave too. Mrs. Reed had bought a house in Torquay and was moving everyone over there. The house in Teignmouth had been sold to a neighbour and now it was time to go. Max wouldn't miss it, too many bad memories. It was a nice house, but it hadn't been a home. Hopefully, the move would be kind to his mother and give her another throw of the dice.

It was March 1978. Max was still going out with Jenny but Rob had finished with Vicky and now he was seeing a girl called Debbie. There was a party at a friend's in Barn Park Road on the Saturday night in Teignmouth and both Max and Rob were going. Although it wasn't that far from where Jenny lived, she'd asked her mother to drop her down as she was reluctant to wear a skirt on the back of Max's bike. He said he'd meet her there.

Max rode from Torquay to Stoke in Teignhead and met up with Rob and together they rode on to Teignmouth.

For some unknown reason, Max felt a little distant from Jenny at the party. It didn't feel right and for the first time since he's asked her out at the end of the previous summer, he suspected that not all was well. He didn't really know how to handle it and not being someone to come running, he sort of left her to it. She talked to her friends and Max talked to his. Come the end of the evening, their indifference was obvious, but she'd kissed Max goodbye and said she'd see him tomorrow, so perhaps he was seeing more into it than there actually was.

Dick was at the party and he'd borrowed his mother's Renault 12, a fabulous looking device, and come the end of the evening, Gods gift to women was offering various girls a lift home. Jenny was one of them. Max didn't for one minute doubt that he would try it on with her. He'd fancied her for ages, but whilst she'd been going out with Max, he was not in the picture.

Max took the view that if Dick by name, Dick by nature, was going to try it on, he'd take Jenny home last, so after the car had disappeared, Max got his gear on and rode up to where Jenny lived and parked his bike a little further up the road. The hallway light was on in the house but he couldn't see any movement, so he guessed she wasn't home as yet. He waited patiently for about half an hour, eventually thinking that Dick had taken her home first, so he went to pick up his helmet and go home, but as he did so, he heard a car in the distance. Max was some way from Jenny's house, but he saw the car park and the headlights go out. And then nothing, no doors opened, no doors shutting and no thank you and goodbye, just silence in the dead of night.

Max could only guess. He was going to look a bit of a lemon if he just got on his bike and rode off, so he decided on something else. He walked up to the car on the driver's side and his intention was to open the door and ask them, 'Is this a private party or can anyone join in?' but it didn't quite work out that way.

Max opened the driver's door and the interior light came on. Dick was all over Jenny. Max reached in and grabbed hold of him and dragged him out of the car. He banged his head on the door as Max gave him the biggest whack he was ever likely to get. And then Max did it again. Dick ran off down the road and Max was having none of it. He caught up with him and was just about to have another go, when he found himself being grappled from behind and being pulled backwards. A voice he recognised was telling him to calm down whilst at the same time he was telling Dick to 'piss off home'.

'It's okay,' Max said holding his hands up as if to surrender and Jenny's dad let go of him.

'I'm sorry about that,' he puffed.

'He got what he deserved, now go on home.'

'Thanks,' said Max, still breathing heavily.

Jenny was standing at the front door with her mother. Max didn't acknowledge her. It was over. *Once bitten and all that*, he thought.

He rode home to Torquay. He wasn't happy with what he'd just done. It was nothing to be proud about. Yes, he vented his upset on Dick but it takes two to tango and if she had any feelings for Max, then she wouldn't have done it. Would he see her again? No, not in a month of Sundays. As for Dick, well he had it coming.

Max woke up the following morning or rather he was woken up the following morning by his mother knocking on the door and then walking in.

211

'I have just had Mrs. Thomas on the phone. She's not very happy with you. What happened?' she asked.

Max told her exactly what he had done.

'You didn't use anything to hit Jonathon with, did you? She thinks you had a bit of wood or something'

'No, I just punched him a couple of times. I don't think he particularly liked it.'

'He certainly did not. Mrs. Thomas says she might go to the police. His face looks like a beetroot, she said, black and blue. You can't be bringing this sort of thing to my door. Whatever next?' She wasn't happy.

Mrs. Thomas rang a few times that day and Max did speak to her and apologise for his behaviour, and she told him she wouldn't be taking it any further. It was a relief. Jenny rang Max that day as well and said she was sorry, but he'd already been hurt and there was no way he was going to let her back in. The first cut is the deepest or so they say. She was a fantastic looking girl but she was also a liability. Every man and his dog wanted to go out with her, and if she was going to behave like that, then there was no point. Life was too short for type of heartache. It was a truly great seven months while it lasted, but there were better days a little bit further down the line. Max wouldn't see Jenny again for another twenty-five years.

Neil came into Max's bedroom and said, 'Mother's just said you whacked Dick.'

'Yes, I did. I don't think he'll be smiling today.'

'Brilliant, well done. I didn't know you had it in you,' said Neil.

'Well there you go. Don't wind me up then.'

The funniest thing about the whole episode was that Dick, whose face had turned black, blue and yellow, had told everyone that he'd had to do an emergency stop in his mother's car and hit his face on the steering wheel. Nobody believed him, they all knew what had happened and smiled wryly thinking 'well done Max, I hope you gave him from me'.

SEPTEMBER 2000

Muzi was sat on the balcony of his plush home looking out over the beautiful surrounding countryside, reading the

212

morning paper with a glass of fresh orange juice in his hand and a round of toast on his side plate in front of him. Tabby sat crossed legged alongside him sipping her coffee flicking through the pages of Vogue magazine.

The telephone rang, it was Max.

'Good morning Max, nice to hear from you,' said Muzi.

'I hope I'm not disturbing you.'

'No, not at all, we were just having a late breakfast.'

It was a Saturday morning and Max had just come off the telephone to Graham Lord.

'What do you think about a 250 GTO or putting it correctly a 330 GTO?' asked Max.

'You mean the four litre car?'

'Yes, that's right, one of three,' said Max.

'Definitely. I know the car you mean. Is it the one that Marese crashed ?' asked Muzi.

'Yes, I believe so.. The story goes that the car did the Nurburgring 1000 km race finishing second, I think, and was then sold to a good customer of Ferrari. Typically, Enzo used the car to test some experimental parts before the forthcoming Le Mans 24 hr race and Marese, Ferrari's test driver crashed the car into a motorway bridge. The car was quite badly damaged.

Enzo Ferrari himself had to speak to the customer to help appease him. The factory didn't have a GTO body at the time, so Ferrari offered a body similar to a 250 SWB, which thankfully for Ferrari, the customer accepted.

'Where's the car now ?'

'I think it's in Japan. I say 'I think' because we're dealing with his agent in the USA, and at this stage he doesn't want to go into too much detail, unless we are serious,' said Max.

'We are definitely serious, you know that, don't you?'

'Yes, of course, but I don't want to appear too eager,' Max replied.

'Okay, that's fair enough. I think you can go ahead and get all the details. Do you know what they are asking?'

'It's going to be around the seven to eight million dollar mark, but obviously we are going to negotiate,' Max confidently replied.

'That's to be expected. I think this is the car that was re-bodied as a correct GTO and sold for the reputed ten million dollars in the dizzy price madness of the early nineties. I thought

213

that one of the big Middle Eastern collectors had it,' enquired Muzi.

'It is the same car. I can't comment on the nineties price but I've heard the same story before so, could be.'

'Max, I would like to buy this car, so get working on it and come back to me as soon as you have more information.'

Muzi put the phone down and went into his study and picked up a book from his desk and fingered the pages until he reached the right page.

'Hey, Tabby, what do you think of that?' Muzi asked.

Tabby looked at the old black and white photograph of a line of old sports racing cars and said, 'Yes, Muzi, very nice.'

She couldn't get that enthusiastic about his passion and continued, 'It means nothing to me darling, I need to see it in the real.'

'Well hopefully, soon, you will.'

Max picked up the phone and dialled Graham Lord's number.

'Hi, I've spoken to my customer on the GTO. I think we could be in business.'

'That's good,' Graham replied.

'We need to confirm the buying price and then I will negotiate with him on the selling price,' said Max.

'The agent I'm dealing with is John Gill. He's direct with the owner.'

'Okay, well if you speak to him and start negotiating a purchase price subject to contract, then we can get things moving. One other thing, have you heard from Majendie about the California Spider?'

'No, not yet,' said Graham. 'I'll get on to it this afternoon. It's too early for both of them now. Give me until about four this afternoon and I should have some news for you,' said Graham.

'Yes, that will be okay, speak to you later.'

Max didn't want to give away too much information about the customer and certainly didn't want to tell him that Muzi had an easy thirty million dollar shopping list, but the first sale could mean such a difference to the business that Max crossed his fingers and hoped that it would happen. There was a lot going on and Max was thinking positively as he picked up the phone from Mike.

'Yes, Mike?'

'It's for you, wouldn't say who he was. I think he's a foreigner though.'

'Put him through.' Max wondered who it was.

'Hi, it's me.'

Max recognised the voice. 'How's it going? Any news?'

'We need some more money. I was hoping to get everything you need, but it's been raining here a lot over the last few days and the last part of the operation hasn't been possible.'

'How much do you need?' asked Max.

'Another five thousand, should do it.'

'Take it off my card.'

'Okay, the weather is due to change tomorrow so we should be able to resume.'

'Okay,' said Max.

'I'll come back to you in seven days,' he cut the connection.

SEPTEMBER 1980

It took quite a while for Max to put Jenny behind him. A couple of times he'd thought about giving her a call but he never did. Time had passed, Max had left South Devon Technical College and was now doing Architecture at Bristol Polytechnic, he no longer had his DT250, he'd bought himself a Yamaha XT500, which he'd left at home. His mother had moved again. She was no longer in Torquay, she had moved to Newton Abbot and Max had bought himself a soft top MGB that he used to get to college in Bristol.

In his last year at South Devon Technical College, he'd become good friends with another Newton Abbot based guy called Martin. His parents spoilt him, but when he was not under his mother's influence, he was great fun. Max had worked for Youngs Seafoods in the summer. He drove one of the seven and half ton fridge lorries from Heathfield up to Bideford every night. He would start work at 10:00 pm and finish at about six in the morning, taking a full lorry up and bringing a different empty truck back. The journey was sixty miles each way and the maximum speed of the lorry was governed to sixty miles per hour. Max used to do it in an hour. He was flat out everywhere. Going down Haldon Hill, he would get up to sixty mph flat out

215

and then knock it out of gear. The speedo needle used to go past the high beam light.

It was a hell of a job, not least because Martin would call for Max at about eleven in the morning and they'd go off down to the beach. Max was burning the candle at both ends, and by the end of the summer he was completely worn out.

Max wasn't enjoying life at Bristol. He was beginning to get fed up with education and wanted to earn some money but didn't know what to do. What he'd really like to do was go motor racing, but he didn't have any money. The thought had been nagging away in his mind on and off but at this stage common sense prevailed.

He'd met quite a few of Martin's friends that summer going to various parties and interestingly he would have met a lot of them before at sporting events when he was in the school sports teams at Buck House. He would have shaken hands with them when he was captain of the football team or rugby team. He didn't remember any of them from then, but he did remember the matches they played against all the local private schools. During conversations, the inevitable, 'do you remember him?' would come out and he suddenly realised that he had a whole new group of friends with a similar background. Max hadn't thought about Buck House for a long time, but it was amazing what he could recall about the schools they went to as the visiting team. They all had a common interest and they were easy to get along with.

Max met them all once at the Highweek Inn at Newton Abbot and strangely, they all had MGBs. It was weird, but it was also a lot of fun.

He was finding it harder at Bristol Polytechnic than he'd expected. It wasn't that the work was difficult, he was tired of having to scrimp and save all the time, and it didn't look like that was going to change for a while. He was working at weekends to afford to run his car, but it wasn't allowing him much free time. He decided that he would carry on until the end of the second year which was the following July and then decide which way to go. At that point, he'd be out on a sandwich year, with a placement in the industry and then back for one more year and then hopefully qualify to finish off.

Max liked the new house in Newton Abbot, it was quite small but it was cheap to run and mother could afford it. Neil was working at Torre Motorcycles as an apprentice and Ferris, now five was at the local nursery school. He was quite a character with all his voices and impressions. Being at Bristol, Max was jointly renting a house, so he was spending less time at home and was beginning to start to go on his own. The gaps between visits was getting bigger and more often.

SEPTEMBER 2000

Harry Thompson was talking to one of his best customers who was based in Jersey.

'What do you want to do with it Matthew?'

'My circumstances are dictating that it's got to go. I haven't used it for several years and it needs work. It hasn't been started for eighteen months, so it will need a new battery and general re-commissioning,' said Matthew.

'Do you want to sell it as it is, or do you want to put it right and sell it as a proper car?'

'I think it would be best to let it go as it is. I don't want to get involved in further cost.'

'Okay, that's all right, but you realise people will knock you on the value?' said Harry.

'Yes, I know that, but if they know the condition and you describe it properly, then it's a straight sale and I don't get any comebacks.'

'Fair enough,' Harry said, 'I can understand that. I've got someone asking about it so I'm going to offer it on that basis.'

'Thanks Harry,' Matthew rang off.

Two days earlier Max had been talking to Harry Thompson about a Jaguar XJR15. Harry had told him that there was the possibility of a car being available and now he was in a position to formally offer Max the car. They talked again on the phone and Harry faxed through the complete details on the car, confirming the current owner as a well-known record producer who had owned the car from new. The car needed re-commissioning, but the price was right at £90,000 and there was the possibility of some negotiation as well. Harry was indicating that the owner would like a quick unfussy sale.

Max didn't have a customer for the car but he knew that Graham Lord was looking for an XJR15 for an American customer. Max had wondered whether the car was for Steve Majendie or one of Steve's customers, but he never asked the question. Graham had agreed that should he have a customer for a car and that if Max found such a car then they would do the deal together, being perfectly open with each other and divide the profit on the car equally. In this instance, Max had the exact car that Graham needed for his customer. Like many, Graham knew Harry Thompson, although he hadn't spoken to him in a while, but he didn't know that Harry had access to this particular Jaguar XJR15. Max passed on all the relevant information to Graham so that he knew exactly which car it was and the basis of the sale. Max hadn't at that stage told Graham who it was that was offering him the car and there was nothing on any of the paperwork that would have indicated that information. Graham was sensible enough not to try contacting the owner direct as that would be a definite no, no.

If it was going to be a deal, it would be fairly simple. The buyer was a Jaguar fanatic and already had a very nice collection of classic racing Jaguars and this car would provide him with a welcome addition to his stable block. Graham told Max that it was looking good.

Max had a lot going on with Graham at the time. His Swiss customer wanted to buy the Ferrari 250 California Spider. Muzi wanted the Ferrari 330 GTO, Graham had a customer for the Jaguar XJR15 and Max looked like he was about to confirm the availability of a new silver Ferrari 360 F1. If all of the cars were to come to fruition, the trading turnover would be nearly seven million pounds and the profit from them would be a significant boost to Velodrome's fortunes. No wonder Max was concentrating so hard in getting the deals done.

SEPTEMBER 2000

Rux picked up his mobile, pressed five two five and the automatic recognition put him straight through.
'Hello.'
'Yeah, it's Rux.'
'Everything all right?'
'Yeah, we got the tap on last night and we're getting transcripts. We'll run it for seven days as agreed,' said Rux.

'That's okay. Have you heard any of it?'

'Yeah.'

'What's it like? It's difficult; there's a few languages. He's fast and it's all over the place.'

'Okay, keep on it.'

'We'll run it for the duration, but we'll let you know if there are any developments.'

'Good.'

Rux cut the conversation.

MAY 2000

Dimo looked at his watch and gave Max a call.

'Hey, Max, how are you?'

'Yeah, fine thanks. How did you get on with Victor?'

'All okay, I have paid the deposits and I'm being told we can have them in September 2000. I've ordered them exactly as the specification you gave me.'

'That's great. I'm just awaiting some news on a new silver 360 F1, so I will need to talk to you if that starts to happen,' said Max.

'Okay, let me know,' said Dimo replied.

'Bye.'

Max put down the phone and thought about the two cars. He hadn't sold them as yet, but he didn't think he'd have any trouble in shifting them when they arrived. Dimo had told Max that he'd got a small discount across the three cars, so Max reckoned he'd make at least £25,000 - £30,000 profit on each car when they arrived and it was only five months to wait.

AUGUST 2008

That first night at Leyhill had been a relatively comfortable one. Max had managed to sleep which he hadn't done at Exeter. He looked around his room, it was a staging post, and next stop would be home. The calendar on the wall had the typical scratched off days marked on it, three weeks down, eleven to go. He still couldn't believe the difference between the two prisons, but at least now he would feel his treatment being more like a human than a wild animal.

The first day of education had been fairly light. There was an appointment at the A Unit Wing office at 8:30 am for an Advice Centre talk followed by a visit to the chaplaincy at nine thirty for ten minutes. The advice centre talk was a short speech on what help could be obtained from the centre and all the chaplain wanted to record was Max's denomination and give him a service timetable for every Sunday. In the afternoon, Max had been taken on a boundary walk, with WPO Redman. The site was fascinating, all the different buildings housing a variety of work alongside education blocks, sports facilities and medical and administration buildings.

Max had quickly realised that this new establishment was going to be a lot easier to get along with. The regime and the petty rules were a nuisance but he could live with that. The important thing was that he would now have Catherine bring the girls with her to visit. He hadn't seen the girls for a month and he missed them enormously. That morning he had managed to fast track an application for a visit on the following Saturday and he couldn't wait to see them all.

There is a huge hole in the system when someone is sentenced for the first time. In most instances, if the prisoner is not expecting it, as was Max, the inmate has absolutely no idea what is going to happen to them and effectively they are completely cut off from the outside world the minute the judge casts his spell. It works both ways too. Those on the outside find it impossible to find out what's happening to their loved one. The frustration is unbelievable. On the outside, Catherine had tried everything she possibly could to find out where Max was going. Having been sentenced in Plymouth Crown Court, he was then taken to Exeter Prison but no one could tell her that and furthermore Max's legal team either didn't care or didn't know, either of which was wholly unacceptable. Those early days at Exeter Prison without any communication were the most harrowing soul destroying days Max had ever experienced. And it shouldn't have happened.

Even when Max arrived at Leyhill where everything was so much more relaxed, the anger in him was still there.

That night he was able to speak to Catherine and the girls in a civilised cubicle without the cacophony of sound from the window warriors behind him. He could have a normal conversation with his family and feel a little closer to them than he had a week earlier. He would go on to ring them every night. Catherine was coping very well, her friends had rallied around and she being a strong girl would get through it. They say it's worse for the people on the outside and in most respects they are right. Catherine had to put up with all the crap, run the house, look after the children and try to remain calm. Max on the other hand just had to do as he was told!

He settled himself into the routine whilst at the same time adding as much to his working day as possible. Breakfast was at 8:00 am, work started at 8:15 am, lunch at 12:00 pm, return to work at 1:00 pm, work through to 4:30 pm, tea was at 5:00 and after that was free time. He could do sport, watch television, play snooker, go to the library, do as much as he wanted. If he filled his day it would pass quickly and that had to be the key to getting out. Once the two-week induction period was over, he could start work within the site and the days, weeks and months would soon pass.

APRIL 1981

It was April 1981. Max had just come home to Newton Abbot for the Easter holiday and his first phone call was to Rob to find out what he was up to. He told Max about his new job at a printing company in Exeter. He was earning money, which was something Max was extremely envious at the time. The guy who he was working for was an architect, but he had the printing firm running alongside as a secondary business. Rob had gone along on a work experience placement at first, then realised there was an opportunity for him and they struck a deal. Max met Rob for a drink at the Jolly Abbot in Newton Abbot and they talked about this and that. Rob had a new girlfriend, which Max wasn't sure about at the time, but from what he could understand, she was stringing him along, but he couldn't see it. He was besotted with her, just like Max had been with Jenny, but Max could see it was going to end in tears. It always does when you're on the wrong end of a relationship.

Max had been out with a few girls since Jenny, but none of them had been serious. Some had lasted a few months, but none had really sparked the flame. Yes, he had some great fun with them but that was all. Nothing lasting and that's the way he liked it.

Rob had been through a few girls too, one of which had been wired up to a machine of some sort. Max never met her, but nonetheless Rob had seen it out for several gruelling months. Neither of them really knew where they were going. Rob probably had a better idea because he'd got himself a job with a very real opportunity of taking it further. Max was in limbo, not knowing what to do, which way to turn and he felt like he was wasting his time.

They'd had a good time catching up, eyeing up all the women in the pub and having a laugh, it was like old times. They talked about school and Max asked Rob if he'd seen anyone from those days. Rob hadn't seen anyone really, although he had seen Vicky from a distance once. He still had a thing for her, Max could see that.

'Have you seen anything of Milly?' asked Rob.

Max sighed, 'Yes, I have.'

'So why the long face?' asked Rob.

'He's asked me to take a friend of his girlfriend out tomorrow to make up the numbers.'

'Oh, where are you going?'

'I don't know.'

'Who is she?'

'What, the friend?' asked Max.

'Yes.'

'I don't know,' said Max, adding, 'All I know is that she's very attractive, slim, nineteen and she's a friend of Milly's girlfriend. He's coming up to my place at two and I'm going to follow him over to Jackie's house.'

'Who's Jackie?' asked Rob.

'Milly's girlfriend, he's been going out with her for about three months.'

'Oh right, well hopefully she'll be all right,' said Rob.

'Hopefully. Only problem is that the description has come from Jackie and girls can't describe girls properly. It's usually exaggerated. She tried to fix me up once before, and that was a complete disaster, so I'm hoping this is not the same,' said Max.

Rob laughed, 'Rather you than me bud.'

Max was having second thoughts too. They finished their drinks and Rob gave Max a lift home. Max's mother was still up when he got back, she was entertaining a new man in her life, Harold. He was a nice guy, a bit older than Celia, but nonetheless a genuinely nice chap. He was a panel beater and repaired cars from a small workshop at the top of Milber. They all sat up and talked for a while and Max thought Harold hadn't a clue what he was letting himself in for. Mrs. Reed had become an absolute nightmare to live with. One day she'd be great and the next day Max would be her worst enemy. When he was younger, he didn't really notice it so much, but as he got older, he was finding it more difficult not to bite back, and really he didn't want to do that. Her Miss Malaprop ways had got worse too.

She was telling Harold about a friend she had in Dawlish called Frank. He was a very good customer of hers when she worked at the shop. Frank was a very big guy, massively overweight and Max's mother said,

'You know Harold, it is very sad when a man is so overweight like that, it's been years since he's seen his gentiles.' She meant genitals, Max and Harold couldn't stop laughing. Max's mother was laughing too, but she had no idea at all.

The following day Max got up early and went into the garage to try to start his faithful motorbike. It hadn't been used for twelve months and he was dreading the thought of trying to start it. Yamaha XT500s are notoriously difficult to start and though he'd got the knack, he'd been in the garage for over half an hour kicking it over without so much as a cough of life. He was thinking of selling it, but it would be no good unless it was running properly. Beads of sweat were running from his forehead, so he said to himself that he'd leave it for another day. The fact was that although he was up against it, he didn't really want to sell his favourite bike. He'd been everywhere on it, competed on it and there are some things that he would have liked to have kept forever and this was one of them.

Milly rang up at midday and told Max that he'd be over just after two o'clock and Max had cross-questioned him about the 'blind date'.

'Have you met her?' asked Max.

'Yes, I have, she's all right.'

'Oh, so she's not slim attractive and nineteen then?' asked Max.

'Well, she's nineteen and she's slim, and yes, she is, sort of, well yes, she is attractive,' said Milly.

This isn't sounding too good, thought Max.

'Look Milly, I'll go along with it. I won't back out, but don't go putting me in an awkward position about another date or anything like that unless I say it's okay first. You all right with that?'

'Yeah, sure, she's okay, though.'

'Not a moose then?' asked Max.

'No, she's not,' said Milly.

'Would you go out with her?' asked Max.

'Well, I can't, I'm with Jackie.'

That answers the question, Max thought. He was going to have a great afternoon. A drive in the countryside to a quiet country pub on Dartmoor with the roof down and a moose in the passenger seat. Great. Ah, but, if he could get his bike running, he could take her on that, he wouldn't be able to speak to her and he wouldn't be able to see her either. Excellent idea. Only problem was that he couldn't get the bloody thing started.

Milly arrived bang on time, ran up to the back door of the house, and tapped on the window.

'Hello Mrs. Reed, how are you?'

'Fine thank you Christopher. Going somewhere nice?'

'Yes, I think we're going to Lustleigh,' said Milly.

Mrs. Reed always called Milly by his proper name as parents invariably do and told him to go carefully. Milly had exactly the same car as Max, only differing in colour and they looked a right pair of cads as they drove over to Jackie's house. Max was only a little apprehensive as he parked his car behind Milly and waited. He fiddled with the cassette player whilst he laughed to himself about whether she would have antlers or not.

His fears were somewhat allayed when he actually saw her though.

'Hi, Max,' said Jackie. Milly had already got into his car.

Jackie continued, 'This is Sonya.'

'Hi Sonya.' She said hello. She didn't look nineteen. Fifteen maybe, he couldn't believe that she was nineteen, but what a body. She had mousey brown straight shoulder length hair, good tits, nice arse and great legs all wrapped up in a close fitting top and spray on jeans with huge high heels and a black leather jacket. She looked a bit tarty. *But hey, what's wrong with a nice tart now and then*, thought Max. She was actually quite pretty, but the make up seemed a little bit overdone. If he'd seen her across the road he'd have thought she would have looked good, but she was a little bit like a piece of modern art. From a distance, she looked pretty good, but up close, she was all over the place.

Anyway, that didn't matter. He kept thinking about that fantastic body. *I can't wait to get my hands on all that lot,* he thought. He drove off following Milly out of Newton Abbot on the Bovey Tracey road and tried several times to get a conversation going with her but she didn't seem to have a lot to say. It was as if the landing light was on but nobody was at home.

Eventually she did warm up and started to string a few sentences together.

'Do you mind if I smoke?' Sonya asked.

Now that's a turn off, thought Max.

'Yeah, that's fine,' said Max, although he thought differently.

'Is there anything in that box down there that you'd like to listen to?' asked Max pointing at the cassettes. She looked through the box and pulled out a tape. Dire Straits. That was okay, Max thought and slotted it into the player.

'I love this song,' she said.

Romeo and Juliet. It was a good song.

She started singing along to it and when it finished she asked Max to wind it back and play it again. That went on more or less all the way to Lustleigh. Her singing got louder, but it was quite funny.

Max pulled into a parking space just up from the Primrose tearooms and switched off the engine. Milly was parked alongside. They'd only been there a couple of minutes when Martin turned up with his girlfriend Hannah and Paul was in his car with Ed. So what was four was now eight.

Now ordinarily Max wouldn't have gone out with a girl like Sonya so now he felt just a little bit uneasy. Max thought that she was definitely the kind of girl that you'd get off with at a party, but you probably wouldn't see her again.

They all said their hellos and made their way towards the tearooms when a beige Toyota 1000 pulled up behind Max's car. Two girls jumped out and said hello. Max looked at the driver. He didn't know who she was, but he wanted to know. It was one of those occasions when he was with a girl but he'd have preferred not to have been.

The other girl sat at a different table to Max and Milly so he didn't get to talk to her and at that time, he didn't know her name either. He looked across at her a few times but never caught her eye so the opportunity, if there was one, passed.

What he did know though, was that she was very beautiful, classically so. She was blonde, blue eyes, five feet six inches, slim, and dressed casually in jeans, cowboy boots and a pale blue Lyle and Scott jumper. She had a lovely smile and she looked easy going and fun. Max needed to find out who she was.

'Hey Martin, what are you up to?' asked Max.

'We're going back to Paul's, you coming?'

'Can't really, I'm with Sonya. She's a friend of Jackie's and I said I'd take her out.'

'Well you could come back afterwards if you like,' said Martin.

'Maybe, where does Paul live?' Max asked having not been there before.

Martin described how to get to Paul's house and Max believed he knew where it was.

'I don't know what we're doing next, so I may see you, I may not. If I don't I'll catch up with you later in the week.'

'Well, just give me a call, I'm not going anywhere,' said Martin.

They turned to go back to their cars and Max caught Martin's sleeve and asked him, 'Who's the girl driving the Toyota?'

'Oh, that's Catherine, Paul's sister.'

'Oh, right,' said Max.

'See you.'

'Yep, bye.'

Max watched the Toyota reverse up from behind him and then drive off up the hill. She was gone.

'Where are we going Milly?' asked Max.

'We'll just go for a drive over the moors and then back to Jackie's.'

'Okay,' said Max, 'I'll follow you.'

SEPTEMBER 2000

Karina tore off the fax sheet that had just come through

226

and walked into her father's office. Josef was sitting at his desk. He read the fax. It was the confirmation of availability of the new Ferrari 360 F1 with all the options listed as per the original conversation that he had with the owner a couple of months previously.

He had several different customers he could sell the car to, but he'd done a lot of business with Max and he was quite happy to offer him this car as well.

He picked up the phone and dialled Max's mobile number. It was nearly ten o'clock Josef's time.

'Hi, Max are you okay?'

'Yes thanks Josef.'

'Good, I have the silver car for you. Do you want it?'

'Yes, of course. Send the paperwork in tomorrow and I'll get the money transferred. I won't be collecting the car, because it's going straight to Japan. The buyer will pick it up direct from the seller. Okay?' asked Max.

'Yes, that's good. You will have the papers by the time you get in tomorrow morning.'

'Thanks, Josef, speak to you tomorrow.'

Sure enough, all the paperwork and payment details were on the fax when Max got into work the following day. After his early morning meeting with Pete, the first job would be to contact Graham Lord.

Most of the competition bike stock had now been sold and the result was a drop in bike stock to a little over £70,000, so Max had told Peter to buy some road bike stock and convert the showroom over to sports bikes, commuters and scooters. It hadn't been easy swallowing the bitter pill, but Velodrome had all their eggs in one basket with the competition off road bikes and they'd suffered because of the foot and mouth disease. Now, they stood the chance of rebuilding the sales and getting moving again. The stock value of £70,000 was not enough to generate massive sales and certainly not enough to gain the profit needed to cover the overheads, but it meant that the bottom of the trough had been met and hopefully Velodrome could start recovering.

Max rang Graham Lord. 'Hi, Graham, I've got a silver 360 for you, new unregistered.'

'Great,' said Graham. 'I'll call my client and let him know and come back to you. Give me ten minutes.'

'Okay,' said Max and put the phone down.

Graham rang his client. 'Don, it's Graham, I've got a

227

silver 360 for you, correct spec, new unregistered, tax free in Germany. Do you want it?'

'Yes, we do. I need that car as soon as possible,' said Don.

'Okay, you'll be buying the car from Velodrome here in the UK and you can collect the car from Stuttgart as soon as the bank transfer is confirmed. If you pay Velodrome for the car, you can pay my commission directly separately. I'll invoice you in the usual way.'

'Have you dealt with these guys before?' asked Don.

'Yeah, I've got a lot on the go with them. If you need to speak to them, that won't be a problem.'

'No, Graham, that shouldn't be necessary. Ask them to fax up a contract with the payment details and we'll get it done,' said Don.

'Okay, I'll take care of that and call you back later.'

Graham put down the phone and immediately called Max to confirm the sale and asked him to fax up the contract, with all Donald Keys company info and car specification and chassis number all written up on it.

On this occasion, Max didn't need Dimo's money to bank the sale as Donald Key was paying up front, so Max would simply take his cut from the sale and then forward the balance on to Josef. Nice easy deal.

Three days later, Donald Key's son, Julian collected the car from Stuttgart and oversaw the delivery to the airport freight forwarding collection so that within a week, the Asian client had his car.

Max was surprised that Donald Key had come to him for a car. It seemed ludicrous, that a company known throughout the world didn't have the contacts to find a new 360. Max wasn't complaining, he'd just made £5000 out of it, but it did seem strange.

Graham Lord rang. 'Max, I now have all the info on the California Spider. Majendie wants one point three million dollars for the car, which includes his commission.'

'Okay, so what are you thinking. One point four, one point four five?' asked Max.

'You know the customer. What do you think you can get?' asked Graham.

'It's the first time I've dealt with him so I'll try it at $1.45M and see how he reacts. We can always come down.'

'Okay, I'll leave it with you.'

'Any news on the Jaguar?' asked Max.

'No, nothing as yet, I'm still working on it.'

'Okay, I'll come back to you later.'

Max picked up the phone and rang Sirol. 'Hi, Sirol, the price on the California Spider is $1.45M. Do you want me to speak to Nino direct or do you want to call him.'

'Max, I'm busy today, I'm testing with the 360 Challenge guys down at Fiorano. Can you call Nino. I'll give you the number.'

Max rang Nino and spent half an hour on the phone with him going through all the details. He would definitely buy the car provided they could agree a price and the car was bonafide. He insisted that the car would need to be inspected and asked Max to see what would be involved. Nino didn't baulk on the price, which was a good sign.

Max waited until the afternoon and rang the dealer at Long Island Ferrari. He needed to find out what sort of cost would be involved to inspect Sangster's California Spider, along with timescale etc. A representative from Ferrari North America would have to do the inspection, then liaise with Angelo at the factory archive department to check all was well. It was just sorting the logistics that would be tricky, especially getting Sangster to drop the car down to the dealership.

For the third time that day, Max dialled Graham Lord's number.

'Graham, it's Max, I've spoken to the Swiss customer about the California Spider and offered it to him for one point four five million dollars. He hasn't flinched at the price, but he wants the car inspected by Ferrari North America who in turn have to liaise with Angelo in the archive department at Ferrari, Italy. I think you need to speak to Steve to get it sorted.'

'Okay, hopefully that shouldn't be a problem with Sangster, but I'll call Steve now and get things moving. Who's paying for the inspection?' asked Graham.

'The Swiss,' replied Max.

'Okay, that sounds positive. I'll get on with it and call you back.'

Max rang off. He needed to speak to Tom McKinney, there was a ticking sound on one of the 355 engines that Max had bought. He'd sold the other two cars so he needed some more stock.

'Tom, it's Max.'

'Hi, all Okay,' said Tom.

'Yes, fine thanks. A couple of things. We've sold two of the 355s and the other one has got a bottom end ticking noise. I need to know how you want to play it.'

'I didn't hear a noise on any of them. Which one is it?'

'It's the 98 355 Spider.'

'That car has only done 10,000 km,' said Tom.

'Yeah, I know. It's probably run out of oil or got low on oil at some stage.'

Max had hit the nail on the head. When Tom collected the car, he had thrashed it back from the German Swiss border and it had run low on oil and the oil pressure had dropped. Tom topped it up, but the damage had been done.

'Can you do it there?'

'We can take the engine out, but it would be better if we dropped the car into Isca Ferrari and got them to sort it out. They do all our work up there and they'll get on with it straightaway.'

'Okay, you do that. You pay for it and I'll credit you on something else,' said Tom.

'Good, that sorts that out. I need some more cars. Have you still got that blue car and the red GTS?'

'I've sold that blue one, but I've got another one here just as good.'

Max agreed a deal on two more 355s and told Tom he'd be up for them.

Max had been on the phone most of the day. Harry Thompson had been chasing him about the Jaguar XJR15. Muzi had called. Steve Majendie had called. Nino had called and he'd missed them all.

He couldn't do much about any of them really, because he was waiting on Graham Lord for a lot of the information especially as Graham was dealing with Steve in Florida, five hours behind UK time.

Pete walked into Max's office. Max was sat leaning on his chair looking out of the window.

'You okay?' Pete asked.

'Yeah. Just thinking, we could do with some luck Pete.'

'I know. Is there anything I can do to help?' he asked .

'Not really Pete, I'm just trying to juggle everything. As long as you can get some sales and revenue on the bikes, hopefully I can pull off a few of the bigger Ferrari deals.'

'How are they looking?' asked Pete.

'I have to say they're looking good, but I need to get them banked. It would be so much easier if one of them came through,' said Max.

'Okay, well I'll see you in the morning.'

'Okay, Pete. Thanks.'

Pete walked out of the office and switched off all the showroom lights as he made his way out. Max got on the phone and started ringing back all his missed calls.

The first call was to Muzi.

'Any news on the 330 GTO?' asked Muzi.

'I'm hoping I could have some info later on this evening,' said Max adding, 'I'm dealing with an American agent so there's a little bit of a time delay so that doesn't help.'

'That's okay. I just wanted to know how you were getting along. And, and, and one more thing. If we managed to acquire the GTO, I will want to run it in the Ferrari Shell Historic Challenge so we will need to make sure it's eligible,' said Muzi.

The Shell Historic was a hugely popular international racing series for classic Ferrari and Muzi wanted the GTO raced in that series. It didn't present a problem to Max. He would simply call Angelo at the factory and get the car ratified.

Max was getting a lot of enquiries for Ferrari 360 Spiders, so he asked Muzi.

'Do you have access to any 360 Spiders?'

'What do you mean? Can I get you some?'

'Yes.'

'How many do you need?' asked Muzi.

'As many as possible, but in an ideal world, I could do with another four right hand drive cars and if possible four left hand drive cars,' said Max.

'Yes, I could probably help you on those, but I will need to come back to you in a couple of days. I have a few friends here and abroad that have them on order. They will only run them around for a few hundred kilometres and then get bored with them. I will see what I can do,' said Muzi.

Max finished the call and thanked him in advance for trying. Sirol rang back on Max's mobile and asked if he'd spoken to Nino. Max had told him that he had and that he was waiting for a response from the California Spider owner regarding his consent to having the car inspected. All is under control Max assured Sirol.

'Okay, I'm happy with that,' said Sirol.

'As soon as I know anything more, I will let you know,' said Max.

'I've passed your details onto Silvio Mazzali, he's a good customer of mine, he wants a 250 short wheel base, but it must be yellow. Everything he has is yellow. Have you got anything?' asked Sirol.

'I saw one a month ago, but I don't know if it's available, I would need to check,' said Max.

'Okay, well if Silvio calls, you will know what it's all about. He's a really nice guy, you'll like him.'

The Ferrari 250 Short Wheel Base was effectively the forerunner to the all-conquering Ferrari 250GTO and as such a highly prized Ferrari to own. Max knew a customer that had a yellow car so he needed to speak to him.

Sirol continued, 'Give me a call tomorrow, I'll be on my mobile.' Sirol rang off.

Max dialled Harry's number and his answer phone cut in. 'Hi Harry, it's Max. Sorry I missed your call earlier today. I'm still waiting for news from my customer on the Jaguar. I'm hoping to hear something tonight. I'll call you again tomorrow. Thanks. Bye.'

Nino dialled Max, surprised that he hadn't called him back.

'Hey Max, it's Nino. Any news for me?'

'Not as yet Nino. I've got the ball rolling and I'm waiting for three different people to come back to me. As soon as I hear, I will call you,' said Max.

'You know Max, this is my all time favourite car, I've loved this car since I was a little boy. If you get me this car, it will be like a childhood dream come true,' said Nino.

It was a story Max had heard many times before, not about a California Spider but Ferraris in general.

'Nino, I will do the best that I can. If we can get the owner to agree, I'm hoping we can have the car inspected next week. I've spoken to Long Island Ferrari so they know what's going on and I've spoken to Angelo at Ferrari and he's faxed the paperwork through to them, so it is happening, but I can't confirm anything definite at the moment.'

'Okay, Max, that sounds good. Let me know.'

Nino rang off. Max rubbed his eyes. The whole business

was so stressful. It was fast moving and then frustratingly slow. Hopefully, it wouldn't be too long and everything would get easier once a few deals were banked.

Graham didn't ring back that night, but did call Max first thing in the morning.

'Hi Max, sorry about yesterday, I was up at Duxford sorting out a few things.'

'That's okay; I was being chased by everyone and you had all the information, so where are we now?' asked Max.

'Majendie has spoken to Sangster who wasn't too happy that we wouldn't take his word for it that the California is original and proper. Steve convinced him that anybody spending that kind of money would want the car checked, so reluctantly Sangster has agreed to drop the car into Long Island Ferrari on Monday. You will need to liaise with the factory and Ferrari North America for the inspection date but it must be done next week because Sangster doesn't want it hanging around in the dealership whilst waiting for Ferrari to get their act together.'

'Yes, that's fair enough,' said Max, 'I'll get that sorted.'

'So the California is in your hands now. The GTO owner has spoken to John Gill and they're due to speak again today, so this afternoon, I'll have a buying price on that car. Have you spoken to your customer?'

'Yeah, he's ready to go. Just one thing. He wants to race the car in the Shell Historic, so we need to make sure it's eligible,' said Max.

'It should be. They won't like it though, because it is a very capable winning car. Those four litre cars were a lot quicker than the three litre cars.'

'What about the Jaguar?' asked Max.

'Can you tell me who you are getting it from?' asked Graham.

Max saw no reason not to tell him. They'd done a bit of business together, and there was a trust between them.

'You know him actually. It's Harry Thompson,' said Max.

'Really, I would never have guessed that. He's normally just Ferraris,' said Graham.

'Yes, I know, but the owner of the car has bought a lot of Ferraris off Harry, but he just happens to have the Jaguar as well,' said Max.

'Okay, well I need to chase that up today, so I'll be back

to you later.'

'Thanks Graham.' Max cut the connection and slowly placed the handset back on the cradle. Unbeknown to him, that was a big mistake.

AUGUST 2008

Day three at Leyhill and there was employment induction. The instructions noted inmates should report to Employment in the Enterprise Unit at 9.00. It would be a short talk for maybe an hour outlining the work available varying from the print shop, recycling, laundry, gardening, painting, stores and kitchen work followed by the optional many courses available within the education centre. Whatever was chosen by a prisoner, they had a choice of two work places or full time education.

Within the working week, an offender could choose up to five half-day sessions of courses, which he could take out of work time subject to the consent of the workplace manager.

The second appointment on that day was at 10.00 and meant reporting for Learning & Skills that was basically an assessment opportunity for the department to find out who was or was not educated and at what level. Max had already been through some assessments at Exeter Prison and had brought all the results with him, so he was excused for the rest of the day.

Max thought that Catherine would be pleased to hear that he had enrolled on the cookery course, something that she had always said he was incapable of doing. He also took up the music option and signed up to work in the print shop.

He'd been to the stores and collected all his prison clothing and footwear, which meant that he could if he wanted do some exercise, rather than just vegetate. After his experience at Exeter Prison, he was still pinching himself about his transfer. It was such relief.

APRIL 1981

It doesn't matter how many times you drive over Dartmoor, it never ceases to amaze you how beautiful and

234

romantic the countryside is. You could drive the same journey twice a day for a year and always see something different, however Sonya was completely indifferent to it.

'It's all right,' she said to Max who in turn thought she still had the landing light switched off.

'What do you like then Sonya?' asked Max.

'I like going to clubs and the pub. I'd like to live in Torquay,' she said. 'I will one day.'

Max was just trying to make conversation with her but it was still very hard work. He smiled to himself as he thought about asking her if she fancied a shag. She'd probably say, yeah all right, so he did and guess what she said.

'Yeah, all right,' so he did. Max found a suitably remote spot out in the middle of the moors somewhere and stopped the car. If she was backward in coming forward with general conversation, she was a Jekyll & Hyde character when it came to sex. One minute she was quiet and dozy and the next minute, she was a sex maniac.

Max was trying to put the roof up on the MG and she was like an octopus. She seemed to have about eight hands and they were everywhere. Max couldn't believe it. Within a few seconds, she was almost completely naked. Max was bug eyed with surprise and she really did have the most fantastic body. At one point, a car pulled up behind Max as if to park, but looking ahead at the sight in front of them, they promptly reversed back out again. Sonya was completely oblivious, Max was lying down in the passenger seat and she was bouncing up and down like she was going off down the garden on a space hopper. Even when the roof blew back down, she was still going unabated. Nothing seemed to stop her. She had an amazing appetite for sex and she was well equipped to deal with it. This must have been one of those illusive nymphos that Max had heard about. It was getting dark by the time the action started to slow down but by any standards, it had been one hell of an afternoon.

Max dropped Sonya back to Jackie's and typically, she didn't say much on the drive back, there again, she didn't need to really with those hidden qualities.

Max had the whole week off as did most of his friends in education, so most days he was out and about visiting different people. It was only Rob that was working at that time, and he was the only one with any money of his own. Mrs. Reed was still seeing Harold so Max got a job in the holiday period working for him. It paid for Max's petrol and gave him a little spending money, not enough but it was something.

He'd been thinking a lot about the girl he'd seen at Lustleigh, Catherine, and was trying to figure out a way of meeting her properly. He'd been up to her house officially to see Paul and saw her there and said hello, but no more than that. He couldn't really go up to Paul's again for another official visit, so he was at a bit of a loss as what to do.

When he'd asked Jenny out three years before, he just went straight up to the front door and asked her. With Catherine, he'd had little or no conversation with her, so it would have been difficult to do that and the fact Max knew her brother could have been very embarrassing if she declined. No, there had to be a better way.

An opportunity arose a few days later. Catherine and her sisters rode horses and they'd been riding with some friends on the moors near Moretonhampstead and would need a lift home. Max went along in his car and met all of the sisters as well. There was no given seat for any of the girls but Catherine had said she would like to go in the burgundy car. Apparently, she liked the colour! Well, that was Max's car.

The drive from Moretonhampstead back to Newton Abbot is a very twisty, mostly single-track road with passing places and would normally take about half an hour, so Max would have Catherine to himself for a while. It was a beautifully sunny day with a sharp chilly wind, but with the heater on full blast, he could still drive comfortably with the roof down. They chatted about horses and music and all sorts of other different things along the route and Max found her really easy going. She wasn't at all stuck up like some classy girls can be. He looked at her in her jodhpurs and riding boots and jacket and thought how lovely she really was, and by the time he'd driven her home he'd offered to take her out that evening for a drink with some of their friends at the Waterman's Arms in Tuckenhay.

Max couldn't take his eyes off Catherine all that evening. She was so engaging. He was completely taken in by her spell, her smile, everything about her and for her part, she probably had no idea at all. One of Catherine's friends, Judy was the daughter of the owner of the pub, so they stayed out a little later than closing time before heading off home just before midnight.

Max changed the tape in the cassette player and put in

Supertramp's 'Crisis What Crisis' album. It was an apt title for Max's life, but he loved the album and one track in particular. As he rounded the bend at the bottom of Catherine's road, he turned to her and asked her out. *A Soapbox Opera* was playing through the speakers. She accepted with a smile. If there was only one thing in his life that he'd got right then that was definitely it. He'd just made the best decision of his life. Whatever happened next was immaterial, nothing could compare with Catherine saying yes. She was everything and at that moment, he knew he wanted to spend the rest of his life with her. He didn't know her, but he just knew, sometimes you do, and he did then.

Max parked the car in her drive and got out to see her in. She stopped at the bottom of the steps and Max kissed her for the first time.

AUGUST 2008

The prison officer came around the corner and onto the 'A' south corridor with his clipboard in his hand. It was 7:00 am, his job was to do a manual roll call check. Some inmates would be up, washing, getting ready for breakfast and that days work, others would still be getting their last minutes of warm sleep.

Being an open prison, Leyhill was used to prisoners absconding so the purpose of the morning tally check confirmed the numbers and identified those that were no longer resident. It all served as a wake up call for those that were struggling to get up.

Max walked up to breakfast on his own and stood in the canteen queue. Everybody seemed very well behaved, there were no raised voices or bravado, all very safe, Max thought. He could have had a hot cooked breakfast but chose to have cereal and toast. It would be easy to get fat and lazy in this prison with three good meals a day and not doing any exercise. The last thing Max wanted to do was return home looking like the Michelin man.

He sat down at a table by the window and looked out across the gardens. It looked like it was going to be a nice day. A guy sat down opposite Max.

'Hi,' he said, 'I'm Raf.' He was a skinny fellow with a few days of stubble probably in his early thirties. He seemed pleasant enough.

'Yeah, hi,' said Max.

Raf looked a bit agitated.

'You okay?' asked Max.

'Yeah, I've just had a call up to do an MDT,' he said.

'They haven't found me yet, but they will.'

Max knew it was a mandatory drugs test. It was usually required by a prison officer if there was a suspicion that the prisoner had been taking drugs of some kind. There were drugs available readily in the prison if anyone wanted them. You just had to know the right people, that's all.

The inmate would need to pee in a bottle and then wait for the results after it had been handed in. If the results were positive, then the prisoner would be shipped out to a category 'B' prison, a bang up prison. There would be no argument, their belongings would be packed up and they'd be off forthwith, and most people wouldn't want that.

'Are you worried about it?' asked Max.

'Wouldn't you be?'

'Yeah, I would.'

'Well, there you go. They're bastards, these screws, they want me out.'

Max didn't have a lot to say about that. It was strange but in prison, men would have the most bizarre conversations. The subject, the details, all of it was based on their experience and their talents. It was as if everything and anything could be said, without fear of retribution. It didn't have to be said in any context. It couldn't possibly be realistic on the outside, but inside it was real and these were the people that thankfully, most never even get close to. These were real life criminals telling real life stories, exactly as it was. No drama, just the cold light of day. They were already serving their time and they wanted get it all off their chest. Some offenders liked telling their story, what they did, how they did it and they liked handing out advice. It was shocking, fascinating and often quite funny. It was very matter of fact, it was everyday conversation, just like any normal person on the outside could have about some menial subject, like going shopping.

'Let me give you a word of advice mate,' said Raf.

'Oh right.'

'If you need to kill someone, don't use a nine millimetre. Make sure it's a two-two. If you use a nine millimetre at close range, it will blow the side of their head off on the exit. If you

238

use a two two the bullet will go into their head, rattle around in there, mush everything up and they'll just keel over. Much better.'

'Right,' said Max.

'I made that mistake. I needed to teach someone a lesson and pulled up next to him at the traffic lights. I got out of the car with a Glock 25, great weapon that, went across to his driver's side and shot him in the head. My mate was sat in the passenger seat and the bullet passed through the wanker and dropped my mate as well. So, I'm in for a double murder. Are you going to eat that toast?'

'No, it's all right, you can have it,' said Max, sitting there in complete astonishment.

'I've got to go, good luck,' said Max.

Raf nodded, stuffing the toast into his mouth, and Max left him to it; he had to be at the Carats drug information advice centre at 8:45 am for another induction talk, this time about drugs, followed by an energy efficiency talk at 10:00 am. He let out a long sigh; he didn't think that anybody had mentioned to him anything like that at breakfast before. It would be one of the many interesting conversations that Max would have with his fellow residents.

The drugs talk was similar to the earlier lecture that Max had received at Exeter. It was designed to highlight those that do and those that don't. Max had never taken drugs so for him he just sat and listened. Those that hadn't, could go, so Max returned to his apartment for half an hour and added a little work to his daily scribe.

SEPTEMBER 2000

Graham Lord picked up the phone and dialled John Gill's number. He needed to know how much the Ferrari 330 GTO was going to cost so that Max could get the deal going. Max had been chasing him and the customer had been calling Max several times too.

'Hi, John, it's Graham, how are you getting on with the GTO.'

'I spoke to the owner yesterday as planned. It's a bit tricky, because there's a finance company and bank included in

239

the sale but I am at liberty to sell the car. We need three point seven five million US dollars for it. The car is in Japan and readily available for inspection.' He said in his Southern drawl.

'What about a contract?' asked Graham.

'Yep, I can issue a contract of sale, that's not a problem. Who will it need to be made out to?' asked John.

'I'll confirm that one and come back to you on it, but in the meantime, could you send me a confirmation email on the description and the price?'

'Yeah, I'll do that for you now. Your guy is obviously serious then?'

'Yes, we think so, but it's not over until the fat lady sings, as well you know,' said Graham.

'Oh, yes, I know that.'

'Get that off to me and I'll speak to the customer and come back to you later this afternoon, okay?'

'Yes, that will be good Graham,' replied John.

So far the description of the car had been fairly light. It was a four litre 330 Ferrari GTO, one of three cars. The car had been comprehensively restored in the late 1980s early 1990s before being sold by a Baron to a Middle Eastern collector. Graham knew the chassis number and had looked through his Ferrari books to determine exactly what the car was, what history it had and importantly if there were any gaps in its history.

The kind of people that buy these expensive cars are usually highly successful businessmen in their own right and they could have inherited wealth or maybe new wealth. Whatever, the underlying trend has to have 'wealth' and wealth means money and 'money' means that they have the capability of instructing legal actions. The last thing Graham wanted was a misquoted description giving rise to a potential claim. The reality though was interesting because Graham was already distancing himself just slightly by considering having Max sign the contract with John Gill rather than Graham sign it himself. The dilemma for Graham was that Max would then know where the car was coming from and give away a contact. Max could also then, effectively cut Graham out of the deal. The upside was that Graham would not be in the loop if things went wrong and the downside would be that he could hand over a contact and potentially lose a significant sum of money.

From what Graham could ascertain, the information

relating to the crash damage on the car in 1963 was fairly well documented. Some chassis parts had been changed and the car had been fitted with a 250 short wheel base style body all at the factory in period. The car had passed quietly between known enthusiasts through the 60s 70s and 80s until it was bought by the Baron and he was well known in the Ferrari world and historic motor racing circles. And then it ended up at Donald Key Restorations. Initially the car was not going to be fully restored, it was going to have a light makeover, but when Donald Key started digging deeper into the project, it was obvious there was a significant amount of rust and previous damage that needed sorting out. The question was whether to continue to do a light makeover or go the whole hog and completely restore the car. Now, bearing in mind its potential value in the early 1990s, Donald Key needed to get his customer in to view the car and make a few important decisions.

Graham knew Don well, he'd been down to Don's place many times, it was only a half hour drive from Graham's High Wycombe base, so it was no surprise he found himself sitting opposite Don that afternoon talking cars. The E-Type had been collected by Steve Majendie's client, the silver Ferrari 360 had gone to Japan and in Don's eyes, Graham was a good man, he had a lot of time for him, he came up with the result that Don needed.

'Tell me Don, what was the story on your man's 330 GTO that you restored?' asked Graham.

'Simple really Graham, I think he bought it in 1988, knowing that it was a GTO even though it was clothed in a 250 SWB body. It didn't look too good, so he bought it here for me to restore, which is what I did,' said Don.

'Okay, so how much did you do?' asked Graham.

'We did everything, the whole car was restored and we put an original style body on it so it now looks like a GTO as well. Engine, gearbox, axles, the lot,' Don said enthusiastically continuing, 'Why do you ask?'

'I have a customer interested in buying the car and I wanted to establish for myself what was exactly done to the car,' Graham replied.

'Well, as I said, we did everything and then the car was sold to Japan.'

'Do you know why the car was sold so quickly after it was bought for such a record price?'

'No, I don't. I didn't get involved with it after it left here,' Don replied.

Graham sensed that Don wasn't telling him the full story. It was just a hunch, but he felt that Don was holding something back. He was.

John Gill emailed Graham and confirmed all the details and specification of the 330 GTO. It would be exactly as Graham expected. John also faxed the details including a dummy copy of the contract for Graham to look over. It would all be ready in Graham's office for when he returned from Don's.

Before Graham left Don's office, Graham asked, 'Just one more question, Don, do you think I need to get the car inspected or is it in the same condition as it left you?'

'I don't think it's been used Graham. It went from here straight to Japan to the buyer, it then sat in his collection for a short while until he sold it to the current owner. The last time I heard about the car, it was owned by a Middle Eastern bank, but I may be wrong on that one.'

'Okay, Don, that's good of you. I'll be in touch.'

Graham got back into his Mitsubishi Evo and sped of towards High Wycombe and home. He was satisfied that Don had answered him truthfully and felt he could now talk to Max about the car with a little bit more certainty. It was a lot of money and Graham didn't want any problems with it. The questions that Graham had asked were all perfectly reasonable questions. It would be the same for almost anyone involved in this type of business to ask for the same type of information. It all builds up a picture of the car, it's history and most importantly, it's credibility. The last thing an owner of a car of such historic significance would want is other owners talking about the car behind his back, deriding it for this or that problem. Worst of all, he wouldn't want a horde of anoraks talking the car down.

What Graham had done, going down to Don's and asking him straight was absolutely right. He'd asked all the right questions, got all the answers but the one question he didn't ask Don was, how original it was. If Graham had asked that question, Don would have been put on the spot and he probably wouldn't have liked that.

Graham sat down at his desk with a coffee in hand looking out over the Buckinghamshire countryside as he waited for his computer to boot up. He read through the faxed copies that John had sent to him and noted that John was selling the car on behalf of the Middle Eastern collector and not the bank. He would need to clarify with John that there was no other secured interest in the car and what the payment instructions would be.

The phone rang at John's office, it was Graham.

'Hi, John, it's Graham. Thanks for the paperwork. That all looks okay. Can you just confirm for me that there is no other financial interest in the car. I'll need that in writing and then I think we can start moving forward.'

'Yeah, of course Graham, that won't be a problem, it's a bit late now, but I should have it tomorrow for you,' John answered.

'Okay, I'll leave it to you and speak to you tomorrow.'

Graham leant forward and pushed down the switch cutting the line and immediately called Max.

'Yeah, Max, it's Graham.'

'Hi, Graham.'

'I've got all the paperwork from the seller for the GTO and I've been down to Donald Key's to ask him about the car as well.'

'How did you get on?' asked Max.

'Fine, no problems, he told me what I already knew and confirmed what was done, so I don't see any problems there. I've asked the seller to confirm that there isn't any outstanding financial interest secured by or in the car and I'll have confirmation of that tomorrow in writing. I assume you're going to back to back the contract?' asked Graham.

'Yes. I will contract to sell the car to my customer on the basis of me being able to buy it and then selling it immediately to him. What's the price?'

'Three point seven five million dollars US.'

'What should we put on it?' asked Max.

'What do you think we can get? Would he take it at double that price?'

'He might, I'd have to ask. It could be a one hit wonder at that price. I don't want to put him off,' said Max.

'No, but it's worth a try,' Graham suggested.

'I'll try him at $7.75 million and see how I get on. I can always come down.'

'Okay, you do that. I'll get the contract made out to Velodrome and get it faxed through sometime tomorrow. You'll need to speak to your customer and let him know that we're getting close.'

'Okay, I'll sort him and let you know. Anything happening with the XJR15?'

'Yes, I spoke to the customer earlier. He's asking about some spares, so I'm trying to source an engine management system and some other bits and pieces for him,' Graham replied.

'How long will it take you to find the parts, I mean will it effect the purchase of the car?' asked Max.

'No, I think he's keen enough on the car and we should be able to sell it without the spares. They can come later if I can find them.'

'I could do with the sale Graham, so the sooner the better.'

'Yes, me too,' Graham answered.

Graham hadn't spoken to the customer that day although he had spoken to Harry. Graham had told him that he was working with Max on the deal so Harry was happy to let Graham have any info he may have needed. It was looking like the deal was coming to a head so Harry was hopeful all would be well. Crucially, Harry didn't check with Max first.

Max dialled Muzi's number and let him know that the 330 GTO deal was coming to fruition and that a copy of the sales contract would be with him the following day. Once he had that in his hands, then he would confirm the price and start drawing up a contract. Muzi was pleased.

The following day Max was on tenterhooks. It was raining. He had a lot to think about. The California Spider was being inspected, the 330 GTO contract would be coming through and he was waiting for his friend to confirm whether the yellow 250 SWB was available. On top of that, he could get some news on the XJR15. He had to be at Andover for 3:00 pm to collect a Ferrari 550 Maranello and the red 355 Spider had been repaired and was ready for collection from Isca Ferrari.

If the 330 came in then that was potentially life changing. If the others came in, it would make life a lot easier and help fill the void left by the blown stock from the foot and mouth disease. Down in the service department, the valet was cleaning another Ferrari 355 ready for its new eager customer's collection. Max was now selling at least one 355 every week plus another high value car as well, so all he needed to do was keep it all going, keep it shuffling along. The bikes were slowly picking up and Pete was working hard to get that show back on the road. A meeting with the bank was imminent and Max was not looking forward to that.

APRIL 1981

The needle dropped onto the vinyl, the hiss of the static and the deep rumble of the turntable drive gave way to the opening bars. The digital peak hold meters flicked yellow and red into the darkness. Genesis. Many Too Many drifted across the room as Catherine lay down on her bed and listened to the album And Then There Were Three. She thought about Max and their going out earlier that night.

It was the first time that someone had actually asked her out properly and it had taken her somewhat off guard. She wasn't expecting it and Max had to ask her again because she didn't hear him properly the first time. She'd been out with other guys before but with them, she'd had sort of fallen into it rather than receiving a bolt out of the blue. She liked it. It was nice being asked out and taken off somewhere. He said he'd call her tomorrow, she was looking forward to it.

She put her head on the pillow and thought of Max in his black jeans, and cowboy boots, red sweatshirt and sheepskin coat and smiled. The music played.

Many too many have stood where I stand
And many more will stand here too,
I think what I find strange is the way you built me up
Then knocked me down again

The part was fun but now it's over,
Why can't I just leave the stage ?
Maybe that's because you securely locked me up
And threw away the key.

Oh mama,
Please will you find the key.
Oh pretty mama,
Please won't you let me go free.
I thought I was lucky

I thought that I'd got it made.
How I could be so blind ?

Catherine drifted off to sleep and the timer switched off the system a few minutes later. It had been a nice evening and she'd gone to bed happy and content. On another day, those lyrics would have meant so much more.

MAY 2004

Jacques looked across the table at his father in law. His wizened features and eighty odd years of wear and tear likened him to something of a bygone age, the kind of image that anyone would suppose to be King Arthur. His almost white hair and long beard constantly distracting him from his thought process as he smoothed himself down.

'You know Jacques, I think we could do something with this guy Max. He knows what he has seen and now he'll be thinking who would buy such a car. I feel comfortable with him.'

'He's a good guy Olivier, he never let me down and he did exactly what he said he would do. Even when he said he was going to come here, he still maintained contact all along.'

'Okay, we're going to need to give him some help to fill in the history, but if he's any good, he will probably know quite a lot by now.'

'We will have to give him better access for when he comes down next.'

'Do you have someone we can trust to help. I'm not up to moving heavy equipment,' said Olivier.

'Yes, I think so. I'll call him and see what I can arrange. We'll have a little more notice than we had this time.'

'I wouldn't count on that Jacques. He's hungry, you can see it in his eyes. Believe me, he wants to do a deal with us and he will, mark my words. Jacques, I need to help the family out and hopefully Max will be the route to that. Make sure you stay in touch with him. Not too often, don't make it obvious, but just keep the dialogue going. If he needs anything or asks, speak to me so that I know what's going on. I don't think this will be a quick transaction. It's going to take some time to sort out the car, all the parts and the paperwork,' said Olivier.

'We should just take it one step at a time Olivier. Get Max down as soon as we can then start moving along. What do you think he'll do now?' asked Jacques.

'My guess is that he will probably speak to someone who knows a lot about the cars. He won't give away the identity or the whereabouts. There would be too much at stake for that. He's going to get some pointers and when he comes down next time, he'll be looking for identifying marks confirming that it is what it is. He needs to be satisfied by his own means that what he has seen and touched is the real thing. Once he's done that, we can move forward. Olivier replied adding, 'I saw him looking at the photograph above the fireplace, he knows he's got something. He's got the ball, let him run with it and we'll see if he's got what it takes. Do you know what I like about him Jacques?'

'No, what?'

'He's polite, he listens, but he doesn't give anything away. That's good for us because he won't be telling everybody about it. Thinking about it, I'm sure he'll come through.'

Olivier stood up, the wooden chair scraped across the random slate floor and he leant on the oak table.

'I have a good feeling about this Jacques, well done.'

Jacques got up from the table and moved towards the door. 'I'll give him a call as soon as I've got someone to come down and give me a hand to shift all that rubbish.'

'Okay, take care,' said Olivier.

Jacques closed the kitchen door behind him and he was gone.

OCTOBER 2000

Therese looked across at her husband, 'Hurry up darling, we're going to be late,' she said, her long brown hair flicked to one side as she looked in the mirror and put on her two carat diamond stud earrings.

'How did it go?' she asked looking this way and that finishing off her perfume spray.

'Yes, we've done it. It's a done deal,' Silvio replied.

Therese went over to him and gave him a light kiss on the cheek. 'Did you get what you wanted?' she asked in her beautiful Italian accent, walking into her dressing room.

'It's worth about seven hundred and fifty, plus various other packages. To be honest, I don't really know how much, because it all sounded so complicated. I think it's one for the accountants to sort out.'

'Sorry darling, what did you say?'

'It's one for the accountants to sort out,' Silvio replied.

'No, before that?' she asked.

'Oh, seven hundred and fifty million dollars.'

'That's fantastic darling, we'll have to celebrate later. She reached down and lifted up the hem of the black close fitting dress to reveal the tops of her stockings.

'No, not now, later,' she said quietly tapping him on the hand.

Silvio had good reason to be happy. He had just sold his company to Pixar for $750,000,000 and the reality was that he'd made so much money, he really didn't know exactly how much he'd made.

He reached into his jacket pocket for Sirol's card, turned it over and looked at the details on the back and picked up the phone.

'Who are you calling? We're going to be late. We're always late.' It would take at least ten minutes to drive to Enrico's restaurant on Lugano's waterfront, she thought.

Silvio walked over to the window and looked out over the beautiful sunny evening setting across the lake and waited for the phone to answer. He caught Therese's eye, 'I'll only be a couple of minutes.'

'Hello, Max Reed.'

'Hi, Max, it's Silvio, how are you?'

'Very well thank you, and yourself?' asked Max.

'Yes, very good. Anything happening with the 250SWB?'

'Yes, it is for sale, we can buy it. The car is completely authentic. I've spoken to Ferrari already and they've confirmed it's all okay.'

'How much do I need to pay?' asked Silvio.

'Eight hundred and fifty thousand euros.'

'Yeah, that's okay, I'll have it. When can I collect it and where?' asked Silvio.

'It's late now, but I'll try to get hold of the seller and call you back. The car is in Belgium, so that's easy enough.'

Silvio looked in the hallway. Therese was standing at the top of the stairs tapping her high gloss fingernails on the banister.

'Okay, don't worry about it now. Call me in the morning. I'll definitely have it.'

'Thanks, Silvio, speak to you tomorrow.'

'No, thank you Max. You've made me very happy.'

Max pressed the red button on his mobile. He thought about how easy Silvio had been to deal with and wondered whether he should have charged him a little more. It didn't matter, he'd made a sale with a decent profit and that would pay a whole months overheads at the garage.

Silvio opened the passenger door of his yellow 550 Marenello and his slinky wife settled in. It took seven minutes to Enrico's at that time of night and he wouldn't be late. He stopped the car by the roped, stainless steel, waterfront entrance and left the keys in the ignition. Two well-dressed Italian men opened the car doors in unison as the driver and his glamorous wife stepped out into a barrage of photographers flashing lights and fast wind shutters.

She was the darling of the Italian press and one of the world's top supermodels and he was a nobody of any consequence that just happened to create an extremely popular Plasticine character that didn't speak. More than that though was the fact that he was a really nice bloke. Max didn't know anything about Silvio at all, Sirol had only told him that he was interested in buying a car.

Two days later, the flight was delayed a quarter of an hour to Skipol and Max was worried that he would be keeping Silvio waiting. The owner of the Ferrari 250SWB was standing in the arrivals hall as Max walked through.

'Good flight Max?'

'Yes, thanks, Francois, a bit delayed, but no problems. Have you seen anyone with a light brown leather jacket and blue faded jeans on, because that will be Silvio?' asked Max.

'No, but that could be a lot of people around here,' Francois replied.

They talked idly whilst they waited for Silvio to arrive.

Max looked across the hall. A short distance away a tall elegant girl was standing near a Hertz rent-a-car sign. Somehow, she looked different. Even though she was in jeans, she just looked expensive. Her jacket, shoes, sunglasses all looked high maintenance. Strangely at odds with the rest of her garb was the headscarf.

Max carried on talking to Francois.

'If it's okay with you, Silvio will transfer the money direct to you if he's happy with the car. It's all been serviced?' asked Max.

'Don't worry, it's all been done,' Francois replied, 'he can drive it five thousand kilometres if he wants.'

'Good, because he probably will,' said Max.

A man walked up to the girl by the Hertz stand with two coffees in his hands. Max could make out a light brown jacket over his shoulder.

'Excuse me a minute Francois,' Max walked across the hallway and said 'Silvio?'

'Yes,' he replied.

'Max.'

Silvio introduced Therese. She lowered her sunglasses without taking them off and said 'hello'. Max beckoned Francois over and did the introductions. They walked and chatted over to Francois' Renault Espace and they all climbed aboard, Max in the front with Silvio and Therese behind.

She undid the headscarf, took off her sunglasses and shook out her hair.

'Sorry about that,' she said. Max recognised her immediately. He'd seen her on the front cover of one of Catherine's Vogue magazines.

Francois drove his passengers to his home, some twenty kilometres from the airport and pulled into his driveway parking halfway around the lily pond alongside the front door. A yellow Ferrari 250 SWB was sat opposite.

'Wow!' said Therese.

'That's it for me!' said Silvio.

They all looked around the car and Silvio just had to have a drive.

' By all means' said Francois adding, ' Max, if you take Silvio out along this road for about five or six km, you can take a big loop and come back. It's a good drive.'

Max hopped into the driver's seat with Silvio getting alongside, but Therese didn't want to be left out so she sat on Silvio's lap.

After an entertaining drive around the local sparsely populated countryside, the three of them cocooned in one of

Maranello's finest pulled into a sandy lay-by. Max jumped out of the driver's seat and Silvio had a go. Therese sat on Max's lap in the passenger seat as Silvio gassed the 1961 Ferrari along the open road. To be fair, Max didn't know what was better, driving the car or having Therese sat on his lap. *Memories are made of this*, he thought.

MAY 1981

He quickly surveyed the instruments laid out in front of him. There was nobody behind him. The rev counter needle had dropped to zero, oil pressure zero, fuel gauge quarter full. The tape player was still blasting away. He dipped the clutch. The car was still rolling fast enough to get to the bus stop a quarter of a mile ahead of him. Max turned down the music and held his breath as his MG crept into the lay-by.

His faithful servant, Hubert had run dry and could deliver no more. On most occasions, Max would hear Hubert clicking away in the boot, signalling the impending doom, but this time there was no warning. 'Hubert' was Max's name for his car's fuel pump. He often spoke to Max as he ran around on empty, frantically searching for the last drops. The fuel gauge had a mind of its own, some days working some days not and on this occasion it obviously wasn't.

He sat in the car looking out of the window, it was 6:45 pm and he was due to collect Catherine at seven. It was a Saturday night and they were going to stay at Judy's in Tuckenhay. He was about five miles from Catherine's house and didn't fancy the walk along the Totnes to Newton Abbot road, but he'd have to do it. He locked the car and started walking, collecting a spare gallon can from the boot as he did so.

Max had worked up quite a sweat speed walking towards the nearest garage when a car drew alongside, and the nearside window slowly unwound. The driver was leaning across the passenger seat.

'Need a lift?'

'Yes, please. I need to get to East Street garage,' Max replied. It was the only petrol station that would be open. Max opened the door, sat in and wound up the window, putting the can on the floor between his legs.

'Thanks, that's very kind of you,' Max said.

'No problem, I'm going that way anyway, and we MG drivers have got to stick together. I'm assuming that was your roadster in the bus stop.'

'Yes, the bloody fuel gauge works sometimes and then not.'

'Probably the sensor, I expect. It's not a difficult job to replace, a bit messy though. Takes about twenty minutes.'

'Okay, thanks. I'm supposed to be picking up my girlfriend at seven, so . . .'

Max was going to say that the driver had been a welcome sight but the man interrupted.

'It's okay. I'll drop you back. I'm only going home from work. An extra fifteen minutes isn't going to make a difference.'

'That's really good of you,' said Max. 'Are you sure?'

'I wouldn't have said it unless I'd meant it.'

'Well, all the same, it's very good of you.'

Max filled up the gallon can and paid the cashier. The driver of the MGB GT was stood casually with his back against the car and his hands in his pockets. Max reckoned he was two or three years older than him and about five feet eleven, maybe six foot tall. Max looked at the number plate of the car, it was supplied by Wadham Stringer, Newton Abbot and it looked new.

'So what do you do?' asked Max as they set off back towards Totnes.

'I work for Wadham Stringer, here in Newton Abbot. I've been down at the Totnes branch today. I'm a car salesman. This is a company car. I'm Chris, by the way,' he said.

'Yeah, I'm Max,' said Max as he looked across at the odometer indicating just ninety miles.

'Is this brand new?'

'Yes, it was only registered yesterday,' said Chris. Approaching Max's car, they slowed to the left hand side of the road and Chris looked in the rear view mirror and did a 'U' turn, booting the accelerator mid way round the bend to get the car to turn tighter.

Max hopped out of the car leaning in through the doorway thanking Chris for the lift.

'Cheers,' he said and thrashed the MG off into the distance.

Max was twenty minutes late by the time he tapped on the back door of Catherine's house.

'Sorry I'm late, I ran out of fuel.'

'It's okay, we don't have to be at Judy's for any given time. I said we'd be there between seven and eight,' Catherine replied.

'Okay, that's all right. Have you got your things?'

Catherine passed Max a bag and he walked back down to the car and placed it in the boot initially, then thinking it might smell of petrol from the can, put it on the shelf behind the seats instead.

He had to stop for fuel again at East Street garage before heading off to Judy's, then they were away. It would be a sign if ever there was one of things to come.

Catherine went off and collected the key of the house next door once they'd arrived at the Waterman's Arms. Judy's parents were away at their holiday home in Fowey and the house they owned next door to the pub was empty.

They spent the evening in the pub with Judy. She was working and on and off helping her elder sister run the place. Judy was a born landlady, she had the rapport and the personality to go with it. She was immense fun and Max could understand why she was Catherine's best friend. They were both at Tech together studying an HCIMA in hotel and catering. Catherine was never going to be involved in the hotel trade but she needed to do something and she didn't want to stay on at Stover School for any longer than she had to. The HCIMA course seemed like an interesting option and gave her the chance of being out in real life. She'd spent most of her education at the highly regarded Stover School for girls. She'd been there since she was seven always one year ahead of her classmates having been accepted a year earlier than the normal starting age. She was exceptionally bright having taken her 'O' levels at fourteen and her 'A' levels at sixteen.

Judy finished work at about eleven and the remainder of the staff were clearing up ready for the following day. Her sister, Pixie, was counting the money, when Judy walked over to Max and Catherine with a large tub of prawns.

'Eat up,' she said and brought over some side dishes and some lemons. It was decadence sat there drinking whatever they wanted, eating prawns, telling funny stories at their corner table. Max placed a few more logs on the open fire and the three of them sat around the hearth looking into the flickering embers, their faces warm with the alcohol and the radiant heat, totally relaxed, a picture of happiness. The conversation had slowed as the drink and the tiredness set in, but like all good friends, sometimes they didn't have to say anything at all, just being with each other was enough.

By half past one, they'd dragged themselves away from the fire and Judy was making her way up to her bedroom above the pub. Max and Catherine had closed the door to the 18th Century Inn behind them and were dawdling arm in arm up the road to the house next door. They stopped at the edge of the road looking up the river, the moon was casting its light across the Dart in the distance and the sounds of the gentle flow of the tributary alongside them slowly making its way downstream. The cold night air had freshened them a little as they unlocked the front door of the house and walked into the hallway, mindful of any muddy shoes on the beige carpet. The house was warm and inviting.

Max caught hold of Catherine's arm and spun her around, holding her close to him, he kissed her passionately on the lips and she responded as he had hoped she would. He held her head in his hands gently caressing her cheeks before running his hands down over her breasts lightly running the backs of his fingers across the thin material covering her nipples.

She broke off and Max stooped down to pick up their bags and climb the stairs. Catherine walked slowly in front of him. He looked at the paintings on the walls as he passed them by and placed the bags on the bed, looking around as he did so. It was tastefully and comfortably furnished. Catherine switched on the bedside light and drew the curtains, kicking off her shoes as she did so, before walking into the bathroom.

She returned a couple of minutes later, 'Now, where were we?'

Max put his arms around her continuing where they'd left off, stroking the soft skin of her arms and slowly unbuttoning her blouse, allowing it to fall to the ground. He felt the warmth of her body against his as he removed his shirt and lay down next to her on the bed. His soft sensual touches along her body sending electrical pulses of pleasure through every part of her very being. He loosened the button of her jeans and slowly removed them, she was all but naked under the soft glow of the light and the darkened shadows it cast across the room. She leant over to the bedside cabinet and switched off the light and they made love.

Max woke up early, it was just after seven, and Catherine was still asleep in his arms with her head resting on his chest. He pulled back the duvet slowly and quietly went over to the window and deftly pulled back the full-length curtains to reveal the outside world. It was a beautiful morning with a wet dew on the grass and the sunlight was beaming its way through the trees of the apple orchard below. The patio door in front of him led to a small balcony overlooking the garden in one direction and the river in the other. He felt the heat of the morning sun on his body as he stretched his arms and back before realising he could be seen by the overlooking pub windows. Displaying himself with nothing on, but a smile, he'd leave to the 'Life of Brian'.

He crept back into bed and snuggled up to Catherine as she quietly slept the last few moments of a waking day.

OCTOBER 1999

'I've got Pinelawns on the phone for you,' said Mike.
'Hello.'
'Hi, it's Rupert Davis here.'
'Hi,'
'We spoke a couple of weeks ago about a blue Ferrari 360 Modena.'
'Yes, I remember.'
'It's being delivered here tomorrow. Is your customer still interested?'
'I need to check, but I think so. I'll call him now and give you a call back shortly. All the details are the same?'
'Of course.'
'Good. I'll come back to you in a minute.'
Max put down the phone and rang Josh at the leasing company.
'Hi Josh, it's Max, do you still need the blue 360 for your customer?'
'Yes, definitely,' he replied.
'It's being delivered tomorrow. Do you want to take it tomorrow?'
'If that's okay?' Josh asked.
'Yeah, it's no problem for me.'

'How do you want paying?' asked Josh.

'I'm getting the car through Pinelawns so the easiest way is for you to get a bank draft made payable to Pinelawns for £126,000 and fax it through to me when you have it. I will send a copy to Rupert Davis, he can get it verified and you can take the car tomorrow.'

'I will need an invoice detailing it as a VAT qualifying car.'

'I'll sort it,' said Max.

Max put down the phone and rang Rupert Davis telling him that the car was sold for £126,000 and Rupert would have to pay Max a £2000 commission as agreed. The funds would be paid by bankers draft and that a copy of the draft would be on his fax later that day for him to verify.

The transaction went exactly to plan. Max met Josh at Pinelawns and Rupert Davis handed over the keys to Max to give Josh a demonstration drive and explain the F1 paddle gearbox. Afterwards, Davis handed over all the correct paperwork along with the VAT qualifying invoice to Josh in return for the bankers draft and off he went. Another satisfied customer Max hoped.

Rupert Davis invited Max back into his office. 'Tea, coffee ?' asked Rupert.

'Yes, tea please, Rupert' Max replied.

All around the room, there were pictures of rally cars, racing cars and the like. Rupert came back into the room with two mugs of tea and sat down behind his large desk. He wrote out a cheque for two thousand pounds.

'Who do you want it made payable to?'

'Velodrome, please Rupert.'

Max took the cheque, scanned it and placed it in his brown leather document case.

'So what do you do the most of Rupert?'

'Racing cars, rally cars, competition, historics, that sort of thing. We do a lot of Ferraris, mainly classic.

'Oh right. We're doing some classic Ferraris as well. I've just supplied a customer with a 250 short wheel base,' said Max eagerly.

'Proper thing?'

'Yes, very much so, fully authenticated by the factory. Sefac hotrod,' Max replied.

'Nice. It's a small world, the Ferrari world. Listen chap.

256

The Ferrari world is like a mountain. The snow at the very peak of that mountain is where all the dealers in the know have their little club. They all know what's going on. It's taken a long time for me to get there, but I could probably help you if you needed anything.'

Rupert lectured Max about his authority on all things Ferrari and how he was the man to deal with. He was flexing his muscles, showing off a little, about how big he was and how good he was, and how much respect he had in the industry.'

'You know Max, a guy once said to me, big hat, no cattle. There's plenty of them out there and you've got to avoid them like the plague. All show and no go. All the dealers in London are the same, ring fenced by the M25. The serious guys like me outside of that fence, we're the ones that make the deals, not them. We're the poachers, they're the prey.'

'Oh right,' said Max, 'I don't get involved too much with the London dealers. I dealt with Chris at Testastretta and Ted Little at Wedgewoods.'

Rupert interrupted, 'Well, he's a wanker if ever there was one.'

'Who?'

'Ted Little. He used to be at Coys. He doesn't know his arse from his elbow let alone a proper car. I know of Chris at Testastretta but of course they've just gone under so that's the end of them.'

'Yes, it is, sadly, because I quite liked Chris, he was a decent bloke.'

'If you're looking for anything give me a call.' Rupert gave Max his card and wrote his home telephone number on the back of his card. 'Anytime,' he said.

'You know, I sold a Porsche 935 recently, proper thing, factory car, race ready, great history, Le Mans car. I was the only guy out there with the balls to give it a go. Nobody else would entertain it. One of my pals is the top man at one of the oldest and most respected auction houses. He lives in California now but we speak a lot and there's all sorts of deals that can be done behind the scenes. Funding, selling, buying, exchanging, it's all going on, you just need to be in with the right people.' Rupert said revelling in his prime position.

It was always going to be difficult in the summer of 1981, Catherine was going off to Colorado for a couple of months and Max would be starting his job on his sandwich year. They would be apart for the first time since they met and things started going wrong right from the start. After a long goodbye at Heathrow airport, Max drove up to London for his work placement in Colindale. On route, the bonnet of the MG blew open and was damaged beyond repair. He couldn't even get it to shut, he had to throw it away at the side of the road.

Colindale was awful. The job was awful and he hated it. He had no friends, no money and with Catherine away too, he was totally miserable. He felt his life had gone from everything to nothing faster than you could say it.

Max wandered into the newsagents on a Saturday morning and read through some of the car and bike magazines before buying a copy of Exchange and Mart and sat in the park reading it cover to cover. One advert took his attention. It read:

Motor Racing. Formula Ford 1600. Twenty trial laps at Brands Hatch. Call for details. Doug 01 etc.

Max walked over to the phone box, dialled the number and gave the guy a call.

'Hello,' he answered.

'Oh, hi, you've got an advert in the Exchange and Mart regarding Formula Ford?'

'Yeah, that's right. I have a couple of Formula Fords. I race myself in the Champion of Brands series. I rent the other car out to help fund my racing,' said Doug.

'Okay; I'm Max by the way.'

'Have you done any racing at all?' asked Doug.

'No, not really. Bike enduro, trials, that sort of thing, but nothing in cars.'

'What about a licence?'

'Yeah, I've got a driving licence,' Max replied.

'A racing licence?' asked Doug.

'No, just a normal driving licence.'

'Well, if you're going to want to have a go, you will need a race licence and some other bits and pieces too. Whereabouts are you?' asked Doug.

'I'm in Colindale at the moment.'

'I'm in Beckenham, why don't you come down and I'll run through everything with you. If it's something you want to do, we'll see what we can do!'

Max put down the phone having agreed to meet Doug at his place in Beckenham the following day. He stuffed the paper in his inside pocket and walked back to his bedsit with a little bit more of a spring in his step. Max noticed a letter in his pigeonhole as he opened the front door, it was from Catherine.

He opened it and sat down on the edge of his bed. It sounded like she was having a great time, riding horses through riverbeds, across ranges and camping out overnight. She was working on a dude ranch in Durango, Colorado she was obviously having a lot of fun. He was pleased for her, but it was a thousand miles away from what he was experiencing in Colindale.

Max pulled up outside the small terraced house in Beckenham and walked to the front door. He didn't need to knock. Doug had beaten him to it.

'Hi, I'm Max.'

'Good to see you Max, come on in, sorry about the mess.'

They walked through to the kitchen and Doug filled up the kettle. 'Tea or coffee?' he asked.

'Tea please,' Max answered looking around.

'So what do you want to do? Have you thought about it?' asked Doug.

'Well, I've always hankered to have a go in the back of my mind, but my circumstances have never really made it possible, then I saw your advert and I thought I'd take it one stage further. If you'd asked me about it the day before yesterday, I probably wouldn't have given it another serious thought,' Max replied.

'Okay, even if you do want to take it further, a taster session is going to help you. I could offer you a test at Brands and we could see if it's the kind of thing you want to do. If you're any good, I'll tell you; if you're not, I'll tell you that too. If you want to do a few races then I could possibly run you in a car if you want,' said Doug.

'What sort of money are we talking about?' asked Max.

'Depends on what you do. If it's testing and I'm there anyway, then the cost would be less. Say you wanted to come down next Wednesday to Brands with me. I've just had an engine rebuilt by Minister and I need to bed it in before next Sunday's race. I could get the other car there and you could have a run out in that.'

'And what would you charge me for that?' asked Max taking a swig from the mug.

'How about seventy-five quid, but you'll have to help with getting the car there, unloading, loading and all that.'

'What about a race licence?' asked Max expectantly.

'You are going to need one, but we should be able to blag that one for testing. I know the guys down there, we should be able to overcome that one. I'll borrow a licence from a friend of mine and stick your picture on it. They won't know any different. Bring a passport size photo with you and don't forget'

'Okay, I'll do it,' said Max. 'I'll give it a go. Once in a lifetime thing really, so I might as well do it now.'

Max went into work on the Monday and asked his boss Roy if he could have the day off on Wednesday and he agreed. He didn't ask why and Max probably wouldn't have told him the real reasons anyway. The first two days of the week dragged.

It was an early start on Wednesday morning. Max had to be at Doug's for 6:00 am so as to get down to West Kingsdown early to collect the cars and be at the circuit for 8:00 am. It would be the first time that Max had been to Brands Hatch. He'd obviously seen the track on the television following the Formula 1 coverage, but this was the real deal and he was both apprehensive and extremely excited at the same time.

The fact that he didn't have any money hadn't stopped him. He was earning £225 per month working with Mowlems in his day job. He could earn another £50 a month with his part time pub job at the Saracen Inn on the Edgeware Road, but his rent was £150 per month, which he had to pay to his robbing landlord. There wasn't a lot left over to make ends meet. The answer was his credit card. He didn't use it very often, but with Doug's offer, Max thought it was too good an offer to pass up.

Max mucked in like an old hand and got the cars and equipment unloaded in the paddock and then moved everything into the pit lane garage behind them. He looked around, recognising parts of the circuit from the television.

'Before we do anything, we've got enough time to walk the circuit, so we'll go out of the pit lane exit and I'll walk and talk you through it.'

260

'Yeah, that would be good,' said Max. 'I don't want to be going the wrong way,' he joked.

The pair of them were getting on really well, as if they'd known each other for years. Max liked Doug. They were a similar build, but Doug was probably ten years older. He'd recently been divorced and was working as a freelance advertising agent, which gave him the time to indulge himself in his passion. He was never going to get to Formula 1, he was too old for that, but he could have done production saloons or other 'tin tops' if he'd wanted to. Maybe if he'd started racing earlier in his life, he could have gone further, but motorsport is all about money and if you haven't got money or access to money, then it's most likely you're going to struggle. Like most , Doug didn't have any money when he was young either.

Both of them walked past race control in the pit lane and out onto the circuit. Max looked at all the grid slot markings back down the start finish straight. It seemed very wide. There were black tyre marks all over the place. On the television, the whole circuit looks flat, but in the real, it was very hilly. The start finish straight was uphill with a sideways slope towards the pit wall. They walked up the left hand side of the track towards Paddock Hill bend. Doug stopped and looked back down the straight demonstrating with his hands.

'Okay, you come off 'Clearways' down there changing from third into fourth just past the wall to the pit lane entrance. Keep slightly more towards the centre of the track, about ten feet off the apex. There's a bump there and it will unsettle the car. Hold fourth gear, you'll probably see five thousand revs on the needle. When you pass this end of the pit lane, you want to be out here on the left of the circuit by this Duckhams Oil sign or roughly where this grandstand starts.'

Max listened intently, trying to take in all the information. It sounded like a lot, but it wasn't really. It just needed to be said.

Doug pointed at the circuit, 'When you get here, you will need to have braked hard and now be in third gear ready for the blind entry into the right hand Paddock Hill bend. If you get this corner right, it is very satisfying, a bit like stepping into an empty lift shaft, it takes your breath away.'

Max was amazed at how steep it was, more like a crater than a corner. They walked on.

Doug continued, 'You want to be clipping the apex

261

here,' pointing at the red and white kerbs as he talked. They walked over to the exit of the corner and stopped, with Doug standing on the painted line with his feet together facing back up to the top of the bend. 'This is where you need to be, and if you look back up there, you can see the curve we've taken. So brakes hard into Paddock up on the left of the circuit going in, foot hard on the throttle into the apex of the bend picking up speed and exit the corner here on the outside of the circuit and snick fourth gear. You'll only be able to hold fourth for one hundred and fifty yards or so.

Max and Doug walked up hill towards the hairpin bend, Druids.

'Okay, stay out here on the left hand side of the track. It would be different if you're racing because they'll all be coming up your inside, but watch out here today because there will be other's testing as well and you don't want to be getting in their way. So, stay out to the left, brake at 150 yards, hook third, brake and then turn in, in second gear. If you lock up on the brakes, get your foot off the brake and then get back on them. Go off here and that sand trap's not going to stop you. It will get expensive.'

They walked around the corner, Doug standing on the outside of the curve gesturing the line.

'Easy corner this one, just hold onto second gear and hug the inside kerb, then let the car drift out towards the opposite side of the circuit as the revs rise and get third gear just beyond the end of the red and white kerbing on the left hand side as you drop down the hill into "Bottom bend or Graham Hill bend", as it's known.'

They walked down the hill some two hundred yards and crossed diagonally from the left hand side to the right hand side. Doug looked back up the hill and pointed out the line.

'See what we're doing?' asked Doug.

'Yes, I see.'

'Here, you want to be out on the right of the circuit about two thirds out as you go past this marshals' post, then turn in for the apex, but watch and aim the car at the exit of this corner which is way over there by the lower paddock entrance.' Doug pointed, 'Do you see where I mean?' he asked. 'That's the exit.'

'Yes, I do,' Max replied.

'This is a long quick left hand sweep and you need to be on the throttle and looking out for the exit, then stay out on the right hand side of the track, and keep off the grass. If you go off there, you going to have a big one.'

Doug indicated to Max where to change into fourth gear and they walked up to the next series of bends.

There were a couple of other lads waiting up in front of them and Doug and Max caught them up.

'Hi, Julian, you all right?' asked Doug.

'Yeah, you out today? Looks like it's going to be a nice one,' he said.

'Yeah, I'll be there, so make sure you don't get in my way,' said Doug.

'Julian laughed and carried on talking to his mate.

Doug walked on and Max followed.

'That was Julian Bailey. He's quick around here. He'll be in the 49s today. Watch out for him he's in a red Lola. If he goes past you, try to follow him, but don't get sucked in.'

Max nodded.

'Okay, this is Kidney,' he said as they arrived at the end of the short straight. If you turn left here, you go out onto the Grand Prix circuit. Today we're only using the club circuit, so brake here, and change down to third and try to straight line these two corners. Go up on the rivets going in over there on the left, then hit the apex over there on the right, then run a straight line to the outside of the corner before turning right. If you're going well, take second gear before you turn right, if not hold third and the revs will slowly pick up as you head back towards clearways and the start finish straight.'

'Simple as that,' quipped Max.

'Yep, simple as that. Add a few more cars and a bit of rain. Carnage.'

They walked across the grass and onto the pit lane entrance, stopping occasionally to talk to other drivers as they made their way back to their pit garage.

'What I think would be best,' said Doug, 'is that if I go out and do a few laps, then come in alongside you and then you follow me around for say, four or five laps?'

'Yes, that would be okay,' said Max.

'And then come back in, have a chat and then go off again and do another five laps.'

Max sat in the Royale RP16 Formula Ford, in a borrowed race suit and his normal motorcycle crash helmet blipping the throttle warming the engine. Doug said, 'warm the car to 80° and then switch off.' Max had done just that. He got out of the car and watched Doug disappear down the pit lane and out onto the circuit in his Van Diemen RF81. Max stood on the pit wall and watched the hornets hurtle past. *This is fantastic*, he thought.

It didn't take long for Doug to do five laps by which time Max was already sat in the Royale, belted up, gloves on and ready to go with his heart beating through his overalls. The mirrors on the car were useless and Max was struggling to see anything behind him as Doug pulled alongside. He lifted the visor on his helmet and gave Max the 'okay' sign, then went down the pit lane with his customer tucked in close behind. The out lap was fairly slow as Doug was keen to ensure that Max didn't take them both off. Clearly, they'd chosen the right time to be on the circuit as they were the only ones out there at that time.

Doug picked up the pace keeping an eye on his other car behind him, and was surprised to see he wasn't dropping off as he'd expected. Doug then pulled over on the start finish straight and let Max go by, putting two fingers up to him as he went by. Max assumed he meant two more laps, then in. He was right.

Max had sat behind Doug quite comfortably, but now he was on his own he had to think and drive for himself. *Two laps*, he thought. *I'm only here once, I might as well have a go.* And he did.

Over the start finish line, 5400 revs, up to the left of the circuit, brake third gear, chuck it in on the power, scream it through the apex, bang it into fourth at the bottom of the hill, hold onto it for 150 yards, third, second, hold onto it, bit of opposite lock turning in, the back wanting to come round, hug the inside of the corner at Druids, exit the corner, 6000 revs down to the Marshall post, left into the apex, aim for the lower paddock entrance, push the throttle through the floor grabbing 4th, holding on for a short while, back to third for the Kidney, up onto the rivets on the left, take the kerb and a bit of grass on the right, brake, brake, brake, second gear, hard right, straighten up on the throttle, third, keep off the hump on the apex of clearways, bury the pedal and back over the line in fourth. Max slowed down and toured around the rest of the lap and then drove into the pit lane. He checked the gauges in front of him, lifted his visor, switched off the engine and unbuckled his harness. The engine crackled as it cooled.

He stood on the seat and got out of the car whilst undoing the catch of his crash helmet. Doug was already out of the car doing the same as he walked towards him.

Doug shouted out, 'Fucking hell, I don't believe it. I couldn't get past you!' Max didn't know that Doug had been trying. He hadn't seen him in the mirrors.

'Oh right,' said Max. 'I just had a bit of a go.'

'And you've never driven competitively or one of these before?' asked Doug.

'No, not at all,' Max replied. 'First time I've sat in anything like it!'

'Unbelievable,' said Doug. 'You want to do everything you can to do this properly. I can't do anything for you. You need to get yourself a car, get some race craft, experience, and I think you could win. You're a fucking winner. I've never seen anyone go that quick for the first time. That was fucking quick, for someone who's never done it before. Believe me, I know.'

Max thought about what Doug had just said as he went off to get two teas. He didn't have any money and this was a rich man's sport. He could hardly afford to live within his means, let alone do a season of motor racing.

That night he got back to Colindale well past midnight. Doug had been telling him all his tales of racing, the people involved and the idea of getting sponsored, what the costs would be, championships etc. Max had something to eat at Doug's and they continued talking until late. There was quite a lot to think about. *Is this the start of something, or just a good day out,* he thought. He didn't know, it always came back to the same old problem, no money and he was getting pissed off with it.

AUGUST 2008

'Still here then Raf?'

'Yeah.'

'What happened?'

'It was okay, they took me up for the test and kept me in all day, but I couldn't go, so they kept me there until I did. I'd had plenty to drink by then so I think I'll be okay. It was nothing heavy anyway, just a bit of weed, so hopefully it won't show up.'

'Close call then.'

'Yeah, you could say that. Did I tell you about the silencer?'

'What silencer?'

'Just in case you ever get caught in this type of situation. If a guy comes at you with a gun, you've got a fifty fifty chance that he's going to shoot you, right? You may not know it, but some of these things don't have any range or accuracy anyway.'

'Okay,' said Max.

'But, if a guy comes at you with a gun and it's got a silencer on it, you can be sure he's coming to kill you.'

Another one of Raf's incongruous bits of advice.

'Okay Raf, I'll try to remember that, but I don't get too many customers with guns. I did have one once though. I stayed on his forty-metre yacht in the South of France and we were sat in the grand saloon up on deck and I asked him what he did for security and he reached behind the sofa and pulled out a small handgun. I don't know what it was though.'

'This'll do the trick,' he said. Needless to say Max didn't get any sleep that night.

OCTOBER 2000

Graham Lord answered the phone; it was Steve Majendie calling about the Jaguar XJR15 in his usual monotone Yankee voice.

'Yeah, Hi Graham, we've got a deal with the Jaguar. My customer would like to go ahead.'

'That's good news Steve.'

'Where do you want me to send the money?' he asked.

'Best if you send it to my account and I'll forward it onto the client,' Graham assured him.

'Okay, you send me a contract of sale for £145,000 and I'll sign and return it. I should be able to get the money into your account by tomorrow, if that's all right with you,' said Steve.

'Yes, that will be good. I'll send the sales contract now and confirmation of my bank details, then that's all done.'

'What about the spare parts?' Steve asked.

'That's all coming. I've organised everything but the bits aren't here yet. As soon as they're here, I'll let you know and you can send the money,' Graham replied.

'And what are we going to have to pay?'

'Twenty-five thousand pounds, plus shipping.'

'The customer will be happy with that price, so that's okay. Realistically, how long is it going to take to get the parts. The reason I'm asking, is I'm wondering whether it would make more sense to ship the car later and put the parts in with the car,' Steve asked.

'I think the best option Steve is to concentrate on getting the car over to you in the USA and if I get the parts soon, then they can go with it, if not, they'll have to go in a later shipment,' Graham replied.

'Okay, Graham, I'll leave it with you, but we must have those parts.'

'No, I understand, I know you need them and I'll make sure you get them.'

'I mean Graham, the car is no good to us without those parts.'

'Yes, I know, you've no need to worry. It will be sorted,' Graham asserted.

'Okay, I'll get that money transferred.'

'Thanks, Steve, speak to you soon.'

The big issue with the Jaguar XJR15 was that it was effectively sold as a non-runner and the end user, a Jaguar collector, needed to be sure that he had some spares for the car especially as it was one of only a few cars made. There would be a limited number of spare parts available on the specialist open market and there was a high probability of the car malfunctioning.

Graham thought about Steve flapping over the parts, but knew at that time, he wasn't able to get hold of them, he'd deal with that later. The important thing for him was that he had sold the car for £145,000 and he had agreed to buy it through Harry for £85,000. It was a nice tidy profit, sixty thousand pounds.

Muzi stood by the fax having just spoken to Max, who had alerted him to the incoming contract for the Ferrari 330 GTO. It ran to four pages with a joint signature for the buyer and seller on the last page. He was reading each page as he pulled it off the machine. It was all pretty standard, he thought. The description was an accurate account of the car's condition as given by Graham Lord and supplied to Max. Donald Key had told Graham exactly what had been done to the car, when it had been in his workshop for the restoration in the late 1980s early 1990s.

Muzi initialled each page in the bottom right hand corner and signed the last page. He'd agreed to buy the car for $7,750,000 USD.

Earlier that day, Max and Graham had a conference call with John Gill in New York. They had confirmed the details of the car, the price and all were satisfied that all was well so that they could proceed with the sale. John Gill had got up early to send a copy of the contract to both Graham Lord and Max and take the calls. He had waited for their confirmation, which took about twenty minutes for Max to sign the purchase paperwork on behalf of Velodrome and return it to him. Max had told John that once he had the US end tied up, he would have his customer sign his copy of Velodrome's contract and confirm the successful sale, which would be later that day.

Max was just a little bit agitated as he waited by the fax machine, pacing up and down in Keith's adjoining office.

'Max, just chill,' he said, 'calm down, it will be okay.' It was a big deal and it could mean so much.

Keith had been Velodrome's bookkeeper for several years and he'd worked with Max closely on all the financial aspects of the business. He was only part time, but he was a valued and humorous part of the team. Several years earlier, Keith had worked for the accountants that Velodrome used, then decided to leave and set up on his own. Max hated all the fuss of the day-to-day ledger work. His view was that if you weren't any good at it, then pay someone that was.

Keith would come in to the office twice a week and input all the information on screen, write the cheques, pay the bills, do the VAT return and liaise with Max. He was a really good guy who was honest and loved his football. He'd often told Max that Velodrome should consider taking on a full time company accountant now that the business was growing so that there could be better information for the bank. It made sense, but Max didn't want to increase the overheads any more than he had to. In hindsight he was right, the foot and mouth disease had seriously effected the business and another wage would not have helped. On the other hand, an on the spot bean counter might have been able to produce enough financial information to ride out the storm. It would have been a difficult call. As it was, Keith was still at Velodrome and was there in the office when

Muzi's signed contract juddered quietly out of the fax machine. He smiled, tore off the sheets and handed them to Max.

'What you wanted?' asked Keith.

'Absolutely.' Max checked through the four pages. 'Hopefully, it's just the start. The first car. Get this one right and we can all sleep at night,' said Max.

'Well done,' Keith said, nodding as he did so.

Max walked into his office and sat down on the leather Chesterfield sofa, crossed his legs and put his arm on the rest. Maybe he could relax a little, he thought. Just get it done, get the money in, tell the bank where to go, lots of things ran through his mind as he sat back and closed his eyes. The original paperwork had to be sent out that night by recorded mail. Max checked the contents of the FedEx package and sealed it ready for the courier to collect.

The fax copies were good enough to show commitment, but Max knew that he needed the originals to make the contract binding. It would come, he was sure of that. He called Graham Lord.

'Graham, it's Max. I've received the signed contract back from my customer. The originals are going out by courier tonight for his signature. All is well at this end.'

'That's brilliant. Well done. What next?' asked Graham.

'Well, once I've got the original documents back, I'll sort out the transfers and get Jeremy at Cars UK to sort out the freight.'

'Where's the car going?'

'Here. All the cars that he wants will come here initially.' Max had made a bit of a slip, he didn't want Graham to know that Muzi wanted more cars just yet.

'What else does he want?' Graham asked.

'I'm not sure what he wants next. He's going to let me know.' Max did know. Muzi wanted a 250 Testa Rossa next, but he thought he would get this one done and dusted first before he launched himself into the next round.

'Hey Graham, what's happening with the Jaguar XJR15?' Max asked.

'Oh, he's changed his mind. He decided it wasn't really what he was looking for,' Graham lied.

'Ah, that's a shame. I thought that was going to be a certainty,' said Max.

'Well, yes, so did I, but it doesn't matter so much now

that we've done the GTO.'

Graham was right, it didn't matter so much. When the dust had settled and the Ferrari was paid for, Max would share $4,000,000 with Graham and he couldn't argue about that. They were still to be paid but it was looking good.

'How are we getting on with the California?' Graham asked, slightly changing the subject.

'I should get a copy of the inspection today or tomorrow. Sangster seems to be playing ball, so no problems there. I hope it's all okay.'

'It should be. Sangster wouldn't have let the car be inspected if it wasn't right. It would be too damaging for him. It would make it look like he's trying to hide something and I don't think he is. There's nothing anywhere in the books that says anything other than that car being correct, so it should be a formality.'

'Well we are going to know very shortly and then I can get it sorted,' said Max.

They finished off their conversation and agreed to speak with each other again the following afternoon.

AUGUST 1981

The summer of '81 was a slow one like it always is when you're waiting for something. Catherine wasn't due back from Colorado until the end of August, which now was only a few short days away. Max had persevered with his job in London however bored he was and however poor he was, but he had been seeing more of Doug. He couldn't afford to go motor racing and drive but he could still be involved, helping, learning and taking it all in. The overriding thing he did notice though was the amount of crooks involved. They seemed to be everywhere, scamming drivers everywhere. Doug was all right though, he made his money selling advertising space or at least that was the way the story went.

Max remembered one Saturday night before a race at Brands Hatch. Doug had said to Max that they'd go out and meet some friends of his. They'd both gone into Dulwich Village in his midnight blue Jaguar E-Type fixed head coupe and arrived at the gates of a spectacular Victorian villa.

270

'You'll have to get out and speak into that box over there, Max,' said Doug.

'Hi, I'm Max and I'm with Doug and we're at the gate.'

A female voice answered and said, 'Come on in.' The gates opened and Doug drove down the pea shingle drive and stopped behind a new Range Rover Vogue.

A man came to the door arms outstretched to greet Doug like a long lost son, obviously pleased to see him. Doug introduced Max.

'Hi, I'm Roy, any friend of Doug's is a friend of mine. Good to meet you come on in.' They walked through the open front door and into a huge hallway, decorated in beige and cream with perfect paintwork. There was art everywhere and obvious money adorned every corner. What did take Max by surprise though were the two dogs, Dobermans. To the left of the hallway there was what could be described as a sizeable alcove about twelve foot wide and seven foot deep and it was secured by a floor to ceiling grill like you'd imagine a prisoner's cell. There was a grilled door to one side to gain access and the two dogs were lying down looking out through the bars. It seemed strangely at odds with the rest of the house.

They walked into the kitchen, which looked like something out of a 'Homes & Gardens' feature and sat down at the island table. Roy's striking young blonde girlfriend asked if she could get them a drink and they all sat around chatting for an hour or so. Doug and Roy went off on their own and Heather made small talk with Max. Apart from the dogs, nothing seemed out of the ordinary. Heather kept Max's attention showing off a lot of cleavage, no bra and criss-crossing her legs every five minutes. With such a short skirt, he was sure she caught him looking once or twice. It was difficult not to with her sat directly in front of him.

Max asked to use the loo and she showed him to the small room and waited outside until he'd finished. That seemed odd too. It wasn't that she was being over attentive, he thought, or was she after him; he didn't know. He overheard quietened voices as he walked past a partly opened door following Heather's fine physique back to the kitchen. He only heard – Kruger Rands. Max thought nothing of it. Londoners, they're a weird lot.

Heather continued crossing her legs and Max was sure she wasn't wearing any or was that just wishful thinking. Roy walked back into the kitchen and slapped Max on the back, 'Heather looking after you properly son?' asked Roy.

'Oh yes, absolutely,' Max replied.

'I've been hearing all about you. Doug says you're a bit quick.'

'Well, I've only been out once so I can't be sure, I need to get amongst them properly,' said Max.

'Keep trying boy. You'll get there. I was you a good few years ago. Keep it on the island. You'll be all right,' said Roy.

'Thanks,' Max replied.

They said their goodbyes, Roy and Heather standing arm in arm at the top of the steps in the open doorway as the E-Type crunched on the gravel, through the open gates and back onto the leafy access road.

'You know who that was?' asked Doug.

'Never mind that Doug, when you were in there with him she was coming on to me. I virtually had a guided tour of her body,' said Max.

'Forget all that. Typical blood racing driver. Two track mind. Sex and speed, probably in that order. No, do you know who that was?' asked Doug again.

'What Roy or Heather?'

'Roy!'

'No, I don't think I've seen him before.'

'That was Roy James.'

'Oh right,' said Max, 'Never heard of him, sounds like a friend of Buck Rogers.'

'I don't think you should be telling him that. He was one of the Great Train Robbers.'

Catherine's father collected her from the airport on her return and drove her back to Devon. Max couldn't get the day off so he'd have to wait a little while longer before he saw her. He was looking forward to it desperately. Of course he'd written to her many times over the summer and she'd written to him too, but nothing beats that homecoming hug. He'd telephoned her four times whilst she was away but it was so expensive that Max spent most of the conversation shovelling ten pence pieces through the slot. It didn't make it easy to concentrate on what he was trying to say.

He called again when she was back home and her mother had picked up the phone.

'Sorry, she's out Max.'

'Okay, I'll try again.'

'Thanks, bye.'

He'd had two or three conversations like that when calling her number and he was beginning to think that something was wrong. Then he thought, *Well maybe not; she's been away for a few months; she's got college to organise and her friends down in Devon to catch up with.* However, the longer it went on, the more he thought things weren't right.

He didn't have to wait long. A few days later he spoke to her on the phone. She was very apologetic about not having spoken to him. So much to do and all that, but the long goodbye at Heathrow really was now the long goodbye. It was over. Max was history. That was then and this is now and Max wasn't part of it. To say he was devastated was a complete understatement. He just couldn't believe it. Her letters, the phone calls, nothing had alerted him to any glimmer of anything wrong. He couldn't understand it, why had she gone from being a loving girlfriend to a cold heartless person, just casting him aside? It didn't matter what he thought; she knew her own mind. She was growing up, feeling her way and she didn't need Max. He was gone, out of mind and that was that. Very matter of fact, but that was that.

The aftermath of Catherine had left a huge void in Max's life. He had thought that one day they would have got married, had children and done all the usual things, but that was not to be. Game over.

Ed had moved to London and was working for a timber company in Erith and he was going to have a moving in party. Everyone would be there, all Max's friends, they'd have a good time. On the day of the party, Max had been down in Beckenham with Doug helping out with his racing, sharing his food and drink. It was great for him to get away from the bedsit in Colindale and Doug had come to look forward to Max's company too. They had all the usual 'when I'm in Formula One', stories to joke about and they'd also spoken seriously about Max doing a championship the following year. Doug would get the sponsorship, Max would work his balls off and somehow they would try to take on the world. The more they talked about it though, the more it seemed like there was a chance of making it happen. They'd convinced themselves. They'd run through the costs and worked out the absolute minimum funding they'd need to do it properly. The obvious choice was the Pre 74 Formula Ford 1600 Championship. It was run by the BRSCC, British

Racing & Sports Car Club and it catered for slightly older Formula Fords. The Royale RP16A that Max had tested earlier was an eligible car for the series. It would make a lot of sense to use that car in that championship. Max had no experience of racing and he needed a year in a racing car where he could learn some race craft relatively cheaply in a Championship not overrun with big budget teams. Doug had said to Max, 'You could win that championship in that car. Okay you may not win straight out of the box, but you could win it, and who knows where that might take you?'

Max drove over to Erith judging he'd get there for around eight thirty. As it happened, he couldn't find the address. He spent an hour driving up and down wasting loads of petrol before he stumbled upon it by accident. The party was well alight by the time he got in through the front door, making his way past a few people he didn't know and getting into the kitchen to pour himself a drink. He chatted with some friends and then had a quick look around. There were so many that he knew from Devon that it took him quite a while before he wandered further on looking around the lounge door to see who was in the room. And then he saw her, right there on the sofa, four feet from him. She was beautiful, but she was with someone else, well and truly ensconced. She stopped what she was doing and looked straight at him. Their eyes said it all as they exchanged a gigabyte of information in a momentary glance. It was Catherine.

Sensing there could be a problem. Nick grabbed Max's arm and pulled him into the hallway.

'Come on, let's go in here.'

Max said nothing. He looked around and he could see his friends looking at him. They were thinking what he was thinking. Is he or isn't he? Well he didn't. He'd been there before with Jenny when he'd punched Dick's lights out and he wasn't about to do that again. Things were different this time and although he still had strong feelings for her, he wasn't about to get involved in something nasty. He was sad, there was no doubting that, but he walked away. It was as it was those few weeks earlier. Game over.

The following weekend Max was down in Devon staying at his mothers. Ferris was growing up fast, eager to jabber to his older brother endlessly about everything he was doing. Neil was around and wanted to go back to London with

Max and kip down on the floor at his bedsit. Max didn't have a problem with that. On the Sunday, Max had reluctantly agreed to meet his father at his home in Dunchideock, it wasn't something he was particularly looking forward to. They were trying to have some kind of reconciliation, maybe a start again situation, wipe the slate clean, but it was difficult. The wounds were still very much open and although nearly seven years had passed, the memories were still as clear as a bell. If it was to work, then his father would have needed to have calmed down and shown that he was a changed man. He was still with Max's mother's ex-best friend and Max didn't enjoy the prospect of seeing her either.

He walked up to the front door with some trepidation. Five minutes earlier he'd dropped Neil off a couple miles up the road and said he'd be back for him later. Neil didn't want to see his father and Max didn't want to stay too long either. The alternator on the MG was not charging the battery properly and the lights would get dim without a proper charge, so he wanted to get back to London in the daylight. He could sort out the alternator during the week. It was his 21st birthday the following day.

Max's father answered the door. He looked older, he'd lost weight, his hair was thinning and going a little grey in places. It had been a long time.

He invited Max in and they sat and talked with Pauline at his side. He still scared the shit out of Max. The reality was that unless Max backed down for an easy life, his father was going to get away with explaining everything away as it being other people's fault. It wasn't. He never remembered the boy's birthdays, even just a card. Christmas, well he obviously didn't celebrate that because he never thought of Max, Neil and Ferris.

For his own safety, Max bit his lip and said nothing. His father hadn't changed and neither had she. It was just the same. The revival of those dreadful memories became all the more clearer as Max listened to his voice.

And then Max said the wrong thing. He told his father he had to go and his father went absolutely berserk. It was like Max had flicked on his father's imaginary psycho switch. When he told close friends afterwards, it was almost unbelievably extreme. He chased Max for all he was worth around the garden with a shovel, and he could have done some damage with that. Thankfully Max escaped any harm, but from then on it was easier to stay away. There was no need for him to subject himself to that sort of frenzy.

Max got back into his MG and drove down the road still feeling a little shaky. Neil stepped out of the hedgerow and got into the car. Max was later than he wanted to be, but he would still get to London before dark he hoped, all being well. They made good time along the A303 past Stonehenge and on towards Andover, following all the returning London traffic out onto the A3. Max looked down at the speedo, they'd been doing a steady eighty to eighty five miles per hour all the way from Devon. Neil was talking about the old man, the radio was on and they pulled out into the third lane to overtake a Rover in front of them in the middle lane. Max came alongside the Rover as he made to pass him, but for some inexplicable reason the driver swerved into Max's path causing the MG to run up onto the central reservation and spear into the underside of the safety barrier. The front of the MG dug its nose under the Armco safety barrier and lifted the back of the car into a series of end-to-end somersaults. The car rolled several times ending up sideways on in the middle of the oncoming traffic. The lights went out.

OCTOBER 2000

Sirol received the fax from Angelo at Ferrari, it was a quarter past five on a Friday afternoon and Sirol was due to run two of his best customers in the Euro 360 Challenge at Magny Cours for the weekend double header. They'd be racing on the Saturday and the Sunday. The ex Ferrari Formula One race trucks were all packed and on their way to the circuit having left Lugano earlier that day. All would be ready for first practice at 10:30 am the following morning.

Sirol put the fax into his briefcase, deciding to read it later when he was with Nino. For now, he had to leave the showroom, go home get changed then drive up to meet Nino at his home in Locarno. It would take about twenty-five minutes to drive in his blue Ferrari 456 demonstrator.

Nino had packed all his race gear into one leather holdall and his everyday wear in a second similar bag. He was a bit anxious about the weekend's racing, but believed he had it in him to give a reasonable showing. He didn't want to show himself up and come last, but then again, he didn't want to stuff the car either. It would be his first competitive race. Sirol had told him to remain calm and be sensible, there was nothing to it.

Sirol pulled up outside Nino's fabulous modern home overlooking the lake and picked up the two holdalls at the bottom of the steps and put them into the boot of the Ferrari. Nino's silver Porsche Carrera 4 sat on the driveway. Sirol caught sight of his passenger jogging down the steps towards him.

'Sirol, how are you, my friend?'

'Busy, Nino, busy!'

'Okay, we go to the airport and park by the clubhouse. All is ready.'

Nino and Sirol nearly always spoke to each other in Swiss. Both spoke Swiss, German, Italian and English, however Nino would be piloting his own jet into Magny Cours and spoke in English often as that is the universal flight language. It would be a ten-minute short drive to the airport and the transfer would take no more than five minutes, it was a small airfield. Nino reckoned they'd be in the air by nineteen hundred hours. He had filed the flight plan earlier that afternoon with the control tower and estimated their time of arrival at Magny Cours for 7.40 pm, 19.40 hours. If they timed it right, they'd be in their hotel and sat down for dinner at 8:30 pm.

Pierre, SLR's race team manager collected Nino and Sirol from the airport and drove them to the hotel and they were sat down ordering their meal at bang on 8:30 pm.

The conversation soon turned to what was happening with the California Spider. Sirol pulled out the fax from his briefcase and read through the information and handed it to Nino.

'Good, that's very good. Max was right,' said Nino.

'He usually is. He supplied a 250SWB to Silvio Mazzali a few weeks back and it is outstanding. We've got it in the service workshop at the moment. Lovely car,' Sirol replied.

'I spoke to Max on the way down here. He said that the California was all okay. Complete numbers matching car,' Pierre added.

'What do you think about the price?' asked Nino.

'That's down to you Nino, there aren't loads of these cars around. It's the right car. I think you will have to pay that sort of money,' Sirol replied.

'Okay, okay; I'll make him an offer first,' said Nino, '...and see how we get along.'

Sirol was almost like a father to Nino who always looked up to him as the dad he never had. He'd often go down to Sirol's home or garage and loiter around. Really, he was a lost soul, trying to find a focus. He was a genius in his business having amassed a multi million-dollar fortune in the thirty-six years of his life, following the design and patenting of unique micro switches used throughout the world in the electronics industry. But his personal life was almost bare. He seemed to have few friends and no lasting girlfriends. It appeared to be a real waste. There would be so much a good woman could have done with him.

Sirol looked back across the table at Nino and put the inspection fax back into his briefcase and said, 'Nino. You asked me to find you a California Spider in red with excellent provenance and that's what Max has found. Please don't go and upset him with a silly offer, not after all the trouble he's gone to.'

'No, I won't do that, of course not.'

'If you do make him an offer, make it close to what he's asking. I know Max, he doesn't put a lot on top, so the price will be near to the owner's selling price.'

'Okay, I understand,' said Nino.

'The other thing is that, at the moment, we are in the front seat to buy the car, but now there will be a lot more people knowing that the car is available. Everyone at Long Island Ferrari will have looked at it and someone over there is bound to say something. We need to be careful and make sure we don't lose it,' said Sirol as tactfully as he could.

'Okay, that makes sense. I'll call Max on Monday when we get back.'

'Hi Graham, it's Max. I've had the result of the inspection from Long Island Ferrari. It's all okay. The chassis number, gearbox number, differential casing back axle number, engine number and the numero interno are all matching, so Sangster was right, it is a proper car. I've tried calling the customer but he's away racing in France, but I have spoken to the race team manager and he told me that Long Island Ferrari had contacted Angelo at Ferrari and confirmed the information by fax. So it all sounds okay.'

'Well that's good. I've just spoken to Steve Majendie

and he's told me much the same. Sangster's jumping up and down though,' said Graham.

'Why?'

'Long Island Ferrari virtually pulled his car apart. Apparently, all the interior, the seats, the carpets, the gearbox tunnel were all out of the car to do the inspection. He turned up unannounced when they were putting it back together.'

'Well, what did he think they were going to do? View it from afar and say, yeah that's okay.'

'It's Sangster, that's what he's like. He'll calm down. It's also Majendie, he panders to him rather than telling him to shut up. I mean for God's sake, we're about to get him the top price ever paid for one of these cars and he's moaning all the time. Steve should put him in his place. Trouble is that he's used to getting his own way all the time,' Graham said.

'Nothing is going to get done over the weekend, so I guess we'll get it finished sometime next week. I'm still waiting for the original signed contract on the GTO. Oh, that reminds me, I need to speak to Angelo about the provenance on the car.'

'I thought the description was agreed?' Graham asked.

'Yes it is, but I said I would check with Ferrari so that he can race in the Shell Historic Series. It shouldn't be a problem.'

'No, it shouldn't,' Graham replied adding, 'Oh, that's right, I knew there was something else I needed to speak to you about.'

'It's not the Jaguar XJR 15 customer changing his mind?' asked Max.

'No, that's definitely dead and buried. I won't get him to change his mind.'

'That's a pity,' said Max.

'Yes it is, but never mind. The other matter was 360 Spiders.'

'What about them?' Max asked.

'When I spoke to you a couple of months ago, you said you had a few coming.'

'That's right, I do. I've got eight cars coming from one source, which are four left hand drive and four right hand drive, then I've got two left hand drive cars and a possible third car arriving soon, and also I have two right hand drive cars coming from Isca Ferrari. I've got a few other customers and dealers that I know have cars coming and I've told them I'd have their cars too. So, quite a lot really.'

'I think I can sell some of those cars for you if you are interested. Have you sold any of them?'

'No, they're all unsold. The thing is, Graham, that I need to make as much money as possible for these cars, because I've committed myself to them. I've told people that I will definitely buy them and they are relying on me to come through.'

'Where are you getting them from?' asked Graham.

'The batch of three are due any day now and they are European cars. Obviously the two right hand drive cars from Isca Ferrari is straightforward enough!' Max replied.

'What about the other eight? Could I have one of them?'

'They aren't due to early next year.'

'No, I need one as soon as possible,' said Graham.

'You are not going to get one Graham. My first cars are coming any day now and they are coming through a very good customer of mine who has some clout at his local Ferrari dealer. All of them are F1 gearboxes, one is blue with tan, one is silver with blue interior and the other one is Giallo Fly yellow with black interior. I won't be able to sell you the yellow one for a while because my guy wants to use the car for a few thousand kilometres, have some fun with it and then sell it, but I will get it at some point.'

'What sort of money do you want for them?'

'The three European cars will be £30,000 over list,' Max replied.

'Do you think you'll get that?' Graham asked.

'Yes, I will. We've had loads of enquiries for them. I could have sold a hundred of them without any trouble at all. People have been offering me money for them for months, but I haven't done anything about it, because it's too far in the distance to tie myself up with a contract.'

'What do you want for the right hand drive cars?'

'Well, I'll be one of the first customers to get them. As far as I know nobody in the country had ordered and paid a deposit for the cars when I placed my order, so I'm expecting two of the first batch of UK cars.'

'What do you want for those?' Graham repeated.

'I've sold both of them Graham. I got £100,000 for one and £110,000 over for the other and the customers have paid a deposit.'

'They must be mad,' said Graham.

When that car comes out and the first ones roll into the

UK, there will be customers out there ready and willing to pay huge premiums for these cars. They won't want to wait two or three years to order a car from Ferrari. They'll want it now and if they've got the money they'll pay the price. As I said, I've had loads of enquiries and not enough cars. I've got a list of potential customers here beside me. All I've got to do is ring them,' said Max.

'Unbelievable. Anyway it's a left hand drive car that I need. Could you do anything with that silver European car coming in now?' Graham asked.

'I don't know Graham. Let me have a think about it and I'll let you know.'

'Okay, I'll do that and speak to you next week about it. Anyway, we've got a lot on, so next week should be good.'

'Let's hope so.'

Max put down the phone having wished Graham a good weekend. Everyone at the time involved in the business was after Ferrari 360 Spiders. Max had resisted the opportunities to sell his cars, for many reasons, but mostly because the nearer it got to the arrival time of the cars, the more money he could make. It made sense that if he had a car coming next week, he'd get more for it from a customer than he would if it was coming in three months once the deliveries had started.

Max had deliberately not told Graham where his cars were coming from with the exception of the two being supplied by Isca Ferrari. He needed to keep that to himself. The cars from Muzi were coming from two different places, four from the USA and four from the right hand drive South Africa market. Dimo's cars were ordered from Sebastien's in Spain. Max didn't want to disclose the details of the supplying dealer because he didn't want to in any way jeopardise any part of the deal. If nobody knew, then nobody could call the dealer direct. The last thing Max would want is the dealer finding out was that he was selling the cars for a vast profit. Whilst it may not hurt him then, it might effect him the next time Ferrari produced a new model and Velodrome's name was on the waiting list. It wasn't worth the aggravation.

Graham put down the phone and immediately called Donald Key. It was late, but Don was in his office and picked up.

'Don, it's Graham, I think I might have a 360 Spider for you.'

'Oh good, my customer will be very pleased. He was the

guy who bought the silver 360 Coupe that we got from Velodrome.'

'Right,' said Graham, going on, 'I've spoken to my contact and he has a silver 360 Spider F1 coming in soon. It was due at the end of September. It's left hand drive, as I said F1 gearbox, blue scurro interior, Scuderia badges, electric seats, blue roof, red callipers.'

'That sounds perfect,' Don replied.

'I'm waiting to hear about price and definite delivery but I will know more next week.'

'Well, keep on it Graham, we'll go for that if we can agree everything.'

They finished their telephone conversation and agreed to speak during the following week. Graham obviously didn't want Don to know where the car was coming from so never mentioned Velodrome.

Graham sat back in his chair and felt pleased with himself. Things were going well and it wasn't costing him anything, just a few phone calls that's all.

NOVEMBER 1981

When Max came around, he could feel someone pushing a needle into his head sewing up a two-inch long gash behind his ear. He wasn't quite focussed, everything was still a bit blurred. He could see the doctors and nurses running around, but he couldn't make out what they were doing or more to the point what he was doing.

He thought he could hear Neil on the other side of the curtain talking to someone but he wasn't sure. He couldn't remember anything about the accident a few hours before. He felt stiff and restricted all over and he had the worst headache he could ever remember. Someone switched off the light.

He woke up the following morning, he was hot and it was stuffy. The orderlies were shunting trolleys and equipment around the ward, making a hell of a noise. His eyes felt heavy. The next time he woke up, it was gone lunchtime and he felt a lot more with it. He sat up in bed, there was a drip in his arm and someone had stuck something up his nose, which felt a bit uncomfortable. Neil was in the next bed alongside him asleep.

I could do with a cup of tea, he thought. The sister walked onto the ward and looked at Max, picking up the clipboard at the end of the bed, then looking at Max again.

'How are you feeling?' she asked.

'My head feels a bit sore, but otherwise okay.'

'You've been concussed. You were out for nearly three hours. We're going to keep you in for a few days and keep an eye on you, okay?'

'Yes, that's okay. Does anyone know I'm here?' Max asked.

'Your parents have been informed, we've told them that you're both okay, a bit battle scarred but you'll be all right. Let me just have a look at that wound.'

She turned Max's head and looked at the stitches, and caught hold of his arm and measured his pulse whilst looking at the watch hanging from her bib. A nurse walked in with a piece of folded paper and gave it to Max. He opened it. The telegram read, Happy 21st Birthday, You just made it. Love Dad. Max read it a few times; he'd forgotten it was his birthday and he'd forgotten about his father chasing him around the garden with a shovel the day before. Things were coming back to him.

'How's Neil?'

'Much the same as you. A few knocks and cuts but nothing much. It looks like you both banged your heads together. From what I hear you were both very lucky to get away with it. I spoke to the ambulance crew who brought you in. Your car was so badly damaged, they didn't know what sort of car it was. Anyway, you're in safe hands now. Just rest,' she said.

The sister and nurse were about to leave , 'Just one more thing. A girl rang this morning asking after you. She didn't leave a name.'

Max said 'thank you' and they wandered off to their next patient. He didn't know who would have called to ask after him. He knew who he'd like it to be, but there was little chance of that. He dozed off.

Sleep gave his body the chance to recharge its batteries. He wasn't badly injured, neither of them were, but the impact had been very hard. They were lucky, they could have easily been killed. They weren't wearing seat belts, driving along in an open top car doing eighty miles per hour, somersaulting and rolling several times before coming to rest in the middle of the road and being hit at seventy mph amidships by an oncoming car. Fortunately nobody else was seriously hurt either. The irony of it was that had they been wearing seat belts, the probably would have lost their lives, because their bodies would have been held upright, where they were actually thrown into the foot wells of the car escaping serious injury.

Max laid in his bed, his eyes closed, lunch was over and there was nothing else to look forward to until teatime. He was thinking. If he didn't have any money before, he certainly didn't now. His car was almost certainly beyond repair. There'd be no racing for him, that was for sure.

He heard the click of heels walking up the corridor and an American girl speaking in her soft Yankee voice. She sounded warm. A nurse walked into the ward and pointed at Max. 'Bed number four,' she said. A tall blonde typically American looking girl stepped in through the doorway and walked towards Max's bed and asked if it was okay to sit on the bed. He thought about saying that she could get in if she liked, but thought better of it. He was perplexed. He had no idea who she was. He'd never met her before in his life and she hadn't introduced herself.

'I've travelled several thousand miles and my best friend has just collected me from Gatwick airport. She thought it would be nice to come and see you.'

Max wondered if she'd got the right patient and was just about to say something when his heart suddenly blipped. In through the ward doorway walked Catherine. She was smiling and quickening her pace as she got closer to him. He smiled and held his arms out to hug her. He didn't know what it all meant, he didn't care, she was in his arms, and that was the best birthday present he could have ever asked for.

MAY 2004

Ralph Sanders listened to the messages on his answer phone and looked at his watch. It was probably a little bit late to call, but he'd give it a try. It was 9:40 pm.

'Hello.'

'Oh, hello, it's Ralph Sanders speaking. I'm just returning your call. Sorry I missed you earlier, I've been out today. How can I help you?' he asked.

'I've stumbled across something abroad that I need your help with.'

'Oh?'

'Yes, I understand you are the main man to speak to in order to get the car verified.'

'Can you tell me anything more?'

'It's a bit difficult at the moment. We've got some friends around and I don't think this is going to be a five minute conversation.'

'I'm intrigued.'

'You will be. Can I ask you. Would you be happy to sign a confidentiality agreement with me regarding the car?'

'Yes, that's not a problem. I wouldn't speak to anyone about inspections or cars that I was working on for other clients anyway, but yes, a confidentiality agreement is perfectly understandable,' said Ralph.

'Okay, I'll call you tomorrow. Any particular time suit you best?'

'I'm out first thing, but I'll be back after ten o'clock,' Ralph replied.

'Okay, I'll speak to you then.'

Ralph put down the phone, with a puzzled look on his face. He'd been around long enough to know that it was a serious conversation. Nobody asks for a confidentiality agreement unless it's important and the way the telephone conversation had run, he felt that it could be interesting. The guy obviously had something or thought he had something and he was laying down the ground rules straightaway. That indicated to Ralph the type of man he was dealing with.

He couldn't stop thinking about it. It could of course be nothing, but what if it wasn't. What if it was a discovery, a long lost gem hidden from the public for decades. What if it was the "find" of the century. Probably not, but it was nice thinking about it. At his time of life and all the history he knew about the cars, the chance of finding a 'lost' car was extremely slim. Anything of any worth pre World War 2 stood little chance of being found now. All the treasure hunters had taken seventy-five years to dig around and all the good stuff had been bagged a long time ago.

The phone call that Max had been waiting for all morning came through just after lunch. It was Nino.

'Hey, Max. How are you?'

'Yes, good. You? Good racing?'

'Yes, very good. I didn't win, but I finished without damaging the car, so I'm pleased about that. I need a bit more speed though.'

'It will come, it just takes a while to get used to these things.'

'I know, Max, firstly thank you for sorting out the California Spider for me. I've spoken to Ferrari and Sirol and I would like to buy the car. I want to make an offer on it. $1.35M. I know it's less than what you are asking but it is a little more than I was expecting to pay.'

'Nino, I can't do it for that. I'd lose money.'

'Okay, is there a price that we can agree here and now?' asked Nino tentatively.

'I'm sure there is.' Max knew there was. Nino wanted the car. He'd made a sensible offer. It was just a matter of pushing him up a little. Max weighed in at $1.4M and accepted one point three seven five million dollars plus shipping. Come the end, it had turned out to be a fairly straightforward deal. Nino had told Max that the money would be transferred from his Credit Suisse bank account once Sirol had the contact with Velodrome sorted out.

Two days later, the money for the California Spider arrived and was forwarded to Sangster's account. The car never left long Island Ferrari so the shippers collected the car direct from the Ferrari dealership.

Nino was pleased. It was the right car and confirms the adage, that money makes money. In the next six years that car had risen in value from an all time record price of $1,375,000 to £6,000,000! They don't come much better than that, you just have to get the right car and some funds!

Max called Graham Lord and let him know that the deal was done. He organised the airfreight forwarding and all the paperwork so that the car would be in Switzerland the following week.

The profit on the deal was split equally between Velodrome and Graham Lord, so Max transferred Graham's money in to his account and effectively closed the deal. Now it was time to concentrate on the 330 GTO for Muzi. Max needed to call Angelo at Ferrari to sort out the issue over the Shell historic paperwork and entry eligibility. Angelo was on holiday for two weeks and no one else was dealing with that type of work at the factory.

Max called Muzi. 'Hi, it's Max, I tried to speak to Angelo at Ferrari earlier regarding the eligibility of the 330, but unfortunately Angelo's away and nobody else can deal with it for me. I'm afraid we are going to have to wait a couple of weeks for confirmation.'

'Don't worry Max, that's okay. It's not going to make a difference anyway. It all looks okay, so we shouldn't have a problem, should we?'

'No, not really.'

'Good, well don't panic. We'll sort it when he returns. We've all got to have holidays you know. I sent the original contract papers back to you this morning, so I guess you'll get those in a few days,' said Muzi.

'Oh good. Thank you. I haven't heard from the sellers today but I'm expecting to later, so I'll give you a call as soon as I know a little more.'

'Then it's the Ferrari 250 Testa Rossa,' said Muzi.

'Yes, I've got something in mind for that one.'

'Good, keep me posted.'

Muzi disconnected the call. Max couldn't believe how easy he was to deal with. It was amazing how matter of fact he was about spending millions of dollars on old cars. He was delighted, of course, so long may it continue.

Graham Lord was back on the phone. Max told him about Angelo being away for a fortnight and not being able to get the eligibility papers, but neither of them were worried about it. Like Graham had said about the California Spider, it was just a formality.

The subject came around to the silver Ferrari 360 F1 Spider due in September.

'Max, my client is keen on your silver 360 Spider. Is there any way we can do a deal with you on that car?'

'Not really, Graham, unless you want to pay me the £30,000 over the list price.'

'I don't think he wants to pay that kind of money. Are you at all negotiable?' Graham asked.

'I don't think so Graham. I need as much as I can for them. I only have a few cars and I'll need to do well out of them.'

'What is the list price?'

'It hasn't been given out as yet, but we are expecting it to be around £110,000 tax paid.'

'Can we buy them tax free?'

'Yes, I think so, I'll have to check. I can call my customer and ask him if you like. Where is the car going? European market or elsewhere?' Max asked.

'I think it's going to the Far East.'

Graham knew it was going to Japan, but didn't want Max to know, just in case he put two and two together. Silver Ferrari going to Japan, sounds familiar.

Graham was desperate to do the deal on the car and Donald Key's Asian client was equally desperate to buy the car, but none of them wanted to pay £30,000 over list. Max wasn't bothered. Yes, he could do with the money but he didn't want to undersell the car, knowing that he would get his price when it arrived. And it wouldn't be long before he had it anyway. Graham would have to pay the price or get one from somewhere else.

There was no doubt that Graham was irritated by Max's stance, but he had to call back Donald Key and see what could be done. Don answered.

'Graham, I'm off on holiday for a week. I can't deal with it whilst I'm away, but you can speak to Julian, he knows all about it.'

'All right Don, I'll liaise with him and the seller and hopefully we can get something done. By the way, where are you going?' asked Graham.

'Oh, Karen and I are doing the Mille Miglia in the 750 Monza.'

'Hey, that sounds fantastic, have a good time. I wish I was coming with you.'

'Well, thanks. Speak to Julian, he'll sort you out,' said Don.

Graham put down the phone and thought about having to speak to Don's son Julian. He thought he was a complete idiot, a cocaine-snorting idiot at that. If ever there was a candidate for blowing away his father's business, it was going to be him. He wasn't looking forward to it.

He sat thinking, he was searching for an angle to prise the 360 Spider out of Max. If he wouldn't sell it for less than £30,000 over list, there had to be a different way of making it work. He didn't want to speak to Julian, but he was going to have to.

He sat back in his chair and put his feet up on the desk, leg stretched out in front of him and laughed to himself. The last time he spoke to Gerry Bayles, another specialist Ferrari dealer, Gerry had referred to Julian as being the industry beach ball. 'What do you mean "beach ball"', Graham had asked, and Gerry had replied, 'Well there's nothing sharp on him!' And he was right, Julian didn't know what he was doing. Everything he did was based on blagging it. He knew hardly anything about what he was supposed to be doing! If a guy was interested in buying a high value Ferrari then he deserved to know that the guy selling him the car knows what he's talking about. Well, Julian didn't.

Both Graham and Max knew plenty of people that had tried to buy a car from Donald Key Restorations where Julian had been involved and it had come to nothing. Basically, Julian put them off. He was the sales director at Donald Key Restorations officially, but unofficially he was the SPO – sales prevention officer!

Looking at it another way, Max had always thought it was a good thing, because if a customer had gone to Donald Key first, then Max thought he had a much better chance of selling a car if the same customer came to him. In a lot of respects, Donald Key didn't know what he had and what he didn't. He could have done a lot better if only he had taken a much closer look at his son's involvement. Don was so preoccupied with the restoration side of the business that he neglected the sales side. Customers were unlikely to tell him. Julian might sell a car now and then and that would justify his being, but the overall impression was poor.

Max had rung him several times about different cars and Julian either couldn't be bothered to ring him back or lost the number or when he did ring back, he came across as an ill-informed babbling fool, and a spoilt one at that.

At twenty two, maybe Julian wasn't mature enough, maybe he was still wrapped up in the Ferrari ego trip thing, but whatever, he didn't take the job as seriously enough as he should have done. It wouldn't be a surprise if his end of term report read, 'Could have done better, doesn't concentrate, if only he would put his mind to it, his work is erratic'. All of it would be right.

Graham had thought of something that might work and called Julian.

'Hi Julian, it's Graham.'

'Hi, Graham, everything all right with you?'

'Yes, thank you.'

Graham didn't offer the pleasantries in return, he hadn't the time to be nice to Julian, and continued, 'We need to sort out the 360 Spider for your Asian client. I've been speaking to my client who has the car coming. Have you got any ideas on encouraging him to part with the car?'

Graham was in fact drawing Julian in. He knew what he wanted Julian to do, but he wanted to suck it out of him as if it was Julian's idea.

'What like paying a deposit?' asked Julian.

Dumbo, Graham thought. 'No, it would need to be more than that. Anyone could pay him a deposit.' Graham replied and carried on,

'No, what we need to do is make the deal irresistible to him. A deposit wouldn't be enough. I think it needs to be more than that.'

'What if we agreed a price and gave him a 50% deposit?' Julian suggested.

'Well, I could try. Would you be happy with that?'

'Yeah, I'd be okay.'

'I'll tell you what, I'll give the client a call and come back to you. Are you going to be around?' asked Graham.

'Yeah, I'll be here. Cheers, Graham.'

'Bye.'

Graham put down the phone. He had no intention of calling Max, he knew what the answer would be. A 50% deposit on a £140,000 car wasn't going to make enough of a difference to justify a significantly lower price. He'd have to do better than that. He thought he'd leave it half an hour or so before he rang Julian back. Make it look like he was doing something.

He tapped out Julian's direct dial number.

'Hi, Julian, it's Graham again.'

'Oh, hi Graham, how are you?'

Graham thought, *what a stupid fucking question to ask.* He'd only spoken to him half an hour ago, how much was he likely to change in that time – idiot!

'Yes, fine thank you. I've just come off the phone to my client.'

He hadn't of course, but it sounded good.

'And we've had a very long talk. Nobody can get hold of these cars, so he doesn't want to accept your offer.'

'Okay, what do you suggest?' Julian asked.

'Well, as I see it, we have two choices. We either make a better offer or we walk away. I think your father was rather hoping you would have it sorted by the time he got back.'

By replying to Julian the way he had, Graham was putting pressure on Julian to perform so that his father would be pleased on his return. The idea of walking away from the deal was not an option. Graham was playing to Julian's weakness.

'What if we agree a discounted price and we pay him up front in full?'

It was the suggestion Graham was waiting for.

'Do you want me to ask my client and call you back?' Graham asked.

'Yeah, do that. Let's see if that will work.'

'Okay, I'll call you back.'

Graham had the offer that he wanted, to go back to Max. He pressed speed dial five and Max answered.

'Max, I've got a deal for you on the 360 Spider.'

'Okay, fire away.'

'I've been talking to my client this morning and he's suggesting that for a small discount on the car, what if he paid up front in full?' Graham held his breath. Max said nothing for a while, he was thinking.

'Max, are you still there?' asked Graham.

'Yes, I was just thinking?'

'Well, what do you think?'

'I don't know Graham. I'm not going to say no, and I'm not going to say yes either. In principle, it's interesting. I just need to give it a little more thought.'

Graham thought Max was either playing it very cool or just being difficult. He hoped it wouldn't be the latter.

'Can I come back to you later on it Max?'

'Yes, give me a couple of days and I'll give it some serious thought.'

Graham realised that Max was half-interested and knew that he didn't need to push him. He would let him reach a decision and hope it was favourable. It would be five thousand pounds in commission if Graham did the deal.

Max thought about the offer. He would still make a good profit and he'd have the money for the car as well. He wasn't sure though. He would rather wait until the car arrived, sell it clean with no fuss. That would be his preferred method, but it was tempting.

AUGUST 2008

The early morning tally at 7:15 am served as a wake up call for those oversleeping. Max was already up. He'd got himself into a routine. Get up at 7:00 am, switch on the radio, get dressed and wander into the kitchen and make a cup of tea. The tea bags needed to be inspected closely as there were two types of bags. One type had larger holes in them and that was the ones Max needed. They at least had some flavour, whereas the others wouldn't taste like anything other than stewed cardboard no matter what you did with them. Once Max's canteen order came on line, he could order PG Tips and some decent milk, but for now he'd have to make do with prison issue.

On a weekday he would then go into the ablutions block for the usual three esses and then wait for the front doors to be opened for breakfast. All the residents or was that ' rodents' on the unit would assemble in front of the doors ready to go and then there would be the usual cow mooing and sheep bleating as the herd moved off outside and up the short walk to the dining hall. He would usually sit down for breakfast at about 8:00 am, mindful not to sit down next to anyone looking at all suspicious. A bit difficult in a prison. He wouldn't want to get labelled as being a nonce by association for sitting down next to one. He also wanted to avoid sitting down near the Taliban corner shop bomb-making department for obvious reasons. Choose the biggest hairy arsed looking thug, sit next to him. That was the advice he'd had right from the start and it usually worked.

It was day five of his induction and he had just one lecture to attend at 9:00 am that morning, namely kinetic lifting and gym induction. The new recruits ambled up to the front doors of the gym and awaited their tour. A Mr. O. arrived. He looked fit. He looked ex military. He was at Leyhill now as a prison officer, but he definitely looked like he'd been in the army

292

or the marines. He had that air about him. He kept it short and to the point, gave us the guide, the safety talk and a whizz around all the equipment and then he was gone. Max was then ushered into another gym area for more form filling and that was it. Finished for the day, which was great news. He could do what he wanted.

Sat 9th August was going to be a good day. It was the first time since July 14th that he would be seeing his two daughters. It had been a long four weeks and he couldn't wait.

The first time he did something at Leyhill it was always with a little apprehension, the rules could easily be misunderstood or forgotten. He never quite knew whether he had followed the correct procedures to arrive at a point that he hoped was where he was meant to be. Max need not have worried. He'd followed the requirements to the letter and found himself in the assembly annexe outside the visiting hall, with his personal belongings sheet in his hand, waiting to be called.

The door was unlocked for the fourth or fifth time and a prison officer returned to sit himself down behind a desk and sifted through a pile of visiting order paperwork. After a twenty minute wait, he heard his name called.

'Reed?'

Max walked into the small room and handed in his identity card.

'Personal belongings?'

Max handed over the personal belongings sheet, that is to say anything that he had on him that wasn't prison issue. As long as it was recorded, he could take items into the visiting hall, but he had to come back out with them. He would be searched on the way out, so if it wasn't on that sheet it would be confiscated.

'Table thirty seven.'

Max went through the door and into the visiting hall. He didn't need to find Table thirty-seven, his two daughters were running up the aisle to see their dad. Catherine was following close behind. It was an emotional moment. The hardest thing for him in prison was dealing with his head. He had to keep it all together and that would be difficult when he was missing his family and friends. They will write and that helps, but the visits make it easier. Max only had a short sentence, but knowing he had a strong loving family on the outside made the time go quicker.

The visiting hall at Leyhill is very family orientated.

There's a children's play area, a coffee snack bar and the prison officers keep their distance. It's a peaceful co-existence. The only problem is that the visiting time is never long enough. Two hours go in a flash and then it's time to say goodbye. Max said his goodbyes and waved to them to the very last moment.

A prison officer shouted out, 'Stay at your seats, put your rubbish in the bins and bring it with you when you're called.'

Time for a reality check, Max thought. *And be treated like a second-class citizen again.*

'Reed?'

Max got up with his rubbish bag and walked back to the prison officer's desk, collected his identity card and stood to one side to be patted down. He said nothing, then walked out through the door he'd come in earlier and returned to his room.

He'd had a great time playing with his children, laughing and joking, and they were happy to see him. His eldest daughter was seven and the youngest was two and a half years old. Catherine looked as beautiful as ever. After twenty-three years of marriage, she still amazed him.

The visit had given Max a boost. It was now a matter of getting his head down and getting through it. He'd collected his sports clothes that morning and thought it was time for a run. He didn't want to run, but he had to do it if he wanted to maintain some kind of fitness.

Ever since 2000, he'd been running usually ten to fifteen miles per week, so having been banged up in Exeter Prison for three weeks, he could now get the chance to stretch his legs. He put on the prison issue sports clothing and then looked at the 'home made prison service' trainers. *How could I possibly run with these on*, he thought. They were like pseudo leather uppers with a huge plastic sole, affectionately known as the Adidas Two Stripes!

With no watch, Max set off on a lap he'd figured out during his many walks to and from the previous day's education courses. He counted the strides and tried to work out how long it took and how far he was running. It didn't really matter, but as long as he was jogging for forty to forty-five minutes, that would be good enough. He started at the A unit office, up the hill, passing the weeping willow and the maize on his left then the small gym on the right, off the path and up to the main road turning right for a couple of hundred yards keeping on the left

294

hand pavement passing the reception on his left. Then turning left, he'd run up the hill to the gym at the top and do a u-turn between the two manhole covers and then run back down the left hand side of the road passing the allotments on his left then after turning left he'd be back on the main road for another couple hundred yards so that he could take the first left up and past the "C" unit blocks and follow the road around the top and back down the other side with the Enterprise Unit and the OMU on his left. He would then rejoin the main road, this time turning right past the tall Russian Oak on his left, over the speed hump for about three hundred yards and then left by the old GPO telephone box. Down the hill passing the back of the kitchens, through the gap between the laurel hedges onto the path leading back to the A unit office passing the Dining Hall on his right. In all he reckoned it was about 0.8 miles per lap and it took him on that first effort forty minutes to do six laps, a seven and a half minute mile or thereabouts. Not brilliant, but he hadn't run for a while, so there was room for some improvement. The Adidas two stripes, didn't help, he could feel every pebble, every surface as if he was running bare feet. Not good.

OCTOBER 2000

Dimo walked into Sebastien Ferrari. He was just passing and wanted to speak to Victor about the three 360 Spiders.

'Ah, Victor, how are you?'

'Well, thank you.'

'And you're looking good too,' said Victor.

'I was just passing. I wondered if you had any news on the 360 Spiders.' Dimo asked.

'I was going to call you. I'm glad you've come in. We've got a little bit of a delay on them at the moment.'

'Oh, why's that?'

'Ferrari have two problems with the car. The roof is proving difficult to manufacture and it's causing production problems and also the xenon lights are burning the paintwork a little. This is not a big problem. Ferrari will sort it, but it means we won't get the cars until Christmas?'

'Are you sure?'

'Yes, I'm sure, you will get your cars at Christmas.'

'Okay, well I'm glad I came in.'

'I would have telephoned you next week Dimo. You've saved me a call.'

'Okay, I'll leave it with you.'

Dimo got back into his Porsche Convertible and headed off towards the marine at Porta Benuiz. It was another beautiful sunny day and the traffic was bumper to bumper along the waterfront. Dimo pressed his sum card into the slot on the dashboard and switched on the comms pack. The display lit up and he trawled through the alphabet to 'R' and then pressed the button to reveal all the contacts listed with 'R' and selected Reed, pressing again to phone Max.

'Hey Max, how are you? Just a quickie. I went into Sebastien's about ten minutes ago and spoke to Victor. There's a delay on the Spiders.'

'How long?' Max asked.

'They won't be here until Christmas, that's what he's saying.'

'Is he sure?'

'Yes, he says definitely.'

'Okay, Dimo. Thanks for letting me know.'

Max put down the phone. 'Bollocks,' he said. He was banking on getting in the sixty thousand pounds profit from the two cars September and now it was going to be late December. Nobody does anything work wise in December, particularly Ferrari, so realistically it would be the first week in January. It was not good news and Max knew it. The bike sales and the Ferrari sales would all slow down in the winter months and he was hoping that the sixty thousand pounds would help the cash flow into the new year. Now he was going to be more on the back foot and he didn't like the thought of that.

Steve Majendie had called Graham Lord several times and had left messages each time asking for Graham to call him back. He thought that perhaps he was away. It seemed strange that he wasn't returning his calls. He never said he'd be away at all. He kept an open mind and rang Max.

'Hey Max, how's it going?'

'Yes, fine thank you Steve.'

'How's your man with the California Spider?'

'Driving it majestically around the Swiss lakes the last

296

time I heard,' Max replied.

'That sounds superb, I was wondering if you could help me. I've been trying to get hold of Graham. Have you spoken to him?' Steve asked.

'Yes, I spoke to him this morning.'

'What number do you ring him on?'

Max read out the number.

'Yes, that's the same number I've been calling. What time did you speak to him?'

'Must have been around ten o'clock.'

'Okay, Max, I'll keep trying. He must have gone out.'

'Yes, I expect so.'

Steve rang off. He was annoyed that Graham hadn't returned his calls. He was getting pestered by his customer regarding the spares for the Jaguar XJR15 and he needed some answers. It was beginning to get embarrassing.

NOVEMBER 1981

Catherine sat on the bed and looked at Max.

'Happy Birthday,' she said. 'Do you know when you'll be getting out?'

'They're saying the day after tomorrow, if I'm okay.'

'What happened?'

'I don't really know. I can't remember much. I was overtaking a car and I remember him swerving towards me. Next thing I was here having my head sewn up.'

'Sorry this is Diane by the way. If you haven't guessed she's my American friend.'

'Yes, I realised that.'

'Hi, Diane, nice to meet you.'

Catherine somehow seemed different. It wasn't like the time when they were at the party. She seemed genuinely concerned. They stayed for maybe an hour. Diane was doing the rounds of the UK, Devon, Stratford, London, the usual and would be staying with Catherine and her parents for a few days before going off to her next destination.

'I'll leave you two for a moment. Catch up with you later,' she said smiling to Max.

He looked at Catherine. 'Thanks for coming. It's good to

see you.' Max didn't know where he was with her so kept it simple.

'I'm taking Diane down to Devon for a few days and then she's off to Stratford to see one of her ancestors,' she joked. 'I thought I'd come up to Colindale,' she looked down, 'and maybe stay a while.'

'Well yes, that would be fantastic. I'll call you when I get out.'

She kissed him and went off with Diane.

MAY 2004

'Okay, so what have you got?'

'Well it's probably better if you ask the questions which are important to you and then I can answer them as best I can. I can tell you that it looks original and I believe it is original. The same family have owned the car since 1932 and therefore it has complete uninterrupted history. I'm not sure how complete it will be, but I'd hazard a guess at ninety five per cent.'

'It's definitely eight cylinder?'

'Yes.'

'Do you know whether it's supercharged or not?'

'Yes, I think it is, only because I know from the owner that the car did not finish at the 1932 Pau Grand Prix because of a supercharger failure. I haven't seen it because the car is so badly stored that I can't get to the right hand side of the car. Thanks for signing the confidentiality agreement by the way.'

'Oh that's okay. I understand. Could you see any numbers on the car?' asked Ralph.

'No, I couldn't see anything. The owner did tell me that the car raced as a factory car on the Targa Florio and that his father bought it direct from the factory.'

'Well this is outstanding. I think I know which car it could be, but I and everyone else thought the car had been lost. I don't want to get your hopes up, just in case it's not quite right, but from what you've told me, it sounds like it's the real thing.'

'I think it is. What I could do with is an indication of where to look for all the confirmation marks and numbers.'

'That's easy enough,' said Ralph, 'what I'd suggest you do, is call me when you are looking at the car and you walk around it whilst I direct you towards the information we need.'

'I'm hoping to go back down to look at it in a couple of weeks. I'll call you the day before I leave and give you a time when I will be with the car and then I can call you on my mobile. How does that sound?'

'Perfect,' said Ralph.

'Good, then I'll speak to you in a fortnight.'

'Bye.'

OCTOBER 2000

Max always hated meetings with the bank and this one was no exception. Nick Salmon had brought a colleague from the Bristol regional head office with him and that didn't bode well. Simon Hughes was Barclays' hot shot commercial regional manager to whom Nick Salmon ultimately answered. If there was a problem outside of Nick's parameter, then it would be Simon Hughes who made the decision.

Initially Max was told that Hughes was with Nick on a fact finding mission, getting up to speed with his portfolio of clients, but it didn't look like that to Max. Keith had prepared all the paperwork and figures the previous week so the bank had plenty of time to read through Velodrome's progress and position.

'How's the foot and mouth disease affected you?' asked Hughes.

'Very badly. As you may or may not know, we were principally an off road competition bike dealer with all the associated stock and service. We've had to change that completely. Our stock has been severely depleted and changed over to road bikes along with the associated stock and services too. The last six months have not been easy,' said Max.

'How much have you lost?'

'In terms of stock, we've probably wiped out over £100,000 of balance sheet stock from the same time last year, but in terms of bike revenue, it's cost us over £150,000 in lost profit. Obviously we've amended some of that by diversifying which has brought in some much needed funds to shore up the company and help fill in the void.'

'Do you think you should have acted sooner?' Hughes

asked quietly.

'Definitely. With the benefit of hindsight, we would have got rid of all the competition stuff straightaway and taken advantage of the spring road bike sales, but as it happened, we didn't know how long the foot and mouth epidemic was going to last and when we did make the decision, the spring bike sale bonanza had gone. There was so much conflicting information at the time, we didn't know where we were. Nobody did. Not even DEFRA. No one person would tell you when the calamity was going to end,' said Max.

'I see. So how have you managed to dramatically increase your turnover?' Hughes knew the answer but he was playing the game.

'We've diversified. We obviously moved into road bikes which are generally more expensive and we've been selling some high value cars,' Max replied.

The cars are something that the bank are not completely happy about and I believe that's been explained to you on previous occasions,' said Hughes firmly.

'Yes, it has, but to be fair, I need to keep my business afloat. I need to be making decisions about making a profit, and if the cars make those profit then I cannot see why you have a problem with it. I'm the one here taking all the risk. If it all fell down tomorrow, the bank would be okay; I wouldn't be, you would.'

'That's all very well, Mr. Reed, but the bank is not keen on the Ferrari sales and we would like you to desist from them. Your projections were all based on motorcycle sales and service and that's why this bank was pleased to support you,' Hughes insisted.

Max was hoping that Hughes would have taken a different view but he was as hard as nails. Max didn't like him. Nick Salmon had said very little in the meeting. Hughes had told Max that the account was being transferred to Bristol under Hughes' direct control although the day-to-day contacts would still be the same at Exeter.

Hughes asked if he could have a look around. Max showed him the parts department and the clothing area with all the accessories. The garage cafe was open with a few customers sat on the bench seating outside.

'Does this work well for you?' Hughes asked pointing at the cafe.

'It keeps us looking busy and it gives bikers somewhere to ride to, so yes it does work. We're never going to become millionaires doing it, but it adds value to what we're doing here.'

'What about your service area? Can I have a look at that?' asked Hughes.

'Yes, okay.' Max knew that the service area would affect him. Max opened the top door for Hughes and Nick Salmon to walk through. They were confronted by a sea of red, with a smattering of blue and yellow. There were eleven Ferraris staring at them. They seemed to be everywhere, double decked on the ramps, one on top, one under, seven 355s of various types, two 308s, a 328 and a 550 Maranello.

'So how are you funding all this?' Hughes asked with some distain.

'We have a good relationship with one supplier for the 355s. He let's us have two or three and we pay for one, which we've usually pre sold, the 550 is here on sale or return as is the 308 GTS. Three cars are sold and paid for, waiting to go out, so we haven't drawn on your support too much.'

Hughes listened but wasn't really interested. He didn't like it. Frankly the swings on Velodrome's bank account were scaring him. With the bikes, the swings had always been low, ten to fifteen thousand pounds one way and then the same or similar in the opposite direction but with the Ferrari sales, the account was swinging one hundred to a hundred and fifty thousand and then back. It would only take something to go wrong, a cash flow blip, a non-payment or something like that and the bank could be looking at a two hundred to two hundred and fifty thousand pounds requirement that the bank would not be prepared to allow. And that could be devastating for Velodrome.

Max finished off the tour, the bike service area and the stores and paused at the door as Hughes was looking at a Ferrari 348 engine on a stand.

'What are you doing here with this?' asked Hughes.

'It's in for repair. The gearbox pinion seal needed replacing so we gave the customer a price and it should be back in the car in a few days,' Max replied.

Hughes looked at the complicated mass of shaped parts and pipes unable to figure out what was what and asked, 'How do you find the expertise to take on this sort of work?'

'It's not complicated. Ferrari would have you believe that it is, but it's not. Motorcycles are far more high tech. If you take a Yamaha YZF-R1, it's a 1000cc rocket, five valves per cylinder producing one hundred and thirty brake horse power easily, and really that is high tech. If you can strip a high performance motorcycle engine with parts as small as a Swiss watch then a Ferrari engine is not a problem.'

Max was pleased to see Hughes get into his car and hopefully drive away as far as possible, but he knew the meeting had marked a watershed in Velodrome's association with Barclays Bank.

'How did it go?' asked Keith.

'I don't know,' Max replied with a sigh, 'they don't like the cars, but we knew that. They're moving the account to Bristol under that other chap Hughes.'

'What about Nick?'

'Yes, we'll still be speaking to Nick as the daily contact, but Nick will probably have to refer to Hughes on some things. I wish we had those two 360 Spiders in and paid for and Muzi's 330 GTO money,' said Max despondently.

'It will come. Don't worry. What have they said about the cars?' Keith asked.

'In a nutshell, don't do them. It's madness.'

'Why?'

'They don't like the swings on the account. It scares them,' Max replied.

'But we're making money on them. What are you going to do?'

Max snorted, 'What I always do,' and smiled, 'take no notice of them, I expect,' adding, 'They're not telling me how to run my business. We'll get the money in from the outstanding cars and then hopefully we won't need to speak to them at all. If we get Muzi's money in, we can stick two fingers up at them.'

'All right, let's get it done and put it behind us. I've done all the cheques with the posting dates on them so all you need to do is sign them and send them. All the input is up to date. Pete's commission is in and done. Don't think there's anything else so I'll see you in two weeks time.'

'Where is it that you're going?'

'Tenerife.'

'Well look, have a good time. Enjoy yourself and don't think about any of this crap.'

'I'll try not to,' said Keith.

Keith left to go on holiday. All his work was up to date

and left neat and tidy. At least Max didn't need to worry about that.

A week later, Max looked at the CCTV monitor in front of him. *Who the hell are they*, he thought.

'Yes Mike,' Max picked up the internal phone line.

'I've got three men here to see you. Won't give me their names. Doesn't look good,' said Mike worryingly.

'Who are they?'

'They won't tell me.'

'Okay, I'm looking at them on the monitor. Is the CCTV on record?'

'I'll make sure it is.'

'Okay, I'm on my way.'

Max put down the phone, and somewhat apprehensively walked out into the showroom and made his way down the central aisle and stopped short of the three huge men, directly between two of the CCTV cameras.

'Can I help you?'

'Max Reed?'

'Yes, that's me.'

'Where's our fucking money. We want it now or we're going to start taking stock. You fucking understand?'

'Hey, hey, hey. What are you talking about?

The men were agitated and looked like they were about to lose it with Max.

'Don't fuck about with us. We've just come down from Rugby and we want our money.'

'Look, just calm down a minute,' said Max.

'Don't you tell me to fucking calm down. I want my fucking money or I want my fucking car back.'

'What car?'

'Are you taking the fucking piss?'

'No, I'm not, just tell me which car, we sell a lot of cars.'

'The 355 you got from that twat at Brooklands.'

'I sold it three weeks ago and I've paid them. They've had their money. What's it to do with you?'

'It's my fucking car and I haven't been paid, that's what it's to do with.'

'Look, I'm sorry but it's nothing to do with me. I bought the car from Brooklands and I've paid for it and that was at least three weeks ago, maybe longer. I can probably prove it to you if you like,' Max offered.

The three men had started to simmer somewhat so Max felt a little bit easier taking them into his office. He picked up his cheque book and flicked back through the stubs and found the Brooklands cheque.

'There you go, the 14th, that's just under four weeks ago,' he said looking across at the calendar, 'fifty seven and a half thousand pounds.' Max reached across to his bank statements file and pulled them down onto his desk leafing through two or three pages to find the correct cheque number.

'There, it went through our account on the 16th. He must have express cleared it.'

'Okay, mate, sorry. He told us that you hadn't paid him, and he told us that you bought it for £5000 less than that. Very sorry about that.'

'It's okay. I'd have taken the three of you on at once anyway,' he smiled.

'Right, let's go and rip his fucking head off.' They left.

Max looked at Pete standing in front of him. 'What was that all about?' he asked.

'Brooklands. They told them, we hadn't paid for that 355 we had off them. Fortunately, we had and I could prove it. They're off up there now and I wouldn't want to be in his shoes.'

'Bloody hell,' said Pete and laughed.

'You know me Pete, I'd have decked them,' he said wryly.

'Yeah,' he laughed.

Catherine had the tea on in the kitchen when Max got home. He kissed her on the cheek.

'Good day?' she asked.

'Yeah, not too bad, you?'

'Yes, we had coffee at Rumours in Totnes this morning with all the girls.' She was rubbing her tummy. 'Little one's been kicking again.'

Max smiled. As soon as he closed those garage doors he completely switched off from work. He wasn't interested in it. His home life was what mattered most. Catherine was expecting their first child at Christmas and they were both looking forward to it immensely. She had given up work in her father's solicitor's office and was having a bit of free time before the offspring came along on the due date of December 25th.

APRIL 1982

The car turned left and up hill onto the flat for several hundred yards before slightly turning right and down hill into the dip, up the other side and into the blind entry Dingle Dell. The driver weaving from side to side in an effort to generate some heat into the tyres. He came out of the woods into the sunshine keeping out to the left before slowing into second gear, then first, creeping towards the marshals waving their flags in front of him. He was fifteenth on the grid on the right hand side of the track. Doug had told him to watch the temperature and angle the car slightly nose down hill to the right to compensate for the sideways slant. Max did just that. It was his first race in proper Formula Ford and Doug was on the pit wall running him. He'd qualified reasonably well all things considered. He only got five minutes practice due to a water pipe fracture, but he'd worked out where he was going. He liked the Grand Prix circuit at Brands Hatch and what a place to have your first race.

He dropped into his grid slot and stopped at the marshal's gesture. Temp, oil, all okay. He could see Catherine on the pit wall with the pit board and Doug chatting to her up ahead. The girl walked across the front of the pack with the thirty second board as the horn sounded. Max's heart was probably beating at two hundred and twenty beats per minute. He lowered his visor to within ten millimetres of closing and checked that the car was in first gear. The red lights on the gantry flashed on. Max counted to three and dropped the clutch. A split second later the lights turned to green. Max was already past the car in front of him and into second gear passing the next row of cars. Doug had told him what to do. He said, 'They won't be watching you back there, just go for it.'

It was an eventful race with carnage on the first corner first lap, and another coming together on the second lap in the same place. Max was up to tenth by half distance as the protagonists were now beginning to string out. Max was slowly reeling in the ninth placed man who was catching the two cars in front of him.

Going over the line for the last lap, seventh, eighth, ninth and tenth could have all been tied together with a shoe lace. Max had got a good run down the hill into clearways and was tucked up behind the other three going over the start finish. Max took the inside line into Paddock driving up the inside of the ninth placed man, squeezing him a bit as he turned into Paddock Hill bend and then running wide on the exit up the hill to Druids. They were weaving all over the track. Max had to cover the inside line and very nearly took out the eighth placed man, but managed to avoid hitting him. It must have put him off though, because he missed a gear coming out of Druids and Max got past him around the outside of Graham Hill bend. He was now eighth and up the chuff of the seventh placed man. The sixth placed driver could just be seen in the distance so there was not much chance of catching him, but seventh was there for the taking. Max followed him at three feet distance out onto the Grand Prix circuit, the pair of them fighting for all they were worth. Max knew he had two chances, one at the blind entry Dingle Dell and the other at Clearways heading onto the start finish. He got alongside him going into Dingle Dell and both cars went through airborne side by side, Max on the right and the other guy on the left. It's a right hand corner, so Max had the inside line and held it along the short straight but his competitor was not giving up either. He now had the inside line for the left hander. They banged wheels on the exit of the corner, side by side with Max having two wheels on the grass with his foot stuck in on the throttle pedal. Absolute madness, but that's youth. They emerged from the darkness of the woods out into the sunlight side by side, Max on the inside for the right hand corner. It was hold your breath time, Max held his line and screamed over the line for seventh, a tenth of a second separating them. He might as well have won, he felt so good. They caught up with the leading pack and slowed, following them back to the pits.

Max got out of the car, Catherine couldn't wait to give him a big hug. Doug was there too, beaming from ear to ear.

'That was brilliant. Absolutely fantastic,' said Max.

'Great to watch Max. We saw you coming down the hill into clearways and we thought that Andy Ackerley had you, but you got him. Brilliant, well done.'

'Who won?'

'I think it was, Bailey, Gugelmin and then Pratt. It was a good race though. You should be pleased.' Max got changed and sat in the pits, soaking it all up. He was on an all time high.

OCTOBER 2000

Tom McKinney was waiting at the railway station in his Ferrari 550 Maranello listening to his favourite U2 CD, humming along to the tune and strumming his fingers across the top of the leather rimmed steering wheel when Max and his driver walked through the exit gate. He wound down the window.

'Hi, all right? Hop in.'

They squeezed into the passenger seat and drove the short ten minute journey over to Tom's house.

'Have you had anything to eat?' asked Tom.

'No, not really,' Max replied.

'Okay, we'll sort the cars later, let's go and get something to eat.' Tom picked up his mobile and dialled Greg's number asking him to meet at the 'Oak Tree Pub'.

Max had known his driver, Paul for the best part of twenty years, in fact since he'd first started going out with Catherine. He'd had his ups and downs in that period but Max had always liked him and was helping him to recover from a recent breakdown. Giving him something to do kept his mind occupied.

Greg sat down at the table next to Jamie Blandford with Tom at the end next to Max. Paul was in between. The conversation was all about cars and bikes.

Max could overhear Paul talking to Jamie.

'So you do a bit of driving for Tom then do you?'

'No, not really, but I said I'd help on this run. I was at a loose end,' said Jamie.

'I collect Max's Ferrari's for him, sometimes deliver them that sort of thing,' Paul mentioned.

'Oh, that sounds good.'

'Yes, it is, keeps me busy,' Paul replied continuing, 'so whereabouts are you then?'

'Blenheim.'

'Oh right,'

'Yes, if you get the chance, you must come along and have a look around,' said Jamie.

'Thanks. The same applies to you if you're ever in Torquay. Look me up. The next time I'm in Germany, I'll give you a call.' Paul said.

Jamie looked at him blankly. Paul had absolutely no idea who Jamie was and it made Max smile eaves dropping on their conversation.

They finished lunch and went back to Tom's house and did all the usual paperwork for the two Ferrari 355s and sat and a cup of tea.

'Tom, can you get hold of a 360 Spider for me? I could do with a tax free car. My customer is based in Monaco?' Max asked.

'When do you want it? I can't get anything this side of Christmas. Early next year is possible.'

'Yes, that would be okay. It must be a new car though, preferably red with black or tan leather and F1 gearbox.'

'Yeah, I can do that. I know of a car coming, so that will be okay. It's red with black, F1.'

'Can I take that as a definite then?'

'Yeah, of course, it's yours.'

'Okay, that's good,' said Max. He was pleased with that. Rick Brady had called him that morning when Max was on the train asking if he could get hold of a red 360 Spider. He wasn't desperate for the car, but he wanted to be sure he could get one. Max would have to take the 360 Modena coupe that he'd sold him earlier in the year in part exchange, but that shouldn't be a problem, he thought. Max trusted Tom to deliver. They'd done a lot of business together and never had any problems. It was easy. They both knew where they stood. Tom found the cars, they were always good cars and Max always bought them.

Paul followed Max out of Essex and around the M25 to the M3 junction and both cars stuck to a steady ninety miles per hour back down the A303 to Newton Abbot.

Graham Lord called Max on his mobile and asked him, 'Have you thought any more about your silver 360 Spider Max?'

Well the answer to that was no he hadn't, but Max had to tell him about the delays anyway.

'Graham, I'm sorry but I won't get the cars until Christmas. My customer went into the dealership last week and he's been told that Ferrari are having problems with the roof manufacturer, and something to do with the lights as well.'

'Oh, that's a pity.'

'Well, it's right across the board, so nobody's going to get a car. They're all delayed, not just ours. You better speak to your customer before we do anything more.'

308

'Okay, I'll call you back.'

Graham sensed the opportunity and so did Max. The thought of being paid up front for a car had become a lot more appealing since Simon Hughes had been down to the garage the week before and now it might be the right time for Max to agree with Graham and do the deal.

Graham called Julian and informed him about the Christmas delivery. Julian said that would be fine.

Max got the call back from Graham.

'Christmas delivery would be okay Max for my client. I've spoken to him and he's perfectly okay with that. He'll still pay you up front in full and you can use the money to buy and sell and make up the amount you would have made if you had waited until it arrived.'

'And the customer knows that?' asked Max.

'Oh yes definitely, it's his suggestion,' Graham replied.

'He's desperate for the car then?'

'Yes, he is, for a number of reasons.'

'Okay, Graham, I'm driving at the moment, and I won't be back in the office tonight, but I will call and sort it out with you tomorrow morning,' Max said.

'That's good. I'll speak to you then.'

'Just one more thing, I knew there was something I needed to tell you. Steve Majendie rang me. He couldn't get hold of you.'

'Well I've been in.'

'I'm just passing on the message Graham,' Max replied.

'When was this?'

'Saturday.'

'Oh, I've spoken to him since then,' Graham said dismissively.

'That's all right then. I'll speak to you tomorrow,' Max rang off. Graham hadn't spoken to Steve Majendie at all. He was avoiding him.

JUNE 2004

'Hey Jacques, it's Max. Are you okay for next week for me to come down again?'

'Yes, that's no problem.'

'Have you managed to clear all that rubbish out of the way?'

'No, but we've moved a lot of it. You can at least now see the car and walk around it. We managed to move the oil tank away from the entrance so it's a lot easier now,' said Jacques, adding, 'Olivier gave the instructions and my friend Michele helped me.'

'Ah, that's good. What about a lead light and an extension?' asked Max.

'Yes, we've got that sorted as well. The only thing that worries us is the end wall over the doors. We'll have to think about that before you take it,' said Jacques.

'Okay, we'll deal with that when the time comes. I've found out a bit more about the car so that's good.'

'Olivier has some old photographs for you as well. Nice old ones of his father with the car outside the front door with some of his racing driver friends in the early 1930s.'

'That sounds good. Absolutely anything however minor could be useful,' said Max.

'What day do you think?' Jacques asked.

'Wednesday afternoon. I'll try to get down in the early afternoon.'

'Okay, ring me before you leave.'

'I will.' Max put down the phone. The plan was coming together. Slowly, slowly catch a monkey.

OCTOBER 2000

'Max, it's Jackie,' said Mike.

'Hi, Jackie, how are you?'

'Max, we've got a problem. Keith had an aneurism on holiday. He was rushed into intensive care. He's not well at all,' she said.

'God, Jackie, I'm so sorry. How is he now?' Max asked.

'Not too good. He doesn't know what day of the week it is. They've put him on Betablockers at the moment and they just knock him out.'

'Is it permanent?'

'We don't know. The blood clot was in his brain and apparently it's not uncommon to have another one. Obviously, he's not going to be in work for a while.'

Pete walked into Max's office being his usual bubbly self, looking at Max inquisitively as he continued speaking to Jackie. He mouthed 'who is it?'

Max wrote 'Keith intensive care' on his blotter.

'Jackie, however long it takes. Is he at home?'

'Yes, but the doctor is monitoring him closely. Probably best not to visit at the moment.'

'Okay, that's understandable.'

Max put down the phone and explained to Pete what had happened. It was very upsetting. Everyone at Velodrome liked Keith and it was such a shame for his young family. *Hopefully he'll make a full recovery, but any problems with your brain is a big deal,* Max thought. Fingers crossed; he'd be okay.

Jackie had sounded tired and worried and she was a nurse, so she should know. Being totally mercenary Max had to think about how it would effect the business if he didn't return, God forbid. It wouldn't be good. Max knew how to input the stock control but he didn't get involved in the purchase ledger, sales ledgers etc. It was another worry Max could do without. He put on a brave face and hoped it wouldn't come to that.

Graham Lord was back on the phone. 'Hi Max. I just wanted to sort out that 360 Spider deal if we can.'

Oh that again, Max thought. He really hadn't thought about it a lot, but it seemed like a sensible deal.

'Okay, Graham, let's do it. Your guy is offering me £120,000 up front for a car that's coming at Christmas. And he knows that I will be using the money to buy and sell so that I can make up the difference between the amount I sell the car for now and what I would have sold it for when it actually arrives?' asked Max.

'Yes, that's right.'

'You're sure?' asked Max.

'Yes, absolutely, a hundred per cent,' said Graham.

'Okay. I will do it on the proviso that the money is in my account no later than seven days from now. If it's not there, I will cancel the order. You need to get that message across,' said Max adding, 'I'll do a contract with all the details on it and fax it to you. If you are happy with it, all that will need to be done, is filling in the customer details. Is that okay?'

'Yes, that's fine. Do the contract and fax it up to me,' Graham replied.

Max didn't do it straightaway. He thought about it for a while, then called Dimo just to be sure that the cars were coming at Christmas.

'Dimo, it's Max. Two things, we've got another 360 Modena going through, so we'll need some funds. There's a 355 GTB coming back in part exchange, so can you roll the funds to cover the 355 as well, because we can retail that. It will stand us in at the right money?'

'Yes, that's okay. Where are you getting the 360 Coupe from? The usual?'

'Yes, it's coming from Josef. I'll collect it next week from Aachen. The part exchange is a yellow 355 GTB with the Fiorano pack on it, a ninety nine car.'

'Sounds good. Okay, just let me know. And the other matter?'

'I just wanted to check that those 360 Spiders are coming in for Christmas?'

'Yes, that's right. That's exactly what Victor has told me.'

'Okay, that's good. I'll give you the details for the 360 in a couple of days.' Max put down the phone satisfied that Dimo was getting the two Spiders at Christmas.

He wrote out the contract for the silver car making sure that it had an overrider on it detailing that the delivery date was subject to the Ferrari factory performing. He felt that covered him, should the car arrive a little bit later. If the customer signed it, then he couldn't say that he didn't know. Max still didn't know who it was.

He faxed the document through to Graham and waited for a response. He got it two minutes later.

'Okay Max, thanks for that. I note the overrider.'

'Well, I've got to protect myself. You know what Ferrari are like.'

'Oh yes, I certainly do. No, that's all okay. I'll run it past the buyer and come back to you.'

'Okay, I'll leave it with you.'

Graham rang Julian and went through the details. It was all okay. Graham confirmed the delivery date and made sure Julian knew that the money had to be in Velodrome's account within seven days or the deal would be cancelled.

Should have guessed, Max thought when he saw the signed contract come back down the fax. Silver car, Japan, should have rung a bell. No worries, the deal was done.

Max pulled out Muzi's file and leafed through the paperwork. The signed original contract was still there that was the main thing. He needed to speak to Angelo.

The receptionist picked up the phone and answered in Italian, and then in English when Max asked to be put through to Angelo.

'Hi, Max, how are you?'

'Very well. Did you have a good holiday?'

'Yes thank you. We went up to the lakes with the family. Very relaxing,' said Angelo.

'Sounds nice.'

'You want to know about the 330 GTO?'

'Yes please.'

'I thought you would. Max it's not good news. We can't accept this car into the Shell Historic.'

'Why?' Max asked with some trepidation.

'Well it's not correct. It's not how it left the factory.

'I know it's had a new body put on it, but it's in the same style as the original, surely that's okay?'

'Max, it's more than that. I can't say what, but it's not eligible.'

Max didn't labour the conversation, he could tell that Angelo was seriously not interested in being convinced otherwise!

He put down the phone and immediately called Graham Lord.

'Graham, Angelo has knocked back the GTO.'

'Why?'

'He says basically it's not how it left the factory.'

'We know that. It's been restored and had an original style body put on it as it would have looked prior to Marese crashing it. I can't see what's wrong with that,' said Graham.

'He's saying there's a lot more to it than that.'

'Do you think Donald Key told you the truth about the restoration?'

'I can't see a reason for him to lie to me. We went through it in detail. It is what it is. A four litre GTO and that's all there is to it. Have you told your customer yet?' Graham asked.

'No, I haven't said anything yet. I need to know some more details before I get him on the phone, otherwise I'm going to look stupid.'

313

'Quite. I'll speak to Donald Key and see if I can find out anything and get back to you. Don't do anything about it until I call you back.'

'No, that's okay, I'm not going to do anything in a hurry,' Max replied and placed the receiver down slowly on the cradle. He sat at his desk, his head in his hands and sighed, thinking to himself that he hoped he hadn't just blown $2,000,000.

SECTION THREE

NEWTON ABBOT, APRIL 1982

Doug took the roof off his Ferrari 308 GTS and jumped in. He was off to Devon for the weekend. He had a couple of stops to make on the way but he'd be at Max and Catherine's before seven o'clock, he was sure. He met up with John Bartelski and Francois Muret to discuss the Willhire twenty-four-hour race they were planning to enter in June, and then it would be a quick stop in Dartmouth to sort out his boat, before blasting back to Newton Abbot. He had a lot going on at the time what with one thing and another.

He dropped down the Old Totnes Road, there were blue flashing lights and a siren behind, beckoning him to pull over. A traffic cop walked up alongside the driver's door of the Ferrari and looked in.

'Your vehicle, sir?'

'Yes,' Doug replied. He didn't like the look of the cop, but he liked the 'sir' bit.

'Had it long, have we?'

Doug thought about saying "what the hell's it got to do with you", but he didn't.

'About six months.'

'Do you know what the speed limit is along here?'

'Thirty mph!'

'That's right, thirty mph. So why were you doing forty mph?'

'I wasn't, I was doing dead on thirty mph.'

'I'm afraid not sir, you were doing forty mph.'

Doug wasn't happy. He was certain he was only doing thirty mph, but he didn't want to get involved in an argument. The traffic was building behind them and Doug didn't want to be late.

'So what do you want to do about it?' asked Doug.

'On this occasion, I'm going to let you go, but mind your speed please.'

Doug wanted to bite back and couldn't resist it. The

traffic cop put his notepad back into his pocket and Doug said, 'I wanted to be a traffic cop.'

'Oh yes, well it's a good job, you know. There was a pause. 'So why didn't you join?'

'Well, I went through all the training, you know. All the usual rubbish.' The cop was nodding his head in agreement. ' I went up to Hendon and did the driving and skid pan course.'

'Oh yes, I know, what year were you there?'

'Oh, '76 or '77 I think.' It was all nonsense of course, but the copper was getting sucked in.

'A bit before me then.'

'Yeah, I passed all the exams and everything, the physical stuff and all that, but never went ahead with it.

'So why didn't you join up, ' the cop enquired.

' Oh that, yes I remember it well. I was called into the office, they found out I'd got a father!'

Doug stuck the Ferrari in first gear and drove off. He hated the police. He hated the petty jealousy of them and the double standards, do as I say, not as I do. He knew that if he'd been driving a Ford Escort or something like that, he wouldn't have been stopped, it was just the green eyed monster that stopped him. The penny dropped by the time the Ferrari was out of sight. Doug laughed. *Wanker*, he thought. However, Doug really couldn't afford to rile the police too much. He had plans and part of those plans were being put into place on that weekend trip.

The meeting with John Bartelski and his sponsor Francois Muret was part business, part pleasure. The pleasure was the motor racing and the business was something totally different. Doug was planning a major voyage. He knew the right people to fund his ideas especially if there was a decent return, and Doug had some big returns in mind.

The yacht moored down on Dartmouth marina was a forty six foot ex ocean race multi hull, well capable of sailing very quickly in the right conditions. Doug had been brought up like Max on the waters edge and spent a lot of his early life by the seaside. He loved everything boats and sails and he could skipper with the best of them. Nothing fazed him, the Atlantic, the Bay of Biscay, he wasn't worried about being alone at sea for weeks on end. It fact he loved it. It was part of life's great adventure, but to do all the great things in his life, he needed money and he was prepared to perhaps deviate from the straight and narrow to get it.

Max always wondered where he got his money from. It wasn't long after Max had been racing with him, that he bought a really nice detached house in Bow near Crediton. He kept his London home and used it whenever he was up that way racing or such like, but spent most of his time in Devon devising his plans.

Max remembered Doug on one occasion collecting him and Catherine from her parent's house. He was in his Rolls Royce Silver Shadow II. It was such a laugh. You only ever see a Rolls Royce being driven slowly and sedately, not Doug, he couldn't care less, he used to thrash his Roller getting the back hanging out, four wheel drifts, it was hilarious.

Doug drove up Catherine's parents drive just after seven o'clock and they swapped cars and drove down to Tuckenhay to their favourite haunt. Max went up to the bar and ordered some drinks and picked up the bar menu and took it back to the table where they were sitting. Judy sat down with them and they talked and laughed until the early hours. Doug didn't want to go and Judy didn't want them to go either. There was a situation developing between Doug and Judy, totally unexpected. Doug was a good ten years older than Judy and he wasn't the type of person Judy usually fell for, but in this instance she had well and truly and so had he, hook line and sinker. It was the start of a real live rock and roll adventure, which would last ten crazy years run at break neck speed across several continents.

OCTOBER 2000

It was an early start for Max, he had to meet Josef at Dusseldorf airport on the 0840 hrs Flybe flight from Bristol International. He asked Paul to accompany him on the way to Bristol and then Paul could drive the car back whilst Max got on the plane.

Josef was waiting in the arrivals hall as Max walked through. The trip to Aachen would take about an hour, so they had time to talk.

'I suppose you've heard about all the 360 Spider delays?' Max asked.

'Yes, it's shit. Ferrari are fucking hopeless. I've got so many cars with deposits paid and now I can't get paid. It's

319

causing me a lot of problems. We'll get through it but I could do without the stress,' said Josef.

Max knew exactly what he meant. He was also getting stressed about it. It was the fear of the unknown. Max just hoped that Dimo's cars would turn up on time.

'How many cars have you got coming Josef?' Max asked.

'A lot, over twenty!'

'Are they all spoken for?'

'What do you mean?'

'Are they all sold?'

'No, I have taken deposits on twelve of them but the others I haven't sold as yet. Are you going to need some? I've got so much trouble with customer's shouting on the phone all the time for their cars and there's nothing I can do about it. They think it's me, but it's not'

'Yes, I probably will. When have they told you that your first cars are coming?'

'Christmas. Probably just after Christmas,' Josef said assertively, 'but you know Ferrari, it's a joke !'

That comforted Max. The story was the same. Roof problems, light problems, resulting in delayed production, and delivery at Christmas. That was good. He felt the weight lift from his shoulders a little.

'What sort of money do you want for them?'

'Around three hundred and fifty thousand Deutschmarks,' Josef replied.

'OK,' said Max. It was a bit more than he was paying for the cars coming from Dimo. It gave him something to think about. At least, he thought, all the dealers appeared to be singing from the same hymn sheet.

They arrived at the garage and Max collected another new Ferrari 360 Modena, fitted his trade plate onto the rear panel recess, waved goodbye to Josef and shot off back to Calais, through the tunnel and home to Newton Abbot before closing time. It had become a boring trip even if he was driving one of the best cars in the world, but now it was just another profit centre and he needed plenty of that if he was to survive the winter. He checked his on line banking account as soon as he got into the office. Nothing from Donald Key he noted. It was early days. In some ways he was hoping that Julian didn't get the money in on time, but on the other hand, the money could be very useful. *Whatever will be, will be*, he thought. He looked through the post laid out on the desk in front of him, seeing if he could recognise any of the envelopes. *I can't be bothered with it now*, he thought. *I'll look at it tomorrow. I'm going home, I've had enough for one day.*

EXETER, SEPTEMBER 2000

A month earlier Sean Williams strolled across the showroom floor at Isca Ferrari with the following year's allocation in his hand. It didn't look good, he was only going to get twelve 360 Spiders and that depended on the company's performance selling the offerings from Maserati as well. If he did well with Maserati, then he might get a few more Ferraris, but it wasn't cast in stone. He needed to reach the targets, then he could bargain, but first he had to shift the metal.

Sean had been brought in to Isca Ferrari to deal with the inadequacies of the previous regime. Sales, service and parts were all just drifting along and they needed a driving force to grab hold of the product and make it happen. There were huge sums of money invested in a high profile business that just wasn't making financial sense. The returns were non existent and even if the range was as prestigious as it was, there was no point in doing it if it didn't make money. The importers had insisted that the showroom be upgraded in line with the brand and the other franchised dealers, so a new site had been acquired and a complete new facility had now become reality as Sean sat down at his desk looking across the shiny tiled floor at the stock laying before him, five cars, two belonging to the garage and three sale or return customer cars. *It's a big ask*, he thought.

When Ferrari was just a Ferrari franchise, in many ways there was less pressure. It wasn't difficult to sell a new car, in fact most of them were pre sold, it was just order taking, the cars sold themselves. But not all the cars sold well especially some of the four seaters, which were generally hugely expensive to buy, wickedly expensive to run and customers were few and far between. The advent of Maserati into the Ferrari fold meant that the Ferrari group could use a lot of the mechanicals within their range and offer them in light disguise in a car badged as a Maserati. Yes, there were more fundamental differences than that, but Maserati were now able to offer with the help of Ferrari's parts bin, a saleable prestigious motorcar in reasonable volume. It was a good potential profit centre for Ferrari dealers, but at first they proved difficult to sell and they were offering discounts to get them out the door, which meant that discounts were cutting into profits. With the exception of the four seaters, all the other new Ferraris were always sold at 'full up' money. Dealers didn't have to discount them, but with Maserati on board, the added costs of running and maintaining the franchise did not make sense, if for one they couldn't sell them in sufficient numbers and secondly couldn't sell them at a decent profit. It took quite a while for Maserati to produce a car that fired up the imagination of the buyer but they had always been difficult to sell and the second hand values have never really held up that well.

Sean's job was always going to be a difficult one. The big profits were with the Ferrari sales and service, but to push that up he needed to sell more new Ferraris. He couldn't sell more new Ferraris unless his allocation was increased and he wasn't going to get a bigger allocation unless he sold more Maseratis, so the pressure was on. What made matters worse was that the importers weren't that reliable either, they could just as easily change their minds too. He had to sell more Maseratis and one way to do that was to sell potential Ferrari customers a new Maserati whilst they were on the waiting list for a new Ferrari. Sean would give the customer a guaranteed part exchange value for the Maserati when the new Ferrari came along subject to the car being serviced and being in the right condition with no more than a certain mileage. It wouldn't work with everyone, but it would work with a lot of customers wanting a new Ferrari. Other customers would be those making up from a different marque, maybe not wanting to leap to a Ferrari in one go.

One problem Sean did have was that the dealership was a relatively new franchise having only been open for a few years and had very little in the way of a customer database. They weren't involved in racing and they had no interest in classic Ferrari, and that is what Ferrari is all about. Heritage. The Ferrari heritage is like no other marque. The staff at Exeter had no knowledge of classic Ferraris or the motor racing side of the brand at all. They weren't enthusiasts passionate about the marque. It was just another car, and Ferrari customers aren't like that. They need to know that their man in the dealership knows everything Ferrari.

When Max first met Sean, he could see that Sean didn't understand the product and for a while he was able to take advantage of that. Max was selling far more used Ferrari than the official franchised dealer, but it was because he was enthusiastic, knew the brand and had the kind of cars people were looking for. Max still had to use Isca Ferrari for most service work in order to get the all important official stamp in the service book, but minor work was carried out at Velodrome.

Sean realised that Max was a speculator in that he'd place deposits on new cars in advance in order to make a profit on the cars when they arrived. Sean didn't like that and he really didn't particularly like Max either. It was a bit of a jealousy thing. He liked the fact that he could dispose of some older Ferrari part exchanges to Max, but the thought of Velodrome collecting a new car and making a £100,000 profit on it, just by driving it out of the showroom door and handing it over to an eager customer, well that was a different matter altogether.

If Sean sold a new car to a customer, then hopefully the new Ferrari owner would keep bringing his car back for servicing and more new cars at a later date, so that Isca Ferrari could maximise their gain over a long period of ownership. If Sean sold a car to Max, then that would be the last they would probably see of that car. There would be no added gain. As such a one hit wonder.

Selling cars effectively to the trade albeit at full retail price actually reduced their opportunities. Sean was stuck with Max. There wasn't a lot he could do about the outstanding Ferrari 360 Spiders due to Velodrome. They were contracted with deposits paid several years before Sean came onto the scene and Max was due to have the first two cars from the allocation. Max was looking forward to it, Sean wasn't and he was looking for a way out.

Typical of Sean Williams, Max wasn't invited to the opening of the new showroom but it didn't bother him too much. Williams was a wanker and he needed Max's business. Max on the other hand didn't necessarily need him. It was a convenience to go to Exeter, that was all. If the relationship became strained, then Max would get the cars serviced elsewhere.

It was several weeks after the new showroom opened that Max wandered in. Williams was sat at his desk, he knew Max was there but he didn't look up. Max had to walk right up to his desk before he acknowledged him. They talked for a while as Max looked around. Right at the front of the showroom was a brand new Ferrari 456 GTA in Tour de France blue with beige leather. Max was looking at it.

'Got a customer for it?' Sean asked.

'No, beautiful car though.'

'Not beautiful enough. We need to see it gone. It's been here too long and it's just about to come up for direct payment out of our stocking loan account,' said Sean.

'How much do you need for it?'

Max could see that the screen price was just under £180,000. Sean had a think about it and returned to his desk to look down his stock list.

'Do you think you could do something with it?'

'It's possible, it depends on the price. You tell me what it owes you and I can try to find a customer for it, if it stacks up,' Max replied.

Sean had a think.

'What if you advertised it as an ex demonstrator with delivery miles?'

'Is it your demonstrator?'

'No, but we could say it was. We could tell Ferrari that it's our demonstrator and get the demo discount. I've got to get this thing out the door.'

'I'd want £3000 for selling the car, that's if I can sell it. How much do you need?'

'If you advertised it for £139,950 as a delivery mileage ex demonstrator and we gave you £3000, that could work,' Sean offered.

'What about Ferrari?'

'They'll never know,' Sean replied.

Max considered what Sean had said. He didn't like him particularly but that wouldn't stop him from making money out of him. The issue with the Ferrari discount was Sean's issue not Max's. If he wanted to lie to Ferrari UK, the that was down to him and his directors.

'Okay, I'll run with that. I'll advertise it in the *Sunday Times* this weekend. Let me have the full specifications and I'll give it a go. I'll put it in at £139,950, but if it sells, I want £3000,' Max told Sean.

'Yes, that's agreed,' Sean replied and they shook hands.

Max finished up his business with Sean and drove the

short journey back to Velodrome in Newton Abbot and immediately booked the advertising space for the forthcoming Sunday. Before he left Isca Ferrari he'd asked Sean how things were coming along with his 360 Spiders and Sean had told him there was no news on any of the cars as yet. Max wasn't expecting any news, but he asked him anyway. It was always the case that the right hand drive market production would take longer to arrive than the left hand drive cars so realistically, if the first European cars were being delivered at Christmas, then the UK cars were going to be a short while after that.

Sean wasn't telling Max the truth of course, because he did have some news. He knew how many cars he would be getting the following year and two of them were Max's orders, but he didn't want Max to know that. He also knew who was having the first car and he didn't want Max to know that either. Come to that, he probably didn't want any of his customers to know the answer to that one.

Max took two calls on the 456 from the *Sunday Times* advert that weekend. One caller he knew. He was a dealer in Cornwall. Max explained the situation, where the car was and how the deal would be done. It was in fact a brand new unused car, but prior to being sold, it would be first registered in Isca Ferrari's name in order for them to get the extra discount. The Cornwall dealer accepted that and agreed to buy the car. He would collect and pay for the car that forthcoming week. Max rang Sean on his mobile.

'Sean, it's Max, I've agreed a sale on the 456 at £139,95, so you give me £3000 and the job's done.'

'Yes, that's good. I'm happy with that.'

Max explained that he would be away on holiday for a week but the buyer would be up to collect the car during the week to pay for it and take it away. The deal was done.

Max put down the phone, pleased that he'd been able to sell the car quite quickly. *All comes down to price,* he thought. £40,000 discount on a new Ferrari. He didn't think that Ferrari UK would be too pleased about that if they found out. Still, that wasn't his problem.

The other caller from the advert was from a number he didn't recognise, but he realised who it was the moment he answered the phone. It was Rupert Davis.

'Sorry Rupert, I've sold it. It's going to the first guy that rang me.'

'Listen chap that's no problem, okay? Let me know if it doesn't go through.'

Max agreed that he would, although he doubted that the deal would fall apart.

'The other thing Max, do you have any 360 Spiders coming?' Davis asked.

'Yes, I've got two right hand drive cars and quite a few left hand drive cars.'

'Are they all sold?'

'No, only one is sold, all the rest will be available. I don't want to sell them just yet. I want to get them here first then let them go. I should have a left hand drive car available just after Christmas. It's a blue car with beige interior, if that's any good to you?'

'Put my name on it chap would you?' Rupert asked.

'Okay, as soon as it's here, I'll let you know.'

Here was the king of the mountain, the man Max should be turning to for all things Ferrari asking Max if he could supply him with a new Ferrari. It was ridiculous, but it was true.

They carried on talking for over an hour, Rupert continuing in his normal domineering style. He didn't talk to Max, he talked at him. He wanted to get his opinions across because to him that's all that mattered. Max mentioned a dealer close by to him.

'Don't go dealing with him, he's a fucking shark if ever there was one. I've known him to be talking to someone about a classic car in another country all meant to be hush-hush and before he's finished the conversation, he's already planning how to get there and buy the car before anyone else,' says Rupert.

'You can't be right, his old man was a great motor racing stalwart, a Le Mans winner. He wouldn't do that surely?' Max said surprisingly.

'He would, he'd take the shirt off your back.'

'Well, you surprise me,' said Max. He didn't know whether it was true.

Rupert was full of his opinions about every dealer and as time went on, Max found out more and more about dealers he should avoid, who could be trusted and who couldn't. Rupert was the self-styled top dog that all others aspired to be or at least that's what he thought.

Max finished the telephone conversation and clicked the red button on his mobile. It was exhausting talking to Rupert, it was always 'full on'. He sighed and put down the phone. He was wondering how Keith was getting on. He didn't want to pester Jackie and he didn't want to appear selfish by giving him a call to find out when he was coming back to work but he was going to need to know fairly soon as the untended paperwork was beginning to pile up. It was Sunday, he tried to forget about it, but it was beginning to get to him. There was so much at stake, Catherine was expecting their first child in a few months and business wise, they were sailing extremely close to the wind. Max was more worried at that point than he had ever been before. If he didn't get it right over the next few months, it could all fall apart. Max likened the business to a ship sailing across the ocean and it was taking on a lot of water. It would only be able to take on so much.

JUNE 1982

The cars slowly drove around Russel Bend, formed up, two by two as they came into view. It was a big grid with a lot of factory supported cars aiming to make their mark. Doug was eighth on the grid making the start, following Max's fastest qualifying class time. It was June 1984 on a sunny Saturday afternoon just coming up to 4 o'clock at Snetterton in Norfolk. It was the start of the Willhire 24 hr race for production sports and saloon cars. The pole sitter was a Porsche 911RS 2.7 hotly pursued by a raft of Ford Capri 2.8s, BMW 323s, Morgans and all sorts. Doug and his team stood a good chance of a result, provided the car hanged together, but 24 hrs in a motor race is a very long time and cars get a hammering. Every part is pushed to its absolute limit and quite often well beyond. Preparation is everything.

The first time Max had sat in the car was when he set his qualifying time. The Vauxhall Astra GTE wasn't a bad car. It was reasonably quick, handled okay and Max could drive the wheels off it, so much so, that the GM Dealer Sport team, the factory cars who Max had out qualified thought Doug was cheating. He wasn't and GM Dealer Sport didn't lodge an official complaint anyway, but it did spice up the race somewhat when it got going.

Max had been racing for three years in Formula Ford

1600, then Formula Ford 2000 and was at that time trying to get a ride in Formula 3, but with very little money it wasn't looking good.

His last two seasons hadn't been as promising as he had hoped. The reality of crashes and the mad costs of racing were a constant downer. He'd said to Catherine that if he didn't get a proper drive in Formula 3 that year, then he was going to call it a day. He knew he could be quick, but that wasn't going to be enough. He needed more than that. He needed a lucky break. It was just a question of whether he was going to get it.

A marketing company were sponsoring the Astra and had all their staff at the circuit supporting the team. ABM Impact was emblazoned across the side of the red and white car as it took the start and ran comfortably in eighth place for the first hour with Doug at the wheel. Catherine and Judy were on the timekeeping when Doug came in for a routine check, taking on fuel and driver change for Max. No problems, all went well and Max rejoined the race. It was a bit like driving a normal road car except it had a little bit more grip and power, but it was an easy car to drive quickly. Like all front wheel drive cars, it under steered a lot, but once Max knew what to do, it was comfortably forgiving. It didn't do anything violently.

The team of Doug, Max, John Bartelski and Francois Muret had all sat down over the lunchtime to discuss the race strategy and they'd agreed to run the race comfortably quick, not out and out quick.

Doug had said, 'Let's get some laps and hours under our belts and see where we are.' It made sense. To finish first, first you must finish. An old motor racing adage, but very true.

The car ran faultlessly for the first four hours allowing all four drivers to get used to the car and the competition, they were leading their class by one lap from the Napolina Fiat team and one lap behind them was the factory Vauxhall GM Dealer Sport team. It was close. One extra pit stop and it would be 'all change'.

By the time Max got his second ride in the car, it was becoming dusk, all the cars had their headlights on with their coloured running lights flickering in the increasing darkness. It was a colourful spectacle.

Snetterton is quite quick, it's got a long back straight into a series of esses, through what is called the bomb hole followed by Coram, a long right hand curve going into a chicane called Russell and then over the start finish into a fast right, then a short straight, difficult sharp right hander leads onto the back straight again. Technically not a difficult circuit, but there were some quick places where you would definitely not want go off.

Max had never won a race although he had come close a couple of times finishing second, but that was all in single seaters. In comparison the production saloon car was a much easier car to drive. For a start you could see where you were going, whereas a single seater being so low to the ground gives a very limited view especially on hilly circuits. Snetterton was fairly flat, which is why it was a US airbase during World War II. Max smiled to himself going down the back straight, it took such a long time, he had the chance to look at the big wheel going around at the fairground on the infield. It was all lit up with its multi coloured lights. Max thought about the view the passengers would have from the top. He fancied a go, then without warning the car coughed and stopped. He was on the outside of the circuit as he pulled onto the grass. He looked at the gauges. All looked okay. He retried the ignition, it spun the starter motor, but nothing, it wouldn't fire. He banged the steering wheel.

'Shit,' he said several times. It was all going so well. It was as if the car had run out of fuel, but it was indicating over a quarter full. He tried the starter several times without any luck. *It was all over*, he thought. A good few minutes passed whilst he tried to sort the problem. With no outside assistance allowed, that was the end of their race. He got out of the car and went around to the fuel cap and released the fuel cap just to see if there was an air lock in it. There was no sudden rush of air, but he did blow into the filler neck just to see if it would start. It did start, but it stopped immediately. Max was certain it was fuel. *The gauge must be knackered*, he thought. He was used to that.

It was bloody dangerous standing behind the car with all the madmen racing past. It was worse than standing naked on the hard shoulder of the M25 at rush hour. The marshals were waving their yellow flags so at least there was no overtaking. Huge flames were shooting out from the exhaust of the BF Goodrich Simmonds Drums Colt Starion as it shut off for the esses. It was all happening. Max ran across to the inside of the track where the team's mechanic, Chris Harrison was standing alongside a race official.

Chris shouted out, 'What's wrong with it?'

'I think it's fuel. It's a quarter full on the gauge. It started a minute ago when I blew into the tank.'

'Okay, you need to keep warm.'

Chris took off his coat to pass it over the fence to Max.

'No, it's all right, I'm okay.'

'Put the coat on, you'll get cold,' he insisted.

'No, honestly, I'm okay. I don't need the coat.'

'Put the fucking coat on, I don't want you getting cold.' He said it slowly and deliberately.

The race official looked on, surprised at Chris's insistence.

'All right, pass it over,' Max said reluctantly. *It's bloody heavy*, he thought. He put the coat on. *Hang on*, he thought. *What's that?* There was something heavy and big in the inside pocket.

'Go back to the car and lift the tailgate. You'll find a fuel pump reset switch in there. Flick that, and see if it will start. The pump might have overheated. Know what I mean?' He winked.

'Yeah.' He didn't know what he meant, but obviously there was something in his pocket that might help. He left Chris with the race official and ran back across the track to the car and opened the tailgate and leant in. He put his hand into his inside pocket and drew out a litre bottle of fuel, being careful not to be seen by the race official. He smiled, and tipped the contents into the fuel tank. It started, Max set off back to the pits, they'd lost eleven laps.

John Bartelski got into the car and fed back out into the race. Chris Harrison walked up to Max and put his arm around him. 'Next time I tell you to put my fucking coat on, I mean put my fucking coat on.'

They laughed.

'I didn't know what you meant about the re-set switch, but it sounded good and that official never twigged.'

'No he didn't, and that's what it's all about. It shouldn't have happened in the first place but there we go, we're still in the game. Go and have something to eat and drink, we're going to run just you, Doug and John through the night. Francois hasn't eaten enough carrots and doesn't like racing in the dark.'

'Okay, that's fine by me.'

Max went off with Catherine. It was such a fantastic atmosphere, a real buzz. The next stint went fine, the car was going like a train, no problems. They were all talking about making the finish. Max couldn't sleep, there was too much going on, too much noise and then he jumped back in the car for the dawn run, the car was still going well when Max turned in left at the Russell chicane. The car was up on the kerbs in the left hand part of the turn and then up on the right hand kerb on the exit of the corner. After fifteen hours, the lower right front wishbone bolt sheared and the wheel detached from the car. It is a very fast part of the circuit and at over 80 mph, Max had his work cut out, not to go off and hit something. Inevitably the car stopped just on the start finish line and Max got out of the car. That was well and truly game over, they weren't going to finish on three wheels. With no outside assistance allowed, the car was not moveable. It had been fun while it lasted.

Max took off his Bell crash helmet and put his gloves inside carrying it in his right hand whilst walking back alongside the pit wall. He stopped a short while and looked into the front wheel arch, it was too dark to see anything. He pulled down the zip of his overalls to let some cool air in. He'd started racing three years earlier racing everywhere in the country more or less every weekend in the season, doing more than fifty races including three 24 hr races and he'd never won anything. He still didn't have any money and his prospects weren't looking too clever either.

A month earlier, he'd asked Catherine's father permission to marry her, but unbelievably he said 'No'. Max wasn't expecting that. It had taken him so much time to summon up the courage to ask him in the first place and then for him to say no was completely bewildering. He said that Max needed to get himself sorted out with some prospects.

As he walked up the grassy verge near the start finish lighting gantry, he pulled out his ear defenders and thought that perhaps this was a good time to call it a day. It was a mugs game. There were better, more feasible ways of making a living. He could always go back to it if he wanted at a later date. It was going to take quite a while for the drug to work out of his system, but maybe now was the right time. The last three years had all been about trying to get to Formula One, everything was based on that belief and it looked as unlikely at that moment as it had on that first day with Doug at Brands Hatch. He'd met some great people, raced against some great drivers some of whom did get to Formula One and he had some fantastic memories to take with him. The more he thought about it, the more he was convincing himself that he needed to get a proper job, earn some decent money and start climbing the ladder.

He jumped over the pit wall where Catherine was still standing with the pit board.

'What's wrong?' she asked.

'Something broke and then there was no drive and not much steering either. We're out'

'Never mind, let's go and get some breakfast,' she said and the team went off to the circuit cafe. They were completely despondent. The thought of packing everything away is so much harder when it's all been a waste of time.

Doug tried to rally the troops. 'Hey, look it's been a good weekend. We've had a good time and some good racing. We haven't finished, but that's the way it goes!' He raised his cup of coffee, 'There's always next year,' and they all tapped their mugs together and laughed.

Max drove out of the paddock taking in all the sights as he did so, before making his way towards the exit. He knew in his mind it would be his last race. Funny how it goes though, the next time he would drive out of that very same paddock, he would have a bottle of champagne and winner's wreath in the back of the car.

OCTOBER 2000

The yellow 355 GTB came into view about a quarter of a mile up the road beyond the railway station as Pete and Max stood at the front of the showroom drinking a cup of coffee. The new 360 Modena that Max had collected from Josef in Aachen was in the service bay ready for its new owner and there he was in the part exchange indicating to turn in right in front of the garage. Max and Pete could hear the wonderful orchestra emanating from the sports exhaust as he blipped the throttle, shut off and stepped out of the car. Unknown to Max at the time, it was a trigger point in Velodrome's history. The Ferrari 355 GTB looked outrageous in Giallo Fly yellow so Max thought he would have no problem in selling it on. It had the desirable Fiorano Sports pack and the F1 paddle gearbox as well so it would all help.

Max shook hands with the new customer and had a good

look around the incoming car, making sure all was as described and then both of them took a short trip around the block to confirm the car's integrity. It was as described, a low mileage one owner 355 in outstanding condition. It needed nothing. A quick clean and it would go straight into the showroom.

Max did all the paperwork in front of the customer and after a short test drive explaining all the mainly familiar controls, the new owner set off back past the railway station and out of view. Max made himself another hot drink and stood again at the front of the showroom looking out. It was mid October 2000, he wondered whether he'd get the yellow car sold before Christmas. If he did, that would be great, if he didn't, then he would still be looking at it in March. He didn't fancy that thought. Sales and enquiries had already started to slow down on what had been a miserable year. Yes, he'd done well selling so many Ferraris but the foot and mouth disease had lost the company so much money that the cars hadn't made up for the year's early losses. If they were lucky Velodrome would break even, which meant keeping costs down as low as possible going into the winter. The juggling continued.

Busy pedestrians wrapped up in their warm coats bustled past the glass frontage some stopping to look at the parked car, some not noticing at all. On a grey day, it stood out like a switched on light bulb in an empty room. *What a fantastic looking car*, Max thought. *But even better looking if it was sold and paid for.*

Standing there watching the traffic passing by, he wondered to himself whether it was all worth it. Was the gain worth the pain? *Probably not*, he thought. No sooner had he gone one step forward when he had to take two steps back. There was always something unexpected, something that he hadn't allowed for. The Ferrari 330 GTO was still unresolved. The car was sold to Muzi, but he couldn't ask him for the money until the issue over the Shell Historic eligibility was solved and that was being dealt with by Graham Lord.

For his part at least, Julian had transferred the money into Velodrome's account for the 360 Spider, which was good news, but all it did at that time was reduce the overdraft down to a less costly level. Max still had to work the money to make the deal worthwhile. The money had come in late, but Max didn't rescind the original contract, it wasn't worth the nuisance. Julian had paid and that was all that mattered.

Keith's condition was becoming an even greater worry. It had been four weeks since he'd gone on holiday and had the aneurism. When Max had last spoken to Jackie, she was hopeful that Keith would be back at work by now, but it wasn't looking good. The doctor was still keeping him off work and he really wasn't anything like himself at home. Max would have to make a decision on that one. It probably wouldn't hurt for another few weeks but it would need dealing with soon after if there was no good news.

It would be the last round of a very much depleted South West Enduro Championship on the next Sunday, Max was entered on his faithful Honda XR230, he'd only need to finish ahead of Chris Dunstall to take the championship in his class for the second time. He liked the course at Pendennis, it was held on a private estate in a lot of forestry and it suited the Honda well. Since he'd stopped motor racing, the enduro racing had filled the competitive hole in his life and he'd been riding successfully for over fifteen years. At this, the last event of the year, Velodrome were running two journalists from 'Bike' magazine so that they could write about the notoriously gruelling event through first hand knowledge. Their two bikes were being prepared by the mechanics in the service workshop and would then be transported to the event on Velodrome's "arrive and ride" programme. The company ran a few customer bikes in exactly the same way and because it was the last round of the year, it had a bumper entry. Velodrome had seven bikes to prepare and deliver to the Lizard in Cornwall for 7:00 am on Sunday morning. It wouldn't be a problem, they were used to it. They knew what to do and they were good at it.

One of Max's tenants spotted him standing in the window.

'Hi, that roof is still leaking. Not so much, but it still comes in when the wind is south westerly,' she said.

'Okay, I'll get the guy to come back and have another look. I'll ring him today.'

'That's nice,' she said pointing at the Ferrari, 'any chance I could borrow it on Saturday night?'

Max smiled and she walked off with a bit of a strut. Above the garage, the building was divided into flats and she rented one of them. She'd been a good tenant, but her flat had a water leak that the builder was struggling to repair. He'd kept saying to Max that the roof needed replacing, but because it was

334

part of six continuous terraced cottages, Max wasn't going to get away with renewing one section, it would have to be the lot. And of course it would be expensive, so Max had asked the builder to keep repairing it, which wasn't really working. Max had bought the building from Nat West Bank when the previous owners, a Vauxhall dealer, had gone bust. He'd got it for the right money, but it had been neglected for so many years that when Velodrome moved in the cost of repairs and renewals to make it habitable was over £40,000 almost immediately. It wasn't unexpected, that was why he got it cheap, but he had hoped that some of the cost could have been spread over a longer period. As it happened, it was easier to do it all at once in order to keep the disruption to a minimum. The one thing that really did need doing next was the roof, but that would have to wait. Maybe if Muzi's deal came off, he could get it done.

Pete walked up to Max.

'Penny for them?' he said.

'Ah, sorry I was miles away.'

'I could see. I've had the tickets for the bike show come in from Aprilia. Are we going to train it up?'

'Yes, I think so Pete. Do you want to sort out the tickets etc?'

'Yep, can do, company credit card?'

'Yeah. Aprilia have got quite a few new models so it should be quite good.'

Every year, Max and Pete would go off to the bike show for a day and view all the latest bikes, accessories and clothing. It was always a good day out. They'd get chance to meet all their suppliers and talk about the latest bit, but the main reason for going was to order the new year models which would arrive into the showroom during December and January.

Pete would give Max an idea of what sort of model mix he wanted and between them they would pre order the new model year range depending on the types of deals that were on offer. Like most motorcycle manufacturers, volume was all important, so dealers were always encouraged to order more than they would normally buy on the basis of discounts and targets. In order for Velodrome to maintain the Aprilia franchise, they had to sell 180 motorcycles and scooters, which wasn't the easiest thing to do especially when some of the models were difficult to sell or Aprilia sent them down in the wrong colour, but any dealer needed to have a new franchise if they were to take advantage of the booming scooter market. Velodrome had the best two franchises in Peugeot and Aprilia and had reached their 2000 target bonuses before the end of September which was good news, because firstly there was a retrospective additional discount which would be credited to their account and secondly it opened up opportunities on some special deals on outgoing models before the end of the year which could increase the profit margin on some bikes. The bike shows enabled Max and Pete to talk directly to the manufacturers and get the best deals possible. It would be an exhausting day but it was always worth it.

Max walked into the service area, it was break time. He sat down with his two long serving mechanics Guy and Steve.

'Want a top up?' asked Guy.

'Oh go on then,' Max replied.

Guy had started working for Max three months after he'd first opened. He was an excellent mechanic and Max trusted him implicitly. In that thirteen years, they'd never had an MOT complaint, not once, because Guy was totally thorough and knew what he was doing. In fairness he wasn't perfect, because Max couldn't put him in front of a customer and expect him to be diplomatic. If the bike was crap, Guy would tell them exactly that and if Max wanted to keep his customers, Guy was not going to be the best man at the front desk. But if Max wanted someone to service a bike properly or prepare a competition bike as it should, then Guy was the man. It would be right, first time.

Steve was a good mechanic too, but not in the same league as Guy. He was a good journeyman and they complimented each other well. Max used to like going into their lair at break times on occasion, passing the time of day with them. He felt it kept them feeling part of the team rather than being cut off from the rest of the staff. It helped keep the common rapport and Max liked it too. It was good to get away from that bloody telephone once in a while.

'Oh well, better get on with it,' he said and returned to his office to call Graham Lord.

'Yeah, hi Graham, it's Max. What's happening with the 330 GTO information? Have you been down to see Donald Key yet?'

Max could have called Don directly but he knew that Don didn't know who was involved in the sale of the GTO because Graham hadn't told him. Ultimately, if Graham didn't sort it out then Max might have to call Donald , but hopefully that wouldn't be necessary.

'No, not yet. I'm hoping to get down there later today or tomorrow.'

'Okay, it would be good if you could. There's a lot at stake.'

Graham wanted the money just as much as Max so when he said he was going down later today or tomorrow then he did actually mean it. Graham was away to Devon for the weekend. He'd agreed to meet Max for dinner where they were staying at Holne Chase Hotel near Ashburton, just on the edge of Dartmoor, so that they would have a better chance to talk. Max still hadn't told him that Muzi wanted a 250 Testa Rossa but if the 330 was going to be a longer term deal to finalize, then maybe it was time to talk about the second car. The seller of the 330 was cool and so was Muzi. The only person jumping up and down at that time was Max because he just wanted to get the deal done and get paid. It would immediately sort out all his worries in one hit. It was incredibly frustrating knowing that he had a customer ready and willing to send $7.75 million dollars of which $2M was going straight to Max, but he couldn't get the deal finished.

Max had thought about hatching a different plan if Graham didn't sort things out. They'd already spoken to John Gill and as far as he was concerned there was nothing wrong with the car and he didn't know why Angelo had said what he had, but very few seller's are going to own up to there being something wrong with the car, even if they did know.

If there was a problem with the car, which effectively was the reason why the car would not be eligible for the Shell Historic Ferrari Challenge, then it had to be something to do with Donald Key, because up to the point Don had the car in his workshop for restoration, it had passed from various quality owners without being touched for over twenty-five years. The supporting documentation and evidence confirmed the history of the car as being completely original from the date it left the factory to its first private owner right up to the late 80's.

Max's view was that, Donald Key would have liaised with Ferrari during the restoration of the car. He would have probably spoken to Angelo about parts and important details, especially if he thought things were missing or had been changed. Although it was original when it arrived at Don's, twenty-five odd years of use including competition would have taken its toll, not least rust. And originality can be difficult to determine. Angelo for his part would have had the factory records on the car and he would have known everything about it from day one. All that Angelo would say to Max was that the car was not eligible, he wouldn't freely comment on anything else. Max didn't own the car, so Angelo was being professional.

The key to the puzzle had to be Don. He knew exactly what he'd done to the car, but for some unknown reason he wasn't telling Graham or more to the point Graham knew but he wasn't telling Max. One of them knew or both of them knew.

Max picked up the phone and rang a friend of his.

'Hi, it's Max, how are you?'

'Yeah good, long time no hear.'

'I've been busy. Are you still racing?'

'Of course, it's in my blood. You can't stop racing.'

'Yeah, I know. If it's not one thing, it's something else,' said Max.

'How's that lovely wife of yours?'

'Beautiful as ever,' said Max.

'You're a lucky bastard Max.'

'Yes, I am in that department.'

'Anyway, what can I do for you?'

'Donald Key. What do you know about him?' Max asked.

'Not a lot really. He has a lot of high ticket clients and he likes to make out he does everything in house, but he doesn't. A lot of it is farmed out and then he reassembles it. I think he's got a good reputation, although I know a lot of people that just won't deal with him . The son's a bit of a wanker though, Julian I think his name is, but you probably know that anyway. Coke and all the rest of it so I'm told. Quite why Don didn't send him somewhere to learn his trade at someone else's expense is beyond me. He comes across as arrogant and completely ill informed. There's a lot of people that have been put off by him.'

'Yes, you could say that,' Max replied.

'I think Don started at Kodak or some film processing firm. It's her money though. She was responsible for making it happen not him and to be fair to her, she's the only one with any sense. He couldn't have done it without her. Rumour has it that she's shagging someone down at the tennis club, but I don't know if that's true or not. I can't say that I could blame her really. I don't know where she got her money from, probably

338

family inheritance or something like that. I've met them quite a few times at different functions and circuits. You know, they're nice people. I certainly don't have a problem with them. Mind you, he's a funny bloke, Don. He used to do a lot of work for one of the big fashion designers and when I say a lot, I mean a lot. Many hundred thousand pounds or more. The story goes that he restored the customer's Jaguar D Type and when the guy came to collect the car, Don ended up arguing with him about the colour they had painted it. Now the thing is, who cares what colour it should or should not have been. You don't argue with a customer as good as that. I mean, what's it going to cost to repaint a car ? A couple of grand ? It's nothing in comparison to losing the guy's business which is exactly what happened. Even if Don was right, which he probably was, sometimes you just have to bite your lip.

'Wow, that's a big stance.'

'There's loads more, but I'll leave that for another day'

It's just that I've got a big deal going through and Ferrari have knocked the car back on the Shell Historic saying it's not eligible and they won't tell me why.'

'Hmm, can I ask what car?'

'It's a GTO.'

'Oh, it is a big deal then.'

'Yes, it is and the problem is that the prospective buyer has the money ready to send and I can't ask him to send it unless I get it into the Shell Historic because he wants to race it. Well he doesn't, he wants me to race it.'

'Double whammy then?'

'Yeah, but the car has continuous known history from the day it left the factory and then it went to Donald Key for a restoration, then it was sold to one of the big Middle Eastern collectors, then he sold it to the guy we're buying it from.'

'I know the car. Four litre?'

'Yeah, that's the one,' Max replied.

'Well, am I not mistaken in thinking that car sold for ten million pounds or a reputed ten million pounds in the early nineties.'

'Yes, I think so. It was a private sale so nobody really knows outside of the loop.'

'Well, let's say it did sell for that kind of money. It would have to be right or at least look right. No, for that money, it would have to be one hundred per cent right. Nobody's going to pay ten million pounds for an iffy car, are they?'

'No, they're not. So why are Ferrari saying it's not eligible?' asked Max.

'Beats me Max, but you need to find out. I do know a guy that has a friend who works for Don. It may be possible for me to ask. I don't know, I'd have to think about it. Obviously, you don't want Don finding out, just in case they're covering up something. Of course, the thing is, at the moment you don't know if something is wrong, you are only guessing. It maybe, the eligibility is to do with some other nonsense, like Ferrari aren't happy with the current owner. You know how pathetic they can be!'

'Yeah, that's true.'

'I'll see what I can do and as soon as I have something, I'll come back to you, okay?'

'Thanks, that's good of you. Any idea how long?' Max asked.

'Give me a few days.'

Max put down the phone and thought about the conversation. The idea of someone on the inside of Donald Key's firm could be extremely revealing.

NOVEMBER 2000

Rux could hear his mobile phone ringing somewhere in his jacket and just managed to catch it before it went to voice mail.

'Yeah, Rux.'

'Hi, have you got everything now?'

'Yeah, I've got it with me, I'm on the road.'

'Official or private?'

'Official. You in GP?'

'Yeah. Can we meet?'

'How's four o'clock?'

'Usual place?'

'Yeah, that's good for me.'

'Good. See you then.'

Rux put down the phone. He had all the information he needed with him. All he had to do was hand it over and get paid. That suited him fine.

PAU, JUNE 2004

Max dialled Jacques number on his mobile. He was half an hour from Olivier's house. They'd already spoken a few times that day and Jacques was expecting him. Ralph Sanders was also waiting patiently for his call. It would come.

'Hi, Jacques. I'm about thirty minutes from Olivier's. Are you already there?'

'Yes, Max, we're all here. Antoinette has come over too. We thought you might like to sit down and have something to eat with us.'

'Yes, that would be very nice, thank you.'

'Okay. See you soon.'

Max put down the phone. He felt quite tense yet excited at the same time. He knew Olivier's car wasn't a fake, it was obvious, he only had to look at it to realise that, but after finding something historically significant which had been lost from public knowledge for over seventy years meant that he had to get it right. He wasn't an expert on the marque so he would need to make absolutely certain that the car was right. The temptation would have been to load the car onto his trailer and drive off back to the UK and sell it. That thought had certainly crossed his mind although he had quickly dismissed it as being too soon and too cheap. What Max had to do was relatively simple. He needed to establish the authenticity of the car beyond question including all its history as best possible. With one elderly long term owner, hopefully it wouldn't be too difficult and that's where Ralph Sanders came into the picture.

Max turned into Olivier's drive. If it looked impressive when he first went there in the dark, it now looked wonderfully idyllic as he drove down the driveway and parked his Nissan Double Cab outside the front door. He looked around, the house had all the looks of faded money. Once a fabulous period house, still a fabulous period house but not now in its best condition. Max could see it needed a lot of work, it was obvious it hadn't had much done to it in a long, long time. The creeping vine had overgrown many of the pale blue slatted shutters, some of which were hanging at different angles. The fascia boards were rotting and split with bits missing. Makeshift guttering spanned two bits of the original directly above the front door. There was a sizeable crack on the end wall, but the French never seem bothered about that sort of thing, so that could have been there for a hundred years. Whatever, it didn't matter, Max wasn't there to buy the house, he was there to have a look at a car and progress the deal a little bit further forward.

In the course of going about his work in the previous weeks, Max had often thought about that first conversation with Jacques when he'd told Max about his father in law's old racing car. It was one of those 'throwaway lines'. Max could have easily not asked him. He'd delivered all but one of his bikes on that trip and Jacques bike was the last and furthest away. Normally, Max would have offloaded the bike, done the paperwork, got paid and blasted back to the UK, but for some reason he stopped a while and chatted passing the time of day. It was funny how things like that happen sometimes.

Olivier shuffled to the front door and welcomed Max with open arms. It was a much warmer welcome than the first time they met and Max sensed he was in. He immediately felt a lot more confident about the deal. Olivier's manner convinced Max that he was being treated like one of the family and it was now a family deal, which they would do together rather than an 'us and them' situation. For Max, he was much more comfortable with everything, because it took away the nerve wracking worry of Olivier or Jacques approaching someone else. Max had potentially the opportunity of a lifetime and he didn't want to lose it. He needed to work with Olivier and find a buyer before Max bought the car. He couldn't afford to buy the car straight out unless Olivier effectively sold it cheap and Max didn't feel he was about to do that. He may have been old but he wasn't stupid and even in his eighties, he surely knew or had a good idea of what the car was worth. It wouldn't have been too difficult to find out the value of a similar car. A quick telephone call to Poulin Auctioneers in Paris mentioning no names or detail would have given him a ball park figure to think about.

They walked into the kitchen, Antoinette stepped forward and kissed Max once on each cheek and commented on how well he looked. He thought she looked pretty good too but didn't say it. Jacques offered Max a coffee.

Olivier pulled out a chair, 'Here, sit yourself down, make yourself at home,' he said in French.

Max caught the "asseyez vous" bit and guessed the rest.

The kitchen was a hive of activity as Olivier's wife and Antoinette went about their food preparation, twittering away in that lovely soft French accent. Everyone seemed so jolly and spirited, it was as if they all knew they were on the verge of something exciting, it was a good feeling.

'We've cleaned everything out of the way so you can walk around the car and have a good look at it. We have found some bits and pieces, we don't know what they are, but they are definitely for the car. Most of the bodywork is in a different barn, which we have now all put together in one place. There are bits missing but Olivier says he can't remember what he's done with them. He's put them away safely somewhere but he just can't remember where. We found some of the small parts in the kitchen drawer,' he laughed.

'You've been busy then,' said Max.

'Well, it's very important for us to get it all sorted out and we didn't want you coming all this way and having the same troubles as last time. That was a bit unfair, but we didn't know at that time how serious you were going to be, so now it's different.'

'That's good. I wasn't looking forward to crawling around on a dirty floor all afternoon.'

'No, you won't have to do that. Sorry about that.'

'That's okay.'

'If you want to bring your coffee out, you can have another look at the car properly if you want and then afterwards we can all sit down and have dinner.'

'Sounds good to me,' Max replied getting up from his chair.

They walked out through the kitchen door and across a small cobbled kitchen yard covered in moss to a gothic arched old wooden door. Max recognised the door, his car was parked on the other side of it.

'I'll just get my stuff,' Max said.

'Okay, I'll go on up and see you up there,' Jacques said as he continued to walk.

'Okay, no problem.'

Max leant into his car and picked up a few things, his mobile phone, a small digital camera, his diary and a pen and walked up towards the old stone buildings further up the drive. He looked around at the grounds. *What a beautiful place*, he thought. It must have been fantastic in its heyday. On the side of

343

the driveway, the lawn stretched for a hundred yards down to a sizeable lake. Ducks were upturned, cleaning themselves in the water, a few more were sat on the grass at the water's edge. Four white Lloyd Loom style chairs and a small white table broke up the infinite shades of green all about him. He couldn't think of a more appealing place to live. It was just so tranquil, so relaxing. He stood there looking out across the lake picturing in his mind's eye, a wonderful garden party with tables of food and bottles of wine, family and friends stood or sat around and kneeling on picnic rugs, children running around playing noisily. The hubbub of chatter, the swish of period dresses. It was Monet, it was Renoir, it was all things French or it could have been straight off the set of Pride and Prejudice. He shook his head and carried on walking.

Olivier and Jacques still hadn't fixed the door into the old building and Max could see why they were reluctant to open the door any further. The oak lintel above must have sagged by at least three inches and was resting on top of the closed door alongside. There were big cracks in the mortar and stonework all the way to the roof. *Best not look at that*, he thought and stepped through the partially opened doorway and inside.

He could now walk to the car quite easily as Jacques had now made a path through the myriad of old rusty farm machinery and associated rubbish and there it was. A skeletal wreck of an old racing car, stripped bare to its chassis, no bodywork, no tyres on its alloy rims, just a huge meccano set of filthy dirty assembled parts. It could have been anything, only the wheels gave it any instant recognition. The long engine sat up front again black with dirt, coupled up to a small biscuit tin gearbox and a large shapely fuel tank with two stacked filters sprouting out of the top.

'I'll leave you to it Max. If you need any help, just give me a call,' said Jacques.

'Thanks, I will,' Max replied glad that he was being left alone to enjoy the moment. He placed his coffee mug on top of the fuel tank and stood back to admire the sight before him. *This is history*, he thought. He ran his hand along the shape of the fuel tank thinking about the people involved in racing the car in the early 30s. They'd all have their white oil stained overalls on, stood around the car. The driver would have his leather scull cap and goggles, the co driver probably the same. The mechanics most likely with flat caps, tools in their hands, some carrying oil cans or huge fuel churns. The owner and his beautiful wife in familiar Charleston fashion. It was a grainy, flickering black and white image of a bygone age of speed, glamour and adventure, and Max liked it.

He walked alongside the car peering in at every nook and cranny, studying the shapes and sizes of all the various parts. Jacques had told Max that Olivier had started to restore the car in the 1950's but had given up and sensibly sprayed the car or covered the car in a thick farm oil, which had had over fifty years of silt and droppings land upon it. Max carefully scraped away a small area revealing a bright shiny metal underneath and realised that beneath its blackened overcoat, it appeared to be like new below. *What a find*, he thought. *Unbelievable*. Even through the grime, he could see it was beautifully made with exquisite detailing. It was more a work of art than a racing car.

Max spent at least half an hour pawing over the skeleton and then reached for his mobile and called Ralph Sanders. The phone hardly rang, before Ralph picked up.

'Hi, Ralph, it's Max Reed.'

'Hello, Max, how are you?'

'Well, I'm here and I'm stood in front of it in all it's glory. There's no bodywork on it, no radiator fitted although the radiator is here on the bench, so I know it goes with the car. It's on it's wheels, but there's no tyres.'

'Okay, good. Is there a forward bulkhead firewall on it?' Ralph asked.

'No.'

'So there's nothing like a flat wall behind the engine stood up vertically?'

'No, nothing there.'

'That's a pity. The chassis plates and maker's plate are fitted to that part which would have made it easier. okay, if you go around to the left hand side of the car or nearside and kneel down as if you are looking at the engine.'

'Yes, I'm there.'

'Okay, it's definitely eight cylinder?'

'Yes, definitely, it's still got the original Champion spark plugs in it, funny looking things.'

'Okay. At the rear of the engine, on your right, there's a support arm engine mount. It's triangular in shape with the more pointed end facing towards you. It's actually part of the sump, but anyway, can you see it?'

345

'Is it flat on the top?' Max asked.

'Yes, it is. What's the number on it? There should be a four digit number stamped into it.'

'Well, there's nothing that I can see, because the whole car is covered in a thick layer of oily dirt.'

'Okay, can you gently rub away, if you can, an area on the top of that mount?'

'It's quite a big part. How large are the numbers?' Max asked.

'They'll be about an inch long in total that's all.'

'Okay, so whereabouts on the mount are they most likely to be, because this dirt is like a layer of burnt jam and it's not easy to get off,' Max enquired.

'I'd say they'd be about a third up from the bottom and roughly in the middle.'

'Okay, I'll have a go.'

There was a piece of wood on the bench which Max picked up and used to gently scrape away the layers.

'Anything?' asked Ralph.

'Nothing,' came the reply.

'Try a bit higher up,' he asked.

'Okay.'

Max cleared an area of dirt about two inches square, it had taken him about five minutes.

'Oh, hang on, I can see something or at least the start of something.'

Max had caught the edge of one of the numbers and worked his way around it to reveal the next followed by two more and read them out to Ralph.

'Are you sure?'

'Absolutely, they can't be anything else. They're as clear as you could possibly hope. No question about it.'

'Can you clear an area to the right of the number?' Ralph asked.

'Yes, it's a bit easier on this bit.' He'd now revealed a bright shiny area the size of the palm of his hand and he could clearly read the number and two other symbols.

'What've you got?' Ralph asked trembling with his eagerness to find out more.

'There's a letter "C" or what looks like a letter "C" but it's on it's side,' Max whispered, still scraping away.

'Anything else?'

'No, not yet, no wait a minute, yes.' With the last scrape, he revealed, 'Yes there's a letter 'T'.'

Ralph Sanders sighed. He'd been involved in these cars since he was in his twenties and it was generally accepted that there wasn't anything he didn't know about the subject. Now, he was confronted with something that he never thought he would have the pleasure to be part of. He looked out across his garden.

'Are you still there?' Max asked.

'Yes, yes I was just thinking. Just thinking what to say next. Max, how authentic does the car look?'

'One hundred per cent.'

Ralph had already formed an opinion in his mind. What Max had in front of him in the location it was found, almost certainly was the real thing. The description Max had given him after that first visit and now again when he's stood in front of the car all lead him to believe that it was the right car.

'Okay, could you have a look around for me?'

'Yeah, no problem.'

'How many fillers does the tank have?'

'Two, sticking up proud at angles,' Max replied.

'Is the magneto fitted onto the back of the cylinder head?'

'Yes, it's a, wait a minute, Scintilla, yes, it's a Scintilla!' came Max's slow deliberating reply.

'Is the gearbox in the car?'

'Yes, it's there, looks like it should house Chocolate Digestives. It looks like an old biscuit tin.'

'Yes, that's the one. Can you rub the top back edge in the middle?'

Max did as he was asked and revealed another three numbers and Ralph wrote them down.

'Can you see the differential at all?' Ralph questioned.

'Yes, I can see it, but I can't get to it. It's a bit of a squeeze under the tank. No, hang on a minute, the tank is loose, I can take it off.'

Max removed the tank and looked at the two shaped wooden rails sitting on top of the chassis. *Amazing*, he thought.

'Yes, I can see the numbers,' Max read them off, it indicated the axle ratio and importantly the part number as well.'

'Okay, just one last thing for now. Can you see the channel at the end of the chassis joining the left rail to the right?'

'Yes.'

'Can you see inside? There should be a number in there.' Ralph assured him.

'Yes, there is. Let me just get that bit of wood again.' He cleared away the surface and read out the number. 'It's upside down.'

'Okay, that's possible.'

Max read it out.

Ralph contemplated all the information written out on the notepad in front of him. He knew, nobody would know all those numbers. It had to be the car. He could feel his eyes welling up, but he tried to temper his enthusiasm.

'Max?'

'Yeah.'

'From what you've told me and obviously I can't confirm this until I physically see the car and inspect it, but I'm almost certain that is the long lost Louis Chiron car. And from what you say, it's probably going to be the most original car in existence. Max, that is amongst 'the finds' of the last seventy-five years. People have looked everywhere for that car. Absolutely everywhere. With the exception of possibly the Monaco winning car, it is probably the most desirable and famous of all of them.' Ralph eulogised.

'Okay, so cutting to the chase, what's it worth?' Max asked, because that's what really mattered to all of them.

'Well, I know of other cars recently sold for between half a million and seven hundred and fifty thousand pounds but they're not in the same league as this car and by the sound of it aren't anywhere near as original. I'm thinking it's got to be well over a million pounds, maybe more.'

The hairs were standing up on the back of Max's neck as he sat down and contemplated what Ralph had just told him.

'Ralph, I'll call you when I get back to the UK, Thanks.'

'Cheerio Max, have a safe trip back,' Ralph replied.

'Yes, thank you, bye.'

Max probably couldn't have hoped for a better response from Ralph. Not only was it the real deal, but it was also historically important too and as a result immensely valuable as well even in its poor part assembled condition.

He needed to look at the bodywork. He would need to speak to Jacques to find out which barn it was in.

Ralph put down the phone. He'd had his fair share of wild goose chases over the years, but he'd never had a gobsmacking find such as this. He wanted to pick up the phone and call everyone and let them know what had been found, shout it from the rooftops, but he couldn't. Max's confidentiality agreement had put paid to that. *No*, he thought. *I'm going to pour myself a nice brandy and sit in my favourite chair and look forward to the time I can see it for myself.* He thought of Max. *What a lucky man; what a lucky man.*

Jacques showed Max to the barn. The bodywork was laid out on the floor mostly and loosely put together. There was a sizeable square roughly cut out of the tail.

'What happened there?' Max asked.

'Oh, we think one of the farm hands must have chopped out a piece to repair the seat on one of the tractors. Olivier vaguely remembers something like that happening,' Jacques replied.

Unbelievable, Max thought. Then he realised, *well, not really, I suppose*. The whole car would have been worth virtually nothing after the war. What was perhaps more surprising was that the whole car hadn't been ransacked for parts. No different to Max cannibalising his father's Atco lawnmower for nuts and bolts to repair his motorcycle when he was sixteen. Same thing really, just on a different scale.

Dinner was fantastic. Olivier's family knew how to entertain. It went on for several hours. Max still had the thought in his mind of having to drive all the way home the following day, but his energy levels had been hugely boosted by Ralph Sanders remarks. After, they all retired to the sitting room languishing in the deep cushioned sofas in front of a huge open fire, their faces glowing, their glasses full to brimming, the stories and laughter ever more louder.

Antoinette stood up and went into another room returning with a couple photograph albums moments later. She sat down on the vacant cushion next to Max and started leafing through the old pictures, pointing out the various members of the family.

Max recognised the house and the grounds, the faces were difficult to determine though especially on the older pictures, but one photo did take his eye. It showed a number of young men in the kitchen a few yards away from where he was sitting. Olivier's father was sat at the head of the table with his only son sat to his right. On his left were three men, leant against each other smiling and gesticulating in good humour. The old black and white photograph was nibbled with the familiar tea stains at the edges, but Max could clearly read the signatures scrawled across the border, Louis, Alberto and Grover. *What a fabulous capture of a moment in time*, Max thought. He could imagine them all in the kitchen feverishly talking racing and women, not particularly in that order. Laughing and joking.

There were more similar pictures in the album, it was an historically important book in its own right. Olivier's father was obviously a very wealthy man in his day and entertained regularly, garden parties, dinner parties, drinks dos, all that sort of thing all frozen in sepia. Max recognised some of the faces but couldn't put a name to them. He'd have asked Olivier if he'd stayed awake but the wine had finally taken a hold of him as he dozed in his chair, head back, mouth open catching flies.

The fire was getting low and the night had marched on all too quickly as it always does when you have a good time, so inevitably sleep beckoned. Max was still thinking of the day's events as he drifted off.

There was a light knock on the door, it seemed like the middle of the night. Max came too and said hello, rubbing his eyes. It was Antoinette, she'd brought a cup of coffee. Max looked at his watch, it was just after eight am.

'Good morning, would you like me to open the curtains?' she asked. 'You sleep okay?'

'Yes to both,' said Max hauling himself up. The sun shone brightly through the old windows, as Antoinette reached for the tie backs and tied them in place. She walked back across the bedroom with the sunlight behind her, probably not realising that the sun's rays rendered her almost completely naked as she did so.

She popped her head back around the door as she was going out onto the landing, 'Breakfast is when you're ready. If you need anything, just ask,' she said huskily.

God, I'd better not answer that question, he thought with a smile.

Max drove out of the gate at around ten o'clock having thoroughly enjoyed twenty-four hours of sincere French hospitality with Olivier and his family. They had managed to agree a way forward that would keep everyone happy. Nobody wanted to lose out, they all wanted to benefit so if they all pulled together it would work. Each one knew what they had to do. Max had to find a buyer, Jacques needed to find the missing

350

parts and Olivier needed to write the history. The car would need to be moved to the UK, but Max would take care of that later. For now, he had a long journey ahead of him and then the serious job of finding someone with deep pockets. The one thing that was now really apparent for Max was that he was no longer under pressure to do the deal quickly and get the car out of its situation pronto. The events of the previous twenty-four hours had slowed down the process. Olivier was happy that Max would do the best for him and Max was happy that Olivier wouldn't pull the rug from under him. Max had convinced Olivier that he could buy the car from him for the best price possible provided he had the time and the information to do it. Olivier and Max had shaken hands on it, so as such, the heat was off. Max could do the job properly, get all the ducks in a row and sell the car without being under pressure to have to sell the car. He knew that if he had to sell it under pressure, he was never going to get as much money for it, whereas if the car was inspected and offered for sale with a full report, all the parts and the supporting history with no time restraints or funding issues, then he could sell it from a position of strength knowing that it was the best available and that was the price. Any prospective buyer could then have the choice, take it or leave it.

Driving long distances on his own, Max had the chance to think through his plans. He didn't need to advertise the car. This wasn't the type of car to hawk around. It would be a collector that bought the car, someone with a passion for originality and historical significance. Something very special for someone sympathetic to this type of car. He had a few ideas on some likely candidates, so he wanted to get home and research the individuals first before he made a move. In the rarefied world of high value cars, collectors all know each other, so the cudos is in the quiet acquisition without other's finding out.

As it stood, he had a fantastic saleable car to offer and he knew he had a lot to gain from it. He thought about Ralph Sanders. He needed to get Sanders to write a report based on the information Max had already given him. He knew that it would have the caveat about him having not seen the car, but that wouldn't be a problem because that would happen later and once Sanders had seen the car, the report would basically be the same anyway.

He mentally ticked the boxes in his mind. 1. Get the

report from Sanders. 2. Select some potential buyers. 3. Bring the car to England. 4. Get Sanders to inspect it. 5. Line up the buyer. 6. Get paid. 7. Go on holiday. When he put it like that, it sounded so simple, but there were a few hoops to jump through along the way. He was confident, that was the main thing. He wasn't wasting his time. He knew that if he did get it right, it was going to be worthwhile. He'd had a rotten previous three years and still had a rain cloud hanging over him but this could hopefully put him back to where he was. There was no rush, it just needed to be done properly.

HMP LEYHILL, AUGUST 2008

Max woke up early on the Sunday and opened the curtains. The sun was trying to find its way through the morning mist surrounding the trees in the distance. A squirrel jerked its way along the top of the low picket fencing whilst a few seagulls were pecking at the ground stretching worms out of their homes. He'd never seen that before. The golden autumn leaves of a young elm tree sat sprinkled around its trunk, glinting in the emerging sunlight as the soft breeze gently moved them to and fro.

There was a heavy dew on the grass and a definite sharpness in the air. The seasons were moving on and that was good news. The quicker it happened, the sooner Max would be back at home with his family. *It would be nice to go for a walk after breakfast; get some fresh air*, he thought.

The prison was a quiet place on a Sunday morning with only a few residents bothering to go for breakfast. Most of them were lying in until later in the day. Max couldn't do that, he had to be up and about despite the fact that the inconsiderate arsehole in the room next to him had kept him up most of the night until Max had banged on the party wall and told him to shut up. He'd stop for a while, then start again. That's drugs for you, probably heroin. They were at it all the time. Max wouldn't have known unless he'd been told by his neighbour, Chris Walton.

'Just look at his behaviour, he's at it. One minute he's up, then he's depressed and quiet. He's just a twat, a fucked up twat. Keep away from him. He's just a Hobbit. Nothing. No value,' said Chris.

352

'How do they do it?' Max asked innocently.

'How do they do what?'

'Well, get the drugs in?'

'Oh that's easy. There's no problem with that. They get it chucked over the fence. It's not difficult here.'

'What about paying for it?'

'Again, fairly easy. He's most likely paying for it through his canteen, buying other people their weekly wants and then passing it over. Or he could be organizing payment on the outside via a mobile phone that he's got access to in here. If someone wants the gear, it's not a problem for them.'

Max wasn't surprised, he often saw suspicious goings on, things being hidden in the roof of the ablutions block, people meeting in the middle of the night, to-ing and fro-ing in different rooms. Unusual activity was the norm. Max hadn't been exposed to drugs or anything like that before, so it was all new to him; even the language was a mystery. Anyway, it didn't matter, it wasn't his problem and he wasn't about to get involved with it. He turned a blind eye and pretended he didn't know or hadn't seen what was going on. It was the best way to be.

He stepped out of the 'A' unit entrance and strolled along the same route he took when he went running. There was more to see at this speed, he thought. Nobody else was out, he was alone and he could have easily walked out the front gate and not be noticed missing for several hours. There was no need though, it wasn't a long sentence, he'd got his head around it and he was now just ticking off the remaining days to go.

The fear he'd had at Exeter was a thing of the past. Gone were the psychos, the plastics, the duppys and the window warriors in their raw state. Now, they were detuned. They were still about, but they were subdued versions of their original wild minds. The stuffing had been knocked out.

The grounds around the prison were originally part of an arboretum and there were so many different species of trees in all shapes, sizes and colours. Max couldn't help stopping and staring at them. It's amazing, he would have never stopped and stared at trees on the outside, but now it was different, he had the time with no distractions. He took fifteen minutes to walk each lap of his running course and six and a half minutes running it. He was still amazed at the difference between an open prison and a bang up. The contrast was vast.

He walked for an hour and a half, stopping to chat with

some inmates every now and then, thinking about all sorts of different things as he did so, what'd he'd be doing if he was at home, what the girls would be doing. It wasn't long now, he thought, and that was what it always came back to. Not long.

He went into the kitchen and made himself a cup of tea and returned to his room. The sun was shining straight in through his window as he looked at the blue cloudless sky. Cards from friends and family stood upright on the window sill as he settled down at his desk listening to Radio Two ready to start his next line. Duran Duran's Ordinary World hit filled the air. He loved the song, he knew Simon Le Bon and had actually spoken to him whilst he was in prison. It is not possible for someone on the outside to ring in, but Catherine had said that Simon had called and that she would get Max to ring him. Max dialled their home number and Yasmin answered the call.

Oh, hi Max, how are you ? She asked.

'Yes, fine thanks. Simon's been trying to get hold of me. I'm away at the moment'.

'Anywhere nice'.

Max had to think about a tactful answer to that one, ' No, not really'.

'Here's Simon for you', she passed the phone over.

'Hi Simon, how are you ?

'Good thanks'.

' Catherine said you called. Sorry, I didn't get back to you, I'm away at the moment.' Max drew a breath.' Well, to tell you the truth, I'm residing at Her Majesty's Pleasure'

They had a bizarre conversation ending in Simon asking Max if he could send anything in, but it wasn't necessary, Max wasn't going to be in for too long.

The acoustic guitar intro played into the lyrics, he listened intently.

Came in from a rainy Thursday on the avenue
Thought I heard you talking softly.
I turned on the lights, the TV and the radio
Still I can't escape the ghost of you
What has happened to it all ?
Crazy, somed say.
Where is the life that I recognise ?
Gone away...

But I won't cry for yesterday, there's an ordinary world,
Somehow, I have to find.
And as I try to make my way, to the ordinary world...
I will learn to survive

Passion or coincidence once prompted you to say
Pride will tear us both apart
Well now prides gone out the window cross the rooftops, run away,
Left me in the vacuum of my heart.
What is happening to me ?
Crazy, somed say,
Where is my friend when you need me most ?
Gone away...

The chorus continued. Max thought about the words, they were so poignant now. He sat at his desk motionless, just thinking. It was hard, so much to say, yet impossible to say it. Four walls prevented that. He sighed, rubbed his hands across his face, he just had to get on with it.

NOVEMBER 2000

Unbelievably for the time of year, the phone hadn't stopped ringing following the *Sunday Times* advert for the yellow Ferrari 355 GTB. Max had taken several calls that Monday morning all asking about the same car, and by the end of the day he'd agreed a deal on selling it. The car would be going to a shipping line owner in Amsterdam and another 355 would be coming back in part exchange. If it hadn't been for the foot and mouth disease, it would have been an exceptional year for Velodrome. All the costs of moving into the new premises and the improvements needed would have easily been covered and the overdraft would have been a lot lower. Okay, the overdraft was low at the present time, but that was artificial due to Donald Key's money being in the pot and that would soon change when his 360 Spider arrived. No, it was a shame that things had happened that way, but that's what it's like in business, it's never plain sailing.

The part exchange coming in against the yellow 355 was one of the first right hand drive 355 Spiders, a 1995 car. It would look good value for money if Max advertised it for £59,950 especially as it would only owe him £51,000 when the deal was done. He was pleased with that, but again he wondered what the chances would be of selling a convertible Ferrari mid winter. That was a risk he'd have to take. All the other callers for the yellow car had part exchanges that Max wouldn't have been happy with trying to retail or trade out at a bargain price. The red 355 Spider was exactly the type of car they sold and it was definitely the right deal to be doing.

A couple of days later, Max found himself walking onto the platform at Newton Abbot railway station with Pete. They were on their way to the Motorcycle Show at the NEC. The journey would take a little over two hours and would give them a chance to talk. It was always difficult to talk at work, there were always too many interruptions and generally too much to do. They sat down at their booked seats.

'Do you know, I've always loved this part of the train journey, between here and Exeter. It's the views from the train, they're so spectacular,' Max said.

'Yeah, they are. Thing is, you don't appreciate it so much when you see it everyday, but imagine what it would be like if you were travelling down from say, Birmingham for the first time. It would be magical, especially for children,' Pete replied.

The railway from Newton Abbot heading towards Exeter runs alongside the River Teign for five miles before it reaches the quaint fishing port of Teignmouth then it borders the beach all along the sea front and cliff edge to Dawlish passing through three sandstone tunnels by Shell Cove. The sea is only a stones throw away and walkers can be seen taking the air on the sea wall pathway. Beyond Dawlish, the sea spray on a stormy easterly day usually cascades tons of foaming sea water all over the track often breaking signs and walls and then further on the train passes through the beautiful sand dunes and pampas grasses of Dawlish Warren. And if that isn't enough, the ride then takes you up the mudflats of the River Exe on the one side and the beautiful parkland estate of Powderham Castle on the other.

The masses of crowds and colours was a stark contrast to where they'd just come from as Pete and Max jumped off the train and having established their bearings quickly walked into the show. Every year it seemed to have become bigger and better and more difficult to see everything they wanted to see, but it was indicative of the popularity of the industry. Motorcycles were booming. The product was better than it had ever been, but strangely the market place hadn't been driven by sales to young people as it had in the past. Now, the buyer in the main was 40 plus. It was the second coming. The boys riding in the mid to late 1970s on their Yamaha FS1Es were now buying superbikes in the 90s. Whereas it was Barry Sheene fuelling the boom in 1976, it was Fogarty, Haga et al twenty odd years later. Fogarty didn't do it for Max, fantastic rider but he just didn't have the charisma of Barry Sheene. Max met Barry once at a race meeting at Donington. They had both gone into the paddock toilet block and it was crowded. Barry had his racing leathers on and promptly stripped to the waist to sort himself out, parking at the urinal next to Max. It was a tight squeeze. Max looked across at him recognising his childhood hero and said , ' small isn't it ?'

Barry replied typically, ' Speak for yourself.' They left together laughing and chatting before going their separate ways.

Aprilia were typically bullish about their new products as the MD of the UK importers showed Pete and Max around each new motorcycle, but they knew what they wanted and stuck to their plan. More discount, same volume, more support and better parts supply, that was the order of the day. Yes, yes, yes, we'll do that for you they'd say and then nothing would happen. Typical. The only point that they could really be sure of was that whatever the number of bikes they ordered, they knew they'd get them. Maybe not the colour, but definitely the volume.

The new March first registration helped a little because the bikes ordered at the show would arrive over the Christmas season and then not need to be paid for until March on the Transamerica stocking loan scheme. It filled the showroom with glittering new motorcycles, tempting some people to part with their money before the spring rush. Velodrome's risk was simple, sell seventy-five new Aprilias before the ninety day Transamerica credit turned into a £200,000 direct debit. No sweat there then!

Pete stayed on at the Aprilia stand whilst Max went over to see the guys at Transamerica, making sure all was okay with them and letting them know the volume of product they'd need to finance for Velodrome on it's Aprilia range then adding another £40–50,000 for the Peugeot franchise as well. It was a courtesy visit really. TA were a faceless facility and Max never really met any one man or kept in contact with anyone. As long as the direct debits were paid, Transamerica never really bothered them – Max was happy with that.

The train ride back was staccato chat as Max and Pete read all the leaflets and brochures they'd taken away with them. Velodrome would have several sales representatives calling for appointments over the following few weeks as companies caught up with their show enquiries.

'It's not as much fun as it used to be, is it?' Pete asked.

'No, it's not. I think that's my fault. Sometimes I let the stress of it all get to me. You know how it is. Keith's worrying me. Jackie's going to call me next week. I hope that's good news. It's been eight weeks since he went on holiday. The doctor is saying he will be fit next week, so all being well, we will have his happy smiling face back in the office. I'll feel much better when he's back,' Max replied.

He didn't say it, but as such Velodrome were flying blind and had been for two months. With no computer input, Max didn't know exactly where he was. He had a good idea. He knew the stock level, the creditors and the bank overdraft but it wasn't the same as pressing a button and being able to read the profit and loss on screen exactly how much Velodrome won or lost last month and he needed to know.

'Got much Ferrari stuff on the go?'

'No, it's slowing, although I have sold the yellow car,' he said, 'so that's good.'

'Is there anything more I can do?'

'I don't think so Pete. You're already doing enough. Just keep it going and I'll try to recover the losses we made earlier in the year. I'm pretty sure I can do it. Just need a lucky run that's all.'

JUNE 2002

Father Abbot steadied himself on the fence post as he slowly walked down the wide paved runway towards the conference centre. He wasn't in the best of health and certain things had been troubling him for some time. He stood at the gate looking ahead. In front of him he could see the octagonal

358

fully glazed modern refectory area. To the left, a large square conference hall and to the right a row of smaller meeting rooms off which were a variety of other linked offices overlooking a narrow leat which fed the woollen mill and twenty-five yards further on, the River Dart. It was a beautiful setting.

He slowed and sat down on the wooden slatted park bench, noting the brass plaque screwed to the top rail of the seat back. It read, 'In memory of our dearly beloved friend Father Augustine 1918–1999', he was 81. The Abbot thought about old Gussy as he was known and smiled.

Life had been good to Father Abbot, he'd lived almost all of his entire adult life at the abbey and he'd achieved more than he could have ever hoped. He'd never considered himself an ambitious man, yet there he was at the top of the tree. All good things come to those that wait.

He looked around at all of natures beautiful things and concluded that whoever said that 'the grass gets greener, the closer you get to the grave', was absolutely right. The beauty of it all had been brought into so much sharper focus as he sat there and soaked it all in. He placed his elbow on the armrest and put his head in his hand. Time had flown by. *Forty years walking these grounds*, he thought. Forty wonderful years since he had first looked around. His mind raced back, the vision of thirty years before, a hazy view, it was a summer evening, all the children were playing, shouting, running around with boundless energy. It was as if it was yesterday, a beautiful time in the prime of his life. Some of the boys were sat with their backs against the low wall opposite, others were playing British bulldog. He looked at the octagonal glazed refectory where once he presided over all the children at the top table, then the large square building which was home to the well equipped gymnasium and then on the other side, the classrooms and store rooms overlooking the leat, which fed the woollen mill and twenty-five yards further on the River Dart. It was a beautiful setting.

'Sir, sir, please, please come and be on our side, we haven't enough players.'

'Max, I can't join in.'

'Yes, you can sir,' the little boy said excitedly grabbing hold of his hand and dragging him over to the lawn area at the end of the classrooms.

'Right, ready everyone?'

'Yesssss,' cried out the reply from the horde.

359

He put his hand up above his head and then dropped it out in front of him as if pointing his sword at the enemy.

'Charge,' he shouted in a prolonged voice and ran towards the opponents.

A teardrop trickled from his eye and rolled down his cheek as he thought about Max, his high-pitched young voice enthusiastically shouting 'sir, sir.' His face locked in his mind. He started to sob and covered his eyes with his hand. He'd done some horrible things. If only he could turn back the clock, so that he could put right the wrongs. It was impossible, he knew that. He'd have to face it in purgatory, he thought; there was no doubting that. Hopefully he would get some credit for all the good he'd done, he didn't know. He dried his eyes, steadied himself as he stood up slowly and walked on, the cool evening air fresh on his reddened cheeks.

The school had long since closed, albeit the landscape was still the same. Father Abbot missed the children, he missed their happy smiling faces beaming back at him. That was all now gone, a fading memory.

NEWTON ABBOT, NOVEMBER 2000

Max stood at the top of the showroom chatting to Pete when the postman brought in the post and handed it over, enthusing over some of the new bikes as he walked back out the front door. It was just after eight am, the showroom lights were still on night light settings as the pair of them discussed their respective weekends.

Max had won the South West Enduro Championship in his class for the second time and he'd also met with Graham Lord on the Saturday. Pete's wife had a successful art exhibition on the Saturday night, so between them they'd all had good weekends and were in a buoyant mood.

Pete walked into Max's office and sat down in his familiar chair. Max switched on all the electrics as he walked through Keith's office into his own and sat at his desk. The usual sound of printers, computers and the fax machine all starting up buzzed, whizzed and whined about them.

They started their daily meeting. Max toyed with the post, one envelope caught his eye. It was obviously from the bank, and it was postmarked Bristol.

The phone rang. It was unusual for that time of the morning.

'I better get this,' Max said to Pete and picked it up. It was Jackie.

'Keith's had another blood clot. He's in intensive care at Torbay.' She didn't have to say anything else. That was enough.

Max asked what he could in the circumstances, but realistically there was very little he could do. He'd put down the phone. Pete had guessed from the way the phone call had gone that it was about Keith.

'Is Jackie all right?' he asked.

'God, I don't know. I think she thought she'd got through the worst of it, now this.'

Max was expecting Keith back at work that day. He took a deep sigh. *I don't know what I'm going to do now*, he thought. Velodrome was already two months and more behind with the accounts paperwork and Keith coming back to work was going to sort out all of that. Now that wasn't going to happen. Max would have to organise an alternative. He was desperately sorry for Jackie and their family but now it was a massive problem for Max too. It was only a few weeks before Christmas and trying to find someone to sort out the back log was going to be impossible.

'Pete, I'm going to need to get on with a few things. Can I leave it at that. If you need me, I'm in all day, just ask.' Max said quickly finishing off their meeting. He certainly had plenty to do, the buoyant start was quickly becoming a stressful morning.

Although it was still early, he picked up the phone and dialled his accountants. The answer phone kicked in and Max left a short message for Ron to call him back as soon as possible. Whilst he was waiting, he trawled through his email messages binning ninety per cent of them. Nino's message was simple, it read Ferrari 250 Short Wheel base, please, call me. There was another from Sirol basically saying the same. Nothing else of any value. Pete brought in a cup of tea and placed it on the desk.

'What are you going to do?' he asked.

'Well, I'm not going to panic. I've just left a message with the accountants, so hopefully I can get something sorted with them. I'll see if I can get them in to input the backlog and then maintain it until we know exactly what's going on, and then take it from there. The reality is that Keith won't be back before Christmas, if at all, so we need to cover our position,' Max replied.

He thought about how stupid he'd been to let it all get into this state, but then thought that most people would have done the same. If they thought someone was coming back to work next week and then that next week became a fortnight, they'd take the view that they'd rather wait and get their own man back in rather than hastily recruit someone else. Given that Keith had been recovering and the doctors had been positive too, it all added to the decision Max had made to hang on and wait for Keith to return. Now, he was nearly in a little bit too deep, at a time when he didn't want to be.

The yellow Ferrari 355 was going out at eleven o'clock, so Max went into the service department just after 9.00 and checked everything was okay; all the instruments were working properly, fuel tank was full and ran the car up for ten minutes until it was properly warm. He left the car running and went around to the back of the car and lifted the engine cover, peering in to check all was well. He was pleased it was exactly as it should be and switched off the ignition closed the driver's door quietly behind him. He looked around at the other seven Ferraris parked in the service area and marvelled at the beauty of them all.

As soon as the deal was done, he'd need to call Dimo and let him know the car was sold and make the payment. Max would not be able to ask Dimo to fund the part exchange as the car was too old for Dimo, so Max would finance it through the bank overdraft until such time that it was sold.

'Max, are you still there?' Guy shouted across the service area.

'Yes, I'm here,' came the reply.

'Nick Salmon's on the line for you.'

'Okay, tell Mike, I'll take it in my office. I'm on my way.'

Max walked into his office and picked up the telephone and answered as he sat down in his swing chair.

'Yes, hi Nick, sorry about that, I was in the service area.'

'That's okay, how are you?'

'Busy chasing my backside. You know how it is.'

'Yes, it's the same here. It's a totally different job to when I started. Now it's all university graduates, young guns.

Plenty of qualifications but no common sense and no experience. I don't know where it's all leading. We used to go on the person now it's all credit score, it's madness, there's no discretion and it's getting worse,' said Nick rather disgruntled.

'I wish I didn't need the bank, but at my stage in business, it's the only way,' said Max.

'Well it is for most people. Look, I don't know if you've had any letters from us yet but Simon Hughes has written a letter direct to you regarding the overdraft facility. He wants it reduced by £50,000 to a maximum of £100,000. Now I know, I've let you run to over £180,000 at times, but with Hughes in control, I'm not going to be allowed any discretion. If you go over the £100,000 limit, I've been instructed to return cheques. The other point is that the cost of borrowing is going up half a per cent to 3.5% over base rate and it's with immediate effect.'

'Why?'

'He thinks your business is a little bit too risky,' Nick replied.

'All businesses are risky. I've been banking with Barclays since 1987, why this, why now?'

'Max, it's not me. I'm just following orders,' Nick said with a sigh.

'This isn't going to do me any good at all.'

'I know, but at least your overdraft is low at the moment,' Nick commented.

Max didn't say anything, but the only reason the overdraft was low was because of Donald Key's money. Now £50,000 of that was being wiped out by the bank.

Max put down the phone and sat back in his chair contemplating the effects of Simon Hughes' funding changes. He was beginning to think, what's the point? but that wouldn't help. What he had to do now was get some deals done, get some money in and fight. *Don't let the bastards grind you down*, he thought.

Ron rang back from the accountants and Max explained about Barclays. Ron told Max he wasn't alone, several of his clients were experiencing the same. That didn't help Max, but at least he didn't think he was being victimised. On a brighter side, Ron had agreed to send around one of his girls from the office to start wading through Velodrome's backlog of paperwork and get it on screen. That was a relief.

The next call came in from the Dutchman buying the

yellow 355.

'Hi, I am extremely sorry, but I can't collect the car today, I have to be in South America for a few weeks. Obviously, I still want the car, so I've sent my son down with my car and a bankers draft for the difference. If it's all okay, I'll collect the new car in the new year and leave you with my car. My son is going to fly back as he's coming with me! All the documents for my car are in the service wallet.'

'That's no problem for me. Provided your car is as you've described, then the deal will be as we agreed on the telephone. When do you think you'll collect the new car?' asked Max.

'Mid to end of January, if that's okay with you?'

'Yes, that will be fine.'

When the car arrived, it was as described, so Max called and confirmed the deal. The part exchange car was in the unusual colour of Barchetta red, which is dark red. It looked different, but in a way a lot more classy than the usual Rosso Corsa racing red. The service department looked quite full when Max parked it indoors and inspected it under the neon light.

The important phone calls were coming in thick and fast. Max had rung Dimo earlier asking if he had any news on the 360 Spider and now Dimo was on the phone saying he'd heard nothing but he'd go into Sebastien's and find out what was happening.

So far it hadn't been too good a day. Keith was back in hospital, the bank had reduced the overdraft by £50,000 and now Dimo was making Max a bit jumpy over the delivery of the 360 Spider. Anyway he had a bankers draft in his hand for 18,000, so he needed to bank that first. He decided to walk up to the bank rather than take a scooter. He needed some fresh air and some time to think.

As Max walked along the pavement returning from the bank he could see up ahead, the Aprilia lorry unloading motorcycle crates on to an already crowded Velodrome forecourt. The workshop staff were busy sliding the boxes into the storage area. It was a familiar sight for the neighbours as the delivery truck blocked one lane of the busy main street of the town, causing traffic chaos as he did so. Max weighed in and helped out.

Dimo rang back. The news was not good.

'I've just spoken to Victor at Sebastien's. He hasn't been

notified of a delivery as yet.'

'Does that mean they're not coming or does that mean, the cars will be here after Christmas?' asked Max.

'I don't know Max. He's going to call me in a couple of days.'

Max lowered the phone slowly and then purposely dropped the last inch or so onto the cradle. He was more than a little bit worried. Dimo had asked about the yellow car and Max had told him it hadn't gone out yet. It wasn't a lie. He was telling the truth, but what he didn't say was that he'd been paid for it. He'd had the part exchange in and he'd been paid the balance. When Max had walked up to the bank, he'd had chance to think things through and although it was against his better judgement, he thought he'd tell Dimo that the car was still with them. It would buy some time over the Christmas break. How right it was to do that especially now that the 360 Spider hadn't arrived was a question he'd answer later, but for now he thought it was the best option.

Carol arrived from the accountants just after lunch. She was pleasant enough. Max showed her all the records and gave her the password to get into the accounts programme.

'I'll file everything first, so I'm assuming these are the current records,' she said, pointing at the records on the shelf.

'Yes. Keith was meticulous with his filing, so it all runs in month order and VAT quarter order,' described Max.

'It should be quite easy. I can see how it all goes. I'll get into the accounts package and see how that works. Is it Sage based, that's what we use back in the office?' she asked.

'No, it's a specialist motorcycle programme called Catalyst.'

'Okay, they're all basically the same, so hopefully it should be all right.'

Max left her to it, relieved that at least something was being done about it. The VAT return was due at the end of the following month so the quarter ended in the current month, which meant all the input needed to be done within the next two weeks. Keith wouldn't have had a problem, because he knew what he was doing. A new data inputter would take a little longer to do all the entries, but Max was confident it wouldn't be an issue.

Max went back into his office, the phone was ringing, he picked it up. It was Graham Lord.

'Yes, hi Graham. Good weekend?'

'Yes, we enjoyed it very much. The hotel was excellent and the countryside is absolutely spectacular. Both Jane and I said we'd both like to do it again. Maybe in the spring if we get chance. It's a very nice part of the world to live,' said Graham.

'We like it, which is why we've always lived here. I went to school, in fact both of us went to school locally and have been born, bred and lived in Devon all our lives. I don't think that I'd have it any other way. You'd like spring, especially when it snows. Dartmoor is beautiful covered in snow .'

'I can imagine.'

'The only problem is the volume of drivers up there testing their skills. Anyway, what can I do for you?' Max asked.

'I've had Donald Key on the phone asking about his 360 Spider. Any news?'

'Not as yet. I'm expecting to hear something in a couple of days,' Max replied.

It wasn't quite true, because Max had spoken to Dimo and he knew that Dimo was told that there was no imminent delivery news. He didn't want to tell Graham that, because it might get Donald Key a bit up tight and at this stage there was no need to say anything negative.

Graham asked, 'What do you think I should tell him?'

'Just say that we've not had anything confirmed as yet and we're waiting to hear. As soon as I know, you'll know,' Max suggested.

The fact that the 360 Spiders hadn't yet arrived would become a very big problem for Max if they didn't appear. Not only would he not benefit from the profit on the second car, but he'd also have all the likely aggravation from Graham Lord's customer Donald Key. It wasn't something Max liked thinking about, because as such, he was not in control. He was at the beck and call of Ferrari and that was not ideal.

'Have you found out anything about the 330 GTO?' Max asked Graham.

'No, nothing definite. I have spoken to Donald Key several times and he always says the same thing, nothing different to when I went down to his office and went through it with him. Thinking about it since, the only thing I do find strange is what happened to the original bodywork. The Middle Eastern customer didn't get it in the original sale and the current owner hasn't got it either. Moreover, we would not be getting it

366

if your customer goes ahead,' said Graham.

'So what are you saying?' Max asked.

'Well, I'm just wondering whether it's worth asking Angelo whether the change of bodywork is the big issue with the eligibility? If it is the bodywork, which we know was replaced when Donald Key restored the car, maybe we could sort it out. I'd have to ask Don the whereabouts of that body,' Graham answered.

'I could call Angelo. See what he says?'

'I think that could be very worthwhile.'

'I'll call him this afternoon,' said Max.

'What's happening with your customer?'

'Oh, he's okay at the moment. He's away on holiday. He's not back for a couple of weeks, but it would be good to get it all sorted out for Christmas.'

'Absolutely,' Graham agreed.

They finished their telephone call and Max thought about the 330 GTO. Right from the start, he knew that the car had crashed when only a month old and still owned by the factory. Enzo Ferrari had sold the car to a customer, prior to it being damaged when they were testing some parts on it for the forthcoming Le Mans 24 hour race. Max knew all that and he was comfortable about it. It had been properly recorded in the various history books so there was no disputing it. The story relating to the replacement bodywork was again fairly straightforward. It was so badly damaged it was beyond repair. The new owner wanted the car quickly and Ferrari didn't have a GTO style body so they fitted a body similar to a 250 short wheel base, which they had in the factory. The new owner accepted the alteration and that is how the car remained until Donald Key's restoration. The Baron however, preferred the GTO style body and commissioned Don to restore the car to look the same as it would have been prior to the 1962 crash with another new body. In other words, exactly as it was first manufactured and also looking the same as all the other 1962 GTO's. Most people would have done the same.

Max called Angelo and asked him the simple question, 'Is it the bodywork that's causing the problem?' and Angelo equally simply said, 'No, it's not the bodywork.'

Well, if it wasn't the bodywork that was the problem, then it had to be either the mechanicals or the chassis. If it was the mechanicals, then something had to be incorrect.

Max called Graham Lord.

'Graham, it's not the bodywork,' he said.

'Okay, well it has to be the chassis, engine, gearbox or back axle, then doesn't it?'

'Well, something's not right and Angelo won't tell me. Can you give John Gill a call and ask him straight out the engine number, gearbox number and back axle numbers. Oh, and the numero interno? It's not as if we have another GTO to offer my customer, otherwise I'd suggest we leave this car alone and go with something else!'

'I'll ring John Gill now and come back to you within the next hour,' said Graham.

'Okay, speak to you later.' Max rang off.

The problem with this GTO was that if the reasons for Angelo not accepting the car were based on the chassis identity then the whole deal was a non runner. Nobody would accept a car of this value having a replacement non original Ferrari factory chassis. If it was a mechanical issue, then it could be that the engine had been replaced, or the gearbox changed or someone had fitted a replacement back axle all of which could be surmountable. The chassis was definitely not something that could be overcome. Donald Key had such a good reputation, it would be unlikely that he had changed the chassis, so Max believed the real problem was the engine. The car possibly had a different engine in it, maybe from a later car and that was at the root of the eligibility problem. If that was the case, then the options open to Max would have been to have found the original engine and fitted it or find an equivalent engine from the correct period to do the job and that would have been feasible.

STOVER, JULY 1985

It was a windy Saturday, the tree tops were gusting fiercely in the south westerly squalls. Hopefully it would blow over by half past two and the sun would come out for a great day.

Rob had been around at Max's flat since about eleven o'clock. They'd talked about how long they'd know each other and all the different things they'd done together. It had been a long and sincere friendship that would probably last for the rest

368

of their lives.

Max walked out of the kitchen with two carnations and gave one to Rob. At the second time of asking, Catherine's father had relented to Max's request to marry his daughter and that afternoon they would walk up the aisle together, four years after they'd first met at the Lustleigh tea room. For both of them, it was everything they had ever wanted.

They had a spectacular day, she looked fabulous and the weather was kind to them and their two hundred guests. Max's father was one of them as was his mother albeit sat at opposite ends of the top table. The rift had not healed even after twelve years. Max had tried to placate both of them on the lead up to the wedding, but a few days before the big day, Max and Catherine still didn't know whether his father was coming. In the end he did, but it was really just another demonstration of his old ways.

It didn't matter, all that did matter was that Catherine and Max were happy and had the best day of their lives. Catherine looked stunning in her white wedding dress, beaming that beautiful smile. Max was a lucky man and he knew it.

They honeymooned in Spain for two weeks and then returned to England to sell Max's flat and buy a home together. They had put an offer in on a three bedroom semi detached house that needed considerable improvement and were hoping that when they got back they would have an answer. They did and it was good news. Max was unemployed at the time, which meant finding a job. Within a couple of weeks he was working as a double glazing salesman by night and renovating their home by day. Rob was helping with the decorating too.

Max had stopped motor racing and was spending all his time either working or doing it yourself. At last, he was earning some decent money and Catherine had settled in working in her father solicitor's practice running the probate department. All was settled and all was well.

Nearly a year later, Max had all but finished the work on the house when a neighbour stopped one day outside. He had told Max that he was going to sell his home and knowing that Max had always admired it, asked him if he was interested. Well yes he was interested but £75,000 in 1986 was a lot of money. He thought about whether he could make it work and after speaking to Catherine decided to talk to an estate agent.

Unbelievably, six weeks later they'd sold the three bedroom semi detached and moved one hundred and fifty yards to a house they still live in today. It was a big risk at the time, but it had turned out to be worth it.

The double glazing job was going well and Max was good at it, so the money was good too which was just as well. He had an appointment to see a customer one night just outside Newton Abbot. Having measured up all the windows and given the customer a price, he sat in their lounge filling out an order form when he noticed a number of photographs of sports cars on top of the fireplace.

'If ever I had the money, I'd have a Ferrari!' Max said.

The customer looked at him. 'I know where there is one if you're interested, it's only five minutes from here. It belongs to a friend of mine. He's either trying to sell it or it's just been sold. I'm not sure. I know he had someone looking at it,' he said.

Max asked him for a telephone number and couldn't wait to get out of the house and give the guy a call. It was a Friday night. The seller was at home and he answered the phone. Max introduced himself and told the seller how he'd come to get his number and they agreed to meet the following morning. Max didn't have enough money to buy the car, but nothing ventured nothing gained. He'd found out that the car was a 1974 Ferrari Dino and that it needed a lot of restoration work. At that stage, Max thought he'd go along, take a look and probably walk away, but things turned out very differently when he met the guy the following day.

Steve had to hold up the large wooden door as he opened the barn and revealed a very sad looking Ferrari Dino. It was in a dreadful state, being almost completely dismantled. The engine and gearbox were out of the car resting on the earthen floor and the interior was also removed. It sat on its four wheels, but there was no glass in it. It didn't look good at all.

'How much do you want for it?' Max asked.

'Eleven thousand,' came the reply.

Max couldn't believe it but he found himself asking Steve if he'd take ten thousand and when Steve said yes, Max was quite taken aback. He didn't have £10,000, but he'd have to find it if he was going to go through with it. He walked around the sorry remains of the car and looked at Steve. Max knew that if the car was all up together, it would be worth at least twice the amount Steve was asking.

'Okay, I'll go with that.' Max stretched out his hand and shook Steve's adding, 'I haven't got any money on me now, but

I'll sort it out on Monday and give you a call. Is that okay?'

Steve agreed, the deal was done, just the matter of paying for it to think about. Max set off home wondering about how he was going to put it to Catherine. It was laughable really but somehow he convinced Catherine and first thing on the Monday morning, he was sat in front of his bank manager trying to convince him too.

The bank manager at Barclays Bank in Newton Abbot at the time was a really nice chap called Peter Howard and he had Max Reed sat in front of him enthusiastically explaining his proposition.

'All I want to do is buy the car for £10,000, take it home, then advertise it for £19,000 in the Exchange & Mart. Hopefully sell it and make a profit,' said Max. He'd bought along a number of magazines showing current values of similar cars in tip top condition to show the car's potential worth.

'And how long will you want to borrow the money for?' asked Peter.

'A month, possibly six weeks,' came the reply.

'And when will you need the money?'

'Today,' said Max adding after a short pause, 'in cash. That's how the seller wants to be paid.'

'Okay, well let me give it some thought and I will give you a call after lunch,' Peter said standing up and walking to the door.

Max was hoping he was going to get an answer there and then. He hadn't thought about the bank manager needing time to make a decision. He went home thinking to himself that he was going to look a bit of a prat if the answer was 'no'. He needn't have worried, Peter Howard called Max just after lunch as he had said and confirmed the cash would be available for him to collect at 3:30 pm. It was the first Ferrari Max would buy and started a life long relationship with the marquee.

The plans to make a quick sale didn't materialise which meant that although Max had done exactly as he had told Peter Howard, the end result was that he still had the car six weeks later. He rang Peter Howard.

'I was wondering if we could have a change of plan on the Ferrari Peter.'

'What do you have in mind?'

'Well, I've had several enquiries on the car but no one as yet has put their hand in their pocket.'

Peter interrupted, 'What about borrowing the money over twelve months?'

'How much would the repayment be?'

'Could you afford £200 per month?'

'Yes, I could do that.'

'Okay, I'll tell you what we can do. I'll set up a loan account in the sum of £10,000,' he was making notes as he talked, 'and you pay back £200 per month by standing order from your M. Reed current account and then we can review it in twelve months time. If you sell the car in between time, then we'll stop the standing order and settle the loan account. How's that?'

'That would be great,' Max replied. It was a good result and gave Max some time to get the car sold. Nearly all of Max's friends who'd seen the car and Catherine in particular thought Max was completely mad. She would say that the car looked like it had been dragged up from the sea bed, but Max hung on to his belief that it was a good deal and that somewhere along the line, there would be a decent profit in it. He was right, but even he didn't expect to make as much as he did in such a short space of time.

The sale of the car came about in a very roundabout way. It started eleven months later with a friend of his giving him a call.

'Hi Max, how are you?'

'Fine, you?'

'Yes, busy as hell. Usual story. What did you do with the Ferrari Dino?' asked Colin.

'I've still got it. I've tried selling it on and off but I only seem to be getting idiots answering the ads!'

'Okay, well this probably won't interest you then, but I'll tell you all the same, because you might know someone that is. There's a guy I know who used to live near me and moved with his job to Virginia in the United States. At the time he had a 1978 Ferrari 308 GTB and he took it with him. Now, he's decided to stay in the States and wants to get a left hand drive Ferrari so the 308 needs to be sold. He only wants £30,000 for it, which seems cheap. Do you know anyone that might be interested?'

'No, I don't, but I'll bear it in mind.' Max put down the phone and thought about it. A good 308 GTB was worth forty to forty five thousand pounds so £30,000 did seem very reasonable.

He wondered about buying the car and then immediately selling it on for say £40,000 and with the profit paying off the Ferrari he had at home. That would make a lot of sense.

He rang Colin back. 'Can you just hang on with that 308 GTB for a moment? I'm going to make a few calls and then I'll call you back.'

'Yes, that's okay with me. I won't offer it to anyone else until I've spoken to you,' said Colin.

Max rang Peter Howard at Barclays Bank and put the scenario to him.

'So let me get this right,' he said, 'you want to borrow another £30,000 to buy a what is it?'

'A Ferrari 308 GTB,' Max replied. It didn't sound good.

'Okay, to buy a Ferrari 308 GTB, which is in Virginia, America and then you want to ship it back to the UK, where you think you'll get £40,000 minimum for it and with the profit, you want to pay off the £10,000 on your loan account. Is that right?'

'Yes, that's about it.'

'How long will it take to ship it back?' Peter asked.

'I've been told about a month, so I'd use that time to advertise and sell the car.'

'I think I've heard that story before, haven't I?'

'Well, yes, but it's a slightly different situation with this car.'

'Okay, I'm not saying yes and I'm not saying no, I need to speak to someone first and then I'll call you back,' said Peter.

Max knew Peter would return the call and he was quite surprised that he hadn't been at all negative. Max thought it was worth a try so what the hell, if Peter said no, Max was no worse off than he was before the call.

When Peter returned from lunch he looked at Max's account and seeing that it had been run properly, he picked up the phone.

'Max, I'm going to have to charge you an arrangement fee of £250, but I will mark it up on your account this afternoon as an overdraft. If you could come into the bank sometime tomorrow to sign some paperwork, that will get everything sorted.'

'Well, thank you for that. I'll be in tomorrow,' Max replied.

'When do you think you'll need the money?'

'I'll have to come back to you on that. If I let you know

when I come in tomorrow. Is that okay?' Max asked.

'Yes, no problem.'

Max put down the phone and immediately called Colin and told him he'd have the car. He was quite surprised. Max organised Rapid Movements to collect the Ferrari from Virginia Beach a few days after the funds were transferred and it arrived back into the UK four weeks later. It had been as easy as one two three, which was just as well because whilst the car was on the water making it's way to Blighty, Max had been trying to sell it and that hadn't produced as much response as he'd expected. He didn't worry about it, because he knew he'd bought it for the right money and there had to be someone out there for it.

Catherine picked up the phone in the kitchen and was talking to someone when Max walked in through the back door.

She shrugged, 'It's an Andy Robertson for you,' and she handed him the phone.

'Hello.'

'Oh, hi, it's Andy Robertson speaking. You left a message on my answer phone a couple of weeks ago regarding a Ferrari 308 GTB.'

Max didn't know who he was and couldn't remember calling him, although to be fair he had called a lot of people.

Andy continued, 'Well, it's just a courtesy call really. I can't say I'm looking for a 308 at the moment, but just wanted to thank you for offering it to me. The 308 is a little bit too new for me, but if you get anything else give me a call.'

'What sort of thing are you looking for?' Max asked.

'I suppose anything really pre 1975. You know the sort of things, Dinos, Daytonas, 275s and all the obvious early stuff.'

'Well, I do have a 246 Dino, if you're interested?'

'Tell me more,' asked Andy.

'It's a 1974 246 GT Dino. It needs a lot of work. It's solid, but stripped out with the engine, gearbox and interior all removed. I bought it locally nearly a year ago. Obviously, I've got the log book and there's lots of parts with it,' Max replied.

'Whereabouts are you?'

'Newton Abbot in Devon.'

'Well, I'm blowed; my family are from Ashburton and Chudleigh a few miles from you. We used to own a lot of land alongside the A38 going up to Haldon Tower.'

'Yes, I know where you mean. So where are you now?'

'Oh, I moved up to Cheshire. Alderley Edge. It's not as

nice as Devon but it's fairly central for what I do. Is there any chance of being able to look at the Dino tomorrow?'

'Yes, that's no problem at all.'

'It'll take me about four hours so if I leave here around eight, I'll be with you somewhere around midday.'

'Great.'

Max gave his address to Andy and put down the phone looking across the kitchen at Catherine and raising his eyebrows in a rather satisfied look.

'What did he say?' she asked.

'He says he's coming down from Alderley Edge tomorrow. Should be here for midday,' said Max.

'That sounds good,' she said.

Both of them had learned not to get their hopes up. Max had sold many bikes and cars over the years and the one thing he knew he could always be sure of was that buyers would almost always let you down. Plenty of talk on a phone but when it came down to parting with the cash they were nowhere to be seen. Fortunately not everyone was like that, but they were definitely in the majority.

It was just before midday when a black BMW 635 CSI nosed its way down Max's drive and parked by the front door. Max noticed the number plate as he walked from the kitchen into the hallway, it read 'Andy'.

'Hi, I'm Max,' he shook Andy's hand. 'You made good time.'

'Yes, it was a good run, no problems. I come down this way quite often, so I knew how long it was going to take.'

Catherine came out onto the driveway and Max introduced her.

'Can I get you a cup of tea or coffee?' she asked.

'Thank you, coffee, white with two would be nice,' came the reply.

Max walked down towards the garage and opened the two hinged wooden doors to reveal the Ferrari Dino.

Andy said nothing. He wandered around the car looking inside it through the unglazed windows and ran his hand along the bodywork. Max just watched him.

'Okay, so where's all the mechanical parts and engine etc?' Andy asked.

'Through here,' Max beckoned him. It had all been laid out for Andy to view.

'And you've got the log book?'

'Yes, I've got all the paperwork inside,' Max replied.

'That's fine. I've seen enough here.' Max was amazed, he'd only looked at it for three minutes or four minutes absolute max.

'Let's get that coffee, I'm parched,' said Andy.

'Yes, okay,' Max closed the garage doors behind him and went into the kitchen thinking, he's not going to buy this.

'How long have you lived here? Nice house.'

'Thanks, just over a year. We like it,' said Catherine.

'I love it down here. It always feels like home, but it's difficult to earn a living,' Andy said with a smile.' Well, a decent living anyway '.

'We've always lived around here so we don't know anything else,' she answered.

'Shall we go and sit in the lounge?' Max suggested.

They all walked into the lounge and sat down. Max opened the Ferrari box file on the coffee table and handed the log book to Andy along with some various other odd pieces of paper he'd got with the car when he'd bought it.

'Okay, that all looks right. I'd like to make you an offer for the car. It's definitely what I'm looking for. If you accept my offer, I'll give you a £10,000 cash deposit now and I'll have my man collect the car tomorrow and pay you the balance by bankers draft,' Andy said assertively.

Max realised straightaway that he'd already covered his cost on the car from the deposit that Andy was prepared to pay. That was a good start.

'That would be okay with us,' said Max, looking across at Catherine and waiting for Andy's next move.

'It's worth £40,000 to me so that's what I'm prepared to offer and I'll give you a £10,000 deposit right now.'

It was a fantastic offer. Max looked at Andy, 'I was hoping I could get a little bit more than that,' he said. He wasn't, he was bowled over by Andy's offer, but he didn't want to give in immediately.

Andy came back at him, 'Well, that's all it's worth to me, so if you want to do it, I'll get the money.'

Max didn't need asking a second time and he didn't need to look at Catherine either. He stood up, stretched out his hand and shook Andy's hand. 'You've got yourself a deal,' he said smiling.

'Thank you. That was a worthwhile trip,' Andy replied.

The BMW reversed back out of the driveway as Max closed the front door having waved goodbye to Andy as he drove off. He looked at Catherine, eyebrows raised with a 'told you so' look. She smiled, shaking her head. Effectively, the 308 GTB came for free. The money that Max had made on the Dino paid for the 308 outright and he still had it seventeen years later.

May 1986 Salcombe

Doug guided the forty two foot multi hull in to Salcombe Estuary being sure to keep within the port and starboard marker buoys. It had been quite a long eleven day journey from the coast of Morocco especially after they had to take shelter twice due to bad weather, but now they were almost home and dry. What Doug was really looking forward to was a nice hot bath and a decent English cooked breakfast. The crew of four including Doug had been away for nearly a month and they were now tired of the sea, the travelling and the cramped living conditions. Although it was a fairly sizeable yacht, it was only sparsely fitted out, because it was an ex-ocean going racer and they would not have had any need for creature comforts on that type of vessel. It was built more for speed.

Doug called up the harbour master on the radio asking permission to moor up on the visitors berth. The response was immediate and affirmative. Ten minutes on the motor and the yacht would be alongside. It was a beautiful day for a Thursday morning in May and Doug took the time to look around as he trickled upstream. It was quiet, just the sounds of the gently splashing water and the light wind in the rigging disturbed the peace. He turned the stainless steel helm slightly to alter course, standing as he did so. The other three crew members were still below deck sorting out their kit for when they went ashore. Doug had enjoyed the adventure, it was like a 'Boys Own' trip with the excitement and the banter all thrown in the mix. He thought about what he would do with his million pound share. It was a nice thought.

He looked around the boat, he was about five hundred yards from the berth. Dave popped his head out of the hatch looking straight back at Doug rubbing his eyes as he did so.

'What the fuck is that?' he shouted.

Doug spun around and looked behind him. It was the customs cutter Endurance. Panic gripped them, they hadn't expected this. It had all gone so well. Doug shouted, 'Get it overboard, dump it, quick, for fuck's sake, get it off the boat.'

Frantically the crew unpacked the cannabis from the secret compartments and tried desperately to dump it over the side. Doug throttled up the engine in a vain attempt to avoid being caught but the cutter was bearing down on them at twenty knots. It was no match for Doug's five knots. They didn't even get a quarter of it off the boat before the cutter pulled alongside and grappled the yacht to a standstill. It was hopeless. Doug thought about diving over the side and trying to make a swim for it, but he knew he didn't stand much chance of that. It was over. Well and truly. Customs had been tracking them for three days at a safe distance since their arrival into British waters, quietly observing them on the radar waiting to see where they would go.

The customs officers jumped onto the yacht and immediately handcuffed Doug and his three crew. He couldn't see how he was getting away with this. Three years maybe five, whatever it was going to be a bloody long time. He thought about Judy. She'd be waiting for him at the quayside. She had probably seen it all happening and wouldn't have been able to warn him. What a mess.

Max sat his kitchen table with Catherine having their evening meal. The six thirty local news was reporting the four million pounds drugs seizure in the Salcombe estuary. Up to that point neither of them were taking much interest, until the reporter mentioned Douglas Harris of Bow, Crediton. So that's how he made his money, they thought. They wouldn't hear of Doug again for another twenty years and then it would be in the most bizarre of circumstances.

GP, SEPTEMBER 2000

The reddish orange dust plume in the distance diverted Rux's attention to the horizon. He could just make out the dirty white four wheel drive Nissan Patrol. It made a change for Leaman to be on time. He pulled up in front of Rux's white and green Landcruiser, reaching over to the passenger seat before opening the driver's door and kicking it open as he straightened himself up.

'Captain Rux, how are you today?'

378

'Ah, just fine,' Rux replied. 'All the better for you to be on time for once.'

'Things to do, people to see, you know what it's like. Got much on?'

'It's quiet at the moment. A few things happening but not much. Your man is still creating some interest, still don't know why, though.'

'What did you make of the taps?'

'Difficult to say,' Rux leant back against the bonnet of his car and lit up a cigarette, flicking the match down on to the earthen road. He took a deep drag. 'You could look at it two ways, he's either currency trading or he's laundering. They're big numbers, I mean huge numbers. I don't know how anybody could make that sort of money.'

'Do you think he's legit?'

'I don't know. Look at the house and the cars. It says wealth but it doesn't scream it, does it?'

'No, not really.'

'Some of the money he's transferring is in billions of dollars. Not millions, or hundreds of thousands, billions,' Rux emphasised. 'I can't even get my head around it.'

'Well, I'll have a look at it all before I pass it on.'

'I think your client needs to be very careful if he does anything with him, that's my advice.' Rux handed over the file and a second package with the telephone tap tapes and the transcripts.'

'There you go Cap.'

Rux took the envelope, looked in through the unsealed flap and said, 'Thanks, always a pleasure.' He flicked his cigarette across the dirt track road and got back into his car. 'Until the next time,' he said nodding and drove off.

Leaman looked through the paperwork before getting back into his car. There was a lot of stuff. Rux was right. He leafed through the transcripts, they were difficult to understand, it was almost like they were spoken in code. Was it code he thought or was it short for something else? He'd need to sit down quietly and try to figure it out. *I guess if you were involved in international finance, then it would be easy to understand*, he thought. But he wasn't and he couldn't really make head nor tail of it.

He opened the car door and jumped in. For a couple of minutes, he sat with his arm hanging out the window thinking about the information he'd just been handed. He wondered if he was a government man, working at arms length. That was a possibility.

He pulled out a piece of paper from the file and studied it intently. It was a copy of the licence application to the Johannesburg Airport Authorities for semi permanent holding for a Global Express registered N74959. *That was a North American registration*, he thought as he looked down at the bottom of the sheet noting the 'Granted' stamp dated two years previously. He slipped the page back into the file and placed it on the passenger seat. He knew someone at Jo'burg airport, he'd give them a call later. He started the car and did a 'U' turn, going off the dirt road and into the grasslands alongside before rejoining the track some thirty yards further on. *Plenty to think about*, he thought.

NEWTON ABBOT NOVEMBER 2000

November 2000, Max had just turned forty and the problems at Velodrome were beginning to unfold all too quickly. It hadn't been a good year. Keith was out of intensive care but not in a position to work which meant that the accounts had now fallen way behind. The bank had lowered the company overdraft by £50,000 without any warning and the two Ferrari 360 Spiders from Dimo had not yet materialised.

It could all still be turned around though and that was the belief that Max had at the time. On the downside was the current position but on the upside, Velodrome had overcome the foot and mouth disease, they had two right hand drive 360 Spiders coming from Isca Ferrari which they would make £210,000 on collectively, Nino was desperate to buy a Ferrari 250 short wheel base which would hopefully bring a decent profit and there was still Muzi's 330 GTO deal and the other Ferrari 360 Spider from Dimo to sell. Max didn't want to dwell on the negatives, all that did was depress him, he needed to get some positive news. Any one of the positive deals would be enough to make a significant difference to the Christmas cash flow period and that's all he could hope for.

Pete was having a good run on the December sales, in fact the best the company had ever had, which was a real surprise. Most of the enquiries had come from the Velodrome website, which was encouraging although they were all at a distance to deliver and as such, the company wouldn't get the benefit of any servicing or accessories from the customer, but nonetheless it was sales and that meant profit. December was traditionally a bad month, Velodrome never made enough money to cover the Christmas overheads. Understandably it was always quiet, nobody is that interested in riding a bike in the freezing cold. The week before the big red-letter day, there was usually a few last minute accessory shoppers, wives and girlfriends, buying the small stocking fillers, but generally, it all started to wind down.

Inevitably, Graham Lord had been on the telephone several times as a result of being pressurised by Donald Key asking about the arrival of his 360 Spider, but Max wasn't able to give Graham any positive information. Dimo had been into Sebastien's and they weren't able to get the delivery information from the factory. Everyone was really starting to wind down. Dimo had suggested that Max call Victor at Sebastien's but there was no point in upsetting the apple cart. Dimo had done what he could, there was little to be gained from someone else chasing Victor as well.

Surprisingly Max sold the barchetta red Ferrari 355 Spider in the first week of December as a straight deal with no part exchange. The customer had seen the car advertised in the *Sunday Times* and had told Max he was buying it for a Christmas present for his wife. They'd agreed a price on the telephone and Max had taken a £10,000 deposit by credit card. It was unexpected, but very welcome. The car was due out three days before Christmas; the customer would catch the train to Newton Abbot and then drive it home and hide the car in his garage until the big day. What a surprise that would be?

Max was talking to a friend in the showroom about doing their usual Christmas ride over Dartmoor on their trail bikes when Mike interrupted their conversation.

'It's Catherine, she's on her mobile.'

Max took the phone 'Hi, are you all right?' he asked.

'I'm in the multi storey car park, my waters have just broke. I'm okay; I'm going home now,' she said.

'Okay, I'll go home now. You sure you're all right?' he asked worryingly.

'Yes, I'm fine,' she replied.

Max went into Pete's office. 'Got to go. I'll leave it all to you. Catherine's waters have broke, so I'll call you later.'

'Yeah, you go. I'll sort this lot out. Good luck,' Pete replied.

Max was gone and out the door. He only lived five minutes from work, but as usual, the Christmas shopper traffic was busy. Catherine was already home when Max walked through the front door.

He smiled and looked at her, reaching across to give her a hug.

'Is this it then?'

'I hope so. I've called the midwife, she'll be here in about twenty minutes,' she said.

'Okay, can I get you anything? Cup of tea?' Max asked.

'Yes, I'll have a cup of tea; that would be nice.'

They weren't expecting to have their first born until Christmas Day, that was the due date, however Catherine had said to Max she didn't expect to go that long.

'What happened?' Max asked handing her a small mug.

'Nothing really, I did some shopping in the market and walked back to the car park and the lift was not working, so I had to walk up the stairs with the bags and bingo!'

'Oh, right, you're okay, though?'

'Yes, but you can put the shopping away for me please.' He'd already done it.

Catherine's contractions were starting when the midwife arrived, so she suggested that Catherine should be admitted into Torbay Hospital. There was no rush; the next couple of hours would be fine. Max collected up her packed bags and drove carefully over to Torquay. They'd both been to all the antenatal classes, which had been quite good, fun, but now this was real and the anticipation was immense. Catherine was fine; she had a few more contractions in the car. He felt for her. There wasn't much he could do other than comfort her.

Over the next three days, it was on, it was off, it was on, it was off. The contractions would start then stop then start again. *They never mentioned this in the antenatal classes*, Max thought. Then in the early hours of Sunday morning, Catherine gave birth to a beautiful healthy little girl, Ellie, weighing in at 6 lb 10 oz. It was a wonderful moment; nothing else mattered. Max and Catherine were elated. He called all the family and friends letting them know the good news and let Pete know that he wouldn't be into work for a few days.

It had been seven days before he returned to work still on a high. Carol was finishing the accounts; she still couldn't make out how to use the software. Max was going to have to pay Catalyst to come down and show her how to use the programme. He told her that he would call them. There was a long list of messages on his desk and a week's worth of post.

Mike brought Max a cup of tea and they stood chatting for a while before Max sat at his desk and started opening the mail. Bills, bills, more bills, the usual blurb and then he opened a letter from Transamerica, the stocking loan finance company. It was a fairly short letter giving Max notice that Transamerica were getting out of the motorcycle financing market place and all indebtedness would be recovered by direct debit within twenty-eight days. Velodrome weren't being focussed as an individual target, Transamerica were withdrawing their facilities right across the board.

Max put down the letter and took a sip of tea. It was a disaster, Velodrome were in to Transamerica for over £100,000. All the new Aprilias that had arrived in the last few weeks following the orders at the motorcycle show were all on TA. Max couldn't just magic up £100,000. He didn't have it. It was only a few days before Christmas, he decided to keep it to himself, there was no need at that stage to tell anyone else. He didn't want to ruin Christmas for the staff, it would be better to fight the cause in the New Year after Max had time to think about how he was going to tackle it. It was a massive problem.

Three days before Christmas, a well-dressed man in his early forties walked in through the showroom stopping every few steps to look at the glittering array of sports bikes and equipment. It was the customer for the barchetta red Ferrari 355 Spider. He'd come to collect the car. Max introduced himself and took him into the service area where the car was all ready to go.

'Just a couple of signatures for you to sign,' said Max as he put the paperwork in front of the customer pointing at the dotted lines. He had telephoned two days earlier and paid the balance with two credit cards. Max handed over the customer copy of the signed contract receipting the amounts paid and gave him the credit card chits as well.

'I hope she likes it,' he said.

'I'm sure she will,' he replied.

Going home for Christmas, Max tried to forget all the problems at Velodrome. He felt like everything was closing in on him. He'd lost £50,000 in funding from the bank, a further £100,000 plus from Transamerica and the 360 Spiders hadn't arrived. He shut the doors to the showroom and thought that's it for another year. Thank God for that. A week off would do him the world of good.

BUCKFASTLEIGH, AUGUST 1985

The letterbox flap clattered as the postman dropped the day's mail in to the Easton household. Leo sprang up out of his chair and eagerly went to collect it. He sifted through the envelopes as he returned to the kitchen table. It was the same anticipation as when he was waiting for his CSE results, a mixture of nerves and excitement. Nervous of failing and the consequences that would have and excitement at the prospect of achieving his goal. The difference with his CSE results was that he could always retake them if he wanted to whereas now, it was unlikely he would be able to take the police entrance exam again. Leo was worried as he looked at the envelope, the blue motif indicating the Devon and Cornwall constabulary on the top showing the sender. His mother looked across at him as he opened it up and looked inside. He unfolded the letter and drew a breath. He looked back at his mother and smiled. He was in. She was so proud of him. He stood up and gave her a hug and his father patted him on the back.

'A job for life son, that's what you've got there. Keep your nose clean and you could go all the way. Start at the bottom, work your way up, you never know; you could be an inspector one day.'

'Thanks Dad,' he replied, chuffed that he'd got in. His CSE results weren't the best, but he'd managed to convince the police panel that he was made of the right stuff. The letter went on to inform him where to report and at what time. The first step would be the police training headquarters where he would be assessed mentally and physically followed by a prolonged period of multi disciplines and procedures. More exams would follow and if all that went well, he would reach his passing out and be detailed to a police station working as a junior colleague on the

384

beat. He was looking forward to it, the money was quite good, it would bring him into contact with lots of new people and he'd be living away from home.

Leo's mother was popping out for an hour. She had to go into the abbey to sort out the last of the flowers for a wedding that was taking place that afternoon and then she thought she'd nip into the village and pick up a cake and congratulations card.

She was so happy for Leo, he was an only child and she'd be sorry to see him go, but pleased that he'd got himself into a steady job with some prospects. They'd always brought him up to be a decent boy who knew the difference between right and wrong and now he was going to go forward and maintain that doctrine. She had hoped that he would have gone into the church and become a priest, but realised many years ago that was not going to be something Leo was going to entertain. He was never particularly interested in the church. It was more of a chore for him to go to Sunday Mass. It got in the way of more important things he could have been doing.

She didn't know how the police force was going to effect his faith, whether or not he would still practice as a Roman Catholic or whether he would give it up as so many before him had. She hoped he'd still keep going to church, but she wasn't going to press him about it. It was up to him. If he felt the need, then he would go. He could always go back to it a later date if he wanted to. It wasn't something that was going to go away.

She bumped into Father Prior walking across the knave and she told him the good news. He asked her to pass on his congratulations to him. Father Prior had known Leo for nearly fifteen years and he liked him a lot. He was a good lad and he knew he would be a good asset to the police force.

HMP LEYHILL, AUGUST 2008

Having completed the two-week induction at Leyhill, Max had been told that it would be at least another two weeks before he was given his work placement. Therefore, he was somewhat surprised when he opened his room door to find a note asking him to report to the laundry at 8:15 am on Monday morning.

When he'd been asked to fill in his work placement

choices in induction, he quite liked the idea of working in the print shop or his second choice, which was working in the gardens. At that point, it had been optional, now it was mandatory. Laundry for four weeks. The first day was an eye opener. Many of the inmates on the same induction had been placed in the laundry too. It wasn't a difficult job and it wasn't continuous either. At least half the time was spent sitting around. All Max had to do was fold track suits and place them in a pile, sometimes it varied, a trolley full of T shirts or blankets would arrive and they were again folded and placed in piles. The time went slowly and he felt guilty if he wasn't doing anything, but that was how it was and he couldn't change it, so he just went along with it.

There was a Welsh guy sitting next to Max and they started talking. Max asked him how long he'd got to go.

'Hopefully, only another two years, depends on probation. You?'

'I've been in for five weeks. I've got another nine weeks before I get out,' said Max.

'Lucky you. I've already been in five years.'

'Bloody hell, what did you do?' Max asked.

'Armed robbery. Yeah, but stupid really. I was desperate for some money and was sat in a pub one night and met a guy who told me he was the manager of a local supermarket. He said he was broke too.'

Max was listening with interest. 'Anyway, he told me that there would be £25,000 in cash in the office on the following Thursday and that if I went in and robbed them, it would be easy. I talked my mate into it and the following Thursday I found myself in this guy's office ready to do the robbery and he wasn't there, it was someone else.'

'So what did you do?' Max asked.

'Well, what I should have done was walked out, but I didn't. I carried on with the robbery. I tied the guy up and stuck him in the cupboard pointing my shotgun at him to get the code for the safe. He'd already wet himself and when I got the safe open, there was only £400 in it. I asked him where the rest of the money was and he said there wasn't any. I kept asking him about the £25,000 but because it had been bank holiday, the wages were coming in the following day. I just legged it with the £400.'

'So how come you're in here?' Max asked with a smile.

'Well, my mate was the getaway driver and stupidly he

told his girlfriend all about it. Sort of bragging really. Then a couple of months later, he split up with her and went off with one of her friends and she didn't like it so she threatened to tell the police. He didn't think she would, but she did. Next thing, we are both being arrested. I got seven years and he got two.'

'Seven years for £400?' Max said.

'Yep, £400. I didn't harm the bloke but he's never been the same since and I don't think he's been able to work. He was in a right state.'

'So you won't be doing that again?'

'No. I'm not proud of it. It was a stupid thing to do, and I'm paying the price.'

A trolley load of blankets arrived for folding. Max delved into the pile and got on with it, some just sat around doing nothing, quite content to let the others do their job. Max quickly learnt not to say anything. One prisoner couldn't tell another prisoner what to do. That was not the done thing. However strongly he felt about the two idle men sat in their chairs, he couldn't do anything to make them work. It went against everything he'd ever earned, but he just had to let it go.

Max was still not getting much sleep, the crack head in the room next to him was beginning to get on his nerves with all his nocturnal habits. It was little things at first like moving his furniture around, dragging the chair across the bare lino floor making it screech, unlocking and locking his door. It was nothing really, but when you start having less sleep, these things irritate.

That first day in the laundry had passed quite quickly even though Max had been doing nothing for half the day. He'd spoken to some different people all in for varying degrees of crime, some organised, some plain stupid. He didn't enjoy it, he wasn't expecting to, but it was another day gone.

Max spoke to Danny on his way back to his room.

'Where did you get placed?' asked Max.

'Market garden.'

'Any good?'

'Yes, it's okay; I buggered off after two o'clock, and went back to my room for a couple of hours then returned in time to hand all the equipment back in,' Danny replied. 'They didn't even notice me gone. You?'

'Folding blankets and track suits all day.'

'Bugger that, I'd rather be outside.'

'Wait 'til winter, everyone will want to be in the laundry, it's warm in there.'

'Well, I'll think about that when it comes to it, but for now I'm happy. After eighteen years in a bang up, this is the great outdoors.'

Danny was in for murder. He was involved in the killing of a super grass. He had been a very dangerous man, hence his sentence. He'd escaped once from HMP Gartree and evaded the police for two years living and working in Tel Aviv. He'd set up a new life for himself running his own building firm with his Israeli girlfriend when one evening he was having a barbeque on the beach in Sharm el Sheik when four backpackers joined them. They got talking and one of the guys said,

'Hang on a minute. Aren't you Danny? Didn't you use to live in Westmede Road?'

Danny immediately went on the defensive. He'd left all that behind, then all of a sudden on the other side of the world, there's a guy asking him if he lived in a road he knew all too well.

'No, not me,' said Danny.

'Yeah, it was you. You lived at number six.'

'No, you're mistaken.'

The guy dropped the conversation and that was the end of it. The backpackers left a few hours later. Danny thought about shutting them up for good, but he didn't want to go down that route.

He hoped they'd go away and forget about him. Unfortunately for Danny they didn't. He'd been on the Britain's most wanted list for two years and the police weren't giving up. Any sightings, any leads, absolutely anything they would follow up until it was exhausted. That's how much they wanted him. It didn't matter about the cost.

He wasn't going to take any chances, so he moved from his apartment and found somewhere off the main street tucked away down a labyrinth of narrow alleys. He always took a different route home, taking time to stop, look at faces, doubling back. It would usually be thirty minutes to do a ten-minute walk. He couldn't be too careful. Then one night he bumped into someone he knew on the main street, just some nobody who he didn't particularly want to talk to and he sort of nonchalantly dismissed him, but what he didn't know was that guy had seen Danny's photograph on a 'Wanted' poster and he followed him.

Danny had prepared the apartment so that if he did get the knock on the door, he could escape out the back, but when the time came, they arrived in numbers and completely surrounded the place. There was no getting away.

The UK police had lied to the Tel Aviv authorities to get him extradited. They'd said that Danny was a drug dealer operating out of their locality. It wasn't true but it worked and soon enough he was on the plane back to another Category A bang up.

They ambled back to the A Unit and went their separate ways to their rooms.

January 2001 Newton Abbot

If the lead up to Christmas break had been stressful, then no matter how good the time off had been, the hard reality of the return to work in the new year was very worrying. Max had tried to forget his woes, but lying in bed at night, his mind was racing with all sorts of scenarios.

Jan 4th 2001. Max opened the doors to the showroom, the familiar smell of polish and new motorcycles hit him as he switched off the alarm. He looked around; it seemed a bit darker. It was, two of the master flood lights were out. He'd sort that out later.

He went through the familiar morning start up routine and sat at his desk taking a piece of paper from his pocket, unfolding it and placing it on the blotter in front of him. He looked at the list he'd written over the Christmas break. It looked impossible. Donald Key, Transamerica, Barclays Bank, Dimo were all on the left hand side of the page and Muzi 330 GTO, Isca Ferrari, Nino and Dimo were on the right hand side. Dimo appeared on both sides because if the two 360 Spiders arrived from Sebastien, then the negative list on the left would no longer have Dimo on it. As he sat there, he tried to get his head around the enormity of the task. He'd lost over £150,000 in funding from Barclays and Transamerica. He wasn't going to be able to do anything about the banks decision, that £50,000 of funding was definitely lost. The TA funding was represented by stock, so that would be offset by sales, but not in twenty-eight days as TA had asked, it would probably take ninety days. He may be able to extend the twenty-eight day deadline; he'd have to try negotiating with them. Otherwise, there would be a big cash flow issue. Back in September, the bank overdraft facility was

£150,000, with the capability of Max taking it to £180,000 if he needed it, now it was £100,000 max. Donald Key's money had reduced the overdraft down from £140,000 at the time to £ 40,000DR, which was fine, but it meant that the operating facility was now only £60,000 and that was not enough to make it all work, and it certainly wasn't enough to pay for Donald Key's car even if it did arrive. Max would need both of the Sebastien cars to arrive at the same time and then with a clever bit of juggling, use the profit from the second car to pay the balance on Key's car. He could make it work, he was confident of that, but if the blue car arrived first rather than Key's silver car then it could be a problem. Max hadn't sold the blue car as yet, so hopefully it would all go to plan, fingers crossed.

Max was definitely expecting Donald Key to get annoyed, but in the circumstances, there was nothing Max could do. If the car hadn't arrived, that wasn't his fault and besides Max had written on the contract that the sale was subject to Ferrari delivering the car. If they didn't deliver it, he couldn't supply it. He thought about it and decided that if Key did get angry then Max was going to dig his heels in and hold Key to the contract.

Pete walked into the office with a mug of tea. They talked about the Christmas holiday for a while then buckled down to the business in hand. Max told Pete about the TA situation and the twenty-eight-day notice period to pay for the stock and between them, they decided to do what they could to discount the stock and minimise the number of part exchanges. What they needed to do was sell each new bike as quickly as possible for any price over the cost price and start reducing the TA exposure. It would be no good taking part exchanges because that would add to the paid for bike stock and that would increase the bank overdraft. Max said he would talk to Deutschebank about their alternative stocking loan facilities, but that was going to be a longer-term situation, and no doubt all the other dealers would be doing the same. Pete knew what he had to do, but the reality was that he was more than a little bit worried. Quite how much, Max hadn't really appreciated, he was more wrapped up in his own concerns. For Pete to sell a load of new bikes in the depths of winter after all the usual costs of Christmas and the likely credit card bills coming in at the end of the month was probably just too much to ask of anyone.

Max logged onto the online banking facility and looked

at Velodrome's balance, it was £27,532 credit. The monthly standing orders had gone through and there was just one TA direct debit going out for a scooter, about £1100. It was a false picture because Velodrome had now been paid in full for the Dimo funded yellow Ferrari 355 GTB. The car was still in the service department, but now that the barchetta red 355 Spider had gone, that deal was now completed. Max owed Dimo £58,000 for the yellow car so the real bank position was £30,468 DR overdrawn if he paid him, not including the £100,000 that Donald Key had paid. Now doing the simple maths, Max knew that the Donald Key car was going to cost him around £92,000 to buy. If he took the real bank position of £30,468 overdrawn and added the cost of Key's car in, he'd be £122,468 overdrawn, so effectively he was £22,468 over the top. If he sold the other Sebastien 360 Spider for a £30,000 premium, he could cover himself. The TA situation was going to be a daily problem to overcome but hopefully that would reduce down daily. If it didn't then Velodrome could be hit for a huge direct debit that they wouldn't be able to meet.

Max picked up the phone and called Dimo wishing him a Happy New Year. He still didn't have any news on the 360 Spiders and he didn't ask about the yellow 355. Dimo knew that sales were slow in January and February and he hadn't expected Max to have sold the car and Max didn't tell him either. Max took the view that whilst the car was still in the service department, he would hold on to the money, then pay for it when it was collected by the customer who as yet hadn't even seen it.

The next call was to Graham Lord. *Head them off at the pass*, he thought. Rather that he rang Graham Lord than Graham Lord rang him.

'Happy New Year Graham, let's hope it's a good one,' Max said.

'Yes, let's hope so; same to you.'

'No news on the 360 Spiders. I've just come off the phone to my customer. As soon as he knows, he'll call me, so if Donald Key contacts you, then you know what to say.'

'Is there any explanation at all?' Graham asked.

'No, nothing. We've just got to sit and wait.'

'Okay, well thanks for letting me know.'

Max was pleased that he made the first move. It settled him down a bit so that he could concentrate on the TA situation and other pressing matters. He looked back at his list and put a tick next to Donald Key's name and Dimo's. He needed to speak to Nino, but he wouldn't do that until later in the day. He had a lead on a Ferrari 250 Short Wheel Base on the East Coast of America and wanted to speak to them first, then he'd call Nino and give him the low down.

He picked up the phone again and called Sean Williams at Isca Ferrari. They went through the usual insincere pleasantries and Max asked him what was happening with his new 360 Spiders.

'I understand that the first cars are coming through in March?' Max asked.

'I don't know anything about that. We've not been told,' said Sean.

'Well, it's what I've been told from Maranello,' said Max.

'Okay, well we will probably hear sometime soon,' Sean replied rather defensively lacking any discernible honesty. Sean did know but he didn't want Max to know. The last thing he wanted was Max on his back.

Max's mobile was ringing so he quickly finished off with Williams and answered.

'Max Reed.'

'Yes, hi Max, it's me.'

'Oh, how are you? Good Christmas? Happy New Year,' said Max.

'Thanks and same to you and Catherine. Yes, we had all the family down. It was a bit hectic at times but we did have a really nice time.'

'It makes it all worth while.'

'Yeah, it does. Anyway the reason for my call is that I spoke to my friend who knows the guy at Donald Key Restorations.'

'Oh, yes. Anything?' Max asked.

'Yes, there is really. I know why Ferrari won't accept that car, and you're not going to like it, I don't think.'

'Okay, well let's have it. Might as well get it all out at once,' Max replied.

'This is what the guy has told my man and it was told in complete confidence, so if this gets out, I don't want people to know that it came from me.'

'That's okay. I wouldn't mention your name and not many people know that I know you. I think if some people did

392

know that, they might treat me slightly differently,' Max assured him.

'Well, that's as maybe, but as long as we both agree, then I'm comfortable.'

'You have my word,' Max said.

'Thank you. The story goes that the Baron bought the car in the mid to late eighties knowing that although it looked similar to a 250 Short Wheel Base, it was actually a 250 GTO but with a 4-litre engine making it a 330 GTO. Now, when he bought it, the car was original, but it was very rusty especially underneath and my guy is saying that he didn't think the buyer knew that otherwise he might not have bought it. But once he had bought it, he was stuck with it. He took it to Donald Key and asked him to restore it, but when they got into it they realised the car was in a far worse state than they'd expected. A lot of the chassis was completely shot especially where the car had been repaired after its factory accident.

'Well, none of this seems to be a problem,' Max interjected.

'It's not. It's what happened next that is a problem. Donald Key rang the Baron and asked him to come and look at the car and between them they decided that the chassis was too far gone to make any good of it.'

'So what did they do?' Max asked.

They stripped all the mechanicals out of the car and supposedly left it as a rolling chassis, and parked it under cover back at Donald Key's home. Then they fabricated a complete new replacement chassis and virtually built up a new car from that point and transferred over the chassis plates from the original car. Obviously, they put a new GTO style body on the car but you know that anyway.'

'Shit, so it's not the original chassis at all,' Max said despondently.

'No. Not at all. It's a fake, that's what I've been told. And possibly a £10 million pound fake at that. Now I have to say, it's what I've been told and there's no good reason for me to believe otherwise. Also. It would explain why Ferrari won't accept it'

'Oh no. What about the engine and gearbox?' Max asked as if he needed to know.

'My man is not sure about the mechanicals, because the car went off site for a while and then it came back, and by that stage everything had been separated.'

'So Donald Key wasn't telling us the full story was he?' Max asked.

'Doesn't sound like it, no. Will your man still buy it, knowing that?'

'I don't think so. In fact, I'm pretty sure he wouldn't. What happened to the original chassis and bodywork?' Max enquired.

'That we are not entirely sure about, but it was still down at Donald Key's house, the last time he knew of it.'

'Do you know if the Middle Eastern collector knew about the chassis etc?'

'Difficult to say, but you'd have to think *almost certainly not*. He wouldn't have paid a supposed £10 million for a fake. Nobody would, would they? Unless it was a scam of some sort'

'No, they wouldn't.'

Max said thank you and rung off. He'd just lost a potential $2,000,000 and he wasn't happy. He wasn't happy at all.

He took a deep breath and went off to make himself a cup of tea. If it wasn't one thing it was something else. *Who the hell would want to run a normal business*, he thought.

He'd have to call Muzi, but he'd leave that for another day. At least he'd paid him for the deposits for the eight 360 Spiders he was getting from him. That £25,000 had long since left Velodrome's bank account. Money was going to be tight, the longer the delays were on the new Ferraris, but for every day that passed, it was another day closer to when they would arrive. It was just a matter of time. He was sure the company would show itself to be profitable by the years' end but he was definitely going to experience cash flow problems in the meantime even if he was ultra careful.

EXETER, NOVEMBER 1986

About six months after the Salcombe estuary debacle, Doug was still on remand in Exeter Prison awaiting trial. He was expecting seven years. That was the best guestimate his barrister could offer. Judy was up against it. She had obviously known what had been going on and she had been facing the potential charges of conspiracy until the police had offered her a deal. Basically, spill the beans darling and you can go free. Realistically, she had no choice. She didn't want to spend her time in jail if there was a way of avoiding it. She wasn't allowed to visit Doug so he was left completely in the cold. Not a nice place to be.

Catherine had been shopping in Marks & Spencers in Newton Abbot when she noticed Judy walking along the aisle.

'Hi, how are you?'

'Yeah, I'm okay. You look well,' Judy said.

'We heard about Doug,' Catherine mentioned.

'Yeah, it's not good. I've had to turn queen's evidence. It's really awful. I'm not looking forward to the trial,' she said.

'Where are you staying?' Catherine asked.

'I'm back with Mum and Dad at the moment. Everything is still up in the air. I don't know where I am with it all.'

It was a short conversation, both of them were in a hurry to be somewhere else. Catherine never heard from Judy again. She didn't know where she'd gone or what she'd been up to. It was a shame, because they were such good friends and basically Doug had spoilt all that. Her parents had sold the pub in Tuckenhay and that's where the trail ended.

TORQUAY, JUNE 1994

Chris Duke had been motor racing most of his adult life and although Max didn't know it at the time, he was the guy that stopped and gave him a lift to the petrol station when he ran out of fuel on his way to Catherine's house. When Max was racing in Formula Ford 1600, they'd met several times even sharing the same sponsor for one season, but whereas Max had stopped racing cars by 1985, Chris had continued in various formulae. Max had always rated him as a driver, because he was quick and he could, given the right equipment, win.

By 1994, Chris was racing in the Production Saloon car championship and part of the ten race series were two one-hour endurance rounds where two drivers were required.

Chris gave Max a call and asked him if he still had his motor racing licence, which fortunately he still renewed every year.

'Do you want to do a two driver race at Donnington?'

Max jumped at the chance. 'Yeah, of course. When?'

Chris gave him the date and the first time he sat in the car was for practice. Chris was racing a Ford Sapphire Cosworth and it was very quick. At Donington, under the Dunlop bridge, the speedo needle used to go off the clock. It was a damp meeting and there was plenty of standing water on the circuit an hour before the start of practice. Max was quite calm and relaxed. It would be just like driving an ordinary car. Chris warmed up the car and sat in line ready to go out for practice. It was business as usual sat on the pit wall with the timing gear. Catherine reflected on the many times she'd stood in exactly the same place waiting for Max to come round. She remembered Ayrton Senna in his overalls stood next to her on the pit wall watching a race that Max was in, they chatted a while. They were good times, if a little fraught.

Chris came back in to the pits at the end of practice, and there was a thirty-minute break before the second drivers were allowed out. They checked everything on the car and put a bit more fuel in and then it was Max's turn. He went out. It was quick, he thought, and it didn't have much grip, either, so it was very lively. Max pulled into the pits at the end of the session and got out of the car. Catherine jumped down from the pit wall and walked across the pit lane to the garages.

'Okay,' she said.

'Yeah, fine. It's quick. It's good fun. What did you get me at?' Max asked looking down at the clipboard.

Before Catherine could answer the question, Chris walked up to them with the official session results and said, 'We've both done exactly the same time. No difference. That's amazing.'

'Where does that put us on the grid?' Max asked.

'Second, yes we're second on the grid. Inside of the front row.'

'That's good. We should be able to do all right from there,' Max said.

The reality was that they should have done but they didn't. Chris had a good start and was running a comfortable second in close proximity to the leader when he came in for the driver change, but when Max resumed, he came out behind a Porsche 944 turbo that was quick in a straight line but slower than the Sapphire in the corners. Max got past him under braking for the chicane and then had to employ Formula Ford style weaving tactics to keep the Porsche behind him along the start finish straight, but after the Craner Curves, Max entered the Old Hairpin and the Porsche just nudged the back of the car enough for Max to go off onto the wet grass. There was no stopping it at that speed and it hit the wall probably without scrubbing off any speed at all, wiping the front of the car clean off. He'd have probably been doing at least 80 mph maybe more. It was not to be their day.

Chris managed with some help from Max to do a body shell change in time for the second one-hour race at Snetterton three weeks later. They all travelled up to the circuit together which is at least five hours from Devon. It's such a long way, Catherine was saying that she couldn't remember how bad it was dragging that racing car all around the countryside, but the journey to Snetterton that day brought it all back to her.

Max remembered once taking the Formula Ford to a motor show, which he knew was being opened by James Hunt. He thought there was a chance of the TV being there and desperate for sponsorship, it was worth a try. He convinced the organisers that they needed his car on show. Max was standing by the car when James Hunt walked up to him and started chatting.

They'd been talking for a few minutes when a film crew from the BBC arrived asking to do an interview with them both particularly in that James had started his career in the same sort of car that Max had on display. It was good publicity for Max as James sat in the Formula Ford ready for the interview. He remembered asking James how he could possibly say on his commentary on the BBC's Grand Prix television coverage that Jean Pierre Jarier had a mental age of two after he had been driving like a mobile chicane in the previous week's South African Grand Prix at Kaylami.

James replied in his typical dry manner, ' Because he has'. They laughed.

Snetterton really is a cold and windy place, but on this particular Sunday at least, the sun was shining and it was good to feel the warmth on your back.

Chris went out for the session one practice and posted a good time and like Donington three weeks earlier, Max went out half an hour later and set his qualifying time. The only difference this time was that Max was just slightly quicker which he was pleased about. When the official practice time sheets were out, their times were good enough for third on the grid, which would be on the inside of the second row. Max had raced at Snetterton more times than at any other circuit. He reckoned that he'd done several hundred laps so he should have known his way around.

Chris got a fantastic start and went straight through the gap between the two front cars to head the race into the first corner and when he came in for the driver change at the halfway mark, he handed Max a ten-second lead. Max rejoined in seventh place and slowly picked off the cars in front of him going over the start finish line for the last lap with a twenty-four-second advantage, but going down the back straight for the last time, the car started coughing. It was running out of fuel. Max weaved the car, trying to get the fuel pick up to find the last drops, almost at the very same point that the Astra GTE had run out of fuel all those years before in the 24 hr race. Max could see in his mirrors the second placed car in the distance closing him down. He was the full length of the back straight behind him. He didn't know if it would be enough. The engine picked up so Max backed off the revs and kept the car in a high gear going through the bomb hole and around the Long Coram Bend but as he slowed for Russel, the engine just cut out, he freewheeled through the left hander and right hander, he was 300 yards from the finish. He dipped the clutch and bump started the car and blasted it over the line, seven seconds in front of the second placed car. He banged the steering wheel with his hands. He'd done it at last. He'd won and that meant a lot to him. He jumped out of the car at the end of the pit lane and celebrated with Catherine and Chris. It was a great moment. Ten years and more of trying and both of them won for the first time in the same car on the same day. They went up together to collect their winner's wreaths and champagne. What a day.

NEWTON ABBOT, JANUARY 2001

The start to January 2001 had been difficult to say the least, but with the plans Max had put in place, they were making progress. The TA bike stock was slowly reducing and the exposure was therefore lessening. Carol had got on top of the accounts paperwork back log and Catalyst, the software provider were scheduled to train her for a day.

Max had collected another 355 from Tom McKinney and whilst he was there he'd asked about the delivery of the red 360 Spider that he was getting for Max and he'd been told to expect that car for March or April. That was fine because Rick Brady was happy to take it then. Max had already paid Tom most of the money for the car. They'd agreed that the £10,000 bill that Isca Ferrari had charged for the earlier Ferrari 355 Spider that had the engine problem would be the deposit. Max had paid the invoice and was going to get a refund or credit from Tom, instead they agreed it would be a deposit for the 360 Spider.

A few months earlier, Max had paid £55,000 into Tom's wife's bank account in cash so in total Tom had already received £65,000 towards the car. Both Max and Tom were happy enough with the arrangement. It was going to be a tax free sale from Germany to Monaco and Max was only paying £82,000 for the car, so as soon as Tom said it was on it's way, Max would collect Brady's Ferrari 360 Coupe and get that sold and then invoice Rick for the balance which would make the deal worthwhile. It was some way off, but at least Max knew there was a decent profit of around £35,000 a little way down the line.

By the third week in January, Pete had sold over half of the TA loan stock, which was exceptional in the circumstances. Velodrome hadn't made a lot of money from the sales but it did prevent Transamerica hitting the company for over £100,000 in direct debits. Now the exposure was less than £50,000 and that was more manageable. Importantly, there were very few part exchanges, which meant that they were mostly straight, and quick deals.

Max had managed to negotiate with TA another twenty-eight days for £25,000 of the loan stock debt, which helped the cash flow position going forward and the customer who had bought the yellow Ferrari 355 GTB, now didn't want to collect the car until some time in February and asked Max to store it for him.

The whole position was looking healthier than that first day back after Christmas even though none of the Ferrari 360 Spiders had yet arrived. Max was able to contain Graham Lord and his bloody irritating customer Donald Key by virtue of the fact that very few other customers were getting their 360 Spiders either. It seemed that only a handful of the cars had reached their eager buyers and that was widely known.

Max had spoken to Muzi about the nonsense with the Ferrari 330 GTO and as expected, Muzi backed off the deal saying that the only way he would still possibly go ahead with the car was if it was significantly cheaper and came with the original chassis and bodywork. In a conversation with Graham Lord shortly after Max had discovered the truth, he'd asked Graham if he had known and Max wasn't entirely satisfied with the way he answered. He felt like Graham did know but wasn't saying anything, although he couldn't be sure.

Some good news on the horizon was that Nino had authorised the go ahead for an inspection of a really lovely Ferrari 250 SWB that Max had found on the east coast of America. The process would be much the same as when he bought the Ferrari 250 SWB California Spider from Sangster, so if that came off, then Max would be able to restore some of the lost revenue he was expecting from the 360 Spiders. He wasn't going to make up for the loss of the 330 GTO sale, but he could still make a sizeable lump and whilst he was selling these types of cars, he wouldn't need too many sales to make a significant difference to Velodrome's financial position.

He went home to Catherine and his five-week-old daughter Ellie, that evening, with a renewed vigour. Whilst he wasn't out of the woods yet, he felt he'd come a long way to overcoming the seemingly insurmountable problems that he was facing before Christmas.

Max was in a good mood when he sat down at his desk the following day. He was in early as usual and there was plenty to be positive about. He started opening the post. Another letter from the bank. It was the annual charge for the valuation of the commercial property that Max owned, which he then rented on a formal lease to Velodrome. *It was a joke*, he thought. The bank was charging him £345 for an independent evaluator to do a drive-by survey of the property and each year the valuation was always the same. Max paid £200,000 for the property in a forced sale situation five years earlier and in a rising market the bank still valued it at the same £200,000. *Madness*, he thought.

The next letter, though, brought him down with one hell of a bump. It was from Barclays Merchant Services. This is the arm of Barclays Bank that runs the credit card facility, so that Velodrome could take credit card sales. Max read the letter three times before he fully understood what he was reading. Essentially, the £49,950 payment on two cards made for the barchetta red Ferrari 355 Spider that went out before Christmas were being disputed along with the three bikes that Pete had sold from the internet enquiries. Another £18,000. In total the sums being disputed were £67,950 and they would be debited from Velodrome's current account within 14 days unless action was taken to prevent it. Max couldn't call them until after 9:00 am, but he needed to sort it out. If he didn't, Velodrome would be in big trouble. Max keyed in the password for the company on line banking and looked at the current account balance, it was £9716 DR debit. There were a few ins and outs going through which would leave the account broadly the same. He still owed Dimo the £58,000 for the yellow 355 in the service department. If Barclays Merchant Services withdrew the £67,950, the account would be close £80,000 overdrawn with Dimo not paid and Donald Keys Ferrari 360 Spider money all gone too. He had to stop the credit card company from taking the money.

It was gone nine by the time Max got through to the merchant services call centre and spoke to the supervisor in control of chargebacks.

'Hi, I received a letter this morning from you concerning some chargebacks on our account and I'm at a loss to know the reason.'

'Have you got your merchant service number id?' she asked.

Max gave her the number and waited whilst she looked through all the details on the screen.

'It looks like you have taken three amounts totalling just under £18,000 before Christmas and all three, by the looks of it, are on stolen cards.'

'Well, how are we supposed to know that?' Max asked.

'Did you get a signature?'

'Yes, I think so. We would have definitely got a signature on delivery,' Max replied.

'How did the transaction take place?' she asked.

'They were all mail order transactions done over the phone and we have the authorisation codes for each one. The goods were three motorcycles and they were paid in full by credit card at the time of the sale. We delivered them to three separate delivery addresses in North London,' Max answered.

'Well I'm afraid all three transactions were done on

stolen cards and we cannot stop the chargebacks which we will debit from your account shortly. If it helps, I have a direct dial telephone number for the police department that deals with this type of offence.'

Max took down the number but didn't think he'd stand much chance of ever finding the bikes again. It was over six weeks since delivery, so they would be long gone by now.

'What about the disputed chargebacks? What's that all about?' Max asked.

'You've got two disputed amounts, one for £38,000 and the other for £11,950. We've had a letter from the customer saying that he had not authorised you to charge his credit card.'

'Well that's madness. The customer bought a Ferrari 355 Spider from us two weeks before Christmas and paid a £10,000 deposit. He then called and paid the outstanding balance a few days before he collected it, and that was done on two different cards. I took the card details for the deposit myself, and one of my colleagues took the balance on the other two cards. He collected the car in person and signed our contract the Saturday before Christmas. He told me that the car was a present for his wife,' Max said.

'Did you get any identification?' she asked, 'did you get a copy of his driving licence or passport or anything like that?'

'No we didn't. All we have is a signed contract and if we looked back, we've probably got him on the CCTV video tapes,' Max replied.

'You should have got some identification really. What's the address on your contract?'

Max read out the details and asked her if she would like him to fax a copy of it up to her.

'Yes, please do that. We can check the signature against the cardholder signature on file and signatures on the letter disputing the amounts. I will put the chargeback for these two disputed amounts on hold for now and I will try to contact you later today or tomorrow after I have spoken to the card issuers. It maybe that our special investigations unit will be calling you. I'm afraid that there's nothing I can do about the £18,000 though. That will be withdrawn from your account in a few days.'

She rang off and Max held the phone against his shoulder for some time before replacing it on the cradle. He looked out the window; it was raining outside; it might as well have been raining inside, he thought. How he was going to overcome this challenge, he just didn't know, but he would start by gathering up all the paperwork on all the chargebacks and dealing with it. He needed to call the police regarding the three stolen bikes and place them on the HP1 stolen register. At least that would alert someone if the bikes were offered anywhere, but realistically they were lost and so was the £18,000 too.

He buzzed through to Pete in his office and asked him to come in. It wasn't Pete's fault; he had done his job. He'd sold the three bikes and Max was trying to establish whether there was anything else that Pete knew which would be useful.

'Remember those three bikes you sold before Christmas? The Yamaha R6, the Honda Fireblade and the Aprilia RS250?' Max asked.

'Yeah,' Pete replied inquisitively.

'Well it looks like we've been the victim of credit card fraud. All the cards were stolen,' Max said.

'You know, and perhaps I should have said this because I definitely thought it, they were very easy deals. Very few questions and they didn't try to beat me down. Even the delivery charge wasn't questioned? What's going to happen now?' Pete asked.

'I'm going to contact the police. Fat lot of good that will probably do though, but the worst is that the credit card company are going to deduct the money from our account, so we've lost the £18,000 we've been paid and the bikes,' Max explained.

'What about insurance? Are we insured for that type of thing?' Pete suggested.

'It's a good point, but I don't think so because we've given them the keys. It's a bit like letting someone test ride a bike. We're not insured if they ride off with it,' Max replied adding, 'look I'm not blaming you, don't think that I am, you were just doing your job, but we will need to put in place some practices that don't let this ever happen again.'

'Absolutely. Such as?'

'We're going to need to get confirmation of identity like a passport or driving licence, that sort of thing. What I'll do is draw up a standard form which will go with all credit card sales over a certain value.'

'Okay, I'm sorry about that. How does it effect us?'

'There's no need for you to be sorry, but £18,000 straight out of our account is going to hurt. It's not as if we're

403

flush with money, what with TA and all the Ferraris not arriving. There is one more thing. I might as well tell you. The 355 Spider customer that collected the car on the Saturday before Christmas. Well, he's disputing that he gave his authority to charge his cards and as with the bikes, the credit card company are threatening to take that money too.'

'How much is that?'

'Oh, only £50,000 or thereabouts.'

'Shit!'

'Yes, exactly.'

'What are you going to do?'

'I've tried contacting the customer, but there's no reply. I've spoken to Barclays Merchant Services and they're investigating it right now, so hopefully they'll have some news later today. In the meantime, I'm going to list the car and the bikes on the HPI stolen register,' said Max.

They finished their conversation and both thought about the problem. Pete could read the expression on Max's face. He knew he was up against it. He knew he was a fighter but he had reservations about whether Max could overcome this.

On a brighter note, the next call into the office was the very early bird from the East Coast of America advising Max that the Ferrari 250 SWB was being taken into Seattle Ferrari for the inspection to be carried out as soon as the representative from Ferrari North America arrived. Hopefully in a few days. Max's mind was rushing ahead to consider how much the deal was worth in profit to Velodrome. Maybe $150,000 if he was lucky. That would go some way to easing the funding problems, but no matter how hard the company tried, they just couldn't hold on to any advantage. As soon as they got ahead, they went two steps backwards. *The roll of bad luck can't carry on; surely it will change soon*, Max thought.

GP, SEPTEMBER 2000

Leaman picked up the phone and dialled the number. His job was now done, all he had to do was get the information posted and he would move on to his next assignment.

Max pressed the green button on his mobile and put it to his ear. He noticed it was a withheld number.

'Max Reed.'

'Hi, it's me.' Max recognised the distinctive South African voice. It was Leaman. He continued, 'Sorry it's taken a lot longer than we expected, but we've now got everything you need.'

'Everything?' Max asked.

'Yes, everything. Full details, tapes, transcripts, addresses, you name it, we've got it.' Leaman replied rather pleased with himself, 'Where do you want me to send it?' he asked.

'Here, yes, send it here, you've got the full details haven't you?' Max asked.

'Yeah, okay, that's it then, until the next time. Thanks for the business.'

'No problem, I'll call you when I receive the package if I've got any questions.'

'Yeah, you do that.' Leaman cut the line, knowing that Max would soon be back on the line when he tried understanding the information.

Max gave Sean Williams a call at Isca Ferrari. He knew the answer would be 'no' but he wanted to make sure Williams had Velodrome at the front of his mind.

'Hi Sean, any news on my 360 Spiders?'

'No, nothing as yet. I'll call you as soon as I hear,' Williams replied.

'Have you had an allocation for this year yet?' Max asked, knowing that he would have done.

'No, not yet,' Williams lied.

'That's unusual, the other Ferrari dealers I've spoken to have had their allocation. Strange that you haven't had yours, don't you think?'

'We all operate independently,' Williams replied.

Max didn't want to push Williams into too much of a corner especially as no cars had arrived as yet. He didn't want to get Williams' back up too much although he sensed that Williams was more than a little irritated. Max didn't believe him, but for the moment he let it go.

'Okay, Sean, keep in touch,' Max said.

'Will do.'

Sean put down the phone. He knew Max was going to be trouble, but he reckoned he could contain him as and when the time arrived.

HMP LEYHILL, AUGUST 2008

Max was pleased, there was a parcel for him to collect from the Reception office at 7:30 pm. Catherine had sent a box of clothes and shoes along with a watch and some other things she knew he wanted. He pulled out his sports kit, pleased that she'd sent his Adidas Climacools running shoes. That would make a big difference. An envelope contained some more photographs along with a nice note signed by the girls too. He felt lucky to have such a loving family. There were so many of his fellow residents that had absolutely nothing outside of the four walls they slept within.

He'd had quite a good day all things considered. The monotony of the laundry job lingered on, but soon that was going to be broken up at least for part of the week. He'd been accepted onto the cookery course which took up two full days a week on a Monday and Tuesday and also he was to start the music course which was all day Thursday.

Now he had a bit of variety in the week. Max had never cooked at home, he'd always done all the washing up, but never really got involved in the cooking. He thought that whilst he had the opportunity, he might as well try to learn something new, if for no other reason than he could maybe cook Catherine a meal when he got out. The music course was a Royal College of Music, Grade 1 exam level, so that appealed too.

As usual, it was the conversations in the prison that were more fascinating than anything else inside. At work in the laundry that day, Max had been moved from the folding area onto the rolling press machine. This amazing piece of equipment took damp sheets in one end and fed them out the other all folded and counted into tens ready for bagging. There were two people tending it, one overseeing the pressing and the other packing the laundry bags. This was a much better job than the manual folding, not least because Max's weekly wages went up to a stunning £9.50 but also because the work was mostly continuous which made the day pass quicker. It was still monotonous though. Max was working alongside Charlie.

They chatted away as they worked, the noise of the machines clacking and rolling along with the intermittent hissing of expelled steam filled the air. The sound of Radio One blaring out the same tracks one after the other struggled in the background.

'Hi, I'm Max.'

'Yeah, I'm Charlie.' He explained to Max what needed doing. It was simple enough, collect, pack and deliver, thirty sheets per bag, two hundred pillowcases per bag, one hundred T-shirts per bag. Nothing to it. Mustn't forget to mark down the numbers and bags on the clipboard, he was told. All the laundry was from various different prisons and had to be stacked on designated racking a short walk away.

Charlie asked where he was from.

'Newton Abbot,' came the reply.

'Oh, I know Newton very well,' Charlie replied.

'How come?'

'I used to live in Torquay. Barton?'

'Yes, I know Barton. I have a friend who used to live up there. A chap called Chris Bartlett,' Max said.

'Yeah, I know Chris, he was in the year above me at school.'

'Audley Park?'

'Yeah, that's right.'

'Did you know Steve Parker?' Max asked.

'Yeah, he was in the same year as Chris Bartlett,' Charlie said.

'Steve was on the same course as me at South Devon Tech.'

'Oh right. I went out with Steve's sister, Alison for quite a long time. I'd love to know what she's doing now.'

'I doubt she'd want to know what you're doing,' Max replied.

'No probably not, but I wouldn't tell her that. I've often thought of her though. I used to get on really well with her.'

'So did you know Toni Duval?' Max asked.

'No, not that I can remember, she went to Audley Park?' Charlie asked.

'Yeah, same year as Chris. Stunning looking girl. I went out with her in I think it was 1978.'

'No, I don't remember her.'

'Where do you live now?'

'St Austell. I got married and moved to Cornwall. I found a nice crime honey pot and I was doing well out of that until I got caught. Do you know Rock?' Charlie asked.

'Yes I do. Quite well. We've stayed with some friends there for a few weekends in the summer holidays over the last number of years. I usually take a boat down and we go waterskiing. The children love it.'

'I did too, but for different reasons. Because it's a holiday home area, a lot of these rich people don't bother locking the house, so I used to go in and help myself. I was doing it for years. Even stayed in some homes for the weekend, made myself welcome and sat down watched the TV or helped myself to a drink from their wine cellar. I made loads of money and nobody got hurt. It was a shame it had to end really.'

'How long did you get?'

'Oh, two years. I'm halfway through now, so I'm on the downward side,' said Charlie.

A guy walked across to Max.

'That's the last of Swansea, the next lot is Eastwood Park.'

'He's No. 1,' said Charlie. 'Nobody takes any notice of him but he thinks he's in control. They all call him No. 1.'

'What was he talking about?' Max asked.

'They've finished Swansea Jail, next it's going to be Eastwood Park. It's a women's jail. You watch all the pervs at the bottom there,' Charlie pointed at the unloading bay at the far end of the warehouse. 'They'll all be hanging around, hoping to find some girls knickers. They'll be wearing them like balaclavas in a minute. You wait and see. Filthy bastards. Nonces, the lot of them.' It was quite funny, watching them in the unloading bay.

No. 1 came back over. 'Ready?'

'Yes sir,' said Charlie. The machine started rolling again, hissing into life.

'What did No. 1 do?'

'Double strike.'

'Double strike?' Max asked.

'Yeah, he murdered his girlfriend and her ex boyfriend in a blind drunken rage. He was the last guy to be convicted at Bodmin Crown Court before it closed. I think he's done more than twenty years. Nice bloke though.'

'Right,' said Max. 'Right.' *Bloody hell*, he thought.

Max looked over at No. 1. Charlie was right, he did seem like a nice bloke, he worked hard, did everything he was supposed to and didn't really bother anyone. It annoyed him that people didn't have the same work ethic as him, but he'd come to accept that side of it just like he'd long since accepted that he was completely wrong in committing the crime that he had. The drink didn't help and of course the hurt and the jealousy at the time completely overwhelmed him.

'There's a very fine line between the anger that I had on that day which was too much and some other people who would have just been able to control themselves, without going too far,' he said.

Max looked at him. He was thirty years old and nineteen stone when he came in to prison, now he was fifty-two and fourteen stone and fit. What had he got outside? Nothing.

'What are you going to do when you get out?' Max asked.

'I don't think I'm going to be allowed out of the country so I'm going to try to see everything I can around Britain, the coast, the mountains, the moors, everything I've dreamt about whilst I've been locked up. I want to do as much as I can in moderation. When I came in here I was nineteen stone. If I'd have continued with the drink like that, I may have made it to sixty. Now I'm fit and healthy with no vices. I've paid for my crime with twenty-two years of my life and not one day goes by without me thinking of what I've done. I'll never forget that, you can't. Being fit, hopefully I can get back those twenty two years and live longer than maybe I would have done.' It was a sobering thought and you really couldn't help but admire his attitude. That took some doing.

The hissing steam and shots of compressed air started again. More sheets were coming through. Max manned his station and got on with the job and soon enough the day's workload was nearly run and soon it would be 4:30 pm. Another working day over, and another chiselled mark in the calendar struck out the day.

ESSEX, FEBRUARY 2001

Tom McKinney sat in the wicker chair drinking a glass of Chateau Neuf du Pape. It was unusually warm for a February and he considered taking off his fleece; then again, he didn't want to catch a chill. He was a fit forty-seven years old, well capable of looking after himself, maybe a little stocky at five feet ten inches, but nonetheless he was a good runner and could easily do a ten-kilometre run in fifty minutes. He had that sort of commando look; short hair and solid looking.

He gazed up at the beautiful house and the majestic gardens thinking how well he had done, but knew all too well that it wouldn't be long before it all caught up with him. If he was lucky, possibly six months, but he wanted to be gone in four . He didn't want to be around when the shit hit the fan. Things hadn't been going too well at home, the marriage had become strained and his wife Laura wanted a divorce. They were still talking but essentially they were leading separate lives. Whatever happened, he was going to give her the house, it was the least he could do for the children. He took a sip of wine.

The taxi rumbled down the driveway and Tom could see it working it's way towards him. It was Max, from the railway station, he'd come to collect another 355. The car was sold, so it would be a fairly fast turnaround. Max just wanted to get back to Devon, clean the car and get paid for it, take his profit and pay Tom. It was the usual fast transaction.

They'd been dealing with each other for nearly two years and as such got on quite well. They weren't going to ask each other's families out to dinner, but they always had a laugh and a joke when they met. It was a typical business relationship, and as long as everything was going okay, then they'd both be happy.

Max sat in the 355 GTS with the door open talking to Tom as the engine warmed through.

'Is it still okay for the 360 Spider? Max asked.

'Yeah, of course. It should be here sometime at the end of next month or early April. They'll let me know and I will call you,' Tom said reassuringly.

'Good, at least I can count on you. All my other 360 Spiders still haven't arrived and it's causing me a bit of aggro.'

'No, you don't need to worry. Your car will be here on time. My people won't let me down, I spend too much money with them,' he said.

Max felt comfortable and reassured with what Tom said and knowing that Rick Brady was a good customer, he was pleased that at least one of the cars was going to be delivered on time. Most of the 355s that Max had bought from Tom had Krell Ferrari stamps in the service book so Max assumed the car was coming from them.

'You don't have to tell me but I assume the car is coming from Krell,' Max said enquiringly.

'Yeah, you're right. How did you know?'

'Most of the 355s have Krell service stamps,' Max replied.

'Obviously, don't go contacting them but yes that's where it's coming from. They've always looked after me, so rest assured, it will be with us at the end of March, beginning of April. You can collect it direct from them if you want,' Tom suggested.

'Okay, well, I'll let you know nearer the time. Thanks, Right. I'd better be getting along, so I'll call you later in the week!' Max drove back down Tom's drive looking at the ever-decreasing image in his mirror before he turned out of the gate and onto the main road. It was the last time he spoke to Tom face to face.

Max was looking forward to going out that night. He was having dinner at one of Rick Stein's restaurants in Padstow with Andrew Ridgeley from Wham. Max had just bought Andrew's Ferrari 308 GTS and they'd become friends. Just after seven, Catherine and Max arrived at Andrew's home in a blue 355 Spider.

'We can all go in my car if you like', Andrew suggested as he introduced his long time girlfriend Kare. Max didn't know who she was and didn't recognise her either. The conversation in the car was interesting. Max and Catherine were in the back whilst Andrew was up front doing the steering with Kare sat alongside.

Kare had said that she was a singer in a band and Max had casually asked her whether he would have heard of the band and she replied, ' I'm in *Bananarama*.'

Max said he was sorry for not recognising her. The fact was that she was a stunner in the real but he hadn't really taken much notice of her whenever one of their pop videos came on. It *was* funny though.

Barclays Merchant Services had been trying to get hold of Max twice during the day. They wanted to make an appointment for the representative Michael Hayes from the Special Investigation Unit to meet at Velodrome to discuss the £49,950 disputed payments. The card issuing bank were pressing BMS for a repayment and Hayes needed to act on it immediately. He had to know who was at fault, Velodrome or the cardholder. On the face of it, the cardholder appeared to be acting fraudulently but until Hayes had met with Max, he couldn't be sure.

Driving home, Max had plenty of time to think things through. Velodrome's position was pretty dire. If he lost out on the credit card fraud, the BMS would instantly deduct the money from the account, which would take them to within a whisker of their overdraft facility. The result of that would be devastating simply because TA would want their money and it wouldn't be there. He thought it through, if they didn't get paid, they would probably go legal which would most likely take months. Maybe he should cancel the direct debit authority on TA's mandate. That would mean they couldn't take the money. He wouldn't be using them again, so any relationship was irrelevant. He couldn't do that with BMS for two good reasons, one being that he needed to continue taking credit card payments and secondly Barclays Bank had put up a £10,000 bond on the account anyway, which would guarantee the first £10,000. That was a non-starter. As soon as Barclays Bank found out that there was going to be a fifty grand chargeback, it would all be over.

The issue was cash flow. He needed to cash flow the problems. If he could get money in, then that would ease the problems, but to get out of the mire completely, he was going to need to cover BMS, Donald Key and Dino and that was nigh on £200,000. If he took Donald Key out of the equation, then he would still need to find £100,000 or thereabouts if they couldn't resolve the barchetta red Ferrari payment.

Nino's deal was looking good on the 250 SWB and that would hopefully bring in $150,000. *That will bridge the gap,* he thought. Max was going to need all his best negotiation skills to slow down all the outgoing payments until such time that the incoming payments materialised. *More juggling,* he thought. It was just cash flow. He made a mental note to make sure he called his accountant first thing in the morning. He wanted to explore the idea of some other alternatives.

PAU, JULY 2006

Jacques sat at the kitchen table whilst Olivier made a coffee. They'd been discussing their comfort zone, how they

412

were going to let go of their potential inheritance to a guy they hardly knew over a thousand kilometres away in a different country. If they had said it was madness, then they would have probably been right, but and there was a big but, they needed Max. They had been dealing with him on and off for nearly two years and he'd done everything he said he would do and more besides. Sooner or later, they were going to have to take the plunge.

In their minds, they knew they had to let the car go if it was going to go to the next stage. They knew Max probably couldn't afford to buy it and they'd all agreed it wasn't a bankable deal in the normal sense, which would have meant Max finding a private investor and that would be another person knowing, and all of them didn't want that either.

'I'd just feel a little bit more comfortable if I had some sort of security,' Olivier said, 'I know he's not going to run off with the car, but something, anything would do. Why don't we call him and see if he has something we can swap?'

'Makes sense to me. Maybe he's got another car or some bikes?' Jacques replied.

Another thousand kilometres towing, Max thought. At least it would be worth it. The Nissan Navara was pretty well loaded with all that he'd need for the trip. The Brian James fully enclosed shuttle trailer was hooked up and he was ready to go.

After a number of telephone conversations with Jacques, Max had agreed with Olivier a simple solution. He would take his AC down to Pau and swap it with Olivier's car effectively leaving it as a deposit. It was a sensible answer for both sides. Max had loaded the car earlier that day and would be with Olivier by noon the following day and then load the trailer and return to the UK thirty six hours later. Well that was the plan, but as usual the French hospitality took over and Max stayed for longer than he had expected, which was okay for him, but for Ralph Sanders, it was agony. He couldn't wait to see the car and having been on tenterhooks for months, he just wanted to put himself out of the agony of it all, get the job done and finally know that what he was hoping it to be was actually what it was.

It only took half an hour to load the car for the return trip, but writing out an inventory list of all the parts had turned into a nightmare. The whole family were involved and because not every part was identifiable, Antoinette and her mother had taken to drawing the parts and then they were arguing about who'd done the best drawing. What should have taken ten minutes took over three hours. In the scheme of things it didn't matter and Max was sure that when he looked back on it in his old age, he'd still find it funny.

The drive home was uneventful but for the first time in several years, he finally felt that there was some light at the end of the tunnel. There was still the dark cloud on the horizon, which may or may not go away but for now he had to get on with his life. If something happened later then he would have to deal with it. For now, he had taken professional advice and he was reasonably happy with their response.

Max was in the kitchen at home when Ralph Sanders rang him on his mobile.

'Hi, Ralph, how are you?'

'Very well thank you. I was just calling to find out how you got on with your trip?' Max thought about pulling his leg a bit and asking him, what trip, but he didn't.

'Yes, very good. The car's here in the garage and I've got a lot of parts as well.'

'What about the bodywork?'

'Yes, I've got all that.' Max was very cool about the discussion, he wasn't worried about its authenticity, and he knew it was the real thing. He knew what he had. It was more than just a car, it was a unique piece of motoring history and as discoveries go, it was up there with the very best of them.

Ralph asked when it would be convenient to come down and they'd agreed that Max would collect him the following morning from the railway station. Ralph put down the phone and rubbed his hands. He couldn't have been happier.

NEWTON ABBOT MARCH 2001

'What's your position?' Ron asked.

'Not good. In fact it's worse than that; it's fucking scary, if you don't mind me saying.'

'It's as bad as that then.'

'Yeah. I don't honestly know if I can hold on to it.' Max paused and looked down at his desk, 'and I'm worried too because this could get bloody messy if I'm not careful.'

Ron looked back across the desk at a man he'd known

414

for the best part of twenty years. He could see the anguish in his face.

'Look Max, run through the scenario with me. How much do you owe?'

'I need to supply a Ferrari 360 Spider to a customer when it arrives, that will cost me £92,000, I owe one of my suppliers £58,000 for a car that we've been paid for and TA are hounding me for £42,000, so that's £192,000 just for those.'

That morning, BMS had deducted the last £49,950 from Velodrome's account for it to sit in a temporary account whilst the matter was being investigated. All being well, Max would get the money back, but for the meantime they didn't have the benefit of the funds.

Max had explained the circumstances in which Velodrome had arrived at this crisis point, most of which he'd known when Max had told him as the events occurred, but he went through it again just to be sure.

'How do I stand from a liquidity point of view? Do I need to do anything drastic?'

'I wouldn't go jumping into anything straight away. How far are you from getting the cars through?'

'I've got one coming this month from Tom McKinney and we've got over £30,000 profit in that one and we've all but paid for the new car. I've got his 360 Coupe coming in part exchange but we shouldn't have a problem selling that fairly quickly, but the others, I just don't know. Dimo's cars were supposed to be here last September, then it was definitely Christmas, now it's March and I still don't know. Donald Key, the customer for one of those Dimo cars is going berserk at me every day on the fucking phone and I've got no answers for him. The cars from Muzi will hopefully start drip feeding through from September, there's eight of those and of course there's the two cars from Isca Ferrari, but the guy up there is such a lying bastard I can't believe anything he says,' Max replied.

'So the only car you can rely on for certain is the Tom McKinney car, but you're sure that those other cars will come through?'

'Oh, yes. It's just time,' said Max.

'Okay, what sort of money are we talking about in terms of profit that you are likely to get from those cars?' Ron asked.

'Obviously nothing from Dimo's first 360 Spider because that money has already vaporised, but the second car from him will give us another £30,000. Tom McKinney's car will give us £35,000 and the two Isca Ferrari cars will bring us £210,000, so that should be £275,000 for those. Then the 360-part exchange from Rick Brady is mostly our money as we've already paid Tom a good deal of the money for that car, so that's another, say £65,000. What's that in total?' Max was writing it down as he talked. '£330,000, we've got another deal on the go as well which should bring us $150,000 and that looks good.'

'From what you've said, it's the classic cash flow scenario. You need to stall the creditors. Take as long as you can to pay on the basis that when those deals come in, you'll be in a position to pay.'

'It's easy for you to say that Ron, but some are people we've been dealing with for years. It's not going to be easy.'

'I never said it was, but you've got to get through it and with no obvious bank option, I think it's your only chance. I'm sorry about Carol by the way; she just upped and left, so we'll have to get someone else to learn the software.'

'As soon as you've got a new girl, let me know and I'll get Catalyst down again.'

'What's your VAT position?'

'We owe them £32,000 or thereabouts and we haven't got the money.'

'That could be difficult.'

'Well, I was hoping to pay them some on account and the balance when Brady's car is all settled.'

'Yes, that's probably the best. How much have you got out in pre payments?'

'There's the McKinney car which is £65,000, we only owe £17,000 to Tom to buy that car, so by the time that comes through and the part exchange is sold we'll be back up to about £100K. We've paid Muzi £25,000 in deposits for the eight cars coming from him plus we've got the deposits paid on the Isca Ferrari cars,' Max repeated.

'In all honesty Max, it's just cash flow. Weather it out until McKinney's car arrives and you should be okay. A hundred thousand back into the pot in the next four to six weeks and possibly the return of the BMS money. You'll be okay. It's just a big squeeze. I know it's going to hurt and I know it's easy for me to say, but I'm sure you'll be all right. You've been through worse than this and come out the other side. Hang on to your hat, that's the best advice I can give you.'

It was good for Max to talk through the problems with Ron. He knew how business worked with all the pitfalls and he'd gone some way to reassuring Max that it was just a blip. It seemed more than that to Max at the time but he also knew that sometimes when it got sticky he just had to hold on tight and see the job through. Just one deal could turn around his whole position and make life a lot easier.

As expected Donald Key was getting more and more awkward, no doubt fuelled by his customer chasing him in exactly the same way. Don had soon dispensed with dealing through Graham Lord, now he was calling Max direct demanding to know the whereabouts of his car or the refund of the money.

Max put it to him straight, 'Don, your car has not arrived. None of the cars have arrived as yet, so it's pointless you hounding me all the time.'

'Well, where's it coming from?' Graham Lord had already told Don that the car was coming from Germany, which was not true. Graham had assumed it was coming from Germany because most of Max's cars were German. Whenever Graham had spoken to Max about the country of origin, he had always referred to Germany. Max for his part had never corrected Graham, as he was pleased that he didn't know the car was coming from Spain. If Graham Lord and Donald Key had started ringing around, then they could ring German Ferrari dealers all they liked, but they'd never find the car and for Max, that was a useful safety net. The last thing he wanted was Graham or Don calling the dealership and asking the whereabouts of the car. All that would do was antagonise the dealer.

'Don, as soon as I know, I will tell you. That's what I'm telling you and that's what I am being told. I can't magic up the car. If it's not here, I can't give it to you.'

'What about the money? Where's that?' Don asked in a more agitated manner.

'Don, we have a contract to supply a car and from my side, that's what I am going to fulfil. When it's here you'll have it.'

Don was not pleased; he said he was talking to his lawyer. He wanted his money back and Max wasn't prepared to give it to him. Velodrome had a signed contract that said the sale of the car was subject to Ferrari delivering the car, so Max dug his heels in. Unbeknown to Don, the money had all gone anyway, so realistically it was the only thing Max could do. Sit it out and wait for the car to arrive. If it didn't arrive within a reasonable time, Max would have to think of something else.

The next few weeks became more and more distraught as the company teetered on the edge of cash flow survival. Everything was hand to mouth, fast and furious. It wasn't pleasant for anyone.

A silver Mercedes E320 pulled up outside the garage. Max was out delivering a bike at the time. Three men stepped out of the car, one small guy and two henchmen. Ferris was living in one of the flats above the garage and just happened to be going out when the three guys walked up to him.

'You, Max Reed?'

'What if I am?'

'Don't fuck with us. Where is he?'

'Can't help you, I don't know.'

They walked into the showroom as Ferris got on the phone to Max. He answered the phone immediately.

'Max, there's three thugs here looking for you.'

'Did they say who they were?'

'No. Just looking for you. They look nasty. The car's a 320 Merc saloon registered RO51XYQ.'

'That's a Reading number. Can't say I know anyone from Reading, but maybe that's no clue. Anyway, thanks. I'll call Pete.'

Max cut the conversation with Ferris and saw the Velodrome number flashing up on the screen.

'Yes, Pete, I know. Ferris has just called me. You okay?'

'Yeah, they're in the showroom waiting for you.'

'Okay. I'll be back as soon as possible. Did they say who they were? Or what they want?'

'No, just that they want to see you. Doesn't look good.'

Pete replaced the receiver. The stress of this was not what he was being paid for. The thugs strutted around the showroom menacingly; they were out to get what they wanted. Customers were coming into the showroom and being put off by these men talking about lifting stock for repayment. Pete needed to get them out but they weren't going. Mike switched on the VCR record button on the CCTV. At least if they were going to kick off then Velodrome would have a record of it.

Max was about forty minutes away when Pete called so it wouldn't be long before he was back at the garage. In the meantime the thugs had made quite a nuisance of themselves, being intimidating to Pete and Mike whilst they lorded around.

One of them reached into his pocket and answered the phone. Pete thought he heard a name but he wasn't sure, then the men hurriedly went back down through the showroom, jumped back into their car, and sped off.

She answered the door. She was more than a little apprehensive when she looked through the opening. Three men stood in front of her and they didn't appear to be making a social call.

The smaller one stepped forward. 'Mrs. Reed?'

'No. Mrs. Reed doesn't live here.'

'What about Max Reed?' he asked.

'No, he doesn't live here either. Never has.'

She looked at the men. She knew they weren't nice people. They were thugs. She didn't like them.

'Do you know where he does live?' one of them asked.

'Yes.' Almost as soon as she said it, she realised that she should have pretended she didn't know, but she'd been caught on the hop.

'Where?'

'Oh, I think it's a little bit further around the hill.'

They didn't say goodbye, they turned and scuttled back down the drive to their car. She watched them leave. She was the daughter of an ex Formula 1 boss and she'd seen their like before. Her house name was very similar to Max's and clearly the men had got the wrong address. They were now hunting down Max at home. He wasn't going to be there either.

They drove past the house then reversed up; Catherine was standing at the front door with her three month old daughter in her arms, talking to a neighbour. The silver Mercedes stopped and the passenger side windows wound down. The thug in the back of the car took out a camera and started taking pictures of Catherine. She didn't like what she could see and went to walk towards them and they sped off.

Five minutes later they were driving back and forth past the garage entrance when Max returned in the van. There was no Mercedes anywhere on the forecourt as he approached, so he thought they'd gone when in fact they'd parked directly behind Max, preventing him from reversing out.

He opened the van door and the three men walked up to him.

'Max Reed?' The small one asked.

'You owe some friends of ours some money and we've come to collect it.'

'Who are you?' Max sneered.

'We're from Donald Key Restorations and they want their money.'

'Well, they're not going to get it and neither are you.'

Max was shaking but he knew exactly where he stood. He had a contract with Donald Key and that was that. It distinctly mentioned the delivery date being subject to Ferrari supplying the car and as yet they hadn't supplied the car. If they had supplied the car and Max hadn't given it to Donald Key, that was a different story, but for now Max was well within his rights.

Max continued, 'Your best bet is to go back to Donald Key and find out what the hell he's talking about, because he sure as hell isn't telling you the full story. You've no business being here behaving like this.'

'We've got every fucking right to be here, smart arse. We'll be back.'

Max walked into the showroom and took a deep breath. Pete walked towards him, he wasn't happy and that was understandable. He'd put up with too much and enough was enough, he didn't need to say anything, he was off. Max didn't try persuading him otherwise, he knew that it was going to get worse before it got any better.

Max picked up the phone and called Donald Key's solicitor, Jim Trent, and told him that his client had just sent thugs down to Velodrome using threatening behaviour to try to obtain money with menaces. He couldn't believe it at first, but having spoken to Donald Key he quickly realised that he could no longer act for Donald and withdrew his services. Don would have to find another solicitor. Interestingly, Don had said to Trent that it wasn't him that had sent the thugs; it was all his son, Julian's, idea. Whatever, Trent could no longer represent him.

Max called Graham Lord and told him what had happened. He couldn't believe it, but later Don had confirmed to Graham that what Max had said was true. Interestingly, the thugs went straight from Velodrome to Donald Key's office and demanded money from Don with the same threatening behaviour. For his part Max could have gone to the police and made an official complaint but he didn't. He knew that when the

360 Spider arrived, everything would be settled and Max knew he'd never deal with Key again. No doubt the feeling was mutual.

A few hours later, Rupert Davis called Max. Was it just a social call or a fishing call? Either way, the conversation soon turned to the events earlier that day.

'Look, chap, Key's just a wanker. Take it from me, I know. And that son of his, he's been crying in his beer too. I've heard all about it. I spoke to him last weekend at a dinner and he was going on about how his dad had taken away his M3 because of the deal he'd done with you. Didn't stop him taking the coke though.'

Max told Davis about the thugs.

'Well if it was me and they did that to me, I'd be telling them to fuck off. Key's in a very dodgy position. If you go to the police, he'll be arrested and that would be interesting. Max, you've got to do it. You can't let him behave like that. We all have problems but we don't send thugs along to sort people out. I'm surprised he even knows people like that. My advice is, go to the police and make a complaint.'

Max had thought about it, but the whole situation was a mess and he didn't want to make it even more so. He didn't trust the police anyway, he'd seen first hand experience of their corrupt ways and he certainly didn't want them fighting his battle. He didn't trust them.

In some respects, Donald Key's actions had now slowed down the whole process. He knew that what he had done was wrong and he was worried about what Max might do. That had told him he ought to be very careful, because should Reed go to the police, Don would be potentially arrested.

Whilst all this was going on, Julian Key was busy rubbishing Max to anyone who would care to listen and in that small Ferrari world, news travels fast. The fact that very few customers had received their cars didn't stop Julian suggesting to all and sundry that Max had ripped him off good and proper. It wasn't true, but it was extremely damaging. What Julian Key didn't realise was that he was just about to cut off his nose to spite his face. He spoke to one person too many.

The deal with Nino on the sale of the Ferrari 250 SWB from Seattle had gone well so far. Angelo had verified the car and all that appeared to have changed from the original car was the differential which had a different number and wasn't really significant. It was still a very good car with some very good competition history so Nino was prepared to go ahead subject to agreeing a price. Max needed to speak to the owner to negotiate a figure first then liaise with Nino and the owner and try to get the deal finished.

BUCKFASTLEIGH, AUGUST 2003

The two men sat on the bench and to those few of the cloth passing by, they appeared to be two old men enjoying the late afternoon sun on a bright wintry day. They were in fact two very worried men staring into a huge black hole of a lifetime's habit. They were the last two standing and they were going to have to face the flock. Stromberg and Gussy had got away with it, by natural means, both having died a few years earlier, but Edmund and Benjamin were younger than the other two and it was looking like time had caught up with them.

The day before, Father Benjamin had been sitting at his desk in his room within the private quarters of the abbey when there was a soft knock at his door, it was Father Anselm. Benjamin opened the door and let him in and he closed the door quietly behind him.

'There are two gentlemen waiting to see you in the public reception. They are policemen and they would like you to accompany them to the police station in Chudleigh to interview about a complaint they've received.'

Benjamin could feel the blood drain from his body as he stood there in front of Anselm. He put his left hand up to his forehead and turned around to look out of the tall narrow leaded window. He didn't know what to say. It could mean only one thing.

Anselm continued, 'They asked to speak to the Abbot first to seek permission to speak to you and Edmund has had to grant that. Edmund has also spoken to the diocesan solicitor and he's on his way here now. We're expecting him in about thirty minutes.'

Benjamin sat down on the edge of his bed and held his head in his hands.

'Edmund will be here in a moment, he's just making sure that we're following the right procedure.'

There was a sharp knock at the door, Anselm let Edmund in.

'Thank you,' he said.

He needed to get rid of Anselm so he sent him back down to the public reception to explain to the two CID officers that the diocesan solicitor was on his way and Father Benjamin will be along shortly. He closed the door quietly behind him.

'I'm sorry, I had no choice. They asked my permission to speak to you. I couldn't say no.'

'It's okay; I understand. Have they said anything?'

'No, they have just said that they have received a complaint and they need to ask you a few questions.'

Benjamin was close to tears. At the age of 67, he hadn't expected this. 'It's all right, I'll deal with it. I won't say anything. I'll keep you out of it.'

Father Abbot put his hand on Benjamin's shoulder and whispered, 'Thank you. I'd better take you down.'

They walked into the public reception office and the two CID officers introduced themselves. There was no sudden rush of handcuffs or anything like that, it was all very civilised. Andrew Tyler simply told Benjamin that he'd like to ask him some questions and would he mind accompanying him to the police station. He wasn't being arrested; he would be helping the police with their enquiries of his own free will.

Benjamin's mind was racing, but the way in which he was being asked lulled him into thinking that perhaps the enquiries weren't that serious. Surely, if the police knew more, they would just arrest him. It made him feel a bit more confident.

Edmund watched Benjamin pick up his coat and put it over his arm as he walked out of the solid oak door accompanied by the two officers and the diocesan solicitor. He shut the door and leant his back against it with his head down. He put his hand up to his face and massaged his eyes simultaneously with his fore finger and his thumb, then dragged his hand back down over his cheeks. 'Oh my God,' he said despairingly, shaking his head as he did so.

The two men didn't speak much, they didn't have to. Edmund was the man at the top and he was the only person entitled to know within the confines of the Abbey, what was happening with Benjamin. Other monks either wouldn't ask or wouldn't know of anything untoward, they were a secretive lot. It helped that Edmund was the Abbot, he'd be able to deal with any issues if they arose and also he'd be the first to know, as was the case with the officer's arrival the day before.

On his return several hours later, Benjamin immediately went to the Abbot's quarters looking for Edmund, he wasn't there. He found him in the grounds ten minutes later.

'You don't have to worry, they never mentioned your name, come to that they never mentioned Guss or Stromberg either,' Benjamin huffed.

'Nothing?'

'No, absolutely nothing. It was all about me. All about where I'd been, who I'd seen, dates and all of that sort of thing.'

'Do you think they know anything?' Edmund asked.

'Yes, I think they do, but I don't know how much. They've got plenty of names that they ran past me and 'you know who', was amongst them. I didn't react any differently when they mentioned his name. I'd managed to compose myself well enough to remain calm.'

'How long was the interview?'

'Three hours. There was a short break, it felt like more. Trouble is Edmund, if they've spoken to all twelve names they've mentioned to me, then effectively it's twelve onto one. They've probably spoken to more, I don't know.'

The two men weren't looking at each other as they spoke, they were looking out over the meadow in front of them; it was like the meeting of two cold war spies, speaking through clenched teeth, meeting in a park. Eyes forward.

'Have I got any options?' Benjamin asked.

'I don't think so, at least not now. If we'd known beforehand, we could have perhaps sent you overseas somewhere, but now that wouldn't be possible. I think you're going to have to deny everything if it gets to that stage and take your chance.'

Benjamin could see his breath in the cooling air as he replied, 'God is my judge, not these people.'

'Yes, ultimately he is. You've lived with it these last twenty odd years, you've served your penance. What's it to do with them?'

'What do you think will happen?' Benjamin asked.

'I've had no experience of this sort of thing, I don't know is the answer, but I think we need to take it one stage at a time. Right now, they haven't got enough to charge you and you haven't been arrested. If that follows, then it may be time to worry. It's possible it might go away.'

Benjamin stood up.

My advice to you, is think things through carefully. Get a picture in your mind, a sequence of events; a story that fits and stick to it. Don't deviate. That's what happened, regardless of what may or may not have been said. You've got to be strong because if they do come back, next time it won't be to ask questions, you can be sure of that,' said Edmund.

Benjamin put his hands in his pockets under the outer cover of his habit and walked back to the Abbey on his own. Edmund sat alone on the bench for a little while thinking about his own situation. He hadn't gone to the extremes that Benjamin had, but nonetheless he'd rather not have to face the same level of enquiry. He may escape it, maybe nobody had made an official complaint against him. He worried about the police trawling through Benjamin's past. They'd be interviewing boys, now in their thirties and forties who just might mention his name. He could possibly get away with it if it was one or two, but if the numbers grew, it could start creating a pattern, and then he might get dragged into it. Bloody Benjamin, why did he have to go so far, he asked himself? Why couldn't he control himself, for God's sake? Bloody idiot, he was getting angry in his mind, there was nothing he could do about it now; it was just a waiting game.

HMP LEYHILL, AUGUST 2008

Come the end of the first week working in the laundry, Max had been in prison for six weeks, three at Exeter and three at Leyhill. Time was definitely going faster, the work in the laundry helped that. It kept Max's mind occupied, it wasn't like counting bricks in Exeter, thankfully that was now long gone. The thought of it still lingered though.

Originally, Leyhill was a lifer's prison with just over a couple hundred prisoners, however the numbers had expanded when it became a category D prison to allow for the increasing volume of criminals coming into the system. Long term residents of her Majesty's pleasure were slowly being released back into the community and the Cat D facilities gradually helped reintroduce prisoners back into civvy street. The learning courses, practical courses and general advisory staff at the prison lead inmates through a series of imaginary gates, ticking the boxes as they did so. It was designed to test the prisoner in all manner of respects, including psychological before letting them out on the general public. Probation staff were constantly interviewing and monitoring residents as they went about their daily grind. In many instances, the freedom that a prisoner had at Leyhill allowed them to do within reason what they wanted and this as such was a reflection of who they were and where they were in their lives. Drugs were a huge problem in the jail and it was plainly evident everywhere screws knew who was on what, heroin, cocaine, cannabis it was all available. A prisoners behaviour, always gave it away, up all night, agitated, sleeping all day, depression and desperation they were all clear signs of drugs abuse. But all the time, this information was being relayed back to probation so they knew that a prisoner had or hadn't changed his ways and stupidly inmates were blind to it. In their minds, they were too discreet, nobody knew what they were doing. How wrong they could be.

The mandatory drugs test would catch a few and they'd be shipped out, but often prisoners would have problems at home. They wanted to see their children, or wanted a town visit or home leave and they were getting knocked back and they couldn't understand why.

At first, all the drugs related issues went completely over Max's head, but as time went by, he began to notice more. Behaviour patterns, ups and downs, reactions, it had become more noticeable. Max's neighbour in No. 3 was a typical example being up all night then trying to sleep all day. He would then wander up and down the corridor asking people for food, have you got any butter, have you got any jam, have you got any milk. Max thought, *have you got any sense*? No, was the answer to that.

The thing with the drugs was that Max, like everyone else turned a blind eye to it. If it didn't bother him, then he wasn't interested in doing anything about it, but when it did start bothering him, he would do something about it.

That night, smack head in No. 3 was darting up and down the corridor, he was loaded up, heroin. It was eleven by the time Max turned in. His neighbour had no intention of going to bed, he was going to stay up all night watching the TV, moving around slamming the doors and by 3 am Max had had enough and went into his room and asked him to be quiet. His answer was, 'What's it got to do with you?'

'Everything,' Max replied, 'I can't sleep, you're keeping me awake.'

Smack head quietened down for a while, but half an hour later he was at it again. Max eventually did get off to sleep but only because he was so tired. This behaviour had been going on for over a week and Max had become more and more irritable. The easy answer would have been to have told the screws, but that was not something Max wanted to do. It would sort itself out one way or another, but Max didn't, at that time, know how.

The visits were the highlight of the week and on the Saturday Catherine and the girls were coming. Max had been looking forward to it and with the weather looking good, hopefully they would all be allowed to sit outside. Max waited in the assembly area listening for his name to be called, it was twenty past one and he'd been stood there for twenty minutes. The prison officer called him forward and checked his personal belongings, gave him his table number and ushered him through to the visiting hall. He opened the door and saw his two young daughters running towards him. He knelt down and picked them both up for a cuddle, it was a great feeling. Catherine walked up and did the same, he was back with his family again, at least for now, if only for two hours.

Like always, the visit went well and all too quickly and soon Max had to say goodbye and watch them disappear back through the visitors' door until the next time.

The usual practice for prisoners after a visit is for them to remain seated at their table numbers until they are called. When Max's name was shouted out, he went to the doorway before being beckoned forward by PO Ricks. When he was ready Ricks waved Max through into the assembly area and did a brief patting down search. He was used to it, he'd had it done to him several times before.

'Put your arms out straight,' Ricks ordered. Max did as he was told.

'Turn around,' Ricks barked and patted Max down from behind. That was it. Job done. Max collected his identity card and walked out of the assembly area and back to his room.

Several hours later, Max was sat in his room thinking about how lovely it was to see his family again, when unusually his name bellowed out of the tannoy. Reed AS4, unit office. No courtesy, just, unit office. Max wondered why he'd be called down to the unit office on a Saturday night. Seemed strange.

He knocked on the door.

'Come in.'

Max opened the door and walked in.

'Shut the door please and sit down,' said PO Wilson.

'You asked for me.'

'Yes, I did. Good visit today?' Wilson asked.

The first thing Max thought was that Catherine might have had an accident at home. Obviously, Max's facial expression gave it away.

'No, it's okay nothing's happened.'

'Oh right,' said Max. 'Yes, I had a great visit.'

'Have you got a problem with authority?' Wilson asked.

'No, not at all, why?' Max asked.

'The officer that patted you down after the visit said you've got a bit of an attitude problem and you didn't like being searched.'

'Well, it's news to me. As far as I'm concerned, I was patted down and walked out. I don't even remember who it was and I don't think I spoke to them either.' Max thought for a moment and continued, 'If I had a problem with someone, I'd probably remember who it was, and I don't, so, no, I haven't got an attitude problem.'

Max wanted to go on to say that perhaps the officer had an attitude problem not him, but he didn't. It did upset him though and it unsettled him. He didn't like the way it was done, Wilson's saying what he had in the manner he did, worried Max. The thought of Catherine having an accident had really struck him. Wilson let him go and said that he would get back to the officer and nothing would be done this time.

Max bit his lip and returned to his room, telling Chris Walton what had just happened.

'Max, they're just wankers, playing with your head. The problem is that you're different. You're not like most of the idiots in here and the screws don't like that. They know you've got a brain and that worries them. Don't take any notice of it. Just laugh at them, they're not worth the trouble.'

Lance looked across the showroom, 'It's Max Reed for you.'

'Tell him I'm out on a test drive,' said Sean.

'It's the fourth or fifth time he's rung.'

'Tell him . . .'

Sean was interrupted as Max walked in through the showroom door with his mobile phone held to his ear.

'Tell him, what Sean. Tell him you're out on a test drive. Tell him you'll call him back.' Max was mad, 'don't do that to me again. Every time I ring you never bother to answer my calls and you never ring me back. What's going on?'

'Nothing. I'm very busy and I haven't been able to call you. You're here now so what can I do for you?' asked Sean sheepishly.

'It's not very good Sean. You're not making me feel very confident about you. I've got two cars on order with you and you're making me feel very jumpy. I've been calling you because for one reason I wanted to find out what was happening with my two 360 Spiders and secondly because I'm interested in the E-Type, you've got there.'

Sean had to back pedal furiously to make himself look like he had any credibility at all. He explained that the Jaguar, a green 1974 V12 roadster belonged to the owner of the garage and he had decided to sell it. He'd owned it for over twenty years, it had complete history from new with only two previous owners and it looked superb.

Max went outside and called Rupert Davis.

'Hi, Rupert, it's Max. Are you interested in a really lovely '74 V12 E-Type roadster?'

'Tell me more,' Rupert replied.

'It's Jaguar racing green, with green leather interior, manual and on steel wheels. It's done 42,000 miles with full history.'

Rupert thought about it. 'What sort of money?'

'Firstly, I want £1500 for the commission.'

'Yes, that's okay.'

'It's up for £28,000 but they'll take £25,000 for it,' Max replied.

'If it's as nice as you say, I'll go for that,' Rupert said adding, 'Where is it?'

'It's at Isca Ferrari. The easiest thing is if you come down. I'll meet you at Granada Services at the end of the M5 and then we can go down to the garage and you can have a look.'

'Okay, I'll go down tomorrow, meet you at eleven; is that okay?' Rupert asked.

'Yeah, that's fine. When you go into the services, park in the top car park and I'll see you there.'

Max pressed the red button on his mobile and walked back into the showroom and had a quick look around the E-Type. Sean Williams didn't move from his desk. He was still embarrassed from earlier.

'Have you got all the paper work on the car?' Max asked looking over the bonnet at Williams.

'Yeah, I'll get it for you.'

Max looked through all the documents. There were a lot of service bills, all the old MOTs supporting the mileage, the original bill of sale from when new. It was all there.

'It's not for me, but I have a customer for it. He's going to come down tomorrow at eleven. If he likes it, and I can't see any reason why he shouldn't, then he'll give you £25,000 for the car and he'll pay me £1500 for the introduction. Are you all right with that?'

'Yeah.'

Max walked back out, Lance rolled his eyes at him as he did so. He couldn't believe the way Williams was running the place. Surely he didn't treat everybody like that did he? Max didn't know, but what he did know was that Williams was not going to make it easy for Max and when the first of the right hand drive 360 Spiders arrived in the country, he was going to have to watch Williams like a hawk. He wouldn't put it past him to sell Max's cars to someone else then tell Max that they hadn't yet arrived. He thought about what he could do to safeguard his position. He could see that Lance wasn't entirely comfortable with the way Williams behaved and to be caught out like that was just too embarrassing for words. Lance knew Williams didn't like Max, but Sean didn't own the company, he worked for it and he should have acted like a manager, not a jealous spoilt kid. It was ridiculous.

Max knew that Williams' predecessor had been moved sideways and he was now working within the group but for a different franchise so he'd be worth talking to and also the former service manager had left under a dark cloud, so he'd be worth talking to as well. A bit of background information might keep Max one step ahead.

Rupert Davis pulled off the M5 exit for the Granada Services and made his way to the top car park and stopped in the most obvious place. He got out of the car and had a quick stretch enjoying the fresh air. Max arrived about three minutes later and parked next to the silver Mercedes CLK55. Rupert was on his mobile chatting away in his usual forthright style. Max thought he'd aged since he last saw him.

'Hi, how are you?'

'Great.'

'Good trip?'

'Yes, thanks. An hour and a half, that's all.'

'I'm not surprised in that.'

'Hop in, we can go in this one and I'll drop you back afterwards,' said Rupert.

Max collected his case and his mobile, locked the car and jumped into the Merc. They chatted along the way about the E-Type and a short while later arrived at Isca Ferrari. Williams, was standing in the reception area talking to the flashy receptionist as Max and Rupert walked in.

The E-Type was just as Max had described, but Rupert took his time to have a good look around the car and satisfy himself that it was correctly described. He spent ages looking through the documentation and then pronounced himself happy. Williams by this time had graced his customers with his presence introducing himself to Rupert as the big wig and sat him down at his desk.

For his part, Williams was selling the car so he wrote out the contract and Davis was the buyer. Both knew that Max was the introducer and would receive £1500 commission for his efforts. The deal went to plan and Rupert asked for Isca Ferrari's bank details in order to send a transfer and also confirmed that his delivery vehicle would collect the Jaguar the following day. It was a simple deal for Max, a quick £1500, but that was because he knew a buyer and the car was under priced. It was a good car and Williams was out of his depth with it. If Sean had been more passionate about what he was doing, he could have made a lot more money for his employer, but to him, he had the mass market mentality of just shifting the metal.

When Rupert dropped Max back at his car, the pair of them sat and talked for an hour or so. Max told Rupert how bad things had become with Donald Key and all the legal letters he was now getting from them and Rupert said, 'Don't pay him back and don't give him his car, not after what he's done to you. He's running you down to everyone. Julian's doing the same. Stick to your guns boy, the ball's in your court.'

Max listened to Rupert but he didn't agree with him. He knew that when the car arrived, he would still hand it over to Don, that was the deal and no matter how hard it was going to be, he would still stick to the contract.

Three weeks later, Max still hadn't been paid by Rupert, so he gave him a call and asked him if he'd overlooked the payment. The invoice from Velodrome had gone off the same day.

'Look chap, when the car arrived here, the tool kit was missing, so I've had to buy a replacement.'

'That's not my fault. You looked at the car and satisfied yourself as to what it was and you agreed to buy the car from Williams.'

'Yes, I did, but the tool kit was not with the car, so I'm sending you an invoice for the new tool kit and a cheque for the balance.'

'Hey, Rupert be fair, that's not what we agreed. I simply introduced you and you're paying me a commission. I've done my bit. You inspected the car and were satisfied, which is why you went ahead with it'

'If you find the tool kit, I'll pay the shortfall, but I'm not doing it now, take it or leave it chap.'

Max was not happy, but he needed the money. He rang Williams and asked about the tool kit. He didn't know anything about it so there was no surprise there. Basically Davis had just shafted Max for a little over £400 and that in truth was the measure of the man.

TEIGNMOUTH, NOVEMBER 2001

Rob arrived a little bit late and the car park was surprisingly nearly full. He drove around and found a space out the back by the playing field and immediately recognised the short number on the black M3 as he parked his Porsche next to it. He got out of the car, shut the door and looked up at the

432

buildings. It had been ages since he'd been here; twenty-five years, in fact. He walked through the grounds, under the portico and down the steps to the walkway. He remembered Max once getting accosted by Grandpa Cresswell before a history lesson. Max had been fully engrossed snogging Michelle Marshall at the time when Cresswell tapped him on the shoulder and said, 'When you do come up for air, perhaps you'd like to come and join us.' Max had then finished his embrace and gone into the history lesson sitting next to Rob, telling him that Michelle had got a tongue like a lizard. Both of them were laughing and Cresswell in a typically understated sarcastic manner said, 'Anything you'd like to share with us Reed, or just Miss Marshall?'

'No, sir.'

'Then it would be ever so nice if you wouldn't mind letting me start,' Cresswell replied.

'Yes, Sir.'

'Thank you. That's jolly good of you.' Cresswell started the lesson.

Rob walked along the corridor towards the school hall and opened the door. The noise hit him like switching the ignition on with the radio at full blast. It was warm and everyone was laughing and joking. Liz and Sarah were at the door taking down everyone's name and immediately Rob felt at home. It was good to see everyone again .The faces had changed a little but generally they were all the same. He could see Max up ahead and made a 'B' line for him. It was a twenty-five year Teignmouth Grammar School reunion. Everyone seemed to be there, teachers, cooks, cleaners and of course all the pupils from the class of that glorious year of 1976.

Rob settled in to the flow and a few faces came and went just like they would have done in period, but a few stayed a little while longer. Vicky took her time to talk to Rob, she was happily married with two kids, just like Rob and all the memories came flooding back and they were good memories too. Max joined in the conversation as they immersed themselves in everything they'd done since school. The way they talked to each other and the animated way they described things was just like it would have been twenty-five years earlier. Things had changed but they hadn't changed, not really. They may have been a little more reserved but they were still the same people.

Max felt a pair of hands cover his eyes from behind.

'Guess who?'

He made to turn around but she stopped him. He'd recognised the voice immediately, like a bolt out of the blue. He hadn't once thought she would have been there and replied.

'I bet you don't wear Charlie perfume any more?'

'No, that was a long time ago.'

She took her hands away and they looked at each other. He kissed her on the cheek and smiling said, 'still as beautiful as ever.'

'You always said the right things.' Her captivating eyes drawing him in.

She looked as fabulous there and then as she had done that time he saw her walk down the stairs in a pair of tight jeans and a white T-shirt. Instant recall. It was Jenny.

'I didn't think I'd be seeing you again.'

'No, we didn't say goodbye.' She paused, thinking about it, then added, 'Properly'.

They talked for hours catching up on all those years gone by. She still had that dangerous feel and the fire hadn't gone out either. It sort of closed a chapter better than it had done the first time, and rounded off everything. Max felt better for that. It finally closed a door that had been ajar for a long, long time.

By midnight the party was coming to an end. Jenny leant forward and kissed Max on the cheek. She looked at him holding on to his hand.

'You know, we did have a good time together didn't we?' She didn't need to ask, it was obvious there was still something there, even after all the years in between had tried to erode the memory.

'Yes, we did,' Max replied.

'It was a shame it ended the way it did.'

'Yeah, well. Things move on.' He cast it aside not wanting to her know how much it had upset him at the time.

'Could have been different,' she said quietly looking down. They could have been the only people in the room.

'Yeah, could have.' He was unsure where this was going, not wanting to get sucked in.

'Are you happy?'

'Yes, very. Same girl since three years after you.'

'That's amazing. I'm pleased for you. It seems like such a long time ago, but I remember it as if it was yesterday. So

434

vivid. It was exciting, I was just so happy.' She said shaking her head.

'You?' he asked.

'Absolutely,' it sounded less convincing. He let down his guard a little.

'Yes, they were good times,' Max replied.

'You know something? I meant it at the time. It could have been different Max.'

'Yes, it could have,' he said trying not to look into her eyes. He knew what she was referring to. His tea making had not had such a dramatic reaction since.

'Whenever I hear that Chicago song. 'If You Leave Me Now', it always reminds me of you.'

'Funny you should say that, because I heard it on the radio the other day and I thought exactly the same. I thought of you immediately. They always say music jogs the memory.' He paused, ' No, they were good times and I do look back on them fondly, but I've been lucky. I've been ever so lucky. I've got the best girl in the world and I don't tell her enough. I've put her through all sorts of crap and she still puts up with me.'

'Well tell her Max, make sure you do, she deserves it.'

Jenny was right, he would.

NETWON ABBOT, MARCH 2001

If Velodrome's fortunes had got worse over the last five months, it was going to be nothing in comparison to what was to come.

Tom McKinney called Max to let him know that the 360 Spider was on its way so there was the part exchange to collect from Rick Brady. That car needed to be sold as quickly as possible. Rick had hardly used the car, it still had less than five thousand miles on the clock so all being well Velodrome would still be able to get a decent price for it.

Donald Key's new solicitors were chasing Max and they needed to be responded to legally which meant that Max had to use his solicitors which was adding to the costs all the time. Max had spoken to Don several times asking him to be patient and wait and it would all be sorted, but Don was having none of it. He was putting on the pressure.

Dimo had been on the telephone asking about the yellow 355GTB and Max had to tell him that the car was sold. It was still in the service area at the garage and had been for several months, but Max could sense that Dimo was getting twitchy. The two 360 Spiders had still not arrived at Sebastien's and worse, Victor had no idea when they were likely to arrive.

Some customers were now starting to receive their cars, so rightfully anyone who had a deposit on a car was now thinking they'd be getting their car soon.

Velodrome's bank overdraft was constantly banging on the limit so Max had to go cap in hand to the bank to ask for a short term fix whilst he waited for Rick Brady's car to be sold and the new car to arrive. Fortunately Simon Hughes was away and Nick Salmon had agreed to a temporary £125,000 limit provided the overdraft was reduced to £80,000 once the money came in. Max had agreed to it. He had to, he didn't have a lot of choice.

Max collected Rick's 360 Coupe from his parent's house in Dartmouth and took it back to the garage to offer it for sale. The weather was changing and Max didn't think he'd have too much difficulty finding a new owner for it.

Max used some of the extra money on the overdraft to send to Dimo. He figured that sending him £10,000 would keep him on side whilst he waited for other monies to arrive. Max had told Dimo what he was doing, but it hadn't gone down too well. Dimo was annoyed that he wasn't getting all his money especially as the car was sold. Max managed to hold onto the situation, by virtue of confirming to him that he still had the car, but it wasn't easy.

Everything Max had dreaded was coming to a head. The only telephone calls were from people asking for money and Velodrome just didn't have it or have access to it. If Max could have borrowed more, he would have done. He'd thought about moving banks but that would have taken too much time and there was no guarantee that he'd get a better deal elsewhere. That morning there was another letter from Customs & Excise, they wanted their money and that was another £32,000.

Realistically Max had to get Brady's new 360 Spider in as quickly as he could. If not, it could all be over.

Max called Tom, 'How are we getting along with the 360 Spider?'

'Next week Max,' Tom answered.

'Thank God for that.'

'Under pressure?'

'Yeah, just a bit.'

'Well, don't worry. It'll be here next week, probably Monday or Tuesday. I'll let you know.'

Max put the phone down. He needed to transport himself into the future by eight days and collect the car from Tom, then he wouldn't have to dodge the creditors. At least by then, he could tell people honestly that he could deal with some outstanding invoices with some degree of sincerity. It wasn't how he wanted to run his business, he hated it but it was the only way he could deal with it at the time.

Max survived the following week unscathed. He'd spoken to the creditors and given them his assurance that all was well and that he just had a cash flow issue. He didn't like having to do it and he certainly didn't want to admit he was in trouble, but he had to stop the calls and prevent any potential writs or summons arriving on the doorstep. That would be extremely damaging.

He was going to need to call Rick Brady to ask for the balance on the new 360 Spider, but he was leaving it until he knew Tom had the car. The balance outstanding was a little under £37,000 so with the sale likely to go through on the part exchange 360 Coupe, Max was expecting about £107,000 into the coffers. Again the *Sunday Times* had produced another eager buyer.

Velodrome were still selling bikes at the same rate as they had previously with Pete running that side of the show, however Max was now working all hours just to keep afloat and it was plainly obvious, that if the problems continued for more than a few weeks, then staff would have to go.

Max sat down at his desk, it was gone seven o'clock at night. He was tired but he needed to finish a few things before he went home. He wanted to do a cheque run and had printed off a list of creditors and figures that had to be paid. He was expecting the funds from the sale of Rick Brady's Ferrari 360 Coupe in the following day and also the balance for the new 360 Spider. He'd promised creditors funds as soon as they arrived and he was going to ensure that he got them off his back. He totted up the list, it came to a little over £95,000 and it didn't include Dimo. He had to be careful because the bank were going to reduce the temporary overdraft down from £125,000 to £80,000 so that was going to knock £45,000 out of the equation straightaway. He juggled the figures allowing himself a £15,000 leeway on his overdraft and made cheques out to pay all the small creditors in full as they were the lifeblood of the company and then made sizeable part payments to the more pressing major creditors. It still wasn't enough to satisfy the problems but it would significantly reduce what appeared to be the endless time wasting phone calls of suppliers chasing £100 or £400 or other small figures. The bigger sums like Dimo and the VAT man were amounts that Max would have to use his best endeavours to re-schedule by negotiation and that was something he wasn't looking forward to. He wrote out all the cheques, signed them and popped them in the envelopes ready to be sent the next day once he had cleared incoming funds.

The next job on the list was more heartfelt, he would have to cut staff. He could no longer afford the luxury of some and they were going to have to go. He had kept them all during the foot and mouth period and now he couldn't continue with such a high wage bill. Max had to put sentiment aside and decide what to do. It was easier to list all of those that had to stay and ultimately the list was a very short one. There was just three people that he could afford to keep on and one of them was him. It would be a miserable decision. He didn't start the business to be sat at his desk late in the evening deciding to get rid of people. They were his friends and he hated himself for it. He hated the incompetence of what had gone before, whether it was his fault or others, it was just fucking awful but it had to be done. If Velodrome stood any chance of continuing, it would have to be with minimal overheads. Yes, it was drastic but Max couldn't see any other options. A year earlier, there was a buzz about the place and fourteen staff were all pulling together and enjoying their work, now it had become more akin to a morgue. Everyone knew Max was struggling, there was no hiding it. People were on the phone asking for money, people were coming in doing the same and the stock level was low. It all looked spartan. None of it instilled confidence and no matter how much Max put a brave face on it, the staff had to be expecting a call into his office.

Max put the envelopes into the night safe, switched off the lights, set the alarm and locked the front doors and went home. He was glad to get away from it.

It was good news the following morning. Max called Tom just after ten o'clock and the new 360 Spider for Rick

Brady was on its way from Germany. Tom had confirmed to Max that he could collect it from his house on Monday after the weekend. Originally Max was going to collect the car from Krell Ferrari in Singen on the Swiss German border but Rick Brady was in the UK at the time and fancied the idea of driving the car straight down to Monaco the following week. At long last, something was going right. The funds had come in for the 360 Coupe and as expected Rick Brady had transferred the balance for his new car. Max felt like a huge weight had been lifted from his shoulder, so he had great pleasure in posting off all the envelopes that he'd written out the night before thinking to himself that he lived to fight another day. The pressure had been almost too much to bear but he was a tough cookie and he believed in himself. He'd always thought he would make it happen.

Brady's Ferrari 360 Coupe was collected by it's new titled owner on the Saturday and Max went home for the weekend feeling a lot better than he had for quite some time. Just before he locked up, he opened the special delivery postmarked GP and pulled out the wad of paperwork. There was loads of it. He couldn't read it there and then, there was too much, it could wait.

HMP LAYHILL, AUGUST

Max looked at the roll call list in front of him and followed the course titles down to the one headed "Domestic Cooking", saw his name and signed in.

The orderly at the desk looked up, checked who was signing and gave Max directions to the kitchens. Off he went in search of a totally different education. In all the years Max had been married, he could count on one hand the number of times he had cooked a meal, so now was his chance to learn something new. The course was a basic level two accredited course run for two days a week over a five week period and it was aimed at people like Max who really didn't have a clue. It got Max out of the humdrum of the laundry for a few days and added a bit of variety to the week. It was something different.

The guy running the course turned out to be a decent bloke even if every other word was the "F" word, but he got everyone to work through the day and by the end of it, Max had cooked himself a Thai Chicken Curry that was actually edible.

The last time he heard the "F" word being used so much in conversation was back in '92 when he was trying to do a deal with Chris Rea to drive his Ferrari 308GT4 in the Maranello Championship. He remembered sitting with his race engineer, Nigel trying to hammer out a cost per race, but it didn't happen for many reasons however that guy could curse with the best of them. Very nice bloke though and great music too.

Needless to say, with six inmates on the course, the stories continued. One guy was in for attempted murder, another for running a cannabis farm, the guy opposite Max was in for fraud, the chap next to him had just served five years for armed robbery and the last guy kept himself to himself so that usually but not always indicated some kind of sex crime. It was quite a mix and the conversations were often funny.

'Have you seen that blind guy?'

'I bet he hasn't seen you!' You know sort of thing, the banter continued.

'What's he in for?'

'Murder.'

'Shit, Who did he murder?'

'He doesn't know.'

'Yeah, he does, he murdered his friend.'

'You wouldn't want to be his enemy then.'

'I was standing in the breakfast queue the other morning and a guy told him he was black. He said he wasn't and the guy said 'How do you know?' Apparently he replied that his mother had told him. This guy said she was lying. He didn't speak after that.'

'He's been working in the kitchens. For Christ's sake, how stupid is that? He could be walking into pointy bits all over the place.'

'They had him going the other day. They were all in the kitchen talking about a shitty screw and the blind guy was giving it both barrels not knowing that the screw had come in and was standing in front of him.'

'Brilliant!'

'They're fucking terrible to him, they pinch food off his plate, give him half measures of milk. It's not funny really. They put things in his pockets to smuggle out of the kitchen. He has no idea about it.'

'I saw him the other day up in the flower bed over by the OMU. God knows what he was doing there. Must have had a steering fault.'

'How old is he?'

'Don't know. I don't think he knows either. He's never seen any presents.'

'You're bastards you lot. Come on get on with the fucking cooking,' Dan said.

'What's that old boy in for? The one with the stoop and the two sticks?'

'I don't know. He looks like he's in his eighties. Always says hello.'

'I think he's the babes in the wood murderer isn't he?'

'I don't know mate. I've seen him about, but I don't know what he did. Can't say I really want to know'

'What's babes in the wood anyway. What's that all about?'

'He's a kiddy murderer. Horrible.'

'Yeah, fucking awful, he shouldn't be on this planet. Kick his sticks if you're passing him.'

Amongst criminals, there is an absolute hatred for sex offenders and child killers. Leyhill is one of the few prisons where all inmates are together. In all other prisons, sex offenders and similar are segregated for their own safety. Depending on who Max talked to, the number of sex offenders at Leyhill were maybe as much as seventy per cent. It was sickening.

Max did his usual run that night, six laps within the boundary. It never seemed to get any easier, it was always a slog and he never found it easy to get himself going either. Of course, he didn't have anything much better to do. The finishing times were usually within thirty seconds of each other, which at least showed some consistency. He didn't know if it was doing him any good, but it did make him sleep better. It passed the time of day and it burnt up a little more of the anger that was still raging away inside him.

CHUDLEIGH, FEBRUARY 2004

Andrew Tyler had seen enough, he'd read enough and as far as he was concerned, he had enough for a conviction, but he

441

was still going to need more if he was to get it past the CPS and make any charges stick. He had talked to his three colleagues working in the team and they'd all agreed that they would need to speak to every child that went to the school. That was about six hundred over a twenty year period. He didn't know whether he was going to be able to get permission to lead the team into that level of investigation but if he was to take it further he was going to need a bit of a break.

He walked into his senior officer Paul Stone's office.

'Morning Andy, how are you?'

'Fine thank you sir.'

'How's your enquiry coming along?'

'I could do with some more hands on the team,' Andrew replied.

'Why?'

'I think we've got a whole can of worms here sir and I want to contact every boy that went to that school.'

'And how many's that?'

'Six hundred.'

'Pull Tim Locke in with you. He'll fit in.' There was a small pause and Steve continued, 'and try contacting Friends Reunited, see if you can do anything with them.'

Tyler went back to his desk and pulled up Friends Reunited on the screen and scrolled through all the information. He might be able to short cut some of the legwork by sending an email message broadcast out to all pupils listed from that school. That would be worth trying.

March 2001 Newton Abbot

Max picked up the phone to call Tom McKinney. It was the fourth time of trying that morning and it was still engaged. He'd tried the home line number and the fax just in case there was a fault but there had been no answer. It seemed a bit odd but he wasn't worried.

He pulled out the wad of paperwork from the large brown envelope. There was a lot of it. He leafed through the many pages and started reading one of the telephone transcripts.

Muzi (American accent): 'What was the day like today?'

Craig (Australian accent): 'It was a pretty nothing day yesterday. I had 'til last night, around midnight I got the last of the coordinates and today I sent you copies of everything. We got the $20 billion B&I. We want to send a BMG coordinate to

442

Spain, the one-five-five. The Citibank one will go to Spain. I arranged that. That's already done that large because I'm doing that one with Skully and Skully sent me the last document that I'd been waiting for. As soon as I give him the coordinates, it will be back in two minutes so that one's all complete. It's just them sending it over to Citibank, which will be today. The other BG and the British Traders Commerce Bank were sending into the Bank of Bahamas and the BOC and the other one, which is the Bankodur Brazil, will go to the coordinates that I give him today. Chris knows all these things and tidies most of the stuff up. However there is a but, there is a local and he's obsessed with the $20 billion that's in Bank Inta and now he keeps writing, ' you have told me nothing', well I've told him exactly what I know and he's now complaining about the whole bloody thing, so much so that this morning in came a little note, signed which is very, very, bloody strange. I don't think he's near. I think he's too bloody scared. To talk, to even talk to them because he doesn't know what's going on.

'I'm saying that not because I hate his guts, but because he is telling us little lies everyday of the fucking week. He says, you are not telling me this, you are not telling me that. We tell him everything that we know and then suddenly he comes up and says we said to him, we want you to get Mr. Echo. If he is going to do so many goody goody things, then he must send the $20 billion to the coordinates. He then says "aagh, I don't think those deals are dead", but like yesterday he is bashing our ear holes. I ask him for the coordinates and he says "Craig, this is the morning, please don't tell me you have answered my question. I have asked daily about the $20 million and you still don't answer. I can appreciate you not knowing, but I promised people something that I was told would happen in hours and this was two weeks ago, the nothing. No one even talks about it. I can't give them no answer at all. I will see what I can do, but I think the deals are dead because I failed to give them answers in two weeks.'

Muzi: 'Tell them to just basically write them back and just ask them in a very short two liner and say please confirm whether these things are dead or not.'

Craig: 'You see what I said, I just told them to tell them what I know. My memo of the 29th makes it clear that he is playing a game because they keep saying that they do not have the instrument. To say that you will ask Mr. Echo to cancel with his bank, will bring it to a hit. Jacko said he has done everything, then we can be assured that they can do a big one. We are unable to get more information on the Bank Inta because the people there are being very guarded. So a push from B&I will help to bring this to an end. You are now telling me you think these deals are dead ? It's very strange that you should be saying this after all the commotion you've been creating. Your logic does not come through and you have everyone on this side turning over backwards and a little more effort would not go amiss. Again, please get Mr. Echo to resend the coordinates that I sent you to bank the pyramid er? One other thing, you made some petty mistake once again by going against people's integrity on the assumption...was discounted. Be very careful what you say or put in print, my friend. I received twenty six pages of written form regarding the two transactions for $50 million and the $100 million. I can't read all the pages because some are blurred. What's it all about ? Not much good sending in paperwork anyway without knowing what the bloody hell is happening.'

Muzi: 'We have to know the size of our commitment before we accept that thing.'

Craig: 'Correct. It pleases him to tell me he can handle this. Well, we want to know what we are handling first and why we are handling it. This time you have not answered my question about the $500 million USD that is B&I. Now I need to know why we are taking this down into a separate bank. There cannot be any confusion at the receiving bank and it will be much quicker. Look if it helps, I will write a letter about the $20 million fiasco. Just le me know if it's needed. I don't know what the problem with this "Young" guy continually winding everybody up.'

Muzi: 'Well. We've got two of those.'

Craig: 'Pardon ?'

Muzi: 'I said we've got two of those.'

Craig: 'Who's the other one?'

Muzi: 'Mr. Yong'

Craig: 'Ha ha. Oh the one that's always sick and tired?'

Muzi: 'Yes.'

Craig: 'It just makes it easy, simple. So that's the situation from now on.'

Muzi: 'So what's the situation on Blice?'

Craig: 'Oh, on Blice, there's no further grounds for

another day or two.'

Muzi: 'All right.'

Craig: 'He calls me everyday.'

Muzi: 'Has George responded to you?'

Graig: 'No.'

Muzi: 'Has Grace responded to your document yet?'

Craig: 'No.'

Muzi: 'Okay, but I need to know what came to what. And the preview?'

Craig: 'He hasn't seen it.'

Muzi: 'Okay, I'm still waiting for a response from George, because he is meant to respond to your letter; isn't he?'

Craig: 'Well, he is supposed to, but of someone wrote me a letter like that I wouldn't be able to get a reply back quick enough.'

Muzi: 'Ja.'

Craig: 'But you see what they did. They got this hairy guy to ring George yesterday morning and Gormay was asking, "Are you happy with Nieman and Nieman? Are they doing the right things for you, blah, blah, blah?" You'd have thought that I'd made all the fucking booboos. So George said, "Hey, I'm quite happy with my dealings with Craig at this stage". I'm the one that's holding things up. The problem is that I'm terribly disappointed that things have been misguided and misdirected. And left it at that. You haven't heard any more?'

Muzi: 'No, but with the…'

Craig: 'Yeah, well I… This stuff that he has just sent me. It can be done, they are bargaining, but as usual we need to know what the commitment is before we jump in.'

Muzi: 'We are not in the discounting business. If we have the money to work with for a while, then Yes. But we are not going to ship money in and ship money out. The answer is no.'

Craig: 'They are not going to do it. That's all there is to it. You know, I have an old fashioned four door Nissan and I know you are much younger and much brighter than I am. My old fashioned thought is that if you are going to discount money, you can walk straight into a bank and get that done in tiny little pieces.'

Muzi: 'Anybody can.'

Craig: 'Yes, so you know. What's the point?'

Muzi: 'No point.'

Craig: 'All right, how are you doing today, apart from just waking up?'

Muzi: 'Well, I will be better. I'm feeling really fine.'

Craig: 'You're fine?'

Muzi: 'Ja.'

Craig: 'You're sure?'

Muzi: 'Ja. Thanks.'

Craig: 'I'm gonna have three to four hours down at the river with Jodie. It's her favourite place. Get the cobwebs out of her system. Sitting around here all night and all bloody day is not funny.'

Muzi: 'Sounds good. You should do like I do now and then: Go shoot some pool. It takes your mind off things.'

Craig: 'Once upon a time, we used to play squash.'

Muzi: 'I used to love that.'

Craig: 'You did?'

Muzi: 'Yes.'

Craig: 'Then we must play again.'

Muzi: 'I haven't played for a few years, but I used to love it. I used to belt the shit out of that little ball. Really take it out on everybody.'

Craig: 'I'll leave you to it. I'm on the mobile if you need me, okay?'

Muzi: 'Okay, speak to you later.'

It was just one telephone conversation and Max must have read it at least five times. He still couldn't make any sense out of it. Three pages, that's all and there were more than a hundred pages in the wad, plus loads of other information. It was fascinating yet almost totally incomprehensible. He put the paperwork down onto his desk and stared at it. He had no idea what they were talking about. It was almost as if it were a different language. They were big numbers and big numbers usually meant big profits. Five hundred million, one hundred million, twenty million, it was all mentioned. Seven million for a Ferrari wouldn't even scratch the surface. He could afford it.

Rick Brady had called asking about collection of his new car, but Max couldn't tell him exactly, so he told him it should be Wednesday. That would give him time to sort the paperwork and get the car all valeted ready to go out. He didn't want to be rushing on the Tuesday, realising that it was unlikely to be arriving on that Monday bearing in mind he couldn't get hold of Tom.

Max eventually managed to speak to Tom but it was gone four when Tom had picked up.

'Yeah, hi ,Tom, it's Max.'

'Hi, you okay?'

'Yes thanks. All right for me to collect the 360 Spider?'

'Not today.'

'Oh?'

'Yeah, we've had a bit of a problem. We had a small bump in the car in London on the way back.'

'What've you done to it?'

'Nothing too much, it's the nearside front wing, bumper and headlight. It sounds a lot, but it's only minor. I've dropped it into the body shop and they're telling me I can have it on Thursday.'

'Okay, what time on Thursday?' Max asked.

'Should be lunchtime. It's nothing much, don't worry?'

Max put down the phone. He was disappointed, not least because he wasn't going to be able to tell Rick Brady the truth. His car was damaged, but he couldn't possibly tell him that it had some minor damage. That wouldn't go down very well at all. *One day won't matter*, he thought. At least it's in the country. He called Rick to let him know that it would be Friday not Wednesday. He was okay with it.

It had been a slow week, the March 1st new registrations had been down on the previous year and the motorcycle boom was definitely on the wane. There was nowhere near the level of enquiries Velodrome took two years previously, which didn't bode well. Still, that was the bikes, Max's concern right now was Rick Brady's 360 Spider.

He called Tom on the Thursday morning fully expecting to collect the car that afternoon. Tom didn't answer. That wasn't a problem, but the dial tone was overseas, it was definitely not UK, and that was little bit strange. He tried again and let it ring until the service provider cut in with their message. It was Spanish. Tom had to be in Spain or at least his mobile was in Spain. He tried again, he was right, it was definitely Spain. The service provider message didn't allow for a message to be left, so Max hung up and thought about it for a while. He tried the landline again, no response. He pulled up the on screen fax programme on his computer and tapped out a message. 'Please call Max ASAP.'

Maybe Tom was away for a couple of days. It was

perfectly possible. He must have gone at short notice. He hadn't told Max he was going, not that he had to at all, but he did say the 360 Spider would be ready on Thursday lunchtime. Max got on with some work, he had plenty to do. He'd try Tom again later.

'Mike, if Tom calls, ask him to ring me on my mobile. I'm just going up to East Street to fill up the truck. Also, can you buzz Guy and ask him to open the rear gates and take the chain lock off the shuttle trailer? Thanks. I'll only be ten to fifteen minutes.'

Max drove up to the filling station and fuelled up the pick up. Whether Tom rang back or not, he was going to get ready to go to Essex to collect the car. Normally, he would have gone on the train and driven back but given that Tom wasn't answering the phone, it seemed better to be taking the trailer. Although he was a little troubled, he was by no means panicking, in fact he didn't want to even dare consider the worst case scenario as he simply thought there had to be a reasonable explanation. He'd been dealing with Tom for nearly two years and they'd done a hell of a lot of business together. Tom wouldn't let him down, no he wouldn't, Max thought.

When he returned to the garage, he reversed into the rear entrance and hitched up the shuttle trailer, then went into his office and tried Tom again. Same response. It rang for a couple of minutes or so then went to the Movistar message. It was nearing lunchtime, surely Tom would remember what they agreed and call him. Max walked across the road to the Park Cafe and bought himself a sandwich. He was staring out of the window when it was his turn to be served. 'Penny for them,' she said.

'Sorry I was miles away,' Max replied.

'Could I have a ham salad sandwich please?'

'Coming right up.'

'Got any new Ferraris coming in. I fancy a test drive.'

'I bet you would,' Max said with a smile.

'So the next red one you get in, come and get me.'

'Okay.'

'One pound ten please.'

'Thanks.'

She smiled, Max had been going to the same shop for years and they were used to all the bikes and cars turning up. It gave them something to look at.

He sat at his desk and slowly ate the sandwich and Mike brought in a cup of tea.

'Thanks.'

'Are you okay?'

'Ask me later this afternoon. Tom hasn't called has he?'

'No, the phone's been very quiet today.'

'Okay.'

'Anything wrong?'

'I don't know. Tom's not answering the phone and it's dialling out in Spain and I'm supposed to be collecting Rick Brady's new car today.'

'Hmmm, that doesn't sound good.'

'Well, that's what I'm thinking, but I'm hoping it's just a communication issue.'

'Yeah, well, let's hope so,' said Mike walking back to his parts counter.

Max ran his fingers through his hair thinking that the consequences of Brady's car not turning up would be disastrous. He didn't think the company could survive that.

He must have rung Tom's number at least another twenty times before closing time and it was always the same response. He tried the landline a dozen times too, no response. Max was starting to get worried. He spoke to Mike before closing time and told him that if he wasn't in first thing, then he would have gone to Essex and that he'd call him later in the morning. Max kept trying all evening and still there was no reply.

Max was up and out the door early with a four hour drive in front of him. He wanted to be at Tom's for around nine o'clock and with the trailer on the back he wasn't going to travel at his usual speed. As soon as he was out on the dual carriageway, he pressed redial on his mobile. It was the same message. He didn't know what to expect when he arrived but he was still trying to be positive. He didn't for one minute think that Tom had stitched him up.

The journey had been pretty uneventful, there had been an accident on the M25, which slowed the traffic for twenty minutes or so, but as he turned into Tom's gateway, he noticed the dashboard clock reading five past nine; he'd made good progress. Now, was the moment of truth.

He parked the car and looked at the beautiful old house in front of him. He couldn't see any movement and there were no curtains drawn. There were no lights on and there were no cars in the drive. It didn't look good.

He stepped out of the car, walked up to the front door and tapped the big brass lion head knocker. There was no response, just an echo. He then stepped back and looked up at the windows all around, nothing. He could see in through the windows downstairs, all the furniture was there and everything seemed to be in its place. *Strange*, he thought. *No outside lights on, no inside lights.* If you were going away, you'd normally leave something on.

Whatever, he decided to stay at Tom's place for at least the morning, just to see if anyone showed up. It may not be Tom, but perhaps the milkman, the postman, anyone might be able to give him a clue as to what was going on.

He finished touring around the outside of the house looking in where he could and then went back to the truck and leant against the drivers door thinking that he'd just wasted his time. Half an hour passed when he thought he could hear a car approaching. He moved away from the truck to look along the driveway and in the distance he could see a black Range Rover coming towards him. It was Tom's car. *Thank God for that*, he thought. However, as it neared him, he could see it was Laura driving; there was no one else in the car. He let her park and get out and she walked towards him.

'Hi, what are you doing here?' she asked in a surprised manner.

'I've been trying to get hold of Tom, but he's not answering his phone.'

'He's gone Max. Got someone else. He's left me and the children and gone to live in Spain with his tart.'

'I'm sorry to hear that Laura, I was supposed to have collected a car from him yesterday.'

'Max, there's been no cars here for a few weeks. He's closed all of that down.'

'Would you like a coffee?'

'Yes, okay.'

'Come on in, I'd just dropped the children off at school, that's why I wasn't here.'

'Oh, right.'

'What car were you collecting?' Laura asked.

'360 Spider.'

'I didn't think Tom could get any of those.'

450

'Unless he's not telling me something, it looks like I've been had. He told me that he collected the car from Krell's last week and had a minor bump on the way home and that the car was at the body shop being repaired and that I could collect it Thursday.'

He hasn't been away for at least a fortnight and he's had no Ferraris here since you collected the last one.'

'Does he have a regular body shop? Max asked.

'No, he collects the cars all done. He doesn't get anything done here.'

'Where's he gone?'

'I don't know yet. He's trying to find somewhere. I had someone else here yesterday asking me similar questions so I guess, he's mislead a few of you.'

Max couldn't take it out on Laura, she was now a single parent. In the circumstances, she'd been pretty calm, he could tell that she was very upset but she had to get on with her life. What Tom had done to Max was nothing to do with her.

Max had plenty of time to think about his position as he drove home. He'd sat and talked with Laura for a couple of hours and she'd told him all about their marital problems, money, children and his business. It was a sorry tale.

A month earlier, Paul, Max's delivery driver had taken a 355 into Croydon DVLA office to get it taxed on the way back to Velodrome. Max had just bought it from Tom who had given Paul all the paperwork to get it done. Paul had been into the vehicle licensing office and obtained the road fund licence and then returned to the car in the car park and as soon as he opened the car door he was surrounded by police and arrested. Now, as it turned out, the car was returned to Paul some hours later and Velodrome heard nothing more about it, but when Max had asked Tom what it was all about, he'd given Max a plausible story about the paperwork being incorrect. It didn't go any further and Max had his mind on other matters at the time so he didn't think of it again, but now with Tom having seemingly ripped off Max for a 360 Spider, it got him thinking.

The big issue for Max there and then was what he was going to say to Rick Brady. If he told him exactly what happened, the next question would be where did Max send the money and of course that was complicated, because £55,000 of the money had been paid in cash into Laura's account and £12,000 had been contra'd against money Tom owed Max.

There was also the chance that Tom would produce the car, unlikely, but not impossible. Max decided that it was not in his best interest to tell Rick the full story but he needed a story and he needed to keep it simple, but before he did that he wanted to buy some time and give him a chance to chase Tom.

Working on the basis that it was better to make the call rather than receive the call, head them off at the pass, Max telephoned Rick and let him know that the car still had not yet arrived. In essence it wasn't exactly true, but he didn't expand on the detail. Rick was busy with his workload so he didn't press Max for any further information and was happy to be called the following week when the car was ready.

By the Wednesday of the following week, Rick was beginning to get sense of humour failure, he'd spoken to Max twice already that day and he sensed that Max was perhaps stringing him along. He was surprised because he didn't think Max was like that, but events just didn't seem to be adding up. He'd paid the balance for the car on the understanding that the car was imminent and now Max couldn't tell him where it was or when he could have it. He was sorry, but he'd lost his temper with Max on that last call and threatened to send 'some friends of his' down to sort him out if he didn't get his car. That was not how he wanted to behave either, but he wanted his car, he'd paid for it and wanted to know why it had now become so difficult to get it for him. His last call went some way to minimise the threat of the heavies although Max was left in no doubt that there would be physical problems ahead if he wasn't careful. Rick just ended the call by saying to Max, 'Sort it out, I'll call you.'

Max still hadn't been able to speak to Tom by Friday. He'd called Laura and she hadn't heard from him either. *It's a fucking mess*, he thought. He'd had so much crap over the last twelve months and now this. When was it going to end ? He walked down the showroom to the front door and looked out across the street. A black BMW X5 pulled up outside the garage and a familiar figure stepped out of the car.

HMP LEYHILL, AUGUST 2008

'Sorry, what did you say your name was?' asked Raz.
'Vincent,' he replied.

452

'Hi, Vincent, I'm Raz and this is Max.'

'Hi.'

'All you've got to do is pack the bags. It's easy man. We'll tell you what to do. We run the machines, you do the bags. How long are you in for?' Raz asked.

'If I get tag, mid October.'

'Okay, that's all right. What you in for?'

'Dangerous driving.'

'We better keep you away from the trollies then!' Raz joked. Vincent was a six ft tall, forty six year old medium build black guy and he looked like the man in the Halifax Building Society advert. In fact, so much so, that after a while nobody called him Vincent, they all called him Howard. He was too nice to be in jail but he was there with the rest of them and he had to get through his time.

'I don't like this laundry,' Vincent said disparagingly.

'Why the hell not?' Raz replied, continuing, ' you've got prospects in here mate'.

'I want to learn to drive the forklift and go on the course to learn that.'

'Hey hang on a minute Vincent. What makes you think they're going to let you drive a forklift?' questioned Raz.

'It's a course. I've put my name down for it?'

'And you think they're going to let you do that do you?' His face opened as he nodded.

'Yeah, why not?'

Raz walked up close to Vincent, 'If I heard you right Vincent, you're in here for dangerous driving.'

'Yeah, so what?'

'So what? Well, I'll tell you what. They aren't gonna let you within a mile of a fucking forklift are they? You're having a laugh, fucking forklift. Vincent, that telescopic forklift thing is three times the size of a car and it has two huge steel poles sticking out the front. They're hardly likely to teach someone in for dangerous driving to drive that, you fucking dickhead.'

'I don't want to talk about it,' Vincent replied quietly.

'Your choice,' said Raz, by now having moved away from Vincent with his arms crossed stood by the folding machine.

Good start, Max thought, Raz's abrasive nature had already upset the guy and he'd only been working in the laundry for five minutes.

453

Raz started up again, 'So you've got a bird on the outside?'

'Yeah.'

'What she called?'

'Rachel.'

'And what's the lovely Rachel look like?' Raz asked.

After a while Vincent replied, 'She looks like Helen Mirren.'

'Helen Mirren?' he exclaimed. 'The last time I looked, she was white and about seventy isn't she? And you're black.'

'She's a good looking woman,' Max chipped in.

'So, I'm allowed to go out with a white woman aren't I?' said Vincent.

'Yeah, of course. Good on you Vincent. So your bird's seventy and she's white?'

'No, she's fifty, but she looks like Helen Mirren.'

'Oh, right so she's aged a bit. Is that what you're trying to tell me?' The conversation was jabby and fast.

'No, she looks like a younger version of Helen Mirren.'

'Oh, I see what you're saying. So how long have you been knocking off this Helen Mirren bird?'

'Rachel.'

'Yeah Rachel.'

'I've been seeing her for nearly a year,' Vincent replied.

'And how's she taken it? You being inside and all?'

'She doesn't know.'

Raz repeated, ' She doesn't know. What do you mean, she doesn't know?'

'I haven't told her.'

'You must have told her something?'

'Yeah. I said I was working away.'

'Where?'

'I didn't say particularly, just the Carribean .'

'So you've been going out with Rachel for a year and now you've told her you're working away.'

'Yeah.'

'So what do you say about work or anything when you ring her?'

'I don't ring her.'

'You don't ring her? This gets better boys' He said turning around realising he had an audience and Vincent was on the ropes.

'No.'

'Vincent, you must be fucking mad. You've got this beautiful bird on the outside and you're not speaking to her. What are you going to say to her when you get out?'

'About what?'

'About not calling her?'

'I'll just say I lost the number.'

'Unbelievable ! What about directory enquiries? She's bound to ask? What about your phone?'

'I'm going to tell her I left it behind.'

'I'm sorry mate but you're gonna have to do better than that.'

'What's this girl do?'

'She works in a solicitors.'

'Well, I think she's probably a little bit more switched on than you might think. She's going to know you're lying to her and then you're history. Bye bye Rachel. Hello Mr. Winkey. Have you shagged her yet?'

'No, and what's it got to do with you.'

'I'm the No. 2 and you need to tell me these things. I need to be kept informed at all times.

Vincent's story didn't sound convincing and Raz was at him like a Jack Russell terrier.

'I tell you what Vincent, you've been in prison for six weeks and you haven't called Rachel, she's going to think you're not interested. You're going to have to tell her because she *will* find out, believe me. And when she does, you're history. You'll just be another wanker !'

'No, she won't find out and please don't talk to me like that !' Vincent replied.

'Okay, Vincent, let's run this one through. You get out of prison and you give her a call. You've been working away for a while and things have been difficult. Hello darling how are you? She says, why didn't you ring me and you reply that you'd lost her number and forgotten her address so you couldn't get her number from directory enquiries and you'd forgotten who she worked for as well. And then she says I tried calling you and you have to say, I know, it was stupid of me, but I left my mobile at home. She goes on to ask you whether you had a nice time and you can't tell her that you were packing two thousand sheets a day in laundry bags, so you make up some bollocks. Then she asks you about the weather and you tell her it was fantastic and fail to mention Hurricane Ike having passed through devastating every building in it's path. Are you getting the picture Vincent, because it's not looking too good is it ?'

'Yeah.'

'And then comes the best bit. You've managed to bullshit your way past everything so far and she asks are you coming around to see me tonight? And you can't, because you've lost your fucking driving licence and you're on a home detention curfew from seven at night to seven in the morning. So, thinking quickly you ask her to come around to yours. She starts getting fruity having not seen you for a while and within minutes you're naked and she looks down and says what's that on your ankle? It looks like a watch.' It's your curfew tag. And you have to tell her what it is because you can't take it off. She gets dressed, you go all limp and she buggers off. Get real Vincent, tell her. At least then you might have a chance of having a girlfriend when you get out, that's of course if she isn't already being rogered blind by Denzil Washington.' Raz finished his onslaught and Vincent quietly retreated into his workload. Max chuckled to himself, the banter helped buck up the monotony of the day.

Max returned to his room and picked up the post on the floor. He flicked through the envelopes, one from his mother and one from Annabel and a couple of internal mail slips. He read through his mother's letter, one sentence from beginning to end. He smiled. It was nice to hear from Annabel, she said some warm things and Max felt better for it. The two internal post letters were instructing Max to present himself for the music course every Thursday and the last note made Max aware that he had an appointment with the OMU probation department on 28th August. Another day over, just another sixty seven to go.

CHUDLEIGH, DECEMBER 2004

Leo Easton hadn't seen Andrew Tyler since they'd been at police training college together and that was nearly twenty years ago. He knew Andy had been transferred to Chudleigh so he'd said to himself that the next time he was passing, he'd pop in and say hello, which is how he found himself sat opposite his old mate that Friday morning.

It had to be said, that Easton had put on a lot of weight, plenty of good living Andy had asked.

'I've always like my food, you know how it is, oh and a few beers now and then. You know, with the lads.'

'Yes,' said Andy.

They were totally different animals. Easton, the overweight, slightly dim shaven headed bulldog and Tyler, the clean living professional investigator. Both had risen to the dizzy heights of detective constable. Easton working within the Economic Crime Unit at Ashburton and Tyler, the more sensitive area of a specialist CID squad.

The truth of it was that neither men particularly liked each other and neither of them would be asking each other out for a quiet drink. Easton was perceived as a man's man and Tyler a family man. They were as different as chalk and cheese.

'So what brings you here,' Andy asked.

'I was just passing and I thought I'd drop in and say hello,' Easton replied. It wasn't true, he had gone from Ashburton to Chudleigh especially to see Andy. He knew what case Andy was working on, one of his mates in the station had told him.

Easton continued, 'It's been a long time Andy. Married yet?'

'Yes, with two children.'

'You?'

'Yes, the same.'

'So are you working on anything interesting?' Easton asked.

'We've got a few things on the go but nothing that we can take a lot further at the moment.'

'I heard you were investigating the Abbey?'

'Well not quite. We've spoken to a few people there but as I said it's not going any further at the moment. We haven't got enough evidence. What about you?'

'I'm between cases right now so we're tidying up the last bits and pieces and then something will come along.' Again it wasn't true, Easton had a file drop on his desk three weeks previously and he was fishing. He didn't want Tyler to know what he was working on at that stage, he'd leave that to a later date. For now, he just wanted to find out how far Andy had got with his investigation and although he recognised that Andy was holding his cards close to his chest, his intuition told him he was telling the truth. The reality was that Easton was right, Andy was telling the truth or at least what little he said was true. He didn't expand on it. They talked for five minutes or so.

'Well, it's good to see you Andy, here's my card. If you're ever down my way, give me a call.'

Tyler took the card and reluctantly returned the gesture and gave his card to Easton as they said their goodbyes. *What was all that about*, Tyler thought. *I never liked the man and he never liked me.* He wondered what he wanted, then dismissed it from his mind.

NEWTON ABBOT, APRIL 2001

Rick pressed the remote locking on the X5 and the indicators flashed as he walked up to the Velodrome showroom, he could see Max walking towards him and he thought how relaxed he looked bearing in mind his was an unannounced visit.

'Hi Max,' he put out his hand and they shook.

'Hello, Rick, how are you?'

'Could be better Max. I'd be a lot better if you had my car.'

'We both would, believe me. Would you like a drink?'

'Yes that would be nice, coffee please, white, two sugars.'

Max organised the drinks and they both went and sat down on the leather chesterfield in Max's office.

'So what have you got to tell me?' Rick asked.

'I'm going to be straight with you Rick. I've paid all but the last small amount for your car and I had done so several months ago and my supplier has now gone off the radar. He's not answering his phone and I've been up to his house and spoken to his wife and she tells me that he's done a runner. I think he's in Spain because that's where the mobile rings out, but he never answers it.'

'Okay.'

'Now the problem for me is that I had been under an enormous financial pressure in the lead up to your car arriving, so last week, when your money arrived and your 360 Coupe was sold, I paid off the almost equivalent value in creditors knowing that I was collecting your car. Now it turns out that the car hasn't arrived and I've lost my money which effectively is yours.'

'What are you going to do about it?' Rick asked.

'Well, I'm going to keep chasing my supplier until I get hold of him.'

'Do you think it was deliberate?'

'I don't know. I spoke to him many times before the car was due to be delivered and he always lead me to believe it was coming. I didn't at any time think that it would come to this. I've been dealing with the guy for a couple of years. I must have spent over two million pounds with him in that time and I never, honestly had any problems with him. Far from it. When I first started buying cars from him, I would pay for two and get three, and pay for the third when it sold. I still can't believe it now.'

Rick was softening as he took a sip of coffee. 'I don't know what to say. I can see your position, but I don't want to be out of pocket. Are you going to survive?'

'Survival's the name of the game Rick, I'll do what I must to make it work.'

'Look, you sort yourself out. Find this guy and do what you have to do and stay in touch with me. I won't chase you for the money but I do want the money back or a car. Get yourself sorted and we'll do another deal at a later date. I know you, you know me, we'll sort it out between us.'

Max looked at Rick and said a sincere thank you. It was unexpected and said a lot about the man he was dealing with. Yes, Max was responsible and he knew that, but sometimes things happen that couldn't be anticipated and couldn't be controlled. Given the circumstances, Max couldn't have foreseen or expected Tom to have done what he had and nothing in the lead up to the collection day in any way indicated anything other than normal. Max would have to find another way of satisfying the outstanding debt to Rick at some time in the future. He was grateful of Rick's gracious gesture, it was a life saver.

Max had been thinking that if Rick Brady had taken legal action it would have probably been time to call it a day and liquidate the company. There was no certainty about the arrival of Dimo's 360 Spiders and he had also asked his solicitors to send Max a warning letter before action. Now, with Dimo, the problem was simple, Max owed him the balance for the yellow Ferrari 355 GTB which was just under £50,000, but he would need to pay that before the 360 Spiders arrived otherwise he wouldn't get them. The legal letter had said that Max had to pay the balance within fourteen days or the lawyers were advised to start recovery action which would most likely involve a statutory demand. If any of the outstanding 360 Spiders arrived, it would make a tremendous difference to Velodrome's position.

A month later, Max still hadn't spoken to Tom, but he rang the number as he had forced himself to do every day and a girl answered the phone.

'Hello,' she said. Max was somewhat taken aback.

'Can I speak to Tom please?' he asked.

'Who's calling please?' she replied.

'It's Martin.' It wasn't Martin, but Max didn't want to let on who it was.

'Hello?' It was Tom.

'Yeah, Tom it's Max. What's going on?'

'Nothing's going on Max,' he said angrily.

'Well where's my car?'

'I don't know about any car Max?'

'Don't come it, Tom, you know what I'm talking about. Where's my 360 Spider? And where are you?'

'Listen to me Max and listen to me good 'cos I want to make sure you understand. I ain't got no fuckin' 360 Spider and I ain't getting one either. Now fuck off and don't ring me again Or.'

'Or what Tom, what are you going to do Tom, eh?'

'I'll shoot you, you fucker, that's what I'll do. Got it?' The phone went dead and Max was only able to speak to Tom once again. He tried several different ways and times to contact Tom but the number was never answered or just rang out to the service provider message. The hard reality of the situation was that the 360 Spider from Tom was lost and the likely chance of recovering any money was unlikely. He called his solicitors and asked their advice, but it looked costly and doubtful. It wasn't a criminal matter, it was a civil matter so going to the police wasn't going to help. It was useless.

Max thought about ringing Rick Brady and letting him know exactly what had happened, but in the end he decided to let sleeping dogs lie. He left it alone. He'd ring Rick a little further down the line. In some ways, the company position was much the same despite their paying off a lot of creditors, because a new larger creditor in the shape of Rick Brady was in the ether. It wasn't on the books, as such, but nonetheless it was there and it was owed. The almost unbelievable company disaster list now

460

had Donald Key's 360 Spider on it at £92,000, the barchetta red 355 Spider credit card fraud at £49,950, the three other credit card frauds for eighteen grand's worth of bikes Dimo's 355 GTB at £49,000 and now Rick Brady's 360 Spider at £107,000 and that totalled over £315,000. Serious money and Velodrome didn't have it.

Donald Key had gone legal and Max was fighting that battle. The credit card companies were looking positive on the return of the £49,950, so when that money came back, Max could at least deal with some of Dimo's demands, but the company had basically lost £315,000 in a little over six months and none of it had been anticipated, expected or intended. It was just a spectacular set of bad circumstances.

With Donald Key going down the legal route, that was effectively good news, because provided Max could afford to pay the solicitors fees, the debt that Velodrome owed could be pushed off into the distance, using the legal process and that could give Max the opportunity to raise cash through sales especially if both of Dimo's 360 Spiders arrived and the two cars from Isca Ferrari turned up. As for Dimo, he would still let Max have the two new cars provided the 355 GTB was paid for, so all Max had to do was keep drip feeding money to Dimo and avoid a possible statutory demand on the limited company. In between all that, the usual cash flow juggling would go on and bike sales would continue slowly but surely. It seemed like an impossible situation to come back from a £315,000 deficit, but with £49,950 likely to come back from Barclays Merchant Services and possibly one or two of the cars, then he reckoned it could be done. It wasn't going to be easy, but there was a chance and that's all he needed.

It didn't help that Julian Key and his father were now calling everyday and hounding Max like there was no tomorrow, but what he didn't expect was Julian Key to speak to the agent representing the owner of the Ferrari 250 SWB that Nino wanted to buy. Julian had really stuck the boot in and savagely described Max as a worthless conman, which was wholly untrue, and the result was that the deal fell to the wayside. If either of the Keys could have seen beyond the end of their noses, they might have realised that by speaking to Max about it, they could have helped themselves and Max get closer to a repayment for all of them. All they needed to have done was discuss the opportunity, agree a proportion of the profit to go to themselves and a deal would have been done so that everybody had a little bit of money and moved on to the next deal. Instead they just blew it out of sheer stupidity and spite. There was a potential $150,000 profit in that car and it had completely evaporated. Max tried everything to get the deal pieced back together but the Keys had done such a good job, that Max could not get it going again.

Despite all the problems and the workload, Velodrome managed to survive the summer of 2001 without incurring any further drastic losses and the Barclays Merchant Service funds had been in part refunded. The company was still £20,000 down on the deal but it was a lot better than being £49,950 down and there was still the chance of the balance being forthcoming as well. The two 360 Spiders from Dimo still hadn't materialised and neither had the two cars from Isca Ferrari, but like before, the longer Max survived, the closer he would inevitably get to taking delivery of all the cars and along with that would come the profits and get the company straight again. It was a painful time, but Max believed he'd get through it and he was determined to do so.

It came as quite a surprise in September 2001 when Rupert Davis called Max. They hadn't spoken since Davis short changed him on the commission due on the sale of the green Jaguar E-Type from Isca Ferrari. Frankly Max didn't want to deal with him, the E-Type deal had left a bitter taste in his mouth. Anyway despite all that, he took the call.

'Hi Rupert, how are you?'

'Okay, thanks chap.'

'Look, I've been talking to Donald Key.'

'Oh yeah.'

'Yeah. Listen chap, I've taken over the debt.'

'What do you mean, you've taken over the debt?'

'Well, the debt is mine to chase and I want the money.'

'Rupert. After everything I've told you and everything you've told me about Donald Key. You honestly expect me to believe you've bought the debt off Donald Key?'

'Well I have.'

'Get real Rupert. This matter is between me and Donald Key and it's got bugger all to do with you.'

'You owe me.'

'I owe you nothing, so don't go asking me for anything. If Donald Key has sold you the debt, then prove it. If you can't, don't bother ringing me. Rupert, I thought you were more than that. I thought you were a decent bloke, but obviously you're not. You're just a Judas, aren't you?'

'Don't get funny with me Max. I want the fucking money and I'm going to get it.'

'Oh, really. Well, we've had thugs down here before Rupert, so we know how Key behaves. Are you going to be doing the same?'

'No, I won't. I have other ways and you *will* pay me.'

'I don't think you could have heard me Rupert. I'm not paying you and that's final. Do what you have to do. Oh, and don't forget, it's a very small place on that mountain peak with all those other Ferrari dealers. I thought you could be trusted and I dare say they think so too. Obviously you can't.'

'The money is due to me and I want it,' Rupert said harshly.

'Don't waste your breath Rupert and don't ring me again.'

Davis never did ring again and Max never heard anything from Donald Key's solicitors saying that Davis now owned the debt. It was ridiculous of Davis to try it on like that, it just made him look stupid and Max couldn't understand why he'd done it, there was no sense in it, no sense at all! Unless, of course, he was just playing the big I am again.

A month had passed since Davis's outburst on the telephone and Max hadn't heard anything more from him so he assumed it was all show, a big hat, no cattle situation. He was standing in the front office looking down the showroom, a well dressed man and woman had walked in and they were looking at a new Honda Fireblade on the rostrum. Max let them look for a while, he figured they might have been killing some time waiting to catch a train. They didn't look like the normal Honda Fireblade customers as he walked towards them and noticed them both carrying briefcases.

'Hello, can I help you?' Max asked expecting them to say, 'Just looking', but instead the woman handed Max a business card and said, 'We're from Customs & Excise, my name is Helen Walters and this is my colleague Adrian Smith and we'd like to speak to Mr. Max Reed, please.'

Max looked at them intently. They looked purposeful. 'You're talking to him,' he replied.

Ralph Sanders had been travelling by train since 5:45 am, he had changed at Birmingham New Street station and was now heading on the last leg of his journey from Bristol Temple Meads towards Newton Abbot. He enjoyed travelling on the train, it gave him the time to catch up with some work and at the same time enjoy the beautiful countryside, which is exceptional in the south-west. He opened up his briefcase and went through the many notes he'd made in the hope that everything Max had said was indeed true. He had no reason to disbelieve him but the chances of stumbling across a car of this magnitude were so slim that it really was a chance in a lifetime opportunity to be involved.

All the information that Ralph had was original or copies of original factory records. A life's devotion to the marque had made Ralph the authority to contact and anybody wanting information on any of the cars would without exception contact him. Yes, there were others that knew a considerable amount but Ralph was the man, there was no doubting that.

Ralph, to be fair hadn't had the best of lives. He had enjoyed life but most of his adult life had been scarred by the scandal and the tragedy of the murder of his first wife. If you asked him, he'd tell you but if you didn't know then he was going to volunteer the information. It was a sad story that led Ralph along an emotional roller coaster over a number of years and ultimately ended in the saddest way possible. She was gone, suffering at the hand of a supposed simpleton and then there was the inevitable national news coverage that went with it. Ralph had struggled to rid himself of those woes in the early days but as time had gone by memories had all but faded away. He looked out of the train window at the rapidly passing view of the many different boats on the River Exe and thought about his life. It could have been so much better if he hadn't been dealt such a cruel hand, but right now, thirty five years later, with his new partner, he couldn't be happier. He was doing a job he thoroughly enjoyed travelling all over the world and he had a good woman by his side. In his retirement, he was about to be involved in his greatest professional moment.

The mixture of tunnels and cliff faces along the coastal section of railway from Exeter to Newton Abbot never ceases to please no matter how many times you've done the journey and it was exactly the same for Ralph. The train whizzed through Dawlish Station passing the Parson & Clark rocky outcrop, then just as quickly raced past Spray Point before slowing to sixty mph to go through Teignmouth Station and then along the beautiful River Teign before finally slowing to a halt at Newton Abbot.

Ralph gathered up his briefcase and overcoat as soon as the station was announced and made his way towards the carriage door as the train rocked and bucked around before finally squeaking to a halt. Checking his step, he climbed down onto the platform and admired the pleasantly decorated old world Victorian station. Up above he noted the exit signs and made his way to the arrivals area at the front of the beautiful period station building. He was looking for a silver Nissan Navara. He didn't know what that was, but the only silver car parked in front of him was a pick up so he assumed that had to be it.

Max looked along the pavement, the train had just pulled out of the station and the exodus of passengers had now spilt onto the forecourt of the station. He screened the possibles as they walked by and then spotted a gentleman in a green wool tweed jacket and similar corduroy trousers and dark brown brogues. He was in his early sixties, probably five foot eight inches tall and about twelve to thirteen stone. He was carrying an old well worn reddish brown leather briefcase. Max got out of the car and walked towards him asking his name as he got close.

'You must be Max. Good to meet you Max.'

'Hi, did you have a good trip down?'

'Yes, thank you,' he answered in a soft Yorkshire accent, and continued, 'the last bit though is so beautiful, I was amazed. It's such a lovely part of the world. I like it where I am, but I can see why people like it so much down here.'

'We haven't far to travel, it should only take us ten minutes or so if the traffic is kind to us.'

'Oh, good. I'm looking forward to seeing it.'

'I thought you would be,' Max replied.

The Nissan creaked as it turned into the driveway and stopped.

'Nice house, Max.'

'Thank you. We like it. We've lived here for twenty-three years. We've thought about moving on occasion but it's

465

just so convenient here that we've never really thought seriously about it.'

Max opened the front door and showed Ralph into the kitchen. Catherine turned around and Max introduced them. She picked up the kettle to refill it and asked if they would like a hot drink.

'Okay, Ralph, this is the moment. I hope you're going to enjoy it,' Max said.

'So do I,' Ralph replied anxiously.

Max opened the side door to the triple garage and went in to switch on the lights. Ralph followed closely behind and looked, but said nothing.

He looked down at the remains. 'I don't have to check it do I?'

'No, it's fairly obvious.'

'My God. I didn't think I'd ever see something like this. It's exactly as you described. Exactly. I didn't expect that. Well, I didn't know what to expect really. I mean, you gave me all the information and I listened to what you said, but there was always some doubt. There had to be after all the time that's passed, but this, well this, I'm struggling for words. I just can't believe it.' He was almost jibbering.

Max said, 'I'll go and get the coffees. You enjoy it, Ralph.'

'I will.'

It took five hours for Ralph to fully inspect and photograph the blackened skeleton of the car before cataloguing all the associated parts for his report. It was an 'extraordinary find' he kept saying and it was. You don't get much better than a works Bugatti Type 35B supercharged sports racing car with Targo Florio history and totally uninterrupted ownership history dating back to 1932. It was the stuff of dreams and both Ralph and Max were living that dream that day.

Ralph checked every part and every number and recorded it against the known factory records. It all checked out. It was what they'd always expected it to be and what they hoped it would be so Max now knew for absolute certain that what he had in front of him after two years of frustration, negotiation *and cunning* was in fact, the golden egg.

Helen Walters and Adrian Smith walked up through the showroom and Max showed them both into the accounts office. They had come unannounced. Usually, the VAT office would ring first to make an appointment, but not this time. It was odd, but Max didn't think to deeply into it. The two Customs & Excise officers advised Max that their visit was a routine VAT visit and that they would like to inspect the company's records. Velodrome had nothing to hide and allowed the VAT officers to go about their work. He showed them where all the records were kept and let them get on with their job. Periodically, he would poke his head around the door to make sure they were all right, but generally didn't take a lot of notice of them. If Keith had been around, he would have sat with them and answered any questions they might have had as they went about their work. In this instance and from a very much depleted staff situation, Max was in the showroom trying to sell motorcycles, so he couldn't do both.

It was gone three in the afternoon when Helen Walters emerged from the accounts office asking Max if they could have a word.

Max sat in his office, whilst Mike looked after the showroom and the two Customs & Excise rustled through their paperwork in front of him.

'Mr. Reed, thank you for giving us the opportunity to go through your records. We've carefully considered all the information and we will be raising an assessment in due course.'

'Assessment?' Max asked. There was always an assessment. They had to show that they weren't wasting their time.

'Yes, Mr. Reed. You owe the revenue a considerable sum of money.'

'Well, I know we owed you £32,000 from the last quarter, but we've been paying that off in lumps and that's now down to £18,000.'

'We're aware of that, Mr. Reed, but the assessment will be far greater than that.'

'Well what do you mean? It can't be,' Max said alarmingly.

'Mr. Reed, your company has sold fifty eight Ferrari motor cars in the last two years and from your records that you

467

have given us now, we can see that you have declared VAT on all of those cars on the margin scheme.'

'Yes, that's right. On all the vehicles we sell, we declare the VAT on the difference between the price we bought the car for and the price we sold it. In other words, we pay the VAT on the gross profit.'

'Yes, Mr. Reed. I know how the margin scheme works.'

'So, that's what we've done.'

'Ah, Mr. Reed, these cars that you have bought from Tom McKinney.'

'Yes?'

'They were bought tax free in Germany.'

'Well, what's that got to do with me? I bought the cars in the UK from a UK home address. The cars were taxed, UK registered with V5 logbooks, and I always bought them on a proper company purchase order, fully detailing the car and getting the sellers signature.'

'Yes, Mr. Reed, we've seen them, but Mr. McKinney hasn't sent you a bonafide VAT invoice to support the sale.'

'I can't see what it's got to do with me. Surely you should be contacting Tom McKinney, not me. He's the one who hasn't paid the VAT not me. He's the one you should be talking to. This is ridiculous.'

'You may think it's ridiculous Mr. Reed, but we are deadly serious. We will be raising an assessment subject to further investigation, but at this stage we have a figure of £267,509, but we expect that to increase as we fill in the details.'

Max watched the two officers walk out the showroom door and immediately called his accountant. McKinney had done a runner and Max was the last man standing.

'Ron, it's Max, I've just had a VAT inspection and they've told me they will be raising an assessment of £267,509.'

'That's madness.'

'I know, but that's what they're doing.'

'On what basis?'

'What they're saying is that all the cars that I bought from Tom McKinney had been bought by him tax free in Germany and that because the VAT has never been paid on the purchase price, I am liable. Ron, you know me. I bought these cars from Tom's house, they were all UK registered with UK log books and taxed and we always got a signed purchase order detailing the car. This can't be right surely?'

468

'No, I don't think it is, but you will have to be very careful how you deal with this. I think the best thing for me to do is pop around to see you tomorrow. I'm going to need to change some appointments, but I'll do that and be with you for ten o'clock. Is that okay?' Ron asked.

Shit, Max thought. This was serious trouble. Customs & Excise have absolute powers and even if they were wrong, they could still cause a lot of grief. He thought through what they had said. Essentially Tom McKinney had bought all the cars in Germany tax free and what he should have done was declared VAT payable on each car as it arrived into the UK and was registered. This should have been done on a form called a C & E 389. Now, the important issue was how Tom had filled in that form. There's a deliberate question on the form, which asks if VAT has been paid on the vehicle and if so, which member country and what VAT number was used ?

As a trader, Tom would have signed the declaration on the reverse of the form giving his VAT number. If he had answered the question, has VAT been paid on the vehicle with a NO, then Customs & Excise in his area would have picked that up and realised that he needed a visit and VAT needed to be paid if he hadn't paid it on his quarterly return. If he answered the question, has VAT been paid on the vehicle with a YES, then he would have to give the member state the VAT was paid to and the VAT number of the trader involved. If he left any of these relevant questions blank on the form, then the DVLA would not have registered the car. So he must have put something on the form and surely Customs & Excise would know that if they checked.

Max went home that evening completely stunned. He couldn't understand why it was that Customs & Excise didn't want to listen to his version of events and now that he'd had time to think about it, he realised that the assessment was made up of only Tom McKinney's invoices. Had the VAT officers just come to check those invoices? If so, did they know more than they were saying and why were there no other assessed figures other than the Ferraris? Why hadn't they not mentioned the outstanding figure that Velodrome already owed? Did they think that Max was involved in some kind of scam with McKinney? He didn't know the answers to any of the questions, but he knew that the implications could cost him his livelihood and now that really was on the line.

Ron kept an open mind walking into the showroom at Velodrome that Friday morning. He'd dealt with many clients versus VAT situations and he'd usually had a good ratio of success. What worried him with Velodrome was the size of the debt and the speed in which the VAT officers had reached their decision. In many respects, it was almost too quick and normally, there would only be one officer and Max had said he had two officers. Unusual to say the least.

'Morning Max. Another sleepless night?'

'Yeah, something like that.'

'You look awful,' Ron said.

'Thanks Ron, at least I know who my friends are.'

Max led Ron into his office and the pair of them sat down.

'I'm not going to bullshit you Max, we've known each other too long for that. You're in the shit, big time. There may be a way out but that's going to take some time to fight and I don't think that the VAT office are going to give you the breathing space. Have you heard of carousel trading?'

'No, what's that?' Max said shaking his head.

'Basically someone sets up a limited company in the UK and buys goods in from abroad net of VAT. The goods are then sold at below the market price but no VAT is *charged or* accounted for on a VAT return. It's usually done with a series of inter-trading limited companies all set up by the same people who trade on import and export either recovering VAT or not paying VAT. Either way it's massive VAT fraud and I think your Tom McKinney is doing it or is involved in it.'

'Yeah, but I've been dealing with him for over two years. Why haven't the VAT people caught up with him before?' Max asked.

'Well, maybe they have, but it's possible he's part of a bigger operation and they're watching him. I don't know. It just seems unusual to me that you had two officers, both of whom have not been here before and from what you've told me, you think they only looked at the Ferrari invoices or Tom McKinney's invoice. That just doesn't sound like a standard VAT check to me.'

'What do you suggest I do?' Max asked.

'Well, first I would like to have a good look at all the paperwork you have relating to Tom McKinney and if it's okay with you, I'd like to take photocopies of those and take them with me. What's the situation with your yellow car you were telling me about?'

'Oh. Dimo. Well, he's issued a statutory demand and it's been advertised in Stubbs so no doubt the bank will see that.'

'What are you going to do about it?'

'I thought I'd drip feed Dimo £5,000 at a time and liaise with his solicitor and him to prevent them from taking it any further.'

'Do you think you can do that?'

'Yes, I think so. Dimo's a decent guy. He just wants to exercise the pressure. We're still on speaking terms and his solicitor is playing ball, so as long as the money keeps going in his direction, he'll be okay.'

'What about the bank? Do they know about the VAT?'

'They don't know about the VAT and I'm not planning to tell them. I should be getting the balance of the credit card fraud Ferrari money back next week so that will help. It's all spoken for, mind.'

'Okay. Let me tell you the VAT assessment is a legal document in itself and Customs & Excise have absolute power. Technically, Velodrome as a limited company is insolvent and as such you have a duty as a director to safeguard creditor's monies so we need to consider that position. I know you've got stock and debtors, so what are those numbers roughly?'

'Stock is roughly one hundred and seventy-five and debtors are minimal. We've got one car coming from Dimo, which still has all the profit in it, and of course there's the Isca Ferrari cars as well. So, say £30,000 from Dimo's second car and £210,000 from Exeter. I've got cars coming from Muzi but they're going to be later, so the only ones I can count on are worth around £240,000 in profit.'

'And you've still got to supply Donald Key's car?'

'Yes.'

'And Dimo's? Sorry, Dimo's yellow car. What do you now owe on that?'

'£30,000.'

'And the big deals, the $2,000,000 and $150,000 ones they've both now gone? And what happened with the two big premium cars, wasn't it £110,000 and £100,000 premiums on the two new cars from Exeter?'

'Yes.'

'Okay. Have you sold Dimo's second car and the two

Exeter cars yet?'

'No, I could easily sell Dimo's second car and take a deposit, but I don't want to have more aggravation if it fails to turn up. I've already had to pay back the deposits on the Isca Ferrari cars because the cars hadn't turned up when Isca said they would. The customers wanted their deposit money back so they could try to find a car elsewhere. I don't want to go through all that again. I'll sell them when they arrive. The problem is that the big premiums are going down as more cars are coming on to the market. The longer I have to wait, the less premium I'm going to make'

'Okay, when do you expect that to happen ? The cars arriving, that is.'

' Well they keep telling me soon, but whilst the clock is ticking, the premium value is going down because as I've said other cars are becoming available on the market. I've told the bank that I'm expecting £210,000 off those two cars, but that was then, when I had two early customers for two early cars. We are just not going to make that kind of money on those two cars now. It's too late, I should have had the cars months ago.'

Ron was writing lots of notes and took some while before he spoke again. Max in the meantime sat quietly looking rather forlorn. There had been times before when it didn't look good, but this really didn't look good.

'I think,' said Ron, 'we need to slow down the VAT process. If I'm understanding you correctly, these other cars are definitely coming?'

'Yes. I would expect all of them before Christmas for certain.'

'Okay, then, we've got about three months to slow them down and I suggest what we do immediately is appeal the assessment. That will mean that they have to go back and rework the figures. It will all be done remotely, they won't be coming back here. If we slow down our replies to their correspondence, we can stretch out the process and give you time to get the company back on an even keel by getting your cars in, sold and banked. It would be better if you could pay the £18,000 currently outstanding to the VAT man, so think about how you could do that.'

Ron went through Max's responsibilities as a director and they both agreed Max was treading a very thin line. He needed to get some money in and he needed to do that quickly.

There were several things that could now trip him up, not least, Dimo's statutory demand, Donald Key's continuous legal assault and now the vat man. All of them had to be kept at bay if Velodrome was to survive. Max didn't worry about Rick Brady because they had shook hands and agreed something for a later date.

'Okay, Max. Get as much in as you can. I'll write to Customs and Excise. You need to speak to your solicitors about McKinney's invoices and see what the legal position is there. I know it's all money but you're on the edge my friend,' Ron said as he got up and shook Max's hand to walk out.

Mike buzzed through to Max's office and told him that Steve Majendie was on hold.

'Hi Steve, long time no speak. You're up early.'

'Yeah, things okay with you?'

'On and off really Steve, it's been a bad year.'

'Still got troubles with Don?'

'Yeah. I don't know at the moment how that's going to resolve itself, but it will, it's just going to take some time, that's all.'

'Have you spoken to Graham recently?'

'Graham Lord?'

'Yeah.'

'No, I haven't spoken to Graham for a few months.'

'Are you likely to be speaking to him or seeing him?'

'Nothing planned, why?'

'I've been trying to get hold of him and he never returns my call.'

'I don't know about that Steve, he used to ring me every day but that's all stopped now and as I say I haven't heard from him in a while.'

'Okay, well if you do, mention to him that I've been chasing him. And if you need anything Max, you've got my numbers, just call.'

'Okay, Steve. Thanks.'

Max put down the phone and didn't give it another thought. He had enough of his own troubles, he didn't want to get involved in other peoples problems as well. Which is why he didn't even ask Steve what it was all about. Perhaps he should have done.

473

Max got in his car and drove up to Exeter. It would have been pointless calling Sean Williams, he wanted to see Williams' face when Max asked him the question. He stopped the car outside the Ferrari dealership and looked across the forecourt and saw a red Ferrari 360 Spider on trade plates. It had to be one of their first batch of cars being delivered, but Max's name was at the top of the list wasn't it?

Williams uncharacteristically walked across the showroom and shook Max's hand saying good morning as he did so. He could see that Max was looking a little bit fiery.

'Is that your first 360 Spider?' Max asked.

'Yes, it's our demonstrator.'

Max thought that sounded a load of nonsense and it was. Sean had rehearsed in his mind several times what he was going to say if Max had caught him 'red handed' with a car and this was just such a moment. It wasn't a demonstrator and it wasn't the first car. It was their fourth. Max didn't know that.

'So mine are next?'

'As soon as they are here Max, we'll be calling you.'

'That's not the question I asked, so when will my car be coming?'

'Soon, Max, but I don't want to commit myself because they're not here yet.'

'Am I going to get them before Christmas?'

'All being well, yes.'

'What's all being well?' Max asked.

'Well, provided we get them. You'll get them.' Even if it was true, Williams was still lying because he had no intention of letting Max have both cars at the same time.'

Max had to take delivery of the cars as quickly as possible if he was going to get the huge premiums they were attracting. The longer it took to get the cars, the more that there would be other cars coming onto the market and as a result the premiums would quickly reduce. There would still be a premium but not at a £110,000 level, it would be more like £30,000 to £40,000, so the more Williams messed Max about, the less money Velodrome would profit from the sale of the cars.

Max as usual wasn't happy with what Williams had told him as he walked out of the showroom, but at least now he was saying 'Before Christmas', which was more definite. He stopped and looked at the 360 Spider on the forecourt paying particular attention to the trade plates covering the car's registration plate below. Without moving the trade plate, he couldn't see what the car's real registration was. He looked up to see if anyone was watching and caught Williams looking at him through the showroom window. Max decided against being obvious and surreptitiously looked at the tax disc in the window. It was a private registration number. In all probability, Williams was lying, he thought; the dealership would not register a brand new demonstrator on a private registration number. He'd leave that little gem to his next visit, he thought. He didn't recognise the number otherwise he might have done some further digging but at that time, he left it and got back into his car. Williams kept watching him. He saw Max look at the tax disc even if he was discreet and he realised that Max knew. Fortunately for Sean, Max hadn't spoken to any of the staff or had seen what was in the transporter. A lucky escape.

August 2008 HMP Leyhill
'Okay, is this your team? You four?'
'Yes Sir.'
'Right so, each team member must do two disciplines.' The PE officer looked at Reed. 'What are you any good at?'
'Running, longer distance preferably, not sprints.'
'Okay, well we've got no one for throwing the hammer and the four hundred relay, so we'll put you down for that, okay?'
It was Leyhill Sports Day and typically disorganised. If it was meant as a joke then it succeeded. Max throwing the hammer? Not a chance in hell, he threw it out of bounds twice and then hit the ground with it before launching it on the third throw so that was no good either.' Max's team came second to last.
The equipment was amusing though. Obviously, the jail was full of murderers, violent offenders and the like so the idea of having a steel ball and chain for the hammer throwing was probably taking the trust level a bit too far so a kit bag on a string with a medicine ball did the trick. And the javelin? Well, that was two plastic corner posts gaffa taped together.
'Where's the proper equipment Guv?' Max heard someone ask.

'It was supposed to have been sent down from HMP Bristol, and it hasn't arrived,' was the reply.

Max thought about the prison officer's reply. Wasn't HMP Bristol a closed 'bang up' prison? Well what the hell would they be doing with javelins and hammers in their stores? What a load of nonsense. They'd hardly likely to be allowed that type of equipment there throwing them up and down the landings. They'd be killing each other with them.

For all that, it was a nice sunny day and it was good to be out on the sports field enjoying the fresh air. There were no records broken that day, but it had been a laugh at times and again it was something different to pass the time of day.

Being in prison for Max was all about increments. The increments of the days would be firstly getting to lunchtime, then getting to tea time, then bed time, another day over and another increment of the week and the weeks become months and so on. On the outside Max would be doing something all the time, so being frustrated made the passage of time seem so much slower.

It's often said that the family on the outside serve a worse sentence than the offender on the inside and so it was for Catherine. She had all the crap to deal with when Max was first taken away from her. The newspapers, the radio and the television had all rammed home their rather one sided story which made it all sound so much worse than it actually was, but on top of that, Catherine had the two children to look after and try to cut through the endless red tape to first speak to Max and secondly visit him let alone deal with solicitors and the day to day running of the business. She was a strong girl and she would cope but Max was more than aware of the strain she had to be going through and he was completely unable to help. It was a horrible situation.

NEWTON ABBOT, DECEMBER 2001

By Christmas 2001, Velodrome had managed to stay in business using their accountants and solicitors to slow down the legal process that had been ganging up on them over the year. Dimo was still keeping the pressure on, Customs & Excise were being kept at arms length and Donald Key had gone quiet. The company hadn't incurred any further debt and was just about holding its own. Sean Williams had told Max that his two cars would be arriving in January 2002, so although it wasn't Christmas as he had said a few months earlier, they were coming. Unbelievably, it had been nearly three years since he had ordered them. Dimo's cars still hadn't arrived and that had been some fifteen months after Max was originally told they'd be delivered. Max had vowed to himself that he'd never get involved in the new car forward orders again in the same way. It was too reliant on others, too speculative and having just gone through the worst two years of his trading life, he didn't want to have to go through anything like that again.

With just three staff, it was a quiet Christmas drink over at the Queens Hotel before closing for the festive break. Max hoped that the New Year was going to be a better one.

It was the Imperial Ball on the Friday night before Christmas, Catherine and Max usually went along. It was either that one or the Holly Ball, that everyone went to and it was a chance to start the wind down to the holiday period. There would be lots of people there that they knew and Catherine always put a table together and they'd have a good fun night out. Max didn't drink a lot at the best of times, so he usually did the driving. The usual band played the usual familiar songs and the usual faces danced and drank haphazardly late into the night. A chance perhaps, if you weren't careful, to make a complete fool of yourself in front of almost the entire local business community.

Come half past one, Max trekked off to get the car to return for Catherine and their friends waiting at the hotel portico entrance. It had been a good night, it was good to see some old friends and catch up. Max drove along his road and noticed that some idiot had parked their BMW on the pavement causing an obstruction. It didn't bother him, but he did notice that the driver was at the wheel. He thought at the time, he must have been waiting to collect someone, which wasn't unusual at that time of year.

Max pulled into his driveway and parked the car. Whilst his passengers were getting out, a man hurriedly walked up to the driver's door.

'Max Reed?' That's all he said.

'Yes,' Max answered.

He handed him a file. By now, it was two o'clock in the morning. As quickly as the man had come, he'd gone.

Max remained seated in the car and opened the file. It

was from Donald Key's solicitors. They had managed to obtain a High Court injunction against Velodrome. It was a freezing order. All of Velodrome's bank accounts would be frozen. It was a shock. Max hadn't seen that coming, but he was well aware of the damage it could do.

He read the contents of the order two or three times, his mind racing as he did so. His first reaction was of extreme worry, but as he read it through more thoroughly, he thought, *Hang on a minute; this is not right.*

Donald Key had lied under oath to a High Court judge in the London Chancery Division that Max was selling the property that he operated his business from and that he was intending to do a runner and not pay him the money he was owed. It couldn't have been further from the truth.

Max thought about it, that was why Key had gone quiet. He'd been planning a coup. Well he wasn't going to get away with that.

It was a weekend and although Max didn't want to trouble his solicitor, he felt that this was serious enough to make an exception. They talked through the paperwork and Max felt more assured after the conversation. Key was way out of order doing what he'd done. The court would take a dim view of Key's behaviour when it was put to them that the injunction had been obtained in a wrongful manner. A judge would have granted the injunction based on an affidavit given by Key, the contents of which would have been completely and wholly untrue. Max's solicitor advised Max not to worry. He said 'You don't need your bank account over Christmas anyway. We'll get this overturned in the first week of January,' and Bertie continued, '...and when we win, which we undoubtedly will, he's going to have to pay our costs and his, and I don't doubt, that will be at least £20,000. Enjoy your Christmas, Max. These things are sent to try us. Key has just spent £10,000 to try to frighten you, that's the way you've got to look at it.'

'Well he certainly managed to do that, when I read it for the first time, but when I understood the content, I could see that it was lies, so I thought we had a chance.'

'Well you've got more than that. He's completely in the wrong and I'm surprised his legal team have allowed him to do this, but who knows? Anyway, as I said, have a good Christmas, forget all this and I'll see you in the New Year.'

Max put down the phone with some relief. He didn't

think for one minute, it would be as easy as Bertie had said, but his cool approach had left Max feeling relatively relaxed over the Christmas break. The reality was that he didn't let it spoil or upset his family's quality time, that would have just played into Key's hands. He made himself forget about it, much like he had done with the debacle of the 360 Spider supposedly arriving the year before. He'd take the time out, recharge and go into battle on his return.

Donald Key was virtually hopping and skipping, knowing that he'd just managed to swing the freezing order injunction on Max's company. He knew it would screw up Velodrome's trading ability, which was ridiculous bearing in mind that if the company went out of business, Don would get nothing, but nonetheless, he thought it was clever. It wasn't and all too soon he had realised it. He had lied on oath to the High Court in the Chancery Division and thought he was going to get away with it. Nothing was going to stop him. First it was thugs, now this.

Bertie returned to his office the first week in January and was looking at a copy of the High Court Injunction on his desk. He was surprised to see that the judge had let it go through. There was no real substance to it at all. It was just one man's say so, and that was the beneficiary Donald Key.

Bertie sketched a response on a sheet of paper and considered the art of his retaliation and it worked. A week later, the freezing order injunction had been lifted. Donald Key had been overturned and his lies exposed and worse for him was that Bertie obtained a costs order against the plaintiffs. The foolish scenario cost Donald Key over £20,000, Bertie was right.

The bank were obviously aware of what was going on and were pleased that Velodrome had got going again but the episode had further highlighted to Simon Hughes how precipitous a path Velodrome were treading. The turnover was massively down on the previous year and there appeared to be more problems ahead. As far as he was concerned, he wasn't going to do anything more to rock the boat. The overdraft was now at a reasonable level and if things did go wrong, Barclays were well covered. They wouldn't lose out.

Ron was keeping a keen eye on events at Velodrome too. He was amazed at Max's ability to keep battling away in the face of extreme adversity, but he was still there, but for how much longer was the question. The statutory demand had been picked up by a number of specialist insolvency practitioners all vying for the opportunity for more business and it seemed like Max was getting letters daily from firms saying that help was just one phone call away. Ron had been fighting the VAT battle on Max's behalf and had staved off action for nearly four months but he was running out of time and good reasoning. Customs & Excise were piling on the pressure. The 360 Spiders from Exeter and Dimo still had not arrived and Max was seriously in danger of flaunting company legislation if he didn't safeguard creditors' monies.

He clung on desperately for another two months. Customs & Excise could have come in at any time and sequestrated a lien on the stock. He didn't want that. If Velodrome were going to go into liquidation then Max wanted to be in control of it, he wanted to appoint a liquidator that would work for him. If the vat man came in, and a compulsory winding up order was made, then Max would be at the mercy of the Official Receiver and he didn't want that.

James Fielding sat down in front of Max as he explained the scenario. It seemed so simple, Max thought. Pay Fielding the liquidator, then he'll take away all the company records, liquidate the company, deal with the creditors and that's it.

Max didn't want to do it there and then. He still believed he had the chance of saving the business. He was wrong. He trusted far too many people. He believed far too many people and a week later he realised that time was up. Customs & Excise were about to deliver the atom bomb and he reluctantly called Fielding.

'James, it's Max Reed.'

'Yes, hello Max.'

'I've just been informed that the vat man's about to take me out.'

'How do you know?'

'One of my distant relatives works at Renslade House in Exeter, which is the local area office and she's told me that they're about to take action.'

'Right, do you want me to come down now?'

'Yes, I think so, in the circumstances.'

480

It was a quiet morning in the laundry, Max was sat on one of the tables looking around. A short and slight man in his early forties walked up to him and sat down next to him on the table. Max had spoken to him a few times. He seemed like a decent bloke.

'The van from Swansea is late this morning, that's why we've got nothing to wash. We could be sat around like this for an hour,' he sighed.

'I can't say I've got anything else to do. At least not in here,' Max replied.

'No, me neither.'

'Have you got long to go?'

'A year,' he replied.

'You?'

'End of October.'

'That's not long to go then. How long have you been in so far.'

'I was sentenced on the 14th July.'

'Ah well, you're a minor offender. I've been in four years already.'

'God, that's a long time. What were you in for?'

'Possession of a firearm with intent. I re-commissioned firearms.'

'What, from display items to fully operational ones?'

'Yeah, you've got it.'

'So how do they decommission them?'

'Usually, the barrel is lined or sleeved and the trigger hammer removed, but it's easy to sort. The sleeve in the barrel can be sweated or tapped out with heat and the hammers are freely available the world over.'

'What about the barrel? Aren't they rifled? Doesn't the sleeve damage them?'

'It can do, but I've got a laser lathe to realign the bore so that's no trouble.'

'And do you have to re rifle them?'

'Some of them, but mostly not.'

'So what does it cost to buy a decommissioned gun?'

'Well something like a Glock 25 would be about £300 to £400.'

'And what could you sell that for as a fully working

unit?'

'Two and half to three thousand pounds.'

'What about the alteration costs?'

'Minimal, £50 maybe absolute maximum £100.'

'So quite a good profit in it then? Better than selling motorbikes, I can tell you that.'

'Yeah, it's pretty good.'

'What about the people you're dealing with?'

'I don't deal direct. Never got involved in that, too risky. No, I've always got someone between me and the end user.'

'Is it just Glocks?'

'No, it's everything really. Kalashnikov's, AK47s, M16s, some older Brownings, but I do sell a lot of Glocks, it's the weapon of choice.'

'So what would you use for what purpose?'

'Glock's the one. It's reliable, it's accurate and it will do the job. The M16, is just a frightener, not much accuracy, but it would frighten the life out of people. It you went into a club or something with an M16 looking for someone, you'd spray the M16 and probably not hit anyone, but when they've all dived on to the floor, you'd pick off your man with the Glock.'

'So what sort of range do these guns have?' Max was interested to ask, not that he was likely to ever use one, but he was unlikely to ever speak to someone again with the same expertise.

'Well, the rifles are very accurate up to a mile, but something like an M16, you'd struggle to hit that guy sat in the chair over there. If it did hit him, it would be more like a bad bee sting. I don't think it would penetrate him. But if they were ten feet away, it would probably cut them in half.'

'What about the Glock?'

'Again not very accurate beyond fifty feet and probably not a killer at that distance. If I was to shoot that guy sat down by the loading bay doors, the paedophile, the one on the right.?

'Yeah, I didn't know he was a paedophile, but carry on.'

'Yeah, well he is. If I wanted to be sure to kill him, it would have to be a rifle and he'd be history. With a Glock 25 even in a steady hand, you'd struggle to hit him, by which time, he's probably legged it.'

'What about forensics and all that?'

'Well, ideally you would carry a granny sock to police the brass.'

'What do you mean?'

'Well, you have a sock that the gun goes into and the spent shell drops into a sock and you take it away with you rather than leaving a full clip of potential forensic identity all over the place.'

'So what about tracing a shell, how do the police do that?'

'Every gun bore and hammer leaves a unique firing imprint on the spent shell so if a gun hasn't been properly cleaned afterwards, the shell can be traced to a particular gun. If you lightly run some soft cloth and valve grinding paste through it, it will alter the imprint so the police can't match the shell to that gun although it may well have been that gun that fired the bullet. The other thing is that, you must wear gloves, because if you don't, you could leave your thumb print on the shell end when you load it into the clip, even the super firing heat won't disperse it.'

The Swansea van reversed up to the loading bay and the day's work started.

'That's the end of today's firearms lesson,' he said with a smile.

CHUDLEIGH, JANUARY 2006

Andy Tyler turned left onto the slip road and made his way onto the A38 dual carriageway quickly increasing his speed up to eighty mph. It was only a seven mile journey to his destination and at this time of day, he was sure he'd be there for ten o'clock. Two of his colleagues were also in the car ready for their work ahead. They'd spent the whole of the previous day running through their strategy, checking and double checking facts, dates and every likely scenario they could think of. There wasn't going to be any trouble, it would be simple text book stuff. Andy flicked the indicator switch downward and slowed towards the Dartbridge exit and stopped at the gateway. A quick look left and right and he set off past the Little Chef eatery on the left hand side and then turned right at the mini roundabout.

If he was honest with himself, he never particularly liked this part of his job and rarely for him did he have to get involved in this type of crime. Whether he'd remain in this specialist sensitive area, he didn't know. What he did know was that the man they were going to see had overwhelming evidence against him if it could be believed and proven to a jury. Andy slowed for the local bus in front of him and thought how scrappy looking the old disused quarry looked on his left hand side. He passed the woollen mill factory on his right and turned left up the hill at the next mini roundabout. It was just a short second gear sprint and then right into the car park. Andy had been there many times before both socially and professionally and he always liked the almost 'National Trust' type feel about it. They all got out of the car, Andy reaching back in to pick up his briefcase. He spoke to his two colleagues across the roof of the car as he blipped the remote and walked around to join them.

'Okay, you both know what you've got to do, what to look for. Keep it calm, we've done it all before. It's just a job. Don't let it get to you.'

'It's okay; we know what we're doing. We've got it sorted,' came the reply.

The two men and their female colleague had over fifty years of experience between them, but Andy was acutely aware that the case was going to be a particularly sensitive and highly publicised inquiry once the ball started rolling and he didn't want any mistakes. They walked through the archway across the cobbled paving between the public restaurant and the gift shop and into the pedestrianised area immediately in front of the main building.

Andy held open the door and beckoned his colleagues inside and approached the lady receptionist sat at the desk. The room had a distinct smell to it, a slightly scented freshly cut wood sort of smell. It was nice, Andy thought; very calming.

'Good morning. My name is Andrew Tyler. I'm from Devon & Cornwall Police and I'd like to see Father Abbot or Edmund Millen if I may?' It was the same person just the professional name as it were and his birth name.

'Yes, of course. I will see if I can get hold of him,' she replied.

There was a short wait whilst she tried to find him within the confines of the Abbey.

'He'll be with you in a few minutes. Can I get you a cup of tea or coffee?' she asked addressing the three.

'No, thank you, we're fine,' Andy answered for all of them.

Father Abbot's heart was beating a little faster as he made his way along the web of corridors and doorways towards the public reception. He'd had plenty of time to think about his position but had no reason to believe the police were there to interview him and despite his holiness, he sincerely hoped that it was not him they wanted to see and that it was just professional courtesy. He was about to find out.

He entered the reception area, surprised to see three people standing there. He gathered himself up and took a deep breath.

'Good morning, would you like to come through?'

They followed him into a small office area behind the outer room and stood talking.

'We are here to arrest Benjamin Coleman, Father Benjamin on suspicion of a number of serious sexual assaults. We would like you to take us to him and we'd also like to search his private room. We have a warrant,' said Andy, handing it to Father Abbot.

'There's no need for that,' he replied dismissing it away with a wave of his hand and thinking to himself thank God for that, it's not me.

Benjamin tried to consider everything as he traced the same steps as Father Abbot had done ten minutes previously towards the public reception area. This was it. Now he was going to face the music. This time, there were no ifs or buts, he would be officially required, like it or not. There were no dramas, no handcuffs. Benjamin simply surrendered himself to the plain clothed officers and was read his rights before being led away to a second unmarked waiting car. The remaining officers took less than half an hour to search his rather spartan room. It was fairly obvious there'd be nothing there, he'd had plenty of time to remove anything incriminating even if there ever was anything and there probably wasn't, at least not now after so many years.

Father Abbot watched the officers complete their search making some polite small talk as he stood in the open doorway and then accompanied them back to where they'd started, showing them to the door and shaking their hands. They hadn't found anything and they hadn't taken anything away and to be fair they'd have been extremely surprised if they had. Edmund folded his arms and held his chin in his hand as he saw the officers disappear out of sight beyond the archway. He turned and looked at Marjorie at the reception desk and said quietly,

'Your absolute discretion Marjorie.'

'Of course,' she replied nodding as she did so, then looking down pretending to get on with some work.

HMP LEYHILL, AUGUST 2008

Another day in the laundry. Max stood next to the folding machine as it hissed and clapped the thousandth green bobbly worn cotton sheet that day.

'Here, did you hear what they did to the blind guy in the kitchens?' Raz asked.

'No, what?'

'Well, they had to take him off the general duties 'cos he kept bumping into things, so they put him in the packing area doing the tea bags.'

Everyday at the evening meal, the kitchen orderly responsible would hand out to each prisoner, a small polythene bag filled with three whiteners, three tea bags and three sachets of sugar, which could be taken back to a prisoner's room. These had to be pre packed and this job had been given to the blind man. Now, there's no end of funnies that could be written here about what was done but Raz continued.

'Well, he's in the stores, on his own, he's got three boxes in front of him with each of the different items and he's quietly getting on with the job and packing the stuff away. A guy walks into the room collects some stuff, doesn't notice him and when he goes back out he switches off the light. Of course, the blind guy has no idea, it's all the same to him. He's working away in the dark anyway, now he's completely in the dark. An hour went by and a prison officer goes into the stores room and switches on the light and gets the fright of his life to find the blind guy carrying on as normal and says, 'Jesus Christ! What are you doing in the fucking dark?'

Max was laughing as two prison officers walked up to him.

'Reed?'

'Yes.'

'ID card?' Plenty of manners as usual.

Max went to his jacket pocket and pulled out his identity card and showed it to the two men. All the inmates in the immediate vicinity stopped working, and turned around to see what was going on. PO Selley, a tall late fifties, overweight officer with short stubby grey hair looked down at Max and read out a legal address informing Max of his rights and the officer's rights to formally demand a mandatory drugs test, supposedly random.

It wasn't a multiple choice answer situation. Max was escorted out of the laundry to the drugs testing facility. There was no courtesy. It was abrupt, arrogant and ignorant. Selley seemed to revel in the shock tactics and the drama. *What an idiot*, Max thought. As they walked from the laundry, Max asked, 'Have you looked at my file?'

'Why should I?' Selley asked.

'Well, you're wasting your time. I've never taken drugs in my life.'

'I don't care. We're testing you and that's that.'

Twat, Max thought but obviously didn't say it. There were so much drugs in the prison, yet the man in charge couldn't seem to see it or be capable of trying to stop it, yet for someone like Max who had no previous understanding or association of drugs, even he could see it everywhere. *Is this man stupid*, he thought. *Or just very stupid?* It didn't matter; Max gave Selley the required sample and an hour or so later was sent on his way. In all the time he was with Selley, he was never once courteous or well mannered. He was rude and ignorant and a lot of people don't respond well to that. Max looked at the sign above the door as he let himself out, it read 'Treat others as you would like to be treated yourself'. It was a joke. The biggest offenders to that were the prison officers themselves and they used their power over the inmates to control them all the time. They were nothing on the outside, nobody would give them a second thought, but on the inside they were all powerful and all too often, they abused that position of trust. It wasn't relevant to all the screws, that would be unfair to say that because there were some decent people there, but eighty per cent of the prison officers were overweight, lazy and rude. It wasn't conducive to getting the best from the residents.

It was too late for Max to return to work, so he made his way to his room ready for the 5.45 tally. The post had come. A card from his good friend Nick. He looked at the front cover black and white picture of two old men sat on a bench seat at a table enjoying a drink and the caption read 'You can't turn back the clock, but you can wind it up again'. Max smiled, how right he was. He couldn't change what had happened, but he knew that when he got out, he would be going out fighting. He hadn't been crushed, his family and friends had stuck by him and that was everything to him. Nothing else mattered.

NEWTON ABBOT, MAY 2002

Ultimately, closing Velodrome hadn't been a hard decision, mainly because the impending likelihood of Customs & Excise closing in on the kill had forced Max's hand. He had to do it, he really didn't have a choice if he wanted to have some say in what happened next.

Fielding had said that he would take all the troubles away from Max so that he could concentrate on getting going again. As far as opening the garage the day after the liquidation, with the exception of the limited company paperwork, absolutely nothing had changed. Fielding was right. Max had done a deal with him to buy back all the stock, the intellectual property and the chattels, the lot. It all now belonged to Max Reed trading as Velodrome. To the onlooker on the outside, Max hadn't, so much as changed a single thing. He didn't need to. Everything now belonged to him personally. The deal he'd done with the liquidator was simple. They agreed values on the stock, good will, chattels and the intellectual property and then further agreed a repayment schedule for Max to buy it all over a period. It allowed Max to sell stock and pay the liquidator as he did so, but at the same time wipe out a mountain of debt and importantly HM Customs & Excise.

In order for Velodrome to continue trading, Max would have to clear some of the limited company's trade supply debt so that he could run the business. That became his first hurdle. He wasn't running away from the Donald Key debt or Rick Brady or Dimo, but what he had to do was stop Customs & Excise and liquidating the limited company was the only way of doing that. Max hadn't gone bankrupt personally, far from it. What he had done, was a legitimate way to stop the angry advances of a government office wrongly pursuing Max for a debt that they knew was not legitimately owed by Velodrome. If they didn't know it, which he doubted, then they were incompetent and shouldn't have been doing the job. If they did know it, which to Max was a forgone conclusion, then they were chasing the wrong man for no other reason other than he was the last man in the chain, the last man standing. Customs & Excise had direct access to Tom McKinney's import paperwork and they would have known what was on the VAT declarations for the imported Ferraris. They would have also known or should have known where McKinney had bought the cars. It might have taken a bit of investigation to have found that out, but ultimately they could have been found out by bank account transfer information etc or copies of the C & E 389 import sheets. Max's paperwork would have shown every car bought from McKinney with all the specific details included so at least they would have been able to match information.

The fact that when Helen Walters and Adrian Smith had walked into Velodrome's office with the express intent of investigating the Ferraris had to mean that the VAT inspection was part of a wider investigation, otherwise why would they have only looked at that information and thinly disguised their real intentions? They weren't interested in the £18,000 Velodrome had outstanding, if Max hadn't mentioned it, they probably wouldn't have. No, Customs & Excise had one intention and that was to come down on Velodrome like a ton of bricks. They thought Max's company was part of a much wider trading fraud, and it wasn't. They couldn't prove it, they were trying it on. By raising the assessment, they would have known the implications and repercussions of such a move, moreover if they had known that Velodrome weren't liable, then surely they were being fraudulent themselves. It was a question Max had asked himself over and over again. Whatever, as far as Velodrome were concerned, Customs & Excise were out of the picture and Max could now get on with sorting out the many problems he'd previously had without the extreme pressure of a government office on his back or at least that's what he thought.

As such a limited company is a stand alone legal entity and although Max was the managing director, he actually worked for the company, he was an employee. The limited company, with the assistance of Fielding had gone into liquidation, down the tubes, and along with it, so had all the unsecured creditors. Max didn't have to pay any creditors and he wasn't obliged to do so, but that wasn't why he was in business and it wasn't the way he carried on.

His priority was to still get the 360 Spiders, supply customers and get the job done. After a lengthy period of negotiation, Donald Key accepted a deal with Max in regard to the monies paid for his customer's Ferrari 360 Spider, and Rick Brady stuck to his word and continued to wait for another deal on another day. So, who were the casualties in the fall out of the limited company's demise? Obviously, the vat man was one and Dimo was the other. Those were the main ones, there were a few other minor creditors that also got caught up in the mess, but mainly it was Dimo and the dreaded VAT.

If Dimo hadn't used a statutory demand as a debt collection facility, then the bank would have been less jumpy. Yes, Max knew that he owed him the money, but given the circumstances when Dimo had become fully aware, he was really using a sledgehammer to crack a nut. He'd always known that when the 360 Spiders arrived, Max would have taken a good profit from them, which would have satisfied his outstanding monies, so it was no big deal really. *God damn it*, Max thought. Dimo had been personally bankrupt twice, once spectacularly, and if anyone should know how it works, it was him.

As for Donald Key, well he'd been a complete nuisance from day one and Max bitterly regretted being convinced by Graham Lord to take Don's money in the first place. He was undecided at the time and if Graham hadn't pushed for the deal, then it was highly likely he wouldn't have done it even if he did need the money. It wasn't that he was worried at the time that the cars wouldn't arrive either, because he didn't know that, it was just that as and when the cars did arrive he would have made a lot more money.

Max had often looked back over that last two years and thought about whether he would have done anything differently and with the benefit of hindsight maybe he would have, but at the time there was no way he could have foreseen the events unfolding. The lack of 360 Spiders being delivered, the credit card frauds, the foot and mouth disease, the bank and the Transamerica stocking finance, Tom McKinney and Customs & Excise. Any one of them in a trading year, he could have fought off and survived, he may have been able to take on two or three and found a way out, but all of them in such a short space was impossible. With the amount of funds of his own and what he had available, it was a hopeless task and ultimately he had to let it go. It was for the best. In the cold light of day it had been a simple commercial decision, but in the real world, it represented the ruination of a lot of hard work and one man's broken dream.

HMP LEYHILL, AUGUST 2008

Jamie worked in the library, he was in for company fraud. Max had spoken to him a number of times and they'd got on quite well, so they would often meet up for lunch or the evening meal. He was on more flexible hours than Max working on a rota which allowed him better access to the facilities like the gym or rugby training and the like whereas Max found that as a result of him wanting to go into the gym at the same time as everyone else, it just became a bun fight, so he didn't bother. He'd said it many times, but Max thought right from the start of the first week at Leyhill that the gym really was the worst organised department in the whole place, so he stuck to his three weekly runs around the boundary and tried to keep his fitness up to a similar level he'd had on the outside.

They were standing in the queue for tea.

'Who's that guy that works with you in the library?'

'Who Colin?' asked Jamie.

'Yeah, Colin. What's he done?'

'I think it's tax evasion, something like that.'

'He's called Colin Bicknell isn't he?'

'Yes, why?'

'For some reason, I think I know him. I don't know why. I think it's from a long time ago. It's the name, it's familiar,' Max said, 'I've heard the name being called on the tannoy a few times and each time I think to myself I know him. I don't recognise him, but it's strange. Where does he live? Where does he come from?'

'Devon, I think. Don't know where, but it's definitely Devon. Jamie came from Tiverton so they'd often talked about the county so he was sure of what he was saying.

'Ah!' Max exclaimed, 'I think the penny's dropped. If it's the same guy, he used to live in Staverton. I remember he used to have a Golf GTI in the early 80s with a CB private registration. Yeah, I'm sure it's him. That's too much of a coincidence. Small world isn't it?'

'Yeah, it is.'

'How long have you been in now?'

'Seven months, another five to go. I shouldn't be here. If I'd had the original judge that I'd had at my earlier court appearances, I wouldn't be here.'

'Why?'

'The judge I was due to have was changed at the last minute and she'd come from a Crown Prosecution Service background and on the day I was sentenced, she'd already put three inside and so she did with me?'

'Which court was that?' Max asked.

'Exeter Crown Court.'

'Oh right, there can't be too many female judges down there?'

'No, I think there's only one. Not sure about that, but I think she is.'

Max thought for a moment. 'I think I know her. If it's the same person that I think it is, she's a customer of mine. I bought an Aston Martin DB7 Vantage Volante off her last year. Quite a tragic story really, because her husband died in a car accident. Not in the Aston Martin, something else, but contrary to your experience, I have to say, I found her a really nice lady. Slightly different situation though,' said Max.

'Yeah. Anyway, there's nothing I can do about it now.'

'No, you're in for the long haul.'

'So, are you going to have a world with Colin?'

'Yes, I probably will. He's from down my way so I expect he'll know a few people that I know. If I get chance, I'll have a chat with him. Oh, I know what I meant to say to you. When I got back from work today, there was a certificate on my bed. Obviously a screw had been in and put it there. It was the result of my MDT test. It was an elaborate sort of thing all printed out as a Certificate of Merit certifying that I'd had a negative drugs test. I presume they're expecting me to hang it on the wall.'

'I know. It's a joke isn't it?' Jamie replied. 'Are you going to the concert tonight?'

'Yes, I think so. It's in the badminton hall isn't it? 6.30?'

'Yeah.'

'Should be good. I heard them practicing when I was in music yesterday. We were helping with the backing vocals on Cockney Rebel's Make Me Smile.'

'Oh yeah. I bet that was quite good fun.'

'Yes it was.'

'What do you actually do in music?'

'Well it's an all day course every week. We do theory in the morning and usually practical in the afternoon. It's good fun and the girl that runs it explains everything well, so it seems easy to understand. It's either that or I haven't got much else to think about.'

'Probably the latter I expect. I think she does the creative writing course as well, doesn't she?'

'Yes, Thursday evenings.'

'Have you shown her your book yet?'

'Yes, I did. I took it to her after I'd been here for a couple of weeks, so I'd only done a few thousand words.

'What did she think of it? I mean she teaches creative writing so she should know.'

'She thought it was really good. I mean she liked what I'd done and wanted to read more, so a good response really.'

'How much have you done now?'

'I think it's about one hundred and fifty thousand words.'

'Bloody hell, I had no idea you'd done that much. All by hand ?'

'Yeah, well, I just get on with it when I can. It's surprising how much you can write.'

' I must have a read at some point. What are you going to do with it?'

'I don't know yet. I want to get it finished whilst I'm here if I can, then I'll make a decision.'

The pair of them sat in the window with their trays of food and idly chatted about nothing in particular. Just passing the time of day.

EXETER, MAY 2002

Sean Williams loosened his tie and undid his top button. He suddenly felt quite warm whilst he stood by his desk looking at the passing traffic along the main arterial road through the business park where he worked. He'd just seen Max Reed's car pass by with its distinctive registration number. *He's going to be in here in a minute and I don't think I can come up with another excuse*, he thought. *I'm going to need to give him a car.* He sighed.

Thirty minutes later, true to form, Max Reed drove up to the showroom stopping less than three inches from the plate glass window. Williams took a sideways glance and didn't move from his spot pretending to be deep in thought as he roved his eyes across the stock. Max marched past the receptionist failing to say hello and was immediately diffused as Williams announced.

'Ah, glad you've come up. I've just had notification from the factory that your first car is on its way'. It wasn't true, but his lies were a way of life.

It somewhat blew the wind out of Max's sails.

'So when will it be here?'

'Three weeks. I'll need your insurance to register it and of course the balance. Do you want me to invoice you or the company?'

Williams was playing the upper hand, he knew Velodrome Ltd had run into trouble and was now in liquidation but he couldn't understand how Max could continue trading exactly as he had previously. It didn't make sense to him.

'Invoice me personally at the garage address please Sean.'

Max looked at the Ferrari F50 in the showroom and asked Williams what was happening with it.

'It's a customer's car and he's asked us to sell it for him.'

'How much do you need for it?' He knew who owned it.

'We've got to return the customer £300,000.'

'And what do you want to get out of it?' Max asked.

'£3000?' Sean asked as a reply.

'Just bear with me Sean, I'll make a phone call.'

Max rang a customer in Dubai, it was late but he hoped he'd pick up. Max walked to the other side of the showroom just as Perez answered.

'Hello.'

'Perez, it's Max, Velodrome.'

'Oh, hello Max.' They went through the usual pleasantries and Max cut to the chase.

'I'm stood next to an F50. Any good to you?'

'Tell me a little bit about it,' Perez asked.

'It's a late car, 1996 in Rossa Corsa red, full Ferrari

494

service history, 6000 km, one owner, recent service, all the updates and needs nothing. It's a late chassis number as well.'

Sean walked across the showroom and mouthed to Max that he had the build book, the cases and the roof pouch which Max in turn passed on to Perez.

'How much do you want for it?' Max turned around, keeping Williams out of earshot and said £335,000.'

'Yes, that's okay.' It was as simple as that.

Max said, 'I'll send you the invoice through and if you transfer the money to my account, I'll have it transported to the garage for your guy to collect.'

Max had dealt with Perez before on bikes and some cars, but he knew he'd been looking for an F50 and this car was exactly what he wanted. It was a done deal. Max agreed the purchase with Williams and two days later the car was sitting in the service area at Velodrome. Max didn't bother asking Sean about the arrival of his second 360 Spider, he was pleased that he was at least getting one car and he now knew that it was the silver one. He had a customer in mind for it, but decided he wouldn't call him until Isca Ferrari sent him the invoice, when he received that paperwork, he'd feel comfortable that it really was on its way.

Williams leant back in his chair with his hands behind his head watching Max reverse out of the dealership car park. He couldn't believe it. He wondered how Max knew these people and shook his head. He was baffled. How does a guy selling motorcycles in a small market town in rural Devon get to know someone who he can call on the other side of the world and in less than five minutes sell him a £300,000 car? He didn't like him, he never had, then again not a lot of people liked Sean either, but what he'd just done was pretty astonishing he thought, and he couldn't help admire that. What surprised him was that there was no emotion, no smile, no nothing. It was just another deal. Sean knew that if he'd just done that, he'd be punching the air with his fist, but with Max he'd calmly said, 'Yes, that's okay,' gave Sean the instructions and got back in his car and drove off.

Max had a meeting with Barclays later that day. He needed to park the old limited company's overdraft and get a repayment holiday on the commercial mortgage. It was a sound plan that Max had taken to Hughes and he readily agreed. The garage had been valued at the same level for the last six years so

Max expected an outside valuation to be much higher than the banks own man and he was right, it was double. In order to pay back Donald Key and others, Max would have to sell the garage, but in order to make it work, the sensible option would be to offer the site with planning consent for a mixed commercial/retail scheme. The local authority was monstrously slow and difficult to deal with, but it would be worth it if the consent was given. The biggest problem again was of course money. Architects fees, engineers, soil reports, demolition costs, it was a lengthy involved and expensive business and the only way to keep paying out was to keep selling bikes and cars. Realistically, Max had just about had enough of it, but he looked at it as a means to an end. He wanted to get away from it, maybe do something different, he didn't know quite what, but he needed a change.

True to his word for once Williams called from Isca Ferrari a few weeks later to let Max know that the silver 360 Spider had arrived and would be available for collection on the Friday evening. Max had now sold the car and taken a £10,000 deposit so the deal was definitely on, and the London buyer was keen to collect his new car later on the Friday evening. Williams sent through the invoice as agreed and Max looked at the figures. It was exactly as he'd expected.

On the evening of the collection Max arrived at the showroom with Catherine, the car was in the showroom ready to be driven out through the glass sliding doors. Max had transferred the balance by telegraphic transfer earlier that day and confirmed with Williams that it had been received. The figure was £3000 short of the invoice total on account of the commission that Williams had promised Max on the sale of the blue Ferrari 456GT the year before and Williams knew that but said nothing. The ' yellow belly ' in him refusing to face the moment.

'The car looks stunning in that colour combination,' Max said to Sean.

'Yeah, it does.'

It was finished in Argento silver with a dark blue leather interior and dark blue roof. It made a change from the usual red. Williams went through the handover with all the paperwork and drawing a deep breath, he said, 'Well, it's just the outstanding £3000.'

'What do you mean the outstanding £3000?' Max said

rather indignantly.

'Well, there's still £3000 owing.'

'Don't be silly Sean. You know about that. You owe me that money for the 456.'

'Yeah, we agreed something, but I don't remember it being £3000.'

'You do Sean and you know it, and in any case why didn't you tell me earlier when I transferred the money?' Max asked.

Sean Williams had no excuse. Basically, when he sold the 456 he didn't allow for Max's commission that he'd agreed. For his part, Max had agreed a deal, shook hands, advertised the car, sold it and Williams got paid. The money was owed, but allowing the silver 360 Spider to go out without the £3000 being paid was outside of Williams' remit. Max had to pay it and he did on his credit card. *Williams is a complete arsehole*, Max thought. At that moment, he didn't know what he was going to do about it, he'd already been messed about for eighteen months and more waiting for the silver car and he had another coming. The last thing he wanted to do was formally fall out with Isca Ferrari, but he was going to have to do or say something.

It's only twenty miles from Exeter to Newton Abbot and Max had already been at the showroom for longer than he'd expected, so it was no surprise to find the buyer waiting outside Max's house when he got home. It had been a nice evening and with the sun shining, the drive back in a new open top Ferrari was very pleasurable. They really were great cars with fantastic handling and loads of ripping performance. And the noise from the two stage exhaust when it opened up was like a banshee wail.

Jez Simmonds looked at the 360 Spider as Max blipped the throttle and barked the engine to a stop.

'What a fabulous looking car,' he said. It was. He looked all around it and Max carried out the almost identical handover that Williams had done to him almost an hour earlier. Jez stopped for a coffee for half an hour and then it was his turn to crank the ignition and blast off into the distance in his new Ferrari. Another one sold. London is three hours away and Jez would have the best three hours he could have imagined, a childhood dream come true.

Max thought about speaking to the owner of Isca Ferrari, but realised that it would be better after he had notification of the next car's arrival. In the meantime, he was going to keep the pressure on and not let Williams forget.

It was Catherine's birthday on the following Sunday and her parents had invited all the family along for a get together. They all got on well especially considering there were so many of them and it wasn't unusual to be sat at the table well after dinner had finished chatting about old times, funny stories, all the usual things families rabbit on about.

Max had mentioned that he'd never flown in a helicopter. He'd flown in light aircraft, many, many times and when he was thirteen he'd had several lessons, indeed his father actually had his private pilot's licence, so the chance to fly in various Cessnas and the like came about nearly every weekend in the early 1970s, but never a helicopter.

It got them all talking.

'Do you remember when we all went to America on holiday and we flew across the Grand Canyon in that helicopter?' Catherine asked.

'Oh yes, I remember that,' said her father.

'I remember, flying across the ground quite low and then suddenly we went over the canyon and there was a huge drop. You could see through the floor at the front of the helicopter, it had small windows. It was really scary.'

They all remembered it and talked about the holiday animatedly for probably half an hour or more, then Catherine's father asked her, 'Do you remember going up in the one with the glass bubble?'

'Oh yes, that was brilliant. I remember I was quite scared at the time. I could have only been about five or six years old,' said Catherine.

Her father continued, 'I remember, I was the Chairman of the Rotary Club at the time and they wanted to do something special. It was fun dressing up as Father Christmas and flying over Newton Abbot. Do you remember flying over the house?' he asked.

'Yes, I do. I kept thinking I was going to fall out. I was hanging on to the seat. I remember all the children waving in the park when we landed,' she said.

Max was listening. There was something strangely familiar to the story.

'When was this?' he asked.

'Oh, it must have been about 1967 or 1968. Obviously just before Christmas.'

'You're not going to believe it,' Max said, amazed by what they'd said, 'I was there. I was there with Neil. We watched you circle around above.'

'That's right,' said her father.

'And then you landed in Courtenay Park and I remember you reaching behind and pulling a little girl out the helicopter and she stood alongside you giving the presents out to the children.'

'Yes, that's right, well, that was me,' Catherine said smiling.

'I remember going up to Father Christmas and he asked me what I wanted, and I think I said I would like Scalextric, and he said he'd like that too. It's funny how you remember these things. I thought Father Christmas was a real good chap because he liked Scalextric.'

Then, in an image that struck him like a passing car, he suddenly recalled a conversation with Caro. It was like instant re-wind. They were in the cornfield at the top of the cliff path, maybe fifty yards from the turnstile onto Cliff Road. He knew exactly where it was and when it was. They were walking back from the fair, they were happy and they were laughing not a care in the world, it was a beautiful warm evening in that glorious summer of '76. The sound of the corn was swishing quietly all around them in the soft breeze, the grass path was flattened and balding in the middle with the passage of walkers and no rain. They were arm in arm and she was wearing her white jeans and a light blue T shirt. He remembered her being cold and him giving her his denim Wrangler jacket and pulling her towards him and giving her a long slow loving kiss. He thought she said something like, have you ever thought if we've already met the person we're going to marry or how close we've been to them or whether we've we passed them on the street? At the time, Max thought she was talking about them both, perhaps she was. He remembered hugging her and feeling the warmth of her body and looking over her shoulder at the estuary in the distant background. He'd just recaptured a truly wonderful moment in time and as he fondly remembered her words, he realised that he'd already met his future wife eight years prior to that moment. He tutted to himself and smiled, he always knew he would never forget her.

The first call Max took on the Monday after the weekend was from Josef. He was looking for a Ferrari F50 for a good

499

customer of his. Max had just sold one and it was still in the service area, but he did know that Harry had a similar car available so he gave him a call.

'Hey Harry, long time no speak, how are you?'

'Very well, Max. And you?'

'Getting through it, you know what it's like.'

'Yes. How did you get on with Donald Key?'

'Well, we've agreed a solution which will take a while to satisfy, but as I say, it's all been agreed.'

'Oh, I am pleased. You don't need all that aggravation and he can be quite difficult if he wants to be. We had a similar problem in South Africa a few years back. We managed to sort it out, but it took eighteen months to do it. Not with Key, I hasten to add, but another dealer and it could have easily got out of hand'

'Well, I think that's how long it will take me, but it would have been a lot better if Don and his son hadn't set out on a destruction course.'

'Yes, I heard about that. In fact a lot of people know and I think it's sort of back fired on them a little bit. The way you were treated was wrong and I think Key realises that now.'

'Anyway, I see you have an F50 advertised. I sold one last week and now I've got an enquiry for another. He is a serious buyer, so we're not wasting each other's time.'

'Sounds good. We supplied the car from new, it's an early chassis number with 1600 km, one owner, all the books etc, it's a very nice car in red and Bob has just serviced it. It's £325,000.'

'Okay, what's the best you can do on that?'

'I suppose £310,000 and we'll let it go.'

'Okay, I'll see what I can do and call you back.'

Harry was just about to say goodbye, when he asked, 'Do you speak to Graham Lord at all?'

'No, I haven't spoken to him for several months. He sort of disappeared when the Donald Key drama started kicking off,' Max replied.

'No, I haven't seen him either. Strange really. Okay, well speak to your man and give me a call. I'll hold on to it until you come back to me.'

Max put down the phone and immediately called Josef and agreed a deal with him on the phone. Max collected the car a few days later and for a short period of time had two Ferrari

F50s in the service area awaiting their new buyers. It was easier dealing with real physical cars, all the forward order cars had been a nightmare. People had said they were getting cars and they were just not arriving. Some of it might have been wishful thinking but most thought their car was on its way and it wasn't. The fact that it affected so many wasn't a coincidence, it was the way that Ferrari used and abused their customers. They appeared to have a total contempt for the customer. It was very wrong and it caused a lot of upset that ultimately cost some people a lot of money.

The next time Sean Williams actually called Max was September 2002. He'd called to confirm the specification of the second 360 Spider that Max had ordered which in turn determined the delivery date for twelve weeks later. The second car was now coming so Max advertised the car and sold it for that delivery date. The premiums Max had made were nowhere near the expected amount because the two cars had arrived so late. There were now too many cars available and the premiums were a fraction of the early contracts.. Although, Max couldn't prove it at the time he was certain that Williams had messed him about. He was sure other people had received their cars before him, effectively jumping the queue. Max would find out, he was determined to, but at that moment, he wasn't sure how. Whatever, Isca Ferrari had cost him nearly two hundred thousand pounds in lost profit and at a time when the company most needed it. In Max's view, Williams had a lot to answer for.

ANSTEYS COVE, JUNE 1999

It had been a glorious weekend. Max and his family had spent the day bobbing up and down on a friend's boat. They were sat at anchor having a drink when Max picked up the Mail on Sunday. He read the front cover page and turned over, there was a full page article on a guy who committed a massive finance fraud on classic Ferraris. There were pictures of the house and all the cars. He read it avidly, but stopped in his tracks at paragraph two. The forty six year old man pleaded guilty at Manchester Crown Court on charges of fraudulent trading and has been sentenced to four years imprisonment. It was Andy Robertson, the guy that had bought Max's Ferrari Dino 246 all those years ago. The same guy.

Max handed it to Catherine and asked her, 'Recognise him?' as he pointed to the picture.

'Yes, vaguely,' she replied and then read the article. *It's a small world*, he thought.

CHUDLEIGH, JANUARY 2006

There was no way out for Benjamin, he'd said very little in his interview with Andy Tyler sticking to his story that he knew nothing about the many serious allegations that were being levelled against him. He was staggered by the amount of questioning Tyler had thrust against him. Living the life he had, prepared him for the onslaught, he knew how to keep quiet and at his age and experience, he wasn't about to be ruffled by Tyler. No way, if Tyler was to take the matter further he was going to have to charge him and go to court. Benjamin was prepared to go all the way if he had to, he didn't want to, but for now he was going to hang on and dig his heels in.

Tyler realised he was not getting anywhere but from the evidence he had, it was more than just one mans word against another. There were several witnesses all of whom had come forward and Tyler suspected more would follow. He'd made his mind up.

Benjamin's solicitor took him to one side and raising his eyebrows, told him that he was about to be charged. Tyler had confirmed his intentions and Benjamin was escorted through to the custody suite to face the sergeant as the charges were read out. Benjamin said nothing as he was bailed to the abbey address. He thought about the publicity; there was bound to be some and worried himself about what he was going to say to his elderly father if he found out. God, what a mess.

Father Abbot had been pretty edgy all day, pacing up and down in his quarters. He was confident that the police weren't interested in him, but Benjamin's investigation could easily drag him in with it and it was that which worried him the most.

There was a quiet knock at his door later that evening after vespers and Benjamin stepped into his room.

'How did it go?' Edmund asked.

'Not good,' he shrugged. 'They've charged me with seven counts, and they're saying there may be more charges to follow.'

'Are you okay?'

'As well as can be expected in the circumstances.'

'What happens next?'

'I have to go to Newton Abbot magistrate's court next week to plead not guilty and then it will be referred to crown court for a later date. Apparently, there's no stopping it now. It will run until the end, until I'm either committed or found not guilty. I'm on bail at this address. It will probably take a year or more before it goes to trial, so I don't know. I didn't think it would come to this.'

'What has the solicitor said?' Edmund asked.

Benjamin put his head in his hands and let out a long sigh, 'He says it doesn't look good and I shouldn't get my hopes up. If it goes against me, possibly ten to fifteen years.'

'Oh my God, Ben, I'm so sorry.'

Edmund stood up, holding his forehead with one hand walking around the room saying, 'I didn't expect that.'

'No, neither did I,' there was a short silence and he repeated, 'No, neither did I.'

NEWTON ABBOT, MARCH 2003

A year had passed, all the Ferrari business had long since gone, Max was due to get the news on the planning application any day soon and that would put an end to the horrendous ongoing professional costs that he'd had to pay out in the last twelve months. There was a lot riding on the outcome of the local authority decision not least that he could finally sell the garage and settle his longstanding dispute with Donald Key.

Max had agreed a sale on the basis of the planning consent so should the outcome be positive, then the conveyance would proceed quickly. It could all be done and dusted in a couple of months. He thought it would mark the end of a rather largely wasted chapter in his life.

Dimo's Ferrari 360 Spiders still hadn't rocked up despite Sebastien's saying that they were due to arrive last month, end of this month and then the next month. The fact was simply that they had no idea when they were coming or they were behaving in exactly the same manner as Max believed Isca Ferrari had been with him. It was despicable.

Like the two years before, the last year had been extremely difficult. Trading had been slow and the profits had been low so paying off the huge backlog of company creditors had taken much longer than expected, nonetheless, by the time Donald Key was satisfied, Max had managed to clear nearly £450,000 in back debt. It took some doing, especially as from a legal standpoint, he didn't have to.

McKinney, in the meantime had shown up, not on the doorstep, but on the national BBC ten o'clock news. A short article had mentioned McKinney, by name having fled the country to Spain after conducting a £7 million VAT fraud. Max never got his money back and the Customs & Excise hadn't bothered coming along to say, 'Oh, sorry, we've got the wrong man.' It was too late for all the bitterness and who knows, they might have actually done him a favour at the time. Perhaps Velodrome could have got in deeper than they already were.

Muzi was still there or thereabouts. Max would usually speak to him at least once a week, but he'd had a hiccup and the once 'life changing' deal that didn't come about because of the cars eligibility really was the only deal that could have been done, because shortly afterwards, Muzi had some major problems of his own.

During the first week of December, the sale of the property finally went through. What a relief that was. Max had never intended to sell it when he started out. It was meant to be a pension for the future, a little nest egg, but push really had come to shove and he had no other realistic way of settling Donald Key, Barclays Bank and a few others, so it had to go. There was no point being sad about it, he thought; it was only a building; you can buy other buildings; better that he cleared the decks and start again. At forty-three, it wasn't something he particularly wanted to do. He was hoping he would have been comfortable by that age, but that's the way it goes sometimes.

It was an early start on the Thursday of the following week, Max had to travel to York for an appearance in the County Court, not as might be expected him owing money, quite the opposite, a former solicitor who had since been struck off owed Max £28,000 and he was going there to fight his corner. There was a very heavy frost and the car had been left running outside warming through for ten minutes or so. Max kept looking out of the window to check if the windscreen had cleared whilst he finished a cup of tea and watched the early BBC news. He could feel the low vibration of the motor, and then unexpectedly it stopped. *That's odd*, he thought. He got up from his chair to look out of the window, he hoped he hadn't run the car out of fuel. There was a knock at the door.

As he walked past the hallway window, he could see two thick set men stood at the door dressed in dark suits. Their very appearance gave them away. They weren't debt collectors, no it was two CID police officers. Max opened the door and looked at the two men, both of them in their mid to late thirties, five eight maybe five ft ten tall, grossly overweight with number one cropped hair. *They could have been twins, Pinky and Perky*, Max thought.

'Good morning, Mr. Reed?'

'Yes,' Max replied.

'Can we come in please?'

'Yes, of course,' Max invited them into the hallway and showed them into the kitchen. The two officers looked around as if they'd never been inside a house before and it was all new to them.

'How can I help you?' Max asked.

The one doing the talking, removed his warrant card from his inside pocket and showed it to Max; there were beads of sweat on his forehead as he did so. Max looked at it carefully, as much as anything to slow things down and remain calm. He wasn't worried, he hadn't done anything wrong.

Detective Constable Leo Easton addressed Max in that typical monotone automaton police delivery.

'Mr. Reed. We are conducting an investigation into the trading activity of Velodrome Ltd and we would like you to accompany us to Torquay Police station where we would like to ask you some questions.' Max said nothing and Easton continued, 'I am arresting you on suspicion of fraudulent trading. You don't have to say anything, but anything you do say may if you do say something, you later rely on.' It got jumbled in his mind and Max didn't catch it all. He'd got the picture. He was shocked.

There was no finger tip search of the property, no handcuffs, nothing like that, Easton merely asked if Max had a stock book, which he readily gave him, and off they went to

Torquay. Max sat in the back of the unmarked police car and said nothing, the two officers trying to engage in some conversation, but Max wasn't up for that. The truth of it was that he really disliked the police. It was a sweeping statement to say they were corrupt and stupid hypocrites, but that was the way he felt and he'd seen nothing to change his mind on that.

The custody sergeant summoned one of the PCs to the desk who then escorted Max to one of the cells. It was cold and stark inside, no comfort, no nothing. His furniture for the day was merely a built in bench bed with a dirty blue vinyl cushion. The slide over the window would open and shut every thirty minutes as the keeper kept a watching eye. Lunchtime came and went as, no doubt, Easton and his buddy dined at the trough, Max thought. Still no interview. Max was beginning to wonder if he was going to be spoken to or not. Even tea time, came and went. Finally, half past six and Easton was ready to talk. Max, by this time, was very pissed off; he'd been kept literally in the dark all day. Why did Easton need to arrest him at eight in the morning and then start an interview at 6:30 pm in the evening? The reason? it had to be that he didn't know what he was doing.

Easton switched on the double tape machine and commenced the formal interview. Max had the duty solicitor at his side as Easton bombarded him with questions relating to customers ordering Ferrari 360 Spiders and not receiving their cars. Max was somewhat bemused, clearly Easton didn't understand the business and he didn't seem to be able to grasp the concept of Velodrome ordering new Ferrari cars that could then be sold on for a profit.

'It's simple,' Max would say, 'a guy wants a Ferrari 360 Spider and he doesn't want to order it from a Ferrari dealer, because if he does that, he'll probably have to wait two to three years and he wants it now or as soon as possible so he comes to me and asks if I can get one for him. I tell him I have one coming and I want £30,000 over list price for it. He says that's okay and they do a deal and the car should arrive on a certain date. But, Ferrari have problems with manufacture and delivery and the car is delayed, so it takes longer to get the car.'

'So why do they come to you?' Easton asked.

'I've just explained that. Because I have a car coming sooner than they'd have to wait if they ordered one from a franchised Ferrari dealer.'

Easton continued with his questioning and rolled out

another of his unique insights into how a business worked, 'I could see your business was in trouble.'

'Oh, yeah, how was that then?' Max asked.

'I've got your bank statements.'

'So you can tell, I was in trouble because you have my bank statements? You've been busy,' Max said with a sarcastic tone.

'Yes, I can.'

'Oh, well, this will be interesting,' Max said calmly.

Easton looked at Max giving him the evil eye. Max wasn't worried, he had quickly realised the total ineptitude of the man.

'I note that on one day in September you were £70,000 in credit and the following day you were £120,000 or thereabouts overdrawn.'

'That's it?'

'Yes.'

'Well, God help us if that's your understanding of a business being in trouble. Have you had any accountancy training? I didn't realise you were an expert.'

'I'm asking the questions.'

'Well, perhaps you should, because you're in no position to offer any sensible comments based on that.'

Max looked at Easton, he was scowling. The sidekick sat with his legs apart and his gut hanging out over his belt recognising that Easton was out of his depth. Max shook his head looking at his solicitor saying, 'this is ridiculous, they don't know what they're talking about, they're wasting my time.' The solicitor nodded but said nothing.

The questioning continued firing backwards and forwards with Donald Key and Dimo's name coming into the fray, then Graham Lord and a bit more on Tom McKinney. *They have plenty of information*, Max thought. *But they don't know what to do with it.* They had arrested Max on suspicion of fraudulent trading but they hadn't touched on it during the interview. If there had been something strange going on at Velodrome, they couldn't figure it out and they certainly didn't have anything to charge Max with.

It was 8:45 pm by the time the two officers took Max home. He was bailed to report at the same police station in three months time.

Typically, Easton and his buddy Ed McGrain needed to

refill their stomachs so stopped at the McDonalds drive in on the way back to Newton Abbot. Max was sat in the back of the car watching them as they drove along the main road, no tax showing in the window, on the mobile phone, eating McDonalds from boxes between their legs, the driver steering with his elbows. *It was a joke*, Max thought. "Do as I say, not as I do".

Catherine was worried when Max walked through the door, it had been a long day, she could see the look on his face. He was angry and she very rarely saw him like that. He told her that he hadn't been charged just bailed for three months whilst they continued their enquiries, but he was concerned mainly because the two officers appeared to be so stupid. They didn't seem to have any idea of how businesses worked, how accounts were run and what it all meant. It was worrying, but for now nothing was going to happen until the bail date. Max had time to think things through, and Easton had three months to get his act together.

No matter how strong Max thought he was, it was difficult to eradicate the dark cloud of the police investigation from his mind. He had to continue with his life but he couldn't let on that he was worried, that would only serve to worry Catherine as well and he didn't want that. He kept casting his mind back over and over again tossing about in his head the many Ferrari transactions he'd done when Velodrome was still in business. He couldn't think of anything that he'd done wrong. Yes, there had been many problems, they were obvious, but nothing stood out as being a criminal activity. He tried to satisfy himself in his mind that there was nothing the police could do. He hadn't done anything wrong, but more than anything else, it was their complete inability to understand what they were talking about that worried him the most. They were dangerous, because they were ignorant.

NEWTON ABBOT, 2006

Ralph Sanders was sifting through all the information when Max called.

'Hi Ralph, how are you coming along with the report?'

'Nearly done, I should have it finished this week and I'll get it off to you,' Ralph replied.

'Have you turned up anything else?' Max asked.

'Yes, it's all good. Lots of photos, period articles plus various confirmation of this and that. There's no doubt as to what it is, so my report will detail that.'

'That's good. I'm looking forward to it.'

Max put down the phone. It had been a long three years getting to this stage and a hell of a lot had happened, some good some bad, but hopefully the door was now going to open so that he could finish the job he'd started. There was still the worry of maybe the cat getting out of the bag, but Max trusted Ralph, so he thought it wasn't likely to come from him. There were only a few people that knew, but it only took someone to overhear a conversation and that would be that. Max had the car and by virtue of that he was in the driving seat. He knew that, and he was confident. All he had to do was hold it together for a little while longer.

GOODWOOD, SEPTEMBER 2009

Max and Catherine stood in the waiting area, it was a beautiful sunny September day. The world war two Spitfires and Mustangs were doing their spectacular and outrageously low fly pasts as Donald Key and his wife Karen walked up and stood next in line. Donald nodded to Max and smiled, saying, 'Good morning'. They were both dressed in 1950's period costume. Max smiled to himself, knowing who they were but also knowing that they had no idea who he was.

The camouflaged WWII Willy's Jeep pulled up alongside them and they all shared the lift into the circuit. They chatted along the five minute journey. It was Goodwood 2009, and Max was helping a friend of his run a couple of 1930s racing cars. He still loved the sport and competed as often as he could in hill climbs and races, but this particular weekend he was just along for the ride, a gofor.

Key had long since forgotten about Max Reed, he'd been paid and the sorry tale was way behind him. If he did think about it, then it was only if he was jogged. Max had gone, for good he hoped. What Max didn't know at that time though, was that it was Key who had made the complaint. He was the one that had gone to the police.

It was a busy meeting, and a long one at that. The first of the transporters had arrived on the Thursday with the last of them leaving on the Monday morning. Catherine enjoyed the motor racing but two days and one night was enough for her so she left early. It gave Max a chance to walk about, chat to people he knew from way back and indulge himself.

Max looked at the Ferrari 250 Testa Rossa in the assembly area waiting to go out for the next practice. Julian Key and his father were stood either side of the car talking across the bonnet. The driver was sat ready with his open faced helmet and Ray Bans reminding Max of the guy in the award winning feature length Honda advert on television. Julian was strutting around dressed like a fifties spiv. Max thought he probably dressed like that every day, the spite was still there.

A dark blue Aston Martin DB4 GT Zagato pulled up and parked on the verge, and a grey haired man in his late fifties, early sixties climbed out of the driving seat. Old Mr Bighat himself. He stood up straight and stretched his back having a good look around as he did so, probably to see who was looking at him. It was a beautiful car, an expensive replica, but nonetheless very nice. Max watched the driver lock the car and walk towards him, his eyes focussed on something or someone behind him. He walked by, no more than three feet distant as he passed. It was Rupert Davis, he hadn't noticed Max.

Ten minutes later, Max was walking through the crowded Ferrari paddock area, Raggy was leaning on six million pounds worth of Ferrari 330 P4, his previous partner had caught Max for £10,000 a few years earlier, Harry Simmonds was talking to some friends a short distance away and over in the far corner Graham Lord was deep in thought looking at a 1964 single seater. They were all there as Max more or less strolled around amongst the celebrities and general public in complete anonymity. It was a strange situation, he felt a little apprehensive, it was almost as if the onset of his next step would be a little unfair considering the amount of water that had flowed under the bridge but all things considered some form of revenge had to be sweet.

510

The busier he made himself, the faster the days, weeks and months passed by. Leyhill hadn't been what his solicitor had told him to expect, but it was a world away from where he'd come. He remembered thinking about having his car bought up to the jail, having his mobile phone with him and spending his days commuting backwards and forwards to and from the prison. His solicitor had said, 'Yeah, it's no problem. You'll be able to come and go as you please, it's business as usual.' How wrong he could have been and how wrong it was for him to not have checked first before he said it.

As the time went by in jail, Max had lots of opportunities to sit and think about what had happened. If he had done wrong, he certainly didn't know it at the time, not that it could have been an excuse, but it showed there was no intent and that was the important issue. There were beginnings of upset in his mind about his representation. Should he have asked more questions? Were they right in what advice was given? Should he have had a second opinion? Some of the more important questions he'd asked, in hindsight he now felt he'd had rather flippant answers to. At the time, the replies seemed reasonable, but now that he knew more, he had reservations about his solicitor and his barrister. The thing about lawyers is that they should know a lot more about what they are doing than you so you have to put your faith in them and trust that they will do right for you. He recalled in his mind one question that he'd asked and it was relevant to a possible confiscation order. The barrister had been quite dismissive about it and Max took that as being a relatively minor issue, but had the barrister fully explained the workings of such an order, who gets what and why, and expanded upon it then Max could well have taken a different path and that would have had a significant effect on the outcome.

Max sat in his room contemplating the days gone and the days yet to do, it was frustration beyond belief. *How can anyone do twenty or thirty years of this*, he thought. They must just surrender to it, resign themselves to their fate. Forget about life outside. It was horrible thinking about it. His mind turned to some conversational snippets of the day.

There's a white man sitting on a table in front of him and they're talking about a muscular black guy opposite who's already been in for seven years for raping a fourteen year old white girl. It sounded like something out of an African war zone, but it wasn't, it was middle England.

The white man continued, 'The thing is Max, do you know what the best thing is about him?' he asked.

'No, what?'

'Every morning, when he wakes up and he goes into the bathroom and looks in the mirror, he's going to have an ugly wog looking at him. The bastard!' It was a hard comment, and he meant it but he wouldn't have been the only one thinking the same.

In music, the day before, Kat the music teacher was talking about film scores and she'd asked if anyone had seen 'Brief Encounter' and the guy next to Max had said in all seriousness 'Of the third kind, Miss?'

He had another visit booked for Sunday, Catherine and the children were coming and Max always looked forward to it every week. It kept them all together despite being apart. It was only fourteen weeks, but that's a long time when you're waiting.

Lots of things were flitting to and fro in his mind. There was the guy who was serving six months for bestiality, they called him the Beast of Bodmin, he'd apparently been caught shagging goats. Another beast was the Barnsley Beast, seven rapes and seven murders and currently in for thirty two years. Why was Max having to be with these people, he asked himself. Perhaps that was the punishment. He had to serve fourteen weeks with the dregs of society, it wasn't the incarceration, it was the association. Not everyone in jail was a murderer, rapist or paedophile, but it just seemed that way at Leyhill because there were so many of them. It put Max on his guard all the time, not because he was scared of them, but because knowing what people have done does have an effect. He was either receptive or dismissive. That's all okay if he'd been told the right thing, but when he first arrived, a similar aged man had spoken to Max many times and had told him he was in for fraud. Max couldn't remember exactly what it was, something to do with mortgages, it wasn't important at the time. Fraud is fraud. Later, it turned out he wasn't in for fraud at all, he'd raped his thirteen year old niece. Max couldn't speak to him after that.

The tannoy noisily announced South and East to the dining hall, no running. Max didn't eat tea on a Friday or Monday and Wednesday. It was his running night. By twenty

512

past five he was looking at his watch and setting off on his six laps of the boundary. It never seemed to get any easier, he was always glad it was over when it was finished. He'd run past the Russian Oak, it had started losing its copper leaves, he was pleased with that. When he'd arrived at Leyhill, the trees were in full foliage and he'd said to himself that by the time all the leaves on the tree had gone, so would he be. He was past the halfway point, he had less to serve than he'd served, so now he was on the downhill side.

CHUDLEIGH, MARCH 2006

Benjamin's investigation had been rattling on for nearly two years whilst every two to three months he'd had his bail extended. He had become accustomed to the stress and strain it had caused him, all the delays and the worry of the outcome. In his mind, he knew what he had done was wrong, but he'd convinced himself otherwise. So much time had passed by that it helped dilute the memory, erode the detail. It didn't seem so bad now, was how he was thinking. Denial was still the way forward and he was determined to stick to that whatever evidence was thrown at him.

Andy Tyler parked in the same space as he usually did when he stopped the car in the Abbey car park and opened the driver's door. It was sharp outside and the wind was gusting in total contrast to when he last visited Father Benjamin.

Tyler's colleagues walked at his side as he passed under the stone archway and across the original car park to the Abbey public reception. He felt a little bit like a stuck record. Same drive, same walk, same talk. He opened the reception door and walked in. The by now, familiar female receptionist was sat at her desk typing some outgoing letters.

'Good morning,' she said looking up over her glasses with a smile.

'Good morning,' the three replied almost in unison.

'Is it Father Abbot you would like to see?' she asked. As before, it was the right protocol, nothing had changed there.

'Yes, please,' Tyler replied. The receptionist rang around chasing the responses until she found him and then let Tyler know that Father Abbot was on his way. Edmund was on the other side of the abbey at the time, which meant it would take a few minutes before he would reach Tyler. He walked quickly whilst his habit billowed behind him. The investigation surrounding Benjamin had been going on for so long that the shock of it had long since gone. Now it was a nagging thought at the back of his mind that every now and then was jerked to the front by happenings such as this. He'd hoped it would have all gone away, but he'd been kept up to date with the happenings, the initial court appearances and the transfers from magistrates to crown level. Now, with the trial only a few weeks away, he assumed that Tyler was paying a courtesy call to let him know of the likely scenario or perhaps he just wanted to talk to Benjamin for one last time.

He opened the internal door in to the reception, holding out his hand to shake Tyler's saying in buoyant mood, 'Good morning everyone, sorry I was a little while. You caught me on the other side of the building. What can I do for you today?' he asked.

'Good morning, Father Abbot. Can we have a word?'

'Of course,' Edmund replied smiling and then ushered them into the small office alongside.

'Do please sit down,' Edmund offered, but soon realised the mood had changed. Tyler looked at Father Abbot, his face expressionless, his steely eyes fixed on Edmund's reaction.

Edmund Millen, I'm arresting you on suspicion . . . Father Abbot watched Tyler's lips moving, but no sound was coming out. He could feel the weight of his jowls in his face as the blood began to drain away. His finger tips were tingling and his palms were clammy. He suddenly felt very dry. He steadied himself against the seat back and sat down on the cushioned chair. Tyler and his colleagues had seen it before, they knew what to expect. The moment when someone's life is about to change forever. Edmund sat quietly, motionless, his head down as he contemplated the very real thought of his fall from grace.

GOODWOOD, SEPTEMBER 2009

The first race in the afternoon was scheduled for two o'clock which meant that if the timetable ran perfectly, Donald Key's client would be out at about ten past three for the third race. All the cars for that race would be required in the assembly area twenty minutes before that.

One of the cars that Max was helping run was out in the first race of the day at 2:00 pm. He knew that the twelve lapper would take under twenty minutes, so he felt he had plenty of time to help recover the car to the paddock afterwards and then watch race three. It was just gone half past twelve as he wandered through the fairground listening to the children's' screams mixed with the sounds of the old fashioned accordion style music boxes. He looked up at the carousel seeing all the girls of all ages sat on or astride horses, elephants and lions going up and down and around in beautiful colour. There was so much vibrancy, music and movement. A World War Two Spitfire flew low overhead banked over on its right hand side displaying it's full underside, a small white vortices streaming from the wing tip. What a sight, he couldn't have been much more than two hundred feet off the ground. There was so much going on. Everywhere Max looked, there was something he wanted to touch, handle or marvel at. For a petrol head interested in classic cars, motorcycles, motor racing, memorabilia and women, this was definitely the place. The spectacle and distractions were endless. It seemed everyone was in pre 1965 dress, what a sight. *If there is a Heaven on Earth, then the Goodwood Revival has to be it*, he thought.

It took ten minutes to walk from the fairground area back to the inner paddock. Max passed a few celebs on the way, Stirling Moss, Rene Arnoux, Patrick Tanbay, Chris Evans, Jackie Stewart, they were all there. It wasn't like the modern Formula 1 circus where all the teams and competitors are cut off from the real world, this was just like it would have been in the golden era of motor racing. A more endearing period with a quintessentially English charm to it.

Max bumped into Murray Walters, he hadn't seen him for a while. The last time they had met was at a BRDC dinner, it must have been around '91 or '92. Murray was sat next to Max and they were talking about Formula 1. The subject came around to Nigel Mansell, again a man Max had met many times and Max asked Murray what he thought of him and he replied,' Well, as a driver, he's a winner, maybe not in the same league as Senna, but he gets the job done. It's typical of the saying that if you do something long enough, sooner or later you're going to do it right. As for Mansell on a personal level, I think he's a very balanced guy. He's got a chip on both shoulders.'

They laughed. Murray finished with a great story about when he was working in the early days at the BBC. He'd been working on the local evening news programme when it had come to the time when the weather girl would give the forecast in front of a map of the region. In those days, there were no computerised graphics, it was all "stick on" symbols. She got to the point where she needed to show that there was fog coming in from the west and placed the letters "F", "O" and "G" on the board. The ' F' promptly fell off. The programme was going out live and the weathergirl finished by giving a quick summary followed by saying that she was sorry about the 'F' in fog.

A few sideshows drifted through the infield, a Laurel & Hardy act entertained as did a typical 1960s road repair crew comprising three Irish navvies with their Mini pick up full of tarmac, shovels and road signs who stopped now and then to put up their barriers, decant their equipment, sit on their makeshift seats and drink mugs of tea whilst passing reasonably polite comments to passers by.

The team's driver had qualified on pole position for the first race, not unexpectedly, he was always quick around Goodwood as was his father before him in the same car. At the end of the first lap, he had a comfortable lead, which he never lost and finally stomped over the finishing line for another Goodwood victory. He extricated himself from the car to accept the applause from the grandstand and surrounding onlookers as Max helped the team push the car back to the paddock, another car well prepared and a race well won.

Apart from standing around and looking the part, if that was possible, Max's weekend was done. There was still the packing away, the loading of the trailers and the decamping of the motor home, but that would all be done later. For now, Max could indulge himself in the various goings on. Race two had just started so the call had already gone out for all race three competitors to make their way to the assembly area.

Max strolled down to the waiting cars and leant against the white picket fencing, the trees providing some welcome shade in what was an uncharacteristically sweltering hot weekend. He folded his arms and looked around; there had to be forty million pounds worth of cars going out to that grid, he thought. Ten feet from him the red Ferrari 250 Testa Rossa sat awaiting its 'Honda advert' owner driver. Donald Key and his son Julian stood with two company mechanics. The whole assembly area was a hive of activity, beautiful people with beautiful cars, the sounds of camera motor winds and distant tannoy commentary echoing all about. It was all big hats, lipstick and sunglasses wrapped in every sensual branded style mixed with the fragrant wafts of Castrol R. *Is there anything better*, Max thought.

His mobile phone rang, it was who he had expected. 'Cream pin striped suit with a cream Panama hat behind the Testa Rossa on the right hand side,' that's all he said and cut the connection. Max put his hands in his pockets.

There was a throbbing roar from the distinctive twittering exhaust as a BSA Rocket Gold Star rolled slowly into the assembly area and parked in front of the red car. The crowds moved aside as the period uniformed policeman complete with off white helmet and huge black leather gauntlet gloves, killed the engine, pushed out the side stand and stepped off the iconic machine. He had quite an audience, as if it were another of the amusing sideshows. He pulled off his gloves one finger at a time deliberating as he did so, and placed them neatly on the seat of the bike and then walked slowly but surely up to Donald Key never once losing his gaze. Rupert Davis was sniggering at his side in anticipation of a joke of some kind.

Don was smiling as the peeler edged closer and asked, 'Donald Key?'

People nearby could hear, but others were watching.

'Yes, that's me.'

The copper reached into his inside breast pocket and pulled out a pale coloured document and handed it to Key.

Key looked at the front cover, his face dropped, realising quickly what it was and just as quickly tucked the High Court Writ into his pocket before all his admirers had chance to see what it was. They didn't need to know, Key's reaction said it all. Whatever it was, it wasn't good and he wasn't smiling. Max watched intently for a few moments whilst Key gathered himself up.. One down three to go.

'And, Rupert Davis, I presume?'

'Yes,' he replied with a beaming smile, eager not to be left out of the source of amusement and not knowing what Key had been given. He was, and they were at top of that snow peaked mountain together, he had to be included. Both of them were revelling in the spotlight, they were big men in a small

517

world. The man in the blue uniform and the three stripes on his sleeves turned his look to Davis and handed him a different document. Davis opened it like a child opening a Christmas present. His face hardened, his cheeks reddened; he was not pleased, Max thought. It was a County Court summons. The peeler had fired up and gone.

Key looked at Davis and said nothing, but both men had a good idea of what the other one had received. It wasn't the content of the documents, it was the embarrassment it caused in front of the assembled crowd that was the real hurt. The knowledge that other people knew that something wasn't quite right about them. They'd been hit in their own back garden.

Max took a seat on a green and white striped deck chair on the grass, overlooking the airfield and ordered a Pimms. *Very relaxing*, he thought, watching the fashion strut by. It was Royal Ascot with more horsepower, a heady mix of avgas and Chanel No. 5, the best garden party on Earth. He stayed a while and soaked up the moment ready for his next move.

He walked back to the pits, briefly stopping to talk to a friend on the way, then showed his pit pass at the security gate entering the paddock, ahead of him were more than £100 million pounds worth of historic sports racing cars taking refuge under the open wooden shelters. He stopped at the original blue Ecurie Ecosse transporter scrutinising the Jaguar D Type parked behind when his mobile rang again. He answered it, the same voice said, 'I'm by your mates Maserati 4CL, they're all here.'

'Do you know who's who?' Max replied.

'No, but I've got a plan.'

'Okay, you know what you're doing.'

Six smartly dressed men had gathered around the wonderfully original dark red 1936 Maserati Formula One grand prix car whilst their informal guide showed them around the paddock. They were special guests of Ferrari UK, each of them being the owner or CEO of one of the official UK Ferrari franchised dealers. The old fashioned copper now with his beat helmet on made his way between the six men and their host giving a wry smile to the guide before removing a pen and paper from his top left hand jacket pocket and promptly addressed the men stood in front of him. It was all part of the atmosphere, they thought, the fun and the frivolity; it was what made the event so special.

'Name?' he asked, looking at the first man on the left.

'Stephen Turton,' came the reply. It wasn't him, he thought. He looked up at the next man and repeated the same question down the line to the end. His man was number four. Inwardly he was smiling to himself as he was able to seemingly completely control these captains of industry. He tapped his pen on his pad, and scanned up and down the line, his prey tittering like a row of excited school girls and then as he put his hand on John Hutching's right shoulder, he said, 'I'm sorry, you're nicked son,' and passed him the paperwork. They all laughed as Hutchings nonchalantly opened the folded A4 sheets inquisitively thinking, these organisers think of everything. Hutchings held the document out in front of him whilst he reached for his spectacles. The others could see exactly what it was, he focussed on the wording of the document, folded it up and placed it in his pocket, his half hearted pretend smile barely concealing his embarrassment. The High Court Writ against Isca Ferrari had been properly served and the peeler had disappeared.

ASHBUTON, 2006

Easton picked up the phone, he was at home and it was late on a Saturday afternoon.

'Hello, darling, mum here, how are you?' she asked.

'Great, thanks, mum, you all right?'

'Yes, dear. The reason I'm calling is that Marjorie has been around this afternoon for a pot of tea and err, well, she's told me in the strictest confidence of course that Father Abbot's been arrested. It's not that I doubt her, but do you know if it's true?'

'Yes, it is.'

'Well, Leo, what's going on? It's like a witch hunt.'

'Yes, I know. It's dreadful. I know who's running the investigation but it's from a different station so it's difficult to know what they've got.'

'We all know Edmund wouldn't be involved in this sort of thing. He's a nice man. He's been a family friend since before you were born.'

'Yes, I know. I find it hard to believe myself. The thing is, they must have something.'

'Look Leo, Edmund would not have done anything like this. He's the abbot for goodness sake. He's devoted his life to God, the church and people like you and me. It's very wrong. Your father's completely beside himself. You know how well they get on. It's making the police force look very stupid. Everyone knows the abbot isn't that kind of person. If this gets out, the whole community is going to be devastated,' she said despondently.

Easton took a long sigh. He knew what his mother was saying was right but he felt powerless to do anything. He couldn't interfere with another man's investigation and it wouldn't be right to suggest another line of enquiry. As far as he could see, he couldn't influence Tyler, but if he had an opportunity, he'd try.

'Mum, I'll see what I can do. I'm not promising anything, but I will try. I promise you that.'

'Okay, darling, thank you. Your father will be pleased,' she replied expectantly.

Easton put down the phone and thought about the abbot's position. He knew Tyler wouldn't have acted on such a high profile arrest unless he was certain of his facts. Whatever Tyler had, it would be good. He toyed with the idea of calling him on some other pretence but thought better of it. Maybe another visit, he wasn't sure. He had time, that was certain, the wheels of justice always turn slowly.

NEWTON ABBOT, JANUARY 2008

Steve Majendie hadn't spoken to Max for more than four years but he still recognised the telephone number when it flashed up on his mobile.

'Hey, Max, fancy you calling me. I was only talking about you the other day. How's it going?'

'Yes, fine thank you. Are you keeping well?'

'Yeah. I'm now officially a geezer. You know, I'm sixty years old, how about that?'

'Well, there's plenty of gas left in the tank, I'm sure.'

'I hope so. Anyhow, what can I do for you?' Steve asked.

'I'm looking for a nice 72 911 RS preferably in white. If

it's got some competition history, all the better, but it's not absolutely necessary. It must be a proper car though.'

'Okay, that's good. I know of a nice car and it's a white one with blue wheel centres, sevens and eights and blue Carrera script. I'll get you some details and call you back in ten minutes.'

'Yes, that would be good. If it's the right thing, I can make a decision quite quickly, so we could get it sorted today.'

'Right, I'll call you shortly,' Steve replied.

Max put down the phone and looked at his reference book on the Porsche 911 and flicked through to the chapter on Carrera RS models. He satisfied himself as to the many details he needed to ask Steve and busily read through the production numbers and specifications.

Sure enough, Steve called back almost on the dot, ten minutes later.

'Hi Steve,' Max answered.

'Yeah, Max, it is for sale. It's a November 1972 Porsche 911 Carrera RS 2.7 in grand prix white with blue script. Interior is black and it has a full bolt in cage, which can be removed if needed. It's a Euro spec car not US, so it was a personal import. The engine and gearbox have recently been fully rebuilt at a cost of nearly $40,000 and it's only done one hours engine running since. It's a comp car and it's won at Daytona, Sebring, Laguna Seca and it's currently owned by a celebrity racer.

'Max it's got the best of everything on it. You don't need to worry. You know how I describe these things. It's right on the money as well. You can buy it for $130,000 all up including me.'

Max thought about it. Every car that Steve had sold him had been right, so there was no need to go into the fine details. He just asked for the chassis number which he checked off and then made Steve an offer of $110,000.

'Sorry, Max, can't do that, but if you can go to $120,000 then we've got a deal.'

'If you can let me have it for $120,000 including delivering it to Chicago, then I'll run with that.'

'The problem I always have with you is that I never make any money,' he said jokingly. What he meant was that he never made as much as he would have liked. Steve agreed to send all the details by email along with copy documents and lots of photographs so that Max would have the full picture. They chatted a while.

'Who's the celebrity?' Max asked. It wasn't important, but it would add a bit of interest.

'Oh, it's a guy called J. Geils. You're probably too young to remember him.'

'Do you mean J. Geils as in the J. Geils Band, My Girlfriend is a Centrefold?'

'Yes, that's him.'

'Yeah, I remember him. I think he was singing that song in '77. I was working in a beach hut kiosk at the time. Crikey, that's brought back some memories. Nice ones as well'

'He does a bit of racing over here and the car is absolutely right. It's been run by the right people, so you've got yourself a good car.'

'Good,' Max replied.

'Hey, do you see anything of Graham Lord?'

'God, no. I haven't spoken to Graham since all that nonsense with Donald Key.'

'No, neither have I. He caused me a lot of problems and my customer a lot of money.'

'How come?'

'Oh, it's a long story.'

'They always are,' said Max.

'Basically, Graham Lord sold me a Jaguar XJR15 which I sold on to a very good customer of mine. He was and still is a proper Jaguar collector. I still deal with him, but it caused a lot of aggravation at the time. We bought the car as a non runner and there was supposed to be a spares package that went with it.'

Max thought, *This sounds interesting and very familiar.* He needed to only ask one question.

'Who's car was it?'

'It was Matt Aitken's car,' Steve replied.

'The bastard,' Max said angrily.

'Who, Aitken?'

'No, not Aitken, Graham Lord.'

'Why?'

'I found that car and I offered it to Graham and he told me that he had a Jaguar collector customer for it. The deal at the time was basically a 50/50 commission on the profit. We'd share it equally. If I remember correctly, I could have bought it for £80,000 ish and that was negotiable.'

'Well, we paid double that!'

'You're joking?'

522

'No, not at all.'

'You obviously got the car?'

'Oh yes, that was okay, but he agreed to sell us a spares package, which included an engine management system and a load of other parts and that was another £25,000. We sent the money and we've never received the parts. We've rung him and written to him too many times to mention and he's basically stung us for the money.'

'I'm sorry to hear that Steve, but obviously he's caught me as well. He should have paid me £40–50,000 on that basis. I wish I'd known back then. I could have done with the money.'

'Yeah, so do I.'

'I think I know where the parts were coming from because I remember speaking to Graham at the time. If I remember correctly, it was a guy living in Scotland, I think he had an orange McLaren F1 and he was a friend of Rupert Davis.' Steve knew Davis but he'd never done any business with him.

'What's your customer done about it?'

'Nothing, for the moment, he's let it go and Lord has got away with it.'

'Well, he won't forever. It's bound to come back around.'

SECTION FOUR

NEWTON ABBOT, NOVEMBER 2006

They finished their phone call with Max agreeing to buy the Porsche and sorting out the payment whilst Steve organised the transport to Chicago. It would be several months before Max would have the car in the UK, but by that time, he had other more worrying developments on his mind.

Max listened to the distinct tones of the continental telephone ringing in the earpiece whilst he waited for Jacques to pick up.

'Hi, it's Max. I've just received the report from the specialist and it's all okay. We have nothing to worry about. The man has thoroughly inspected it, and everything Olivier said was exactly right.

'What happens now?' Jacques asked.

'Well, I need to make a few phone calls and see what sort of reaction I get.'

'Okay, that sounds good. You know who to speak to?'

'Yes, I've been thinking about that for a long time.'

'And what sort of reaction do you think you'll get?' asked Jacques.

'I don't know for sure. If I can get through to the main man and get the chance to describe the car, then that will be our best shot. I can but try.'

'Okay, well you know what you're doing, so I'll leave you to it. I'll let Olivier know you called.'

'As soon as I hear anything positive, I'll call you.'

Max put down the phone, he couldn't tell Jacques everything, it would take too long and probably confuse him, but basically Max knew someone close to the potential buyer. If he could convince him, then either Max would speak to the buyer or the middle man would.

Three hours had passed since the conversation with Jacques, when Max picked up the phone and dialled the US number, it rang seven times before Maurice answered.

'Hi, it's Max Reed.'

'Oh, hello Max, how are you?'

'Fine thanks.'

'How's the family?'

'Yes, great, and you?'

'All's well.'

'Good.'

'What can I do for you?' asked Maurice.

Max explained in detail what he had, how he came upon it, where it was located and the results of Sander's report. Maurice was stunned.

'I can't believe you've got that.'

'Well, I have,' said Max, 'and it's sitting here in my garage awaiting a new excited owner.'

'I know the man for the car.'

'I thought you did,' Max replied.

'What can you let me have? I am going to need some pictures, history and a copy of Sander's report. Can you do that?'

'Yes, that's possible. What about confidentiality?'

'I'll get an agreement over to you on the email to cover that,' said Maurice adding, 'I have one man in mind for the car, whom I'm guessing you already know.'

'Yes.'

'Okay, crunch time. What do you want for it?'

'As much as I can get.'

'Well that's obvious, but where do you see its value?'

'Sanders says between one and one and a half million pounds.'

After a short pause, he answered, 'Yes, he's probably right. I'll have to pitch it at the right price. I wouldn't want to frighten them off.'

'How would you want paying?'

'I would need to speak to my partner first but if we agree an offer price, then we can also agree a fixed commission fee, and take it from there. What's your email address?'

Max gave Maurice all the details he needed so that in the first instance the confidentiality paperwork would be sent over. On receipt of that, Max would then fire off all the info Maurice wanted in order for him to approach the potential buyer. It was all very simple which was how Max wanted it. He'd known Maurice for many years, not as close friends, but well enough to know that he could trust him and that's what he needed now above all else. He would probably only ever get one chance of selling such a 'fantastic find', and he didn't want it to be messed up by some half wit.

Max put down the phone, he had been talking with Maurice for over half an hour. He felt comfortable, and now it was down to some one else's efforts. All he could do for now was sit and wait. How long? He didn't know. In the scheme of things it didn't matter either. Yes, he could do with the money, as could Olivier and Jacques, but it was a rising market. Within reason, and all other things being equal, the longer it took, the more they would get for the car. It had taken nearly three years to get to this juncture, a little while longer was not going to be a problem.

TORQUAY, JUNE 2006

The three months had quickly passed since Max's first interview with the police. Leo Easton's interview had been worrying, not least because of his ineptitude, thought Max, but now he was answering bail and was expecting another assault on his memory banks. It didn't happen. Bail was extended another three months whilst further enquiries were being made. Max couldn't believe it. *What enquiries*, he thought. He was only selling cars and bikes. What more could they be investigating? he said to himself. Max's solicitor couldn't offer any advice. It just seemed such a complete waste of time. Of course, there was a positive side and that was that the police clearly didn't have enough to press charges. Nonetheless, the anxiety would continue.

Easton knew that Max was answering bail that day, but he wasn't on hand to deal with it in person. He was wading through the thousands of sheets of company paperwork that he'd seized from Velodrome's liquidator, but he couldn't find enough to bring any charges. The clear fact was that Max hadn't been fraudulently trading. There was no evidence of it. He couldn't find anything within all the paperwork that suggested a fraud, but he kept looking. That was what he was being paid to do. That was his job. He had people to answer to and in this case, it wasn't just his senior commanding officer, it was further up the line. He was under pressure to find something one way or another.

Easton had another three months before Max would answer bail and in that time, he wanted to gather up as much dirt as possible to throw at him and see if anything stuck in his next interview. He was seriously running out of ideas, but that wouldn't stop him. He was going to get his man whatever it took.

NEWTON ABBOT, JANUARY 2006

Max stood by the back door for a while feeling the early morning warmth of the sun on his body, then walked along the path to his office, unlocked the door and walked in switching on the overhead light and the computer at the same time. The familiar sound of the Microsoft welcome prompted him to click onto Outlook Express and see if there were any messages for him. He tapped his fingers on the desk as he waited for the inbox to download. Six messages, he read them. No, I don't want a bigger penis. Delete that. No, not interested in another watch. Delete that. No, can't be bothered with just another survey. Delete that. eBay, your watched item is finishing. No. Delete that. Friends Reunited, you have a message. Come back to that in a moment, and lastly a current stock list from Josef. *I'll keep that*, he thought.

He clicked onto the Friends Reunited email and followed the links to the site. He read, 'You have a personal message under the Buck House Preparatory School banner and opened the message at the prompt.

'If you attended Buck House Preparatory School between the years 1968 to 1987, we would like to hear from you. We will be contacting every pupil in due course in relation to an ongoing investigation and would appreciate your assistance. Please telephone DC Andrew Tyler on the following number at Devon & Cornwall Police.

Max read the message again. He knew what it would be about, but he didn't really want to get involved. He had enough problems of his own with the police, he didn't want to add to someone else's. He closed the Friends Reunited site, switched off the computer and thought no more about it until he received a call a few weeks later from Andrew Tyler. He announced himself and explained loosely what he was investigating and asked if Max would be prepared to help. The fact was that he didn't want to, he didn't want to get involved and he told Tyler just that.

If nothing else, Tyler was persistent and he rang again a week later and said to Max, 'If this was happening to one of your children, you would want to stop it wouldn't you?'

Max agreed, 'Of course,' he said.

'Well, we can't stop it, unless we get help from people like you. You were there, you know what was going on and it shouldn't have happened, but it did. Your parents put you in a school with people they thought they could trust and you know that some of them couldn't be trusted, don't you?'

Max said nothing. Tyler was just supposing. He didn't know whether Max knew anything at all, he was just trying his luck. The comment about Max's own children struck a nerve with him. He was teetering on the edge of saying something, when Tyler sensed an opportunity.

'Max, I only need half an hour of your time. I just need to ask you a few questions that's all. Nothing too demanding. I need to know some information about a few of your old teachers that's all. It won't take long and then you can be on your way. I can go to you or you can come to us, we have a safe house in Powderham Road.'

Max thought about it. If it only took half an hour and he could be of some help, then maybe he should go. On the other hand, his experience of the police with Leo Easton was so negative that he didn't know whether he wanted to help. Ultimately, Tyler convinced Max to go along to the safe house and have a chat, not a formal interview, just an open unrecorded conversation with Tyler and one of his colleagues present. It was the least he could do.

It was proving extremely difficult for Tyler to ask potential witnesses to step forward. It was very sensitive and it was a long time ago. A lot of water had passed under the bridge. A lot of memories had been wiped and now there seemed little point in dragging up the past. Why? What was the point? They were questions most people would ask if prompted and understandably they'd rather forget. There was, of course, the other factor which was that the Catholics, the church, call it what you like, they had closed ranks and they were going to stick together, say nothing and hope it would go away, brush it under the carpet, like they had done on numerous occasions before, the world over, down the centuries.

HMP LEYHIL, SEPTEMBER 2008

He was a fairly normal looking guy, but there was something different about him, Max thought. He didn't know quite what it was, but he stood out as being slightly at odds. Maybe it was the woollen black scarf. Why would anyone wear a scarf in September, Max asked himself? He continued looking at the man who was quiet, reserved, didn't look up much and didn't ask or answer any questions. He was in his early fifties, probably five feet ten inches and weighed around twelve to twelve and a half stone. Max supposed he'd be described as medium build with dark hair receding somewhat.

Max had never spoken to the man, so he didn't know what he had done or how long he was in for. What he did know was that statistically there was a more than fifty per cent chance he was a sex offender. Max's mind flicked between the music teacher's ramblings and the man sat opposite him. He was wearing his own clothes, not prison issue, which meant he was particular and he didn't mind standing out. Okay, the clothes were a dreary grey but they were his own and that said something. Max was sure the campus psychiatrists would make something of that. If he had to put money on it, Max would say the man was definitely a sex offender.

All day Thursday each week at Leyhill, Max was on a music course. It was a chance to get away from the laundry, have a break from the drudgery and do something different. In the mornings, Kat would teach theory and then the afternoons were given over to practical. It worked well. Max could play a bit of piano or listen to others gigging in the hall as a full band, usually playing heavy metal with out of tune vocals. At times, it was quite funny and it helped Max take his mind off the thought of the remaining days. Whilst his head was occupied with being taught music, he wasn't thinking about his home life. When he was on his own, it was all he thought about. The television or the radio would distract him, but then suddenly he'd get a reality check and look around him and see where he was and why he was there.

At eleven thirty, he returned to his room for the eleven

forty-five morning tally. He opened his door and noticed some mail on the bed. A letter from Annabel, another from Jo and Duncan, and confirmation of his upgraded status to Enhanced prisoner. It didn't mean a lot, a bit more personal money to spend on the weekly canteen and perhaps a little more status with the psychoanalysts at CMU. It was nothing really, but Max was playing the game, towing the line, getting everything right so that when the time came for him to go, nothing was going to stand in his way. He wanted to be a model prisoner, keep his head down, stay out of trouble, do his bird and go.

He stood at his door waiting for the PO to walk the corridor and check off the tally. The Welsh guy diagonally opposite to Max's room was standing in the doorway of the smackhead next door in ASL03. Max looked at him as he leant backwards and said, 'You wanna watch it mate, you're making enemies.'

'Oh yeah, first I've heard of it,' Max replied.

'Don't get funny mate, I'm telling you, you're making enemies.'

Max looked at him. Andy was a smackhead too but he never troubled Max. He never had a lot to say for himself and Max hadn't really spoken to him either, so he was surprised that he was now teaming up with the guy next door. Max ignored him for that moment, he had no reason to get involved in a confrontation, but he did need to handle himself properly. He didn't want to be ridiculed in front of the other prisoners, but there were ways of dealing with it and he needed to think about it if it got worse.

Daft as it may seem, Max was eating more, but losing weight. He was a good stone lighter since his sentence date yet, he had three good meals a day with maybe five or six slices of bread as well. He didn't think it was the running alone as he had done that before he went in, so it had to be that he wasn't grazing so much. The irritation of the lunchtime queue, up back, up back in the line up, watched over by the overweight prison officers was tedious. Three different choices, he went for the chilli, it looked good.

Lunch passed without incident and Max went back to his room, a bit of free time before returning to music at a quarter past one. He realised that he'd left his laundry for collection, so quickly ran off to retrieve his washed clothes and then having deposited them back in his room, he made to return to music.

He'd noticed Andy's door was at a jar as he walked down the corridor coming back from the laundry so as he set off, unexpectedly he knocked on Andy's door. He didn't wait for an answer, he just walked straight in and stood in front of Andy as he sat in his chair alongside his bed below the window.

Andy was early thirties, six feet two, well built, fit and confident with it. Max would be a pushover, if it came to a straight fight.

'Andy, I haven't got a problem with you. I couldn't care less whether you're on this or that. It doesn't interfere with me. You don't cause me any problems. The guy next to me does. He keeps me up all night making a racket being totally inconsiderate to me and anyone else that can hear him and it's not on. I went in there last night and I told him to shut up, so if he's the enemy, I couldn't care less.'

Andy took a slow deep drag on his roll up, remained sat in his chair and looked up saying,

'Look, he says that you've been telling people in the laundry that he's a tosser.'

'Oh, I know who's said that, Phil down the end?'

'Yeah, that's him.'

'And what? He's overheard or supposedly overheard something I've said and he's told him.'

'Yeah, something like that,' Andy replied.

'Andy, I can tell you that I didn't call him a tosser.'

'Well, that's what they're saying.'

'I said he was a fucking tosser because he is.'

Andy snorted and smiled and then put his hand out to shake Max's hand. 'You haven't got a problem with me lad,' he said in his Welsh valley accent and they laughed. Max knew it was always better to confront than be confronted and effectively he had knocked out one of his neighbour's allies. In the scheme of prison life, it was a minor skirmish, but it was important for Max to make sure that his neighbour didn't have the support of others around him. If Max could get them onto his side, then sorting him out would be easier.

Andy had been in for little over four years and had a four year old daughter he'd never seen. Each Christmas had come and gone and he wasn't there for her. He was a broken man. A stupid, senseless crime, committed whilst he was high on crack cocaine had deprived him of one of life's great gifts and he knew it. He needed some money and violently robbed a Spar store getting away with about four hundred pounds to feed the next jab, but got caught. He was due for release six weeks after Max, provided he stayed clean.

NEWTON ABBOT, JULY 2006

The interview with Tyler had been pretty harrowing for Max, it brought back memories of a time he would rather forget and it had made him feel uneasy. He didn't need to say anything, but the manner in which Tyler had kicked off the questions clearly put the onus on Max to come forward as a decent citizen and prevent similar things happening again. Tyler had said right from the start that, 'You wouldn't want this to happen to your children would you?' It was a 'no brainer' answer to respond.

Max had agreed to meet Tyler at the so called 'safe house' in Powderham Road as it was a little more friendly than the police station at Newton Abbot. It was embarrassing enough for Max to talk to anyone about it, let alone do it in front of an audience of Britain's finest loose tongued, investigative minds, but he'd agreed and was happy to answer the questions, get it done, walk away and store it back in the lost memory banks of his mind.

The questioning was informal as Max had sat on a comfortable settee in the lounge. Tyler and his colleague sat opposite in armchairs.

'We just need to know what was going on at Buck House when you were there, that's all,' asked Tyler.

'Anything in particular?' Max replied with a question.

'Well, what can you tell me about Father Benjamin?'

'I didn't have a lot to do with Benjamin, he was Brother Benjamin back then and I think he taught geography as I remember. I don't think he was at the school for very long when I was there. We maybe only crossed over for about a year or two.'

'Did he take you for any other lessons?'

'Not that I remember. He possibly took us for sport, but not as the main man, that was Father Gabriel, so he may have been a support master on the sport side. As I say, I didn't have a lot to do with him.'

'Why? Because you didn't like him?'

535

'No, not at all. He was a nice chap. He was young in his twenties at the time and maybe a little more approachable than some of the other masters. He wasn't overly strict, so no it wasn't that I didn't like him, it was just that I didn't come into contact with him that much.'

'What about other boys? Did they like him?'

'I can only speak for myself when I say that I liked him, but I can't remember other boys saying they didn't like him. There certainly were masters who were not liked, but Benjamin wasn't one of them.'

'Were you aware of any abuse of other boys in the school by Benjamin?'

'No, I wasn't aware of that and if it had been happening, I'm sure I would have known, especially towards the end of my days at Buck House.'

'Why?'

'Well, as you get older, you become more knowing and aware of what is going on around you. You ask more questions and have more sensible conversations. It's a growing up thing.'

'Would it surprise you that we have been approached by several former pupils of the school with allegations of abuse to children over a long period?'

'No.'

'Why?'

'Because I knew it went on. Everyone at the school knew that it went on. It was an accepted part of school life. Nobody talked about it except in jest, but we knew who was that way inclined.'

'But you said earlier that you were unaware of any abuse by Father Benjamin.'

'That's right, I didn't know that he was like that. He certainly didn't make it obvious to me at the time, maybe he became that way after I left, I don't know.'

'Okay, so you know that there was abuse going on, but you weren't aware that Benjamin was involved, so it begs the question, who was?'

Max thought for a while before answering the question. If they knew that there was abuse at the school, then they must have some evidence, but was that evidence solely relating to Benjamin or did they have other potential suspects too; he asked himself. What he didn't want to do was drop someone in it by responding quickly without any thought. It would be better if the

536

police gave him a bit more information first.

'You most likely already know the answer to that question, don't you?'

'Well, we're asking you.'

'Okay, but I'm here of my own free will encouraged by you to come forward and help. If you have suspects then I will confirm my knowledge of them, but I'm not prepared to point the finger. That's not what I'm here for. I'll help you, but I don't want to start accusations.'

'Very well. You were at the school from 1967 to 1974?'

'Yes, that's right.'

'You're not a Roman Catholic though are you?'

'No, I was one of maybe five children who were Church of England.'

'And you were a boarder?'

'Yes, both in dormitories in the main building with Father Bennett as the housemaster at the time and then afterwards at 'Avila' with Father Augustine.'

'What was "Avila"?'

'It was the dormitory house up the road from the abbey. It was generally called the "Lobster Pot".'

'Ah right, that fits together. We've had witnesses mention the Lobster Pot but not Avila, but obviously it's one and the same.'

'Yes, that's right.'

'So was there any abuse going on under the housemaster, Father Bennett, in the main building?'

'Not as far as I am aware. No, I think he was having it off with the matron,' Max laughed.

'So, it was all going on up at the Lobster Pot?'

'There was certainly some bad things happening there on occasion, yes.'

'And it was Father Augustine that was responsible for some of those bad things.'

'Yes, it was.'

'Would you like to tell us, what sort of things? I know this might be difficult so take your time.'

'It's not difficult, it's simple. Father Augustine or Guss as he was known, used to go into the shower rooms when we were naked and take photographs of us all. He would do it quite regularly. At the time, we thought nothing of it, but now, you'd have to ask the question why? He used to tell us that he had his own dark room and could develop the pictures himself. Now we know why, but at the time, it just seemed like a master pursuing his own interests, which of course he was, but not in the manner we were thinking.'

'How often did he take the photos?'

'It was many times, but I can't remember numbers.'

'Do you know what he did with the pictures?'

'No, but I can guess.'

'Yes, I think we all can. Was Father Augustine responsible for any other abuse?'

'No, I don't think so, but who knows, I don't. He was very strict and would whack us six of the best fairly often, but nothing else. The photograph business became common knowledge because one of the boy's parents who was a successful race horse trainer, in fact, Grand National winner, found out from him that Guss was taking pictures in the showers. There was a bit of a storm and Guss was removed from the Lobster Pot, but it didn't last because as soon as the storm had passed through, Guss was back in charge up there. If the headmaster didn't know what was going on beforehand, then he certainly did after that episode and really he had a duty of care to look after the children which clearly he neglected. I think he had an opportunity at that point to stop the rot, but he didn't and that was quite a failing.'

'What about Stromberg? Were you at the Lobster Pot at the same time as him?'

'Yes, I was. His room was directly opposite mine across the landing.'

'Were you aware of anything untoward about him?'

'Not at Buck House, but there was some talk of something untoward happening when he was a music teacher in Stockholm. I can't say I knew very much about him. He was a good teacher. Music at the school had never been so good as it was when Stromberg was there. He was a very clever guy. He played numerous instruments and spoke many languages fluently. As I remember he was also a keen radio ham. I liked him, he was interesting with all his travels and adventures.

'Are there any other masters we should be asking you about?'

'As I said before, you tell me?'

'What about Father Abbot?'

'I never knew him. I don't think I ever met him. I saw

him take the Sunday Mass on occasion, but I had no dealings or cause to come into contact with him.'

'But he taught you in the school.'

'No he didn't. As far as I know, he very rarely came to the school.'

'Father Abbot?' Tyler turned to his colleague with a rather quizzical glance.

'Yes, he wasn't a teacher, at least he certainly wasn't at the time I was there.'

'Father Abbot is . . .' Tyler was confused, he was gathering himself up. He wasn't expecting Max's response to be so dismissive.'

'Ah, no, no, no,' Tyler continued, looking at his notes. 'Father Abbot would have been Father Prior or as such Father Edmund back then. He's Father Abbot now, but at the time you were at school he would have been Father Prior. What about him? Were you aware of any abuse that he was doing to children?'

'Yes, yes I was.' Max took a breath and took some time before he continued, 'Yes, I was aware that he was abusing boys. If that's what you want to call it. He was doing it all the time that I was there. Of course, we wouldn't have called it abuse at the time and we wouldn't have mentioned it to our parents. Not because we didn't want to, but because it wasn't important. We probably had better things on our minds than telling tales.'

'Do you know the extent of the abuse by Father Prior?'

'What, how many boys? No.'

'No, do you know exactly what he did?'

'Yes, I did in some instances.'

Max sat through the interview for more than three hours and told Tyler exactly what he'd seen. It wasn't good, in fact it was pretty damming. What Max had said was an almost carbon copy of the statement made by one of the complainants and it was supported by numerous other witnesses having given similar accounts, all of whom Max hadn't spoken to in more than thirty years. Max had witnessed, quite by accident an incident carried out by Father Prior on one of the complainants and it was this information that Tyler wanted. Yes, he wanted to know about, Guss, Stromberg and the rest but Max's eye witness account of events relating to one of the complainants was exactly the same.

Tyler looked at Max and then again at his colleague and said, 'I'm sorry to have to put you through all this, but can you

539

remember who it was that Father Edmund was abusing?'

'Yes, I can,' Max replied and gave him the name.

It was the complainant. Tyler was satisfied that Max's version of events was enough to charge Father Prior, although he didn't say anything at the time. All the witnesses interviewed up to that point by Tyler had confirmed that there was *widespread* abuse at the school, but only Max had witnessed what was going on that summer's evening at the Lobster Pot. It was only the three of them that would be able to testify those happenings.

'Would you mind giving a statement to that effect?' Tyler asked.

'Well, yes, I haven't got a problem with that,' Max replied not realising at the time that by doing so he was in fact signing away his own destiny. It was a simple honest decision but the implications of it were to be massively disruptive and Max would not have thought at the time how damaging it was going to be for his life too. If he had known what the future had in store, then he would not have agreed to Tyler's interview let alone a statement. What was to come would be shattering and beyond belief as someone else was then able to capitalise on Max's helping hand.

Tyler wrote out the statement based on the facts Max had given. He didn't seem to be a bad bloke, Max thought; too nice to be a policeman. He knew that Max was being investigated by the Ashburton office but he only mentioned it once in passing and never said anything more about it. He placed the pages of the handwritten statement on the glass table facing Max and asked him to sign at various points. It was done.

The fresh breeze on Max's cheeks cooled him as he walked home from Powderham Road, he neither felt good or bad about what he'd just done. It was just a statement of fact about happenings a long time ago. No more, no less.

SLOUGH, SEPTEMBER 2009

Donald Key shuffled around his office, he had plenty to do, but he was deep in thought. He went over to the window and looked outside not seeing anything. He was troubled. The document that had been given to him at Goodwood was a worry. It wasn't that it was just another legal document, that could be

540

dealt with at arms length by a professional. No it wasn't that, it was the accompanying paperwork and that Max Reed was not going to let it go. He wasn't going to simply shut up shop and let sleeping dogs lie.

Don thought about Rupert Davis and the document that he'd received at the same time. Clearly, they had to be linked. Why did Davis get something as well, Don kept asking himself. He didn't want to ring Rupert, or at least not at that moment, but he definitely wanted to know what was in Davis's paperwork. There was a whisper too that someone from Ferrari had also been given some paperwork in much the same way and from the account he'd been given, by the same policeman. He hadn't recognised the man dressed up in the bobby's uniform. Was he the man or just the messenger? He didn't know, but what he did know was that whoever it was, he knew a lot. He knew too much and that was dangerous. Was it going to stop at just that or would there be more and what did the guy want? He pulled the paperwork from the top drawer of his desk and read it again for the umpteenth time. It was accurate and it was true but more than fifteen years had passed since his involvement so what good would it do anyone now? He walked over to the window overlooking the workshops and wondered if there was someone there before him, the enemy within, someone in his own camp torturing him this way. He didn't think so, but he would keep an open mind.

A hundred miles away on a leafy road just off the M3, Rupert Davis was surveying his stock neatly parked in parallel diagonal lines under the chicken shed roofs. He was less worried than Donald Key, but he couldn't say he wasn't concerned. He'd seen the look on Key's face when he'd realised what had been handed to him and judging by his reaction it didn't look good. Whatever it was that Don had, it couldn't have been the same as Rupert's papers, unless Don had totally over reacted, which he didn't think was the case. As far as Rupert was concerned, the papers meant nothing but why someone would go to the lengths they had to serve the papers baffled him and above all else it was *that* question which was repeatedly running through his mind.

Seventy-five miles north east of Davis, Graham Lord was also pondering over the contents of his Goodwood envelope. The copper had found him leaning over the pit wall when he had said, ' Mr. Lord ?'

'Yes, why ?'

'Mr. Graham Lord ?'

' Yes, that's me ' Graham replied.

'I thought it was' came the response and a brown C4 envelope was handed over.

Of the three of them, Graham, Rupert and Don, Graham was probably the most concerned but he didn't show it. He was carrying on as before, telling himself that nothing had happened and that he wasn't in any way to blame. He didn't know who had sent the papers although he thought he had a pretty good idea, but he was wrong. He didn't ask himself the simple question, Why? Why would he do it that way rather than contact him direct? If he had asked himself that question, he might have arrived at a different person.

There was of course a fourth recipient of the paperwork at Goodwood, and that was John Hutchings. He'd felt acutely embarrassed by the episode and kicked himself for not seeing it coming. It wasn't even a bad joke, it was real and in front of onlookers too. Not just a fly in the ointment of what was otherwise a really good weekend. He was completely unaware that there were three others who also received similar documents and in any case that would not have influenced him. Did Hutchings know the other three? No he didn't. He might have come across one of them, but in reality he was far too removed from the shop floor to be involved with the day to day goings on of his business. He had a group of companies to run, the Ferrari franchise was just one of them and not a particularly successful one at that. Had he strolled into his Ferrari dealership and had a casual conversation with his sales manager or just picked up the phone and talked to him direct, he could have asked a few questions that might have generated some answers worthy of concern, but he didn't and that was a mistake.

NEWTON ABBOT, JUNE 2007

Not a day went by when Max thought about the ongoing police investigation. Every idle moment, the thought was never far from his mind, yet outwardly he always remained calm in the hope that it would all go away. It didn't stop his heart missing a beat, the longer it went on, even though he'd become more used to it. He was angry, very angry. He was angry at Easton. He couldn't believe that Easton could be so thick as to not understand what Max had been doing in business. Max had thought that, surely any reasonable person could understand that, but Easton? No, he was looking for an angle, a reason, a crime. A crime that didn't exist.

Max's solicitor called. He was the new specialist criminal lawyer that Bertie had suggested several months before, William Phillipps.

'Hi, Will, how are you?'

'Very well thanks, Max, and you?'

'Bearing up, business is quiet at the moment, but life goes on.'

'Yes, I've had a letter from Easton. They're looking for confirmation of the cars you ordered from Muzi Kweyaka.'

'Okay, what do they want exactly?' Max asked.

'Do you have any copies of order forms or payments, emails, anything really that confirms you ordered them from him?'

'All the paperwork was taken by the liquidator, so no I haven't got anything, they should have it all. Didn't the police say that they'd collected all the company paperwork from the liquidator?'

'Yes,' said Will.

'Well, the police already have the information they are asking for. They probably can't be bothered to look for it. I remember the liquidator came in on the day we closed the limited company, boxed everything up and took it away. I haven't seen any of it since.'

'Did you pay any monies over to Kweyaka, deposits or balances?'

'Yes, I did. We ordered eight cars, four left hand drive and four right hand drive,' Max answered, 'and if I remember rightly, we paid twenty-five thousand pounds as deposits.'

'How did you pay the money?' Will asked.

'I can't remember exactly, it was a long time ago, but it should all be in the files they already have.'

'They're saying that they don't have anything relating to Kweyaka at all,' said Will.

'That can't be right. I was in the office when the liquidator took it all. Kweyaka's information was in there too.'

'Did you keep any records at all?'

'Well, I kept some stuff, but only minor documentation

that's all. Nothing that the police would want. There should be a record of the payments though. As I said, I can't remember exactly how I paid him, but I definitely did, so the money would have come from our current account at the time.'

'Would you have paid the money in one lump sum?'

'No, I think we did it in a number of smaller payments, totalling twenty-five thousand pounds. Actually, now that I'm talking about it, I think we paid some money to him through Western Union. There would be a receipt in the file for that. There could have been others too.'

'Okay, well, I will ask them to look into that. What about those order forms? Are there any copies that you might have of those?'

Max thought about what Will was saying and reading between the lines wondered if there could possibly be some paperwork somewhere. He finished the phone call with Will and thought about their conversation. Easton was checking out the validity of Max's claims that he'd ordered several cars from Kweyaka, but according to Easton there was no record of it. The only trace of a record of the orders would be from money paid over or copies of the order forms, both of which Easton says he doesn't have. Max knew that Kweyaka had been interviewed by the police because Muzi had told him, so as far as Max knew, Muzi had confirmed that he'd agreed to sell the eight cars to Max and that the deposits had been paid. He had no reason to doubt Muzi, but something somewhere didn't seem quite right. Max thought about it for a while and decided he'd give Muzi a call. Max could sound him out, get a feel for where the land lied, but he also remembered that he had kept a file on Muzi. Somewhere amongst the masses of company paperwork, there was indeed, a file on Muzi Kweyaka and Max would need to find it. There was an outside chance that the deposit receipts were in that file along with possibly copies of the order forms. He needed to find them. He could remember what the file looked like, but he couldn't remember what was in it. He hadn't seen it for probably six years or more, but now it was part of a more crucial need. Max was puzzled by Easton's insistence that there was no paperwork, no record of any correspondence or payments to Kweyaka. There would have been several thousand sheets of paper that the liquidator would have boxed up. How could Easton be sure that there was no Kweyaka paperwork, files, receipts, faxes etc? The simple answer was that he hadn't found them, that's of course if he had made the effort to look, but the worrying thought was whether he had found them. Max was being cynical, he thought, surely that wouldn't happen here, in this country in this age, would it?

CONNECTICUT, JUNE 2007

Maurice picked up the phone and dialled Matt's number. It was going to be a crunch call. Matt had been chewing over the idea of the Bugatti for a few days and Maurice had agreed on a day and date for a return call. That time had now arrived as Matt answered the incoming line.

'Hi, Matt, it's Maurice, everything okay with you?'

'Yes, thank you Maurice. I've been thinking long and hard about the car and I think it would fit in well with the rest of our collection, so I would like to take it further. A few things that I would need to cover, price, inspection etc, but I think we have something that we can proceed with.'

'Well, that's great news,' Maurice replied enthusiastically. 'How do you want to move forward?'

'The way I'd like to play it is firstly get a second opinion. I know we have Sander's report, but I think a second report by a leading specialist would doubly confirm Sanders'. There's a guy in France, Pierre Leblanc, an absolute anorak, but I would like to instruct him to check the car. I can sort him from my end, so I would need you to arrange a convenient time with the vendor. Perhaps we could liaise on that one later today. If Leblanc confirms Sander's opinion, then I will fly over to the UK and lay my hand on the car. Somewhere in between all that, we will need to agree a price.'

Maurice could see that Matt was more than just interested. Indeed, he had a sale on his hands and having dealt with Matt before, he knew his client, how he worked and what made him tick. That was what Maurice was being paid to know.

They finished their phone call and Maurice immediately fired off an email to Max informing him of the potential buyer's intentions. When Max read it a few hours later, the joy of the moment was being overshadowed by the misery of the day. Easton was beginning to push harder and it was looking more likely that charges were going to be brought against him.

Max read through the email again. It had taken three years to do the deal and now he was right on the edge of making it happen. He smiled to himself. Despite Easton, he was still able to compose himself, keep moving forward and outwardly appear as normal as possible. He wasn't going to let the bastards grind him down.

He wrote a quick three line reply to Maurice confirming his acceptance to allowing Leblanc to inspect the car as and when, then stood up, stretched his back and walked into the kitchen. Catherine was preparing the evening meal.

'Looks like Maurice has got a buyer for the Bug.'

'Who is it?'

'I don't know, he hasn't said. He's just sent an email asking if it's okay to have the car re-inspected by someone called Leblanc.'

'Who's he?' Catherine asked.

'I don't know. I've never heard of him?' Max replied. 'I guess he's a Bugatti expert, probably from France, with a name like that.'

'It's not a problem is it?'

'No, not at all. If they want a second opinion, it can only be good. Sanders has put his name on it, so nothing has changed. They're paying for the guy to come over and I'll get a copy of the report, so if they don't buy it, at least I will get something out of it. The reality though, is that Leblanc will confirm what Sanders has already said. You can't argue with numbers and age. When he sees it, he will know, just like Sanders when he came here. It's just another hoop to jump through, but it looks like we're getting closer.'

'When is he coming?'

'I don't know yet. Maurice is going to ring later and give me some details. I'll sound him out when he calls.'

'Well, that will be good.'

It was a huge understatement. A deal like the Bugatti was a 'once in a lifetime' opportunity. Two hours later, Maurice called and confirmed the details.

'It's simple Max. If Leblanc accepts Sander's findings and we agree a price, the car is sold.'

Max took a moment to reply to Maurice as he thought about him sat at his desk looking out across a blue sky day from his blue glass office. He had no idea of the agony and the ecstasy that was going through Max's life.

546

'Well done Maurice. Good work.'

'It's all about knowing the right people. It's not done yet, but I can't see that Leblanc will say anything different to Sanders, so hopefully it will just be a formality. My client has asked Leblanc to inspect the car as soon as possible and it's looking like Tuesday or Wednesday next week.'

'That's fine with me,' Max interrupted.

'He's driving over from Reims, so I guess he'll take the tunnel and stay overnight on Monday. I'll give him your telephone numbers and get him to call you direct. He'll probably need a hotel etc.'

'Yeah, I can sort that. Ask him to call me and we can make the arrangements.'

'Okay Max, good to talk to you. The finish line is in sight.'

'Thanks Maurice, speak to you soon.'

Max put down the phone and pondered over events. He would need to speak to Jacques and Olivier, but that was probably best left until after Leblanc had been. He thought about how happy they would all be. He was looking forward to telling them. It was the reward for the trust they'd all shown each other.

Max had done many big deals with some of the world's finest cars, selling them to hugely successful people, but the Bugatti was different, because it was more family in that it was a lifetime association and all the history, good and bad, that went with it. When Sangster sold Max the Ferrari California Spider it was a cold mercenary deal, there was no love there. Sangster was a hard nosed businessman that wanted it all his own way and it was hard work. When the sale went through, it was just another sale, whereas the Bugatti and everyone that were involved would stay a lasting memory. Something warm to look back on.

NEWTON ABBOT, JUNE 2007

Tyler dialled Reed's number to give him the news.

'Hey Max, it's Andy Tyler speaking. I just thought that I'd let you know that we've charged Father Abbot Phillip Millen. Fourteen counts I'm afraid to say.'

'Fourteen counts?' Max repeated.

'Yes, he's been charged. You will be required to come to

547

court at some point to give evidence if, as it would appear, he is going to plead, not guilty. He will appear before the local magistrates in a few days time where he will answer his name and enter a plea before the bench, but it will be directed to Crown Court so that will take a few months. You don't have to do anything. We will write in due course.'

'Okay,' said Max. He couldn't understand how as a man of the cloth, he could plead not guilty. He shrugged and thought about what a mess to get into at his age. Prison is not a place to be in your latter years. Just when you're thinking that it's time to wind down a bit, take a back seat, the last thing you'd want would be to face the anguish behind bars. It wasn't something Max cared to think about. His own anguish was still rolling in. He didn't think he'd be going down that route, but Easton, well he just didn't trust him. And it wasn't just the trust, it was Max's lasting impression that Easton just didn't understand, didn't want to understand and really didn't know what he was talking about.

The news about Father Abbot was now widely known throughout the police force. They all knew, as did Easton, but and it was a big but, Easton knew that he could do something about it. He knew that a little intervention, all very above board could work. It wouldn't get the Abbot off, but it could seriously reduce any sentence if what he knew was true. What he needed to find out first was how accurate his information was and how best he could use it.

Three months earlier, Easton had taken Max's paperwork to the Crown Prosecution Service and it had been knocked back for the second time of asking, not enough evidence. It was 2007 and Easton had been working on the case since 2002. Max had been arrested in 2004, some two years after Easton's first contact with the Velodrome papers being dumped on his desk and here they were five years later and effectively Easton had nothing of any worth that the Crown Prosecution Service would take on.

The reality was that Easton had come too far, the investigation had gone on for too long. If he stopped it now, he'd look more stupid than he already was. But if he pushed on and still couldn't get it past the CPS, then someone from high above was likely to come down on him like a ton of bricks. He had to do something and do it fast.

It was late in the evening, just Easton and Ed McGrain were sat in their office. The rest of the department had gone home. It was warm, a bluebottle was irritatingly conducting bombing runs out of arms reach above Easton's sweaty head. His top button was undone and his tie loosened, but still his neck spilled out over the collar. They were like Tweedle Dee and Tweedle Dum, mirror images of each other. A gathering of potato heads.

'We need to get this sorted,' Easton said quietly, raising his eyebrows at McGrain, 'Know what I mean?'

'Yes, but how?'

'He's relying on certain paperwork, isn't he?'

'Yeah.'

'Well, if it's not there, he can't use it. Look, we both know he's as guilty as fuck, but we can't prove it. We need to lose some paperwork.' McGrain didn't necessarily agree.

'Right, I know what you mean, but why haven't we mentioned this to CPS before? Aren't they going to think there's something odd?'

'I don't think we need to worry about it. They've got loads of cases being put to them every day. They can't remember everything. All we have to do is get it past the post. It's simple, Reed was taking deposits for Ferraris and he's saying that suppliers have let him down. We can't lose Isca Ferrari's contracts, 'cos they've definitely screwed him over.'

'He doesn't know that though, does he?' McGrain interrupted.

'No, he doesn't, but there's too much supporting info on that. I think we could lose the contracts on the cars from the African. That could do it. No contracts, no proof.' Easton opened his eyes wide, clenching his lips tight.

'What about the deposits he paid on them? Twenty-five grand?'

'He paid it through Western Union. He could have paid it to anyone for anything. There's no proof that the African got it.'

'I don't know. It looks pretty thin to me. For what it's worth, I think he's clean. Yeah, he's sailed close to the wind, but I think he's been shafted by all and sundry.'

'Well, that's as maybe, but that ain't going to help us.'

'No, you're right there,' McGrain answered slowly.

'What do you think?'

McGrain shrugged and nodded. 'It's worth a try. Let's see what happens.'

'If CPS go with it, we've done our job. If it gets kicked out at a later date then it's not our fault. We're not going to look like idiots,' stressed Easton.

'Okay, you know best,' McGrain quietly replied. He stood up and pulled his jacket from the back of the chair and threw it over his left shoulder. 'A quick half?'

'Yeah, why not,' Easton smiled as he switched off the fluorescent strip lighting and closed the door behind him. The electric fan still blowing on maximum as it arced from side to side across Easton's office. It didn't matter, he wasn't paying for it.

Unknown to McGrain, Easton had already sent a letter to Reed's solicitor, Will Phillipps asking for copies of the African contracts. He was working on the basis that had McGrain not agreed with his plan, he would simply tell Phillipps that he'd found the paperwork and not to worry. As it was McGrain, was none the wiser. What Easton couldn't have expected though was the knee jerk reaction from Reed which would seal his fate.

LEYHILL, OCTOBER 2008

As the end of September drew nearer, Max could almost see the end of his sentence in sight. If he counted it down in weeks, it was four to go, four weekends, possibly eight visits from Catherine five or six of which could be with the children, twenty nine days, everything was ticking down. He looked at the calendar on the wall, the blocks of strikes through the days of the months darkened the A3 sheet. He'd served a good deal more than he had left to go. He thought about those who had been inside for years and wondered how they would return to any form of normality afterwards. It was going to be difficult enough for Max, but he had no idea how people were going to react to him and how he himself was going to react to them. Was it going to be a question of thinking that people would be saying that he was the guy that did this or that. He went to prison, you know. He must be guilty. His mind was clogged up with all the negatives, but really it was going to be down to him and how he was going to deal with it. What other people thought was up to them. He was going to need to rebuild his life, rebuild his business and try to make the best of what years he had to live. If he let the whole sorry mess get him down, then that was not going to work. He needed to pick himself up off the floor, dust himself down, straighten his cap and walk forward, face it, conquer it and live to fight another day.

In ten minutes, Catherine would be sat opposite him in the visiting hall. His heart missed a beat as he thought about seeing her again but it was tainted by the damage he'd done. Now he realised that keeping all the crap to himself for all those years really hadn't done him any good at all. He confided himself in that he'd behaved like that to protect Catherine from all the day to day worries that were darting in and out of his life, but a problem shared would have been a problem halved. It may have been easier. He didn't know, he couldn't turn back the clock and in any case he had no idea that it would have come to this.

He changed into his visiting clothes and made his way up to the hall, it only took a few minutes and it was a nice day. He faced the usual queue of prisoners awaiting their call forward.

'Reed?' a voice shouted out.

Max stepped forward, handed in his personal belongings sheet, raised his arms out level and stood to one side as he was patted down before being allowed through the door to a smiling Catherine. She looked fantastic, as she always did. It was the highlight to the week. She was on her own this time, the children were at school and it gave them chance to talk. There was no doubting she was really hurt and Max knew that she had every right to be. It wasn't the so called crime, it was that Max hadn't confided in her, he'd taken on the burden himself, he hadn't talked to her about it and she was struggling with that. She knew he wasn't a criminal, he wouldn't have been criminal with any intent. He might have been bloody stupid, cutting a few corners and not paying attention to the detail, but as for doing something deliberate, no, that wasn't Max. If it was, she would have left him and that would have been that.

At the end of the hall on a raised platform sat the Governor Hill in all his glory, stomach hanging out over his trousers lazily slumped in his chair, hardly the image one would expect, but it reflected the regime. He cloned everyone he managed, power crazed slobs dictating to the yobs.

No sooner had the visit began when it was time to say goodbye. Always hard, the sudden change from almost normality

551

when Max could speak to Catherine ignoring his surroundings to the moment she passed through the visitors exit door craning her neck to meet his gaze as long as possible.

'Stay seated in your chairs gentlemen. Put your rubbish in the plastic bags provided and bring it with you to the door when I call your name.'

Governor Hill extracted himself from his chair like Jabba the Hutt in a scene from Star Wars and rippled off the podium to oversee his staff carry out random body searches as the prisoners were called one by one. In stark contrast it was now almost eerily silent. Five minutes earlier, it had been noisy and busy, people moving around, children shouting, a couple sat opposite each other cross armed saying nothing, others in passionate embraces, an old woman shaking her finger at her imprisoned son, a couple to Max's left with the inmate's hand up his girlfriend's short skirt. It was all going on and it was mad, but now it was quiet. The prisoners sat around the room heads down or propping themselves up on their chin. Others looked outside, a distant view but saw nothing. For now, this was reality. Do as you are told and don't step out of line. Say as little as possible, bite your lip, patience. Max's name was called and he made his way to the exit and dumped his rubbish. He went straight through the open doorway and made his way back to his room, nodding at a couple of guys as he passed by the old rattan bobber parked in the flower bed.

Max thought about Catherine. She probably wouldn't have said exactly how she felt. She most likely would not have wanted to upset him. They both had an intolerable situation, but Max knew they'd get through it and come out the other side a lot stronger. They had to, anything else didn't bear thinking about.

Jim walked across, 'Good visit?'

'Yes thanks, you?'

'Yeah. Mother rabbits on and the old man doesn't want to be here, but yeah it was okay.'

'Was that your missus?'

'Yes.'

'Lucky you.'

'Yes, I am,' Max smiled.

'Are you running tonight? I'll come with you if you like?' Jim asked.

'Yeah, okay. Half five, quarter to six, outside 'A' doors.'

'Okay, I'll be there. See you later.'

'Cheers.' After that night's run, Max would have just eleven more runs remaining, sixty six laps, about sixty miles and five thousand calories. By the end of the week it would be nearer forty five miles, it was all about counting down to a better life. *Roll on*, he thought. Let's get this done.

NEWTON ABBOT, FRIDAY, 13 FEBRUARY 2009

Over the last six months, Max had been developing a plan in his mind. Most of the pieces had been slotted together. Now was the time that he could start getting his own back. It was time for other people to start paying for what they had done and just like a terrier, Max was not going to let it go. He'd been through a lot, a hell of a lot, whilst the real perpetrators were laughing. *Time to wipe the smiles off their faces*, he thought. He dialled the number for Isca Ferrari and asked for John Hutchings.

'I'm sorry but Mr. Hutchings is on the other line at the moment,' came the receptionist's reply, 'can I ask him to return your call?' she asked.

Max could picture her in his mind, young, attractive, well dressed in a tight pencil skirt, always shades of grey. She'd worked at Isca Ferrari for years and always looked down her nose at him whenever he had drifted by so often, nine years before. He had recognised her voice as she had also done with him but she still asked the question.

'Who's calling please?'

'It's Max Reed.'

'Oh, hello Mr. Reed, I will ask Mr. Hutchings to call you. What number is best?'

Max gave her the number. It was Friday 13th and the call was deliberately made to coincide with that day. The receptionist told Max that she would pass the message on. It was just after ten in the morning. Max wondered how long it would take Hutchings to return the call, but it wasn't long. Barely half an hour had passed and Hutchings was talking on the phone to Max.

'Max Reed?'

'Yes.'

'It's John Hutchings here. I'm returning your call, how can I help you?'

'Mr. Hutchings, I would like to set up a meeting with you to discuss my company's involvement with yourselves between the years 1997 to 2003.'

'What do you mean?'

'At the time, I ran a company called Velodrome and I bought a number of vehicles from you and sold a few for you as well. I would like to discuss some of those dealings with you face to face.'

'I see. Well, I'm free on the 25th. Is that any good to you?'

'Yes, that would be okay. What time?'

'Two thirty.'

'That's good for me too. May I suggest that you take the opportunity to look over some of the paperwork before we meet so that we both know what we are talking about.'

'Yes, of course.'

Hutchings put down the telephone slowly with a frown and ran his tongue along the front of his teeth as he thought about Reed's comment. What the hell is all that about? he asked himself. Well, sure as eggs are eggs, he was going to find out and he wouldn't have to wait long.

Max picked up the phone and dialled the number on the internet screen in front of him. The connection rang three times and then diverted to a mobile.

'DPI,' came the reply.

'Oh, hi,' said Max. 'I was wondering if you could help me.'

'I'll try,' the man said.

'I need to find the addresses for both home and work and also the telephone numbers, home, work and mobile for someone,' said Max.

'Yes, we can do that. Do you have any previous information, contact numbers etc?'

'I have a previous telephone number which is a land line and a mobile. I haven't tried the mobile but the land line is discontinued. I have not had an address, but I do know or I have been lead to believe that the guy lived in the High Wycombe area.'

'Okay, that should be enough.'

'What's it going to cost and how long will it take?' Max asked.

'Two hundred quid, which I will want up front by credit

card and you can have the info by the end of the week.'

Max agreed and gave him the credit card details and the previous known telephone numbers.

'And what's his name?'

'Graham Lord.'

'Graham Lord,' he repeated and confirmed the spelling. 'Okay, leave it with me and I'll get back to you.'

It didn't take to the end of the week to find out. Two days later, Max had all the information that he'd asked for, so now all he had to do was choose a time. DPI had said that other info was available at a fee but Max declined. He had enough for what he wanted to do. He thought that at this stage anything more would have been a waste of money.

The Porsche 911 2.7RS that Max had bought from Steve Majendie almost a year earlier had now been sold to a customer in Monaco and part of the deal required Max to deliver the car to London and meet with one of the Cars Motorsport trucks for it's onward journey to the sunny climes of the south of France. Being in the area, Max thought it would make sense to doorstep Graham Lord completely unannounced, the element of surprise adding a little more shock to the situation. For certain, Graham Lord would not be expecting it and that's exactly what Max wanted. If all went to plan, Max would deliver the Porsche and then drive the forty minute journey around the M25 motorway to Lord's house and talk things through.

The phone rang in Max's pocket. He fumbled around to find it and then answered it.

'Yeah, hi Darren. How are you?'

'Good thanks Max. I got your email so I'm just responding to that.'

'Okay,' said Max.

'All the websites are up and running. All the links are done and everything is pointing in the right direction. The email capture is finished, so the only outstanding items are the wording on the front page and the name.'

'Okay,' Max replied, adding, 'I'm not a hundred per cent sure on the wording as yet. I need to get a few things finished, but the general feel looks good. The words will only change a little. But I'm fairly certain the name will be real and not as it is at the moment.'

'Okay, well that's something that will only take a few minutes.'

Max was pleased. He'd been working away at different ideas and the internet was just one of them. Darren had been trustworthy and relatively inexpensive in setting up the websites so now Max had one of the biggest marketing tools at his disposal. *The internet*, he thought. *What a great weapon. You can type in someone's name and get all manner of information on them.* What a thought. He had that look on his face of someone who had seen it all, been through it all and was now quietly and calmly retaliating. A sense of imminent satisfaction, maybe misplaced, maybe not. Time would tell. He knew he would have to be careful. There's one thing asking for money that's legitimately owed to you, but it's quite another if Max was to use it for extortion. What he wanted to do was get paid and be recompensed for all the money owed to him and what he had been through, but there were ways and means of doing it properly and still causing the most embarrassment. The internet was definitely one of them.

Max pulled into Heston Services on the M5, it was a quarter to eight in the morning. The huge articulated Cars Motorsport transporter was there waiting for him. He parked alongside and unloaded the Porsche 911 RS. *It was a great car*, he thought as he inched his way up into the back of the truck. A quick blip of the throttle, cut the ignition, everything off, in gear and the hand brake on. That was it, another car sold and away to another happy customer.

Max returned to his pick up and opened his brown leather bag and pulled out the sheet of paper with all Graham Lord's details hand-written on it. He looked for the postcode and then typed it into his satellite navigation. It analysed the route and then gave out the information, twenty seven miles and forty two minutes. It wasn't very far at all. The delivery driver passed Max the receipted paperwork for the Porsche. All was done, now the real work would begin.

Max stopped a mile from Graham Lord's house and looked at the sat nav screen in front of him. He was mindful that he had a large covered trailer on the back and he didn't want to get stuck down a residential road. It looked okay. If he turned into Lord's road, there was a cul de sac at the bottom of the road on the left hand side. He could back into there and turn around.

Having exited the main road and then heading towards Lord's place at first was quite encouraging. Many of the houses were large detached 1920s style properties, but that quickly disappeared as Max turned into Lord's road and lined out before him on both sides were rows of mid sixties semi-detached three-bedroomed Wimpey houses. It was more than disappointing, it was pathetic. When they first met, Lord had told Max that his father was high up in the Bank of England and that he himself had been one of the founders of Apple Computers. *What a load of bollocks*, Max thought. *The guy's a fucking liar. You don't live in a place like this if you've got that kind of money.* It was all an illusion. It was exactly what Lord had wanted to create. He wanted Max to think that he was monied, lived in a grand house in the rural countryside, was self made and all the rest of it. He spoke well with his public school accent, but Max was now thinking that perhaps even that was a 'put on'. The guy just had to be a fake, but why? Max wouldn't have thought any different of him if he had told the truth about who he was and what he did. It didn't matter. What did matter at the time was that between them, they could have made a lot of money. Certainly, half of that did work, because between them they did make a lot of money, it was just that Lord had kept it and not told Max.

Graham Lord's house was the fourth one up on the left hand side. Max drove past and had a cursory glance as he did so. No cars on the drive, a postage stamp sized front lawn and a muddy brown painted garage door. That just about summed it up.

Max turned around at the end of the road and then parked on the opposite side of the street about fifty yards clear vision from Lord's front door. Max sat in the driver's seat thinking as he looked across. A white Volkswagen Polo pulled up outside the house and two elderly people stepped out, taking their time to walk the short distance to Lord's front door. *This will be interesting*, Max thought. Which it was but not in the way Max had hoped. He was thinking that Lord was going to come to the door, but he didn't because, rather than press the door bell, the two old folk simply put the key in the lock and let themselves in. Well, they had to be his parents, they couldn't be anyone else. Lord wasn't married so there were no in laws. It had to be his parents, he thought, and then it dawned on him. Lord lived at home with his parents. That was why he told the 'big I am', story about the Bank of England and Apple Computers. It was all bollocks. Everything; complete bollocks. An inadequate. Max was beginning to wonder whether anything Lord had said to him was true. The Spitfires, the aeroplanes that he and his brother had, all the cars that they raced, the deals that he had done. All of it could be crap, Max puzzled and the things that kept coming back into his mind was the single thought that had nagged him right from the start. The public school voice, the knowledge, the dress, the big talk yet he drove a white Mitsubishi Evo. Many may think differently, but for Max it just didn't add up, it looked strangely at odds with everything Lord was supposed to be. Maybe he didn't have a brother, maybe it was his brother that had all those things and Graham hadn't achieved anything. The reality was that the chances of getting any money from Lord looked slim to say the least, unless he had completely misread the situation. He hoped so, but he didn't think so.

A blue Mercedes ML drove towards Max and parked in the driveway of the house Max was looking at. It was Lord, no doubt about it. Even for that short moment that he passed, Max recognised him. He'd lost a bit of weight and the hairline had receded in the seven years since Max had last seen him, but yes it was definitely him.

Max stepped out of the car and strolled across to Lord's driver's door and looked in. He was talking on the hands free. Lord opened the door.

'Can I help you?' he asked in a rather abrupt offish manner. He hadn't recognised Max.

'Well, as a matter of fact you can. My name is Max Reed.'

'Just a minute.' Lord finished his call and got out of his car ushering Max towards the pavement.

'Graham, I've taken the trouble to come and see you face to face because there's a few things which we need to sort out and that couldn't have been done on the telephone and besides, if I had called you, you would have probably avoided it. So I am here.'

'You've come here especially to see me?'

'Yes, that's right.'

'Well, I could have saved you a lot of trouble. I would have answered your call.'

'I don't think you would have Graham, so . . .'

Lord interrupted, 'Can you make this quick. I have an appointment with my builders right now and I haven't got time for this.'

'That's okay, Graham; I can wait until you get back. How long are you going to be?'

'An hour or two.'

Max knew it was bullshit. Lord got back into his car, reversed up and sped off. He was rattled. Why hadn't he gone into the house, you don't normally drive home, park in your driveway and then speed away. Lord had gone off on the pretence of meeting his builders. That was a 'red herring'. Graham was being his usual self. He was trying to make Max think that he had a house elsewhere and that this house where Max was standing was nothing to do with him. Max didn't believe him as he walked back to the car and locked it. What was he going to do for an hour or two? Well he could go and have a cup of tea with Lord's parents, that would be enlightening or he could take a walk. He decided on the latter.

He'd only made it the one hundred and fifty yards or so to the junction at the end of the road when the blue Mercedes ML appeared again. It was Lord. He stopped the car alongside Max and beckoned him to get in.

'We can go and get a coffee if you like and talk things over.'

'Yeah, that's fine with me,' Max reached into his top pocket and switched on the miniature dictaphone. Lord hadn't noticed.

Graham was clearly agitated. Max's doorstep surprise had definitely got to him. He'd been found out, he wasn't who he made out he was. Driving off like that wasn't to see the builders, it was to give himself some time to think about what he was going to do, but there was one thing for sure, he couldn't leave Max parked outside his parents' house just in case he walked up to the front door. Better that he confronted Max, attack being the best form of defence and try to fend him off.

The waitress smiled and asked, 'What can I get you?'

'Coffee for me please,' replied Graham.

'And I'll have the same,' said Max.

They sat for twenty minutes or so and Max told Graham exactly why he was there. He wanted the money from the sale of the Jaguar XJR15 and he wanted it within seven days or he was going to the police.

'The police won't be interested. It's nothing to do with them. I didn't buy that car through your chap, I bought it from a fellow in Norfolk,' Graham angrily replied.

'Graham, I gave you all the details, the price, the condition, the whereabouts, the phone numbers and you told me you had a buyer, a Jaguar collector in America. We had an agreement. Then after several weeks, you told me that the buyer was no longer interested and was not going ahead. That was a lie, but you're quite good at that, because you lied to the police as well.'

'I most certainly did not. You've got a fucking cheek coming here and suggesting that.' They remained seated.

'Graham, you told the police that when I sold the 360 Spider to Donald Key, that I asked Julian Key for the whole contract price up front and you know that's not true. I never asked for the money up front, you said Julian was offering that to me as a deal to get the car, because you knew I didn't particularly want to sell the car until it arrived. The thing is Graham, Julian Key whilst being a complete idiot, didn't offer that deal either did he? because you were playing one off against the other. You were telling me that Julian was offering the money up front and you were telling Julian that I would do the deal if the money was paid up front. You were telling us both different stories, playing us both, because it was in your interest to do so. You were getting a £5000 commission from me and the same from him. And you needed the money' There was a pause and neither of them said anything as they sipped their coffee.

Max continued, looking up, and said, 'So that's why you lied. For the money, simple wasn't it?'

Graham said nothing. Max had surmised that was what had happened. He'd read Julian Key's statement and whilst he may have been stupid, it was clear that he had been offered a deal to buy the car if he paid in full, "up front". Julian himself hadn't made that offer and neither had Max. Graham had engineered it that way and the fact that he hadn't retaliated in any way at Max's suggestion, convinced Max that he was right. Graham Lord was responsible.

'Graham, I don't want to cause any fuss, I just want my money.'

'Well, you're not going to get any, you're not due it,' said Graham.

'We both know that's not true. I almost forgot just one more thing. I bought a Porsche RS2.7 last year from Steve Majendie and he asked after you. He asked me if I had seen you or was likely to. I asked him why and he told me that you ripped him off and his customer for £25,000 for some spare parts for a Jaguar XJR15. Do you remember Graham, because they want

560

their money too, because you took their money, lied to everyone involved and they never got their spare parts, but you knew that anyway, didn't you? There are probably others too I suspect. I mean, why stop a winning formula eh Graham ?'

Max noticed Graham take a big gulp. He wasn't expecting that. They finished their coffees and walked to the car and drove back to the junction at the end of Lord's road where he stopped to let Max out.

'I thought we were supposed to be friends?' Graham asked.

'We were, Graham, but that ended when you stabbed me in the back. Seven days, Graham, seven days.' Max shut the door as Lord sped off up the road, the private registration bearing no relevance to his name.

Two days later, Max stepped smartly into Isca Ferrari's showroom, the receptionist looked up and smiled, 'Mr. Reed, I will let Mr. Hutchings know that you are here. Can I get you a cup of coffee?'

'Yes, why not?' Max replied. 'White, one sugar please.' He sat down on the red settee and looked at all the black and white racing pictures adorning the yellow painted walls.

The receptionist returned with the coffee and said, 'Mr. Hutchings can see you now.'

'Thank you,' Max replied and followed her to Hutchings's office, where she beckoned him in.

'Ah, good morning, Mr. Reed, pleased to meet you.'

You won't be, Max thought.

'Thanks for taking the time to see me,' Max said as he sat down in the comfortable chair, and continued, 'there's a few things that I would like to discuss with you.'

'Okay,' said Hutchings. 'Fire away.'

'You may be aware that I was a good customer of yours from 1997 onwards, both on the sales side and the service side. At that time, most of the cars were 355s and 348s and generally we had a good relationship. I was selling a lot of 355s and you were doing all the service and preparation work for me. I think it's fair to say that, at the time, I was probably your biggest customer. On one occasion, I remember seeing only my cars in your service bays.'

There was a pause as Max took a sip of coffee and began talking again.

'You may also remember that in 1999, Ferrari

introduced the 360 Coupe which was a great car, and I thought at the time, that it was highly likely that Ferrari would make a convertible version, so I spoke to your sales manager Richard Rippon and asked him if it would be possible to order such a car. He told me that I could pay a deposit and if Ferrari decided to produce a car, then yes, I could have one. Well, I was so convinced that Ferrari would make a 360 convertible that I paid two deposits for two cars in my name, there and then. If my memory serves me correctly, that would have been March 1999. Richard told me that no one else had placed a deposit for such a car and that if Ferrari did manufacture a 'Spider' version of the 360, then I would get my cars in late 2000 or early 2001. I have to say I was very pleased with that. In other words, I would get the first two cars.

'From 1999 onwards, you had several changes. The original service manager was replaced, as was the Ferrari sales manager twice, culminating in Shaun Williams taking over the running of the Ferrari sales and of course, you moved premises twice.

'I continued to do business with you both on the sales side and the service side, but generally we started to do more service work in house at Newton Abbot so that began to taper off a bit. As a result, I was not up here as often as I had used to be. By July 1999, Richard Rippon had confirmed to me what I already knew, which was that Ferrari were going ahead with a 360 Spider. He also told me that I would be the first to get my cars because, naturally, I was the first to order one and pay my deposits. Richard then wrote to me and confirmed my order, however, it is worth saying that you had cashed my deposit cheque for both cars some four months earlier.'

Hutchings shifted uneasily in his chair, saying very little other than nodding, or shaking his head, but he could see where this conversation was going and more uncomfortably, he knew who had been given the first car. He could also see the clarity in Max's mind, the sequence of events, the details and he'd consciously made up his mind to say the very least possible, which was just as well because Max was recording every last word, just like two days earlier with Graham Lord.

'Over the course of 1999 and early 2000, your succession of sales managers ended with Shaun Williams as I've already said and to be fair I don't think Williams particularly liked me, for whatever reason. You bought him in to a loss

562

making business to shift the metal and that's exactly what he was – someone to sell units. He had no passion about the marque and I don't think he knew the history or the significance and what's more I don't think he really cared.'

Hutchings still said nothing, but was now propping his head up on his hand with his elbow on the table looking just a little bit irritated.

'I was aware that left hand drive 360 Spiders were becoming available on the continent in small numbers so I had started asking Shaun about my cars. He kept telling me that he had no news, but would tell me something as soon as he heard. Over the months that followed, I persistently asked Shaun about my cars, but he always gave me a variation of the same story. I had to believe him because I had no other means of finding out anything different. Now Richard Rippon knew as did Shaun Williams, that I was a dealer, a speculator so it was clear that I was going to simply buy the cars from you and then sell them on. Can I ask you, were you aware that when the first right hand 360 Spiders came onto the market, they were attracting premiums in excess of £100,000?'

'Yes, I was aware of that,' Hutchings nodded.

'Well, the thing is Mr. Hutchings, that I sold one of my cars for a hundred thousand pounds over list price and the other car for one hundred and ten thousand pounds over list price, so I know for certain that those kind of figures were being achieved, but and it's a big but, it was only for the first few cars. And of course, I was due two of those first few cars. And what's more, my customers never got their cars.' There was a pause. 'From you, Mr. Hutchings, from your company, Isca Ferrari.'

Hutchings declined to comment as Max was goading him; but whilst he wasn't going to admit it he knew what had been going on.

'I don't know if you know, but last year I went to prison as a result of a lengthy investigation into my dealings with Ferraris and I hold your company partly responsible for that. During the police investigation into me, they were following up their lines of enquiry which also lead to your door. The police took statements from Williams and several others here and Ferrari UK and the first chance that I had to read those statements was when the Crown Prosecution Service served them on my defence team, which was April last year, 2008, nearly twelve months ago. It is clear that there was no collusion between the sales staff as they told their story exactly as it was. As it happened.

'In relation to my cars arriving, your staff have said in their statements that they consistently lied to me, that they fobbed me off, that they knew that I was a speculator and that they didn't want me to have any cars because they would rather sell the cars to one of your own customers. This is the same message in all the statements Mr. Hutchings and on top of that, if that wasn't enough, you deliberately did not order my second car.

'Now, I am a reasonable man, but the reason I am here today is that I want to be compensated for all this aggravation.'

Hutchings still said nothing, but looked like he was boiling within.

'As I see it, at the very least, I have a significant claim against you in the civil courts for breach of contract, but in doing what you have and the way that you have done it, I think you have acted criminally as well.'

Hutchings stood up abruptly, quickly strode around his desk and opened his office door. 'Meeting's over, see you in court,' he said.

Max got up out of his chair, 'What a shame,' he said, 'there was so much more to say.'

There were no formal goodbyes, Hutchings just quickly escorted Max off the premises and shut the door behind him. As for Max, he walked back to the car jumped in and pulled the discreet recorder from the top pocket of his jacket and pressed 'end'. He rewound a few seconds, pressed 'play' and listened. Perfect.

It was obvious that Hutchings was not going to keel over and say to Max, yes, here's your money, so it was going to need to be done the hard way. Max dialled Will Phillipps and asked him if he knew a good no win, no fee civil lawyer. They'd spoken about it a few times before, so Will was ready to give Max the guy's name. Simon Tait. Max was pulling out of Isca Ferrari's car park as Tait got on the phone.

'Max, I've had copies of the statements and related paperwork from Will and in my opinion, you've got one major problem, which is the six year statutory limitation rule. You cannot sue for breach of contract if the time limit is beyond six years after the breach, and clearly the breach in this instance would be at the latest 2001. Here we are in 2009, some eight

564

years later.' He continued with great emphasis, 'However, having looked at the law relating to these matters, there are three distinct reasons why the six year rule can be overturned. I will write to you and detail this more fully, but essentially, if we can show fraud, concealment, concealment for profit or mistake then that would be grounds for wiping out the six year statutory limitation. My belief is that we clearly have concealment for profit which means that we could issue proceedings against them and given the context of their own staff's statements, I cannot see where they would have a defence, although no doubt, they would try something. '

'That sounds promising,' Max countered.

'Yes, I think you have a very good chance of success here. We need to get a barrister on board and get his opinion, so I have a chap in mind who I've worked with several times, so I will get in contact with him and fix up an appointment. Max, it's important that you were not aware at any time during your relations with Isca Ferrari that you knew they were telling you lies.'

'The first time I knew that they were doing what they were, was when I read their statements. As mad as I was about not getting my cars, I still believed at the time what they were telling me,' Max replied.

'Well, that said, the breach would run from the date of that supposed first car delivery, probably late 2000, early 2001 but the statutory limitation would run from the date that you were given the Crown Prosecution Service papers in April 2008, which means you would be well within your rights to commence action. In regard to the first car, there could be some argument as to Isca Ferrari's legitimacy with the contract, although very weak, but in relation to the second car, where they hadn't even ordered it, the breach of contract is clear cut. Let's see what the barrister has to say and we can take it from there.'

Max put down the phone and thought about Hutchings's last defiant words. 'Meeting's over, see you in court'. *Yes, you bastard, I fucking will*, he thought.

REIMS, AUGUST 2007

Leblanc packed his car, being sure to have all the

565

paperwork he'd amassed. Bugatti was his domain. He knew everything about the man and the machines. He was the kind of guy that would win Mastermind, step down from his seat and return to the bench hardly showing any sign of a smile. Like a lot of French, he was well dressed, slim and particular with straight brown hair parted at the side and a thin moustache. He looked like he was in his late thirties, early forties. He reminded Max of the strange keyboard player in the 1970s pop band 'Sparks'. The journey from Reims to Newton Abbot would take Leblanc about eight or nine hours in his Peugeot. He didn't need to race down, he was being well paid for doing the job he loved. It wasn't his full time career, although he would certainly have liked it to be, because his day job was as an administration director at National Hôpital du Reims. He'd been working there since he left university, he was single and lived in a small apartment overlooking the river boats a mere twenty metres from his comfortable lounge wrought iron balcony. Everywhere you looked in his flat, there were books, more and more books, on the floor, on tables, windowsills, cabinets, all over the place. And where there weren't books, there were magazines. All motoring related. Biographies, histories, technical, they were all there.

On the wall, to the left of the television hung a beautiful old oil painting depicting a Bugatti Type 35B racing alongside the huge arched brick viaduct at Pau. Everyday he had looked at that painting, knowing that he'd spent so much time and effort to track it down without success and had always wondered what had happened to it. Almost all of the great Bugattis were accounted for, but that one eluded him. Even with the help of all the historic records from the factory and great collectors, he still hadn't been able to piece together its whereabouts. He'd resigned himself to thinking that it was gone, probably scrapped for parts in World War II or stolen by the Nazi's. Whatever, it was a lost piece of history.

Interestingly, in the early Nineties, someone had pronounced themselves as being the owner of the car and proudly displayed it for everyone to see, but inevitably, the hope was dashed by the lack of provenance and hardly any original parts. It was a reproduction, nothing more. Someone simply realising that there was an opportunity for a lost car to become a found car, but it didn't work. They neither had the integrity of the car or the historical background to make it valid. It was a fake, nothing more.

As Leblanc sat down in the driver's seat of his Peugeot and made himself comfortable, he thought about his conversations with the man paying his fee to do the job. He was one of the foremost collectors in the world and had been for a long time. This didn't have the hallmark of a wild goose chase. This seemed to be the real thing. He knew Sanders and he knew that Sanders knew the difference between what was real and what was not, so Leblanc's second opinion was merely a comforting stand alone confirmation of what had already been reported by his English friend. Whatever, Leblanc had all the factory numbers for all the parts and he was going to do his job to the last detail. It was only what was expected of him.

It was just after 8:00 am when Leblanc left Reims and he'd agreed with Max that he would telephone him when he arrived on British soil. The plan was for him to stay at a local hotel that evening, have dinner with Max and then inspect the car in the morning.

For Max, the inspection was a concern. The car was exactly what it was supposed to be and Sanders had proven that beyond doubt, but there was always the worry that another inspection would throw up a doubt, maybe something trivial that perhaps Sanders had overlooked. To say Max was on edge, would have been a gross understatement. Until now, despite all the bad things going on around him, he had still managed to stay calm and relaxed. Now that the time was nigh, he was most obviously more than a little anxious. If Leblanc put the buyer off, then not only would it scupper the sale but equally it would cast a shadow over the car and that wouldn't be good. If one expert says one thing and another says something different, it would be enough to worry potential buyers into looking elsewhere. Their view would be that there would be little point in buying something which has an element of doubt.

Max knew that Leblanc had been looking for the car, and in fact Leblanc had spent several summer holidays quietly foraging for his prey, but obviously he hadn't been successful. What he hadn't realised was that he had been so close. Like most treasure hunters, there is always an element of luck, a good pointer here or something unwittingly said there, but Leblanc had been on the right track, but took the wrong fork. A little more time and he would have found the car.

From the instant that Maurice had told Max about

Leblanc, Max had made the decision to find out as much about the man was he possibly could. He didn't want some Froggy to ruin his day.

By the time that they had met in the bar at the Passage House Inn, Max felt more comfortable, he had seen sense in what was a mad time. Sander's report was conclusive, Leblanc could only really agree with it.

They sat down for dinner overlooking the River Teign and the colourful variety of small boats tied up alongside the jetty. Max quickly realised that Leblanc wasn't on a crusade to differ from Sander's opinion, he was there to enjoy the moment and be part of the car's history. Max was immediately at ease. They chatted until late and looked forward to meeting again in the morning. Sanders was due to arrive by rail at Newton Abbot station at 10:32 am, so by 11:00 am they would all be staring at the same subject matter shaking their heads in disbelief.

CARDIFF, JULY 2007

Will Phillipps looked at the paperwork in front of him. There were the original orders for the two Ferraris from Isca Ferrari, there was the faxed confirmation of the specifications for the two cars coming from Spain, two contracts of sale that matched the Exeter cars and similarly two further contracts of sale for the Spanish cars. Furthermore, there were two purchase contracts for the four cars coming from Kweyaka in Africa along with the original receipts for the deposits for those cars. It looked convincing. Easton wanted confirmation that Max had ordered the cars and what laid before Will Phillipps seemed to be enough. He was confident that the whole mess would just slip away and be another NFA – no further action. It had been a long investigation which had started with an arrest, five years earlier, on suspicion of fraudulent trading and despite all the police efforts it was clear that Max had not been involved in anything fraudulent. Far from it, if anything he had been on the wrong end of some other peoples' fraudulent activity and they were people he had trusted.

Phillipps faxed through the paperwork to Easton's office as agreed, duly thinking that would be the end of it. Outside, it was a beautiful July summer's day. Max didn't have to answer bail until September 5th. It would be almost seven years to the day since Max had signed the sale contract with Julian Key. Will had said, 'Go on holiday Max as planned. Enjoy the time with your family and forget all this rubbish. When you get back, hopefully all this will be over.' Max had taken some pleasure in hearing those words, but it wasn't over until it was over and still the nagging anxiety niggled away inside him.

Come September 5th, Max met Will Phillipps outside the police station at Torquay not least with some apprehension. The moment had come. It was either going to be charges or you're free to go.

They walked into the reception area and Phillipps introduced themselves to the less than helpful WPC behind the glazed screen. They waited and waited. Twenty minutes passed by and still nothing. Max was trying to remain outwardly calm but deep down, he was boiling over. If they were going to let him go, he thought, surely they would just leave a message at the front desk telling them they were not needed. It would be another typical waste of time, but this agonising wait was something else. It was mental torture.

Alongside them, the crisp fast sound of a mortise turning in its lock and the handle reaching the end of its travel revealed a uniformed officer on the other side of the opening door beckoning Will Phillipps and Max into the inner waiting area where they were asked to be seated. Max looked at Will and raised his eyebrows.

'This is it,' he said.

Will nodded. 'Looks like a straight charge, Max. I'm sorry.'

Max held his head in his hands in bewilderment. Another officer walked through to them asked if they would follow him. Fluorescent lit, institutional beige painted, narrow corridors lead the three of them from one set of steel grilled gates to another until they reached the custody suite.

From his elevated position, the custody sergeant looked down on Max and confirmed his name and address followed by three charges of deception. It was ridiculous, Max thought. He was sickened to the pit of his stomach. Will said that it wasn't going to come to this, but he was wrong. The whole process took twenty-five minutes. Sign here, sign there, the usual crap. The officer handed over the paperwork and Max gave it to Will. They retraced their steps back down the corridors and chatted on the steps outside.

'Look, Max, it's three charges on what is effectively a technical deception. It's nothing. They've charged you with the lowest of the low after having investigated you thoroughly for five years,' Will said. 'It's all they could get on you,' he continued.

'God, what am I going to do now?' Max asked, not expecting an answer.

'The first charge relates to Donald Key's car and we know all about that. The second and third charges are effectively one and the same and relate to Rick Brady's car. I'd be worried if we didn't have any answers to this, but that's not the case. We do have answers and we have justifiable reasons why you did what you did.'

'I know,' said Max, 'but this just seems so stupid.'

'Right, firstly your bail continues as previously, but you will now have to attend Plymouth Magistrates Court next Wednesday,' Will confirmed adding that he would be there too.

'Why Plymouth?'

'I don't know. I assume Plymouth is the local area for Easton's office. Ignorant of him to not be there today, don't you think?'

'Well, he is what he is. A stupid fat twat,' Max was mad.

'All that's going to happen now is, you will go to the magistrates court next week and enter your plea, not guilty and the case will be referred up to the Crown Court. We will probably have two or more preliminary hearings at Crown Court before it goes to trial and I wouldn't see that happening much before next summer. We will need to get a good barrister on board, but that won't be necessary until we get full disclosure of all the documents from CPS – Crown Prosecution Service. Then we will know exactly what they have on you.'

Max was shaking his head as Will continued, 'For the record, I think what has happened is that Easton has probably gone so far with this that he's managed to get it past the CPS so now if it fails, it's not down to him. He's done his job. The fact that he's spent five years wasting the public's money is neither here nor there. It doesn't matter. What does matter is that he doesn't lose face.'

'How can they charge me over Donald Key's car when I paid them back?' Max asked. 'It doesn't make sense.'

'Well, that's something we will have to deal with, but as

I said earlier. At least we have answers to all this. It's not like we have to find them.'

'Yeah, but we've got answers and we've given those answers and yet they've still charged me. It doesn't add up.'

The two of them went their separate ways. Will back to his office and Max home to Catherine. *What the hell am I going to tell her*, he thought. Did he have to tell her anything at all? He knew he would have to, but there would have to be the right moment. However he did it, there was going to be tears and upset and he really didn't want that. If being in business can come down to this, then who in their right mind would contemplate such madness?

The following Wednesday, Max passed through the security checks at Plymouth Magistrates Court and looked through the listings to see which court he was in. He read his name amongst what seemed to be a never ending list for Court 3. Will Phillipps briefed Max before they went in to the hearing just after eleven fifteen am. Max stood in the witness box and read the words on the card held out in front of him. *This is real*, he thought.

The process took no more than ten minutes. The CPS read out the charges, suggesting there might be more to follow, Max entered his pleas and the bench gave directions to move the case to the Crown Court for a preliminary hearing two months later. The CPS handed over twenty two box files. There would be more when full disclosure was given. It was an enormous amount of paperwork for what seemed like a fairly trivial charge according to Will, but it had to be remembered that what the investigating officers had set out to prove had now changed. What was the serious accusation of fraudulent trading had been downgraded to a much lesser charge of deception and a technical deception at that. It was all they could find.

Easton was pleased, in fact it was more than that, he was gloating. He knew he had succeeded on two counts plus he had a further ace up his sleeve. He was playing the game as best he could. McGrain still wasn't happy about it, but he was going along for the ride. If the shit hit the fan, then it was Easton's name at the top of the list, not his. The two of them had sat in court like two Mr. Potato Heads as Max had wondered how on earth anyone could take them seriously. Surely, even at this late stage, Max would get a reprieve. Someone had to see sense somewhere along the line. Maybe the guy with the wig and gown would see through it all at the next hearing. *Who knows*, Max thought. *It's just a bloody farce.*

HMP LEYHILL, SEPTEMBER 2009

It takes a while to sort yourself out when you get locked up, especially if you are not expecting it. Simple things like, money, telephone, laundry, books, music etc. It all takes time to organise. At Exeter, it just didn't happen and with such a short stay, there was little time to join clubs, find out who does what etc. Leyhill was different. There was more time, because you aren't locked up. You have the freedom to move within constraints. Getting what you want is a simpler process. If you need a radio, you go to the church, pay the deposit from your prison account, sign the release note and bingo, you've got music. You want CDs, join the library and rent CDs.

The time passed quickly in Leyhill if you could manage yourself properly. Max always made himself busy. He wasn't one to loiter and wait for things to happen. Some just closed their doors and slept their way through their sentence, which was fine if that was best for them, but Max realised that by pushing himself in the day, he'd be tired at night and he'd sleep.

The weeks had become a routine, he knew exactly where he had to be at any time of the day, what he had to do and how long he could do it for. The only variables were meals and intervention. On the whole, the food was good, but the queuing was irritating. On the right day and being in the right frame of mind, the banter in the queues could be very funny, but on other days it was a monotonous grind, easier to cop out and give it a miss. And that's exactly what Max did. He only had one meal on a Monday, Wednesday and Friday which coincided with his running days and towards the end of his sentence he'd started missing out on one meal of a Sunday. Sometimes, he just couldn't face the thought of having to go and eat again, stand in the queue for ages whilst being watched continually by three generally overweight guards slobbing out on their plastic school chairs. And as for sitting opposite someone who was shovelling food into their mouth like they hadn't eaten for months, well sometimes it was just too much. Better to sit outside in the late afternoon sun on one of the many park benches and soak up the rays, forget life for a while and think of all the wonderful things to go back to. It would be quiet, just the birds for company whilst all the animals were eating. With his eyes closed, he could be wherever he wanted to be, doing whatever he wanted, it was a million miles from reality, but there for the moment it brought a smile to his face and gave him the strength to beat the bastards.

The nights were beginning to draw in, the days getting shorter, Max wondered if by the time he was ready to go whether or not he'd be running in the dark. He wondered as to whether the prison changed its rules on outdoor activity when the nights pulled in. As it happened, it didn't matter, he'd be gone before the clocks changed. Max was thinking, the funny thing is, that when you are deprived of your freedom, everything on the outside is so much more vivid, more colourful. The grass is greener, the sky is a more beautiful shade of blue and the simplest things seem so much more interesting. Max thought about how good it would be to ride a bicycle again, feeling the wind in his face, eyes streaming, T-shirt flapping like a breached sail, as he blasted off the top of Haldon Moor, through the sleepiness of Holcombe Down, arms tucked in, flashing in and out of the sunlight beneath the trees, and into the back of Dawlish. He'd done it loads of times before when he was a kid some thirty five years earlier, but somehow now it seemed all the more pleasurable. He convinced himself that was one of many things he was going to do when he got out. When he was twelve years old, he and his good friend Mark enjoyed football and all the things boys do. Their friendship stood the test of time as they went through school, swapping girlfriends amongst other things, but Mark was a sportsman as was Max always competitive and the pair of them had a totally different relationship to Max and Rob. In those youthful days it was Max and Mark that used to cycle for miles and miles between Teignmouth, Dawlish and Exeter, one always trying to push the other. It was a long time ago, a distant but happy and vibrant innocent memory that could never have foreseen where they would both be thirty five years on. One a successful London lawyer and the other sat on a park bench in the middle of rural Gloucester in a pair of ill fitting grey track suit bottoms and a wine red T-shirt with HMP Leyhill emblazoned upon it. Max looked down at the ground in front of him and laughed out loud as he thought, *Some things never change*. He was wearing a pair of black Adidas Samba training shoes, exactly the same as the pair he would have been wearing thirty five years ago. He stood up, stretched his arms and strolled back to the apartment, smiling to himself as he did so thinking there's been times before and there will be times again. All was quiet save the distant sound of Rachmaninoff's Concerto No. 2 eerily drifting across the camp from an open first floor window on the 'C' wing. Bizarre.

CHUDLEIGH, AUGUST 2007

Tyler was a realist. He knew that the abbot was as guilty as Benjamin, but he also realised that without Max as a witness, then he wasn't going to be able to make the main charges stick. It would be the victim versus the accused, his word against another's.

Tyler flicked through the pages of his contact list and dialled the number for Max. They went through the usual pleasantries and Andy said, 'Look, Max, it's simple. We cannot, or rather the prosecution have said that we can't go ahead with you as a witness.'

'Why?' asked Max, although he wasn't particularly fussed about it anyway.

'Obviously, we know that you've been charged in connection with a deception and whilst we don't know the details about it, we can't take the risk of having you in the witness box, because the defence will have a field day with you.'

'Okay,' Max replied quietly.

Tyler continued, 'They will have the information about you and they will do their best to discredit you, whether you are guilty or not. And the potential is for our case against the Abbot to fall down around our ears. Obviously we don't want that to happen, but you being charged has resulted in us having a huge hole in our case.'

'Well, I'm sorry about that, but believe me, I wasn't expecting it.'

'No, I'm not blaming you. It's not your fault. These things happen. The abbot is going into court next week and I think we'll end up doing a deal. We'll drop the more serious charges and accept a changed plea of guilty on the lesser offences. He'll still go inside, but probably only two years rather than five or six if we had made the other charges stick.'

Max sighed but didn't say anything in response. In truth, he was more worried about himself than he was about the abbot.

'I suppose you read about Benjamin in the paper,' Tyler enquired.

'Yes, I did. Seemed a lot,' Max replied.

'No, not really, eleven years was what we expected. He'd ruined someone's life and no amount of years behind bars is going to wipe that from the victims mind. It would have been similar for the abbot, but again as I've said, without you we can't do it. Not to worry.'

Max put down the phone and that was the last he thought of it. Tyler did end up doing a deal with the abbot the following week virtually on the steps of the court. He was sentenced to two years and two months. Quite a fall from grace. Max read the article in the local newspaper and thought about his days at Buck House. He'd had a great time there but it would never be remembered for that, it would be remembered for something totally different.

A splodge of strawberry jam dripped onto Easton's shirt as he lounged in his desk chair whilst tucking into his second doughnut. He scraped off the gooey substance with the side of his finger and licked it clean. He was pleased with himself, he knew that if he charged Max, he would be helping the abbot. He wasn't going to get him off, but he could help and that's exactly what he had promised his mother. He knew what he was doing, one rule for one and one for another. Tyler didn't have a case without Max, that was obvious. All Easton had to do was remove Max from the proceedings and the abbot was almost home and dry. All very easy and the best thing about it, Easton thought, was that his hands were clean. That's the way we like it, he said to himself and pondered for a nano second on whether to have the last doughnut. He deserved it. Another time in another place, things would be very different.

BRISTOL, MARCH 2008

Max shut the car door, pressed the remote locking and placed his brown leather bag under his arm. It was just a short walk to Arthur Bailey's chambers in Corn Street. Will would be there with his personal assistant waiting patiently. Max was twenty minutes late and a barrister's hourly rate is not cheap. The response from the intercom asked Max to push open the door and walk in, take the lift and go to the third floor and someone will meet you. He did as he was told.

A grey haired man in his late fifties greeted Max as the lift doors parted. He held out his hand.

'Arthur Bailey,' he said, 'Good to meet you Max.'

'Hi,' said Max.

'Please follow me and I'll take you through to the conference room.'

'Sorry to keep you waiting, I didn't allow myself enough time,' Max said politely.

Will Phillipps stood up from his chair and shook Max's hand. His PA smiled as she leant across the table and did the same.

'Okay, so we're all here, I think we had better take a good look at what we have,' said Arthur. He shuffled through various files laid out in front of him as Will's PA poured the teas and coffees.

Arthur looked up and faced Max, steepling his fingers in front of him as he did so.

'I'd like to go back over your circumstances. I've spent quite some time looking through these files. It is clear that the start of the police investigation was far more intense than what transpired to be the eventual charges. And it's also clear that the investigating officers have gone to considerable lengths to make all this stick.' He was pointing to all the files as he was talking, stopping for a short while before continuing.

'It's obvious to me that you were simply running a business at the sharp end, spinning lots of plates and unfortunately for you, some of those plates started tumbling down, and when they did, the repercussions were rather harmful to your ability to trade. I don't see any malpractice or intent. Like many businesses out there, you were running hard and I understand that in the real world, that is what it's like. Buy today, sell tomorrow, but what it doesn't allow for is buying today and not selling tomorrow. That's when things start to go wrong.'

Max nodded as he listened intently. The barrister's opinion would set the course for the trial and Max needed to be sure that Arthur understood exactly what had happened and why it had happened. It was encouraging that he'd made reference to various points along the way that Max felt comfortable about and particularly important that the barrister realised that Max wasn't a criminal, merely a cog in a bigger wheel that ultimately stopped turning.

'Look Max, if we take the three charges of deception, then I think we have a good defence. The prosecution will try to muddy the water with all the various dealings but I think we have enough in our favour to deal with that. If it came to a trial, the jury should be able to understand what you were doing. It's interesting yet quite beyond me as to why the prosecution appear to have made absolutely no attempt to reel Tom McKinney into the caper. I cannot find anything relating to him at all,' he looked at Will as if asking for support.

'No, I haven't seen anything either,' Will remarked.

'Well.' Arthur removed his gaze to Max, 'You gave McKinney the full payment for the second car, someone you trusted having dealt with them for several years and to coin a phrase, the man did a runner.'

'Yes, that's right. I think he's now in Spain on the Costa del Crime evading his creditors and not least HM Customs & Excise,' Max interjected.

'Hmm,' Arthur coughed. 'You've been well and truly had. I've seen it before and no doubt I will see it many times again. And you repaid the victim in relation to the first charge,' there was a pause, 'Donald Key?'

'Yes, that was dealt with through the civil courts, albeit it got a bit rough along the way. Key sent some thugs down to sort me out, then he lied in the High Court to get a freezing injunction, but it was eventually sorted. Settled in full and final payment,' Max answered.

'What about this character Dimo something?'

'He was funding cars for me and he was the chap behind the orders to Sebastien Ferrari in Spain for the two new Ferrari 360 Spiders. The left hand drive cars that is.'

'Okay. And he's the man you sent the fax with the specifications you required for the cars you were getting?'

'Yes, one blue car and one silver.'

'So in relation to Donald Key's car, you were getting that car from Sebastien Ferrari in Spain and it had been ordered through this Dimo chap and he told you that the car would be available at Christmas 2000, to the specification as per the fax you had sent him?'

'Yes, that's right.'

'When did those cars arrive?' Arthur asked himself.

'According to the police witness statements,' Will said, 'they didn't arrive until late 2003.'

'By which time, I assume it was too late for you Max?'

'Yes, I sold the car on the basis that it would arrive at Christmas 2000, and it didn't. It wasn't Dimo's fault, it was either Ferrari, the factory or Sebastien.'

'Hmm,' said Arthur. 'Looking at the witness statements, I rather think it was the dealership, Sebastien. Dimo Dacari states that he was continually being mucked about although he did eventually get the cars. Do you know if the cars arrived in the specification you ordered?'

'I believe so,' said Max.

'Okay, so there's little doubt that the cars you ordered through Dacari were eventually supplied, but as I said earlier, far too late for you to satisfy your customers.'

'Yes, that's right.'

'It is clear that Dimo Dacari had ordered the cars. They were in the specification as per your fax and they eventually arrived in that same specification, but it is also clear that Sebastien's were also time and time again, putting him off. Dacari says in his statement that the cars should have first arrived in September 2000 and then December 2000, which concurs with both your statement to the police and of course the timing and the reason for your contract of sale with Donald Key.' There was a pause as Arthur considered the information. 'And that of course didn't happen, because Sebastien Ferrari didn't supply the cars until late 2003, which was no good to you.'

'I was completely buggered. I couldn't get another car from somewhere else at short notice. I had several cars coming, but none of them were due soon enough to sort Key.'

'And of course, you'd been paid in full up front?'

'Yes, that's right.'

'Why was that?' Arthur asked.

'Well, I was dealing with Graham Lord who was the agent between me and Donald Key's son Julian and basically they were desperate for a car for their Asian client. I had already sold them another car successfully a few months earlier and now they wanted a new 360 Spider and I had one coming. Graham Lord knew that I had a car due, because I had told him. He tried to get me to do a deal with him, but I was holding out for the best deal which I thought I'd get if I waited until the car arrived. Graham was constantly at me over several weeks to get me to sell the car to Key and I'd always said no. However, his final offer was that Julian Key said he would pay all the money up front for a small discount if I agreed. Key had told Graham Lord, that I could use the money to "buy and sell" during the period up to when the car arrived. I didn't agree to it straightaway. I told Graham that I would come back to him. I didn't. He rang me and I agreed. On reflection, I wish I had stuck to my guns, but the offer was such a good one that I couldn't refuse.'

'Indeed,' said Arthur continuing, 'What do we know about Graham Lord? I've read his statement, but it mentions nothing of the lead up or the manner in which this deal was done. Lord simply says that you had a car for sale and that he acted as a commission earning agent to sell the car on your behalf to Donald Key's company. There's nothing about the protracted negotiations, or any offers to pay up front. It appears that Lord was being paid a commission of £5000 from you and the same amount from Julian Key. Ten thousand pounds is quite an incentive to get a deal done wouldn't you say?'

'Yes, it is. I didn't know he was getting paid by Key as well. I guess I never really thought about it,' said Max.

There was quite a long pause as Arthur Bailey scribbled a few notes, with his elbow on the table whilst he massaged his forehead. He slid his hand down his face and clenched his fist as he rested his chin on his knuckles.

'It's fairly damning evidence that both Graham Lord and Julian Key say in their statements that you asked for the money to be paid up front, yet you are categorical in saying that Key offered you the money' . He paused for a while, deep in thought and then continued, ' Has it ever occurred to you that Graham Lord was lying?'

'No,' said Max, after a deal of thought. 'No, not at all. In what way?' he asked.

'Well, ten thousand pounds is a pretty big incentive. What if Lord realised that you had a car coming and Key was desperate for a car and realising that he was getting nowhere with you wanting to sell the car, he simply said to you that Key was prepared to offer you the full amount up front, whereas he told Key that you had said that you would do a deal if all the money was paid up front? Both you and Key would think that the other had made the offer, when in actual fact, neither of you had made the offer. Lord had played you both. If you read both your statements to the police and Julian Key's statement, both of you are adamant that the other made the offer, yet neither of you actually spoke to each other during the course of the negotiation, it was Lord that did all the negotiations. Now if you go back to Graham Lord's statement, he makes absolutely no mention at all about protracted negotiations or payment made up front offer. According to him, it was a straightforward sale of a car from you to Donald Key's company. It is my view that Graham Lord lied. Neither you or Julian Key made that offer, it was in fact Graham Lord!

'Now, when or if this goes to trial, the prosecution will say that you deliberately asked for the money up front, because your business was in difficulty and furthermore Julian Key's and Graham Lord's statements will support them. They will say that your statement bore a false account of what actually happened. Also, the prosecutions' whole case is based on what they think is a deliberate deception and they are going to interpret everything that you have done in a dim light rather than the actual reasons. This is not about right or wrong, it's about what the prosecution can convince the jury. They will try to present a convincing story and blacken your name as much as possible. Conversely, it's our job to convince them otherwise, and I think, not to put too fine a point on it, we are going to have an uphill struggle. It's definitely not going to be easy. The prosecution have masses of information that they can use to twist the interpretation in their favour.

'What are you saying?' Max asked worryingly.

'I think that we are going to have a hard job convincing the jury.'

The sudden realisation of what Arthur was saying sent a shockwave right through Max's body. He suddenly felt cold yet sweaty. He looked down at the table and started thinking of the implications. They didn't bear thinking about.

'But you said earlier, 'when or if' this goes to trial. I had in my mind the thought that maybe you were thinking there was the possibility of there not being a trial and it's all over.'

'Well, not quite. By 'when', I am meaning that in the normal course of events we proceed to the trial, but by 'if', I mean that perhaps we do a deal with the prosecution.'

'Well, what do you mean by that?'

'We plead guilty to some of the offences,' replied Arthur.

'You must be joking. I'm not going to plead guilty to something I haven't done. I'd have to be bloody mad.'

'Well, I think you need to hear me out on my next point before you make that decision.'

Max looked across at Will as if to say, what the bloody hell's going on, but Arthur started up again.

'I'd like to talk to you about the cars coming from South Africa and in particular Mr. Kweyaka. How well do you know him?'

'Well, he's been a customer of mine since August, September 2000. He contracted to buy from me a very expensive Ferrari for more than seven million dollars which ultimately came to nothing, but he had said to me that he could supply me with some Ferrari 360 Spiders. South Africa being a right hand drive market was good news because I only had two right hand drive cars ordered, which were coming from Isca Ferrari. Kweyaka's four cars would have made me a very good return – at least £200,000. He also told me that he could supply me with some left hand drive cars from some of his contacts, so I agreed to buy four left and four right hand drive cars,' Max explained.

'And you entered into a contract with Mr. Kweyaka for the supply of all these cars?'

'Yes, there were two contracts with four cars listed on each. One for left hand and one for right.'

'And you paid deposits for the cars?'

'Yes, in total, I paid £25,000 in deposits, and I've given Will the original receipts for the payments.'

'Yes, I've seen them,' Arthur commented.

'Okay,' said Max, wondering where all this was leading to.

'And what about the contracts?'

'You have them.'

Arthur was looking down at the paperwork in front of him. He didn't lift his head, he just looked up and said, 'Do I? That's the question. Do you mean these?' asked Arthur waving them loosely in his right hand.

'Yes, that's them.'

'Hmm,' he replied. There was a short pause. 'But they are not the originals are they Max?'

'No,' he let out a long sigh and continued after a while,

581

'I couldn't find the originals, despite looking everywhere for them, so I did what I thought was the next best thing I rang Kweyaka and asked him if he had his original copies and after a couple of days, he came back to me saying he hadn't. I mean, it's been eight years. Why would you keep those documents for that length of time? The simple answer was to rewrite them, which is what we did. I didn't have a problem with it and neither did Kweyaka, so we rewrote them as per the originals. Duplicates'

'And you dated them September 2000?' stated Arthur.

'Yes, I think that's what we did.'

'Well, my friend, I'm afraid that was an extremely costly mistake. Up until that part, I think we would have had a struggle on our hands to convince the jury, but I would have pursued it with all the vigour you deserve. I'm certain that you did not have any intent to deceive whatsoever in what has happened with the sales, purchasing and supply of these Ferraris, but in doing what you have with Mr. Kweyaka, rewriting the contracts, dating them as per September 2000, I think you have done yourself a great injustice. The prosecution believe that by remaking those contracts, you have tried to pervert the course of justice.'

'Well, I haven't, I've just rewritten the originals. Call them duplicates if you like. There would have been originals, but we cannot find them. This is ridiculous.'

'Max, believe me, the prosecution is right. For whatever reason that you rewrote the contracts, it's immaterial. The fact is that you have tried to pass them off as the originals. If you had said that these documents,' Arthur held them out in front of him and continued, 'were duplicates of what you believe were the contract and description of the originals and you had said that openly, then it would be different, but not saying anything, however innocent you believed your actions were, could be easily construed as 'perverting the course of justice' of which the court would take a very dim view. And the punishment would be at least five years imprisonment.'

On the drive up to Corn Street, Bristol from Newton Abbot, anybody could have been forgiven for thinking that Max didn't have a care in the world, such was his ability to contain his problems. He felt he was completely innocent. Okay, he might have sailed close to the wind, but in business, sometimes that happens. Usually, you get through it, come out the other side and sail on. This, however, was not what he'd bargained for. All of a sudden, things were looking very nasty.

Max pondered over what Arthur had said and asked, 'Where does that leave me?'

'In short. Between a rock and a hard place. I don't see that you really have a lot of choice if you are sensible about it. The prosecution are saying that they will bring further charges against you in relation to perverting the course of justice unless you plead guilty to the three charges already brought. The implication of that is that if you go to trial as per your 'Not guilty' plea at present, and we lose, then you could go to prison for five years.'

'I don't bloody believe this. It's mad. I haven't done anything wrong. I was running a business that had cash flow problems. I wasn't running a criminal organisation.'

'I know, but let's stick to the facts. However hard you might find this, it is the way it works. This is how the police operate. You need to think very seriously about where we go from here.'

There was a long period of silence, just the sound of the outside traffic filled the air.

'I'm not saying I would plead guilty, but what if I did?' Max asked finding it difficult to believe that he would be asking such a question.

'If you change your plea to guilty. Firstly you will get a reduction in any sentence for doing so at the earliest opportunity. Secondly, any sentence would be drastically reduced and thirdly, the prosecution will withdraw the perverting the course of justice charge.'

'But, drastically reducing any sentence. What do you mean by that?'

'It depends on the judge of course, but it is my view that this would be the type of offence that should attract a suspended sentence or community service order maybe even a combination of both. There is a chance of a custodial sentence, but I think it more likely that a suspended sentence would be appropriate.'

Max couldn't believe what he was hearing. All the stress and anxiety over the last seven years had now come down to this. Realistically, he didn't know what to think. Were these people in front of him friends or foes. Who could he trust ? He didn't know. There didn't seem to be any fight in them, no answers. Even they realised that Max hadn't done anything with any intent but they seemed powerless to intervene. It was almost as if it was an everyday occurrence, next please.

'I just feel like I've been completely shafted,' Max said despondently.

'Well you have. Sebastien, Graham Lord, Tom McKinney, Isca Ferrari, Donald Key and the rest. They've all shafted you. People you have trusted have completely taken advantage of you and all of that would come out if we go to trial. And I fully believe that you have an extremely strong case against some of those if you were to pursue them through the civil courts, but that's a different matter altogether and not one that I can get involved with. This case is all about money and in particular cash flow. You didn't have any cash flow for numerous reasons all legitimate, but you had plenty of customers and plenty of orders. It was just that you couldn't fulfil them. Had Sebastien, Isca Ferrari or Tom McKinney come through with the cars as expected when you ordered them, I don't think we'd be here today and you would probably still have a successful business.'

Max nodded. 'I need some time to think this through. When do we have to go back to the prosecution with an answer?'

'Some time later on next week should be okay,' Arthur replied.

Max stood up and went to the window looking out over the ageing rooftops of the proceeds of Bristol's industrial revolution. Intricate details, dentil mouldings, corbels, all signs of bygone wealth and prosperity laid out in front and below him.

'You know,' said Max turning around to look at Arthur, 'I've absolutely no faith in all this. It's all trickery. It's as if the police have a set pattern and they try to manoeuvre themselves into a strong position by suggestion. It's not how it happened that counts, it's what they can take advantage of as professionals dealing with people like me who really haven't got a clue what all this is about. It's not about a crime, is it?' Max asked, but continued answering his own question.

'It's about money.' Max stooped his head, put his hands in his pockets and walked away from the window. 'It's about money,' he repeated.

'I'm afraid so,' Arthur piped up.

Back in Ashburton, Leo Easton was rubbing his hands together like an old miser. He'd played his ace and he knew what the result would be. Against the fickle Justice Barlow, nobody in their right mind would want to run the risk of pleading 'not guilty' to perverting the course of justice. A deal would be done.

He could almost hear the defence squirming in their chairs.

'So to recap,' Max asked, 'what's my position?'

'Plead guilty to the three deception charges and you'll most like get six to twelve months suspended sentence and or community service and that will be it. All this will go away. Or plead not guilty and the prosecution will charge you with perverting the course of justice as well. If you win, you walk free. If you lose on all counts, which you could, then you may get a five year sentence. In both instances, there will be a confiscation order most likely awarded against you too,' Arthur said shrugging his shoulders.

'And what's that going to amount to?'

'I don't know, it will be up to the judge. Max, I know it's difficult, and life isn't fair, but you must think about your family. If you got five years, that's a long time.'

They'd all been in the conference room for over two hours and it was that last sentence that Arthur had said that convinced Max to plead guilty. It was completely against everything he stood for, but in simplistic terms, he really had no choice.

'If I do go 'guilty', what happens next?' Max asked reluctantly.

Arthur sat back in his chair, putting his hands on his head, 'We change your plea, which will be at the earliest opportunity. Prosecution drops the potential perverting charge, you go to court in April and the case will be adjourned for pre sentence reports. You will need to see probation and they will send their findings into the court.'

'That's all I need, a load of commy, sandal wearing do gooders.'

'That's as maybe Max, but you need them and you need to get them on side. What they say to the court and what they recommend will affect you. So, best behaviour and keep your thoughts to yourself.'

'Just one more question before we break up the meeting ?' Max asked.

'Anything', Arthur replied.

Max stood by the window, he looked tired. The last few years were beginning to take their toll. He spoke quietly . 'Who made the complaint to the police ?'

Arthur looked across at Will with a somewhat resigned look on his face and replied, ' Donald Key'.

There was a short pause, nobody said anything and then Arthur added stoically, ' After you paid him back !'

Max never drove at sixty miles per hour on the motorway, it was nearly always half as much again but that day he did. The meeting had broken up with Arthur telling Max that he's speak to him again after the weekend, but in truth, the decision had been made. There was only one decision to make. He felt numbed, the last seven years had really knocked the stuffing out of him. By the time he appeared in court in April, he would only have a few months at best and then he'd be in the final hearing. It was a fearful countdown. Up to now, there had been absolutely no publicity, but Max knew that anything with the word 'Ferrari' in it was going to attract the attention of the media. By pleading 'guilty', he was basically saying 'yes I did it', when in truth, he hadn't, but they wouldn't want to know about that. The media never do, they just want the scandal to sensationalise their stories. Max could read the headlines in his mind. 'God, what a fucking mess,' he said to himself.

What mattered now was the next four months to the final hearing date. There would be no trial, so the public wouldn't know the true story, they'd only know what they could read in print. Max resigned himself to his most likely fate, twelve months suspended sentence, a hundred hours community service and public humiliation, but that was a few months down the line. In the meantime he had a holiday booked, his daughter's second birthday and there was still Olivier to sort out. He wanted to live every day to the max, enjoy the moments with his family and friends because he knew that life after the hearing would never be the same as before it. Quite how it would affect him, he didn't know. He could hazard a guess, but if you haven't been through it before, then how could you possibly have any real idea. If he was lucky he would get four months between April and sentencing, if he was unlucky it would be just two. It depended on how busy the courts were, that's all.

HMP LEYHILL, SEPTEMBER 2008

Max walked back to his 'apartment' as he called it. A truck load of new holiday makers were signing on at the front desk. One stood out from the crowd, he was five foot ten, five foot eleven, thin with pale skin. He had masses of hair with a full beard and moustache hanging down like Merlin, but jet black rather than silver grey. He reminded Max of a guy he used to work with at Churston Go Karts back in the summer of 1978. Max had started working there in the July and had his feet under the table when this rather unusual looking guy walked through the door announcing to Keith, the manager that he was the new recruit. He was probably in his mid twenties and Max just seventeen and his likeness to Rasputin made the name stick. In fact, Max never knew his real name, he was only known as Rasputin. He was a weirdo. Silly little things, like when he had his lunch, he covered his food, nobody knew what he was eating, he sort of hid it from view and sat awkwardly, all tightly together, his arms tucked in, feet together, knees together and crouched.

It had been a blisteringly hot day and there were no toilets or facilities on site, so when the time came, Max would tell Keith and off he would trot to the pub up the road. If, however it was just a pee, then a quick trip up to the end of the circuit, through the gate and behind the hedge would do the trick. There was a guy working at the track called Jimmy, he'd been working on the go karts for years. He'd gone off for a pee and he was one of life's great characters. He could tell a story like no other.

There was a huge commotion at the bottom of the track, Jimmy was shouting and jumping up and down trying to attract someone's attention. Naturally they all ignored him, but after a while, some drifted over to see what all the fuss was about. And there it was in all its glory. It was enormous, a leviathan, like a fallen tree basking in the sunshine, Max had never seen one so big. It was about eighteen inches long and must have been at least two inches in diameter along its picnic bar length and pointed to a tip at both ends. It had flattened the long grass either side. It was very dark, almost black and had a distinct pinch mark about one third from the most pointed end. There was a line of parallel shuffled forward footprints in front of the sharp end, the flattened grass clearly indicating the direction of travel. It was massive. Before long, all the staff were stood around it at a safe distance completely agog at what lay before them.

Jimmy summed it up, 'I bet that made his fucking eyes water!' There was one guy missing, it was Rasputin.

Max shook his head and smiled, leant forward and tied

587

the laces on his running shoes. It had started to rain, but it didn't matter, there would only be five more runs, thirty laps and two thousand five hundred calories as the time eked its way towards the finishing post.

Tim patted Max on the back as he walked past his room, 'Do one for me,' he shouted. The familiar tune blaring from his room was still reverberating around Max's head as he climbed the steep hill from the old red telephone box up to the gym at the top of the site. 'I don't like prison, Oh no, I hate it', Dreadlock Holiday. Graham Gouldman's lyrics just slightly changed by Max's version of the mid Seventies song by 10CC. With little over two weeks to go, the Russian Oak was shedding its leaves fast. Max would probably be right. He passed a few people out walking in the rain, their conversations still the same, no change there. What had changed was Max's mind. The desperation to be free as it edged closer was being tarnished by the worry of how things might have changed. The mental torture was still there too. The system that he had lived with since July filled him with apprehension. It would be the governor's decision to let Max go. What the governor said, the rest followed. Okay, Max hadn't stepped out of line, he complied with everything he was supposed to, but there was always the chance that someone, somewhere along the line might deem a longer stay at Her Majesty's pleasure. Just like the judge that put him away, the whole system was fickle. He never really knew exactly where he was. Would they let him out, he hoped so, but with Easton in the background still rumbling on, anything could happen.

A few days earlier, Will Phillipps had visited Max in prison. He'd come to go through some paperwork relating to Max's assets. The confiscation order would need to take into account every financial transaction over five hundred pounds that Max had done in the previous six years. Both personal and business accounts, absolutely everything including gifts, property, vehicles, the lot. It ran to twenty six lever arch files covering more than three thousand financial movements. It was difficult enough at that time trying to remember what happened yesterday, let alone recalling the details of a motorcycle bought by someone in London six years earlier. For Will, it had been the culmination of six months work started shortly after the April 'guilty plea' hearing.

Max worked through the paperwork and duly signed the affidavit in the space provided. To the best of his knowledge it was correct, but no doubt the prosecution would try to punch holes in it.

'What do you reckon it's going to cost me?' Max asked Will.

'A hundred, a hundred and twenty. It's difficult to say.'

'Do you think we could do a deal. Say, make them an offer of £50,000?'

'We can try.'

Unbeknown to Max, the reality was that Will was completely unaware of the potential penalty, like he had been about a lot of things. Yes, he was there doing his job, but he didn't really know how it all worked. He was a criminal lawyer, yet he had mislead Max so many times and it wasn't until Max had to confront certain situations that he had realised that Will didn't really have a clue what he was talking about. He was too flippant, too ready to give an answer.

Will had visited Max once before, when he was in Exeter prison. He'd been there a couple of weeks when a guard had come to the cell door and oiked Max out for a legal visit. At the time, the stress of living in those conditions was quite telling and Max needed to know that he was going to be transferred. Will should have known that Max could only be held at Exeter for three weeks, but he didn't. Will just kept saying that he would write to the governor and get Max out of there, which really just continued the anxiety. It was the 'not knowing'.

'Look Max, we will have you transferred as soon as we can. They're going to get you moved to Leyhill. It's an open prison. You will be able to come and go as you please, as long as you sign out at seven in the morning and sign in at seven at night.' Will assured Max.

'Can I take my car?'

'Yes, you can come and go as you please. Business as usual.'

'What? To and from Devon every day?' Max asked.

'Yeah. Whatever you want,' Will replied.

At the time, it seemed almost too good to be true and like most things too good to be true, they normally aren't. Okay, Leyhill was a million miles from Exeter's twenty-three hour day lock up, but it wasn't easy come, easy go either. Max was still contained in a strict regime. The thing is that, the prison service is all about control, and they do it in all sorts of ways but the mind games were something else. Max needed to keep his mental strength. Will's flippant comments had got Max's hopes up, only to be completely dashed at a later date by reality. It was those kind of things that made Max constantly on guard, wary of what was said, disbelieving of any potential good. His constant worry was always of a last minute change of plan. He'd heard too many stories of others being held back to feel confident that his release day was actually going to be as given. He wasn't sure of anything.

PLYMOUTH, APRIL 2008

Max made the now familiar journey to Plymouth. He parked the car and took the short walk into the Crown Court. April had come around quite quickly. Will Phillipps, Arthur Bailey and his personal assistant all turned to greet Max as he passed through the revolving doors. Court No. 2 was the destination as all four made their way past the court usher and into the silent room. Max took his seat in the witness box and waited.

A flurry of activity went on before him. The prosecution and defence barristers, chatting and smiling as if they were old friends.

'Court rise,' a voice rang out.

Max stood up and watched the ageing judge take his time to be seated. It wasn't a long hearing, maybe only thirty minutes at most. Max listened to the charges being read out by the clerk and stood for his response.

He had to answer 'Guilty', to each of the three counts and each time it became progressively more difficult to answer. It was galling beyond belief. He looked across at Easton bathing in his glory. Quite a lot of things came to Max's mind and none of them were good. He resigned himself to his hopeless position. There weren't that many in court that day. Apart from the court staff, the defence and the prosecution, there were only two other people sat at the back. One turned out to be the probation officer and the other was Easton's pocket journalist. Max didn't know it at the time, but that's how it was. Everything that happened, all the details, timings, privileged information, all going back to the journo.

Max walked out of court in deep thought. It wasn't a

huge weight lifted from his shoulders. Far from it, but it was a milestone. A no going back situation. From here on in, he was in the hands of the probation and the judge. He would have little or no influence on the outcome.

Inevitably, Arthur Bailey and Will Phillipps were fairly upbeat, but that was their job. Their lives didn't depend on the decision. They would still go home to their wives and families even if they got it wrong.

Apart from the anxiety of the lead up to July 14th, Max was starting to notice more than a number of strange goings on. Someone came to read the meter at his home. Max was outside, as was the meter. The guy flashed an ID card, which Max didn't take much notice of, but the guy read the meter too quickly. He couldn't have taken in the information as fast as he had made out. He closed the meter cupboard door and tried to make conversation with Max as he scanned the contents of the garage alongside. He wasn't there to read the meter, he was on a fact finding mission, probably sent by Easton. The guy walked out of the drive, jotting down something on his clipboard as he did so. Obviously feeling a little ill at ease, Max followed the guy discreetly and watched him get into a car some one hundred yards away and drive off. Strangely, he didn't read any other meters. It didn't happen once, it happened several times with different people. Most certainly, on another occasion, Easton had used a parcel delivery courier to do another check and a civvy dressed police officer as well. There were abnormal cars parked nearby Max's house with a lone occupant sat at the wheel. It wasn't paranoia, it was happening.

Easton needed to find out about Max's current dealings. He wanted to check with a number of customers exactly how much money Max had made and how he made it. Nearly all the customers were taken aback by Easton's approach. He was hard hitting, no nicety. He liked to dupe them, say something to get their backs up, something supposedly said by Max. It was Easton's style, that's how he got his results. It was the same when he was conducting the interviews with witnesses prior to Max being charged. He'd dupe them first, then provoke them into saying something. Not all of them wanted to be interviewed and some in particular gave Easton the short shrift he deserved. But Easton got the information he needed, not that he always liked it and discovered there really was no criminal dealings. Everything was above board with cars and bikes bought and sold, over two thousand of them. Easton did his best to muddy the water, but it didn't wash with everyone. They could see through him and the means to an end.

Easton's shock tactics approach made him few friends. His lies reeled off his tongue to perfection. On one occasion, he walked into a workshop where one of Max's cars was being repaired, fronted up to the proprietor and announced that he was from the fraud squad and those were the two words he used. He wasn't, but it sounded good. Easton said, 'Hey look, we don't want to cause Max any harm, we just want to get our job done, but as a matter of interest he's going to get at least two years.' It was all a load of bollocks, he just couldn't stop lying. That was his M.O.

The few months run in to July went quickly as the stomach acid increased for Max. There was no stopping the wheels of justice. With few days to go, Max had a full calendar to fulfil. He was racing his 1935 MG at the Silverstone International meeting over the fifth and sixth, so the car had to be prepared. He has several bikes being readied to go abroad plus there was the James Bond Ball to go to as well. By now, all Max could think about was the bloody court case. The same old story on and on and on. If he looked at it on the bright side, then he'd say to himself that at least it would all be over, but he just couldn't have realised how wrong he could be.

The previous week, he had the lengthy interviews with probation. They'd been exactly as expected, sandal wearing, lefty do-gooders. Nice enough people, but Max couldn't see the point. They had little or no idea of what had happened, why Max was charged and why he pleaded guilty. They were more used to simple theft, grievous bodily harm, drugs, that sort of thing. Even the probation officer in charge of doing the report admitted that she didn't understand the case. Nevertheless, she wrote the report and made her recommendations resulting in a twelve month suspended sentence or two hundred hours community service.

Max read the report and looked at the suggested penalty of two hundred hours community service and wondered how on earth he was going to fit it into his busy life. Two hundred hours working in a charity shop. It didn't bear thinking about, but it would be that or a twelve month suspended sentence.

Max walked out of the probation office not for the last time and called Will Phillipps letting him know how the probation report had gone.

'That's great Max. That's what we expected. You obviously didn't call them sandal wearing lefties then?'

'No, I wouldn't do that. I gave her all the information, answered all her questions and that was that,' Max replied.

'Okay, so two hundred hours community order or twelve months suspended sentence?'

'Yes, that's right.' He sighed.

'Well, I know how you feel about it all, but that has to be a good result. What will happen now is that probation will file the report with the court and the judge will go along with it. Okay? I'll speak to you between now and then, but you've got over the worst of it, so now it's just a rubber stamp exercise,' Will assured Max.

Somehow, Max wasn't completely at ease with Will's comments, but hey, he was the lawyer, he knew how it all worked, didn't he? The fact was that it was still up in the air, there was nothing definite and whilst Easton was running wild out there, anything could happen.

SILVERSTON, JULY 2008

It was the weekend of the 5th July, Max pulled into his allocated parking area behind the pits at Silverstone. He'd been there many times before tooing and froing for more than twenty seven years. It still filled him with the same excitement, that gladiatorial feel duelling in front of the assembled crowds. It was always fun at the start not always at the end, but that was motor racing. A mad mix of emotion. Max got himself sorted, unloaded the car and went off to sign on. It was the same routine at every meeting. Say hello to people he knew and take a cursory look at what else was about, then start the car, warm it through getting everything up to temperature, checking the gauges and with all okay wander on down to scrutineering. No matter how many times Max went through scrutineering, it was always the worst moment of the meeting, the anticipation of something wrong being found. As it was, he needn't have worried, the car sailed through, the 'passed' tag confirming the cars eligibility to race along with the drivers overalls and helmet. He could relax, there was more than a couple of hours before practice. Time to get a cup of tea and a bacon sandwich and forget about all the crap for a while.

The MG Max was racing was what is known as a Triple MMM car, a pre war two seat, supercharged sports racing car, complete with cycle wings, aero screens and a fish tail exhaust. It was quite quick too with its four cylinder 930cc engine producing about one hundred and fifty horsepower combined with a lightweight aluminium body made it great fun to drive. It was all over the place even in a straight line, but that's old cars. When Max had tested a Formula Three car at Silverstone back in 1984 with RD Motorsport, that car was like it was on rails. The MG couldn't have been more different. Narrow wire wheels, soft suspension, no seat belts plus steering and brakes that needed more than a little anticipation. For all that, it was a great car and Max loved racing it.

Practice had been pretty eventful. Max had rolled out onto the circuit, all temperatures at their normal operating levels, but two laps in, the water coolant was pressurising out of the radiator cap making it difficult to see as the spray showered him with hot water. Backing off seemed to help, but two laps later, he was in the pit lane. The claxon sounded as Max crawled past the pit lane garages to a halt. It was best left to cool down and take a look. It didn't matter how many times it was checked before the meeting, but if it's going to happen, it always will in practice or a race. It was a beautiful day, a bit windy, but a good racing day. Max jumped onto the pit wall along the start/finish straight and watched the rest of practice, noting the cars in his class and timing some of them loosely on his wristwatch. There wasn't a lot to be learnt from watching them all drone by on the straight, but he could see that two in his class were reasonably close. The opening gap between them along the straight indicated that the front car had a 'great' advantage and the fact that they were close together down by the start meant that the following car was probably quicker in the tight section of the complex. The six cylinder MGK3 led the way whilst the lightweight aluminium bodied special scrapped behind it. All good stuff.

Max took the car back to the paddock after practice and started investigating the fault. He had plenty of time, the race wasn't until the following day and right then it was just before three in the afternoon. Having checked all the usual possibles, hoses, water pump etc, it was looking increasingly like the radiator was blocked. Max stripped down the front of the car and set about attempting a repair but it was useless, nothing could be done there and then. Being the biggest meeting on the MG calendar, there were masses of stalls and shops all over the infield, so a search resulted in a brand new aluminium radiator and seven hundred quid less in his pocket. It was a bit of a fuss trying to get everything to fit, but with some help he managed to run it up before he lost the daylight.

A good clean up later, Max picked up a copy of the practice times, surprised to see that he had qualified eighth overall and fastest in class. The two protagonists he'd been watching earlier from the pit lane wall would sit behind him on row five for the start.

It had been a long day and with so much going on, the thought of the court hearing had not crossed his mind once, but now alone in his motor home, he could think of nothing else.

Back in the early eighties, Catherine would have gone to all the meetings, been chief gofor, pushed the Formula Ford, passed the spanners and then slept in the back of the car afterwards, but she wasn't at Silverstone that weekend, the children had her occupied helping out at a birthday party hence Max was on his own, just like Billy Nomates.

Come the following day, Max got up early and tested the radiator, all seemed well, but for the race under racing conditions, who knows what would happen. It was really untried, but there wasn't much else he could do as he sat in the assembly area waiting for his race to be called.

No matter how many times Max had raced, he still got the ticker pumping. It wasn't as rapid as it was on the grid in Formula Ford, because racing historics was much more relaxed, but he still skipped a beat now and then. The race official waved the cars forward and Max held back a little to give himself a bit of a gap simply to have enough room in front of him to give the car a quick blast and check the radiator cap. He did just that and there didn't seem to be a problem. All the needles sat comfortably as Max drew slowly up to his grid position alongside the club secretary's six cylinder MGK3. A similar car would be directly behind him and the lightweight next.

Max made a useless start getting swamped off the line, but managed to recover through the first corner, Copse and regain his starting grid position by the time he reached Becketts before the right turn onto the back straight down to Abbey. For a while he thought he could continue ripping through the grid, but

595

they were slower starting coming up to speed whereas Max had to go quickly immediately because of the bad start. The cherry red MGK3 and the lightweight special were all over the back of Max going into Abbey which was a pattern that lasted the whole race. All three of them in close action, wheel to wheel lap after lap, sometimes swapping places two or three times in the space of a few corners. It was thrilling stuff.

Max was leading the class on the final lap, running seventh overall as they went into Beckett's for the last time, all three eager to win. Max looked in the mirror, there was nothing in it. The lightweight was up the inside and the K3 was trying his luck on the outside. Max held the left third of the circuit and braked as late as he dared for Abbey being careful not to collect the lightweight steaming up his right hand side. In defending the corner, Max lost a little bit of momentum as he started the uphill climb towards Bridge. A bit of race craft was needed. From Abbey up to Bridge Corner, the K3 and the lightweight were definitely quicker. Max took the centre of the track up the hill moving slowly further towards the right to stop the lightweight, but the more powerful K3 stomped past Max and took the apex at Bridge. It was a brave move at close quarter. Into the left hander at Priory, all three ran nose to tail and again played follow the leader through Turn 15 of the GP circuit. Then, it was just a short straight into the right hand corner at Luffield before the blast back onto the start/finish straight. Max followed the K3 up into Luffield but knew that if the leading car held his line at the apex, onto the final run down to the flag, Max couldn't win. Instead, the K3 did exactly what he thought he would do, but Max took what is considered the wet line on the outside of Luffield. Instantly, the lightweight special jumped into the vacant space behind the K3. It's a longer curve on the outside at Luffield but Max knew he could get on the throttle earlier, which worked to perfection as he went around the outside to take and win the class. The three of them went over the line barely a tenth of a second apart. Okay, it wasn't as thrilling as the final lap of the 1978 Transatlantic with Sheene doing the same to Roberts as they edged towards the grass, but it felt like it.

Any thoughts of the impending doom awaiting him a little over a week later were for a short while at the back of his mind, but the long journey home would soon ignite those worries. For now though, he had a prize giving to attend.

The last two weeks at Leyhill had flown by. Keeping himself occupied had shortened the days and the hours hadn't dragged. It was Friday 25 October and it was his last working day in the laundry. He wasn't going to miss it when he was gone, the thought of Raz and what he'd done, but he would look back on his time there with mixed memories, some good, some bad. The good would come from the camaraderie and the humour whilst the bad would be some of the terrible stories he heard about some of those he had to work with.

Back in August, Max had met with his on site probation officer in OMU. It was a sounding out exercise, how are you and all that, but also Max was given the discretionary dates for his release. Although, he couldn't figure out exactly how they came to the 29th October date, he nevertheless had it confirmed again. It was the same date as given to him in Exeter, which at the time he thought was a mistake. It would still need the governor's signature, but if he kept out of trouble, the date would stand.

'You will get a confirmation of your release date from us two weeks before you go,' the probation officer had said. In actual fact, he only received the confirmation paperwork five days before his release. Even this was more mental torture. Max had told Catherine that he would know for sure when he'd be released two weeks before he was going out the door, but it didn't happen that way. Max had to put in an application to the OMU to chase them up. It was a tense time.

Five days before leaving, he got the confirmation papers, duly signed by the OMU and the governor. It looked like he was getting out. He read through the information. He was being released on licence. He would have to wear a tag bracelet on his ankle and remain on curfew at his home address for three months between the hours of eight at night and eight in the morning. No travel abroad, plus weekly meetings with the local probation office. Abide by the conditions and stay out of trouble was the order of the day or failure to do so would result in Max being collected and sent straight back to a lock up prison and he certainly didn't want that. In some ways he really did think for the first time that he was going to get out as the emotional pressure was welling up inside him.

Max finished in the laundry at just after half past two that day and had the rest of the day off. They always finished early on a Thursday and Friday, so he went back to his room. There was a note under the door. He picked it up and read it. He smiled, it was from Kat, the music teacher. She was also responsible for the Creative Writing club and her note simply asked if Max would like to read out some sections of his book to the members that evening. He looked across at his desk, the reams of handwritten manuscript neatly stacked in the corner. Three hundred thousand words in eleven weeks. That was a lot of ink.

He opened his locker and looked at his provisions. Just enough to ride out the weekend. He pulled out his beaker and made himself a cup of tea and sat on the end of the bed. He picked up his pen and wrote down the last line, it had been a long time coming.

Being a Friday meant that he would skip the evening meal and go running. Like so many other things now, it would be for the last time. It had come down to the last six miles. He would have normally run on the following Monday, but because he was going to be released on the Tuesday, then all his personal belongings would be bagged up and held in the custody office as from 2:00 pm on Monday.

He had renewed vigour in his step running those last six miles. The effort came easily, it wasn't hard work, he'd broken the back of it. Coming down the hill from the top of :C" wing, passing the OMU office, he looked up at the old tall Russian oak before him. It was all but bare, just as he had thought. He sprinted the last three hundred yards as if his life depended on it. It was over, no more.

The creative writing club was held once a week for an hour in a small room annexed to the library. It was a two minute walk from Max's room. He sat down, nodding to a few that he knew and waited for the stragglers to arrive, or 'stranglers' as someone said.

The hubbub of conversation died as Kat stood up and started, 'Hi, everyone. Thanks for coming. I've asked Max to come along this week and read a passage from his book. He came to me when he first arrived here a few months ago and asked my advice. I read the first few pages and I was hooked. I wanted to read more. It's called 'Another Day in Paradise'.'

A few snorted down their noses as they smiled, nodding in acknowledgement. They knew what it meant.

Max read a passage and then stopped. Kat looked around at everyone. No one said anything. It was a bit disconcerting. He needn't have worried.

'You wrote that?'

'Yes,' Max replied.

'I don't think I'm ever going to be able to write like that.'

Max smiled. One by one, they all added their bit. It was good, they all liked it, he just hoped the paying public would think the same.

'Go on then, read us some more,' so he did.

EXETER, APRIL 2009

John Hutchings along with his company chairman, Brian Furlong and the longstanding company solicitor Robin Moore sat waiting patiently in the reception area of their Exeter based barristers chambers. Whilst Brian and Robin quietly chatted about some totally un-associated subject, John pulled out the solicitors letter from his brief case and familiarised himself with the content. He'd read it a dozen times before, but one more time wouldn't hurt.

'*We act for the above named.*

Our client has previously, from around January 1996 to December 2004 purchased from you various Ferrari motor vehicles, parts and servicing.

In March 1999, our client placed two orders with you for two Ferrari 360 Spider motor vehicles ('Vehicles'). By way of a receipt he paid the sum of £1000 in respect of each of the Vehicles. Our client's purchase of the Vehicles was evidenced in your order forms, a copy of which is attached. Our client dealt with your then sales manager Richard Rippon who informed our client that he could expect delivery of the Vehicles in late 2000.

At the time of placing the order for the Vehicles, our client was informed that he was the first person to do so.

On the strength of placing orders for the Vehicles with you, our client at a later date then sold on each Vehicle to his customers at a premium. You were well aware of this practice by

599

our client, knowing him to be a vehicle 'speculator'. You would also have been aware that the premiums would have been substantial. In fact, the Vehicles attracted premiums of £110,000 and £100,000 respectively. In that respect, our client entered into written contracts with both of his customers and took a £1000 deposit from each customer in respect of the Vehicles.

You will be familiar with the practice of vehicle speculators, which relies on the speculator being able to obtain one of the first few vehicles produced.

We understood that ownership of the Ferrari dealership was subsequently acquired in or around 1999 by the Lisk Group and that Mr. Rippon was replaced by Mr. Desmond Law as sales manager and then afterwards by Shaun Williams.

When our client had not received either of the Vehicles by September 2000 he started making enquiries with your sales staff, most notably Shaun Williams and Lance Mills. We are instructed that on every occasion, whether by telephone or personal visits, he was given various and numerous reasons as to why the vehicles had not been delivered. These included delays at the factory, production problems, allocation issues, lack of Maserati sales etc.

Our client eventually took delivery of the first of the Vehicles ('First Vehicle') in July 2002. However, owing to the delay in the delivery of the First Vehicle, he had by this time lost his original buyer and refunded his deposit. Although our client found a new buyer for the First Vehicle, he was only able to realise a premium of £20,000.

The second of the Vehicles ('Second Vehicle') was not received until January 2003 and, again, our client had by then lost his original purchaser and refunded the deposit to him. In respect of the Second Vehicle ultimately our client was only able to realise a premium of £15,000.

At the time that our client was awaiting delivery of the Vehicles, he had no reason to suspect that you had deliberately taken steps to delay their delivery to our client.

Pursuant to an investigation into our client's business activities, in 2005, witness statements were taken by the police from employees of yours, namely Shaun Williams, Lance Mills and Nick Pelling. Copies of the statements are enclosed for your attention. Those statements came into our client's possession in March 2008.

It is clear to us from an examination of the enclosed

600

witness statements that you deliberately breached your contracts with our client in respect of the orders of the Vehicles. The First Vehicle should have been delivered to our client in early 2001, when the initial allocation of Ferrari 360 Spiders was delivered to you. The date of that allocation can be checked with Ferrari UK should the need arise. However, it is clear from the statements of Shaun Williams and Lance Mills that in order to conceal the delivery dates of the Vehicles, that they continually lied to our client over a considerable period of time, informing our client that the Vehicles had not arrived.

With regards to the Second Vehicle, which should also have been delivered in early 2001, it is apparent that you significantly delayed the process by not having ordered the Vehicle in the first place, despite giving our client assurances that this vehicle was also due to be delivered.

As a result of the above, you were in breach of contract with our client on both occasions. Accordingly our client lost the opportunity to fulfil his order to his first original customer on the First Vehicle which he had sold for a premium of £110,000. Our client also lost the opportunity to fulfil his order to his second original customer for the Second Vehicle which he had sold for a premium of £100,000.

Our client was not aware of your breaches of contract until his receipt of the enclosed statements. In that regard, we therefore consider that the provisions of Section 32(1)(b) of the Limitation Act 1980 are applicable.

As an aside, our client visited your dealership on one of many occasions in early 2002. At the time, you apparently had a new blue Ferrari 456GTA for sale in the showroom at an asking price of circa £179,000. The vehicle had apparently been unsold for a considerable period of time. Mr. Williams asked our client whether he had a customer for the vehicle; he said that he did not. However, Mr. Williams apparently suggested to our client that he could offer the car for sale at £139,950 and receive a £3000 commission if sold. We understand that Mr. Williams was able to offer this car at an advantageous price because he intended to inform Ferrari UK that the vehicle would be put on as a demonstrator and therefore attract the considerable demonstrator discount available. Our client duly advertised the car in The Sunday Times *the following weekend and found such a buyer who duly completed the purchase of the vehicles from you. Mr. Williams informed our client that he would credit our client's account in relation to the balance of the monies due on the First Ferrari 360 Spider, which he still had not yet received. Despite assurances from Mr. Williams, we are instructed that our client never received the agreed sum of £3000.*

On the basis of your clear breaches of contract, our client has suffered losses equivalent to the difference between the premium that he was due to make on the Vehicles and the premium that he did in fact make. That loss amounts to £175,000 plus interest plus damages. Our client would also like to be paid the outstanding commission due for the sale of the Ferrari 456GTA plus interest.

We look forward to receiving your proposals in relation to the above claim within the next fourteen days, failing which our client will have no alternative other than to bring proceedings against you in that respect.'

Hutchings looked at his name as the addressee and the client's name below, Max Reed. He folded up the letter and placed it back into his brief case letting out a long sigh as he did so.

Moments later, all three men were sitting in front of their barrister. The usual pleasantries aside, Walter Sprowell started his advice.

'Gentlemen, I'm going to be straight to the point with you on this one. I would advise that you reach a compromise and settle this quickly. Interest is running as are fees. My view is that whilst we could make a stand, I think ultimately we would fail.

'There are areas which we could explore in relation to the Statutory Limitations, but they would be very weak and I don't see us having any real chance of overturning the claim. If you want me to sketch out a battle plan to try to put them off then it maybe worth a try. It depends on how deep his pockets are and how much you want to spend as well.'

'With regard to the statements made by your employees, each appears to concur with the other, therefore it seems clear to me that what has been said was in fact true.

'Your only hope in this case would be to knockout the six year statutory limitation period, in other words the claimant should have made a claim within six years of the breach of contract. However, he is saying he didn't know about any breach of contract, which again according to your staff appears to be correct, because by their own admission, they were indeed lying to the claimant.'

Sprowell paused for a while and consulted his statute reference book, reading out loud the claimant's point.

'The provisions of section 32(1)(b) of the Limitations Act 1980 state that the six year ruling can be dismissed if it is adjudged that there was 'Concealment' and the part (b) adds the potential for 'profit'. Having read the papers Robin sent to me, I believe that the court would find in favour of the 'Concealment for profit' element of their claim and therefore allow the proceedings against you in regard to the breaches of contract to go ahead.

'It follows that your employees witness statements support the claims of Mr. Reed and that, I believe would be very difficult, if not impossible to overcome.

'In short, you're on a very sticky wicket, which is why my advice would be to settle.'

Hutchings rubbed his forehead and looked across at Brian Furlong, both realising what a bloody mess they were in. It wasn't just the breaches of contract, it was the whole debacle. It could soon get out of hand if they were not careful. Ferrari UK could be drawn in and possibly the factory too. There was also the matter of the £40,000 demonstrator discount that they had falsely claimed. There could be others too. The last thing he wanted was for this to get out. Bad publicity like this would be pretty damaging and anything with the word Ferrari in the headline would grab attention.

Furlong and Hutchings walked side by side from the barrister's chambers in Southernhay Gardens, back to their car.

'He's got us by the balls,' Brian said despairingly.

'Yeah, I think he has, but we've got more money,' Hutchings slowly replied thinking to himself that maybe he should have been a little less cocksure when they had met.

HMP LEYHILL, 28 OCTOBER 2008

The last full day at HMP Leyhill was a busy one. The technical term is 'walkabout'. It was time to hand back everything that Max acquired during his stay. The CD player needed to be returned to the church, books back to the library, clothing to the stores and start signing out of the system. By the end of the day he would have a virtually bare room and the

603

clothes he was standing up in. All else would be waiting for him at Custody or have been given back to the appropriate department. It was a simple system which gave Max plenty of time to get his exit card stamped and signed ready to go, but absolutely everything had to be signed off. If anything was missed, then route one out would be closed. There were a few goodbyes to be said to those genuine people that Max had met and a little bit of guilt that he was the one leaving whilst they stayed behind, but the number one priority in prison is every man for himself. It was now Max's turn to go and whilst he felt sorry for those he liked, it was time for him to return to his family and try to put the sorry tale behind him. That was never going to be easy which is why he was on the one hand ecstatic about leaving yet on the other hand, full of apprehension as to what would happen next.

It was just after 7.00 pm, Max's room was empty. Photographs, cards, letters all gone from the walls. The chisel like carvings in the calendar marking off the dates inside, all gone. There was nothing, the room echoed with his every move. It was now down to hours. Looking back, it would have been easy to say that it had all gone so quickly, but that would have been rose tinted glasses and it wasn't. There were times when he struggled to get through the day and often the nights. The thoughts would stay with him, might even haunt him at times, he didn't know. There were two teabags left, one for a cup at 8:00 pm and the other for when he got up in the morning.

There was a quiet knock at the door. Max got up from his chair overlooking the meadow and opened it. The old habit of putting his foot behind it still there. It was Jim, with two mugs of coffee and a packet of Hobnobs. He was the first of many that night, notably Chris, Danny and Tim, all knowing Max was on his way. They were all hard men, fraud, drugs, assassin and murder all in that order. It didn't bear thinking about what some had done, but underneath that, in that environment, Max could enjoy a couple of hours of laughter, telling jokes, hearing stories no doubt embellished and winding out the last few hours. There was a camaraderie, united in their position, giving one of their friends a send off. Max hadn't expected it, but it showed that he had some standing even when he was in a totally different environment to the norm. These were hardened criminals, men that he would not have normally come across, but here they gave him some respect. Max had stuck to his principles, steered a neutral course and stood up for himself when he had to. As far as they were concerned, Max shouldn't have been there, such was the difference between them, but they had grown to like him and would probably think about him now and then when he was gone just like he would of them.

It was gone ten, Danny was the first to go, he didn't like goodbyes, Max could see it in his face. Were his eyes watering, it certainly looked like it. Max wondered if they were for him or the sudden realisation yet again, that it still wasn't his turn. Max watched him to the corner at the end of the corridor and disappear out of sight probably never to see him again. And that was it really, friends for a moment. When you are kids changing schools, moving on, you take it in your stride, but later in life, you think so much more about it and it affects you more.

They'd all gone. Max switched off the light and rested his head on the pillow. He thought about the evening and was trying to remember who said it, because it sounded so real. 'A flash of anger, a lifetime of regret, it's still murder though'. It was a chilling thought, which no doubt would ring a few bells with some.

He turned over and closed his eyes. *I'm not going to miss this bed*, he thought.

14 JULY 2008

The day started badly. Max had a restless night's sleep, constantly turning this way and that. Inevitably, the thought of the day ahead and how it would all unfold.

The telephone rang at 7:05 am, it was Catherine's father. He was up early as always and had the radio on in the kitchen as he made the morning tea.

'Max, I've just been listening to the local news, they're saying you are to appear in court today on charges of deception and . . .' he paused, he didn't know what to say, 'is it true?'

'Yes, it is. I'm sorry. I can't explain it all now, but I will talk to you about it later.' Max put down the phone.

'Who was that?' Catherine asked.

'Your dad.' Max held his head in his hands. 'It's all over the radio.'

'Oh, no,' Catherine replied, knowing that was the last

thing they needed. Max could hear the sorrow in her voice as she said it. He hadn't wanted it to come to this and he'd done everything he could to protect his family from it, but now it was out of his control. And guess who was pulling the strings, revving everyone up. It was Easton. He had them all eating out of his hand and he loved it.

Max reversed out of his driveway and watched his family wave back at him as he drove off towards Plymouth. 'I'm not sure what time I'll be back, but I'll call you when I get out of court.' It was the last thing he'd said before leaving. It was a fifty minute journey to Plymouth at that time of the morning. The barrister and Will Phillipps had asked Max to be at court by 9:30 am. He was there on time, but he hadn't expected the reception. There was a television crew and reporters blocking the entrance to the court. He watched them from a distance for a while thinking surely this can't be for me? Abruptly, the cameraman had been distracted and in an instant Max slipped through the entrance way passing the reporters and was on his way upstairs to the first floor Crown Courts.

Arthur Bailey stood in the foyer with his secretary as Max walked in to say hello. Surprisingly, Will Phillipps wasn't there. He sent his apologies. Max wasn't impressed.

They walked through to a briefing room and Max asked, 'So what's the format?'

Arthur Bailey looked over his glasses in his usual style, remarking that, 'we will go into court, you will stand in the witness box whilst the charges etc are read out. The Crown Prosecution Service will say a few words for a couple of minutes and then I will respond asserting the plea.'

It seemed so simple. Bailey continued, 'The judge will either respond with his summing up and sentencing at that point or he will retire for a while and come back in to sentence a little bit later.'

Arthur came across as being rather dismissive of it all. It was just a formality. Another day in the life of . . . Max was worried. It was more than that. For some reason, he just didn't seem to have the confidence in Arthur Bailey that he really should have had. And why wasn't Will Phillipps there? He'd been with Max from the start and now on the day of reckoning, there was no sign of him and no word from him either. Max didn't know whether paranoia was creeping in, but it seemed like too much was ganging up on him.

Easton and McGrain walked past with Rick Brady. 'What the hell was Rick doing here?' Max asked.

'They can bring whoever they like,' Bailey replied, 'but it's of no consequence because he's not taking part in any of the proceedings.'

Max looked at Brady and realised that Easton must have 'turned' him.

The court usher called forward the case and everyone shuffled quietly through to their places. It took a while for everyone to be seated. Max sat in the witness box flanked either side by Reliance Security guards. He looked around the room, there were a lot more than at previous hearings. There were four or five reporters at the back, notepads in hand or laptops busily being tapped. Easton's pocket journo' happy to take every last word.

The formalities of the court session opening aside, the barrister for the CPS stood up to give his version of events. Twice he was interrupted by the judge as he heaped vitriol on what had happened and proceeded with a forty five minute character assassination. Max was fuming. If he could have leapt over the witness box and beat the hell out of the barrister and got away with it, he would have done. He was so mad. Bailey said the CPS would get up for a couple of minutes and say their bit. That's not what happened. Max was now genuinely fearing for his situation. Not only had Bailey been wrong about the CPS, but now he'd replied with a very weak response pleading with the judge to exercise some leniency. This wasn't at all like Bailey had led Max to believe. The judge needed to retire for a while and consider his verdict. The usher directed the court to rise and moments later Max was outside again in the foyer. He caught sight of Bailey walking towards him. He looked sheepish as if he knew something Max didn't.

There was a sharp, frank exchange of words between them as Max let Bailey know exactly how he felt. There didn't seem to be one thing that Bailey had said would happen, actually did. It was all going wrong. The sudden change of position from six to twelve month suspended sentence or a community order to the very real possibility of going to prison was altogether shocking. It took Max's breath away.

It was an agonising forty five minutes waiting for the judge to arrive at a decision. Meanwhile, Easton was running around like a headless chicken setting up all his pocket reporters.

It was a world away from how Max thought all these things worked. Max had lost faith not just in his barrister, but in the whole justice system. The judge didn't appear to give the case enough consideration. The investigating officers hadn't once interviewed Max's accountant and this was a fraud case and they themselves had absolutely no accountancy training. None of it made any sense. The CPS barrister seemed too venomous and the police bent every rule if they could to justify a result. And as for Arthur Bailey, who was supposed to be on Max's side, he just keeled over and waved his legs in the air. It didn't matter to him, it wasn't his life on the line.

There was so much more Bailey should have said. He was woefully weak on his advice. He should have said more, expanding on scenarios and outcomes, Max thought. He'd never once prepared Max for a situation like this. In the eight years that Max's probation officer had been doing her job, a judge had never acted outside of her recommendation. What she had suggested had generally been accepted and applied.

Forty agonising minutes passed and the court was back in session, the judge making his address. As he spoke, Max could sense an air of inevitability in his tone. By then the fear had taken over in Max's body, a cold sweat, his hearing getting weaker and weaker until he could hear no more.

By the time the judge had said to Arthur Bailey that, 'he left him no choice other than to pass a custodial sentence of . . .' Max was on the floor. Passed out.

Easton looked at McGrain, 'I don't think he was expecting that.'

No, he certainly wasn't. When he came around, he heard the decision second hand. Fourteen months.

'Take him down.'

Outside, a white Reliance van awaited him.

The female security guard to the left of Max asked him the time. He raised his wrist in response and she cuffed it. It worked every time.

NEWTON ABBOT, AUGUST 2007 2007

Sanders wanted to see the look on Leblanc's face when he walked through the workshop door. He heard his footsteps

608

walk down the driveway and the distant conversation. The door opened and in walked Leblanc. He hadn't noticed Sanders standing on the far side as he eyes absorbed in disbelief the beautiful old remains of the racing Bugatti sat before him. He knelt down and ran his hand along the top of the rocker cover, deep in thought.

'Beautiful, isn't it?' said Sanders.

'Ah, Ralph, how are you? I didn't see you.'

'That's understandable.'

'C'est magnifique,' Leblanc said, shaking his head.

Max made the coffees as the pair of them buried themselves in every detail of the car. Photograph after photograph, details, numbers, shapes and sizes. It was all recorded over a five hour period leaving nothing uncovered.

It was late in the afternoon, Sanders and Leblanc's work was finished. The telephone rang in Leblanc's jacket pocket as he fumbled for it.

'Allo, Leblanc.'

It was the Russian. He was the buyer. He simply needed to know if it was what it was supposed to be.

Leblanc answered, 'In my opinion, this is without doubt the most original Bugatti Type 35B ever to have been found and I agree totally with Ralph Sanders report. It is unbelievable and fantastic all in one.'

Leblanc looked at Max. 'He wants to speak to you.'

Max took the mobile, 'Hello, Max Reed speaking.'

'Hi, I think we have a deal don't we?'

'Yes, I think so.'

'Okay, let me have your banking details and I'll get the monies wired over. I'm not sure what we're gonna do with the car just now, but if it's okay with you, can it stay at your place for a couple of weeks?'

'Yes, that's fine with me.'

'Good, I'll be in touch.'

That was it. The end of three years work. The Russian did exactly what he said he would do and he bought the car. A piece of automotive history as he called it.

Sadly, the euphoria of the moment was cut drastically short by the impending conclusion to another long term investigation which was something Sanders and Leblanc had no idea about. Max had managed to stay calm throughout and do the deal regardless of his own personal problems and to that end he succeeded. Unfortunately, the trade off was much worse than he could have expected. Some you win, some you lose. It's all about a sensible balance.

HMP LEYHILL, 29 OCTOBER 2008

Inevitably, it was bound to be. Max woke up early. It was dark outside and the orange of the camp lights flashed across the room as he opened the curtains to look outside. It was snowing very lightly and there were signs of it settling in places around the meadow in front of him. He looked at his watch, 5:45 am. He got back into bed and dozed for a while. Today was the day.

He could hear people shuffling around upstairs and along the corridor. The noisy clicking of the starters on the fluorescent tubes indicating that someone had set off the automatic lights. The distant sound of the flush, taps and doors opening and closing confirming the slow waking of the prison.

Max rolled out of bed and headed for the kitchen, where he dunked his last teabag. He placed his beaker on the desk in his room, gathered up his wash bag and went to the ablution block. Minding his own business, he cleaned his teeth as he watched people in his peripheral vision come and go. Eyes straight ahead, but watching all the time. Now, it was second nature.

The shower started running, and a voice shouted across the room.

'Would you like me to sing you a song Max?'

'Yeah, why not,' he replied.

It was Tim, 'I'm coming home, I've done my time. And I've got to know what is and isn't mine. A simple yellow ribbon…'

He sang the whole song from start to finish. It was sort of corny, but it happened. A huge muscular black guy, who'd already served more than ten years for murder was there singing, 'Tie a Yellow Ribbon' to Max at 7:15 am in the morning. Nothing failed to amaze him, even on the day he was leaving.

Even though Max had the exit papers and had cleared his room, the apprehension of the moment was still immense. He had maybe four hundred yards absolute maximum for his walk to freedom. There would be three staging posts along the way, the first being the unlocking of the 'A' unit doors, the second being the custody Reception/Discharge office and lastly the security officer at the gatehouse. It was nothing, yet it was everything. The clock ticked agonisingly slow towards the "Go" time of 7:45 am. Max closed his room door for the last time and flipped over the name tag on the door. The night before, he had written on the back of it, a message for the guards. It read, 'Please find the biggest, most violent, hairy arsed prisoner to take my place in this room and see how he likes being kept awake all night, signed Max Reed, 29.10.08.' It was a parting shot for the crack head next door.

Max slowly walked down to the 'A' unit main doors, by the office, a small number had already gathered waiting for the doors to open, so they could drift up to the canteen for breakfast. The guard emerged from the office, his stomach appearing first. He stood for a while, waiting until the radio confirmed the roll call numbers were correct and then slowly unlocked the exit. A swell of prisoners crammed through the three foot space and out into the cold fresh air. It had stopped snowing and it was light but the orange camp lights were still ablaze. The reception building was only a couple of hundred yards. Up ahead, Max could see three new recruits being escorted down the path. They must have arrived on the early tour bus. He wanted to run, but it would have made no difference. He looked around as he passed the miniature maze on his left hand side, the guard with his three prisoners now in focus a stones throw away. Max looked at them all knowing what they were thinking as he had done before them. He looked at one, the nearest to him, he was quite old, but somehow he seemed strangely familiar. As he passed Max, shoulder to shoulder, they looked straight at each other, their heads rotating holding the gaze as they walked forward. Max walked backwards for a few steps continuing to look back down the path at the new recruit. Max was certain he knew him, but couldn't place him. He wanted to go up to him and ask him who he was, satisfy himself that it was either someone he did or didn't know, but he didn't, he was going home and it didn't matter. He still had the picture of the man's face in his mind as he pushed open the door to the Reception building and stood up against the wall. Five others were also going out, Max knew two of them from working in the laundry. They nodded, a token hello.

The guards called them in one by one. A little

conversation broke out.

'Christ, I'd have thought you'd have a happier face than that,' a guy said to Max.

'I will, when I get out that gate,' is all Max said. The moment was tense, the last few minutes of the guards' control.

Reed's name was shouted out, he turned and went into the discharge office. Three prison officers stood around lazily whilst the governor sat behind his desk. Max walked up to him.

'Sign here and here and collect your stuff in there.' It was all Max wanted to hear from him. 'And then wait outside.'

Max did as he was told. Two down one to go. Whilst he was waiting for the others to go through the same procedures he had time to think about the night before. Jim had asked him what he was going to do when he got out. All the usual answers and suggestions came out, but in particular he'd asked about Max's book.

'Hopefully, I'll find a publisher and make it all worthwhile.'

'Yeah, but are you going to do it in your own name or someone else?' Jim asked.

'The jury's still out on that one,' Max replied.

'What about getting back at them all? How are you going to do that?'

Max thought for a moment. 'Oh that's the easy bit, when I get the book published and I've got them in my hands, then I'll send each one of the individuals a copy. If they start reading it, at first they won't know what it's about, but as they get further into the book, there'll be snippets of information which will make them think, "that's something like I did". They'll read on thinking, "that sounds familiar" and then it will dawn on them that the book is about them. They may well be thinking that they'd got away with it, but they won't because everyone will know.' Max smiled and continued, 'A lasting testament.'

The thought of the conversation was overpowered by the image of the man's face he'd seen ten minutes earlier. Who was he? He was sure he knew him.

From where he stood Max could easily see the gate house, the red and white pole was all that kept him from the outside world. He could hurdle it, if he had to. The guard stepped out onto the pavement by which time all were ready to go.

'Okay lads, keep to the path, single file and present your discharge sheet to the gatehouse. Stay out of trouble.' No one said anything. It was no more than one hundred and fifty yards. There were two guards to pass en route, watching. Max took the walk, feeling like a cold war spy being handed over at checkpoint Charlie, not knowing if he was going to make it to the other side.

He passed the first guard, expressionless. He had nothing to say to him. Max had already had one "run in" with him at the mandatory drugs test. He hadn't liked him then and nothing had changed his mind. The face reappeared in his mind, he shook his head, he knew who it was now. There was no mistaking, a little less hair, a little more weight and thirty four years wear and tear. It was Prior!

He passed the next guard, he was clear through to the gatehouse, he took a breath, he was all but there. A firm hand dropped onto his shoulder. Max turned. *Surely not*, he thought.

'You dropped your discharge sheet mate. You'll need that,' he smiled. Max could feel the sweat on his hands, as he stood at the gatehouse looking out across the entrance for Catherine. He couldn't see her, or her car. She wasn't there.

NEWTON ABBOT, SEPTEMBER 2007

Max wasn't surprised when he received Jacques' phone call. It was only three days after the sale had gone through on the Bugatti and it was a lot of money to be thinking about, but the call wasn't what he'd expected. There was no talk of how much and when, what they would be spending it on, there was no frivolity, no joy. Max could tell immediately from the tone in Jacques' voice that something was wrong, tragically wrong. Olivier had died, and in the best possible way if there was one. He had sat in his chair down by the lake on that fine summer's day. He had just finished a light lunch, a green salad with a homemade bread roll and a glass of local red wine. He sat back and rested his head, closed his eyes and listened to the soft breeze in the reeds and the two or three ducks flitting about at the shoreline. He drifted off in the tranquillity of it all and never woke up.

Max could picture it exactly. The thought of Olivier going peacefully was a pleasant one. He'd always been very understanding, easy to get along with, a proper gentleman in an old school way. Yes, it was sad, but in a strange sort of way, it made Max smile. It was a fitting end to a grand life, notable for the extreme highs of the early good times and the dark lows of the second world war, yet through all that, he had remained a charming and beguiling, trusting and charismatic head of a family that Max was unlikely to meet the likes of ever again. It was and always would be a nice thought.

CHRISTMAS DAY 2009

Donald Key woke early, the family were all due to descend on him by lunchtime for the traditional Christmas turkey. He went downstairs slowly, rubbing his eyes and made a cup of tea and some toast to take back up for Karen.

John Hutchings was still away with the fairies as was Rupert Davis. With the children having grown up and left the nest, Christmas wasn't quite the same without them .Graham Lord was awake but still under cover. He could hear his father shuffling around in the bathroom, the same avocado bathroom suite they had all shared since Graham was born. Tom McKinney was on holiday in Marrakesh without a care in the world despite a posse of Customs & Excise, police and creditors still on his tail and Leo Easton was sat on the throne wincing as he regretted his intake from the night before. Their Christmas presents awaited them.

Ten days earlier, Max had taken delivery of fifty books for his own use. He knew who he'd be sending them to, some for nostalgic reasons, some for family and friends and the remainder to those who had played their part. He carefully wrapped each book firstly in Christmas paper and then in plain brown paper for posting, each book bearing a handwritten message. He'd been thinking of this moment for a very long time and now it was happening, the end of one very hard journey. Exposing some and serving as an explanation to others, it nonetheless covered half a lifetime and taught Max much, not least to be careful of those he had trusted so easily.

Taking the parcels into the Post Office, he felt like a huge weight had lifted from his shoulders as he passed each book through the till. *Now it was someone else's turn.* He walked across the road into the bank with a small box under his arm and asked Customer Services for directions to the safety deposit area. Moments later, accompanied by the bank official, he filled the small safe. It wasn't a lot, but it was important. The original handwritten manuscript, the orginal statements from those that had helped and the real names, addresses and contact details of the five.

Sam made two milky coffees and went into the lounge to sit down next to his wife in front of the open log fire. There was a hard frost outside, not untypical for a bleak Northumberland Christmas morning. He handed her a sack of small presents and like an excited little girl, her eyes lit up and sparkled. It was unusual for Sam to be home at Christmas, a lifetime in the forces meant he was often away. He watched her delve into the sack and pull out a small brown paper wrapped parcel and saw her peer at the handwriting trying to recall the style. She didn't recognise it and the postmark was smudged too, so she didn't know from what area it had come.

'Oh, that arrived for you the other day,' Sam said as he noticed her starting to unwrap it.

She ripped open the festive covering to reveal a paperback book and stared at the title for what seemed like an age. Her eyes drifted down the front cover as she locked onto the author's name at the bottom.

'I used to go to school with a Max Reed,' she said to Sam, thinking *it couldn't be could it ?*

'Yeah, I remember, he was in your year wasn't he?,' he replied looking over.

She didn't answer, she was too engrossed as she opened the book and looked inside. On the first page, a simple message read:

To Caro,

Happy Christmas.

Fondest memories,
Max

THE END

615

About the Author

The author was born in November 1960 and has spent the whole of his life within a twenty mile radius of his birthplace, Exeter. His childhood was spent with his brother on the back beach at Teignmouth amongst the boats and fishermen, tourists, friends and beach huts.

On reflection, the time spent at Teignmouth Grammar School really was a wonderful period of his life, especially that glorious summer of 1976. Reaching the age of sixteen, gave him the start of his love of motorcycles and motorcars which ultimately lead him into his business career.

He is a keen sportsman having played five a side football with his old school friends for more than twenty-five years ; he keeps fit, running ten to fifteen miles a week, enjoys cycling and motorsport.

The idea of writing a book started as long ago as 1992 when he wrote 30,000 words entitled *'Through the Hoop'*. Due to pressures at work and time restraints, he put the book down one evening with the intention of continuing the story, but it never happened. Over the ensuing years, the thought of writing was always there, but not that seriously until that fateful day of July 14th 2008.

What drove him to pick up the pen again was the burning rage and anger within him to tell his story. On the first night in HMP Leyhill, he sat down and started handwriting the manuscript, *'Another Day in Paradise'*. It took eleven weeks to write 250,000 words using the limited free time available within the confines of the prison. There were passages that made him cry and others that made him laugh, but overall the feeling of satisfaction was immense.

With so many distractions, once free from incarceration, the last chapters were the most difficult to write, however two weeks prior to Christmas 2008, Raider Publishing International offered a contract which was finally agreed on July 4th 2009.

He lives with his wife Katie and two daughters, Ellie and Beanie.

The title, *'Another Day in Paradise'*, comes from the often used sarcastic greeting used by prisoners.

What happened next ? Find out in the sequel entitled '
Through the Hoop'.

The story begins where *'Another Day in Paradise'* finishes. How
do the ' Five' react and what do they do ? Who's going to pay
the price and who's going to hear the door slam behind
them?

Keep informed :-

Web : www.throughthehoop.co.uk or Email :
info@throughthehoop.co.uk

Lightning Source UK Ltd.
Milton Keynes UK
23 October 2009

145318UK00001B/13/P